a festschrift
for
morris halle

Morris Halle

a festschrift for morris halle

Edited by

Stephen R. Anderson
Harvard University

and

Paul Kiparsky
Massachusetts Institute of Technology

Holt, Rinehart and Winston, Inc.
New York   Chicago   San Francisco   Atlanta
Dallas   Montreal   Toronto   London   Sydney

Copyright © 1973 by Holt, Rinehart and Winston, Inc.
All Rights Reserved
Library of Congress Catalog Card Number: 73–186
ISBN: 0–03–086595–6
Printed in the United States of America
3 4 5 6   071   9 8 7 6 5 4 3 2 1

pReface

The editors and contributors did not originally intend that this volume should commemorate any particular occasion in Morris Halle's career, but because of various delays it now seems that it will appear close to his fiftieth birthday. This fact should be taken to be accidental; it would indeed be presumptuous for us to mark some special terminus now in Morris' life. Rather, the volume marks a stage in our own careers as his students and colleagues. Enough of us have by now spent enough time in collaboration with him to warrant some sort of accounting of his influence on us.

Morris Halle's work has laid the foundation for an impressively wide range of new areas of research and introduced productive new lines of research in familiar areas. His books and articles on acoustic phonetics, Slavic studies, metrics, and especially phonology and morphology are already classics. Less known is his interest in syntactic and semantic problems, but until very recently almost everyone who studied at M.I.T. had his views in this area shaped originally by Morris' beautifully taught introductory course, and he has often had as many students working on syntax as on phonology. The extent of this influence is reflected in the number of papers on such topics that appear here.

Morris' contributions to the field of linguistics have certainly not been limited to his own publications. His primary influence on just about all of us, in fact, has been his contribution to our work. Most of us would probably own up to having published at least one idea that was basically Morris', and we have all in one way or another gotten from him more than is easily acknowledged, through arguments, comments on papers, conversations, and so on. The particular value of his classes, also, has been not so much in the factual material they convey (which could, after all, be conveyed in other ways) as in the fact that they genuinely make you think. What Morris says in class and on other semipublic or private occasions is often outrageous, but it sets off something productive in his listeners, and of course in himself. And the ensuing arguments, which may be a long time in maturing, invariably lead somewhere useful. It is impossible not to get excited in Morris' classes, and this more than anything else has created the sometimes peculiar life style connected with graduate study in linguistics at M.I.T.

A paradox of Morris' teaching has always been the fact that with this ability to produce creative thought in others he couples an unrelenting insistence on disciplined argument, on the difference between devices that work and solutions to problems. Few, if any, of the excesses that have appeared in the field from time to time can be blamed on him, and he can be credited with having headed off more than one of them. An index of Morris' own understanding of the relation between creativity and discipline can perhaps be found in the fact that, however incredible some of the things he has said to some of us at times, he has seldom been wrong or trivial in print.

We must not neglect the contribution Morris has made through his administration of the linguistics program at M.I.T. It is absolutely certain that without Morris' uncanny ability to keep everything going and everyone reasonably happy, the whole thing would have fallen apart long ago. How he manages to keep such a close watch on everything while getting his own work done is a perpetual mystery—but however it's done, it works.

For reasons both intellectual and practical, then, Morris has been largely responsible for the special quality of life that has characterized linguistics at M.I.T. since its beginning. By this we do not denigrate the contributions of the many others who have been essential to the life and growth of the department. But everyone will agree that things would have been very much less interesting without Morris, even if there had been someone else around to write his papers.

Many people have passed through the department by now, as students or related in other ways to Morris' work, and it seems appropriate that they express a little appreciation. In this spirit, the editors sought to limit the contributors to this collection to three categories—those who have written dissertations that were directed primarily by Morris, those who have been part of the regular linguistics faculty at M.I.T., and those who have collaborated with him on some major piece of research. A few others, related to him particularly closely in other ways, were added, but we tried to be absolutely fair in adhering to these limits. Had we set out to include all those whose work Morris has influenced or who wish to show him their appreciation, this would rapidly have become just another of those 2500-page Festschriften that no one can afford to buy. Some toes have doubtless been stepped on, but we hope their owners will understand; it seems safe to say that there will be opportunities in the future for all. Some of those who were asked were unable to contribute, primarily because of the pressures of time which we attempted to impose on the production of the volume. Compelling personal reasons prevented Professor Gunnar Fant from contributing a paper, and he asks us to express his regret.

The resulting group of papers gives, we think, a fair picture of the sort of influence Morris has had and continues to have. They cover a suitably wide range of topics and reflect most of his interests. We are sorry that there are not more papers of a primarily phonetic character, for phonetics has always been one of his principal preoccupations and was the area in which many of his first major scholarly contributions were made. Otherwise, however, the range is broad. The papers vary considerably in length, because few of them were conceived specifically for this volume; rather, most represent whatever people happened to be working on when they were asked to contribute, which is the kind of sample we wanted.

With such a range of topics, scopes, and styles, the editorial problems have been substantial, and we wish to express our special appreciation to Florence Warshawsky Harris for the time and effort she put into this volume. Had she not assumed most of the burden of its production, it would not have been possible.

Most of all, of course, we want to express our appreciation to Morris for making it necessary.

Cambridge, Massachusetts

Stephen R. Anderson
Paul Kiparsky

contents

pARt 1

pARt 2

Contents

publications by morris halle

(1951) "The Old Church Slavonic conjugation," *Word, 7*, 155–167.

(1952) [with R. Jakobson and C. G. M. Fant] *Preliminaries to Speech Analysis*, Technical Report 13, M.I.T. Acoustics Laboratory; fifth printing, M.I.T. Press, 1963.

(1953a) "The German conjugation," *Word, 9*, 45–53.

(1953b) Review of H. Koneczna and W. Zawadowski, *Przekroje rentgenograficzne głosek polskich*, in *Word, 9*, 394–396.

(1953c) [with R. Jakobson and E. C. Cherry] "Toward the logical description of languages in their phonemic aspect," *Language, 29*, 34–46.

(1954a) "The strategy of phonemics," *Word, 10*, 197–209.

(1954b) "Why and How Do We Study the Sounds of Speech?" Georgetown University Monograph on Languages and Linguistics No. 7, 73–83.

(1955a) Review of H. Lullies, *Physiologie der Sprache und Stimme*, in *Journal of the Acoustical Society of America, 27*, 391.

(1955b) Review of *Miscellanea Phonetica II*, in *Journal of the Acoustical Society of America, 27*, 621.

(1956a) Review of C. F. Hockett, *A Manual of Phonology*, in *Journal of the Acoustical Society of America, 28*, 509–511.

(1956b) [with N. Chomsky and F. Lukoff] "On Accent and Juncture in English," in *For Roman Jakobson*, The Hague: Mouton.

(1956c) [with G. W. Hughes] "Spectral properties of fricative consonants," *Journal of the Acoustical Society of America, 28*, 303–310.

(1956d) [with R. Jakobson] "Phonology and Phonetics," in *Fundamentals of Language*, The Hague: Mouton.

(1957a) "In Defense of the Number Two," in *Studies Presented to J. Whatmough*, The Hague: Mouton.

(1957b) [with G. W. Hughes and J.-P. A. Radley] "Acoustic properties of stop consonants," *Journal of the Acoustical Society of America, 29*, 107–116.

(1957c) [with R. Jakobson] "Phonology in Relation to Phonetics," in L. Kaiser, ed., *Manual of Phonetics*, Amsterdam: North Holland.

(1958) Review of G. Herdan, *Language as Choice and Chance*, in *Kratylos, 3*, 20–28.

(1959a) "O nezamečennom akrostixe Deržavina," *International Journal of Slavic Linguistics and Poetics, 1/2*, 232–236.

(1959b) "Questions of linguistics," Supplemento al *Nuovo Cimento*, vol. 13, serie X, 494–517.

(1959c) Review of C. K. Thomas, *An Introduction to the Phonetics of American English*, in *Journal of the Acoustical Society of America, 31*, 86.

(1959d) *The Sound Pattern of Russian*, The Hague: Mouton.

(1959e) [with R. Jakobson] "Supplementary Note to E. Petrovici: 'La distinction phonologique en trois sortes de N et de L,'" *International Journal of Slavic Linguistics and Poetics, 1/2*, 192–194.

(1959f) [with K. N. Stevens] "Analysis by Synthesis," in *Proceedings of the Seminar on Speech Compression and Processing*, vol. II, D-7, Bedford, Mass.: Air Force Cambridge Research Center.

(1960a) Review of R. I. Avanesov, *Fonetika sovremennogo russkogo literaturnogo jazyka*, in *Word, 16*, 140–152.

(1960b) Review of *Materialy po mašinnomu perevodu*, in *Language, 36*, 112–117.

(1960c) [with G. W. Hughes] "On the Recognition of Speech by Machine," in *Proceedings of the International Conference on Information Processing*, Paris, Munich, London: UNESCO.

(1961a) "On the role of simplicity in linguistic descriptions," *American Mathematical Society Proceedings of Symposia in Applied Mathematics, 12*, 89–94.

(1961b) Review of R. Fahtechand's chapter, "Machine Recognition of Spoken Words," in F. L. Alt, ed., *Advances in Computers, I*, in *Information and Control, 4*, 88–91.

(1961c) Review of H. H. Waengler, *Einführung in die Phonetik des Deutschen*, in *Journal of the Acoustical Society of America, 33*, 364.

(1961d) [with M. Eden] "The Characterization of Cursive Handwriting," in E. C. Cherry, ed., *Information Theory*, London: Butterfield.

(1962a) "Phonology in generative grammar," *Word, 18*, 54–72; reprinted in J. A. Fodor, J. J. Katz, eds. (1964), *The Structure of Language*, Englewood Cliffs, N.J.: Prentice-Hall.

(1962b) "Speech Sounds and Sequences," in *Proceedings of the 4th International Congress of Phonetic Sciences*, The Hague: Mouton.

(1962c) [with R. Jakobson] "Tenseness and Laxness," in R. Jakobson, *Selected Writings, I*: The Hague: Mouton; reprinted in fifth printing (1963) of R. Jakobson, C. G. M. Fant, and M. Halle, *Preliminaries to Speech Analysis*, Cambridge, Mass.: M.I.T. Press; reprinted in D. Abercrombie et al., eds. (1964), *In Honor of Daniel Jones*, London: Longmans.

(1962d) [with K. N. Stevens] "Speech Recognition: a Model and a Program for Research," I.R.E. Transactions of the P.G.I.T., IT-8, 155–159; reprinted in J. A. Fodor, J. J. Katz, eds. (1964), *The Structure of Language*, Englewood Cliffs, N.J.: Prentice-Hall.

(1963a) Foreword and "Essay on the Relationship between Russian Sounds and Letters," in S. Folomkina and H. Weiser, *The Learner's English–Russian Dictionary*, Cambridge, Mass.: M.I.T. Press; also in B. A. Lapidus and S. V. Shevtsova, *The Learner's Russian–English Dictionary*, Cambridge, Mass.: M.I.T. Press.

(1963b) "O pravilax russkogo sprjaženija," in *American Contributions to the 5th International Congress of Slavists*, The Hague: Mouton.

(1963c) "Phonemics," in T. A. Sebeok, ed., *Soviet and East European Linguistics*, Vol. I, Current Trends in Linguistics, The Hague: Mouton.

(1964a) Review of Claes-Christian Elert, *Phonological Studies of Quantity in Swedish*, in *Journal of the Acoustical Society of America*, 36, 2429.

(1964b) [with R. Jakobson] "The Term *kanaan* in Medieval Hebrew," in *For Max Weinreich on His 70th Birthday*, The Hague: Mouton.

(1965a) "*Akan'e*: The Treatment of Nondiffuse Unstressed Vowels in Southern Great Russian Dialects," in *Symbolae Linguisticae in Honorem Georgii Kurylowicz*, Krakow: Polska Akademia Nauk.

(1965b) [with N. Chomsky] "Some controversial questions in phonological theory," *Journal of Linguistics*, 1, 97–138.

(1966a) "On the metrics of pre-Islamic Arabic poetry," *Quarterly Progress Report of the Research Laboratory of Electronics*, 83, M.I.T., 113–116.

(1966b) [with S. J. Keyser] "Chaucer and the study of prosody," *College English*, 28, 187–219.

(1966c) [with V. J. Zeps] "Survey of Latvian morphophonemics," *Quarterly Progress Report of the Research Laboratory of Electronics*, 83, M.I.T., 105–113.

(1967a) "On the modern study of speech sounds," *International Social Science Journal*, 19, 17–27.

(1967b) [with S. J. Keyser] "Les Changements phonétiques conçus comme changements de règles," *Langages*, *8*, 94–111.

(1967c) [with S. J. Keyser] Review of John Hart's works on English orthography and pronunciation, 1551, 1569, 1570: Part II, Phonology, in *Language*, *43*, 773–787.

(1967d) [with K. N. Stevens] "Remarks on Analysis by Synthesis and Distinctive Features," in W. Wathen-Dunn, ed., *Models for the Perception of Speech and Visual Form*, Cambridge, Mass.: M.I.T. Press (proceedings of a symposium sponsored by the Data Sciences Laboratory, Air Force Cambridge Research Laboratories, Boston, Mass., November 1964).

(1968a) "Žirmunskij's theory of verse: a review article," *The Slavic and East European Journal*, *12*, 213–218.

(1968b) [with N. Chomsky] *Sound Pattern of English*, New York: Harper & Row.

(1968c) [with S. J. Keyser] "What Do We Do When We Speak?" in P. A. Kolers and M. Eden, eds., *Recognizing Pattern: Studies in Living and Automatic Systems*, Cambridge, Mass.: M.I.T. Press.

(1969a) "How not to measure length of lexical representations and related matters," *Journal of Linguistics*, *5*, 305–308.

(1969b) "Impressions of Japan and Japanese" (an Interview with S. Kawamoto), *The Study of English* (Tokyo), *58*, 4–11.

(1969c) "An Instance of Linguistic Rules," in D. Ploog and T. Melnechuk, *Primate Communication: Neurosciences Research Program Bulletin 7*, 483–485.

(1969d) "Some Thoughts on Spelling," in K. S. Goodman and J. T. Fleming, eds., *Psycholinguistics and the Teaching of Reading*, Newark, Del.: International Reading Association, 17–24.

(1970a) "Is Kabardian a vowel-less language?" *Foundations of Language*, *6*, 95–103.

(1970b) "Markedness," in *Proceedings of the 6th International Congress of Phonetic Sciences*, Prague: Academia.

(1970c) "A Note on the Accentual Pattern of the Russian Nominal Declension," in R. Jakobson and S. Kawamoto, eds., *Studies in General and Oriental Linguistics*, Tokyo: TEC Company.

(1970d) "On Meter and Prosody," in M. Bierwisch and K. E. Heidolph, eds., *Progress in Linguistics*, The Hague: Mouton.

(1970e) "A survey of modern English accentuation," *Sciences of Language* (The Journal of the Tokyo Institute for Advanced Study of Language), *2*, 139–159.

(1970f) "What is meter in poetry?" *Sciences of Language* (The Journal of the Tokyo Institute for Advanced Study of Language), *2*, 124–138.

(1971a) "Frontiers in Linguistic Theory," in *Linguistics in the 1970's*, Washington, D.C.: Center for Applied Linguistics.

(1971b) "A Minor Accentual Rule of Contemporary Standard Russian," in R. Jakobson, L. L. Hammerich et al., eds., *Form and Substance*, Copenhagen: Akademisk Forlag.

(1971c) "Remarks on Slavic accentology," *Linguistic Inquiry*, *2*, 1–19.

(1971d) "Word Boundaries as Environments in Rules," *Linguistic Inquiry*, *2*, 540–541.

(1971e) [with S. J. Keyser] *English Stress: Its Form, Its Growth, and Its Role in Verse*, New York: Harper & Row.

(1971f) [with S. J. Keyser] "Illustration and defense of a theory of the iambic pentameter," *College English*, *33*, 154–176.

(1971g) [with K. N. Stevens] "A note on laryngeal features," *Quarterly Progress Report of the Research Laboratory of Electronics*, *101*, M.I.T., 198–213.

(1971h) [with V. J. Zeps] "Outline of the accentuation in inflectional paradigms of literary Lithuanian with an appendix on the accentuation of nominal derivatives," *Quarterly Progress Report of the Research Laboratory of Electronics*, *103*, M.I.T., 139–158.

(1972a) "Entretien de Morris Halle avec Jean Paris, M.I.T. 11 Mai 1970," in R. Jakobson et al., *Hypotheses*, Paris: Editions Seghers/Lafont.

(1972b) "On a Parallel between Conventions of Versification and Orthography; and on Literacy among the Cherokee," in J. F. Kavanagh and I. G. Mattingly, eds., *Language by Ear and by Eye: The Relationships between Speech and Reading*, Cambridge, Mass.: M.I.T. Press.

(1972c) [with K. N. Stevens] "On Phonetic Features," presented at 1972 Conference on Speech Communication and Processing, sponsored by the Institute of Electrical and Electronics Engineers, Inc., and the Air Force Cambridge Research Laboratories.

(1973a) "The Accentuation of Russian Words," *Language*, *49*.

(1973b) "Prolegomena to a Theory of Word Formation," *Linguistic Inquiry*, *4*, 3–16.

a festschrift
for
morris halle

part
1

u-umlaut
and skaldic verse[1]

Stephen R. Anderson

Harvard University

The well-known rule of *u*-Umlaut in Scandinavian (discussed for Modern Icelandic in Anderson (1971)) is responsible for alternations between *a* and a (rounded) vowel which is written ǫ in Old Norse and *ö* in Modern Icelandic. The appearance of this vowel, which will be written *ö* in all cases here, can be shown to be conditioned by the presence of the vowel *u* in the syllable following an *a*. Thus, for instance, alternations such as those in (1) appear:

(1) (a) *barn* 'child'
       börnum 'children' (dat)
    (b) *svangt* 'hungry' (nom sg neut)
       svöngu (dat sg neut)
    (c) (*ég*) *kalla* '(I) call'
       (*við*) *köllum* '(we) call'

On independent grounds, all instances of apparently non-Umlauting *u* can be shown to be due to later epentheses, and apparently unconditioned Umlaut can be shown to be due to the syncope of *u*. The Umlaut Rule can accordingly be formulated, both for Old Norse and Modern Icelandic, as (2):[2]

---

[1] I would like to thank Morris Halle, Paul Kiparsky, Wayne O'Neil, and Calvert Watkins for comments and suggestions on earlier versions of this paper. They are not, of course, to be held responsible for my use of their assistance. It is a pleasure to be able to dedicate this paper to Professor Halle, whose work on abstract metrical patterns was its inspiration.

[2] The formulation (2), while adequate for the purposes of this paper, is significantly oversimplified. In Anderson (1971) it is argued that, both in Old Norse and in Modern Icelandic, the rule should simply convert *a* to /ɔ/ in the Umlauting environment. Modern Icelandic has additional, independently motivated rules that convert this /ɔ/ to the surface form [ö]; in Old Norse, /ɔ/ was realized as [ɔ].

(2) Umlaut   a → ö / ____C_0u

This rule interacts with another rule which is responsible for the syncope of certain final-syllable vowels before vocalic endings, as in the examples in (3):

(3) (a) *hamar* 'hammer'
       hamri (dat sg)
    (b) *fífill* 'dandelion'
       fífli (dat sg)
    (c) *morgunn* 'morning'
       morgni (dat sg)

The exact conditions under which the rule in question applies are not relevant here. An approximate formulation, which would require refinement, is given in (4):

(4) Syncope

$$[+\text{syllabic}] \rightarrow \phi \ / \ C\begin{bmatrix} \overline{} \\ -\text{stress} \end{bmatrix} \begin{bmatrix} +\text{coronal} \\ +\text{sonorant} \\ \left(\left\{ \begin{bmatrix} +\text{continuant} \\ -\text{voice} \end{bmatrix} \right\} \right) \end{bmatrix} + V$$

This rule deletes an unstressed vowel between a consonant and a dental sonorant (*r*, *l*, or *n*) or *s* before an inflectional ending beginning with a vowel.

To determine the relative ordering of rules (2) and (4), let us consider some forms to which both apply. These are given in (5):

(5) (a) *ketill* 'kettle' (underlying /katil+r/; cf. dat sg *katli*)
       kötlum (dat pl) (underlying /katil+um/)
    (b) *regin* '(the) gods' (underlying /ragin+ϕ/; cf. gen pl *ragna*)
       rögnum (dat pl) (underlying /ragin+um/)
    (c) *alin* 'ell (of cloth)'
       ölnum (usually *álnum*) (dat pl)

In the derivation of these dative plural forms, we can see that rule (4) must precede rule (2), since it is only after rule (4) has deleted from the stem the final-syllable vowel, which is not *u*, that rule (2) is satisfied.

Note, however, the forms in (6), consisting of a root plus one of the stem-forming suffixes *-ul*, *-un*, which also show an interaction of rules (2) and (4):

(6) (a) *böggull* 'parcel' (root = /bagg/; cf. *baggi* 'bundle')
       böggli (dat sg)
    (b) *jökull* 'glacier' (root = /jak/; cf. *jaki* 'piece of ice')
       jökli (dat sg)
    (c) *jötunn* 'giant' (root = /jat/, from /et/; cf. *eta* 'eat')[3]
       jötni (dat sg)

In these examples the *u* of the suffix produces Umlaut in the root, even though it is itself deleted by the operation of the Syncope Rule. But then it cannot be the case that the Syncope Rule precedes the *u*-Umlaut Rule in all derivations, though the forms in (5) seemed to indicate that this was so.

Since the forms in (5) and (6) seem to require contradictory orders of application of the rules (2) and (4), we must look for some way to reconcile these facts with linguistic theory. In the usual approach of generative phonology, rules are assumed to apply in a single linear order (see Chomsky (1967)). Hence, the facts at issue here

---

[3] N.B.: Giants eat people.

cannot be accommodated within such a theory without either duplicating the statement of one of the rules (here the Umlaut Rule) or denying that both rules apply in the derivation of all of the forms in (5) and (6). The process of Umlaut appears to be the same in both cases, which leads us to reject the duplication of the rules; therefore, we turn to the possibility that one of the rules (2) and (4) does not apply in some of the forms in (5) and (6). It seems obvious that Syncope has applied in all of these forms; it is also fairly clear that Umlaut has applied at least to the forms in (5), where an *a/ö* alternation appears. The only reasonable solution of the sort we are seeking, then, would be to deny that rule (2) applies to the forms in (6). Since these words show the vowel *ö* in all paradigmatically related forms, one might argue (along the lines of Kiparsky (1968a)) that their underlying representations should contain this vowel as well. Although the vowel *ö* could be produced by umlaut from an underlying *a* in these forms (assuming we can solve the ordering problem), one could argue that such a derivation from an abstract segment should be prevented in any case like this, where it is not required to explain an actual alternation in the shape of the form in question.[4] Of course, if the forms in (6) have the vowel *ö* in their underlying forms, no ordering problem arises at all, and the rules can simply be applied in the order (Syncope, Umlaut).

Denying that the forms in (6) are derived from representations with underlying /a/ is not particularly appealing, however. As pointed out in (6), these forms are more or less clearly related to other forms with the vowel *a* by productive morphological processes, and it is clearly desirable to be able to derive, say, both *jökull* and *jaki* from the same root. Since it seems implausible to include in the grammar a "Reverse *u*-Umlaut" rule to derive *jaki* from a root /jök/, we seem to be forced to derive both from /jak/, with *jökull* undergoing *u*-Umlaut.

But, in the facts of rhyme in Old Norse Skaldic verse, there is clearer and more compelling evidence that forms showing *ö* throughout their paradigms should be derived from underlying forms with /a/. While these facts do not apply directly to Modern Icelandic, the rules of *u*-Umlaut and Syncope are in all relevant respects identical in the two stages, and the ordering paradox under investigation arises in the Old Norse of the Skaldic poets as well as in the modern language. Accordingly, evidence for the abstract derivation at one stage is indirectly applicable to the other as well.

The metrical tradition of Skaldic verse was undoubtedly developed as an elaboration of the earlier, freer meters of early Germanic and the verse of the Eddic poems. Though there do appear a few lines in early runic material which may be Skaldic in form, the type appears to emerge nearly fully formed in the work of Bragi hinn gamli, a Norwegian poet of the middle of the ninth century. The style was variously elaborated, especially by Égill Skallagrímsson (*ca.* 910–990), and is regarded as fully matured in the verse of Sighvatr þorðarson (*ca.* 995–1045). As a medium for the composition of occasional praise, heroic description, magical incantation, love poetry,

---

[4] Two forms of an anti-abstractness position must be distinguished here. One, which is explicitly defended by Kiparsky in his paper, would prohibit a derivation from an abstract source just in case no related form shows a different result which could serve to motivate an alternation and thus a nonphonetic source. A stronger form of this condition would require that a form show an alternation in paradigmatically related forms (and not just in derivationally related or alternate forms) in order to motivate an abstract derivation. It is this second, and stronger, condition that is required if the application of rule (2) in the forms in (6) is to be denied since, as shown, these forms are related to other forms in other paradigms that could provide motivation for abstract derivations even within the confines of Kiparsky's constraint. But if such derivations are allowed, then the ordering problem discussed in the text remains.

and so on, it flourished for the next several centuries. In about 1223, Snorri Sturluson, who felt that the art of versifying was being practiced less skillfully than before, wrote a treatise on poetics which was designed to enlighten his contemporaries as to the correct bases of Norse poetics. This work, the *háttatal* or account of meters (part of the *Snorra Edda*), is still one of the most valuable studies of Skaldic verse, fundamental to later descriptions. More will be said shortly concerning its influence.

Since Skaldic verse was primarily practiced by professional poets, whose livelihood depended in many instances on their ability to compose a well-turned stanza or two in celebration of a patron's deeds, it quickly became highly intricate and conventionalized, especially in its syntax. Sentences were interwoven in incredibly complex ways in a stanza, and Skaldic syntax remains a murky and little-understood field. The complexity of the meters employed in the verse was such that versification was a highly conscious, reflective art; accordingly, the forms were generally quite strictly adhered to. This makes it likely, in most cases, that apparently irregular lines of verse are actually characterized by hitherto unnoticed regularities, and the evidential value of this material for deciding phonological questions has long been recognized.

A Skaldic stanza was divided into two metrically identical half-stanzas, each consisting of two couplets or long-lines. Each long-line, in turn, consisted of two half-lines; the latter unit, the *visuorð*, is the basic building block of the poetry. Within the long-line, the two half-lines had to be related in particular ways by alliteration. The structure of the half-line, and especially the distribution of stress and length over it, has been studied in considerable detail. The structural tendency is clearly toward a trochaic line of three feet, the downbeat of each foot being a long syllable. But there are a large number of exceptions to this pattern, and scholars (especially Sievers (1878–79)) have catalogued these and attempted to present rules for the composition of the line. Such encyclopedic treatment, however, while compendious and probably complete, seems often to miss the essential point: the pattern of the verse as determined by strictly metrical considerations is basically rather simple, with many of the complexities found by Sievers and others arising from the interaction of the structure of the language with the requirements of alliteration and rhyme. Though it is well beyond the scope of this article to demonstrate this claim, the abstract pattern of the verse (see Halle (1970) and Halle and Keyser (1971) for the present usage of this notion) appears to be as in (7):

(7) WW WW S

In this formula, W is realized in general by a single syllable, with the following exceptions: (*a*) the first W may be realized optionally by two short syllables not separated by # or by a short syllable followed by an unstressed monosyllable; (*b*) any W may optionally be realized by two of three consecutive vowels. The S in the formula is realized by two syllables at the end of a word, of which the first is long and the second does not bear stronger stress than the first. Because of the structure of the language, this will almost always mean that the second is short and unstressed. There is, in addition, a requirement that at least two instances of main (that is, primary or secondary) stress occur within the four W's.

Variations on this formula involve the addition of either another W or an S* (a single stressed long syllable) between the two groups of W's in (7) or variations in the realization rule for S (for example, S may be made the same as S*). This basic pattern is similar to that of the Latvian trochaic folk songs and some traditional Serbo-Croatian poetry (see Jakobson (1952), Zeps (1963), and Halle (1970) for some discussion), with the difference that these other forms have an S* equal to S. While these patterns are of course very general, simple arrangements of patterning units, the fact is that other Indo-European poetic traditions, such as Sanskrit, Greek, and Latin poetry, have used considerably different patterns. Furthermore, it is not only the pattern (7) but also the mapping rule for S which is duplicated in Scandinavian, Slavic, and Baltic verse. These facts perhaps point to some interesting community of poetic tradition, including Slavic, certain Baltic languages, and the earliest distinctively Scandinavian verse. Such a community would not be unlikely in light of the extensive explorations of Scandinavians in Russia and the Baltic area at approximately the appropriate time.

Added constraints of a rather restrictive type are superimposed on the pattern. In addition to the alliteration already mentioned, there are requirements of internal and external rhyme. In regular *drottkvætt* (the commonest meter), the first half-line of each long-line must contain a stressed syllable within the W's with the same final consonantism as the first syllable of the S but different vocalism (called *skothending*); in the second half-line, there had to be such consonant rhyme in syllables with the SAME vocalism (*aðalhending*). Further complexities, illustrated in the *Snorra Edda*, include stricter rhyme within the line and end rhyme (*rundhending*). With regard to phonological analysis, the principle utility of these restrictions comes from the required identity of vocalism: when two syllables appear in rhyming position, it can be inferred that their vowels were (in some sense) identical. This fact has been used in numerous studies to support various claims about the similarity or dissimilarity of particular vowel segments.

Of course, if a line does not appear to exhibit the required identity, it may simply be that the poet has produced a metrically deviant line. Unfortunately, such a thing is possible, especially where constraints are as narrow as they frequently are in Skaldic verse. If the "deviant" lines fall into reasonably defined classes, however, we can consider the possibility, suggested previously, that they constitute a special sub-regularity, and we can attempt to relate this regularity to the structure of the language in general. An example of this kind of argument is found in Kiparsky (1968c), where it is shown that certain apparent deviations in the lines of the *Kalevala* can be accounted for if we assume that the meter is defined on a representation to which some but not all of the rules of the phonology have applied. The representation which appears to be metrically significant is neither phonetic nor phonemic (in any sense of this term) but an intermediate level with no other known systematic properties. A similar argument is found for Latvian in Zeps (1963) and for Sanskrit in Kiparsky (1972).

A very large class of exceptions to the Skaldic rules of internal rhyme consists of lines in which one of the apparent rhyming syllables has the vowel *a* and the other has *ö*. In a representative corpus of approximately 4,000 lines of Skaldic verse from throughout the period (Jónsson (1929)), approximately 94 percent of the "unmetrical" lines violating *aðalhending* were of this type, consisting of rhymes like *allvaldr/sköldum*. This type of rhyme is very common and clearly constitutes a well-defined class of exceptions. Thus, if the rule of regular rhyme is to be preserved, we must look for some level of nonphonetic representation at which the vowels in such forms are identical. In this case, such a level is not hard to suggest: if, in fact, all instances of *ö* in these rhymes are derived from *a* by the *u*-Umlaut Rule, then the metrically relevant level of representation is simply the level prior to the application of this rule.

The level in question cannot simply be that of underlying representation, as shown by rhymes like *skjöldum/aldri*, for the vowel in *skjöldum* is underlying *e* (cf. *skildi* (dat sg), for example). The /e/ is converted to *ja* by the rule of Breaking, and *ja* in turn Umlauts to *jö*. The level of identical vowels, then, can be placed after the application of Breaking but before *u*-Umlaut. Incidentally, the fact that vowels in words like *skjöldum* rhyme with *a* but never with *o* is evidence in favor of this account of Breaking, as opposed to an alternative occasionally proposed in which the development is *e* > *jə* > *jo* > *jö* (see Anderson (1971) for discussion and Jónsson (1906) for the facts concerning rhymes of *jö*).

Such an account appears quite satisfactory, so long as all instances of rhyming *ö* can be derived from *a*. However, the proposal to eliminate all abstract derivations (and hence, all derivations of *ö* from *a*) except in cases where they are necessitated by an alternation in the paradigm would seriously restrict the applicability of this explanation. Any rhymes between nonalternating *ö* and *a* or alternating *ö* would remain unaccounted for. Such rhymes do in fact exist, in approximately the expected proportion, given the frequency of the relevant words in the language. In rhymes like *knörr/varrar* and *öndur/landi*, the first member of the rhyme in each case is a word showing the vowel *ö* in all forms of its paradigm. The strongest form of the anti-abstractness position, then, which is the form one must maintain if one is to deny that the Umlaut Rule (2) applies in forms like those in (6), would say that these forms have the vowel *ö* underlyingly and at all subsequent points in the derivation. In the second member of these rhymes, however, the vowel *a* appears throughout the derivation; accordingly, the identity required by the rhyme rule will not be met at any point. Forms like *knörr* and *öndurr*, like the forms in (6), are related to other forms with the vowel *a* although the latter do not occur in the same paradigm. Thus, the weaker form of the anti-abstractness position, which is argued for in Kiparsky's paper, would allow the derivation of these forms with *ö* from a source with /a/. In this case, the required identity could be satisfied at the point after Breaking and before *u*-Umlaut. A rhyme like *öngull/hangi*, however, is different: *öngull* 'fishhook' is a completely isolated form, and no related forms exist to motivate a root /ang/. Accordingly, even Kiparsky's version of the anti-abstractness position would prohibit the derivation of this form from /angul+r/ and predict the impossibility of this rhyme. Given their extreme rarity in the language, completely isolated forms like *öngull* appear to participate in *ö/a* rhymes as freely as other words with *ö*.

Another kind of problem for the solutions without abstract derivations is presented by rhymes like *juföl/dvöldu, örleiks/jörlum*. If the metrically relevant point in the derivation is to be exactly "after Breaking and before *u*-Umlaut," a nonabstract account of these rhymes will fail. Here, again, the first member of each rhyme is a word with nonalternating *ö*, which must accordingly be represented as underlying /ö/ if abstract derivations are prohibited. The second member of each of these rhymes, however, has an instance of *ö* alternating with (and accordingly derived by rule (2) from) *a* within the paradigm. Unless the *ö*'s of forms like *juföl* and *örleiks* are derived from *a*, then, these rhymes will not meet the identity condition at the level after Breaking and before *u*-Umlaut.

We seem, therefore, to be left with two alternatives: either we accept abstract derivations and represent all instances of *ö* as underlying /a/, whether or not they alternate with *a*, or we give up hope of explaining the *ö/a* rhymes. If we accept the abstract derivations, we can preserve the unity of the rhyme constraint as one requiring identity at a certain abstract level of representation. If we do not, we must add an ad hoc rider to the constraint, saying that while identity is generally the basis of rhyme, *a* and *ö* rhyme regardless. We may be forced into this second type of account, but we would then miss the fact that precisely the two vowels related as exceptions are also related in a nonarbitrary way by a highly productive rule of the phonology of the language. We should prefer a statement that avoids this.

To determine whether the ad hoc exception solution to the problem of *a/ö* rhymes is appropriate, we can consider the other "exceptional" rhymes and see whether it is appropriate for them as well. If we find that such a solution is not, in general, available, we should probably reject it in this case also: if a solution which preserves the "identity of vowels" formulation of the rhyme rule is available in other cases, whether violating an abstractness condition or not, we would be led to adopt a solution for *a/ö* rhymes which involved abstract derivations of *ö* from *a*. Cases that would be decisive here are of the following sort. Suppose there is a vowel V* in the language which is derived from two (or more) different underlying sources, say, V_1, V_2, etc. Then suppose that in addition to V*/V* rhymes, there are rhymes of V* with V_1, V* with V_2, etc. Now, if all of the instances of V* that rhyme with V_1 are in forms in which V* is most plausibly derived from V_1 (rather than from V_2, etc.), it appears that what is involved is a condition of identity of representation at some level. If, on the other hand, instances of V* that are derived from V_1 rhyme not only with V_1 but also with V_2, etc., then it cannot be the case that identity of representation is involved: rather, it must be that the rhyme rule includes the ad hoc statement "V* rhymes with any of V_1, V_2, etc., while other vowels must be identical." Notice that if the first situation obtains (that is, only V* from V_1 rhymes with V_1), such an ad hoc statement will not be possible since it predicts that any V* can rhyme with any source of V*.

In fact, there are three possible vowels in Old Icelandic that look as if they might give rise to a situation that would allow us to test the problem—*e*, which can be either basic /e/ or derived from /a/ by *i*-Umlaut; *ø*, which can be either the *i*-Umlaut of /o/ or the *u/v*-Umlaut of /e/; *y* (= [ü]), which can be either the *i*-Umlaut of *u* or the *u/v*-Umlaut of /i/. With regard to the first vowel, *e*, Benediktsson (1966) has shown that, while the two kinds of *e* have coalesced in the modern language, they were probably phonetically distinct earlier. The absence of rhymes of *e* from /e/ with *a* or with *e* from /a/ is thus not of interest, and this case provides no evidence either way. In both of the other cases, however, evidence does exist pointing to the impossibility of the ad hoc statement approach and requiring the principle of identity at some stage of the derivation.

Kahle (1892) noted the rhymes involving *ø* from the two possible sources /o/ and /e/. Forms with *ø* from /o/, such as *før*, rhyme freely with words with *ø* from /e/, such as the forms of the verb *gør(v)a*, but only the latter can rhyme freely with words like *sver*, with /e/. Kahle interprets this as indicating simply that the vowel of *gør(v)a* was not rounded at this point (historically), but such an approach is clearly inconsistent with the fact that during the same period *gør(v)a* rhymes with *før*, for example, which clearly had a rounded vowel from underlying /o/. The only way to deal with these facts in a coherent manner is to say that the rule which rounds /e/ to *ø* may create new rhymes but forms which rhyme before its operation are also metrically correct. In other words, the rhyme constraint is to be stated not as a constraint on a single level of representation, but rather as the requirement that the vowels in question be identical at SOME level after the operation of rules like *i*-Umlaut and Breaking and either before or after *u/v*-Umlaut.[5] It would be impossible here to deal with the "irregular" rhymes of *ø* from /e/ with *e* by an ad hoc rider to the effect that "*ø* rhymes with *e*" because only some instances of *ø* can rhyme with *e*, namely, those that have /e/ as their abstract source.

---

[5] Notice that by allowing rhyme to be stated as a constraint that must be met at at least one of a defined set of stages of the derivation, rather than at exactly one stage, we remove the problem that rhymes like *örleiks/jörlum* pose for a solution prohibiting abstract derivations. In these cases, even though identity may not exist before *u*-Umlaut, it does exist after this rule has applied.

The other vowel which might possibly bear on the question, *y*, was discussed by Jónsson (1921). He adduces the seven or eight examples in early Skaldic poetry of *y* from /i/ rhyming with (original) *i* and also examples of *y* from /i/ rhyming with *y* from /u/ (by *i*-Umlaut) but notes that there are no examples of *y* from /u/ which rhyme with *i* (or *y* from /i/ which rhyme with *u*) until the introduction of the (historically late) rule unrounding all *y*'s to [i]. For instance, *hryggr* (with *y* from /u/) is cited as rhyming with *tryggir* (with *y* from /i/), while *trygg-* (again with *y* from /i/) is also cited as rhyming with *þriggja*, with *i*. Rhymes such as **hryggr/þriggja*, however, do not occur at this period. Accordingly, the situation is the same as that with *ø*: an ad hoc rider "*y* rhymes with *i*" is not possible since it would predict rhymes like **hryggr/þriggja*; however, the solution stating the rhyme requirement as one of identity of vowels at some point either before or after the *u/v*-Umlaut Rule covers the observed facts completely and elegantly.

Notice that the rule which rounds /e/ and /i/ to *ø* and *y*, respectively, is clearly related to the rule which rounds /a/ to *ö* (= [ɔ]), and the two rules can be identified as the *u/v*-Umlaut Rule. Accordingly, the fact that this rule is involved in the statement of the rhyme conditions for *ø* and *y* lends plausibility to the suggestion that it is also involved in the statement of the rhyme condition of *ö*. The vowel *ö* has only one plausible source, /a/, and hence does not lend itself to arguments like the ones given for *ø* and *y*. These arguments, however, are certainly sufficient to show that the device of ad hoc rhyming statements is not, in general, appropriate for Skaldic verse and that the statement of rhyme should be as suggested previously, namely, as given in (8):

(8) (*aðalhending*)
Two syllables rhyme if they have the same final consonantism and the same vocalism at a point in their derivation either immediately before or after the operation of the rule of *u/v*-Umlaut.

If this statement is to be maintained, however, we must relax the constraint on abstract derivation so as to permit the derivation of nonalternating *ö* in words like *knörr* and *örleiks* from underlying /a/. To do so, of course, implies that all instances of *ö* in productive morphological categories (nouns, verbs, and adjectives) should be derived from /a/ and that the *u*-Umlaut Rule should be allowed to play a role in the derivation of forms like *bögull/böggli*, *jökull/jökli* since morphologically identical words like *öndurr*, *öngull* are found to rhyme with forms in *a* like *landi*, *hanga*.

To conclude this discussion of Skaldic poetics, a few historical observations are in order. Benediktsson (1960) has discussed the same facts concerning the rhymes of *a* with *ö* and has attempted to give an explanation which would avoid the purely ad hoc statement that "vowels have to be identical except that *a* rhymes with *ö* as well as with *a*." His explanation was in terms of the taxonomic phonemic status of the vowels involved. He claimed that while the other phonemic vowels of Old Norse were (more or less) completely opposed to one another, the opposition between /a/ and /ö/ was completely neutralized in a very common position, namely, before /u/ in the next syllable. The neutralization is due (in our terms) to the operation of the *u*-Umlaut Rule, of course. Because of this widespread neutralization, the taxonomic opposition between these two phonemes was significantly weakened, and they were particularly likely to be identified.

Benediktsson further notes the following. In the work of Snorri Sturluson and virtually all later poets, there are no more instances of *a/ö* rhymes than would be explicable simply as unmetrical lines. It is furthermore the case that the neutralization of /a/ and /ö/ before /u/ in the next syllable was eliminated at a certain point: a rule creating certain instances of epenthetic *u*, ordered AFTER *u*-Umlaut, was introduced into the language. Since these epenthetic *u*'s did not cause Umlaut, a contrast between *a* and *ö* in syllables before *u* was established, and the opposition of the taxonomic phonemes /a/ and /ö/ was reinforced. If this event could be directly correlated with the loss of *a/ö* rhymes, Benediktsson would have found a very important piece of evidence for his theory of such rhymes (and, indirectly, for the theory of taxonomic phonemics on which it depends).

The two events were not simultaneous, however. As Benediktsson observes, both the loss of *a/ö* rhymes and the appearance of epenthetic *u* are susceptible of reasonably precise dating, and there is a period of about 75 years separating the former from the latter. Since there are no *a/ö* rhymes during this period in which the opposition of /a/ and /ö/ is still neutralized before C_0u, this would seem to be a major objection to Benediktsson's theory, one for which he has no explanation.

However, another explanation for the loss of *a/ö* (and, incidentally, *e/ø* and *i/y*) rhymes in the poetry of Snorri Sturluson and later poets is available, namely, the influence of Snorri's work itself. Snorri was concerned to produce a manual for poets that could be followed more or less mechanically to turn out (formally) correct stanzas: he was concerned (in characterizing the rules of the poetry) with giving a set of generalizations about the surface forms of such poetry. By becoming reflective about the surface generalizations to be extracted from it, he lost sight of the more abstract components of the grammar of the language that had guided earlier poets, whose skill was largely unconscious. As a good Norse linguist, in any event, he was probably inclined to a view of language that notably prefigured that of taxonomic phonemics. While he cannot be identified with the so-called first grammarian, whose work was undoubtedly the earliest and clearest example of a straightforward taxonomic phonemic analysis on record (see Haugen (1950)), he was no doubt influenced by the same attitudes. It was precisely his codification of the rules for writing Skaldic verse that resulted in the elimination of one of its (linguistically) interesting features: since Snorri could not see how rhymes like *a/ö*, *e/ø*, and *i/y* could be considered regular, he ruled them out, and since his word was the basis of all later poetizing, these rhymes perforce disappeared from the verse.

Returning to the ordering paradox posed by the application of rules (2) and (4) to the forms in (5) and (6), we see that the solution based on denying that rule (2) applies to the forms in (6) is ruled out by the evidence of Skaldic rhyme. If, as we have argued, it is necessary to assume a derivation of *ö* from /a/ in order to state the rhyme constraint in a unified way, it will be necessary to derive the forms in (6) from forms with underlying /a/, using a rule which is indistinguishable from rule (2). Unless we are willing to accept the possibility that the same rule can appear more than once in the grammar, we will be forced to admit a paradoxical ordering of the two rules. We must therefore look for a different kind of resolution.

As has already been pointed out, a situation in which two rules apply in both of the possible orders is inconsistent with the standard theory of rule ordering in generative phonology, since this theory requires the rules to be arranged in a single linearly organized list and applied in sequence. It is possible to envision alternatives to this conception of rule ordering, however, and a different theory, the theory of *local ordering*, has been proposed in a series of recent publications (Anderson (1969; 1970; 1971; 1972; forthcoming)). In such a theory, ordering relations are not confined to a set of statements "rule *A* precedes rule *B*" constrained by requirements of transitivity, nonirreflexivity, asymmetry, and so on. In particular, rules are allowed (in many cases) to apply in a "natural" or "unmarked" order (see Kiparsky (1968b) and Anderson (forthcoming)). This means that rules can apply in whichever order leads to their maximum utilization in the derivation. In such a case the actual ordering is not given as a particularity of the grammar but, rather, is predicted by general principles of the theory of grammar.

Such a solution can readily be made use of in the case of rules (2) and (4). Consider the forms in (5), where it is the application of rule (4) that permits the environment of rule (2) to be satisfied. In such forms, the ordering (4), (2) allows both rules to apply, while the ordering (2), (4) allows only rule (4) to apply. Accordingly, if the grammar specifies that these rules are to apply in the "natural" order, this is to be interpreted as the ordering (4), (2) for these forms. In the forms in (6), however, a different condition prevails. Here the application of rule (4) precludes the application of rule (2); hence, the order (4), (2) allows only rule (4) to apply, while the order (2), (4) allows both rules to apply. In these forms, then, the "natural" order must be interpreted as (2), (4). A theory which allows statements such as "rules *A* and *B* apply in the natural order" as well as statements like "rule *A* precedes rule *B* (in all forms)"[6] is thus able to encompass the facts of rules (2) and (4) as they apply to forms like those in (5) and (6). The demonstration that both (2) and (4) must apply in both sets of forms, and hence that the paradox noted must arise, gives considerable support to any theory of ordering that allows the apparent conflict to be resolved. The facts just cited, then, constitute evidence of a very important sort for the correctness of the theory of local ordering. It should additionally be noted that an important aspect of this theory is the definition of "natural" order of application as being relative to a particular form. Previous discussions of the notion have assumed that it could be defined for a given pair of rules in such a way that the same order would be "marked" or "unmarked" for every form in the language. This example shows that an order which is unmarked for one class of forms may be marked for another class and hence that the notion "natural" is one defined in terms of a triad composed of two rules and a particular form. It is this fact which makes the theory of local ordering interestingly different from the theory of linear ordering as supplemented by a metric for evaluating the naturalness of the orderings imposed.

---

[6] The necessity of explicit, "extrinsic" ordering statements of this second sort seems to me beyond question, contrary to various recent suggestions that all ordering relations can be predicted by natural ordering principles. Consider, for example, the rule of *u*-Epenthesis referred to in the text. Since the *u*'s inserted by this rule do not cause Umlaut, it seems inescapable that the Umlaut Rule must be prohibited from applying to the output of the Epenthesis Rule. This result, while perfectly plausible, and in accord with the history of the two rules, is nevertheless completely inconsistent with the requirement that natural ordering predict all ordering relations since it is precisely a "feeding order" that must be prevented here. Insofar as we have any evidence about the principles determining natural ordering, this evidence would suggest that "feeding orders" are natural. In that case, it seems clear that some orders are *not* natural and must be stated explicitly in the grammar. The observation that many ordering relations can be predicted by general principles does not entail the proposition that *all* orderings can be so predicted, and indeed this seems to be false. Notice that this example also argues against an approach like Chafe's (see Chafe (1968)), which divides rules into those that are linearly ordered and those that are "persistent" or "anywhere" rules. Such a theory makes the claim that any rule applying both before and after some other rule must be able to apply at any point whatsoever in the derivation. We have seen that *u*-Umlaut applies both before and after Syncope, and it must thus be a "persistent" rule for Chafe. But this makes incorrect predictions: we have also seen that *u*-Umlaut cannot apply after Epenthesis. We must therefore conclude that a rule can be freely or naturally ordered with respect to some rules of the grammar but explicitly (or extrinsically) ordered with respect to others, and that a division of the rules into linearly ordered rules and anywhere rules is incorrect.

REFERENCES

Anderson, S. R. (1969), "An outline of the phonology of Modern Icelandic vowels," *Foundations of Language*, *5*, 53–72.

Anderson, S. R. (1970), "On Grassmann's Law in Sanskrit," *Linguistic Inquiry*, *1*, 387–396.

Anderson, S. R. (1971), "Icelandic *u*-Umlaut and Breaking in a Generative Grammar," in *Festskrift for Einar Haugen*, The Hague: Mouton.

Anderson, S. R. (1972), "The Vowel System of Faroese," in M. K. Brame, ed., *Contributions to Generative Phonology*, Austin: University of Texas Press.

Anderson, S. R. (forthcoming), *The Organization of Phonology* (revision of Ph.D. dissertation, M.I.T.).

Benediktsson, H. (1960), "Phonemic neutralization and inaccurate rhymes," *Acta Philologica Scandinavica*, *26*, 1–18.

Benediktsson, H. (1966), "Old Norse short *e*: one phoneme or two?" *Arkiv för Nordisk Filologi*, *79*, 63–104.

Chafe, W. (1968), "The ordering of phonological rules," *IJAL*, *34*, 115–136.

Chomsky, N. (1967), "Some general properties of phonological rules," *Language*, *43*, 102–128.

Halle, M. (1970), "On Meter and Prosody," in M. Bierwisch and K. H. Heidolph, eds., *Progress in Linguistics*, The Hague: Mouton.

Halle, M., and S. J. Keyser (1966), "Chaucer and the study of prosody," *College English*, *28*, 182–219.

Halle, M., and S. J. Keyser (1971), *English Stress: Its Form, Its Growth, and Its Role in Verse*, New York: Harper & Row.

Haugen, E. (1950), *The First Grammatical Treatise: The Earliest Germanic Phonology*, *Language* monograph no. 25.

Jakobson, R. (1952), "Studies in Comparative Slavic Metrics," in *Selected Writings*, Vol. IV, The Hague: Mouton.

Jakobson, R. (1963), "On the so-called vowel alliteration in Germanic verse," *Zeitschrift für Phonetik, Sprachwissenschaft und Kommunikationsforschung*, *16*, 85–92.

Jónsson, F. (1906), "io:io i Norsk-Islandsk," *Arkiv för Nordisk Filologi*, *21*, 244–253.

Jónsson, F. (1921), *Norsk–Islandske Kultur- og Sprogforhold i 9. og 10. Årh.*, Copenhagen: Bianco Lunos Bogtrykkeri.

Jónsson, F. (1929), *Carmina Scaldica: Udvalg af Norske og Islandske Skaldekvad*, Copenhagen: Gads.

Kahle, B. (1892), *Die Sprache der Skalden*, Strassburg: Trübner.

Kiparsky, P. (1968a), "How Abstract is Phonology?" unpublished ditto, M.I.T.

Kiparsky, P. (1968b), "Linguistic Universals and Linguistic Change," in E. Bach and R. Harms, eds., *Universals in Linguistic Theory*, New York: Holt, Rinehart and Winston.

Kiparsky, P. (1968c), "Metrics and Morphophonemics in the *Kalevala*," in C. Gribble, ed., *Studies Presented to Professor Roman Jakobson by His Students*, Cambridge, Mass.: Slavica; reprinted in D. C. Freeman, ed. (1970), *Linguistics and Literary Style*, New York: Holt, Rinehart and Winston.

Kiparsky, P. (1972), "Metrics and Morphophonemics in the *Rigveda*," in M. K. Brame, ed., *Contributions to Generative Phonology*, Austin: University of Texas Press.

Rask, R. (1830), *Die Verslehre der Isländer*, Berlin, Reimer.

Reichardt, K. (1928), *Skalden der 9 u. 10 Jahrhunderts*, Leipzig: Mayer und Müller.

Sievers, E. (1878–79), *Beiträge zur Skaldenmetrik*, Halle: Karras.

Snorri Sturlusonar (ed. 1954), *Edda Snorra Sturlusonar*, Akureyri: Prentverk Odds Björnssonar.

Zeps, V. J. (1963), "The meter of the so-called trochaic Latvian folksongs," *International Journal of Slavic Linguistics and Poetics*, *7*, 123–128.

on stress assignment in two arabic dialects[1]

Michael K. Brame

University of Washington

1. INTRODUCTION

In this paper some stress and related phenomena in two Arabic dialects are investigated. The discussion will bring to light an apparent anomaly in the phonology of Maltese and of Palestinian.[2] The explanation which will be advanced supports and confirms an interesting phonological mechanism proposed in Chomsky and Halle (1968), namely, the transformational cycle.

2. MALTESE

The examples in (1) will serve as a general introduction to the stress-assigning mechanism of Maltese:[3]

(1) *ḥátaf*   'he grabbed'   *béza'*   'he spit'
     ḥátfet 'she grabbed'   *bés'et*   'she spit'
     ḥtáft   'I grabbed'   *bzá't*   'I spit'

[1] I would like to thank Alfred Cauchi, whose dialect of Maltese is described in Section 2 of this paper. Thanks are also due to George Saad for confirming the examples found in Section 3. Finally, I want to thank C. L. Baker for reading and commenting on a preliminary draft. Some of the research that went into this paper was made possible by a grant from the National Science Foundation (NSF-2468), for which I am grateful.

[2] The terms "Maltese" and "Palestinian" are somewhat misleading in that each covers numerous dialects. Even referring to Maltese and Palestinian as "dialects" of Arabic could be called into question as the languages are to a large extent mutually unintelligible. For lack of more appropriate terms, however, these will be employed.

[3] The following symbols will be used in this paper. The symbols *ḥ* and *ʕ* represent voiceless and voiced pharyngeal spirants, respectively. The symbol *a* is used to represent phonetic æ in Palestinian, a vowel which is slightly higher and backer than the vowel of English *bad*. The symbol *a* should be given its usual interpretation for the Maltese data. Glottal stop is represented by the symbol '.

If one takes *ḥataf* and *beza'* to be the stems underlying these forms, followed by the person markers φ 'he', *et* 'she', and *t* 'I', it is possible to give a plausible account of the alternations listed in (1). The presence or absence of the stem vowels will be accounted for by the rule of Syncope (2):

(2) Syncope $\begin{bmatrix} V \\ -\text{stress} \end{bmatrix} \rightarrow \phi \ / \ \underline{\quad} CV$

This rule specifies that unstressed vowels are syncopated before CV sequences. The stipulation that the eliding vowel be [−stress] is required to prevent elision in cases such as *séna* 'year', *jóbon* 'cheese', and *nísa* 'women'. This condition accounts for the absence of elision in the case of *ḥátaf* and *béza'* in (1).

Rule (2) is quite general and is needed elsewhere in the grammar—for example, in the plurals of the imperfective conjugation, which will be encountered at a later point in the exposition. For the moment it suffices to note that rule (2) will convert first person *ḥatáf+t* and *bezá'+t* into *ḥtáf+t* and *bzá'+t*, as desired. The third person feminine forms of (1), *ḥátfet* and *bés'et*, will be derived from the more basic *ḥátaf+et* and *béza'+et* by Syncope. In examples such as these third person feminine forms, stress must have been placed on the antepenultimate syllable. In examples such as *ḥátaf* and *béza'*, on the other hand, penultimate stress is required. Finally, *ḥtáft* and *bzá't* display ultimate stress. In view of these observations, the rule assigning stress in Maltese can be formulated as (3):

(3) Stress Assignment $\quad V \rightarrow [+\text{stress}] \ / \ \underline{\quad} C_0((VC)VC_0^1)]$

Schema (3) abbreviates the disjunctively ordered rules in (4):

(4) (a) $V \rightarrow [+\text{stress}] \ / \ \underline{\quad} C_0 VCVC_0^1]$
　　(b) $V \rightarrow [+\text{stress}] \ / \ \underline{\quad} C_0 VC_0^1]$
　　(c) $V \rightarrow [+\text{stress}] \ / \ \underline{\quad} C_0]$

The forms in (1) may now be generated as shown in the derivations in (5):

(5)

ḥataf	ḥataf+et	ḥataf+t	beza'	beza'+et	beza'+t	
—	ḥátaf+et	—	—	béza'+et	—	Stress (4a)
ḥátaf	—	—	béza'	—	—	Stress (4b)
—	—	ḥatáf+t	—	—	bezá'+t	Stress (4c)
—	ḥátf+et	ḥtáf+t	—	béz'+et	bzá'+t	Syncope (2)
ḥátaf	*ḥátfet*	*ḥtáft*	*béza'*	*béz'et*	*bzá't*	

Case (4a) of Stress Assignment (3) exhibits the longest environment and as a consequence is the first case to be invoked. Stress on intermediate *ḥátaf+et* and *béza'+et* is correctly assigned by this case, but the abstract representations *ḥataf*, *ḥataf+t*, *beza'*, and *beza'+t* are not affected because of their failure to meet the environmental conditions. Case (4b), with the second longest environment, accounts for the stress patterns of examples such as *ḥátaf* and *béza'*. Underlying *ḥataf+t* and *beza'+t* are unaffected by this case since, again, the environmental conditions are not fulfilled. The examples of (5) which at this stage are of the form *ḥátaf+et* and *béza'+et* do meet the environmental conditions of (4b), but they fail to undergo this particular case of the rule as a result of the disjunctiveness principle; that is, since stress has already been assigned by case (4a) of (3), none of the later cases can apply.[4] Next, the two forms in (5) still without stress undergo case (4c). Finally, Syncope applies where it can to produce, with one exception, the forms in (1).

---

[4] See Chomsky (1967) and Chomsky and Halle (1968) for discussion of disjunctive ordering.

The one form of (1) which is not adequately generated in (5) is the third person feminine *bes'et*, which has *s* where its alternating third person masculine and first person forms have *z*. Phonetic *s* can be accounted for by the rule of Voicing Assimilation in (6):[5]

(6) Voicing Assimilation $[-\text{sonorant}]^n_1 \rightarrow [\alpha\text{voice}] / \underline{\hspace{1cm}} \begin{bmatrix} -\text{sonorant} \\ \alpha\text{voice} \end{bmatrix}$

This rule will assimilate the feature of voicing across any number of non-sonorants, the final nonsonorant being the determining segment. That (6) actually affects more than a single segment will be illustrated later. For now it is sufficient to note that this rule accounts for the change of *béz'et*, which occurs in the output of (5), to *bés'et*.

One additional set of forms can be brought forward in support of the rule of Stress Assignment postulated here. These forms are represented by examples such as those in (7), all of which have long vowels:

(7) *ḥáres*   'he observed'   *sultán*   'king'
    kmámar   'rooms'   *ḥayyát*   'tailor'
    ḥdúra   'greenness'   *'attús*   'cat'

If long vowels are derived from sequences of two (in some cases perhaps more) morae in Maltese, the examples of (7) are assigned stress properly by (3). A lower-level rule might then be required to turn sequences of short vowels into a single long vowel. Representative derivations are given in (8):

(8) ḥaares   ḥayyyaat
    ḥáares   —   Stress (4a)
    —   ḥayyáat   Stress (4b)
    ḥáres   *ḥayyát*   Lengthening

Another rule which will be relevant to the ensuing discussion is Vowel Reduction, which reduces unstressed *i* to *e* in a word-final syllable. Consider the third person feminine singular person marker which shows up in (1) as *et*. Actually this ending derives from *it*, as suggested by the following alternating forms: *ḥatfítkom* 'she grabbed you (pl)', *bes'ítlek* 'she spit at you (sg)', *ma ḥatfitkómš* 'she did not grab you (pl)', *ma bes'itlíkš* 'she did not spit at you (sg)'. Here the feminine subject marker shows up as *it*. Notice, furthermore, the alternation between *ek* and *ik* in the second person singular indirect object. Also motivating Vowel Reduction are pairs of examples like *zífen* 'she danced', *sfínt* 'I danced'. All these vowel alternations are accounted for by rule (9):[6]

(9) Vowel Reduction $\begin{bmatrix} i \\ -\text{stress} \end{bmatrix} \rightarrow e / \underline{\hspace{1cm}} C_0 \#$

---

[5] In Maltese *ḥ* neither affects nor is affected by Voicing Assimilation. Thus, for example, *nízboḥu* does not become *níspḥu* (see (11d)). Voicing Assimilation can be altered to take account of this. The precise choice of feature is not immediately obvious, however. It is not clear whether the rule should be complicated or whether sonorants and *ḥ* crossclassify in such a way as to make feasible the substitution of some common feature for [−sonorant] in (6).

[6] Vowel Reduction could also be stated as follows:

    $i \rightarrow e / \acute{V}C_0 \underline{\hspace{1cm}}$

This is the formulation given in Brame (1972). Evidence favoring one of the two possible formulations of the reduction process is not easy to find. Note, however, that the *e* of examples such as

Representative derivations are given in (10):

(10) zifin   zifin + t   beza' + it
      zífin   zifín + t   béza' + it   Stress (3)
      —   zfín + t   béz' + it   Syncope (2)
      zífen   —   béz' + et   Reduction (9)
      —   sfín + t   bés' + et   Assimilation (6)
      zífen *sfínt*   *bés'et*

With the foregoing rules in hand, it is possible to turn now to the rule which will figure crucially in the main argument of this section. This rule will be motivated by examples drawn from the imperfective conjugation of Maltese. Examples of this conjugation are given in (11):

(11)

	I		II	
(a)	*níkteb*	'I write'	*nígdbu*	'I write it'
	tíkteb	'you write'	*tígdbu*	'you write it'
(b)	*níkšef*	'I uncover'	*níkšfu*	'I uncover it'
	tíkšef	'you uncover'	*tíkšfu*	'you uncover it'
(c)	*nízbor*	'I prune'	*nízbru*	'I prune it'
	tízbor	'you prune'	*tízbru*	'you prune it'
(d)	*nízboḥ*	'I paint'	*nízbḥu*	'I paint it'
	tízboḥ	'you paint'	*tízbḥu*	'you paint it'

These forms indicate that *ni* and *ti* are prefixes marking the first and second persons, respectively, and that the suffix *u* is the object pronoun. Further, the singulars

---

ḥáres in (7) derives from *i* (cf. *ḥarískom* 'he observed you (pl)'). In order to derive the phonetic *e* utilizing the rule given in this note, it is necessary that the low-level rule of Lengthening (see (8)) apply before Vowel Reduction. That is, the following derivation is required:

ḥaaris
ḥáaris   Stress (4a)
ḥáris   Lengthening
ḥáres   Vowel Reduction

If the formulation of Vowel Reduction as in (9) is employed, however, there is no reason for a crucial ordering with Lengthening. My feeling is that Lengthening is a late rule and is not crucially ordered with respect to other rules, but this is no more than an intuition, at the moment unsupported by evidence.

Spanish exhibits alternations analogous to those in Maltese. Compare the following forms of Spanish:

(a) *hablámos*   'we speak'
    háblan   'they speak'
(b) *comémos*   'we eat'
    cómen   'they eat'
(c) *vivímos*   'we live'
    víven   'they live'

These examples exemplify the three verb conjugations of Spanish, the examples in (a) representing the first conjugation, the examples in (b) the second conjugation, and the examples in (c) the third conjugation. The first, second, and third conjugations exhibit the theme vowels *a*, *e*, and *i*, respectively, in abstract representations, as seen in the first person plural forms. The third person plural forms also retain the theme vowel, but in the example in (c) *i* has been changed to *e*. The rule which effects this change is apparently quite similar to the Maltese rule I have been referring to as Vowel Reduction. Harris (1969) states this rule of Spanish as our rule (9), generalized to apply to back vowels.

reveal a stem vowel in *e* or *o*. (There are other stem vowels as well, which are discussed in Brame (1972).) The stem vowel *e* derives from basic *i* by Vowel Reduction, as proven by related forms such as *ma niktípš* 'I do not write' and *niktíblek* 'I write to you'. Given these observations it is possible to infer that the column II examples of (11) are represented at a more abstract level by *ni+ktib+u, ti+ktib+u, ni+zbor+u, ti+zbor+u*, etc. The rules of Stress Assignment, Syncope, and Voicing Assimilation will then yield the desired results, as shown in the sample derivations of (12):[7]

(12) ni+ktib+u   ni+zbor+u
      ní±ktib+u   ní+zbor+u   Stress (3)
      ní+ktb+u   ní+zbr+u   Syncope (2)
      ní+gdb+u   —   Assimilation (6)
      nígdbu   *nízbru*   •

Consider now the examples in (13), which should be compared with those in (11):

(13)   I   II
    (a) *nítlef*   'I lose'   *nitílfu*   'I lose it'
        títlef   'you lose'   *titílfu*   'you lose it'
    (b) *níšrob*   'I drink'   *nišórbu*   'I drink it'
        tíšrob   'you drink'   *tišórbu*   'you drink it'

Examples such as these are quite common in Maltese. The forms of column I present no problem. The forms of column II, however, are not parallel to those listed under II of (11). The abstract representations for the column II examples of (13) are presumably *ni+tlif+u, ti+tlif+u, ni+šrob+u*, and *ti+šrob+u*, very much like the abstract representations for the column II examples of (11) (see (12)). Stress should then be assigned to the antepenult, giving *ní+tlif+u, tí+tlif+u, ní+šrob+u*, and *tí+šrob+u*. Following the example of (12), Syncope should eliminate the vowel of the penultimate syllable, but the column II forms in (13) retain this vowel. Apparently, there is yet a further rule of Maltese that is operative here. This is indicated by the fact that patterns similar to those of (13II) are found only in cases where the post-tonic consonant in phonetic representations is a member of the class *r, l, m, n*.[8]

The suffix *u* is also the plural marker for the imperfective conjugation. Corresponding to *nídneb* 'I sin' and *tídneb* 'you sin' one finds *nidínbu* 'we sin' and *tidínbu* 'you (pl) sin'; corresponding to *nítlob* 'I pray' and *títlob* 'you pray' one encounters *nitólbu* 'we pray' and *titólbu* 'you (pl) pray'. In all other cases, one finds that the pattern exemplified in (11II) holds.

These facts suggest that there is a rule of metathesis which gives rise to the examples in column II of (13) and that the segments *r, l, m*, and *n* will be crucial in triggering this rule. Let us sidestep the question of what feature or features cross-classify this set and adopt the symbol R to designate any member of the class. The new rule may then be stated as (14):[9]

(14) Metathesis   CRVCV → CVRCV

---

[7] Several of the ordering relations are unimportant. For example, Voicing Assimilation can precede Vowel Reduction.

[8] I have argued elsewhere (see Brame (1972)) that ʕ, the voiced pharyngeal spirant, is also a member of this class in the synchronic grammar of Maltese.

[9] Such rules are usually stated in a transformational format. However, since I am unable at present to determine whether it is V or R that is moved, or both, I will sidestep the issue by adopting an informal notation.

The rule will convert $ni+tlif+u$, $ti+tlif+u$, $ni+šrob+u$, and $ti+šrob+u$ into the desired canonical representations of (13)—$ni+tilf+u$, $ti+tilf+u$, $ni+šorb+u$, $ti+šorb+u$. This result is desirable, as it allows for a generalization of both sets of column II examples, those of (11) and (13), to the more abstract pattern $Ci+CCVC+u$.

However, there is one obstacle standing in the way of this seemingly natural approach. If Syncope precedes Metathesis, the metathesizing vowel will be deleted and it will not be possible to invoke (14) at a later point in the derivation. That is, $ní+tlif+u$, $ní+šrob+u$, and so on will become $ní+tlf+u$, $ní+šrb+u$, and so on by Syncope, whereupon (14) is inapplicable. It will not be possible to predict the stem vowel of the column II examples of (13) by a rule of epenthesis since the relevant vowel may be i or o. On the other hand, Syncope could be required to follow Metathesis. This seems reasonable since stress actually falls on the strong cluster, that is, on the metathesized vowel, of the column II examples of (13). Syncope must follow Stress Assignment by virtue of its inclusion of the feature [−stress]. And if Metathesis feeds Stress Assignment, that is, if it creates the environment for the assignment of stress—which is to say that Metathesis precedes Stress Assignment—it follows from a theory of linear ordering that Metathesis precedes Syncope. This new hypothesis may now be tested on $ni + tlif + u$ and $ni + šrob + u$ to determine its feasibility. The rule ordering under consideration gives us the derivations in (15):

(15) ni + tlif + u   ni + šrob + u
      ni + tilf + u   ni + šorb + u   Metathesis (14)
      ni + tílf + u   ni + šórb + u   Stress (3)
      n + tílf + u   n + šórb + u   Syncope (2)
      *ntílfu   *nšórbu

Observe that here, too, the incorrect surface representations are generated. This new possibility, then, will not do: it solves one problem while creating another. The problem is not insuperable, however. By shifting attention to the prefixal vowel, it is not difficult to recognize that this vowel, which we do not wish to lose to Syncope, is just the vowel that would be stressed if Stress Assignment preceded Metathesis. That is, $ni+tlif+u$ and $ni+šrob+u$ would be stressed $ní+tlif+u$ and $ní+šrob+u$. What is needed, then, is for Stress Assignment both to precede and to follow Metathesis. This would allow for the utilization of stress to prevent elision of the prefixal vowel and for correct placement of the primary stress in the surface representations. A cyclic approach to Stress Assignment will produce just the desired results. This attack on the dilemma is embodied in the derivations of (16):[10]

(16) [[ti + tlif] + u]   [[ti + šrob] + u]
      tí + tlif   tí + šrob   Stress (3)
      ───
      tí + tilf + u   tí + šorb + u   Metathesis (14)
      tì + tílf + u   tì + šórb + u   Stress (3)
      —   —   Syncope (2)
      tìtílfu   tìšórbu

It is significant that there is a natural labeled bracketing associated with all relevant examples which squares nicely with administering Stress Assignment in a

---

[10] There is a question as to whether an intermediate stress actually shows up on the prefixal vowel in phonetic representations. If it does not, a further rule is required to eliminate it.

cyclic fashion. All other rules relevant to this discussion will apply at the level of word, as is the usual assumption in generative phonology. These facts from Maltese, then, provide strong evidence for the existence of the transformational cycle.

3. PALESTINIAN

The stress rule of Palestinian Arabic is essentially the rule needed for Maltese, as we see from the examples in (17):

(17) *símiʕ* 'he heard'   *fíhim*   'he understood'   *kátab*   'he wrote'
     símʕit 'she heard'   *fíhmit* 'she understood'   *kátabit* 'she wrote'
     smíʕna 'we heard'   *fhímna* 'we understood'   *katábna* 'we wrote'

Again, it is possible to postulate underlying stems of the shape CVCVC for these forms. Thus, *simiʕ* and *fihim* will underlie the perfective of the verbs for 'hear' and 'understand', and *katab* will underlie the perfective of the verb for 'write'. The stem *katab* is unaffected by any phonological rules other than Stress Assignment. However, as in the case of Maltese, a rule of vowel elision must be posited to derive the correct surface representations from the more basic stems *simiʕ* and *fihim*. We give this rule as (18):

(18) Syncope $\begin{bmatrix} V \\ + \text{high} \\ - \text{stress} \end{bmatrix} \rightarrow \phi \ / \ \underline{\hspace{1em}} CV$

Rule (18) differs from the Maltese rule of Syncope (2) in that it applies only to high vowels. This accounts for the lack of vowel elision in cases of stems such as *katab*. Note that the vowel to be syncopated by (18) must be specified as [−stress] to allow for the fact that the initial *i* of *símiʕ* and *fíhim* is not dropped. In this regard the Palestinian rule and the Maltese rule are identical.

Long vowels in Palestinian may be treated as sequences of identical morae, again as in Maltese. Thus, words such as *ktáb* 'book', *tájir* 'merchant' will be stressed in a manner similar to that of the words with long vowels in Maltese.[11] For facility of reference, we state the Palestinian rule of Stress Assignment as (19):

(19) Stress Assignment $V \rightarrow [+\text{stress}] \ / \ \underline{\hspace{1em}} C_0((\text{VC})\text{VC}_0^1)]$

This rule is of course identical to the Maltese rule of Stress Assignment (3). It, along with Syncope, allows for the derivations in (20):

(20) simiʕ   simiʕ+it   simiʕ+na   katab+na   taajir
     símiʕ   símiʕ+it   simíʕ+na   katáb+na   táajir   Stress (19)
     —   símʕ+it   smíʕ+na   —   —   Syncope (18)
     símiʕ *símʕit*   *smíʕna*   *katábna* *táajir*

As in Maltese, it is assumed that a lower-level rule of Lengthening takes *táajir* to *tájir*.

The examples in (21) will now be investigated:

---

[11] There is some indication that many of the long vowels derive from a more abstract representation. However, this is irrelevant to the present discussion as the vowel clusters are created before Stress Assignment becomes applicable.

(21) (a) (i) *'ábil*   'before'
      (ii) *'ábilna*   'before us'
   (b) (i) *táḥit*   'below'
      (ii) *táḥitkum*   'below you (pl)'
   (c) (i) *ḥíbir*   'ink'
      (ii) *ḥíbirkum*   'your (pl) ink'
   (d) (i) *míliḥ*   'salt'
      (ii) *mílihna*   'our salt'

The (ii) examples of (21) appear to contradict the rule of Stress Assignment: given (19), one would expect stress to fall on the closed syllable. The forms in (21) should now be compared with those in (22):

(22) (a) (i) *'íbil*   'he accepted'
      (ii) *'bílna*   'we accepted'
   (b) (i) *málik*   'king'
      (ii) *malíkna*   'our king'
   (c) (i) *mállaḥ*   'he salted'
      (ii) *malláḥna*   'we salted'
   (d) (i) *šírib*   'he drank'
      (ii) *šríbna*   'we drank'

The (ii) examples of (22) exhibit stress patterns that are in accord with the rule of Stress Assignment (19). The problem to be confronted is that of accounting for the difference in stress patterns between the (ii) examples of (21), which run counter to the Stress Assignment Rule, and the examples in (22), which are predicted by Stress Assignment. There is in fact a straightforward way of predicting the stress patterns in (21) as well as those in (22). To this end the phonological rule in (23) will be utilized:

(23) Epenthesis $\phi \rightarrow i \ / \ C\underline{\quad} C \begin{Bmatrix} C \\ \# \end{Bmatrix}$

Given this rule of Epenthesis, it is possible to make the assumption that the unstressed *i*'s of (21) are not present in underlying representations. If Stress Assignment is applied before Epenthesis, all the examples of (21) will be accounted for. Some representative derivations are given in (24):

(24) taḥt   taḥt+kum   milḥ   milḥ+na
    táḥt   táḥt+kum   mílḥ   mílḥ+na   Stress (19)
    táḥit   táḥit+kum   mílih   mílih+na   Epenthesis (23)
    táḥit   *táḥitkum*   *mílih*   *mílihna*

The examples of (22), on the other hand, unlike those of (21) but like those of (20), do possess a corresponding *i* in underlying representations. Consequently, this *i* is stressed in the (ii) examples.

If this analysis is correct, the (ii) examples of (21) are not counterexamples to Stress Assignment. Rather, the strong clusters of these cases are brought about as the result of a later rule, namely, the rule of Epenthesis.

The set of examples in (25) appears at first glance to be anomalous:

(25)   I   II

    simíʕkum   'he heard you (pl)'   *ma simíʕiš*   'he did not hear'
    fihímna   'he understood us'   *ma fihímiš*   'he did not understand'
    šríbha   'he drank it (fem)'   *ma širíbiš*   'he did not drink'

First, the fact that stress falls on the penultimate syllable in the column II examples must be explained. Here, rule (23) may again be utilized if *š* and not *iš* is taken to be the negative particle. Accordingly, *ma simiʕ + š*, *ma fihim + š*, and *ma širib + š* will receive stress on the appropriate syllable, becoming *ma simíʕ + š*, *ma fihím + š*, and *ma širíb + š*, whereupon Epenthesis will account for the final unstressed *i* of the phonetic representations. Thus, the stress of these examples is accounted for in the same way as that of the examples listed in (21), as illustrated in the derivations of (24).

There is still another problem that arises in conjunction with the examples of (25). Why is it that the initial *i* of all these examples does not elide by Syncope? In this regard, the examples of (25) should be compared with the first person plurals of (17), namely, *smiʕna* 'we heard' and *fhimna* 'we understood', where the initial stem *i* has been dropped. An explanation for the apparently anomalous cases of (25) can now be given, one that is similar to that offered for the Maltese data. If the rule of Stress Assignment is applied in a cyclical fashion, as in Maltese, the appearance of the initial *i* in the examples of (25) is accounted for, as can be seen from the derivations in (26) and (27):[12]

(26) [[simiʕ] + kum]
      símiʕ   Stress (19)
      ────────────
      sìmíʕ + kum   Stress (19)
      —   Syncope (18)
      —   Epenthesis (23)
      sìmíʕkum

(27) [[širib] + š]
      šírib   Stress (19)
      ────────────
      širíb + š   Stress (19)
      —   Syncope (18)
      šìríb + iš   Epenthesis (23)
      šìríbiš

Here, as with the Maltese case, the bracketing needed to bring about the desired phonetic representations finds a natural syntactic interpretation.

In the Maltese examples (see (16)), the person markers were considered to be part of the first cycle scansion whereas the object pronoun markers were analyzed as being included on the second cycle. The same analysis is given for the Palestinian data (see (26) and (27)). If the subject pronouns are assumed to be present on the first cycle in Palestinian, the difference between *fhímna* 'we understood' (see (17)) and *fihímna* 'he understood us' is predictable, as shown in the derivations in (28):[13]

(28) [[fihim + na]]   [[fihim] + na]
      fihím + na   fíhim   Stress (19)
      ────────────   ────────────
      fihím + na   fìhím + na   Stress (19)
      fhím + na   —   Syncope (18)
      —   —   Epenthesis (23)
      fhímna   fìhímna

[12] The remark made in note 10 applies here as well.

[13] As mentioned in notes 10 and 12, if the reduced stress of *fìhímna* is not actually present in phonetic representations, a lower-level rule can be postulated to eliminate it.

The rules of Syncope (18) and Epenthesis (23) are not applied until the final cycle; therefore, they never apply to a bracketed string embedded within a word. The relative ordering of these two rules, namely, Syncope before Epenthesis, was assumed in (26)–(28) without justification: the opposite order could have been employed with the same results. There are, however, crucial examples proving that the order adopted in these derivations is correct. A form such as *tiktib* 'you write' will take a suffixal *u* in the plural. There are dialects for which the result of this suffixation is *tiktbu* 'you (pl) write', as might be expected in view of the fact that *ti+ktib+u* is susceptible to Syncope. However, there are also dialects, including the one under investigation, for which the phonetic representation emerges as *tikitbu*. Here, it is the rule of Epenthesis which creates the unstressed strong cluster. But it is the rule of Syncope which creates the environment for Epenthesis, confirming the claim that Syncope precedes Epenthesis and not vice versa. The requisite derivation is given as (29):

(29) ti+ktib+u
     tí+ktib+u   Stress (19)
     tí+ktb+u   Syncope (18)
     tí+kitb+u   Epenthesis (23)
     tíkitbu

It is possible to assume a previous cycle at which point *ti+ktib* alone is analyzed. The result will be the same since stress will be assigned to the first syllable on both cycles.

Before terminating this section, one additional set of examples should be considered. This is given in (30):

(30) *fihmítkum*   'she understood you (pl)'
     širbítha   'she drank it (fem)'
     ma'iblítiš   'she did not accept'

These forms are all third person singular perfectives with suffixal material. As can be seen from the representative derivations in (31), they are all generable without recourse to the transformational cycle:

(31) fihim+it+kum   'ibil+it+š
     fihim+ít+kum   'ibil+ít+š   Stress (19)
     fhm+ít+kum   'bl+ít+š   Syncope (18)
     fihm+ít+kum   'ibl+ít+iš   Epenthesis (23)
     fihmítkum   *'iblítiš*

With the assumption of an extra cycle, the same results are obtained, as shown in (32):

(32) [[fihim+it] +kum]   [['ibil+it] +š]
     fíhim+it   'íbil+it   Stress (19)
     ——————————   ——————————
     fìhim+ít+kum   'ìbil+ít+š   Stress (19)
     fìhm+ít+kum   'ìbl+ít+š   Syncope (18)
     —   'ìbl+ít+iš   Epenthesis (23)
     fìhmítkum   *'iblít+iš*

Although the results are the same, the claims implicit in the two approaches are different: by (31) it is claimed that the first *i* of *fihmítkum* and *'iblítiš* is epenthetic;

by (32) it is claimed that this vowel is an underlying vowel which has not been altered. Both sets of derivations give the desired phonetic results, but this is accomplished by differing intermediate stages. It would seem that the approach used in (32) is to be favored over that in (31) because of the fact that, as we have seen, the cyclic application of Stress Assignment is required elsewhere to explain other phenomena.

At this point it is appropriate to note that a similar situation arises in Maltese. In motivating the rule of Vowel Reduction (9) in the preceding section, examples such as *ḥatfítkom* 'she grabbed you (pl)' and *bes'ítlek* 'she spit at you (sg)' were mentioned. If Stress Assignment in Maltese is not cyclic, one would expect the derivations in (33) to obtain:

(33) ḥataf + it + kom   beza' + it + l + ik
      ḥataf + ít + kom   beza' + ít + l + ik   Stress (3)
      ḥtf + ít + kom   bz' + ít + l + ik   Syncope (2)
      —   bz' + ít + l + ek   Reduction (9)
      —   ps' + ít + l + ek   Assimilation (6)
          *ḥtfítkom   *ps'ítlek

In Maltese there is no possibility of a derivation analogous to (31) since there is no equivalent to Epenthesis (23). (There is a rule of epenthesis in Maltese—see Brame (1972)—but its formulation differs from that of the Palestinian rule (23).) Moreover, even if (23) were included among the phonological rules of Maltese, it could not be utilized to predict the vowels absent from the phonetic representations generated in (33) since the vowel quality differs from case to case. In fact, it is always the underlying vowel which shows up in phonetic representations, proving that this vowel was never syncopated in the first place. In other words, for Maltese, there is a direct proof that derivations analogous to those of (32) are required. In place of (33), then, the derivations of (34) are proposed:[14]

(34) [[ḥataf + it] + kom]   [[beza' + it] + l + ik]
      ḥátaf + it   béza' + it   Stress (3)
      ───────────────   ────────────────
      ḥàtaf + ít + kom   bèza' + ít + l + ik   Stress (3)
      ḥàtf + ít + kom   bèz' + ít + l + ik   Syncope (2)
      —   bèz' + ít + l + ek   Reduction (9)
      —   bès' + ít + l + ek   Assimilation (6)
          ḥàtfítkom   bès'ítlek

4. CONCLUSION

It is of some interest that the stress rules of both Maltese and Palestinian can be demonstrated to apply in a cyclical manner. These so-called dialects of Arabic are geographically far removed and are mutually unintelligible. And yet, the stress-assigning mechanisms of both languages are alike in manner of application as well as in their formal statement. Thus, the analyses presented here are of interest not only in that they support the principle of the transformational cycle as advocated by Chomsky and Halle, but also, in the more constricted domain of Arabic dialectology, for the fact that they bring out some rather basic and deep-seated similarities between two languages which derive from a common source.

[14] See note 13.

As noted previously, the bracketing needed to assign stress correctly in both Maltese and Palestinian correlates with a natural syntactic bracketing. The particular instantiation of this bracketing is of some interest. In the Maltese case (see (16)), the object pronoun was not scanned until the final cycle. This was also true of the Palestinian example (see (26)). However, in the Maltese examples not only was the stem of both cases taken into consideration on the first cycle but also the subject pronoun. One might have expected the subject pronoun, like the object pronoun, to be analyzed on the final cycle instead. That this is not so is quite natural. The object pronoun is less closely associated with the stem than the subject pronoun and is probably incorporated into it by a low-level syntactic rule. One can produce stems devoid of object pronouns, but stems must bear a subject pronoun (with the exception of the third person masculine singular perfective, where 'he' is reflected by the lack of an explicit subject pronoun). Thus, it is not surprising that subject pronouns are analyzed on the first cycle and object pronouns, negative particles, and so on on the final cycle. Also of concern here is the plural marker of Maltese. As remarked previously, this is identical to the third person object pronoun *u*. The plurals corresponding to the column I examples of (11) and (13) turn out to be identical to the forms listed in column II. Apparently, then, derivations similar to those of (16) are needed for plurals. This indicates that the plural marker is analyzed on the final cycle, a result which is somewhat surprising.

REfERENCES

Brame, M. K. (1972), "On the Abstractness of Phonology, Maltese ʕ," in M. K. Brame, ed., *Contributions to Generative Phonology*, Austin: University of Texas Press.

Chomsky, N. (1967), "Some general properties of phonological rules," *Language*, *43*, 102–128.

Chomsky, N., and M. Halle (1968), *The Sound Pattern of English*, New York: Harper & Row.

Harris, J. W. (1969), *Spanish Phonology*, Cambridge, Mass.: M.I.T. Press.

e muet: fiction graphique ou réalité linguistique?[1]

François Dell

Centre National de la Recherche Scientifique

Le développement récent de la phonologie générative a introduit dans l'étude des systèmes phoniques un bouleversement dont il est sans doute superflu de souligner l'importance dans un volume dédié à Morris Halle. A la notion centrale d'opposition distinctive s'est substituée celle de règle. Ce brutal changement d'éclairage a rendu presque méconnaissable un paysage où l'oeil formé aux perspectives structuralistes avait cru s'être assuré des repères stables. Des lignes de clivage fondamentales comme celle entre phonologie et morphologie ont été déplacées, et les non initiés ont bien souvent du mal à distinguer dans l'amas de détails secondaires (mais nécessaires) les quelques idées simples qui font la fécondité de l'approche générative. Les lecteurs français sont particulièrement mal placés à cet égard. Les travaux ne manquent pas qui exposent la démarche nouvelle et comparent ses mérites avec ceux de théories plus anciennes, mais ils sont pour la plupart rédigés en anglais,[2] et traitent de faits linguistiques que les Français ne connaissent souvent que de seconde main. Dans l'étude qu'il a consacrée à certains aspects de la phonologie du français (Schane (1967b; 1968a)), Schane n'a pu s'arrêter qu'occasionnellement à discuter des fondements de sa démarche, pressé qu'il était de rendre compte de l'essentiel des faits.

En rédigeant le présent article, nous avons avant tout voulu faire oeuvre pédagogique à l'usage des lecteurs français. Partant des alternances de genre en français, faits familiers et qui ont déjà fait l'objet d'innombrables discussions, nous nous sommes attachés à reconstruire pas à pas la démarche qui conduit à postuler des représentations phonologiques relativement abstraites liées aux représentations

---

[1] L'auteur a eu la chance et l'honneur d'être pendant trois ans l'élève de Morris Halle et de rédiger sous sa direction une thèse de doctorat dont la première partie traite du comportement de schwa en francais.

[2] Nous pensons notamment à Chomsky (1964), Chomsky et Halle (1965; 1968), Postal (1968). Une exception notable est Halle (1962), dont une traduction française a paru dans Schane (1967a).

phonétiques par un système de règles ordonnées. Nous avons concentré notre attention sur le caractère abstrait des représentations phonologiques (i.e. leur éloignement relatif des données phonétiques), laissant délibérément au second plan ou passant complètement sous silence d'autres problèmes essentiels comme ceux posés par l'ordre d'application des règles ou le rôle des traits distinctifs.

L'analyse à laquelle nous tenterons d'amener progressivement les lecteurs s'inspire directement de celle proposée par Schane (1967b; 1968a).[3] Notre souci de justifier soigneusement chacun de nos pas nous a conduits à tirer de l'ombre et à montrer comment se regroupent naturellement un certain nombre de faits qui sont expliqués par la théorie de Schane, mais dont il n'a pas lui-même fait usage. En cela nous espérons aussi apporter avec le présent travail une contribution aux études de phonologie française.

1. LES ALTERNANCES DE GENRE DES ADJECTIFS

1.1. Sous le titre "Formation du féminin dans la langue parlée," Durand (1936, p. 25) écrit:

> La question est fort différente selon qu'il s'agit d'étudier la langue écrite ou la langue parlée ... à part quelques détails de redoublement de consonnes finales ou l'adjonction d'accents à la voyelle de la syllabe finale, la règle de formation orthographique du féminin est la suivante: la féminin en français se forme en ajoutant un *e* muet après la dernière lettre du mot sous la forme masculine.
>
> Cette règle enseignée dans les écoles, dès les classes élémentaires, est la seule dont nous ayons conscience en ce qui concerne la différence des genres et l'on ne songe guère à rendre conscientes les règles inhérentes à la langue parlée. Que les lois de notre langue n'aient pas été l'objet du travail des grammairiens et qu'un explorateur rétablisse les règles grammaticales d'après la langue parlée, il n'aurait certainement pas l'idée de dire, d'après ce qu'il entendrait, que le féminin se forme en ajoutant un *e* muet à la fin du mot sous sa forme masculine.

Et elle continue (p. 32):

> Le féminin se forme en ajoutant des phonèmes au masculin pris pour base et ce phonème est une consonne, ce qui permet d'énoncer un premier résultat: le féminin, en français écrit ... est caractérisé par une désinence vocalique, alors que, dans la langue parlée, il est caractérisé par une désinence consonantique.

Pour illustrer les propos de Durand, il suffit de mettre les prononciations [pətilivr], [pətitru] en regard des graphies correspondantes *petit livre, petite roue*. Tandis que dans la prononciation on passe du masculin [pəti] au féminin [pətit] en ajoutant un [t] final, on passe de la graphie *petit* à la graphie *petite* en ajoutant la lettre *e*.

Nous nous proposons de montrer que le divorce entre prononciation et graphie n'est qu'apparent, et que pour rendre compte des alternances de genre dans toute leur généralité, les représentations phonétiques des adjectifs féminins doivent être dérivées de représentations plus abstraites qui se terminent par un certain phonème vocalique, appelons-le pour l'instant /x/. Le phonème /x/ a ceci de particulier qu'*il ne lui correspond en général aucun son au niveau phonétique*. C'est ce phonème /x/

---

[3] Schane (1967b) est une adaptation française du premier chapitre de Schane (1968a). Chaque fois que nous voudrons faire référence à des choses contenues dans ce premier chapitre, nous donnerons simultanément les renvois dans les deux éditions.

que l'orthographe traditionnelle représente par un *e* muet. En fin de mot, *e* muet ne se prononce en général pas, et indique simplement que la consonne représentée par la lettre précédente doit, elle, être prononcée.

Cette analyse n'a rien d'inédit.[4] Mais si les auteurs qui l'ont proposée ont montré qu'elle "collait" avec un certain nombre de faits, ils sont en revanche restés assez discrets sur les raisons qui la leur ont fait préférer à telle ou telle autre également compatible avec les mêmes faits, comme par exemple celle de Durand. Nous nous proposons précisément de comparer les mérites respectifs de diverses analyses et de montrer en particulier que lorsqu'on élargit progressivement le champ des faits considérés, l'analyse de Durand (ou d'autres identiques dans leur principe)[5] ne peuvent être maintenues qu'au prix de complications croissantes qui obscurcissent certaines régularités.

1.2. Durand (1936, pp. 73–104) a dressé une liste de quelques 5600 mots susceptibles d'alternances de genre (noms et déterminants de noms), d'où on peut tirer une table exhaustive des diverses alternances phonétiques par lesquelles le français marque le genre. Comme les noms et les déterminants de noms sont soumis au même système d'alternances phonétiques et que les noms ne sont susceptibles d'alternances de genre que sporadiquement, nous simplifierons la discussion en la limitant au cas des déterminants de noms, des adjectifs principalement.

Certains adjectifs n'ont pas la même représentation phonétique selon qu'ils dépendent d'un nom masculin ou féminin. Par exemple *vert* se prononce [vɛr] dans *un plat vert* et [vɛrt] dans *une tasse verte*. On dit que *vert* s'accorde en genre avec le nom dont il dépend, et qu'il a la forme masculine [vɛr] et la forme féminine [vɛrt]. D'autres adjectifs ont au contraire la même représentation phonétique lorsqu'ils dépendent d'un nom masculin et d'un nom féminin. *Bleu* se prononce [blö] aussi bien dans *un plat bleu* que dans *une tasse bleue*. Plutôt que de distinguer deux classes d'adjectifs, ceux comme *vert*, qui s'accorderaient en genre et auraient une forme masculine et une forme féminine, et ceux comme *bleu*, qui ne s'accorderaient pas et auraient une forme unique, nous supposerons que tous les adjectifs sont sujets aux règles d'accord et ont une forme masculine et une forme féminine, mais que ces formes ne sont pas toujours distinctes phonétiquement.[6] Comme Durand, nous partirons des seules représentations phonétiques, de ce qu'entendrait un ethnologue ignorant de nos traditions orthographiques. Nous distinguerons donc entre les adjectifs "invariables" (ceux dont la représentation phonétique est la même au masculin et au féminin) et les autres:[7]

[4] Elle a encore été exposée récemment, avec des divergences de détail, dans De Félice (1950), Schane (1967b; 1968a) et Valdman (1970). Au moment de signer le bon à tirer, nous découvrons que certains des arguments développés ici l'ont déjà été dans Schane (1968b).

[5] Pour deux autres exemples particulièrement nets, cf. la préface de Nyrop (1903) et Blanche-Bénéniste et Chervel (1969, pp. 131, 139, 180).

[6] Comparer avec le fait que certains verbes ont des formes distinctes pour l'indicatif présent et le subjonctif présent (*savent/sachent, sont/soient*), et d'autres non (*lavent/lavent*). Ou avec l'homonymie du nominatif et de l'accusatif des noms neutres en latin (*templum*).

[7] Nous emploierons tout au long du présent travail les abréviations suivantes: "v" représente les voyelles non nasales, "ṽ" les voyelles nasales, "V" toutes les voyelles sans distinction de nasalité, "C" toutes les consonnes (yod inclus), "N" les consonnes nasales, et "B" les consonnes bruissantes (en anglais "obstruents"), i.e. toutes les consonnes qui ne sont ni des liquides ni des nasales ni des semi-consonnes.

Nous avons laissé de côté un petit nombre d'alternances (*neuf/neuve, sec/sèche, beau/belle*) qui ne sont pas centrales à notre propos, ainsi que les alternances V/VBB (*suspect/suspecte, distinct/distincte*). Sur ces dernières, cf. Dell (1970, pp. 66–67).

(1) ADJECTIFS INVARIABLES
    (a) v/v   modèle *flou* [flu] / *floue* [flu]; *carré, abruti, poilu*[8]
    (b) B/B   modèle *vide* [vid] / *vide* [vid]; *atroce, unique, triste, fourbe*
    (c) N/N   modèle *jaune* [žon] / *jaune* [žon]; *terne, sublime, calme, digne, borgne*
    (d) autres   *seul, pareil, rare, souple, pauvre*

(2) ADJECTIFS VARIABLES
    (a) v/vB   modèle *plat* [pla] / *plate* [plat]; *froid, laid, gros, jaloux*
    (b) Vr/VrB modèle *court* [kur] / *courte* [kurt]; *fort, pervers, lourd*
    (c) ṽ/ṽB   modèle *grand* [grã] / *grande* [grãd]; *long, saint, blanc, profond*
    (d) ṽ/vN   modèle *plan* [plã] / *plane* [plan]; *plein, fin, brun, bon*

Supposons que notre ethnographe entreprenne de rédiger une grammaire et un dictionnaire du français. La grammaire consistera en un certain nombre de règles, et le dictionnaire sera un répertoire de formes, chaque forme faisant l'objet d'un article où sont décrites toutes celles de ses propriétés qui ne peuvent pas être déduites de règles, telles que son sens, des propriétés syntaxiques comme "adjectif," "transitif" et certaines caractéristiques morphologiques. Nous ne nous intéressons ici qu'à la partie morphologique des articles de dictionnaire.

Pour nous faire une idée générale de ce en quoi peut consister la partie morphologique d'un article de dictionnaire, examinons rapidement le cas des verbes latins. Pour conjuguer un verbe en latin, il faut connaître la liste des désinences qui sont accolées au thème verbal aux divers temps, modes, voix et personnes, et éventuellement les modifications phonétiques subies par le thème dans ces combinaisons. Ceci représente un total d'environ cent cinquante formes fléchies pour chaque verbe. Ceci ne veut pas dire que pour être en mesure de conjuguer correctement *n* verbes latins il faille auparavant avoir rencontré et mémorisé individuellement *n* × 150 formes. En fait il suffit de connaître quelques formes conjuguées pour être capable d'en déduire toutes les autres. Les grammaires latines répartissent tous les verbes du dictionnaire entre un petit nombre de CLASSES FLEXIONNELLES ou "conjugaisons": "première conjugaison, modèle *amo, amare, amavi, amatum*, deuxième conjugaison, modèle *deleo, delere, delevi, deletum*," et ainsi de suite. Les dictionnaires latins se contentent de fournir pour chaque verbe la prononciation du thème, des indications qui permettent de reconnaître sa classe flexionnelle, ainsi que certaines particularités imprévisibles par règle; par exemple l'article de *video* "voir" indiquera que ce verbe appartient à la deuxième conjugaison, mais que le parfait est *vidi* et non **videvi*. Cette façon de rédiger les dictionnaires n'est pas simplement un procédé qui permet aux éditeurs d'économiser le papier. Elle trouve un corrélat proprement linguistique dans l'aptitude des locuteurs à produire et à comprendre des formes fléchies qu'ils n'ont encore jamais rencontrées.

Les passages de M. Durand cités plus haut semblent suggérer que dans la grammaire confectionnée par notre ethnographe les adjectifs français seront distribués en autant de classes flexionnelles qu'il y a de consonnes qui peuvent être ajoutées en guise de désinence du féminin, plus la classe des adjectifs invariables, où nous poserons une désinence zéro (φ). Il y aura par exemple la classe des adjectifs qui prennent au féminin la désinence /d/ (*lourd, grand, laid*, etc.), celle des adjectifs qui prennent au féminin la désinence /s/ (*faux, pervers, gras*, etc.) et ainsi de suite. Dans le dictionnaire l'article correspondant à chaque adjectif aura la forme d'une paire (M, K), où M est la

---

[8] Les formes terminées par une voyelle nasale sont extrêmement rares. Durand n'en donne que quatre en tout et pour tout: *marron, grognon, ronchon, gnangnan.*

représentation phonologique[9] du thème nu qui apparaît au masculin, et où K est un symbole indiquant que l'adjectif appartient à telle ou telle classe flexionnelle. La paire (M, K) représente l'ensemble des propriétés qu'il est nécessaire de connaître pour pouvoir fléchir correctement l'adjectif considéré. Plutôt que d'indiquer les diverses classes flexionnelles K par des marques arbitraires, nous les représenterons directement par les consonnes auxquelles elles correspondent. Les adjectifs invariables seront indiqués par le symbole φ. Les articles *doux/douce*, *tout/toute* et *flou/floue* contiendront par exemple les représentations lexicales (/du/, /s/), (/tu/, /t/) et (/flu/, φ). La grammaire contiendra la règle (3):

(3) Un adjectif de représentation lexicale (M, K) a la représentation phonologique /MK/ au féminin et /M/ au masculin

Dans cette perspective, il y a entre le *s* final du féminin [dus] *douce* et le *t* final du féminin [tut] *toute* une relation de même nature qu'entre le *e* final de l'infinitif [grave] *graver* et le *ir* final de l'infinitif [gravir] *gravir*: ce sont deux variantes (allomorphes) d'une même désinence flexionnelle ("féminin" dans le premier cas, "infinitif" dans le second), variantes dont le choix est déterminé par la classe flexionnelle du thème. Voilà une analyse qui donne à la morphologie des adjectifs une allure un peu insolite, mais qui a pour elle de partir de la réalité phonétique plutôt que de l'orthographe, et d'être conçue avec méthode.

2. FORME COURTE ET FORME LONGUE

2.1. Si la grammaire et le dictionnaire confectionnés par notre ethnographe n'en disaient pas plus, on serait en droit de supposer que la classe flexionnelle K d'un adjectif et la structure phonique de son thème M sont deux variables complètement indépendantes l'une de l'autre, c'est-à-dire que dans l'ensemble des flexions en genre permises par la structure de la langue, n'importe quelle désinence peut être combinée avec n'importe quel thème. Or Durand (1936, p. 140) note que "tout [adjectif] terminé au masculin par une consonne quelconque *r* excepté est invariable quant au genre." Seuls peuvent recevoir une désinence autre que φ les adjectifs dont le masculin est terminé par /V/ ou par /Vr/. Cette restriction remarquable sur la forme des paires (M, K) doit faire l'objet d'une mention spéciale dans la grammaire. Nous écrirons la règle de redondance lexicale suivante:

(4) Pour tout adjectif (M, K) où M ne se termine ni par /V/ ni par /Vr/, K = φ

En examinant la table donnée en (2), on notera d'autre part que les seules consonnes qui puissent jouer le rôle de désinence du féminin sont les bruissantes. Les adjectifs terminés au féminin par des liquides ou des semi-consonnes sont en général

---

[9] Nous avons en tête une transcription phonologique comme celles que prônent les structuralistes Américains ou les linguistes de l'école de Prague, et qui sont essentiellement des représentations phonétiques épurées des redondances phonétiques les plus superficielles. Pour une discussion générale, cf. par exemple Chomsky (1964) et Postal (1968). Dans le cas du français, il s'agit d'un mode de représentation qui permette de grouper sous un même phonème le *k* de *qui* et celui de *cou*, le *r* voisé de *gros* et le *r* sourd de *carte*, le *i* de *scie* et le yod de *scier*, mais qui attribue à deux phonèmes différents le [t] de *diplomate* et le [s] de *diplomatie*, le [s] de [grosami] *grosse amie* et le [z] de [grozami] *gros ami*, ou le [ə] de [arsəle] *harcelez* et le [ɛ] de [arsɛl] *harcèle*. On en trouvera des exemples dans Martinet (1960) et Blanche-Benvéniste et Chervel (1969).

invariables.[10] Quant à ceux terminés par des consonnes nasales, cf. infra section 4.5.

2.2. Dans les mots dérivés d'adjectifs, c'est presque toujours la forme féminine qui apparaît devant le suffixe dérivationnel : *étroit* [etrwa] / *étroite* [etrwat] / *étroitesse* [etrwatɛs]; *jaloux* [žalu] / *jalouse* [žaluz] / *jalousie* [žaluzi]; *gros* [gro] / *grosse* [gros] / *grossir* [grosir].[11]

C'est encore la forme féminine qui apparaît lorsqu'un adjectif MASCULIN singulier précède immédiatement un substantif qui commence par une voyelle (phénomène dit de "liaison"). *Petit écrou* se prononce [pətitekru] et non *[pətiekru]; *petit ami* et *petite amie* sont homophones : [pətitami].[12]

En parlant de la consonne finale de [pətit] *petite* comme d'une désinence du féminin, on a l'air de suggérer qu'elle est spécialisée dans l'indication du féminin. Or les faits dont il vient d'être question montrent qu'il n'en est rien : cette même consonne apparaît dans *petitesse*, où le problème du genre de *petit* ne se pose pas, et dans *petit écrou*, où l'adjectif est masculin puisque s'accordant en genre avec le nom *écrou*. Plutôt que de forme masculine et de forme féminine, mieux vaudrait parler de forme courte et de forme longue[13] par exemple. Appelons "consonne latente" la consonne dont l'addition à une forme courte permet d'obtenir la forme longue correspondante, et "adjectifs sans consonne latente" ceux dont la forme courte et la forme longue sont identiques. La forme longue d'un adjectif n'apparaît pas qu'au féminin. Elle apparaît aussi dans la dérivation et dans les formes du masculin singulier sujettes à la liaison.

2.3. Avant d'aller plus loin, remarquons que l'alternance d'une forme courte et d'une forme longue obtenue par addition d'une consonne n'est pas un phénomène particulier aux mots susceptibles d'alternances en genre. Nombreux sont en effet les mots non susceptibles d'alternances en genre où une consonne intercalaire apparaît dans la dérivation : *débarras* [debara] / *débarrasser* [debarase], *mât* [ma] / *mâture* [matür], *tard* [tar] / *tarder* [tarde]. L'apparition de cette consonne est soumise exactement aux mêmes restrictions que celles qui gouvernent la distribution des consonnes latentes des adjectifs (règle (4)). Nous pouvons poser la règle (5) :

(5) Soit U un mot non susceptible d'alternances en genre; une consonne intercalaire ne peut apparaître dans les dérivés de U que si U se termine par /V/ ou /Vr/ lorsqu'il est prononcé devant une pause

Nombreux sont aussi les mots non susceptibles d'alternances en genre à la fin desquels apparaît une consonne faisant liaison avec la voyelle initiale du mot suivant :[14]

---

[10] Il y a des exceptions, dont la plus notable est celle des adjectifs en *-ier/-ière*, comme *premier, dernier, entier, droitier*. Pour d'autres, cf. Schane (1967b, p. 51; 1968a, p. 11).

[11] Il y a en effet des exceptions : par exemple *noire* [nwar] / *noircir* [nwarsir]; *nue* [nü] / *nudité* [nüdite].

[12] Nous laissons de côté certaines alternances de voisement : *faux* [fo] / *fausse* [fos] / *faux ami* [fozami]; *grand* [grã] / *grande* [grãd] / *grand ami* [grãtami]. Voir là-dessus Schane (1967b, p. 42; 1968a, p. 127).

[13] Nous empruntons ces termes à Blanche-Benvéniste et Chervel (1969, p. 131).

[14] Pour qu'il y ait liaison entre deux mots, il est nécessaire mais non suffisant que le second commence par une voyelle. Il faut en outre qu'ils soient dans un rapport syntaxique suffisamment étroit. Par exemple dans *il en a vendu trois à mes trois amis* [ilãnavãdütrwaametrwazami], on fait la liaison entre la seconde occurrence de *trois* et le nom *amis*, mais pas entre la première et la préposition *à*. Lorsque le rapport syntaxique des deux mots ne permet pas la liaison, le premier se prononce comme devant une pause. Dans *il en a vendu dix à mes dix amis* [ilãnavãdüdisamedizami], la première

vous se prononce [vu] dans *c'est à vous* [sɛtavu] et *vous partirez* [vupartire], mais [vuz] dans *vous arrivez* [vuzarive].

Notons pour couronner le tout que lorsqu'un même mot non susceptible d'alternances en genre peut apparaître alternativement comme base dérivationnelle ou en liaison avec le mot suivant, c'est la même consonne intercalaire qui apparaît dans les deux cas. *Trois*, par exemple, appelle la consonne *z* dans un cas comme dans l'autre:

(6) *trois fils*   [trwafis]
    troisième   [trwazyɛm]
    trois amis [trwazami]

2.4. Le parallélisme entre les faits discutés en 2.2 et ceux discutés en 2.3 montre qu'indépendamment des alternances de genre, de nombreuses unités[15] oscillent entre deux réalisations différentes dont l'apparition est conditionnée par le contexte: une forme courte et une forme longue qui s'en distingue par l'addition d'une consonne bruissante finale. La forme longue apparaît dans la dérivation et la liaison, la forme courte partout ailleurs. Le mode de représentation lexicale adopté pour les adjectifs en 1.2 peut être étendu à toutes les unités. On leur associera donc une paire (M, K), où M est la représentation phonologique de la forme courte, et K une consonne telle que /MK/ soit la représentation phonologique de la forme longue correspondante, ou le symbole φ (pour les unités sans consonne latente). *Lit* aura donc la représentation lexicale (/li/, /t/), cf. *alité*, *fard* la représentation (/far/, /d/), cf. *farder*, *trou* la représentation (/tru/, φ), cf. *trouer*, et ainsi de suite.

Si on remarque que la quasi-totalité des suffixes dérivationnels du français commencent par une VOYELLE, on ne peut manquer d'être frappé par le parallélisme entre l'apparition de la consonne latente dans la liaison et son apparition dans la dérivation: *la consonne latente d'une unité apparaît chaque fois que cette unité est étroitement liée à un mot (liaison) ou à un morphème (dérivation) suivant commençant par une voyelle.*

Récapitulons brièvement ce que nous avons dit jusqu'ici. Le lexique est une liste d'unités représentées par des paires de la forme (M, K), où M est une certaine représentation phonologique et K, soit une consonne latente soit le symbole φ. La gram-

---

occurrence de *dix* se prononce [dis], comme dans *il en a vendu dix* [ilãnavãdüdis], et non [di] comme dans *dix vélos* [divelo]. Ces faits montrent que pour les besoins de la description phonologique du français il est nécessaire de distinguer au moins deux sortes de frontières entre mots: les frontières "faibles," qui permettent la liaison, et que nous noterons #, et les frontières "fortes," qui ne la permettent pas, et qu'il est commode de noter # # (sur les liaisons facultatives, cf. Milner (1967) et Dell (1970, pp. 68–69)). Dans notre premier exemple par exemple, les frontières se distribuent comme suit: # # *il* # *en* # *a* # *vendu* # # *trois* # *à* # *mes* # *trois* # *amis* # #, comme on peut s'en assurer en examinant les liaisons dans *vous en avez offert un à mes autres amis*, qui a même structure syntaxique: [vuzãnavezɔfɛrɛamezotrəzami]. La description systématique des principes syntaxiques qui régissent la distribution des frontières faibles et fortes dans la phrase reste à faire.

En règle générale, les mots se prononcent de la même façon devant une frontière forte et devant une frontière faible suivie d'un mot commençant par une consonne. *Trois* se prononce [trwa] dans *il en a trois* # et dans *trois* # *vélos*. Les mots qui comme *dix* font exception à cette règle sont rarissimes. Afin de ne pas compliquer la discussion nous ne traiterons que du cas général.

[15] Au sens où nous l'entendons ici, "unité" englobe à la fois les mots et les morphèmes. Nous introduisons ce terme pour la commodité de l'exposition. Il permet de faire abstraction des différences syntaxiques (non pertinentes pour notre propos) qui séparent l'occurrence de *petit* dans *petit ami* et l'occurrence de *petit* dans *petitesse*, et de les réunir sous une désignation unique.

maire G1 contient les règles en (7)–(9), qui valent pour toute unité U de représentation lexicale (M, K):[16]

(7) Devant une frontière # ou + elle-même suivie d'une voyelle, U se réalise comme /MK/

(8) Si U est un adjectif féminin, elle se réalise comme /MK/

(9) Si U ne tombe sous le coup ni de la règle (7) ni de la règle (8), elle se réalise comme /M/

Des règles comme (7), (8) et (9) établissent une correspondance entre la représentation syntaxique d'une phrase considérée comme un certain arrangement linéaire de morphèmes lexicaux et grammaticaux, et sa représentation phonologique. A chaque morphème de la représentation syntaxique elles associent, en fonction du contexte, une certaine séquence de phonèmes (un allomorphe). La représentation lexicale d'un morphème donné doit contenir la somme d'information nécessaire pour permettre à ces règles de spécifier l'allomorphe particulier qu'appelle n'importe lequel des contextes où ce morphème est susceptible d'apparaître. Par exemple l'adjectif *petit* est représenté dans le lexique par la paire (/pəti/, /t/). Il se réalise comme l'allomorphe /pətit/ dans *petit+esse* [pətitɛs] et *petit#ami* [pətitami] en vertu de la règle (7), comme /pətit/ dans *petite fille* [pətitfiy] en vertu de la règle (8), et comme /pəti/ dans *petit pied* [pətipye] en vertu de la règle (9).

La grammaire G1 contient d'autre part la règle de redondance lexicale (10) obtenue en rassemblant les généralisations partielles exprimées par les règles (4) et (5):

(10) Pour toute unité (M, K) où M ne se termine ni par /V/ ni par /Vr/, K = φ

3. LE PHONEME SCHWA

3.1. Jusqu'ici nous n'avons encore à proprement parler rien dit qui contredise la position de M. Durand. Nous avons simplement montré que l'addition d'une consonne finale n'est pas un phénomène limité aux seules alternances de genre. Pour un adjectif donné, une consonne finale identique à celle du féminin apparaît aussi dans la liaison et la dérivation, et on ne compte pas les unités non susceptibles d'alternances en genre qui font apparaître une consonne finale dans la liaison et la dérivation. Nous avons donc introduit la notion de consonne latente, applicable au lexique tout entier. Nous avons également vu que la restriction (4) n'était qu'un cas particulier de la restriction (10), valable pour le lexique tout entier. Mais *dans la grammaire G1 les alternances de genre gardent leur caractère spécifique.* Elles font l'objet d'une clause spéciale: alors que les autres règles s'appliquent à toutes les unités lexicales sans distinction, la règle (8) ne s'applique qu'aux adjectifs, et elle est apparemment irréductible aux autres règles. Au fond, le seul reproche qu'on peut faire pour l'instant à M. Durand, c'est d'avoir isolé arbitrairement les alternances de genre, d'avoir voulu en rendre compte sans faire voir qu'elles s'insèrent dans le réseau plus général des phénomènes décrits par les règles (7), (9) et (10).

C'est arrivés à ce point que nos routes se séparent. Nous pensons en effet que l'irréductibilité de (8) à (7) n'est qu'apparente. Imaginons en effet que pour former le féminin de n'importe quel adjectif, on ajoute au thème une désinence consistant en une certaine VOYELLE /x/ qui a la particularité de se réaliser phonétiquement comme

---

[16] Le signe + symbolise une frontière entre deux morphèmes qui appartiennent au même mot, comme par exemple entre *long-* et *-eur* dans *longueur* ou *lav-* et *-ez* dans *lavez*.

zéro la plupart du temps. Par exemple le féminin *petite* a la forme (/pəti/, /t/) + /x/. Du coup, EN VERTU DE LA RÈGLE (7), la consonne latente /t/ apparaît devant la voyelle /x/ de la désinence du féminin, au même titre que par exemple devant la voyelle du suffixe dérivationnel -*esse* dans *petitesse* [pətitɛs]. La règle (8) n'a donc plus aucune raison d'être, puisqu'elle fait simplement double emploi avec la règle (7) dans le cas des adjectifs féminins. Nous proposons donc d'adopter la grammaire G2, obtenue à partir de la grammaire G1 en supprimant la règle (8), en reformulant la règle (9) comme (13), et en ajoutant les règles (11) et (14). Les règles (7) et (10) restent inchangées: nous les redonnons ici sous les numéros (12) et (15) respectivement:

(11) (a) Tout adjectif prend le genre du nom dont il dépend
     (b) La forme du masculin est le thème nu A, et celle du féminin A + /x/
(12) Devant une frontière # ou + elle-même suivie d'une voyelle, une unité U = (M, K) se réalise comme /MK/
(13) Si U ne tombe pas sous le coup de la règle (12), elle se réalise comme /M/
(14) La voyelle /x/ se réalise toujours phonétiquement comme zéro
(15) Pour toute unité U = (M, K) où M ne se termine ni par /V/ ni par /Vr/, K = φ

L'opposition entre les représentations phonétiques [pəti] et [pətit] est donc la manifestation superficielle d'une opposition sous-jacente entre les représentations (/pəti/, /t/) et (/pəti/, /t/) + /x/. La voyelle /x/ ne laissant en vertu de la règle (14) aucun vestige direct au niveau phonétique, sa présence n'est signalée que de façon indirecte, par la présence de la consonne finale caractéristique de la forme longue. Dans le cas des adjectifs sans consonne latente comme *flou*, l'opposition entre la forme masculine (M, φ) et la forme féminine (M, φ) + /x/ n'est manifestée par aucune différence au niveau phonétique. Les formes (/flu/, φ) et (/flu/, φ) + /x/ se réalisent l'une et l'autre comme [flu]. La forme courte et la forme longue étant identiques, il ne reste en surface aucune trace, même indirecte, de la présence de la désinence /x/. L'invariabilité de ces adjectifs est somme toute un phénomène assez superficiel, qui n'a rien à voir avec leur comportement syntaxique ou flexionnel. Comme tous les autres adjectifs ils s'accordent en genre avec le nom dont ils dépendent (règle (11a)), et comme eux ils prennent au féminin la désinence /x/ (règle (11b)). Un concours de circonstances particulier empêche simplement la flexion de laisser une marque matérielle dans la chaîne parlée. C'est un peu comme lorsqu'un corps est soumis à deux forces égales et de sens opposés; les effets de ces forces s'annulent et le corps reste immobile comme s'il n'était soumis à aucune force.

On pourrait vouloir attribuer l'invariabilité de ces adjectifs à des causes plus profondes, par exemple en supposant qu'ils ne sont pas sujets à la règle syntaxique d'accord (règle (11a)). Dans cette hypothèse il faudrait rendre compte du fait que les adjectifs qui ne s'accordent pas en genre avec le nom dont ils dépendent sont précisément ceux qui ne font pas non plus apparaître de consonne latente dans la liaison et la dérivation. En d'autres termes la grammaire devrait stipuler que la classe des adjectifs qui ne s'accordent pas en genre coincide avec la classe des ajectifs dont la représentation lexicale est de la forme (M, φ). Mais cette restriction est superflue puisque par définition la forme des représentations lexicales (M, φ) garantit que ces adjectifs ont la même forme phonétique au masculin et au féminin.[17]

---

[17] Une telle hypothèse introduit aussi des complications lorsqu'on fait entrer en ligne de compte l'accord en nombre. Il faudrait par exemple considérer tous les adjectifs en -*al*/-*aux* comme ne s'accordant en genre que lorsque le nom dont ils dépendent est au pluriel: *un temps égal* [ε̃tãegal] / *une part égale* [ünparegal], mais *des temps égaux* [detãego] / *des parts égales* [deparegal]. Il serait impossible de faire apparaître la similitude formelle profonde de l'accord en genre et de l'accord en nombre.

3.2. Tout ce que nous savons pour l'instant du phonème /x/ dont nous avons postulé la présence dans la désinence du féminin introduite par la règle (11b), c'est que c'est une voyelle. Mais nous ne savons rien de son timbre, et il serait sans doute difficile d'être mieux renseignés si, comme l'affirme la règle (14), /x/ se réalisait TOUJOURS comme zéro. Mais (14) n'est en fait qu'une première approximation. Lorsqu'un adjectif féminin précède immédiatement un mot à "h aspiré,"[18] /x/ se réalise comme la voyelle [ə]. On dit par exemple *grosse outre* [grosutr], *grosse poutre* [grosputr], mais *grosse housse* se prononce [grosəus], et non *[grosus]. La voyelle [ə] qui apparaît dans ces cas-là correspond bien à un phonème particulier, et n'est pas simplement une voyelle épenthétique qui serait insérée automatiquement chaque fois qu'une consonne précède immédiatement un mot à *h* aspiré: on comprendrait mal sans cela pourquoi un [ə] apparaît dans *quelle housse* [kɛləus] et pas dans *quel hêtre*, qui se prononce [kɛlɛtr] (comme *quel être*) ou [kɛlʔɛtr] avec une occlusion glottale, mais en tout cas pas *[kɛləɛtr].[19]

Si le français possède un certain phonème qui se réalise tantôt comme zéro et tantôt comme [ə], phonème que nous noterons désormais /ə/, il serait étonnant que ce phonème n'apparaisse jamais que dans la désinence du féminin. De fait il est d'autres contextes où l'on constate la présence d'une voyelle [ə] qui ne peut être prédite mécaniquement à partir de l'entourage phonétique. Considérons par exemple les verbes *secouer* et *skier*. Lorsque le mot précédent est terminé par une voyelle, le /s/ et le /k/ se prononcent à la file: [marisku] *Marie secoue*, [mariski] *Marie skie*. Lorsque le mot précédent est terminé par une consonne, il y a apparition d'un [ə] entre /s/ et /k/ dans *secouer* mais pas dans *skier*: [filipsəku] *Philippe secoue*, mais [filipski] *Philippe skie* (jamais *[filipsəki]). La même différence existe entre *pelouse* et *place*. On dit [lapluz] *la pelouse* et [laplas] *la place*, où /p/ et /l/ se prononcent à la file. Par contre on dit [sɛtpəluz] *cette pelouse* avec un schwa intercalaire, mais [sɛtplas] sans schwa intercalaire. La prononciation *[sɛtpəlas] est absolument exclue. On pourrait multiplier les exemples. Pour rendre compte de ces faits nous ne voyons pas d'autre solution que d'attribuer respectivement à *secoue*, *skie*, *pelouse* et *place* les représentations phonologiques /səku/, /ski/, /pəluz/ et /plas/, et de poser la règle (16):

(16) Lorsque le phonème /ə/ est précédé d'une seule consonne à l'initiale de mot, il se réalise phonétiquement comme zéro si le mot précédent se termine par une voyelle, et comme [ə] si ce mot se termine par une consonne[20]

Le développement qui précède montre que les alternances de genre ne sont pas les seuls faits dont il faille rendre compte en postulant l'existence d'un phonème /ə/ qui se réalise tantôt comme [ə] et tantôt comme zéro. En un point de la chaîne, la

[18] On appelle traditionnellement mots à *h* aspiré les mots qui commencent phonétiquement par une voyelle mais ont sur le mot précédent le même effet que s'ils commençaient par une consonne (cf. Schane (1967b, pp. 45–46; 1968a, pp. 7–8) et Dell (1970, pp. 83–93)).

[19] La réalisation de /x/ comme [ə] est obligatoire devant un mot court comme *housse*, mais facultative seulement devant les mots plus longs comme *hongroise*. Un [ə] n'apparaît d'autre part jamais lorsque le phonème précédent est une voyelle: *jolie housse* se prononce [žolius] et non *[žoliəus]. Sur le détail des facteurs qui conditionnent le comportement de schwa devant un *h* aspiré, cf. Dell (1970, pp. 86–90).

[20] Lorsqu'un phonème se réalise phonétiquement comme zéro dans un certain contexte, nous dirons que ce phonème "tombe" ou "s'efface" dans le contexte en question. On prendra garde qu'il s'agit ici de termes qui ont un statut dans la description SYNCHRONIQUE, où ils caractérisent une certaine relation entre les représentations phonologiques et les représentations phonétiques d'une langue à un moment donné. On se gardera de confondre avec les cas où ces termes s'emploient dans un sens diachronique, lorsqu'on compare les représentations phonologiques ou phonétiques de deux états successifs d'une même langue.

réalisation de /ə/ comme [ə] ou comme zéro dépend non seulement des caracté-ristiques phonétiques du contexte environnant (comme par exemple le nombre de consonnes qui précèdent), mais aussi de sa position dans le mot. La règle (14) ne vaut que pour les schwas situés en fin de mot, ce que nous exprimons en la reformulant de la façon suivante:[21]

(17) EFIN: /ə/ tombe devant #

La règle (17) est loin de rendre compte de façon satisfaisante du comportement de tous les schwas finaux. Mais le propos du présent article est simplement d'établir l'existence du phonème /ə/, et non d'examiner en détail les règles qui régissent la distribution de ses variantes. On trouvera une description détaillée de ces règles dans Dell (1970).

4. LA TRONCATION DES CONSONNES LATENTES, PROCESSUS PHONOLOGIQUE

4.1. Dans la perspective que nous avons adoptée, chaque unité répertoriée dans le lexique a le choix, dans la chaîne, entre deux variantes consistant chacune en une certaine séquence de phonèmes, variantes que nous avons baptisées forme longue et forme courte (ces deux variantes sont confondues dans le cas des unités sans con-sonne latente). Rien de plus répandu dans les langues que ce genre d'alternance entre plusieurs variantes (allomorphes): le thème du verbe *aller* se réalise par exemple comme /al/ dans *vous allez* [vuzale] et comme /ir/ dans *vous irez* [vuzire]. Mais il existe une différence essentielle entre l'alternance /al/–/ir/ et celle entre les variantes /lurd/–/lur/ de l'adjectif *lourd*. La relation entre /al/ et /ir/ est ARBITRAIRE en ce sens qu'elle est isolée et n'entre dans aucune série d'alternances analogues. Aucune règle générale ne permet de passer de /al/ à /ir/ ou inversement. Au contraire /lurd/ et /lur/ ont en commun la tranche /lur/ et ne se distinguent que par le /d/ final, et une similitude partielle de même type se retrouve entre la forme longue et la forme courte de nombreuses unités. Bref, la relation est RÉGULIÈRE. C'est précisément cette régularité qui nous a permis de donner aux représentations lexicales la forme de paires (M, K), où M est la représentation phonologique de la forme courte, et K, non celle de la forme longue tout entière, mais seulement un résidu qui permet de la retrouver.

Si la relation était arbitraire, les sujets qui apprennent la langue devraient retenir séparément la forme longue et la forme courte de chaque unité, de la même façon

---

[21] Sous EFIN, lisez "schwa final." Les schwas des monosyllabes (*le, ce, je, te,* etc.) sont régulièrement sujets à (16), et non à EFIN, ce qui n'apparaît pas clairement dans la formulation volontairement simplifiée adoptée ici. Notez d'autre part que la règle EFIN ne dit rien des cas où le mot suivant a un *h* aspiré. C'est que *h* aspiré empêche aussi de tomber les schwas normalement sujets à d'autres règles, comme par exemple (16). Conformément à (16) on prononce *Philippe le dit* [filiplədi] et *Marie le dit* [marildi]. Mais contrairement à ce que cette règle laisse attendre, *Marie le hisse* se prononce [mariləis] et non *[marilis]. Les restrictions que *h* aspiré apporte au fonctionne-ment de la règle EFIN ne sont donc qu'un cas particulier d'un phénomène plus général, que nous n'étudierons pas ici (cf. Dell (1970, p. 88)).

On notera enfin que la règle EFIN permet aux schwas en fin de mot de tomber quel que soit le nombre de consonnes qui précèdent. Par exemple la prononciation [kurt] de *courte* provient de la chute d'un schwa précédé de deux consonnes. Ailleurs qu'en fin de mot, schwa ne peut en général tomber que lorsqu'il n'est pas précédé de plus d'une consonne (voyez par exemple la règle (16) et la note 25).

qu'ils doivent retenir séparément les variantes /al/ et /ir/ de *aller*.[22] L'existence de cette régularité facilite grandement l'apprentissage en réduisant le fardeau mémoriel. Une moitié seulement des formes doit être mémorisée. L'autre peut ensuite s'en déduire par règle. Dans le cas qui nous concerne, quelles sont les formes mémorisées, et quelles sont celles qui en sont déduites par règle?

En mettant les représentations lexicales sous la forme de paires (M, K), nous avons implicitement suggéré que les locuteurs construisent les formes longues à partir des formes courtes correspondantes par addition de K, qui est considéré comme une sorte d'AUGMENT. Mais on peut aussi bien concevoir la situation inverse, où les locuteurs ne mémorisent que les formes longues et en déduisent les formes courtes par TRONCATION (soustraction) de la dernière consonne.

Les deux théories se valent à première vue. Car quelle différence y a-t-il au fond entre apprendre séparément les deux membres de la paire (/lur/, /d/) et former ensuite /lurd/, et apprendre la forme unique /lurd/ et en déduire /lur/ par troncation de la consonne finale? Apparemment aucune. Mais il nous faut une fois de plus prendre du recul et replacer cette alternative dans le cadre plus vaste du système phonique pris dans son ensemble.

Formulons d'abord de façon plus précise la théorie de la troncation. Dans cette théorie, chaque unité U est représentée dans le lexique par la séquence phonématique qui correspond à sa forme longue, appelons-la /Z/. Il faut distinguer deux cas, selon la nature du dernier phonème de /Z/. Si ce phonème est une bruissante,[23] la forme courte est la séquence obtenue en amputant /Z/ de cette bruissante: /lurd/ → /lur/ (*lourd*), /gros/ → /gro/ (*gros*). Si ce phonème est autre chose qu'une bruissante, c'est-à-dire une consonne sonante ou une voyelle, la forme courte est /Z/, comme la forme longue: /rar/ → /rar/ (*rare*), /flu/ → /flu/ (*flou*).

Tâchons maintenant d'intégrer cette théorie de la troncation à la grammaire G2 présentée à la section 3.1. Les règles (12) et (13) doivent être reformulées comme (12′) et (13′):

(12′) Devant une frontière # ou + elle-même suivie d'une voyelle, une unité U = /Z/ a pour allomorphe la séquence phonématique /Z/

(13′) Dans les cas où U ne tombe pas sous le coup de la règle (12′):
  (a) si la séquence /Z/ se termine par une bruissante, U a pour allomorphe la séquence phonématique obtenue en amputant /Z/ de cette bruissante
  (b) si la séquence /Z/ ne se termine pas par une bruissante, U se réalise comme /Z/

Dans l'énoncé de (13′), le membre de phrase "dans les cas où U ne tombe pas sous le coup de la règle (12′)" signifie exactement la même chose que: "dans les cas où U se trouve devant une frontière # ou + elle-même suivie d'une consonne ou d'une pause." On peut remplacer la paire de règles (12′)–(13′) par la paire (18)–(19), où (18) dit sous une autre forme la même chose que (13′a), et (19) la même chose que la combinaison de (12′) et (13′b):

(18) Devant une frontière # ou + elle-même suivie d'une consonne ou d'une pause, une unité U dont la représentation lexicale /Z/ se termine par une bruissante a pour allomorphe la séquence phonématique obtenue en amputant /Z/ de cette bruissante

---

[22] Il est remarquable que la flexion en genre des adjectifs ne présente aucun cas de suppletion totalement arbitraire comme /al/–/ir/.

[23] Cf. en fin de section 2.1. Sur le cas des adjectifs "invariables" terminés par une bruissante, comme *riche*, *atroce*, *moite*, cf. infra section 4.3.

La règle (19) traite des unités qui ne satisfont pas aux conditions qui doivent être remplies pour que (18) soit applicable, soit qu'elles se trouvent devant une frontière suivie d'une voyelle, soit que leur représentation lexicale /Z/ se termine par autre chose qu'une bruissante:

(19) Toute unité U qui ne tombe pas sous le coup de la règle (18) se réalise comme /Z/

Examinons maintenant en quels termes la théorie de la troncation rendra compte des faits exprimés par la règle (15) dans la théorie de l'augment.

4.2. Pour bien saisir la signification de cette règle, il faut la rapprocher de contraintes d'ordre très général que la structure des morphèmes impose aux combinaisons de consonnes en français. Qu'on nous permette une digression sur ces contraintes et les "règles de structure morphématique."

On peut répartir la totalité des amas de consonnes qui apparaissent dans les représentations phonétiques entre les catégories suivantes:

(*a*) amas à cheval sur deux morphèmes; ces amas naissent du contact de deux mots ou de deux morphèmes appartenant au même mot: [rštr] dans *il marche trop vite* [imarštrovit]; [sž] dans *tasse jaune* [tasžon]; [tr] dans *cette roue* [sɛtru]; [ksp] dans *expirer* [ɛkspire]

(*b*) amas dont les éléments appartiennent à un même morphème, mais qui résultent de la chute d'un schwa, comme en témoignent les formes données entre parenthèses (cf. règle (16)): [žl] dans *nez gelé* [nežle] (*patte gelée* [patžəle]); [mz] dans *la mesure* [lamzür] (*une mesure* [ünməzür]); [db] dans *vous serez debout* [vusredbu] (*vous êtes debout* [vuzɛtdəbu])

(*c*) amas que nous appellerons "primaires" par opposition aux amas "secondaires" des catégories précédentes; ce sont les amas dont les éléments appartiennent à un même morphème et ne sont séparés par aucune voyelle dans les représentations phonologiques: [sk] dans *Marie skie* [mariski]; [tr] dans *trou* [tru]; [rt] dans *carte* [kart]

La classe des amas secondaires est d'une richesse et d'une variété qui décourage toute tentative d'inventaire raisonné qui ne se fonderait pas sur un examen préliminaire de la classe des amas primaires. La classe de ceux-ci est assez réduite, et on a tôt fait d'en dresser un répertoire exhaustif et d'apercevoir que les combinaisons de consonnes y sont soumises à un système de contraintes rigides. Notre propos n'est pas d'examiner ce système en détail. Nous prendrons simplement quelques faits particuliers. Aucun amas primaire ne peut par exemple contenir une consonne géminée. Lorsque deux occurrences d'une même consonne se suivent dans les représentations phonétiques, on peut toujours montrer qu'au niveau phonologique elles sont séparées par une frontière et/ou un schwa, comme dans *faute terrible* [fotteribl]. A l'exception de /sf/ (*sphere, phosphore*) toutes les séquences de bruissantes fricatives sont interdites; il n'y a pas de morphème qui contienne des amas primaires comme */sž/, */šf/ ou */vz/. Les interdictions dépendent souvent de la position à l'intérieur des morphèmes. Ainsi les groupes qui consistent en une liquide suivie d'une consonne quelconque ne sont interdits qu'en début de morphème. Il y a par exemple des morphèmes comme *lucarne* [lükarn], *étourneau* [eturno], mais pas de morphème qui commence par /rn/. Le groupe qui apparaît dans *des renards* [dernar] est un groupe secondaire, comme le montre la forme *quel renard* [kɛlrənar].

Il ne s'agit pas de lacunes accidentelles. Pour former la face matérielle des morphèmes, les phonèmes se combinent en se conformant à certaines règles, qu'on appelle les "règles de structure morphématique." Circonscrire, dans l'ensemble de toutes les combinaisons de phonèmes concevables a priori, le sous-ensemble de celles qui se conforment aux règles de structure morphématique du français, c'est définir la notion de morphème possible en français (cf. Chomsky et Halle (1965; 1968, pp. 416–418)). C'est en particulier aux règles de structure morphématique que les français tâchent de se conformer lorsqu'ils empruntent en les remaniant des mots étrangers, ou créent de toutes pièces des mots nouveaux.

En interdisant d'ajouter un augment consonantique à des formes courtes se terminant par autre chose qu'une voyelle ou un *r* immédiatement précédé d'une voyelle, la règle (15) garantit que les seuls amas de consonnes nouveaux (i.e. n'appartenant pas déjà aux formes courtes) qui peuvent être formés par son entremise sont de la forme /rC/. Or les amas primaires /rC/ sont monnaie courante dans les morphèmes qui ne sont pas susceptibles d'alternances entre forme longue et forme courte, comme *fardeau* [fardo], *tarte* [tart], *bourse* [burs]. Bref, *les formes longues des morphèmes à alternance ne violent aucune des contraintes combinatoires dont on peut montrer indépendamment qu'elles sont nécessaires pour caractériser adéquatement la notion de "morphème possible en français."* S'il n'existe pas et ne saurait exister en français d'adjectif dont la forme courte ait la représentation phonologique /riš/ et la forme longue la représentation phonologique /rišt/ (addition de l'augment /t/ à une forme courte terminée par /š/), c'est que la séquence /rišt/ ne fait pas partie de l'ensemble des morphèmes possibles en français. Dans la théorie de la troncation, la représentation lexicale d'un morphème à alternances est la représentation phonologique de sa forme longue; l'impossibilité de l'alternance */rišt/–/riš/ découle automatiquement de celle de la représentation lexicale */rišt/, qui ne se conforme pas aux règles de structure morphématique. Les contraintes sur la forme des paires (M, K) exprimées par la règle (15) font en grande partie double emploi avec les règles de structure morphématique.[24]

4.3. Nous opterons donc pour la théorie de la troncation, telle qu'elle est formulée dans les règles (18) et (19). Nous les redonnons ci-dessous pour la commodité du lecteur, ainsi que les règles EFIN et (16) (numéros (20) et (21)):

(18) Devant une frontière # ou + elle-même suivie d'une consonne ou d'une pause, une unité U dont la représentation lexicale /Z/ se termine par une bruissante a pour allomorphe la séquence phonématique obtenue en amputant /Z/ de cette bruissante

(19) Toute unité U qui ne tombe pas sous le coup de la règle (18) se réalise comme /Z/

(20) EFIN: /ə/ tombe devant #

(21) VCE: /ə/ tombe lorsqu'il est précédé d'une séquence /V#C/[25]

---

[24] En grande partie, mais pas complètement. Tout amas de consonnes interdit par les règles de structure morphématique l'est aussi par (15), mais la réciproque n'est pas vraie. La règle (15) interdit en effet certaines alternances qui sont apparemment permises par les règles de structure morphématique. Par exemple l'alternance [rist]–[ris] est impossible, quoique l'amas primaire /st/ soit très bien attesté (cf. *histoire, poste*).

[25] Sous les initiales VCE, lire "voyelle-consonne-schwa." Cette règle ne concerne que les schwas qui ne sont pas du ressort de EFIN (cf. la note 19). Elle constitue un cas particulier d'une règle plus générale qui veut qu'un schwa intérieur tombe lorsqu'il est précédé d'une seule consonne, mais se maintienne losqu'il est précédé de deux consonnes à la file ou plus. Comparer *ficeler* [fisle] et *harceler* [arsəle], *amener* [amne] et *malmener* [malməne], ou le comportement des deux schwas de *breveter* [brəvte]. En fait la chute de schwa n'est que facultative derrière une séquence /V#C/, mais ce point n'est pas pertinent pour notre propos. Pour une formulation précise de cette règle, assortie d'une discussion détaillée des faits, cf. Dell (1970, pp. 13–18).

Les règles EFIN et VCE n'ont pas le même statut que les règles (18) et (19). EFIN et VCE spécifient les réalisations phonétiques d'un certain phonème. Elles établissent une correspondance entre les représentations phonologiques et les représentations phonétiques. Les règles (18) et (19) spécifient les réalisations phonologiques (les allomorphes) de certaines unités lexicales. Elles stipulent que telle unité lexicale se réalise comme telle séquence de phonèmes dans telles conditions. Elles établissent une correspondance entre la représentation syntaxique d'une phrase considérée comme un certain arrangement linéaire de morphèmes lexicaux et grammaticaux, et sa représentation phonologique. Bref, les premières relèvent de la PHONOLOGIE, et les secondes de la MORPHOLOGIE.

Soit par exemple à rendre compte de la prononciation [sɔ̃ptine] du syntagme *son#petit#nez*. L'adjectif *petit*, qui a la représentation lexicale /pətit/, s'y réalise au niveau phonologique comme l'allomorphe /pəti/ en vertu de la règle morphologique (18), d'où la représentation phonologique /#sɔ̃#pəti#ne#/. Cette représentation phonologique est ensuite convertie en une représentation phonétique par les règles phonologiques, qui attribuent à chaque phonème une certaine réalisation phonétique. En particulier, la règle VCE s'applique, associant au schwa de /pəti/ la réalisation zéro, d'où finalement la représentation phonétique [sɔ̃ptine].

Le passage de la représentation lexicale /pətit/ à la représentation phonétique [pti] s'est fait en deux étapes: on passe d'abord de /pətit/ à /pəti/ par troncation (morphologique) de /t/ final; on passe ensuite de /pəti/ à [pti] par effacement (phonologique) de /ə/. Mais après tout, *pourquoi cette distinction de niveau entre la soustraction de /t/ et celle de /ə/*? Pourquoi ne pas dire plutôt que le /t/ final de *petit* se réalise phonétiquement tantôt comme [t] et tantôt comme zéro? Les diverses réalisations phonétiques de *petit*[26] ne dériveraient plus de deux représentations phonologiques distinctes /pətit/ et /pəti/ liées entre elles par les règles morphologiques (18) et (19), mais d'une seule représentation phonologique /pətit/. Le mécanisme qui régit la chute et le maintien des bruissantes finales n'est pas différent dans son principe d'une règle comme EFIN ou VCE. Après tout, on peut donner de la règle (18) la formulation (22), qui est strictement équivalente du point de vue descriptif:

(22) TRONC: Une consonne bruissante tombe devant une frontière # ou + elle-même suivie d'une consonne ou d'une pause

Puisque nous avons admis que pour rendre compte de phénomènes que tout le monde s'accordera à considérer comme relevant de la phonologie, comme l'alternance [səku]/[sku] *secoue*, il est nécessaire d'introduire des règles d'effacement dans notre arsenal théorique, il n'y a aucune raison qui nous empêche d'en tirer parti pour rendre compte des alternances entre forme longue et forme courte. Du coup, seules relèvent encore de la morphologie des suppléances vraies comme ***all-ez/ir-ez***, les autres morphèmes ayant une représentation phonologique unique confondue avec leur représentation lexicale.

Soit par exemple le syntagme *joli petit trou*, qui a la représentation phonologique /#žoli#pətit#tru#/. Le schwa de *petit* tombe en vertu de VCE, puisqu'il est précédé de la séquence /i#p/, et le /t/ final tombe en vertu de TRONC, puisque c'est une bruissante et qu'il précède une frontière # suivie de la consonne /t/. D'où la représentation phonétique [žoliptitru]. Au contraire dans /#žoli#pətit#ekru#/

---

[26] A savoir: [pti] comme dans [sɔ̃ptine] *son petit nez*; [pəti] comme dans [šakpətine] *chaque petit nez*; [ptit] comme dans [laptitfiy] *la petite fille*; [pətit] comme dans [šakpətitfiy] *chaque petite fille*.

(*joli petit écrou*) la règle TRONC ne peut pas effacer le /t/ final de *petit*, puisqu'il se trouve devant une frontière qui n'est suivie ni d'une consonne ni d'une pause. Ce /t/ se maintient donc,[27] d'où finalement la représentation phonétique [žoliptitekru]. Enfin dans / # la # pətit + ə # ru # / (*la petite roue*) la règle TRONC ne peut pas effacer le /t/ final, puisqu'il est séparé de la frontière # par la voyelle /ə/. La règle VCE efface comme précédemment le schwa de la première syllabe de *petite*, et la règle EFIN efface le schwa final, d'où la représentation [laptitru], où la séquence [ptitru] est identique à celle dérivée plus haut pour *petit trou*.

Considérons enfin un adjectif "invariable" comme *lisse*, qui se prononce toujours [lis]. Si sa représentation lexicale était /lis/, le /s/ tomberait au masculin et on aurait l'alternance [li] / [lis] parallèle à *las* [la] / *lasse* [las]. Il faut plutôt lui attribuer la représentation lexicale /lisə/, avec un schwa final qui fait partie intégrante du thème. Au niveau PHONOLOGIQUE, *lisse* a donc la structure /CVCV/, et son /s/ n'a pas plus de raison de tomber que celui de *lassé* [lase] (de /las + e/). Ainsi toutes les unités dont la représentation phonétique se termine par une bruissante "ferme" (i.e. qui ne tombe jamais) sont-elles terminées par un schwa au niveau phonologique;[28] comparez /bardə/ (*barde*) et /bavard/ (*bavard/bavarde*), /muatə/ (*moite*) et /druat/ (*droit/droite*), /bãdə/[29] (*bande*) et /grãd/ (*grand/grande*). Comme les autres, ces adjectifs prennent la désinence /ə/ au féminin. *Lisse* a donc la forme masculine / # lisə # / et la forme féminine / # lisə + ə # /.

La discussion qui précède suggère que les règles phonologiques comme TRONC, EFIN et VCE peuvent être considérées de deux façons. On peut d'une part les envisager comme des ASSERTIONS qui établissent une relation entre les propriétés des représentations phonologiques et les propriétés des représentations phonétiques correspondantes: "tout énoncé dont la représentation phonologique possède la propriété P a une représentation phonétique qui possède la propriété Q." Par exemple la règle VCE affirme que tout énoncé dont la représentation phonologique présente une occurrence de /ə/ précédée d'une séquence /V # C/ a une représentation phonétique où ne figure, à la place correspondante, aucun son.

On peut d'autre part considérer une règle phonologique comme un ensemble d'instructions qui indiquent comment effectuer une certaine OPÉRATION. Cette opération produit, à partir de toute représentation (input) qui est soumise à la règle, une autre représentation (output) obtenue en y effectuant certaines modifications: "à toute représentation phonologique W qui a la propriété P correspond une représentation phonétique W' obtenue en modifiant W de telle et telle façon." Dans le cas de VCE, la propriété P est l'existence d'un /ə/ précédé d'une séquence /V # C/, et la transformation à effectuer, l'effacement de ce /ə/. Bref, la règle VCE est une opération qui associe à tout input de la forme /XV # C∂Y/, où X et Y représentent

---

[27] Rappelons que notre analyse s'inspire directement, en la simplifiant pour la commodité de l'exposition, de celle de Schane (1967b; 1968a). Dans cette analyse la liaison résulte simplement du maintien de la consonne finale devant la voyelle initiale du mot suivant. Nous avons montré dans Dell (1970, pp. 65–72) que ce maintien résulte en fait d'une permutation avec la frontière de mot qui suit, et que la règle de troncation doit être formulée différemment. Mais ces différences ne sont pas pertinentes ici.

[28] Il faut faire exception pour certaines unités comme *sept*. Si *sept* avait la représentation /sɛtə/, on s'attendrait à ce que le schwa final soit maintenu devant un *h* aspiré. Or *sept housses* se prononce [sɛtus] ou [sɛtʔus], mais pas *[sɛtəus], qui est la prononciation de *cette housse*. Force est donc d'admettre que certaines bruissantes sont des exceptions à la règle TRONC. Reste à distinguer en général entre les bruissantes qui ne tombent pas parce que protégées par un schwa final et celles qui font exception à la règle TRONC. Pour un début de discussion cf. Schane (1967b, pp. 46–49; 1968a, pp. 8–9) et Dell (1970, pp. 59–64).

[29] Sur la représentation phonologique des voyelles nasales, cf. section 4.5.

des séquences quelconques, la séquence (output) obtenue en y effaçant /ə/, soit [*XVCY*]. Par exemple la représentation /#žoli#məlɔ̃#/ est de la forme /*XV*#C*ə**Y*/ avec *X* = /#žol/, *V* = /i/, *C* = /m/ et *Y* = /lɔ̃#/, et la règle VCE lui associe la représentation [žolimlɔ̃].[30] D'un phonème comme le schwa de *melon* dans *joli melon*, qui répond aux conditions requises pour pouvoir être affecté par VCE, nous dirons qu'il est DU RESSORT DE la règle VCE. Le /i/ de *joli* et le /m/ de *melon* ne sont pas du ressort de VCE. Dans le passage de l'input à l'output, une règle n'affecte que les phonèmes qui sont de son ressort. Aux autres phonèmes, ceux qui ne sont pas de son ressort et qu'elle laisse intacts, nous dirons qu'elle s'applique "trivialement."

Dans les cas où une séquence input W n'a en aucun point la propriété P requise pour être modifiée par une règle, plutôt que de dire que la règle ne s'applique pas, il est commode de considérer qu'elle s'applique "trivialement" à W sans lui faire subir aucune modification, associant à l'input W l'output identique W. Ainsi la séquence /#kɛl#məlɔ̃#/ (*quel melon*) ne contient aucun phonème qui soit du ressort de VCE, puisque le seul schwa qu'il contienne est précédé d'une séquence /C#C/. VCE s'applique donc trivialement à cette représentation phonologique, lui associant la représentation phonétique [kɛlmәlɔ̃].

L'opération par laquelle on dérive la représentation phonétique correspondant à une représentation phonologique donnée est à proprement parler la composition simultanée, en chaque point de l'input, des applications (triviales ou non) de toutes les règles phonologiques à la fois. Chaque règle modifie les phonèmes qui sont de son ressort et laisse les autres intacts. Soit par exemple à obtenir la représentation phonétique (24) à partir de la représentation phonologique (23) (*la petite brise*):

(23) /#la#pətit+ə#brizə#/
(24) [laptitbriz]

On examine (23) du point de vue de chacune des règles phonologiques pour y repérer les phonèmes qui sont de son ressort, puis on effectue les modifications correspondantes. La représentation (23) ne contenant aucun phonème qui soit du ressort de TRONC, cette règle s'applique trivialement partout. VCE s'applique trivialement partout, sauf au schwa de *petite*, qu'elle efface. Enfin EFIN efface les schwas finaux de *petite* et *brise* et s'applique trivialement partout ailleurs. D'où (24). Il va de soi que nous avons présenté les choses de façon très schématique. Il y a une règle qui stipule que le [i] de *brise* est plus long que celui de *petite*, une autre qui a pour effet de voiser légèrement le [t] final de *petite* sous l'influence du [b] de *brise*, etc., de sorte qu'en pratique il n'existe pas de phonème des représentations phonologiques qui ne soit pas affecté par une règle ou une autre dans le passage aux représentations phonétiques.

4.4. Pour mener notre analyse jusqu'à son terme, nous avons procédé en deux grandes étapes. Dans un premier temps (section 3), nous avons examiné les propriétés du contexte qui gouvernent l'alternance entre la forme longue et la forme courte, considérées comme des variantes contextuelles (allomorphes) d'un même morphème. Nous avons montré que si on postulait un schwa sous-jacent à la fin des adjectifs féminins, tous les cas d'alternance se ramenaient à un principe P unique dans la formulation duquel n'entrent que les notions de voyelle, de consonne, et de frontière de mot ou de morphème (cf. règles (12)–(13)). Bref, nous avons montré que les facteurs qui déterminent l'apparition de l'un ou l'autre allomorphe sont typiquement de

---

[30] Nous supposons l'existence d'un dispositif qui efface automatiquement toutes les frontières de mot et de morphème lorsqu'on passe aux représentations phonétiques.

ceux que les phonologues font entrer en ligne de compte lorsqu'ils s'attachent à décrire les propriétés du contexte qui conditionnent la distribution des variantes contextuelles d'un PHONÈME.

Dans un deuxième temps (section 4) notre attention a quitté les faits de contexte pour se porter sur la relation formelle qu'entretiennent entre eux les allomorphes d'une même unité, et nous avons fait la constatation C: on obtient un allomorphe en amputant l'autre de sa consonne bruissante finale, s'il en a une. Pour pouvoir faire cette constatation, il n'était pas nécessaire d'avoir tiré les mêmes conclusions que nous (i.e. le principe P) des faits de contexte examinés au cours de l'étape précédente. Mais seule l'acceptation du principe P et de l'analyse de schwa qu'il implique permet de donner à C sa véritable signification, et de voir que l'alternance entre forme longue et forme courte est la manifestation d'un processus phonologique de troncation qui affecte les bruissantes finales (règle TRONC). Car si on ne voit pas que les adjectifs féminins se distinguent des adjectifs masculins par la présence d'une voyelle finale, à l'action de quel facteur PHONIQUE peut-on attribuer la chute de la consonne latente dans ceux-ci et son maintien dans ceux-là? Voyez par exemple ce qu'en disent Blanche-Benvéniste et Chervel (1969, p. 131), qui ne reconnaissent pas l'existence d'un schwa final au féminin:[31]

> Dans *un petit enfant*, on a un enchaînement sur la syllabe /tã/. Dans *un petit garçon*, le *g* initial interdit l'enchaînement, mais entraîne de plus la disparition du /t/. On a donc pour un même mot *petit* deux formes alternantes en distribution complémentaire /pti/ et /ptit/; la forme brève apparaît devant consonne. ... L'existence pour un même mot d'une forme longue et d'une forme courte est un fait de morphologie. ... On a appelé "consonne latente" la consonne propre à la forme longue. L'expression est équivoque: elle suggère que dans *le* /pti/ *garçon*, le mot /pti/ se termine par un /t/ qui est présent quoique caché. C'est admettre que le /t/ est sous-entendu et que des raisons d'ordre phonétique l'empêchent d'apparaître. Rien n'est plus faux, puisque le /t/ précède le /g/ dans: *la* /ptit/ *garce*. En fait la forme masculine de *petit* est soumise à une variation morphologique. L'écriture a généralisé la forme longue, ce qui est sans doute à l'origine de la notion de "consonne latente."

L'absence de réalisation phonétique directe n'est sans doute pas la seule raison qui explique la répugnance instinctive de nombreux linguistes à admettre la présence de schwas finaux. Il faut aussi tenir compte du fait que les formes comme *petite* se conduisent, au regard de certains processus phonologiques, comme si elles se terminaient par une consonne. Si on exige que les traits du contexte qui conditionnent les variantes combinatoires d'un phonème soient toujours définissables au niveau des représentations phonologiques, *petite* devrait toujours avoir sur les phonèmes du mot suivant le même effet qu'un mot à finale vocalique comme *joli*.

Examinons par exemple le syntagme *la petite mesure*, dont la représentation phonologique et la représentation phonétique sont données en (25) et (26):

(25) /#la#pətit+ə#məzür#/

(26) [laptitməzür]

Le schwa initial de *petite* est effacé par la règle VCE, puisqu'il est précédé d'une séquence /V#C/. Par contre on constate que celui de *mesure* se maintient nécessairement. On ne peut pas dire *[laptitmzür]. S'il ne peut pas tomber, c'est qu'il est précédé de deux consonnes à la file *t* et *m*, comme le suggère la représentation phonétique (26), et que dans ce contexte il n'est pas du ressort de VCE. Mais à ne considérer

---

[31] Cf. pp. 139, 180. *Un petit enfant, un petit garçon* et *la petite garce* se prononcent respectivement [ɛ̃ptitãfã], [ɛ̃ptigarsõ] et [laptitgars].

que la représentation phonologique (25), VCE devrait pouvoir effacer le schwa de *mesure* de la même façon qu'elle efface celui de *petite*, puisque ce schwa y est précédé de la séquence /ə # m/. Ainsi, pour expliquer que le schwa de *mesure* n'est pas susceptible d'être effacé par VCE, il faut tenir compte du fait que EFIN efface de son côté le schwa final de *petite*. Mais cette information ne figure pas dans la représentation phonologique (25). Bref, il semble que pour appliquer une règle à une représentation phonologique donnée, il faille parfois faire entrer en ligne compte, outre la forme de cette représentation, les autres règles qui sont susceptibles de s'y appliquer (de façon non triviale).

Un autre fait vient d'ailleurs renforcer notre conviction que le maintien du schwa de *mesure* est dû à la présence de l'amas de deux consonnes que EFIN crée en effaçant le schwa final de *petite*. C'est que le schwa de *mesure* tombe normalement dans / # žoli + ə # məzür # / (*jolie mesure*), qui se prononce [žolimzür]. Dans ce cas, l'effacement du schwa final de *jolie* ne crée pas d'amas de consonnes devant le schwa de *mesure*, et VCE peut prendre effet normalement.

Si nous tenons absolument à ce que les propriétés du contexte qui sont responsables du maintien du schwa de *mesure* dans (25) (i.e. les propriétés qui font que ce schwa n'est pas du ressort de VCE) soient manifestes dans la représentation phonologique, il n'y a que deux solutions.

Nous pouvons conserver la représentation phonologique (25) telle qu'elle est, et reformuler la règle VCE comme suit :

(27) /ə/ tombe lorsqu'il est précédé d'une séquence /V # C/, SAUF dans les cas où il est précédé de /C + ə # C/

Avec la formulation (27) le schwa de *mesure* est du ressort de VCE dans *jolie mesure* mais pas dans *petite mesure*, et on peut en conséquence dériver les représentations phonétiques cherchées. Mais cette analyse traite comme pure coïncidence le fait que la restriction apportée à VCE vise très précisément les mêmes voyelles qui sont de toutes façons effacées par EFIN, et dont la disparition crée un amas de consonnes.

L'autre solution consiste à supprimer purement et simplement le problème en décidant qu'il n'y a pas de voyelle finale dans la représentation phonologique de *petite*, qui se termine par une consonne. Il reste alors à proposer une analyse de rechange qui rende compte aussi naturellement que la nôtre de tous les faits examinés jusqu'ici.

Pour sortir du dilemme, il faut abandonner l'idée que les règles phonologiques appliquent DIRECTEMENT les représentations phonologiques sur les représentations phonétiques, et introduire des niveaux de représentation intermédiaires. En général, une règle n'opère pas sur des représentations phonologiques, mais sur des représentations qui en dérivent par application d'autres règles. Ainsi, on soumettra à la règle VCE, non pas la représentation phonologique (25), mais la représentation (28) qui est dérivée de (25) en y effaçant tous les schwas qui sont du ressort de la règle EFIN :

(28) / # la # pətit # məzür # /

Dans (28) le schwa initial de *petite* est encore dans un contexte qui lui permet d'être effacé par VCE, mais plus celui de *mesure*. En appliquant la règle VCE à une représentation phonologique préalablement modifiée par application de EFIN, nous exprimons le fait que, *quoique terminé par une voyelle au niveau phonologique, le mot* petite *doit être considéré comme terminé par une consonne du point de vue de la règle VCE, et que ceci est dû à l'action de la règle EFIN.* On dit que l'application de la règle EFIN PRÉCÈDE celle de la règle VCE. Le mot "précéder" indique ici une priorité d'ordre logique, non d'ordre chronologique.[32] En appliquant une règle *A* avant une règle *B*, nous utilisons simplement un dispositif qui a exactement les propriétés formelles requises pour refléter le fait que la règle *B* doit prendre en considération des facteurs qui dépendent de l'action de la règle *A*.

On se convaincra aisément que EFIN et VCE ne sont pas les seules règles qui doivent s'appliquer dans un certain ordre. Prenons par exemple le cas du syntagme *gros melon*, dont la représentation phonologique est donnée en (29), et la représentation phonétique en (30):

(29) /♯gros♯məlɔ̃♯/
(30) [gromlɔ̃]

La représentation (30) montre que le schwa de *melon* peut tomber, quoique dans (29) il ne soit pas du ressort de VCE, puisque précédé d'une séquence /C♯C/. En fait on constate que schwa peut tomber chaque fois qu'il est précédé d'une séquence /C♯C/ dont la première consonne est du ressort de TRONC. S'il ne peut pas tomber dans *quel melon* [kɛlmələɔ̃] ou dans *sept melons* [sɛtmələɔ̃], c'est que la consonne finale du mot précédent n'est pas du ressort de TRONC. Dans le premier cas c'est une liquide, et dans le second c'est une bruissante, mais qui fait exception à TRONC (cf. note 28). Bref, quoique terminé par une consonne dans la représentation phonologique, *gros* doit être considéré comme terminé par une voyelle du point de vue de la règle VCE, et ceci est dû à l'action de la règle TRONC qui efface le /s/ final. On soumettra donc à la règle VCE, non pas la représentation phonologique (29), mais la représentation qui en dérive par application de TRONC, soit /♯gro♯məlɔ̃♯/.

L'introduction d'un ordre dans l'application des règles nous oblige à remanier considérablement l'organisation de la grammaire que nous avons esquissée à la fin de la section 4.3. Pour associer à une certaine représentation phonologique la représentation phonétique correspondante, on applique successivement les diverses règles selon un ordre fixé à l'avance, chaque règle s'appliquant à l'output de la règle précédente, et produisant un output qui est soumis à la règle suivante. Dans le cas qui nous occupe, les règles phonologiques doivent s'appliquer dans l'ordre suivant: TRONC, EFIN, VCE.[33] Nous donnons en (31) la séquence des opérations qui associent aux représentations (25) et (29) les représentations phonétiques correspondantes (26) et (30). Dans la ligne correspondant à chaque règle figurent les représentations qui sont l'output de cette règle.[33]

(31) /♯la♯pətit+ə♯məzür♯/   /♯gros♯məlɔ̃♯/
      /♯la♯pətit+ə♯məzür♯/   /♯gro♯məlɔ̃♯/   TRONC
      /♯la♯pətit♯məzür♯/   /♯gro♯məlɔ̃♯/   EFIN
      /♯la♯ptit♯məzür♯/   /♯gro♯mlɔ̃♯/   VCE
      [laptitməzür]   [gromlɔ̃]

---

[32] L'application des règles dans un certain ordre reflète la structure synchronique d'un état de langue donné, et cet ordre est en droit indépendant de la succession des changements phonétiques qui ont amené à l'état de langue en question. Sur la relation entre l'ordre (synchronique) des règles et la chronologie relative des changements phonétiques, cf. Halle (1962) et Kiparsky (1967).

[33] Si EFIN s'appliquait avant TRONC, les schwas finaux seraient impuissants à protéger une bruissante précédente de la troncation, puisqu'ils auraient disparu dans les représentations produites par EFIN et soumises à TRONC: /♯plat+ə♯/ (*plate*) aurait la représentation [pla], comme /♯plat♯/ (*plat*).

La séquence ordonnée des règles qui permettent de passer des représentations phonologiques aux représentations phonétiques constitue ce qu'on appelle la composante phonologique de la grammaire. Les règles présentées ici ne constituent qu'un petit fragment de la composante phonologique du français. Schane (1968a) et Dell (1970) ont examiné d'autres règles de cette composante, et montré que certaines doivent s'appliquer avant TRONC. Les représentations qui figurent dans la première ligne de la table (31) ne sont donc pas à proprement parler des représentations phonologiques, mais des représentations intermédiaires qui sont le produit de règles dont l'application précède celle de TRONC.

L'introduction de niveaux de représentation intermédiaires entre le niveau des représentations phonologiques et celui des représentations phonétiques n'est pas le résultat d'une décision a priori. Ce n'est qu'un corollaire de notre décision d'appliquer les règles dans un certain ordre. Dans la théorie esquissée à la fin de la section 4.3 toutes les règles phonologiques étaient de la forme: "à tel phonème, situé dans tel contexte dans la représentation phonologique, correspond tel son dans la représentation phonétique." C'est-à-dire qu'il n'y avait que deux niveaux de représentation: celui de l'input des règles (représentations phonologiques) et celui de leur output (représentations phonétiques), toutes les règles s'appliquant en même temps aux représentations phonologiques. Mais nous avons vu quelles complications il fallait apporter à la formulation des règles pour pouvoir les appliquer toutes en même temps. Nous avons par exemple vu que si on veut que la règle VCE fasse passer directement de la première ligne de la table (31) à la dernière ligne, il faut en donner la formulation (32):

(32) /ə/ tombe lorsqu'il est précédé d'une séquence /V ♯ C/ sauf dans les cas où il est précédé de /C + ə ♯ C/; il tombe aussi lorsqu'il est précédé d'une séquence /B ♯ C/ sauf si la bruissante B est marquée comme une exception à la règle TRONC

Si on veut conserver à la règle VCE toute la généralité de la formulation (21), et qu'on admette (explicitement ou implicitement) un schéma théorique où chaque règle relie directement les représentations phonétiques aux représentations phonologiques, on est tout naturellement amené à se donner comme représentations phonologiques des représentations où *petite* se termine par une consonne (comme *seul*), et où *petit* se termine par une voyelle (comme *joli*). Ce niveau de représentation correspond à la troisième ligne de la table (31), et est en gros celui adopté par les phonologues structuralistes. Notre objet a été de montrer que rien en fait ne justifiait cette persistance à fixer la frontière entre phonologie et morphologie si près du niveau phonétique, car les règles qui permettent de passer de la première ligne à la troisième ligne ne sont pas différentes dans leur principe de celles qui font passer de la troisième ligne à la dernière ligne.

4.5. Le comportement des nasales nous semble corroborer notre analyse de façon particulièrement frappante.[34] Nous avons jusqu'ici laissé de côté le problème posé par les unités dont la forme LONGUE se termine par une consonne nasale, comme *plane* [plan] / *plan* [plã], *plafonner* [plafɔne] / *plafond* [plafɔ̃], *baigner* [bɛɲe] / *bain* [bɛ̃]. Ici la chute de la consonne finale s'accompagne toujours de la nasalisation de la voyelle précédente. Dans la logique de l'analyse que nous prônons, le féminin *plane* a

---

[34] Certains des arguments développés dans la section 4.5 sont repris de Dell (1970, pp. 56–59). Nous laisserons de côté le comportement des nasales dans la liaison, qui a été discuté en détail dans Dell (à paraître).

la représentation phonologique /#plan+ə#/, de laquelle on dérive sans difficulté la représentation phonétique [plan] en appliquant la règle EFIN. Le masculin *plan* doit avoir une représentation phonologique qui ne diffère de celle de *plane* que par l'absence de la désinence du féminin (cf. règle (11b)), soit /#plan#/. Pour en dériver la représentation phonétique [plã], il est nécessaire, non seulement d'effacer le /n/ final,[35] mais aussi de postuler l'existence d'une règle qui nasalise toute voyelle précédant une consonne nasale située en fin de mot:

(33) NASAL: Toute voyelle précédant une séquence /N#/ se nasalise

La présence d'un schwa final dans la représentation /#plan+ə#/ sous-jacente à [plan] (*plane*) se manifeste donc de deux façons: elle empêche le /n/ de tomber, puisqu'elle en fait une consonne intervocalique, et elle empêche le /a/ précédent d'être du ressort de NASAL. Le schwa du féminin a, quoiqu'il n'ait pas de manifestation phonétique directe, exactement le même effet que la voyelle /e/ dans /#plafɔn+e#/ (*plafonner* [plafɔne]), par opposition à /#plafɔn#/ *plafond* [plafɔ̃].

La règle NASAL nous permet de ramener les alternances [plan] / [plã] et [plat] / [pla] (*plate/plat*) à la formule unique /A+ə/~/A/, c'est-à-dire qu'elle nous permet de conserver à la règle (11b) toute sa généralité. Elle nous permet d'autre part d'expliquer pourquoi il n'existe pas et ne saurait exister d'adjectif qui ait la forme féminine [plan] et la forme masculine [pla], parallèlement à [plat] / [pla]. Cette règle garantit en effet qu'une consonne nasale finale caractéristique d'une forme longue ne peut tomber sans nasaliser préalablement la voyelle précédente. Dans une analyse où on obtient les formes longues à partir des formes courtes en leur ajoutant une consonne finale, il faudrait une clause qui stipule que seules les formes courtes terminées par une voyelle nasale peuvent recevoir une consonne nasale. Cette clause permettrait des représentations lexicales comme (/plã/, /n/), mais interdirait celles comme (/pla/, /n/). Afin de permettre la dérivation de la représentation phonétique [plan] à partir de la représentation phonologique obtenue en ajoutant /n/ à la droite de /plã/, il faudrait d'autre part une règle (34), qui est en quelque sorte l'image inverse de la règle NASAL:

(34) L'adjonction d'une consonne latente nasale à une forme courte entraîne la dénasalisation de la voyelle finale de cette forme courte

Tandis que NASAL décrit un phénomène d'assimilation qui est abondamment attesté dans les langues du monde, les cas de dissimilation semblables à (34) sont à tout le moins rarissimes.

Une analyse fondée sur la théorie de l'augment se heurte d'autre part à des difficultés dues à ce que l'application de NASAL a pour corollaire des ajustements de timbre qui entraînent certaines neutralisations. Par exemple [i] a pour contrepartie nasale, non pas [ĩ], mais [ɛ̃]: *fine* [fin] / *fin* [fɛ̃], *latine* [latin] / *latin* [latɛ̃], *câline* [kalin] / *calin* [kalɛ̃]. La grammaire doit donc contenir la règle (35):[36]

(35) La voyelle /ĩ/ (obtenue par application de NASAL à /i/) se réalise phonétiquement comme [ɛ̃]

---

[35] Il n'est pas nécessaire de remanier la règle TRONC de façon à lui permettre d'effacer les consonnes nasales (qui ne sont pas des bruissantes). Nous verrons en effet que la chute des consonnes nasales est imputable à une règle qui n'opère pas seulement en fin de mot, mais derrière toutes les voyelles nasales, quelle que soit leur position dans le mot (règle (37)).

[36] Sur le détail des ajustements de timbre après nasalisation, cf. Schane (1968a, pp. 45–50).

Or [ɛ̃] est par ailleurs la contrepartie nasale de [ɛ]: *saine* [sɛn] / *sain* [sɛ̃], *pleine* [plɛn] / *plein* [plɛ̃], *moyenne* [mwayɛn] / *moyen* [mwayɛ̃]. Etant donné le timbre de la voyelle non nasale qui figure dans une forme longue, on peut toujours prédire le timbre de la voyelle nasale de la forme courte correspondante, MAIS PAS INVERSEMENT: à une même voyelle nasale peuvent correspondre dans les formes longues plusieurs voyelles non nasales. Ainsi [i] a toujours la contrepartie nasale [ɛ̃]. Mais à [ɛ̃] correspond dans certains cas [i] (*fin/fine*), dans d'autres [ɛ] (*sain/saine*), dans d'autres encore [ü] *un* [ɛ̃] / *une* [ün]). Si la représentation lexicale de *fin* est la paire (/fɛ̃/, /n/), et celle de *sain* la paire (/sɛ̃/, /n/),[37] aucune différence formelle entre les deux représentations n'indique que le résultat de la dénasalisation de /ɛ̃/ doit être [i] dans la première forme et [ɛ] dans la seconde. Ainsi le cas des formes à nasale finale montre qu'il ne suffit pas toujours de connaître la forme courte M et la consonne latente K pour pouvoir prédire exhaustivement la forme longue. Il faut aussi connaître la voyelle qui, dans la forme longue, correspond à la voyelle finale de M. Il faudrait donc répartir les représentations lexicales en deux types formels distincts, selon que la consonne latente est nasale ou non.

Notre analyse évite toutes ces complications. *Sain* y a la représentation lexicale /sɛn/ et *fin* la représentation /fin/. Les formes féminines [sɛn] et [fin] dérivent des représentations phonologiques /#sɛn+ə#/ et /#fin+ə#/ par application de EFIN. Les formes masculines [sɛ̃] et [fɛ̃] dérivent de /#sɛn#/ et /#fin#/ par application de NASAL (et de (35) dans le cas de *fin*), et par effacement du /n/ final.

En écrivant la règle NASAL, nous affirmons que CERTAINES voyelles nasales dérivent de séquences phonématiques /VN/: celles qui alternent en fin de mot avec [vN] dans les représentations phonétiques. Mais que dire de celles qui n'entrent pas dans de telles alternances, par exemple celles de *hareng* [arã], *selon* [səlɔ̃], *lent* [lã] / *lente* [lãt], *blond* [blɔ̃] / *blonde* [blɔ̃d]? Rien ne laissant jamais supposer la présence d'une consonne nasale, nous n'avons à première vue aucune raison de ne pas les faire dériver d'authentiques phonèmes /ã/ et /ɔ̃/. Dans cette perspective [marɔ̃] dérive de /#marɔ̃+ə#/ dans *une jupe marron* et de /#marɔ̃#/ dans *un chapeau marron*, tout comme [blö] dérive de /#blö+ə#/ dans *une jupe bleue* et de /#blö#/ dans *un chapeau bleu*. Il est curieux de constater à quel point les adjectifs "invariables" terminés par une voyelle nasale sont rares, tandis que ceux terminés par une voyelle non nasale sont monnaie courante (cf. (1a)).

Supposons au contraire que l'inventaire des phonèmes qui apparaissent dans les représentations lexicales ne comprend que des voyelles non nasales, et que TOUTES les voyelles nasales qui apparaissent au niveau phonétique dérivent de séquences phonématiques /VN/ (Schane (1968a, pp. 142–143, note 37)). Les séquences /VN/ se réalisent comme [ṽ] non seulement devant une frontière de mot, mais aussi devant une consonne. La formulation de NASAL donnée en (33) laisse place à la formulation plus générale (36). La règle (37) rend compte de la chute des consonnes nasales après nasalisation de la voyelle précédente:

(36) NASAL: Toute voyelle précédant une séquence /N#/ ou /NC/ se nasalise
(37)   Une consonne nasale tombe lorsqu'elle est précédée d'une voyelle nasale

La représentation phonologique de *lent* est /#lant#/, où /a/ se nasalise en vertu de NASAL, d'où la représentation intermédiaire /#lãnt#/. Le /n/ tombe ensuite en vertu de (37), d'où /#lãt#/. Le /t/ tombe en vertu de TRONC, d'où finalement la représentation phonétique [lã]. Tout amas [NC] qui apparaît dans une représentation

---

[37] Par opposition à celle de *saint* [sɛ̃] / *sainte* [sɛ̃t], qui serait (/sɛ̃/, /t/).

phonétique dérive d'une séquence /NəC/. Car si la consonne nasale avait été au contact de la consonne suivante dès le niveau phonologique, elle serait tombée après avoir nasalisé la voyelle précédente. Ainsi la représentation lexicale de *canneton* [kãtɔ̃] est /kanətɔn/, tandis que celle de *canton* [kãtɔ̃] est /kantɔn/.

Comme les adjectifs prennent normalement la désinence /ə/ au féminin, il ne saurait y avoir de formes féminines terminées phonétiquement par une voyelle nasale, puisque toute voyelle nasale dérive d'une séquence /VN/, et que /VN/ ne peut pas se réaliser comme [ṽ] lorsqu'une voyelle suit. La représentation phonologique de *marron* doit être /#marɔn#/ dans *une jupe marron* aussi bien que dans *un chapeau marron*. Si *bleu* et *marron* sont des adjectifs "invariables," ce n'est pas pour les mêmes raisons. *Bleu* est invariable parce que les règles phonologiques associent la même représentation phonétique [blö] aux représentations phonologiques /#blö+ə#/ et /#blö#/. *Marron* est invariable parce qu'étant une exception à la règle (11b), il ne prend pas la désinence /ə/ au féminin et a en conséquence la même représentation phonologique /#marɔn#/ aux deux genres. L'invariabilité de *bleu* n'est que le résultat du fonctionnement normal des règles morphologiques et phonologiques. Celle de *marron* témoigne d'un comportement aberrant du point de vue morphologique.[38]

L'impossibilité d'avoir des adjectifs qui soient régulièrement soumis à la règle morphologique (11b) et dont la représentation phonétique se termine par une voyelle nasale au féminin doit être rapprochée du fait général suivant : au niveau phonétique, le français n'admet pas à l'intérieur d'un mot de séquence de deux voyelles dont la première soit nasale. Il existe des séquences comme [ea] (*béat* [bea]), [eã] (*séance* [seãs]), mais il n'existe pas et ne saurait exister de séquence *[ẽa] ou *[ẽã]. En effet, si à l'intérieur d'un mot toute voyelle nasale [ṽ] dérive d'une séquence /VN/ située devant une consonne, une séquence [ṽV] ne saurait dériver que d'une séquence /VNCV/ où C est tombée après nasalisation de la première voyelle et chute de N. Or il n'existe en français qu'une seule consonne qui puisse tomber entre deux voyelles, *h* aspiré, qui n'apparaît que très rarement au milieu d'un mot. En dehors de ce cas, illustré par le seul exemple de *enhardir* [ãardir], les mots français ne comportent pas de séquence [ṽV].

5. CONCLUSION

Pour conclure, une remarque qui nous ramène à notre point de départ. Comme le fait remarquer Schane (1967b, p. 58; 1968a, pp. 16–17), les graphies traditionnelles sont très proches de nos représentations phonologiques en ce qui concerne le traitement des consonnes latentes et des schwas finaux, beaucoup plus en tout cas que les transcriptions phonologiques prônées par les linguistes structuralistes (cf. note 9). Comme nous n'avons à aucun moment tiré argument des faits de graphie pour étayer notre analyse, cette remarque n'a aucun caractère de nécessité logique, et il s'agit d'une constatation empirique. Elle n'a rien qui doive intriguer si on partage l'opinion communément admise que le principe des écritures alphabétiques est de "coller" phonème par phonème aux représentations phonologiques, et que l'adéquation d'une écriture à la langue qu'elle note se mesure à la constance avec laquelle elle se conforme à ce principe. Encore faut-il se mettre d'accord sur ce qui compte comme une "représentation phonologique" du français. Si à propos de graphies comme *plate*

---

[38] Il n'est pas rare d'entendre des enfants ajouter la désinence /ə/ au féminin et dire **une robe marronne*.

([plat]) et *plat* ([pla]), Blanche-Benvéniste et Chervel (1969, p. 139) s'étonnent de "cette pratique paradoxale qui consiste à écrire une voyelle pour faire prononcer une consonne [... et qui] crée une situation fictive où la consonne est traitée comme si elle se trouvait à l'intervocalique dans le mot, et non à la finale," c'est qu'au terme de leur analyse il y a les représentations phonologiques / ⧣ plat ⧣ / et / ⧣ pla ⧣ /. En généralisant le *t* de la forme longue, ce qui lui permet d'associer à toutes les occurrences du morphème *plat* la séquence graphique invariante P-L-A-T, l'orthographe française aurait selon eux recours à un procédé caractéristique des écritures idéographiques, qui transcrivent toutes les occurrences d'un morphème à l'aide d'une unité graphique unique, sans tenir compte des variations phoniques qui peuvent les séparer. Nous avons au contraire essayé de montrer que les représentations / ⧣ plat ⧣ / et / ⧣ pla ⧣ / n'ont qu'un statut intermédiaire et dérivent de représentations plus abstraites / ⧣ plat + ə ⧣ / et / ⧣ plat ⧣ / par application des règles TRONC et EFIN. L'invariance de la représentation orthographique du morphème *plat* reflète l'invariance de sa représentation phonologique.[39] Les défauts de l'orthographe actuelle ne se comptent pas, mais on est forcé de reconnaître que sur ce point au moins elle offre un reflet fidèle de la réalité linguistique.

RefERENCES

Blanche-Benvéniste, C., and A. Chervel (1969), *L'Orthographe*, Paris: Maspéro.

Chomsky, N. (1964), *Current Issues in Linguistic Theory*, The Hague: Mouton.

Chomsky, N., and M. Halle (1965), "Some controversial questions in phonological theory," *Journal of Linguistics*, 1, 97–138.

Chomsky, N., and M. Halle (1968), *The Sound Pattern of English*, New York: Harper & Row.

De Félice, T. (1950), *Eléments de grammaire morphologique*, Paris: Didier.

Dell, F. (1970), *Les Règles phonologiques tardives et la morphologie dérivationnelle en français*, unpublished Ph.D. dissertation, M.I.T.

Dell, F. (forthcoming), "Two Cases of Exceptional Rule Ordering," in M. Bierwisch, S. Kiefer, and N. Ruwet, eds., *Generative Grammar in Europe*, Dortrecht: Reidel.

Durand, M. (1936), *Le Genre grammatical en français parlé*, Paris: D'Artrey.

Halle, M. (1962), "Phonology in a generative grammar," *Word*, 18, 54–72; reprinted in Schane (1967a) as "Place de la phonologie dans la grammaire générative."

Kiparsky, P. (1967), "A propos de l'histoire de l'accentuation grecque," in Schane (1967a).

Martinet, A. (1960), *Eléments de linguistique générale*, Paris: Armand Colin.

Milner, J.-C. (1967), "French truncation rule," *Quarterly Progress Report of the Research Laboratory of Electronics*, 86, M.I.T., 273–283.

Nyrop, K. (1903), *Grammaire historique de la langue française*, Vol. 1, Copenhagen: Bojesen.

Postal, P. (1968), *Aspects of Phonological Theory*, New York: Harper & Row.

Schane, S., ed. (1967a), *La phonologie générative*, *Langages*, 8, Paris: Didier-Larousse.

Schane, S. (1967b), "L'Élision et la liaison en français," in Schane (1967a).

Schane, S. (1968a), *French Phonology and Morphology*, Cambridge, Mass.: M.I.T. Press.

Schane, S. (1968b), "On the abstract character of the French 'e muet'," *Glossa*, 2, 150–163.

Valdman, A. (1970), "Competing Models of Linguistic Analysis: French Adjective Inflexion," *The French Review*, 43, 606–623.

[39] Notre analyse prédit que les écoliers ne devraient éprouver aucune difficulté particulière à maîtriser les règles orthographiques qui veulent que *plate* se lise [plat] et *plat* [pla], puisque ces règles ont pour contrepartie exacte les règles EFIN et TRONC.

assimilation of phonological strength in germanic

James Foley

Simon Fraser University

1. INTRODUCTION

1.1. Assimilation of Phonological Strength

Assimilation is of two types, (*a*) phonetic, and (*b*) phonological. The phonetic type is well known; an example is Latin *dictus* > Italian *detto*, where *k* assimilates in position to the following dental. The phonological type of assimilation is perceivable only within a theoretical system that includes the concept of relative phonological strength.

There are many types of assimilation which are nonphonetic in nature and must receive a phonological interpretation. In Norwegian, for example, *s* becomes *š* before *l* but not before *n*, as illustrated in (1):

(1) (a) *slem* [šlem] 'bad'
    slå [šlo] 'beat'
    Oslo [ošlo] 'Oslo'

   (b) *snakke* 'talk'
    snø 'snow'
    snar 'quick'

The conversion of *s* to *š* cannot be attributed to phonetic influences since *l* and *n* are both dentals, and in any case conversion of dental *s* to palatal *š* looks more like dissimilation than assimilation. In short, there is no phonetic explanation for the palatalization of *s* before *l* but not before *n*. But there is a phonological explanation: *l* is phonologically stronger than *n*, and *s* is strengthened by proximity to *l* but not by proximity to the relatively weaker *n*; the strengthened *s* then manifests itself as *š*.

Evidence for the relative phonological strength of *l* and *n* comes from observation of phonological phenomena. Note, for example, that the Indo-European cluster *ln* assimilates to *ll* in English and Latin, as illustrated in (2):

(2) IE (LITHUANIAN)   ENGLISH   LATIN
   pílnas   *full*   (*plenus*)
   kálnas   *hill*   *collis*

The direction of assimilation here is worthy of attention. Since *n* is in a stronger (syllable-initial) position, we should expect **funn*, **hinn*, analogous to *dictus* > *detto*. However, since *l* dominates *n* even when *n* is in a stronger position, *l* must be inherently stronger than *n*, in fact strong enough to overcome its weaker position.

By arguments of this nature it is possible to construct a scale of relative phonological strength of phonological elements as in (3), where *t* stands for oral stops, *s* for continuants, *n* for nasals, *l* for liquids, *w* for glides, and *e* for vowels, and where a higher number represents greater relative strength:

(3) t   s   n   l   w   e
   ————————————————————————————→
    1   2   3   4   5   6
   relative phonological strength ρ

As noted with regard to (1), the conversion of Norwegian *s* to *š* before *l* but not before *n* illustrates assimilation of phonological strength: *l* is phonologically stronger than *n*, and this strength is passed on to the preceding *s*, which when strengthened in this case becomes *š*. We have, then, the situation sketched in (4):

(4)   s $\rightarrow$ s$^+$ / ____l   (s$^+$ $\rightarrow$ š)
      BUT
      s $\rightarrow$ *idem* / ____n

Although many languages manifest assimilation of phonological strength, we shall be concerned primarily with Germanic.

1.2. The Situation in Germanic

In Germanic there are several instances of certain phenomena occurring in the vicinity of dentals but not labials or velars. We shall look at three such cases. First, in Anglo-Saxon *z* becomes *r* before dentals, as shown in (5):

(5) GOTHIC   ANGLO-SAXON
   huzd   *hord*   'treasure'
   razda   *reord*   'speech'
   mizdo   *meord*   'reward'

Second, as shown in (6), in the third person singular of German verbs the thematic vowel is elided when preceded by a labial or velar but not when preceded by a dental:

(6) (a) **bebet* > *bebt*
      **saget* > *sagt*
      **folget* > *folgt*

(b) *arbeitet* > idem
wartet > idem
regnet > idem

Third, the Germanic diphthong *au* monophthongizes to *ō* in Germanic when followed by a dental but not when followed by a labial or velar. We illustrate in (7):

(7)   GOTHIC   GERMAN

  (a) *dauþus*   *Tod*
     rauþs   *rot*
     auso   *Ohr*
     hausjan *hören*

  (b) *augo*   *Auge*
     auk   *auch*
     haubiþ *Haupt*
     hlaupan *laufen*

There is no phonetic explanation for these three phenomena, and we must search for a phonological explanation.

2. THE ESTABLISHMENT OF THE RELATIVE PHONOLOGICAL STRENGTH OF GERMAN OCCLUSIVES

It is first necessary to show that among Germanic occlusives the dentals are the strongest. Evidence comes from (*a*) the High German consonant shift, (*b*) the conversion of final *m* to *n*, and (*c*) the conversion of English *t* to ?.

2.1. The High German Consonant Shift

In the High German consonant shift all dentals shift (8a), some labials (8b), but no velars (8c), illustrating nicely the relative phonological strength of German occlusives:

(8) (a) t → ts   *tooth/Zahn*
      d → t   *door/Tür*

    (b) p → pf   *pipe/Pfeife*
      b → *idem* *bed/Bett*

    (c) k → *idem* *corn/Korn*
      g → *idem* *grave/Grab*

In a strengthening process inherently strong elements are first to strengthen and show the greatest extent of strengthening, just as in a weakening process the weakest elements are first to weaken and show the greatest extent of weakening. Thus, from the patterning of the High German consonant shift, we can establish a scale of relative phonological strength of Germanic occlusives as in (9):

(9) k   p   t
    g   b   d
    ŋ   m   n
    ‾‾‾‾‾‾‾‾‾‾→
    1   2   3
relative phonological strength α

Further evidence for velars being weaker than labials or dentals comes from North German *g* > *γ* (*sagen* > *saγen*), but *b* > idem (*beben*) and *d* > idem (*baden*).

Southern German dialects provide additional evidence for the relative weakness of velars and labials since, according to Prokosch (1916), medial *b* and *g* are dropped, as shown in (10):

(10) *habest* > *hāst*
     gibest > *gīst*
     magister > *Meister*
     meget > *Maid*
     stegil > *steil* (*steigen*)
     Nägelchen > *Nelke*
     laicus > *Laie*

2.2. Auslautsverhärtung

Evidence for relative strength among consonants comes from changes that occur in strong position: if a consonant in strong position changes to another consonant, then we conclude that the second consonant is stronger than the first. Thus in Gothic, where final *m* becomes *n*, as illustrated in (11), we conclude that *n* is stronger than *m*:

(11) LATIN   GOTHIC
     quum   *hvan*
     tum   *þan*

The conversion here is an instance of *Auslautsverhärtung*, or strengthening of a consonant in final position. The usual example is the devoicing of voiced stops sketched in (12):

(12) g,b,d → k,p,t / ____ #

The phonetic devoicing is a manifestation of a phonological change: voiceless stops are phonologically stronger than voiced stops. Note as further evidence that in the High German consonant shift voiceless labials shift (*pepper/Pfeffer*) but voiced labials do not (*bid/bitten*). We therefore have the scale of relative phonological strength in (13):

(13) d   t
     b   p
     g   k
     ‾‾‾‾‾‾→
     1   2
relative phonological strength β

The *Auslautsverhärtung*, following its name, is not essentially devoicing, but rather strengthening, as sketched in (14), with the phonetic manifestations indicated in (15):

(14) $C \rightarrow C^+ /$ ___ #

(15) (a) $d^+, b^+, g^+ \rightarrow t, p, k$ (increase of strength on β scale)
    (b) $m^+ \rightarrow n$ (increase of strength on α scale)

2.3. The Conversion of English *t* to ʔ

When consonants are strengthened, they convert to stronger consonants. If the consonant being strengthened is already the strongest, it cannot manifest itself as a stronger consonant; therefore, it appears instead as the weakest consonant.

In English *t* becomes ʔ in strong position (after a stressed vowel and before a syllabic *l* or *n*), whereas *p* and *k* do not shift in this position. We illustrate in (16):

(16) (a) *fountain*
       mountain
       Latin
       bottle
       kitten
       mitten

    (b) *beckon*
       pickle
       nipple
       weapon

Since *t* becomes ʔ in strong position, this shift must represent a strengthening. Since, however, *t* is already the strongest occlusive and thus cannot manifest itself as a stronger one, it appears as the weakest one on the same scale, that is, the scale shown in (17):

(17) ʔ k p t
$$\xrightarrow{\hspace{3cm}}$$
   1 2 3 4
relative phonological strength α (revised)

The weakest (most unspecified) occlusive is ʔ, just as the weakest (most unspecified) vowel is ə.

We have thus seen in this section that (*a*) the widespread shifting of dentals but not of labials or velars in the Germanic consonant shift, (*b*) the strengthening of *m* to *n* in final position, and (*c*) the strengthening of *t* to t^+ (manifesting itself as ʔ) indicate that in the Germanic languages the dentals are the strongest occlusives.

3. PHONOLOGICAL ASSIMILATION TO STRONG CONSONANTS

The concept of relative phonological strength, in particular the concept of greatest relative phonological strength, provides an explanatory framework for certain nonphonetic assimilatory phenomena of Germanic.

3.1. Anglo-Saxon Strengthening of *z* to *r*

The Anglo-Saxon shifting of *z* to *r* before dentals (*huzd* > *hord*) is here interpreted as the strengthening process (18):

(18) (a) Assimilation of phonological strength
$$z \rightarrow z^+ \ / \ \underline{\qquad} \alpha \ strength \ 4$$

     (b) Phonetic manifestation
$$z^+ \rightarrow r$$

Thus *z* assimilates the strength (just as in Latin *dictus* > Italian *detto*, *k* assimilates the position) of the following strong consonant (which in Germanic is a dental).

There is no phonetic reason for the rhotacism of *z* in this particular environment, but there is a phonological reason within a system of relative phonological strength.

3.2. Elision in Third Person Singular Verb Forms

The vowel *ə* (original thematic *e*) is dropped if preceded by a labial or velar but not if preceded by a dental. The rule is given in (19):

(19) Assimilation of phonological strength
$$ə \rightarrow ə^+ \ / \ \alpha \ strength \ 4\underline{\qquad}$$

The segment *ə* assimilates the strength of the preceding strong consonant. Then *ə*, but not *ə*$^+$, is elided by rule (20):

(20) Elision
$$V_n \rightarrow \phi$$
     where *n* = a sufficiently small value
     here *n* = 1

Thus *ə*, the weakest vowel (with a value of 1), drops, but *ə*$^+$, with a value of 2 (inherent value of 1 plus acquired value of 1), does not. We have, then, derivations like those in (21):

(21) sagət   arbeitət
              arbeitə$^+$t   rule (19)
    sagt   rule (20)
    sagt   *arbeitət*

A parallel situation exists in Latin, where we have the forms in (22):

(22) *sum*   *sumus*
     es   *estis*
     est   *sunt*

The underlying forms for (22) are those in (23):

(23) *səm*   *səmus*
     səs   *sətis*
     sət   *sənt*

And the relevant rules are those in (24) and (25):

(24) Assimilation of ρ strength

    ə → ə$^+$ / ____*nasal*

(25) ə → φ

The results of these rules on the forms in (23) are shown in (26):

(26) *səm > sə$^+$m > sum*
    səs > ss
    sət > st
    səmus > sə$^+$mus > sumus
    sətis > stis
    sənt > sə$^+$nt > sunt

Where *ə* has been deleted, a prosthetic *e* is inserted, giving the forms in (27):

(27) *ss > ess > es*
    st > est
    stis > estis

3.3. Monophthongization of *au* Before Dentals

Within a phonetic system there is no reason for diphthongs to monophthongize before dentals (*dauþus/Tod*) but not before labials or velars (*augo/Auge*). But such a restriction is to be expected within a theoretical system with the concept of assimilation of phonological strength.

The monophthongization occurs in the two stages shown in (28) and (29):

(28) Assimilation of phonological strength

    au → au$^+$ / ____α *strength 4*

(29) Increase of bond strength

    au$^+$ → ō

First the diphthong assumes the strength of the following strong consonant (rule (28)). Then the unit of phonological strength acquired by the diphthong binds the components together more tightly, creating a monophthong (rule (29)).

Monophthongization does not occur contiguous to a relatively weak consonant (labial or dental) since here no prior assimilation of phonological strength has occurred.

4. SUMMARY

Among Germanic occlusives, dentals are strongest, velars weakest. This order is indicated by the widespread shift of dentals but not of velars in the High German consonant shift, the *Auslautsverhärtung* of *m* to *n*, and the strengthening of English *t* to ʔ.

The establishment of dentals as the phonologically strongest occlusives in Germanic provides a principled explanation for the following phenomena occurring under the influence of dentals: (*a*) the strengthening of *z* to *r* in Anglo-Saxon, (*b*) the retention of *ə* after dentals in German third person singular verb forms, and (*c*) the

German monophthongization of *au* to *ō* before dentals. Such phenomena are uninterpretable in a phonetic system but receive a natural interpretation within a theoretical system that includes the concepts of relative phonological strength and assimilation of phonological strength.

References

Foley, J. (1970a), *Systematic Morphophonology*, unpublished monograph.
Foley, J. (1970b), "A systematic phonological interpretation of the Germanic consonant shift," *Language Sciences*, 9.
Foley, J. (1970c), "Phonological distinctive features," *Folia Linguistica, IV*.
Malm, I., and A. Sommerfelt (1959), *Teach Yourself Norwegian*, London: English Universities Press.
Prokosch, E. (1916), *Sounds and History of the German Language*, New York.

on the order
of certain phonological rules
in spanish[1]

James W. Harris
Massachusetts Institute of Technology

1. INTRODUCTION

I will discuss here two sets of exceptional forms in Spanish that bear on the theory of the ordering of phonological rules. It will be argued that the only descriptively adequate account of these forms attributes the exceptionality of each set to the reversal of the normal order of two rules. This sort of phonological description, as is well known, is not permitted by the rule ordering theory that has been one of the cornerstones of generative phonology in the last decade, namely, the theory in Chomsky's "Some general properties of phonological rules" (1967) and Chomsky and Halle's *The Sound Pattern of English* (1968). On the other hand, rule order reversal is permitted by the rather radical revision of ordering theory proposed in Stephen R. Anderson's *West Scandinavian Vowel Systems and the Ordering of Phonological Rules* (1969). But I will argue that Anderson's theory, too, fails to provide the basis for a satisfactory account of the Spanish data.

Stated briefly, the problem presented by this material is that surface uniformity in paradigms, traditionally attributed to the regularizing force of analogy, is not necessarily reflected in the simplicity or naturalness of generative phonological

[1] This paper was written in 1970. Portions of it were read at the 1970 Winter meeting of the Linguistic Society of America under the title "Paradigmatic Regularity and Naturalness of Grammars."

A large part of whatever I know about linguistics, and a lot else, is due to my enormous good fortune in having had Morris Halle as my teacher, friend, and *schatchen*. I gratefully dedicate this study to him.

grammars, under any presently known evaluation metric. The material to be covered here suggests, however, that paradigms are a real part of language, not an artifact of the linguist, and that paradigmatic relationships play a role in the organization of grammars, both synchronically and diachronically, and therefore must be incorporated into linguistic theory.

2. THE VERB CASES

It is an easily observable fact that the same stem-final consonant appears in every form of any given regular verb in Spanish, regardless of the desinential vowel that follows this consonant in phonetic representations. Indeed, this is one of the defining characteristics of "regular" verbs. Consider, for example, the illustrative forms in (1) of the verbs *cocer* 'to cook (especially by boiling)' and *proteger* 'to protect':

(1)   cue[s]o   prote[x]o   (1st pers sg, pres indic)
     co[s]emos   prote[x]emos   (1st pers pl, pres indic)
     co[s]amos   prote[x]amos   (1st pers pl, pres subj)

The stems here are /kok-/ and /proteg-/, respectively, as shown by the nouns *co*[k]*ción* 'cooking' and *prote*[k]*ción* 'protection'. (Stem-final /g/ of the latter form is assimilated in voicing to the following voiceless obstruent by a general rule.) The phonetic representations of the verb forms can be accounted for, in part, by the operation of the rules in (2) and (3):[2]

(2) Velar Softening $\begin{bmatrix} k \\ g \end{bmatrix} \rightarrow \begin{bmatrix} s \\ x \end{bmatrix} / \underline{\hspace{1cm}} \begin{bmatrix} -\text{consonantal} \\ -\text{back} \end{bmatrix}$

(3) Truncation $V \rightarrow \phi / + \underline{\hspace{1cm}} + V$

The operation of these rules is illustrated in the sample derivations in (4) (in which $/+e+/$ is the "theme vowel" of the second conjugation, $/+o+/$ is the marker for first person singular for all conjugations, and $/+a+/$ is the marker for present subjunctive for the second conjugation):

(4)   /proteg+e+o/   /proteg+e+mos/   /proteg+e+a+mos/
       x   x   x   Velar Softening
         φ   φ   Truncation
  prote[x]o   prote[x]emos   prote[x]amos

As can be seen from (4), the presence of the theme vowel, that is, the front vowel *e*, at the level of derivation at which Velar Softening applies accounts for the appearance of the "softened" consonant in all forms of the verb, before back vowels as well as front vowels in phonetic representations.

Consider now the irregular verbs *hacer* 'to do' and *decir* 'to say'. *Hacer* is second conjugation (theme vowel *e*), like *cocer* and *proteger*, and *decir* is third (theme vowel *i*,

---

[2] Several of the rules that appear here have been simplified slightly, with details not immediately relevant having been omitted for the sake of clarity. (Fuller discussion can be found in my *Spanish Phonology* (1969).) Velar Softening, as stated in (2) for illustrative purposes, is actually a summary of the effects of several rules. All that is really relevant to the present argument is the first of these rules, which palatalizes *k* to *č* and *g* to *j* before a front vowel or glide.

In so-called "Castilian" Spanish the result of "softened" /k/ is [θ] rather than [s]. I will ignore this henceforth.

but otherwise like the second). Ignoring vowel alternations and other irrelevant details, let us assume that the underlying representations of the stems are /hak-/ and /dik-/. If these verbs were regular, then we should expect the forms shown in (5):

(5) *ha[s]o   *di[s]o   (1st pers sg, pres indic)
 ha[s]emos   de[s]imos   (1st pers pl, pres indic)
 *ha[s]amos *di[s]amos (1st pers pl, pres subj)

Instead, the actually occurring forms are those in (6):[3]

(6) ha[g]o   di[g]o
 ha[s]emos   de[s]imos
 ha[g]amos   di[g]amos

We may begin to account for the irregular forms *hago, hagamos, digo, digamos* by observing that the grammar of Spanish contains a rule with the effect of (7):

(7) Lenition $k \rightarrow g \ / \ V\_\_\_V$

Thus it is apparent that the *g* of the forms in (6) is simply the "unsoftened" but lenited reflex of underlying *k*. In other words, if the rule of Velar Softening is somehow prevented from applying, then the normal phonological processes of the language produce the correct irregular phonetic shapes. This is illustrated in the partial derivations in (8), where the underlying representations are perfectly regular but where it is assumed that the application of Velar Softening is excluded:

(8) /hak+e+o/   /hak+e+a+mos/   /dik+i+o/   /dik+i+a+mos/
     φ   φ   φ   φ   Truncation
     g   g   g   g   Lenition
   hago   hagamos   digo   digamos

The underlying representations of the regular forms *ha[s]emos* and *de[s]imos* are /hak+e+mos/ and /dik+i+mos/, which have no +V+V sequence to which Truncation can apply. It can be seen, then, that the "unsoftened" consonant *g* appears (in *hago, hagamos, digo, digamos*) in precisely the environment in which Truncation deletes the front theme vowel that would otherwise condition the application of Velar Softening, while "softened" *s* appears (in *ha[s]emos, de[s]imos*) where Truncation does not delete this vowel. In short, the nonapplication of Velar Softening to *hago, hagamos,* etc., is not totally arbitrary and accidental, but is instead directly related to the application of Truncation. This generalization can be expressed readily and naturally by allowing Truncation to apply before Velar Softening, as illustrated in (9):

(9) /hak+e+o/   /hak+e+mos/   /hak+e+a+mos/
     φ   φ   Truncation
     −   s   −   Velar Softening
     g   g   Lenition
   ha[g]o   ha[s]emos   ha[g]amos

[3] Actually, intervocalic *g* is changed to the velar continuant obstruent [ɣ] by a general rule. I will ignore this for typographical convenience.

Hacer and *decir* are irregular in paradigms other than the present indicative and subjunctive. While these additional irregularities present several unresolved problems, they seem to have no direct bearing on the present discussion.

It must now be argued that the account of *hacer* and *decir* just outlined is the descriptively adequate one. Note first of all that it cannot be said that the irregular forms of *hacer* and *decir* are simply idiosyncratic or suppletive: a regularity has been demonstrated. Nor can it be claimed that the stems themselves are regular but the phonetic peculiarities are due to the absence of the front theme vowel in underlying representations, such as */hak + o/, */dik + a + mos/: whatever machinery is invented to generate such representations simply duplicates the work of Truncation and is thus ad hoc. Furthermore, one cannot argue that the stems in question are lexically marked as exceptions to Velar Softening: Velar Softening does apply, in all forms to which Truncation is inapplicable. Finally, to claim that just the forms that do not undergo Velar Softening are somehow marked as exceptions to Velar Softening would be empty (and ad hoc as well, since these forms are identifiable in any event as those to which Truncation is applicable). In short, it is apparently the case that any alternative to the solution suggested here must involve ad hoc additions to the grammar whose only function is to deny that linguistically significant generalizations are expressed by the application of Truncation and Velar Softening in the order (Truncation, Velar Softening) as in (9).

Recall now that the order (Velar Softening, Truncation) is required for regular verbs, as was shown in (4). We might speculate, then, that exceptional *hacer* and *decir* have some sort of lexical requirement that the normal order of the pair of rules in question be reversed.

3. THE STRESS CASES

With the exceptions to which we turn directly, the same vowel is stressed in singular/plural pairs of Spanish nouns and adjectives, as illustrated by the pairs in (10):

(10) *teléfono/teléfonos*   'telephone(s)'
     consonánte/consonántes   'consonant(s)'
     sonído/sonídos   'sound(s)'
     fonológico/fonológicos   'phonological'
     abstrácto/abstráctos   'abstract'
     sonóro/sonóros   'voiced'

In the examples in (10), both members of each pair have the same number of syllables. But, as can be seen from (11), stress appears on the same vowel even in nouns and adjectives whose plural has one syllable more than the singular:

(11) *papél/papéles*   'paper(s)'
     lápiz/lápices   'pencil(s)'
     órden/órdenes   'order(s)'
     débil/débiles   'weak'
     palatál/palatáles   'palatal'

These facts concerning stress placement are among the various consequences of rules (12) and (13), which apply in the order shown:[4]

---

[4] The identity of the vowel diacritic [ˇ] (the opposite value of which will be represented as [ˉ] in a few subsequent examples) is a matter of considerable interest but need not concern us here. For discussion see Harris (1969, pp. 116–122).

(12) Stress $\quad$ V → [1stress] / ___$(C_0(\breve{V}C_0^1)V)C_0 \# \#|_{N,A}$

(13) Apocope $\quad$ e → φ / V $\begin{bmatrix} +\text{coronal} \\ +\text{voice} \end{bmatrix}$ ___$\# \#$

It is easy to see from (14) why Stress and Apocope must apply in that order:

(14) /papēle/ $\qquad\qquad$ /papēle/
$\quad$ papéle $\quad$ Stress $\qquad$ papēl $\quad$ Apocope
$\quad$ *papél* $\quad$ Apocope $\qquad$ **pápel* $\quad$ Stress

The fact that the same vowel is stressed in singular/plural pairs, in the sense illustrated in (10) and (11), is so familiar and unremarkable that it is easy to lose sight of the fact that it is not logically necessary. There are, in fact, five Spanish nouns that behave differently. These are listed in (15):

(15) $\quad$ *carácter/caractéres* $\qquad$ 'character(s)'
$\qquad$ *régimen/regímenes* $\qquad$ 'regime(s)'
$\qquad$ *espécimen/especímenes* $\qquad$ 'specimen(s)'
$\qquad$ *júnior/junióres* $\qquad$ 'junior(s)' (special religious sense)
$\qquad$ *ínterin/intérines* $\qquad$ 'interim(s)'

One might take the position that these five nouns are simply idiosyncratic oddities about which there is nothing of any general interest to be said in a synchronic description of Spanish. This would not be unreasonable given the quite marginal status of these nouns.[5] It is something of an embarrassment to this position, however, that these forms are not in fact totally idiosyncratic. That is, stress is not assigned in an arbitrary fashion, as in, say, **caractér/cáracteres*, **regimen/regimenés*. Rather, in every case, stress is found farther to the right in the plural, the form with an additional syllable on the right. There is thus an intimate connection between the observed "stress shift" and the Apocope Rule, which deletes this extra syllable in all the singular forms.

Note that the phonetic representations of the singular forms in (15) end in the voiced dentals *r* and *n*, members of the class of consonants after which Apocope deletes final *e*. Thus, if the underlying representations of these stems had a final *e*, this *e* would be deleted in the singular forms by the same rule that operates in all other cases in the language in which the plural contains one syllable more than the singular. Strikingly, the connection between the "stress shifts" of (15) and Apocope can be expressed directly by allowing Apocope to apply before Stress, to completely regular underlying representations:

[5] It is easy to feel uncomfortable about the validity of these examples. I share this feeling fully, but can find no rational basis for it. *Júnior* and *interin* (particularly the plural of the latter) are not commonly used, but the first three examples are certainly in the active vocabulary of all educated speakers. It might be objected that these forms are somehow "Latin" rather than Spanish. They are all erudite borrowings from Latin (*júnior* is not borrowed from English), but so is an extremely high percentage of the total lexicon of modern Spanish, as can be seen simply by flipping through the pages of a dictionary. Thus it is not clear in what sense any of the forms of (15) is any more "Latin" than countless other words. Most of them—[rréximen], [espésimen] or Castilian [espéθimen], [xúnior] —differ radically in pronunciation from their respective etyma. More importantly, aside from the "stress shift" at issue, none violates any regularity of Spanish, syntactic, morphological or phonological. This last fact sharply differentiates these examples from obvious Latinisms like *déficit, ad hoc, a fortiori.* Let me stress that *carácter/caractéres*, etc., are certainly peculiar; this is not at issue. What is at issue is what else is to be said.

(16) (a) /caractēre/   /caractēre + s/
         caractēr   Apocope
         carácter   *caractéres*   Stress

     (b) /regĭmĕne/   /regĭmĕne + s/
         regĭmĕn   Apocope
         régimen   *regímenes*   Stress

     (c) /junĭōre/   /junĭōre + s/
         junĭōr   Apocope
         júnior   *junióres*   Stress

Let us see what support can be found for alternative proposals. It might be claimed that the appearance of final-syllable *e* in the plural only is due to mild suppletion, rather than to the operation of Apocope. That is, we would have underlying representations like singular /caracter/, /regimen/ as opposed to plural /caractere + s/, /regimene + s/. This is ad hoc: there is no other case in the language of singular/plural suppletion in nouns and adjectives, not even in learned borrowings like *stigma/ stigmata* in English. (The plural of Spanish *estigma* is *estigmas*.) Thus such ad hoc underlying representations as /caracter/ versus /caractere + s/ are nothing but an otiose restatement at the lexical level of the effect of Apocope, which must be in the grammar in any case.

It might be argued that, unlike the examples in (11), the peculiar cases in (15) have no stem-final *e* in underlying representations of either singular or plural and the final-syllable phonetic *e* of the plurals is due to an epenthesis rule that inserts *e* between voiced dentals and + *s*. But this move would be made at the cost of adding a totally unmotivated rule to the grammar, a rule which must repeat (a more complicated version of) the environment of the Apocope Rule.[6]

Since no Spanish word is stressed farther to the left than the third syllable from the end (there are no words like **régimenes*, **espécimenes*), some hitherto unformulated principle(s) might be proposed whereby stress is first assigned as in **régimenes*, **espécimenes*, for example, and then shifted to *regímenes*, *especímenes*. But this is both inadequate and ad hoc. It is inadequate in that it does not account for the "shift" in *carácter/caractéres*, both of which are stressed on the penultimate syllable. It is ad hoc in that the fact that stress cannot appear more than three syllables from the end of a word is already built into the Stress Rule. The case of *júnior/junióres* is perhaps even more compelling: if the orthographic *i* is syllabic when stress is assigned (which is arguable), then we have, as in no other example, a two-syllable jump. But this is exactly the result predicted by the Stress Rule, as shown in (16). In short, it would be extremely odd and implausible to maintain that some other new and unknown principles of stress assignment are at work in these examples: such principles would have to duplicate exactly the effects of the Stress Rule already in the grammar of Spanish.

There seems to be, then, no factual support for denying that the forms in (15) are stressed by rule (12) or that their underlying representations have final-syllable *e* which is deleted by rule (13) where applicable. Thus it must be the case that the rules Stress and Apocope apply to singular *carácter*, *régimen*, etc., in the order (Apocope,

---

[6] An epenthesis rule of the type mentioned has been proposed in Saltarelli (1970), but for regular cases only. I have argued in Harris (1970) that this proposal is untenable, independently of the examples of (15). Saltarelli mentions these examples only to say that they are "idiosyncrasies."

Stress), as shown in (16). This order is the opposite of that in (14), the order necessary for all other imparisyllabic nouns (and adjectives) in the language. Thus, we might again speculate, as we did in the preceding section, that the exceptional cases have some sort of lexical marker whose effect is to reverse the normal order of the pair of rules in question.

To conclude this section, I would like to attempt to forestall a possible objection. It might be argued that I have sneaked into the discussion illicit assumptions concerning "simplicity," assumptions based on intuitions about phonological theory. Specifically, the argument goes, I have preferred the ordering solution over others because I assume the lexical ordering-marker to be "cheaper" than whatever machinery is required by other solutions. In answer to this objection, I would agree that the use of such assumptions is indeed illicit—one cannot possibly have a priori intuitions about simplicity—but I would deny that anything of the sort has played a role in the discussion. We have been concerned with the discovery of linguistically significant generalizations in an area of Spanish phonology, not with evaluating the machinery used in the formalization of these generalizations. I see it as a significant generalization that the examples in (15) are stressed by the same rule as every other noun in the language and that the absence of final *e* in the singular forms is due to the operation of the same rule that accounts for $e \sim \phi$ alternations in all o her nouns and adjectives in the language. Any disagreement at this point can stem only from the denial that these are significant generalizations. Of course, *mutatis mutandis*, similar remarks can be made concerning the verb cases discussed in the previous section.

4. MARKED AND UNMARKED ORDERS OF RULES

The peculiarities of certain forms of two highly irregular verbs are, in themselves, of very little interest. The odd stress patterns of the singular/plural pairs of five nouns are of even less intrinsic interest, because of the marginal status of these nouns. It is of considerable interest, however, to discover that the various peculiarities of these two apparently unrelated sets of examples can (and probably must) be subsumed under the single higher-level principle that the normal order of a pair of rules can be reversed in exceptional cases. If this is correct, then the cases discussed in the two preceding sections constitute important disconfirming evidence for the theory of phonological rule ordering formulated most comprehensively in Chomsky (1967) and Chomsky and Halle (1968), a theory which underlies virtually all of the work in generative phonology of the last decade. It is for this reason that I have taken some pains to argue in the preceding sections that only rule ordering can capture the generalizations relevant in each case.

Anderson (1969) has presented a number of similar cases, in widely unrelated languages, and has proposed a new theory of "local ordering" of phonological rules. It is important, then, to investigate the bearing of the Spanish data on this more recent theory. Anderson has proposed a set of universal principles in terms of which certain pairwise orders of rules may be reckoned as more highly valued than others. Oversimplifying somewhat, the more highly valued orders, the "unmarked" orders, are those which permit maximal application of a pair of rules in a given derivation. Less highly valued, or "marked," orders are those that do not permit maximal application. To illustrate, I repeat as (17) the derivations of *protejo* and *protejamos* given previously in (4):

(17) /proteg+e+o/   /proteg+e+a+mos/
    x   x   Velar Softening
     φ   φ   Truncation
  prote[x]*o*   *prote*[x]*amos*

In these derivations, both Velar Softening and Truncation in fact apply. This is maximal application: thus, in these derivations, the order (Velar Softening, Truncation) is an unmarked order.

Now consider the derivations of *hago* and *hagamos* given previously in (9), which I repeat here as (18):

(18) /hak+e+o/   /hak+e+a+mos/
    φ   φ   Truncation
   −   −   Velar Softening (fails)
   g   g   Lenition
  ha[g]*o*   *ha*[g]*amos*

In (18) (Truncation, Velar Softening) is a marked order. The two rules could, in principle, both apply here, just as they in fact do in (17); but in the empirically correct order, the prior application of Truncation removes the environment of Velar Softening so that the latter can no longer apply. This is not maximal application.

So far, on this theory the notion of marked and unmarked orders distinguishes the "regular" derivations of *protejo*, *protejamos* (unmarked order of Velar Softening and Truncation) from the "irregular" derivations of *hago*, *hagamos* (marked order of Velar Softening and Truncation). Consider, now, forms of regular first conjugation verbs like *marcar* 'to mark' and *pagar* 'to pay', shown in (19):

(19) *mar*[k]*o*   *pa*[g]*o*   (1st pers sg, pres indic)
     mar[k]*amos*   *pa*[g]*amos*   (1st pers pl, pres indic)
     mar[k]*emos*   *pa*[g]*emos*   (1st pers pl, pres subj)

Although stem-final *k* and *g* are followed by the front vowel *e* in the phonetic representations of the subjunctive forms in (19), Velar Softening has not applied to give *mar[s]*emos*, *pa[x]*emos*. As shown in (20), this is accounted for with underlying representations and derivations parallel to those of the "regular" forms in (17) (in the case of the first conjugation, /+a+/ is the theme vowel and /+e+/ is the subjunctive marker):

(20) /mark+a+e+mos/   /pag+a+e+mos/
    −   −   Velar Softening (fails)
    φ   φ   Truncation
  mar[k]*emos*   *pa*[g]*emos*

Now observe that both Velar Softening and Truncation could, in principle, apply to the underlying representations in (20): if Truncation applied first, the result would be *mark+e+mos*, *pag+e+mos*, to which Velar Softening could then apply to give *mar[s]*emos*, *pa[x]*emos*. This would be an unmarked order (of maximal application). Thus the empirically correct order shown in (20), in which only Truncation can apply, is marked.

We can now see that the principles of marked and unmarked orders of rules fail to differentiate consistently between the two orderings in question: the order (Velar

Softening, Truncation) is unmarked for some cases (forms of regular non-first conjugation verbs like *cue*[s]*o, co*[s]*amos, prote*[x]*o, prote*[x]*amos*) but marked for others (forms of regular first conjugation verbs like *mar*[k]*emos, pa*[g]*emos*), while the opposite order is also a marked order for irregular forms like *hago, hagamos, digo, digamos*. For reasons to be given in the next section, it seems to me to be an unfortunate result that the markedness principles lump together some regular verbs (*cocer, proteger*) not with other regular verbs (*marcar, pagar*) but rather with irregular *hacer* and *decir*. However, I should stress that the classification of verbs according to the traditional definitions of "regular" and "irregular" is not the issue. We are concerned, rather, to find some set of general principles which characterizes all and only the forms subject to a particular ordering of a pair of rules. This the markedness principles fail to do in the present case.

Let us turn now to Stress and Apocope. Evidently, these two rules cannot possibly interact so as to render either of their two possible orders either marked or unmarked by the principles proposed by Anderson. This follows from two facts: (*a*) every noun and adjective is stressed on some syllable, whether or not Apocope also applies, and (*b*) Apocope applies wherever it is applicable, regardless of the position of stress. The second point can be clarified: the feature [stress] is not mentioned in the Apocope Rule (13) and need not be since Stress cannot assign stress to the final syllable of polysyllabic words, the only forms to which Apocope can apply (there is no Spanish word consisting of one or more consonants alone). In short, the principles of markedness provide no way at all of distinguishing between the order (Stress, Apocope) illustrated in (14) and the order (Apocope, Stress) illustrated in (16).[7]

5. PARADIGMATIC UNIFORMITY

Although the notion of marked and unmarked orders of rules fails to differentiate between the orderings in both of the sets of examples (14) and (16), there exists a property that makes the relevant distinction quite clearly in the verb cases, albeit less so in the stress cases. Verb forms that must be subject to the order (Velar Softening, Truncation), like the forms of *marcar, pagar, cocer, proteger* discussed previously, are "paradigmatically uniform"; those that must be subject to the order (Truncation, Velar Softening), namely, the forms of *hacer* and *decir*, are not "paradigmatically uniform." With respect to verb forms, "paradigmatic uniformity" is intended to refer to the fact that the phonetic representation of a given stem is invariable (except for stress, which follows a simple fixed pattern) in all of the forty to fifty (depending on dialect) inflected forms that comprise the various paradigms of each verb. For example, the stem /mark-/ appears only as [mark-] and /proteg-/ only as [protex-] before all of their forty or so respective inflectional desinences. The overwhelming majority of Spanish verbs are paradigmatically uniform, in the sense just described,

[7] Anderson (1969) defines a "contingent" ordering as one that specifies an order not given by universal principles (either both marked or unmarked or neither marked or unmarked). Thus, both the regular order (Stress, Apocope) and the exceptional order (Apocope, Stress) are "contingent" orders since neither is marked or unmarked. However, Anderson states (pp. 163–164) that "one would not expect to find a situation in which one contingent ordering restriction applied to one (unsystematic, language-particular) class of forms, while the opposite contingent order applied to another." But this seems to be precisely the situation we have found in Spanish.

but *hacer* and *decir* are not, with *ha*[g]*o* versus *ha*[s]*e*, *di*[g]*o* versus *di*[s]*e*, and so on.[8]

Spanish nouns are inflected only for number (singular and plural) and adjectives only for number and gender (masculine and feminine). Thus noun paradigms have a maximum of two distinct members and adjective paradigms have four. With so few forms to consider, the notion of paradigmatic uniformity is much less meaningful in connection with nouns and adjectives than with verbs. Consequently, nouns and adjectives will not be discussed further in this context.[9]

I would like to put forward the claim that it is not an accident that all but a vanishingly small minority of Spanish verbs (not to mention nouns and adjectives) are paradigmatically uniform, in the sense just described; that is, that paradigmatic uniformity is in some way more natural and more desirable than paradigmatic irregularity. (For example, perhaps the regular verbs of Spanish are more easily acquired by first—or *n*th—language learners than verbs whose stems vary in phonetic representations. This is obviously not logically necessary.) If this is correct, then greater surface regularity in the paradigms of a language should be correlated with greater naturalness and simplicity of the grammar of the language. In other words, an empirically supported evaluation metric must be found that rewards grammars for producing regular paradigms.

Before examining evidence in support of the privileged status of paradigmatic uniformity, let us see that current phonological theories fail, in general, to reflect this status. First, observe that the material discussed in the earlier sections of this paper falls entirely outside the scope of the "standard" phonological theory of Chomsky and Halle, which, unlike Anderson's theory of "local ordering," provides no motivation and no mechanism for evaluating one order of rules more highly than another. Now let us look at Anderson's theory in the context of paradigmatic uniformity. Consider the derivations in (21):

(21)		UNMARKED	MARKED	
Indic	Indic	Subj	Subj	
(a) /mark+a/	/proteg+e/	/mark+a+e/	/proteg+e+a/	
		marke	protega	Truncation
	protexe	marse		Velar Softening
mar[k]*a*	*prote*[x]*e*	**mar*[s]*e*	**prote*[g]*a*	
(b) /proteg+e/	/mark+a/	/proteg+e+a/	/mark+a+e/	
protexe		protexea		Velar Softening
		protexa	marke	Truncation
prote[x]*e*	*mar*[k]*a*	*prote*[x]*a*	*mar*[k]*e*	

---

[8] A sizable number of verbs deviate from total uniformity only in that unstressed *e* and *o* alternate with stressed *ie* and *ue*, respectively, as in *coc-émos, coc-ian, coc-iste, coc-iérais,* etc., but *cuéc-e, cuéc-es, cuéc-en.*

[9] It seems reasonable, however, to maintain that all Spanish nouns and adjectives are paradigmatically uniform except for the five cases in (15) and hence that this property successfully distinguishes the two orders of the two rules in question. Except for (15), phonetic representations of singular/plural pairs of nouns and adjectives differ only in the final *s* of the plural and the deleted final *e* of those singulars to which Apocope applies. In other words, both the location of stress and the segmental composition (except for final *e*) of these stems are strictly invariable. I think it can be plausibly argued that this *e* is an inflectional class marker (like the *-o* and *-a* of, say, *tío* 'uncle', *tía* 'aunt', and *loco* (masculine) / *loca* (feminine) 'crazy') rather than part of the stem proper; thus, there need be no exception to the absolute invariability of noun and adjective stems, aside from those in (15). I will not press the point, however, since it will not enter into the remainder of the discussion.

The grammar of (21a), with the order (Truncation, Velar Softening), has one marked-order derivation and one unmarked, and it produces irregular (and incorrect) paradigms. The grammar of (21b), with the order (Velar Softening, Truncation), also has one marked-order derivation and one unmarked, but this ordering produces regular (and correct) paradigms. Thus, on Anderson's theory, the correct grammar is not more highly valued than the incorrect one; that is, the correct grammar is not rewarded for producing regular paradigms.[10]

Let us see now what support can be found for the contention that paradigmatic uniformity is more natural than lack of uniformity. The history of Spanish verb forms is a rich source of evidence, providing many examples of the interaction of changes in paradigms and changes in grammars. As will be seen in the examples to be cited, although general sound changes may introduce irregularities into paradigms, there is a strong tendency for paradigms to regularize themselves in one way or another and to resist the introduction of irregularity. Of particular interest are the last three examples to be discussed, in which paradigmatic uniformity is bought at the cost of additional complexity in the grammar, as measured by current phonological theories.

In the sections to follow, first the examples will be cited, with only a few explanatory comments. Then, after all the data have been accumulated, general observations will be made and some conclusions drawn.

5.1. The ancestor of the regular modern verb *cocer* was at one time irregular, with underlying stem-final /k/ alternating in phonetic representations between g and the dental affricate [d^z], as shown in (22):

(22)

EARLY STAGE	LATER STAGE	
co[d^z]*er*	*co*[s]*er*	(inf)
cue[g]*o*	*cue*[s]*o*	(1st pers sg, pres indic)
co[d^z]*emos*	*co*[s]*emos*	(1st pers pl, pres indic)
co[g]*amos*	*co*[s]*amos*	(1st pers pl, pres subj)

Although the change from d^z to modern s is part of a general sound shift (the well-known "medieval sibilant" changes), the changes affecting g are not, being traditionally ascribed to "analogy." There is, however, a straightforward explanation for the regularization of the paradigms of *cocer* in terms of rule ordering. Consider the derivations in (23). (As shown, at the early stage, the "softened" reflex of k was t^s, to which Lenition could apply.)

(23) (a)

/kok+e+mos/	/kok+e+a+mos/	
	kokamos	Truncation
kot^{s}emos		Velar Softening
kod^{z}emos	kogamos	Lenition
co[d^z]*emos*	*co*[g]*amos*	

(Continued)

---

[10] It could conceivably be argued that the correct grammar (21b) is much worse, since first conjugation verbs (like *marcar*), which require the marked order, outnumber by an enormous margin non-first conjugation verbs (like *proteger*), which undergo the unmarked order. The first is the only productive conjugation; new coinages and borrowings are invariably assigned to it. Thus, every verb entering the language would have to be subject to the marked order of the rules in question.

(b) /kok+e+mos/ /kok+e+a+mos/
    kotˢemos   kotˢeamos   Velar Softening
                  kotˢamos   Truncation
    kodᶻemos   kodᶻamos   Lenition
    co[dᶻ]emos *co[dᶻ]amos*

It can be seen from (23) that the regularization of the paradigms in question is reflected in a change in the order of Truncation and Velar Softening (which is, incidentally, a change from a marked to an unmarked order).

5.2. The ancestor of the modern Truncation Rule made its first appearance in the prehistory of Latin, and its effects are easy to spot in Classical Latin. Classical Latin Truncation applied to some conjugations—in particular to the first—but not to others, as suggested by the partial synchronic derivations in (24):[11]

(24) NO TRUNCATION   TRUNCATION
     Second Conjugation   First Conjugation
     Indic   Subj   Indic   Subj
     /deb+e+o/   /deb+e+a+mus/   /am+a+o/   /am+a+e+mus/
                                                ϕ ϕ Truncation

     debeo   *debeamus*   *amo*   *amemus*

The ancestor of the modern rule of Velar Softening entered late Latin or early Romance centuries after the first appearance of Truncation.[12] For convenience, we may assume that the original effect was to change velar k before a front nonconsonantal segment to $č$ (although some other output, say, the dental affricate t^s, would serve our purpose just as well). As the standard literature is careful to point out, Velar Softening applied without morphological restriction, except for stem-final segments of first conjugation verbs. (Only the subjunctive is relevant here since the indicative does not supply the appropriate environment.) Thus, consider the examples in (25):

(25) (a) Noun (nom, acc pl)
         pakes → *pačes* (CL *pāx, pācis*)
         Non-first conjugation verb (pres indic)
         fakes → *fačes* (CL *făciō, făcĕre*)

     (b) First conjugation verbs (pres subj)
         pakes → *pakes*, not *pačes (CL *pācō, pācāre*)
         kerkes → *čerkes*, not *čerčes, *kerkes (CL *cĭrcō, cĭrcāre*)

We have, then, phonetic minimal pairs like *pačes* (noun) versus *pakes* (verb). As the last example in (25) shows, Velar Softening did apply to velars not in stem-final position in first conjugation verbs. The explanation universally given in the literature for the unique inapplicability of Velar Softening to stem-final position in first conjugation subjunctives is that k is retained by analogy with paradigms in which this

---

[11] Classical Latin Truncation applied also to third conjugation "*e*-stems" (indicative *tego*, subjunctive *tegam*), but not to third conjugation "*i*-stems" (*capio, capiam*) or to fourth conjugation forms (*audio, audiam*). In modern Spanish, Truncation applies to all conjugations.

[12] Velar Softening should not be confused with two other changes, the palatalization of dentals and of velars before the glide *y*, which antedate Velar Softening by a considerable period. Velar Softening is distinct from the earlier processes not only in date, segments affected, and environment, but also in effect in several Romance areas.

velar is followed by a back vowel, like present indicative *pako, pakas, pakat* or *čerko, čerkas, čerkat.*

In a synchronic grammar of ordered rules, how might we account for forms like *pakes* and *čerkes*? It could be proposed that the rule of Velar Softening is inserted into the grammar so that it is ordered before Truncation, the chronologically earlier rule. This would give derivations like those in (26):

(26)
NOUN		VERBS		
/pak + es/	/pak + a + es/	/kerk + a + es/		
č	–	č –		Velar Softening
	φ	φ		Truncation
pačes	*pakes*	*čerkes*		

The phonetic outputs are correct, but the antichronological insertion of Velar Softening before Truncation results, in Anderson's terms, in a marked order. Such insertions are presumably extraordinarily rare, if they exist at all.

Alternatively, Velar Softening could be added to the grammar after Truncation if there is also added, perhaps by some sort of redundancy rule, a condition that stem-final velars of first conjugation verbs are exempt from Velar Softening. The awkward and ad hoc character of this condition should be emphasized, however: velars not in stem-final position do undergo Velar Softening in verbs, as in *kerk-* → *čerk-*; and stem-final velars undergo Velar Softening in nonverbs, as in the noun *pak-* → *pač-*, which is presumably the same stem /pak-/ that occurs in the verb *pakare.*

I do not know what the correct grammar is here, in terms of current phonological theories. It seems inescapable, however, that paradigmatic uniformity—the phonetic integrity of first conjugation stems—must be paid for, under any evaluation metric presently known, with some kind of additional complexity in the synchronic grammar.

5.3. In Latin, stress was assigned to verbs by the same principles that assigned stress to other lexical categories. A few details aside, these are the well-known principles embodied in the modern Stress Rule (12), to which the notions "strong cluster" and "weak cluster" are fundamental. (Unlike the Latin rule, however, the modern rule does not apply to verbs.) Consider, now, the Vulgar Latin paradigms of regular first conjugation *amō, amāre* given in (27). (For convenience I identify these paradigms according to their function in Spanish rather than in Latin.)

(27)
Imperfect Indicative		Past Subjunctive -*ra*- form		-*sse*- form	
amába	*amābámus*	*amára*	*amārámus*	*amásse*	*amāssémus*
amábas	*amābátis*	*amáras*	*amārátis*	*amásses*	*amāssétis*
amábat	*amábant*	*amárat*	*amárant*	*amásset*	*amássent*

Future
Subjunctive
amáro/e	*amárĭmus*
amáris	*amárĭtis*
amárit	*amárent*

In all but the last paradigm, all forms are penultimately stressed; in the last, the first and second persons plural are antepenultimately stressed, all in conformity with the weak cluster/strong cluster principle of the Latin stress rule. At a very early date, however, in the Latin of Spain these arrangements of stress are replaced by those shown in the paradigms in (28). (I now give Old Spanish forms; all consonant and vowel changes are due to general "sound laws.")

(28) *amába   amábamos*   *amára   amáramos*   *amásse   amássemos*
     amábas   amábades   *amáras   amárades*   *amásses   amássedes*
     amába   amában   *amára   amáran*   *amásse   amássen*

                        amáro/e   amáremos
                        amáres   amáredes
                        amáre   amáren

Now all four paradigms have the same pattern: stress has been retracted one syllable in the first and second persons plural of the imperfect indicative and past subjunctive.[13] This change cannot be explained on the basis of a supposed shortening (laxing) of the vowel in the affixes -*bā*-, -*rā*-, and -*ssē*- since there is no evidence at all for this and, as we shall see directly, it would have no effect in any event.

We now turn to another set of examples, in which we see two patterns of stress in a single paradigm in Latin. Consider (29), which shows the present indicative of *castīgo* (long penultimate vowel) and *renĕgo* (short penultimate), both regular first conjugation verbs:

(29) *castī́go   castīgắmus*   *rénĕgo   renĕgắmus*
     castī́gas   castīgắtis   *rénĕgas   renĕgắtis*
     castī́gat   castī́gant   *rénĕgat   rénĕgant*

All the forms of *castigo* are penultimately stressed, but *renego* has both penultimately and antepenultimately stressed forms. The latter pattern was replaced at an early date in Spain by one of uniform penultimate stress, as shown in (30):[14]

(30)   EARLY   MODERN
     renĕ́go   renĕgắmus   *reniégo   renegámos*
     renĕ́gas   renĕgắtis   *reniégas   renegáis*
     renĕ́gat   renĕ́gant   *reniéga   reniégan*

The modern forms in (30) show that the change to uniform penultimate stress cannot be attributed to a lengthening of the penultimate vowel before stress is assigned by the Latin stress rule. Short *e* diphthongizes to *ie* under stress, but long *e* does not. Thus this vowel must be short at the time stress is assigned.

At this point, all connection between length (tenseness/laxness) of vowels and verb stress has been severed. There are unstressed strong penultimate syllables

[13] Some dialects retained the Latin stress pattern, as, for example, in Galician *cantabámos*, *falasémos*.

[14] Some qualification may be necessary. A few antepenultimately stressed present tense forms are found as late as the thirteenth century, for example, *signífica*, *sacrífica*. I do not know whether such forms enjoyed an unbroken existence from Latin times to the Middle Ages as a special erudite class, or whether they dropped out of use entirely in Vulgar Latin, to be reintroduced later as learned borrowings. In any event, after the thirteenth century, their stress became penultimate (*significa*, *sacrifica*).

A few other details have been omitted from the discussion here, details having to do largely with deletion of pre- and post-tonic vowels and coalescence of Latin conjugational classes. As far as I can see, this simplification of a complex and somewhat obscure picture does not affect the crucial points of the discussion.

(*amábāmos, amárāmos*) and stressed weak penultimate syllables (*renégo, renégas*). The rule that has come to replace the Latin stress rule for stress assignment in verbs (and which continues to operate to the present day) can be given essentially as in (31):

(31)
$$V \rightarrow [1\text{stress}] \; / \; \begin{cases}]_{\text{STEM}}\text{---}C_0VC_0VC_0 \# \#]_V & \text{(a)} \\ \text{---}C_0VC_0 \# \#]_V & \text{(b)} \\ \text{---}C_0 \# \#]_V & \text{(c)} \end{cases}$$

(32) $V \rightarrow [1\text{stress}] \; / \; (\langle]_{\text{STEM}} \rangle \text{---} \langle C_0 V \rangle C_0 V) C_0 \# \#]_V$

Rule (31a) assigns antepenultimate stress to forms with a two-syllable inflectional ending (*am + á-bamos, am + á-ramos*); (31b) assigns penultimate stress to all other polysyllabic forms (*amámos, amábas, amáron, áman, ámo*); (31c) applies to monosyllables (*dás, vé, sóy*). In (32) the three rules of (31) are collapsed into a single schema. The net effect of (31) = (32) is that stress is invariably assigned to the theme vowel in all paradigms except present indicative and subjunctive, where polysyllabic forms have uniform penultimate stress.[15]

In short, the uniformization of the location of stress in Spanish verb forms illustrated in (27) through (30) has required an increase in the complexity of the grammar. The Latin stress rule continues to assign stress to nonverbs, but verb stress is now controlled by (31), in which the "strong cluster/weak cluster" principle of the Latin stress rule plays no role.[16]

Certain substandard dialects of Spanish have gone further in the uniformization of stress placement within paradigms. In these dialects, stress placement in the present indicative remains uniformly penultimate, as in the standard dialects. I illustrate in (33) with regular first conjugation *amar*, regular second conjugation *comer*, and irregular third conjugation *venir*.[17] (I enclose second person plural forms in parentheses since they are not used in all dialects.)

(33)
ámo	*amámos*	*cómo*	*comémos*	*véngo*	*venímos*
ámas	(*amáis*)	*cómes*	(*coméis*)	*viénes*	(*venís*)
áma	*áman*	*cóme*	*cómen*	*viéne*	*viénen*

[15] In the present indicative and subjunctive, stress is assigned to the theme vowel in some forms but not in others. In the latter case the theme vowel is deleted prior to stress assignment (*am + a + e + mos* → *am + e + mos* → *amémos*; *am + a + o* → *am + o* → *ámo*) or is in the final syllable of a polysyllabic form (*am + a + s* → *ámas*; *am + a* → *áma*). We might thus paraphrase (31) informally as "stress the theme vowel if you can find it in a nonfinal syllable; otherwise stress the penultimate vowel, or in monosyllables stress the only vowel."

In a few cases in other paradigms, later rules may disguise slightly the fact that stress is assigned to the theme vowel. To illustrate, I give on the left the representations of the preterit of *amar* to which the stress rule applies, and on the right the actual phonetic forms:

am + á + i	am + á + mos	*amé*	*amámos*
am + á + ste	am + á + steis	*amáste*	*amásteys*
am + á + u	am + á + ron	*amó*	*amáron*

[16] There are, to be sure, examples of stress shifts in nouns and adjectives, but the uniformization of stress placement in verbs cannot be related to the former, as, for example, the shift from the first to the second of two contiguous vowels (*muliere* → *muliére*) and the addition of CL to the set of consonant sequences that form a "strong cluster" (*íntegro* → *intégro*). Furthermore, modern Spanish, whose stress rules had to come into existence at some point, provides a wealth of evidence that verbs and nonverbs are stressed by different principles: there are literally hundreds of noun/verb and adjective/verb pairs like *plática/platíca* 'chat', *catálogo/catalógo* 'catalog', *contínuo/continúo* 'continuous'/'continue', *válido/valído* 'valid'/'validate'.

[17] *Venís* is "penultimately stressed" because it is derived from *ven + i + is*: compare *am + á + is*, *com + é + is* in (33) and *am + é + is*, *com + á + is*, *veng + á + is* in (34).

In standard Spanish, the corresponding subjunctive forms also have uniform penultimate stress, as shown in (34):

(34) *áme*   *amémos*   *cóma*   *comámos*   *vénga*   *vengámos*
     ámes   *(améis)*   *cómas*   *(comáis)*   *véngas*   *(vengáis)*
     áme   *ámen*   *cóma*   *cóman*   *vénga*   *véngan*

In some substandard dialects, however, stress is uniformly on the stem in the present subjunctive (unlike the present indicative in the same dialects), as in (35):[18]

(35) *áme*   *ámenos*   *cóma*   *cómanos*   *vénga*   *vénganos*
     ámes   *(ámeis)*   *cómas*   *(cómais)*   *véngas*   *(véngais)*
     áme   *ámen*   *cóma*   *cóman*   *vénga*   *véngan*

Other substandard dialects have uniform penultimate stress in the first conjugation subjunctive (as in the indicative) and uniform stem stress in the second and third conjugation subjunctive (unlike the indicative):

(36) *áme*   *amémos*   *cóma*   *cómanos*   *vénga*   *vénganos*
     ámes   *(améis)*   *cómas*   *(cómais)*   *véngas*   *(véngais)*
     áme   *ámen*   *cóma*   *cóman*   *vénga*   *véngan*

The uniformization of stress placement within paradigms illustrated in (35) and (36) obviously imposes considerable complexity on the stress rules of the dialects in question though I will not attempt to express these rules formally here. It is worth noting that it is the first conjugation and present indicative that have proved most resistant to uniformization. That is, these forms provide the only instances in which stress is not assigned to the same vowel in all members of a given paradigm in all dialects. We may speculate why this should be so. It is well known that in Spanish the first conjugation contains astronomically more verbs than the second and third conjugations combined, has virtually no irregular forms (only *estar* and *andar* have any irregular forms at all), is the class to which new verbs and nonce inventions are assigned, and is the basis of most of the productive deverbal derivation in the language. In other words, the first conjugation is the model conjugation *par excellence*. As for the present indicative, statistical counts have shown that it is used with considerably greater frequency than all other paradigms combined.[19] It is a widely accepted tenet of traditional historical studies that, in general, the forms that hold on to their irregularities most tenaciously in the face of analogical pressures are the forms that speakers are most familiar with and use most often. This is just what we have witnessed in our brief sketch of the history of verb forms from Latin to modern Spanish.

5.4. The material presented here seems to me to lend considerable support to the view that paradigms are "psychologically real" and that paradigmatic relations play a role both in phonological change and in the organization of synchronic gram-

---

[18] See Espinosa (1930, pp. 53, 345–349).
Antepenultimately stressed first and second person plural present subjunctive forms have not always been considered substandard. They were used, for example, by the noted nineteenth-century writer Espronceda.
[19] See Bull (1947) and Rolfe (1968).

mars.[20] The problem which must be faced by current theories of generative phonology, which do not provide for paradigmatic reference in either diachronic or synchronic contexts, is that the question of the paradigm is multiderivational. That is, information relevant to the derivation of a given form may be found in the paradigms of which this form is a member, rather than in the representations of the form itself. Furthermore, if it is correct that paradigmatic uniformity is more natural than paradigmatic irregularity, then an empirically supported evaluation metric that rewards grammars for producing regular paradigms must be found.

To conclude, I raise the question of counterexamples. Not surprisingly, Spanish has a handful of irregular, more or less idiosyncratic verbs.[21] There is, however, only one kind of departure from uniformity in the phonetic representations of verb stems among and within paradigms that is tolerated on a large scale. This is illustrated, with *renegar*, in the right-hand column of (30), where we see an alternation between the simple vowel *e* and the diphthong *ie*. The distribution is predictable: the diphthong appears under stress, the simple vowel otherwise. We have seen a similar alternation in the forms of *cocer*, in (1), for example, where the unstressed simple vowel *o* alternates with the stressed diphthong *ue*. Spanish has a very large number of verbs with these two alternations, as well as a large number in which *e* and *o* do not alternate with diphthongs (plus a few in which the diphthongs *ie* and *ue* do not alternate with simple vowels).

There are a number of ways of drawing a formal distinction between this unique type of nonuniformity, generally tolerated in Spanish, and other types, which are strongly rejected. However, I have no idea which, if any, of these distinctions are of genuine significance. It is an interesting problem for future research to determine whether there exists a general characterization of those types of paradigmatic irregularity that tend to be accepted and those that tend to be rejected in all highly inflected languages.

[20] A striking example is presented in Vennemann (1968), where a condition on the application of a synchronic phonological rule in German is stated as follows: "The suffixal /ə/ of the 2nd and 3rd Person Singular Present Indicative forms of strong verbs with root-final /t/ or /d/ is syncopated if and only if a contrast exists between the radical vowel of these two forms and that of the remaining forms of the Present Indicative paradigm of the same verb" (p. 7). Vennemann leaves no stone unturned to argue that this condition is the only adequate statement of the generalization in question.

[21] The major classes of irregular verbs in Spanish have been studied in Harris (1972).

REFERENCES

Anderson, S. (1969), *West Scandinavian Vowel Systems and the Ordering of Phonological Rules*, unpublished Ph.D. dissertation, M.I.T.

Bull, W. (1947), "Modern Spanish verb-form frequencies," *Hispania, 30*, 451–466.

Chomsky, N. (1967), "Some general properties of phonological rules," *Language, 43*, 102–128.

Chomsky, N., and M. Halle (1968), *The Sound Pattern of English*, New York: Harper & Row.

Espinosa, A. M. (1930), *Estudios sobre el español de Nuevo Méjico, Parte I, Fonología*, Biblioteca de Dialectología Hispanoamericana, Tomo I, Buenos Aires.

Harris, J. W. (1969), *Spanish Phonology*, Cambridge, Mass.: M.I.T. Press.

Harris, J. W. (1970), "A note on Spanish plural formation," *Language*, *46*, 928–930.

Harris, J. W. (1972), "Five classes of irregular verbs in Spanish," in J. Casagrande and B. Saciuk, eds., *Generative Studies in Romance Languages*, Rowley, Mass.: Newbury House.

Rolfe, O. (1968), "Grammatical frequency and language teaching: verbal categories in French and Spanish, " *Word*, *24*, 410–417.

Saltarelli, M. (1970), "Spanish plural formation: apocope or epenthesis?" *Language*, *46*, 89–96.

Vennemann, T. (1968), "On the Use of Paradigmatic Information in a Competence Rule of Modern German Phonology," paper read at the Summer meeting of the Linguistic Society of America.

tense/lax alternations among the low vowels[1]

Samuel Jay Keyser

University of Massachusetts at Amherst

1. INTRODUCTION

It is a well-known observation among phoneticians that tense vowels differ from their lax counterparts not only in duration but also in vowel quality. For example, in modern English the tense vowel in the word *beat* is a higher and more fronted vowel than its lax counterpart in *bit*. Similarly, the tense vowel in *gate* is higher and more fronted than its lax counterpart in *get*. When we turn to the back vowels, a similar relationship can be seen. The tense vowel in *food* is higher and more backed than its lax counterpart in *foot*. We represent these relationships in (1) by arrows connecting the appropriate vowels as they appear in the vowel triangle on page 1 of Kurath and McDavid's *Pronunciation of English in the Atlantic States* (hereinafter PEAS).

The [i] in *beat* appears in the upper left-hand corner of the triangle while its lax counterpart appears in the same block of the diagram but somewhat lower and more toward the center. The [u] in *food* and the [ʊ] in *foot* are similarly related, the lax vowel being lower and more centralized than its tense counterpart. And again, the [e] in *gate* appears in the upper left-hand corner of the second block while its lax counterpart appears in a lower and more central position in the same block.

[1] This work was supported in part by a National Science Foundation Grant No. GS 2005 to Brandeis University, Waltham, Massachusetts, and by a National Science Foundation Grant No. GS 35283 to the University of Massachusetts, Amherst, Massachusetts.

Having collaborated with Morris Halle for a good part of the last ten years, I feel that this work is also a part of our collaboration and acknowledge that debt here. Based on that collaboration and on my long friendship with Morris Halle, I would like to observe that, though his hair has thinned a bit in the last decade, Morris Halle remains a Gargantua among phonologists.

(1)

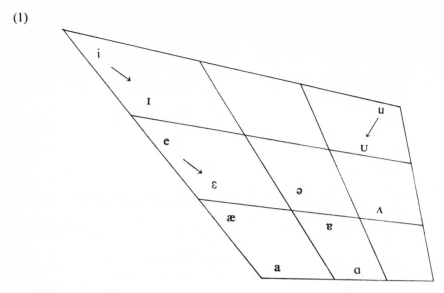

This relationship between tense and lax vowels can be found in many other languages of the world (see Chomsky and Halle (1968, p. 324) and Lehiste (1970, pp. 30 ff)), and very probably we are dealing here with a linguistic universal on the phonetic level. There is, however, a question raised by the triangle in (1), namely, what, if any, are the lax counterparts of the low vowels listed in the bottom block? A certain amount of light is thrown on this question if we consider the phonetic data recorded in PEAS from the perspective of the treatment of diphthongs as underlying tense vowels in Chomsky and Halle's *The Sound Pattern of English* (hereinafter SPE).

To begin our discussion we must first look at the symbols which appear in PEAS. They are drawn from the finely graded phonetic alphabet used by the Linguistic Atlas of the Eastern United States, on the collections of which PEAS is based. The purpose of the alphabet was to provide the Atlas workers with a recording instrument of great flexibility since the goal of the collections was to preserve as accurate a phonic record as possible. The result is that the phonetic array which appears in the PEAS synopses is, on the surface at least, extremely chaotic, and it is rather difficult to see any sort of meaningful pattern. Consider, for example, the synopses in (2):[2]

(2) (a) Baltimore, Md. (99)

five	ɑ^{<·ɛ}	*down*	æ˙ᴜ
twice	ɑ^ɪ	*out*	ə˯<ᴜ<
wire	ɑ˙ɛə	*flower*	æ˙ᴜə

   (b) Baltimore, Md. (98)

five	ɑɛ>	*down*	a^˙ᴜ
twice	ɑ<ˆɪ	*out*	a^ᴜ
wire	ɑ˙ɛə	*flower*	a^ᴜə

The diacritic system employed in PEAS and illustrated in (2) in effect multiplies the number of symbols that appears in (1) so that beside [ɑ] we must include [ɑ^], [ɑ[<]], and [ɑ_∧[<]]. Similarly, beside [a] we must include [a^]. The net effect of these symbol differentiations is to widen the gap between the two Baltimore dialects represented in (2) rather than narrow it.

In the face of this proliferation of symbols, it is natural to ask whether it is possible to reduce their number in some interesting fashion. For example, it is conceivable that the [a^] in (2b) should be identified with the [æ] in (2a), and such a reduction would bring the two dialects closer together. It is also conceivable that the [ɑ^] in (2a) is identical to the [ɐ] in (1), and this equation would make (2a) resemble a great many other dialects of the Atlantic states, as we shall see. It would, in addition, relate the Baltimore dialects in (2) in a fashion which will be seen to be typical of several other Atlantic states dialects.

In the discussion which follows, an attempt will be made to bring about a reduction in the number of symbols and, consequently, a reduction in the distance between the dialects synopsized in PEAS. In keeping with recent work in phonology, the symbols in (1) will be assumed to represent configurations of distinctive features. The particular features are, to a large extent, implicit in the vowel diagram itself and are, in any case, well known. Thus, the horizontal lines in (1) divide the vowels into three heights, namely, high, low, and mid. In terms of binary features we represent these three heights with two features, high and low, in the following fashion: [+high] = high, [+low] = low, and [−high, −low] = mid. The vertical divisions in the chart suggest a three-way division into front, central, and back vowels. In what follows here, however, we use only two dimensions, namely, front and back, and therefore only one binary feature: [+back] = back and [−back] = front. In discussing the dialects in PEAS we will see that a front/back division is all that is required.

In order to distinguish [i] from [ɪ], [e] from [ɛ] and [u] from [ʊ] we set up a feature of tenseness (see note 7): the first member of each pair is [+tense], the second [−tense]. Finally, the feature [round] plays a role in distinguishing [u] and [ʊ], which are [+round], from all of the other vowels in (1), which are [−round].[3] All of the vowels are assumed to be [+syllabic], as opposed to glides, for example, which are [−syllabic].

Though we treat all of the vowels in (1) as abbreviations for configurations of distinctive features, we do not assume that they all share the same theoretical status. It has been common to view phonology as composed of an abstract systematic phonological level and a less abstract systematic phonetic level, together with a set of phonological rules which map configurations of the former into configurations of the latter. It has also been common to assume a third level, below the systematic phonetic one, within which entities are specified by numerical values instead of the simple binary specifications of the other levels. At this level we suppose a scale numbered from 1 to n where each integer along the scale indicates the precise degree of backness, lowness, highness, and so on. For example, *five* appears in (2a) as [fɑ[<]ˈɛv]. We can interpret [ɑ] as the configuration [+low, −round, +back] at the phonetic level. (We shall see later that its phonological representation is quite different.) We take the diacritic [[<]] as indicating a particular degree of backness to be represented by some integer along the backness scale ranging from 1 to n. In fact, these numerical values will in general reflect the diacritic system utilized in PEAS.

In attempting to interpret and wherever possible reduce the symbols which appear in (1) and in the synopses of PEAS, it is important to keep in mind that the

---

[3] The feature [round] does not figure in the discussion to follow. It is mentioned here only for the sake of completeness.

use of a finely graded phonetic alphabet will not be uniform from one recorder to another nor, even, from one recording to another by the same recorder. It is perfectly conceivable, then, that the symbol [ʌ˅] which appears in PEAS is, in certain instances, equivalent to the symbol [ɑ˃] which also appears there. A decision in this regard cannot depend on any absolute empirical standard but must rest on one's theoretical view of what is going on in the relevant dialects. In interpreting the results of a finely graded phonetic alphabet, it is also important to keep in mind that a symbol like [ʌ˅] can actually represent, at the phonetic level where values are numerical, the extreme end of the [+low] scale, perhaps resulting from a raising rule where a [+low] vowel has been raised to the extreme degree. In other instances this same symbol can represent, more straightforwardly, the [−low, −high] phonetic configuration in English words like *cut*.

We have established a rudimentary feature representation for the vowels in (1). It is apparent, however, that given the feature representation just outlined there will not be a one-to-one mapping of the vowels in (1) into these features. For example, the feature representation assumes only three heights, but in (1) there are apparently four phonetic heights, represented by [i], [e], [æ], and [a]. Similarly, though our feature representation has only two vertical dimensions, namely, front and back, the chart in (1) treats [ə], [ɐ], and [ɑ] as central vowels. In what follows we shall attempt to demonstrate that the empirical data of PEAS provide us with grounds for treating the relationships of the vowels in (1) in a somewhat different fashion and that the resultant relationships are expressed very naturally in the distinctive feature system we have outlined.

2. THE ARGUMENT

Let us begin by considering the vowels [ɐ] and [ʌ]. In the chart in (1) they are obviously distinct. The PEAS synopses in (3) suggest, however, that these two vowels are in fact simply very low-level phonetic variants of each other and should be identified as the same vowel at a more abstract level:

(3) (a) Georgetown, S.C. (131)

five	ɑ˃·ɪ	*down*	ɑ·o
twice	ɐ^ɪ	*out*	ʌ˂ᴜ
wire	ɑ˂·ə	*flower*	ʌ˃·ᴜwə

(b) Columbia, S.C. (142)

five	a˃·ə	*down*	a˃·o
twice	ɐɪ	*out*	ʌ˂ᴜ
wire	a˃·ɪə	*flower*	ɑ·wə

In (3a) and (3b) it is a rather straightforward matter to predict the occurrence of [ɐ] and [ʌ]: the former appears before front glides and the latter before back glides. Since the matter of which variant appears is determined by the immediate phonetic environment, we shall assume that the difference between [ɐ] and [ʌ] is not a systematic one at a more abstract level. That is, these vowels are contextual variants, produced by an assimilation rule, of the same more abstract vowel.

Let us now examine the vowels in (1) which are symbolized as [a] and [ɑ]. Consider, first, synopsis (3b). The occurrence of [a] before the front glide in *wire* and [ɑ] before the back glide in *flower* suggests that these vowels are also contextual variants of the same more abstract vowel and are differentiated only by a very low-level assimilation rule. A similar relationship can be seen in the synopsis in (4a), where the same alternation appears in *wire* and *flower*:

(4) (a) Atlanta, Ga. (157)

five	a$^{>}_{\wedge}$˙ə	*down*	æ˙o	
twice	a$^{>}$ɨ	*out*	æˇo	
wire	a$^{>}_{\wedge}$˙ə	*flower*	ɑˆ˙oə	

(b) Litchfield, Conn. (35)

five	ɑɨ	*down*	ɑo	
twice	aɨ	*out*	au	
wire	ɑɪəʳ	*flower*	ɑuʷəʳ	

In (4b) the occurrence of [a] before a front glide (in *twice*) and [ɑ] before a back glide (in *out*) is apparently limited to environments in which the glide is itself followed by a voiceless consonant. Nonetheless, the assimilation corresponds to that of (3b) and provides further evidence for the identification of these vowels.

In the light of what has just been discussed, we now modify the vowel chart (1) as in (5):

(5)

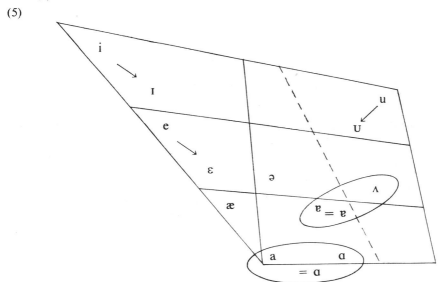

It is assumed that the vowels connected by a circle in (5) are in fact the same vowel, at a more abstract level, with the particular realization in each case determined by the environment. As indicated in (5), we shall represent the vowel underlying [ɐ] and [ʌ] as [ɐ] and the vowel underlying [a] and [ɑ] as [ɑ]. Furthermore, since we are assuming that [a] and [ɑ] are variants of a back unrounded vowel, we draw the line which separates front from back so that [a] is now categorized as a back vowel. Since we do not consider the additional division in (1) to be theoretically important, we indicate it in (5) as a dotted line for reference only.

Having made these correspondences, let us return to the dialectal evidence in (3). The obvious fact about these dialects is that there is a correlation between the occurrence of [ɐ] (∼ [ʌ]) and its environment, namely, some version of this vowel occurs before a glide just in case a voiceless consonant follows the glide. We can account for the occurrences of the various versions of [ɐ] in (3) if we make the three assumptions in (6):

(6) (a) The surface diphthongs in *twice* and *out* (as well as those in *five*, *down*, *wire*, and *flower*) are derived from underlying tense vowels
   (b) There exists a diphthong laxing rule which laxes the first element of diphthongs before voiceless consonants
   (c) [ɐ] and [ʌ] are lax vowels

We shall not attempt to justify (6a) directly but shall first assume its correctness and summarize briefly the treatment of the vocalic nuclei in *five*, *twice*, *wire*, *down*, *out*, and *flower* in terms of SPE. According to SPE the phonetic diphthongs in these words are actually surface realizations of the tense vowels in the underlying forms /fīv/, /twīs/, /wīr/, /dūn/, /ūt/, /flūr/. SPE argues that such underlying forms are necessary in order to account for vowel alternations in such pairs as *divíne/divínity*, *obscéne/obscénity*, *profáne/profánity*, *hármony/harmónious/harmónic*.[4] The rules which map the underlying tense vowels into surface diphthongs are those summarized in (7):

(7) (a) DIPHTHONGIZATION: places a homorganic glide immediately after an underlying tense vowel
   (b) VOWEL SHIFT: shifts all underlying high vowels to low vowels, all underlying mid vowels to high vowels, and all underlying low vowels to mid vowels
   (c) UNROUNDING: unrounds all back low vowels which have been vowel shifted
   (d) BACKNESS ADJUSTMENT: backs all tense low vowels which have been vowel shifted

Since we shall have reference to Backness Adjustment in our discussion, we shall state it formally here as (8):

(8) Backness Adjustment

$$\begin{bmatrix} +\text{low} \\ +\text{tense} \\ V \end{bmatrix} \rightarrow [+\text{back}] \;/\; \underline{\hspace{1cm}} \begin{bmatrix} -\text{syllabic} \\ -\text{consonantal} \end{bmatrix}$$

Let us now consider the derivation of *five* and *down* in (9) in terms of the rules in (7):

(9) /fīv/   /dūn/
    īy   ūw   Diphthongization
    ǣy   ɔ̄w   Vowel Shift
    –   ā̄w   Unrounding
    āy   –   Backness Adjustment
    [fāyv]   [dāwn]

Ignoring the obvious differences in the offglides, we see that the PEAS synopsis for Pittsfield, Mass., in (10) provides phonetic data consistent with the derivation in

---

[4] See SPE, pp. 178 ff. We shall follow the practice of SPE in using the macron (‾) to indicate underlying tenseness in the derivations to follow.

(9), assuming that [ɑ] in (10) represents a tense vowel (which we shall justify later):

(10) Pittsfield, Mass. (37)

five	ɑɛ	*down*	ɑo
twice	ɑɛ	*out*	ɑo
wire	ɑɛə	*flower*	ɑoə̞

It is instructive to compare the synopsis in (10) with the two synopses combined as (11):

(11) Billerica, Mass. (8)
(= Newport, R.I. (17))

five	aɪ	*down*	aʊ
twice	aɪ	*out*	aʊ
wire	aɪə	*flower*	aʊə

The difference in (11) is that the first element of the diphthong is realized not as [ɑ] but as [a], the slightly more fronted variety of the low vowel. But since we have already concluded that the differences between [a] and [ɑ] are not systematic underlyingly, we can conclude that the dialects in (11), like the dialect in (10), are consistent with the derivations in (9). The difference is in the degree of backness with which low, back, unrounded, tense vowels are realized: Pittsfield (10) realizes them farther back while Billerica and Newport realize them farther forward.[5]

We take assumption (6a), then, to be justified in terms of the treatment of tense/lax alternations among vowels as outlined in SPE and summarized here. We shall now attempt to justify the remaining assumptions, (6b) and (6c), in the light of the data already presented.

The existence of a Diphthong Laxing Rule of some sort (assumption (6b)) has been suggested by several linguists and is by no means an innovation.[6] The data in (3) give us a clue as to how the rule should be stated, and we formulate it as in (12):

(12) Diphthong Laxing

Low vowels which are the first elements of diphthongs are laxed just in case their glides are followed by a voiceless consonant; formally,

$$\begin{bmatrix} +\text{low} \\ V \end{bmatrix} \rightarrow [-\text{tense}] \ / \ \underline{\hspace{1cm}} \begin{bmatrix} -\text{syllabic} \\ -\text{consonantal} \end{bmatrix} \begin{bmatrix} -\text{voice} \\ C \end{bmatrix}$$

We are now in a position to account for the occurrence of [ɐ] (~ [ʌ]) in the dialects of (3). Given the assumption (6c), namely, that [ɐ] and [ʌ] are lax vowels, and the Diphthong Laxing Rule (12), we may postulate the derivations in (13) for both (3a) and (3b):

---

[5] Although specific alternations of [a] and [ɑ] can be accounted for in terms of assimilation to an immediate environment, no such explanation is feasible for the dialects in (10) and (11). We shall assume, therefore, two modes of execution of the low, back, unrounded, tense vowel and an apparently arbitrary choice by dialects as to which mode is basic. This seems more natural than treating (10) and (11) as cases of assimilation.

[6] See SPE, p. 342, and Joos (1942).

(13) /twīs/   /ūt/
        iy   ūw   Diphthongization
        ǣy   ɔ̄w   Vowel Shift
        —   āw   Unrounding
        āy   āw   Backness Adjustment
        ɐy   ɐw   Diphthong Laxing
        ɐy   ʌw   Assimilation
    [twɐys]   [ʌwt]

Hence, both dialects in (3) exhibit Diphthong Laxing. The occurrence of [ɐ] (~ [ʌ]) in (3) is a direct consequence of the operation of Diphthong Laxing and of the assimilating influence of the glide following the laxed vowel. If we return to the chart in (5), we see that this consequence is, in fact, a natural one. Thus, the arrows in (5) and (1) are meant to draw attention to the fact that the lax counterparts of high and mid tense vowels tend to be lower in quality and more centralized with respect to position of articulation. We can now integrate that observation with the results of the derivations in (13), in which the lax counterparts of low tense vowels tend to be higher in vowel quality and articulated more toward a central position. Taken together, the raising of tense low vowels when laxed is part and parcel of the same phenomenon that lowers and centralizes the lax counterparts of the high and mid tense vowels.

The picture which emerges thus far (and which will be enhanced in the discussion to follow) is one in which the lax vowels gravitate toward the center of the diagram. If we suppose that the articulatory analog of the center of diagram (5) is, in fact, the neutral position assumed by the tongue prior to speaking (in which the body of the tongue is raised to about the level required to articulate the English vowel [e]—see SPE, p. 300), then the significance is quite clear. The low tense vowels, like their high and mid counterparts, are simply articulated farther from the neutral position of the vocal tract than are their lax counterparts.[7]

Let us turn to yet another synopsis, in (14):

---

[7] This discussion assumes that all low vowels are intrinsically tense vowels, although it leaves open the interesting question of what the articulatory correlate or correlates of the feature [+ tense] might be. In Perkell (1969) the following observation appears: "A correlation of the feature *tense* with vocal-tract behavior for vowels is observed for measurements which reflect tongue movement toward the direction of articulation. In comparison of the behavior of these measurements for tense and lax vowels, the tense vowels are generally characterized by attainment of a steady state. In contrast the lax vowels are characterized by motion or instability. My hypothesis is that tenseness in vowels implies contraction of extrinsic, tongue-positioning musculature to a more complete extent than for lax vowels. This could result in attainment of a steady state and greater movement of the tongue away from a neutral position." The relationship of tense to lax low vowels we have described is clearly consistent with Perkell's hypothesis of the articulatory correlate of the feature [tense]. There is, however, a second model suggested to me by K. Stevens, according to which tenseness is correlated with a specific articulatory gesture, namely, a constricted pharynx. (For some discussion see SPE, pp. 324 ff.) The front wall of the pharynx is made up of the tongue root. Thus, a retracted tongue root, which results from positioning the tongue for low vowels, may conceivably operate to constrict the pharynx, and this would account for the automatic tenseness of the low vowels. It may well be that both mechanisms are operating, one for the low vowels and one for the nonlow vowels. This very interesting question must, unfortunately, be left open here.

For a criticism of Perkell's view of tenseness and a possible reinterpretation see Lieberman's (1970) very favorable review of Perkell (1969).

(14) Harrisburg, Pa. (75

five	aˑɨ	*down*	æ˅ˑu˅
twice	aɨ	*out*	æˑu˅
wire	aɨəʳ	*flower*	æ˅ˑuəʳ

Since we are not making a distinction between [a] and [ɑ], the rules in (7) will account for the first element of the Harrisburg diphthongs in *five*, *twice*, and *wire*—that is, those with an underlying /ī/—provided that realization of the more fronted variety of the low, back, unrounded, tense vowel, that is, [a], is assumed. However, in order to account for the first element of the diphthong which derives from an underlying /ū/, it is necessary to modify the rules in (7). In particular, the Backness Adjustment Rule (8) must be replaced by a new rule which has the joint effect of backing [+low] vowels before [−back] glides and fronting [+low] vowels before [+back] glides; in other words, the rule is one of dissimilation. We can state the modified rule as in (15):[8]

(15) Backness Adjustment₂

$$
\begin{bmatrix} +\text{low} \\ V \end{bmatrix} \rightarrow
\begin{cases}
[+\text{back}] \ / \ \underline{\quad}
\begin{bmatrix} -\text{syllabic} \\ -\text{consonantal} \\ -\text{back} \end{bmatrix} & \text{(a)} \\[2em]
[-\text{back}] \ / \ \underline{\quad}
\begin{bmatrix} -\text{syllabic} \\ -\text{consonantal} \\ +\text{back} \end{bmatrix} & \text{(b)}
\end{cases}
$$

We now illustrate the operation of rule (15) in the derivations in (16) for the Harrisburg dialect in (14):

(16) /fīv/ /dūn/

īy	ūw	Diphthongization
ǣy	ɔ̄w	Vowel Shift
–	ā̄w	Unrounding
āy	–	Backness Adjustment (15a)
–	ǣw	Backness Adjustment (15b)
–	–	Diphthong Laxing
[fā̃yv]	[dæ̃wn]	

Two points need to be mentioned here. First, we have indicated in the derivations of (16) that the new Backness Adjustment Rule (15a) yields the fronted [a] rather than the backed [ɑ] which we have encountered in Pittsfield, Mass. (10), Litchfield, Conn. (4b), and Georgetown, S.C. (3a). Second, the data with respect to Diphthong Laxing is quite clear for Harrisburg. Since the first element of the diphthongs in *twice* and in *out* has not been raised, Diphthong Laxing must not have applied.

We now consider in (17) another set of synopses from PEAS which throws additional light on the question of tense-lax alternations among the low vowels:

[8] The rule is stated in this uncollapsed form for expository purposes. It is clear, however, that a more concise statement is required, and, indeed, the rule is stated in SPE (p. 189) as follows:

$$
\begin{bmatrix} +\text{low} \\ V \end{bmatrix} \rightarrow [-\alpha\text{back}] \ / \ \underline{\quad}
\begin{bmatrix} -\text{syllabic} \\ -\text{consonantal} \\ \alpha\text{back} \end{bmatrix}
$$

(17) (a) Richmond, Va. (111)

five	ɑ^{<·ɛ}	*down*	æU
twice	ɐɨ	*out*	ə^U^
wire	a^{>ɛə}	*flower*	æ[>]Uə

(b) Richmond, Va. (112)

five	a^{·ə<}	*down*	æ^·U
twice	ɐɨ	*out*	əU^
wire	a^ɛə	*flower*	æ·Uə

(c) Norfolk, Va. (114)

five	a[>]·ɛ	*down*	æU
twice	ɐɨ	*out*	ə^U^
wire	a[>]·ɛə	*flower*	æUə

(d) Alexandria, Va. (103)

five	a^{·ə>}	*down*	æ·ʊ
twice	ɐɨ	*out*	ə[<]U[<]
wire	a^{·ɛə}	*flower*	æ·ʊə

The most striking feature of the synopses in (17) is that they exhibit two different mid-central vowels, namely, [ə] and [ɐ]. There are, moreover, certain suggestive correlations in these data, which we list in (18):

(18) (a) [ɐ] appears only in diphthongs which derive from underlying /ī/
(b) [ə] appears only in diphthongs which derive from underlying /ū/
(c) Every dialect cited is subject to the Backness Adjustment$_2$ Rule: (15a) produces the more fronted variety [a] of the [+low] vowel; (15b) produces the [æ] which appears before the back glide

The fact that the dialects in (17) contain [ɐ] in the environment of the rule of Diphthong Laxing strongly suggests the operation of the rule here. We must suppose, then, that [ə] is also the lax counterpart of a low tense vowel. Since we already have identified [ɐ] (~ [ʌ]) as the lax counterpart of [ɑ] (~ [a]), we must look elsewhere for the tense counterpart of [ə]. That this must be [æ] is indicated by the fact that the Backness Adjustment Rule (15) has operated in these dialects and has, as a consequence, interacted with Diphthong Laxing. Thus, we have the derivations in (19), which are characteristic of all of the dialects in (17):

(19) /twīs/   /ūt/

īy	ūw	Diphthongization
ǣy	ɔ̄w	Vowel Shift
–	ā̄w	Unrounding
āy	–	Backness Adjustment (15a)
–	ǣw	Backness Adjustment (15b)
ɐy	əw	Diphthong Laxing
[twɐys]	[əwt]	

What is desirable about this result is that we are now able to explain the raising and centralization of [æ] to [ə] in precisely the same way that we account for the centralization of the lax counterparts of [i], [e], [u], and [ɑ], namely, as a result of the general tendency of lax vowels to be articulated more centrally than their tense counterparts.

We can now modify (5) as in (20):

(20)

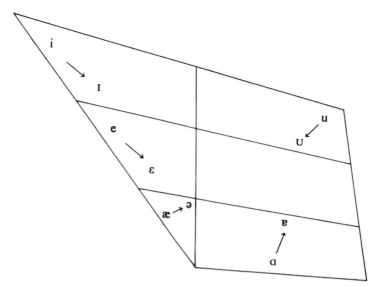

We began our discussion by attempting to realign the relationships among vowels in (1) in a fashion consistent with the facts of diphthong laxing and assimilation in the dialects of PEAS. We suggested that the resultant realignment would be expressible in a natural fashion in terms of the distinctive feature configurations outlined at the beginning of our discussion. The realignment is shown in (20), and the phonetic distinctive feature table in (21) indicates how this is to be expressed:

(21)

	i	ɪ	e	ɛ	æ	ə	ɑ	ɐ	u	ʊ
high	+	+	−	−	−	−	−	−	+	+
low	−	−	−	−	+	+	+	+	−	−
back	−	−	−	−	−	−	+	+	+	+
tense	+	−	+	−	+	−	+	−	+	−
round	−	−	−	−	−	−	−	−	+	+

In terms of (21), then, neither [ʌ] nor [a] has any abstract phonetic status. Rather, each of these symbols represents a low-level variant of one of the phonetic configurations in (21). Returning to our earlier notion of using integers to represent degrees of a property along a scale, we would describe [ʌ] as a backed and raised version of /ɐ/, raised to degree n as a result of the assimilating influence of the following glide. Similarly, we would describe [a] as a fronted version of /ɑ/, fronted to the degree m, although here the degree of fronting appears to be an arbitrary choice of various dialects.

If the results given here are correct, then it follows that there will be no dialect which exhibits the operation of the Backness Adjustment Rule (15) and the Diphthong Laxing Rule and which does not exhibit [ə] before the back glide in such words as *out*. In this regard consider the synopses in (22):

(22) (a) Fayetteville, N.C. (123)

five	a[>]ˑɛ	*down*	æ^ᵛʊ
twice	ɐ^ᵛɨ	*out*	ɐ[<]ʊ
wire	a[>]ɛə	*flower*	æ_ᵛ[>]ʊə

(Continued)

(b) Lynchburg, Va. (118)

five	a˙ɛ	*down*	æ˙ʊ
twice	ɐɪ	*out*	ɐU
wire	a[>]ɛə	*flower*	æ˙Uə

In (22a) we seem to find a counterexample since it appears that both Backness Adjustment and Diphthong Laxing have operated and yet the vowel before the back glide in *out* is [ɐ], not [ə]. However, this counterexample is more apparent than real. The diacritic marks indicate that [ɐ] in *twice* is lower than it is in *out*, suggesting [ɐ ˅] = [ɐ] and [ɐ ˂] = [ə]. There are no diacritics in (22b), but it is quite possible that here the expected [ə] has been assimilated to the following back glide, yielding [ɐ]. In this instance, the dialect will have a derivation which includes Backness Adjustment (15), Diphthong Laxing, and assimilation.

3. A POSSIBLE COUNTERARGUMENT

We have argued that all of the [+low] vowels in the forms discussed are [+tense]: [æ], [ɑ] ~ [a]. When these are laxed, they must automatically be raised to yield [ə], [ɐ] ~ [ʌ], respectively. Recall now that we adopted the SPE solution to tense/lax alternations in words like *profane/profanity*. According to this solution, the underlying vowel in the stressed syllable is /ǣ/. In *profane* this vowel undergoes all of the rules in (7) to yield the surface diphthong [ēɪ]. However, in the form *profanity* no surface diphthong appears. To account for this, it is postulated in SPE that a rule of Trisyllabic Shortening applies, prior to Vowel Shift, which laxes the underlying /ǣ/. Since in general Vowel Shift applies only to underlying tense vowels, it is prevented from applying to *profanity*. Thus, from underlying /prɔfǣn + iti/, Trisyllabic Shortening gives /prɔfæn + iti/. This, however, is inconsistent with the preceding discussion since it is a case of a low tense vowel which undergoes laxing but does not also undergo raising. We would predict the incorrect form [prōfə́niti].

Notice, however, that elsewhere in SPE it is pointed out that certain occurrences of phonetic [æ] behave as if they were in fact tense. The crucial examples are the words *pellágra, Alabáma, Koála,* and *panoráma* (SPE, p. 152). In all of these words the penultimate vowel is lax and yet it receives primary stress. This is an impossible situation in terms of SPE: only strong syllables receive stress, and the penultimate syllable in these forms (and others, such as *banána, bandána, cabána*) can be strong only if the vowel is tense. In the face of this, underlying forms with /ā/ are postulated in SPE: /pVlāgræ/, /ælVbāmæ/, /koālæ/. The vowel /ā/ does not undergo Vowel Shift since it does not agree in the features [back] and [round] (see SPE for details). However, the vowel is tense and therefore attracts the stress. In order to obtain [æ], a rule is now proposed which shifts the vowel from back to front and simultaneously laxes it: /ā/ → /æ̆/. It is suggested in SPE (p. 189) that such a rule should fall together with Backness Adjustment in the version (15).

On this approach, the fronting of /ā/ involves two separate processes, namely, fronting and laxing. Let us suppose, contrary to SPE, that the fronting rule is simply /ā/ → /ǣ/, that is, laxing does not occur. Then the falling together of this rule with Backness Adjustment (15) is even more natural: both rules involve a shift of backness, as opposed to the SPE approach where a rule which shifts backness is collapsed with a rule which not only shifts backness but also causes laxing.

This, however, still leaves the [æ] in *profanity* as a problem. It will now be necessary to suppose a low-level rule which operates to tense all stressed low vowels. Thus the [æ] in *profanity* will be tensed and therefore prevented from raising to [ə]. Such a rule could be collapsed with the Diphthong Laxing Rule as in (23):

$$(23) \quad \begin{bmatrix} +\text{low} \\ +\text{stress} \\ V \end{bmatrix} \rightarrow \begin{cases} [+\text{tense}] & \qquad\qquad\qquad\qquad\qquad\qquad (a) \\ [-\text{tense}] \ / \ \underline{\quad} \begin{bmatrix} -\text{syllabic} \\ -\text{consonantal} \end{bmatrix} \begin{bmatrix} -\text{voice} \\ C \end{bmatrix} & (b) \end{cases}$$

This solution is formally equivalent to that proposed in SPE. Whereas SPE supposes a rule of low vowel laxing, we propose a rule of low vowel tensing. It is simply a question of whether to lax the penultimate vowel in *Alabama* or tense the antepenultimate vowel in *profanity*. Since both vowels are phonetically identical, the proper solution cannot be based upon the phonetic facts. If we adopt the SPE solution, however, we lose the generalization noted here that the lax counterparts of all tense vowels are articulated closer to the neutral position. If we adopt some version of the solution formalized as (23), we can maintain this generalization. Since the generalization appears to be such a natural one and since the two solutions proposed are formally equivalent, some version of (23) seems preferable to the laxing rule of SPE.

4. POSTSCRIPT

Implicit in the discussion in this paper has been a criticism of the representation of data in the fashion of PEAS, namely, that the presentation of synopses in finely detailed phonetic transcription obscures the underlying processes of the dialects. Such presentations, in other words, fail to give a true picture of the relatedness among dialects.

If the discussion in the preceding sections is correct, then the results in (24) obtain:

(24) (a) There exists a Diphthong Laxing Rule which some dialects share
   (b) Evidence of diphthong laxing is the occurrence of lax, centralized vowels before glides followed by a voiceless consonant; if a dialect does not exhibit such vowels, then diphthong laxing has not occurred
   (c) Dialects differ as to which Backness Adjustment Rule is operative, (8) or (15); however, all dialects have one or the other
   (d) There exist two varieties of low, back, unrounded, tense vowels, namely, [a] and [ɑ]; dialects differ as to which variety they adopt, though specific occurrences of one or the other is strictly a function of phonetic environment

Given these results, we may now consider replacing synopses by tables which indicate which processes have occurred in which dialects. Two such tables are presented in (25) and (26). In these tables the + indicates that a rule has applied, the − that it has not; however a − entry under Backness Adjustment indicates that (8) has applied instead of (15). All of the synopses appearing in PEAS have been included to give a more complete picture; those specifically discussed in the preceding sections appear in the tables in italics.

Early in this paper we noted that the use of a finely graded phonetic alphabet tended to widen the gap between dialects represented in the PEAS synopses and we illustrated this with the Baltimore dialects in (2). Let us now reconsider these dialects in

(25)

Dialects with [a]

Backness Adjustment (15)	+	+	−	−
Diphthong Laxing	+	−	+	−

Annapolis, Md.(100)	Harrisburg, Pa.(75)	Columbia, S.C.(142)	Billerica, Mass.(8)
Alexandria, Va.(103)	Charleston, W. Va.(91)	Savannah, Ga.(147)	Plymouth, Mass.(13)
Wicomico Church, Va.(108)	Georgetown, D.C.(102)		Newport, R.I.(17)
Richmond, Va.(111)	Edenton, N.C.(119)		New London, Conn.(19)
Richmond, Va.(112)	New Bern, N.C.(120)		Providence, R.I.(21)
Petersburg, Va.(113)	Charlotte, N.C.(128)		Springfield, Mass.(25)
Norfolk, Va.(114)	Asheville, N.C.(129)		Northampton, Mass.(27)
Lexington, Va.(117)	Atlanta, Ga.(157)		Middletown, Conn.(30)
Lynchburg, Va.(118)			New Haven, Conn.(32)
Wilmington, N.C.(121)			Poughkeepsie, N.Y.(41)
Fayetteville, N.C.(123)			Port Edward, N.Y.(44)
Raleigh, N.C.(126)			Utica, N.Y.(45)
Augusta, Ga.(153)			Binghampton, N.Y.(48)
			Manhattan, N.Y.(60)
			Manhattan, N.Y.(62)
			Brooklyn, N.Y.(63)
			Jersey City, N.J.(65)
			Reading, Pa.(76)
			Williamsport, Pa.(79)
			Brookville, Pa.(82)
			Wheeling, W. Va.(88)

90

(26)

Dialects with [ɑ]

Backness Adjustment (15)	+	+	−	−
Diphthong Laxing	+	−	+	−
	Baltimore, Md.(99) Winchester, Va.(105) Fredericksburg, Va.(107)	Philadelphia, Pa.(72) *Baltimore, Md.*(98)	*Georgetown, S.C.*(131) Beaufort, S.C.(138)	Boston, Mass.(11) *Litchfield, Conn.*(35) *Pittsfield, Mass.*(37) Burlington, Vt.(39) Rochester, N.Y.(53) Cassville, Pa.(80)

the light of our later discussion. The relevant data are repeated here for convenience as (27):

(27) (a) Baltimore, Md. (99)

five	ɑ<ε	*down*	æ˙ʊ
twice	ɑ^ɨ	*out*	ə̬<u<
wire	ɑ˙ɛə	*flower*	æ˙ʊə

   (b) Baltimore, Md. (98)

five	ɑɛ>	*down*	a^˙ʊ
twice	ɑ̬<ɨ	*out*	a^ʊ
wire	ɑ˙ɛ̬ə	*flower*	a^ᵗʲə

The dialect in (27a) can be treated as an [ɑ]-variety dialect which exhibits both Backness Adjustment (15) and Diphthong Laxing if [ɑ^] is interpreted as equivalent to [ɐ], a not unreasonable equation. Similarly, the dialect in (27b) can be considered as a dialect exhibiting Backness Adjustment (15) without Diphthong Laxing if [a^] is uniformly interpreted as [æ].[9] In other words, (27b) differs from (27a) in that the latter has simply added a rule, a familiar means of dialectal differentiation but one which brings out the relationship between the dialects.

We see, then, that a representation of the dialects of the Atlantic states synopsized in PEAS in terms of phonological processes enables us to superimpose a rather simple order on what otherwise appears to be a wildly disordered array of phonetic facts. PEAS constitutes a vast improvement over the presentation of data in the New England Dialect Atlas. The intent of this postscript is to suggest that still another refinement can be made, namely, that dialects can be presented in terms of the phonological processes that underlie the phonetic data.[10]

REFERENCES

Chomsky, N., and M. Halle (1968), *The Sound Pattern of English*, New York: Harper & Row.

Joos, M. (1942), "A phonological dilemma in Canadian English," *Language*, 18, 141–144.

Kurath, H., and R. McDavid, Jr., eds. (1961), *The Pronunciation of English in the Atlantic States*, Ann Arbor: University of Michigan Press.

Lehiste, I. (1970), *Suprasegmentals*, Cambridge, Mass.: M.I.T. Press.

Lieberman, P. (1970), Review of Perkell (1969), *Language Sciences*, December, 25–28.

Perkell, J. S. (1969), *Physiology of Speech Production*, Cambridge, Mass.: M.I.T. Press.

[9] In making the assignments in (25) and (26) equivalences of this sort were often assumed. The details have not been discussed here since the tables are meant to be illustrative rather than definitive. It is worth noting, however, that some thirteen synopses have been left out because the phonetic data make an assignment indeterminate or because other processes have taken place to further modify the data and make assignment either difficult or pointless. These dialects are Nobleboro, Me. (3), Portland, Me. (5), Concord, N.H. (6), Deerfield, Mass. (28), Albany, N.Y. (43), Buffalo, N.Y. (56), Pittsburgh, Pa. (85), Farmington, W. Va. (89), Roanoke, Va. (115), Charleston, S.C. (135), Charleston, S.C. (136), Newberry, S.C. (144), Greenville, S.C. (146).

[10] An interesting correlation emerges from the data in (25) and (26) for which I have no explanation. Backness Adjustment (8) and the absence of Diphthong Laxing (12) characterize the majority dialect in PEAS. The next most frequent dialect, however, is that in which Backness Adjustment (15) occurs with Diphthong Laxing (12). It appears as if Backness Adjustment (15) favors Diphthong Laxing (12) while Backness Adjustment (8) does not. It also appears from the data in (25) and (26) that the fronted variety of /ɑ/ is far more common than the back variety. Again, it would be interesting to know why.

"elsewhere"
in phonology[1]

Paul Kiparsky

Massachusetts Institute of Technology

The purpose of this paper is to investigate the conditions under which there is disjunctive ordering of rules in the phonological component of a grammar. I will present some evidence to show that disjunctive ordering is independent of the use of abbreviatory notations like parentheses or angled brackets, and I will defend a formal condition not involving any abbreviatory notations which seems to come close to being an empirically adequate necessary and sufficient condition on disjunctive ordering.

Let us begin by recapitulating the familiar example of English stress. For verbs like *édit*, *cóvet*, *devélop*, *rélish*, in which the last syllable has a lax vowel followed by no more than one consonant, there must be a rule like (1) stressing the penult:

(1) $V \rightarrow [1\text{stress}] / \underline{\quad} C_0 \breve{V} C_0^1 \#$

Elsewhere, the final syllable is stressed. An enumeration of these "elsewhere" environments would be complex and would miss the point that the totality of "elsewhere" environments is exactly the complement of the cases in which (1) applies. Instead of having various rules putting final stress on verbs with a tense last vowel (*refráin*, *caréen*, *eráse*), verbs ending in two or more consonants (*elápse*, *corréct*, *respéct*), and monosyllabic verbs (*rún*, *hít*, *sée*), we should be able to have simply a rule like (2), which stresses the final syllable *wherever* (1) is inapplicable:

(2) $V \rightarrow [1\text{stress}] / \underline{\quad} C_0 \#$

Rule (2) is quite general and subject only to the restriction that it does not apply when (1) applies (lest we get **edit*, **develop*, and so on). This relation between (1) and (2) is what Chomsky and Halle (1968) term "disjunctive ordering."

[1] This paper was supported in part by the National Institutes of Health (Grant No. 5 T01 HD 00111-08) and the National Institute of Mental Health (Grant No. 2-P01-MH 13390-06).

93

The relation of disjunctive ordering is obviously not one which needs an ad hoc specification for each pair of rules between which it holds. For example, it seems reasonable to assume that (1) and (2) must be disjunctively ordered because of their intrinsic nature, not because of some accidental facts about English stress. We may conclude this from the fact that rule pairs of the general type represented by (1), (2), which are very frequent in languages, have always been found to apply disjunctively. We would not expect to encounter a dialect of English with (1) and (2) not ordered disjunctively, that is, a dialect that has *edit, develop*, but otherwise the stress system of regular English. For this reason it makes sense to look for a general principle that will assign disjunctive ordering to rules like (1) and (2).

The ideal result would be the discovery of some sufficient and necessary condition K which would have to hold for rules to be disjunctively ordered. Chomsky and Halle (1968, p. 77) propose that K is abbreviability by means of parentheses (and angled brackets, which can be regarded as discontinuous parentheses). The reason for the disjunctive ordering of (1) and (2), then, would be that they can be collapsed by parentheses, as in (3):

(3) $V \rightarrow [\text{1stress}] / \underline{\quad} C_0 (\breve{V} C_0^1) \#$

However, there is a rather different way of looking at the disjunctive relation between these stress rules: we have here a *general* case (final stress) which is limited by a *special* case (penultimate stress in the environment $\underline{\quad} C_0 \breve{V} C_0^1 \#$). We might say, then, that it is this general/special relationship which constitutes the required condition K which induces disjunctive ordering. We can state the condition more precisely as in (4):

(4) Two adjacent rules of the form

   $A \rightarrow B / P\underline{\quad}Q$
   $C \rightarrow D / R\underline{\quad}S$

are disjunctively ordered if and only if:

(a) the set of strings that fit *PAQ* is a subset of the set of strings that fit *RCS*, and
(b) the structural changes of the two rules are either identical or incompatible[2]

For example, the two stress rules (1) and (2) are disjunctively ordered because any input subject to (1) is necessarily also subject to (2).

Let us term (4) the "Elsewhere Condition." A version of this condition is consistently employed in Pāṇini's Aṣṭādhyāyī.[3] And S. Anderson (1969) has also suggested one.[4] Furthermore, a similar principle is referred to in Koutsoudas, Sanders, and Noll (1971).

---

[2] This excludes cases where the two rules have nothing to do with each other, where the ordering must be conjunctive. For example, suppose that obstruents are voiced in the environment V$\underline{\quad}$V and palatalized in the environment $i\underline{\quad}i$. Clearly, we expect /iki/ → [ig,i], with both rules applying. Here the subset relation holds, but the structural changes are neither identical nor incompatible and therefore one rule is still not a "special case" relative to the other.

[3] The Elsewhere Condition is explicitly formulated in the Mahābhāṣya (for example, ad P. 6.1.89 *etyedhatyūṭhsu*; see Kielhorn (1960, vol. 3, p. 69) and constitutes Paribhāṣā LVII of the Paribhāṣenduśekhara: *yena nāprāpte yo vidhir ārabhyate sa tasya bādhako bhavati* ("a rule which is given [in reference to a particular case or particular cases to which, or to all of which] another [rule] cannot but apply [or in other words, which all already fall under some other rule], supersedes the latter"—Kielhorn's translation).

[4] However, Pat Wolfe has pointed out to me that there are some problems with the Middle English example which Anderson cites.

In the English stress example involving rules (1) and (2), Chomsky and Halle's condition and the Elsewhere Condition have the same outcome. But the conditions are by no means equivalent generally. I will try to establish here that there are, on the one hand, cases of disjunctively ordered rules which cannot be abbreviated by means of parentheses or angled brackets and, on the other, cases of rules which must be abbreviated by means of parentheses or angled brackets but are not disjunctively ordered. In both classes of examples, the Elsewhere Condition gives the right result. On this basis I will argue that the Elsewhere Condition is to be preferred over Chomsky and Halle's principle for disjunctive ordering.

A simple type of situation requiring parentheses but not disjunctive ordering is the following. Karok (Bright (1957)) has a rule turning *s* into *š* after a front vowel or *y*, where a consonant may optionally intervene. Examples are given in (5):

(5) *mu*   'his'
     múspuka   'his money'
     išpuka   'money'

     ʔu   'he'
     ʔúskak   'he jumps'
     iškak   'jump'

     níkšup   'I pointed'
     yê·pša   'good ones'

We have, then, the rule in (6):

(6) $\text{s} \rightarrow \check{\text{s}} \ / \begin{bmatrix} -\text{back} \\ -\text{consonantal} \end{bmatrix} (\text{C}) \underline{\qquad}$

But the two subrules must apply conjunctively, as is clear from examples like *ʔiššaha* 'water' versus *vássih* 'back'. As opposed to Chomsky and Halle's convention, the Elsewhere Condition correctly predicts conjunctive ordering since one subrule is not a "special case" of the other in the sense of (4).

A common type of situation which calls for the Elsewhere Condition but does not involve parentheses is a disjunctive relation between assimilation and deletion processes. A typical case is the treatment of word-final *-k* in Finnish. In western Finland this segment is assimilated to an initial consonant in the following word and deleted before vowels and pauses (see Itkonen (1964)). In some dialects the assimilation is optional or inapplicable in certain environments (for example, *h, f,* or clusters). The scope of deletion is then correspondingly greater. Synchronically, *-k* must be present as a consonant in underlying representations (see, for example, Wiik (1969)). (One might argue that it has been reanalyzed as /h/, but this is of no importance for the point at issue.) Some examples are given in (7):

(7) *menek # pois*   →   *menep pois*   'go away'
     menek # alas   →   *mene alas*   'go down'
     menek #   →   *mene*   'go'

The rule for final /k/ (or /h/, as the case may be) would now have to be stated as in (8):

(8) (a) $\text{k} \rightarrow \text{C}_i \ / \underline{\qquad} \# \text{C}_i$

    (b) $\text{k} \rightarrow \phi \ / \underline{\qquad} \# \begin{Bmatrix} \text{V} \\ pause \end{Bmatrix}$

In the dialects where Assimilation takes place in a more restricted environment, Deletion has to be modified accordingly. For example, Itkonen (1964, pp. 59–60) notes that many speakers have Deletion rather than Assimilation before clusters (/huomauttaak # professori/ → *huomauttaa professori* 'remarks the professor'). For these speakers the rules would be stated as in (9):

(9) (a) $k \rightarrow C_i / \underline{\hspace{1cm}} \# C_i V$

$$\text{(b) } k \rightarrow \phi / \underline{\hspace{1cm}} \# \begin{Bmatrix} V \\ CC \\ pause \end{Bmatrix}$$

Additional complications in both rules would have to be made for dialects which delete instead of assimilating before *h* and/or *f*.

What the rules in (8) and in (9) miss is that their environments are complementary. They represent as accidental the fact that (b) applies wherever (a) does not apply and vice versa; yet, as the dialect variation shows, this is not an accidental fact but a systematic one. The present theory of phonology can only use conjunctive ordering to express this kind of complementarity. But conjunctive ordering, as illustrated in the rule in (10), will not work in this case:

(10) (a) $k \rightarrow C_i / \underline{\hspace{1cm}} \# C_i$
     (b) $k \rightarrow \phi / \underline{\hspace{1cm}} \#$

Rule (10) would wrongly delete the final *-k* before an initial *k*. For example, in /menek # kotiin/ 'go home' we would, after (vacuously) applying (10a), get **mene # kotiin* by (10b). Nor can we put *k*-Deletion first and reformulate Assimilation as an Epenthesis rule: *k*-Deletion would wipe out the underlying distinction between words that end in /k/ and words that end in a vowel so that Epenthesis would wrongly apply to the latter.

Now, given the Elsewhere Condition, we can simply write (10) and have it apply correctly, for (10b) will be automatically interpreted as applying only where (10a) does not apply. Since in /menek # kotiin/ (10a) does apply, albeit vacuously, (10b) will not apply to delete the final *k*. Any change in the scope of (10a) will automatically be reflected in the interpretation of (10b).

A more elaborate example of the same general type is consonant sandhi in Diola-Fogny as reported by Sapir (1965). As Sapir notes, the basic situation is this: "Consonant reduction is achieved by eliding the first two adjacent consonants. If the first consonant is nasal it assimilates where possible without eliding (p. 16)." Examples are given in (11). (The palatal nasal, which Sapir transcribes inconsistently, is here written *ɲ* throughout.)

(11) (a) *ni+gam+gam*   *nigaŋgam*   'I judge'
         pan+ji+maɲj   *paɲjimaɲj*   'you (pl) will know'
         ku+bɔɲ+bɔɲ   *kubɔmbɔɲ*   'they sent'
         na+tiːŋ+tiːŋ   *natiːntiːŋ*   'he cut (it) through'
     (b) *na+miːn+miːn*   *namiːmmiːn*   'he cut (with a knife)'
     (c) *takun+mbi ...*   *takumbi ...*   'he must not ....'
     (d) *na+laɲ+laɲ*   *nalalaɲ*   'he returned'
         na+yɔkɛn+yɔkɛn   *nayɔkɛyɔkɛn*   'he tires'
         na+waɲ+aːm+waɲ   *nawaɲaːwaɲ*   'he cultivated for me'

(e) *lɛt+ku+jaw*	*lɛkujaw*	'they won't go'
ɛ+rɛnt+rɛnt	*ɛrɛrɛnt*	'it is light'
na+maɲj+maɲj	*namamaɲj*	'he knows'
(f) *kutɛb ⧻ sinaŋas*	*kutɛsinaŋas*	'they carried the food'
ɛkɛt ⧻ bɔ	*ɛkɛbɔ*	'death there'
ban ⧻ ɲa	*baɲa*	'finish now'
(g) *napum ⧻ kuɲilak*	*napuŋkuɲilak*	'he pushed back the children'
najum ⧻ tɔ	*najuntɔ*	'he stopped there'

In the current framework we can state the two rules as in (12):

(12) (a) Assimilation

$$\begin{bmatrix} C \\ +\text{nasal} \end{bmatrix} \rightarrow [\alpha\text{place}] / \underline{\hspace{1cm}} + \begin{cases} (⧻)[+\text{obstruent}] & \text{(i)} \\ [+\text{nasal}] & \text{(ii)} \end{cases}$$

(b) Deletion

$$\begin{bmatrix} C \\ +\text{nasal} \end{bmatrix} \rightarrow \phi / \underline{\hspace{1cm}} \begin{cases} + \begin{bmatrix} -\text{nasal} \\ -\text{obstruent} \end{bmatrix} & \text{(i)} \\ ⧻[-\text{obstruent}] & \text{(ii)} \\ CC & \text{(iii)} \end{cases}$$

$$\begin{bmatrix} C \\ -\text{nasal} \end{bmatrix} \rightarrow \phi / \underline{\hspace{1cm}} + (⧻)C \qquad \text{(iv)}$$

By ordering Assimilation after Deletion, we can simplify Assimilation somewhat, as shown in (13):

(13) (a) Deletion

$$\begin{bmatrix} C \\ +\text{nasal} \end{bmatrix} \rightarrow \phi / \underline{\hspace{1cm}} \begin{cases} + \begin{bmatrix} -\text{nasal} \\ -\text{obstruent} \end{bmatrix} & \text{(i)} \\ ⧻[-\text{obstruent}] & \text{(ii)} \\ CC & \text{(iii)} \end{cases}$$

$$\begin{bmatrix} C \\ -\text{nasal} \end{bmatrix} \rightarrow \phi / \underline{\hspace{1cm}} + (⧻)C \qquad \text{(iv)}$$

(b) Assimilation (revised)

$$\begin{bmatrix} C \\ +\text{nasal} \end{bmatrix} \rightarrow [\alpha\text{place}] / \underline{\hspace{1cm}} (⧻)C$$

But this description is still not very enlightening. It completely fails to bring out the basic complementarity between Assimilation and Deletion that Sapir's verbal statement of the rules emphasizes. The formal consequences of this weakness include the fact that each one of the rules must mention the feature of nasality on the left of the arrow and also the fact that Deletion is divided into two separate parts which, in spite of their similar form and function, cannot be collapsed by the notations that the theory of Chomsky and Halle (1968) provides.

The Elsewhere Condition, on the other hand, enables us to write the rules in a way that closely corresponds to Sapir's evidently correct verbal formulation. Leaving the original Assimilation Rule unchanged, we can radically simplify the Deletion Rule as in (14b) so that it essentially deletes consonants "elsewhere":

(14) (a) Assimilation

$$\begin{bmatrix} C \\ +\text{nasal} \end{bmatrix} \rightarrow [\alpha\text{place}] \; / \; \underline{\hspace{1cm}} + \begin{cases} (\#)[+\text{obstruent}] & \text{(i)} \\ [+\text{nasal}] & \text{(ii)} \end{cases}$$

(b) Deletion (under Elsewhere Condition)

$$C \rightarrow \phi \; / \; \underline{\hspace{1cm}} + \begin{cases} (\#)C & \text{(i)} \\ CC & \text{(ii)} \end{cases}$$

The inputs to both branches (i) and (ii) of the Assimilation Rule are proper subsets of the inputs to branch (i) of the Deletion Rule. Therefore, by the Elsewhere Condition, Assimilation will be disjunctive with branch (i) of Deletion. The rules now say: assimilate, and if assimilation is inapplicable, delete.

A different and somewhat surprising piece of evidence for the Elsewhere Condition, which is of some methodological interest in its own right, comes from metrics. Recent work has shown that there are poetic traditions in which the metrical form of a line is determined not on the basis of its pronunciation, but on the basis of an intermediate representation, or set of representations, in the phonological derivation. In Kiparsky (1972) it is shown that the metrical requirements on a line in the *Rigveda* are allowed to be satisfied either before or after the rules for Vowel Contraction and Glide Formation apply. For example, [ayugdhuam] can be scanned either as four syllables, in accordance with its pronunciation, or as three syllables, in accordance with its morphophonemic representation, which is /a+yug+dhvam/. Conversely, [śacyā] can be scanned either as two syllables, in accordance with its pronunciation, or as three syllables, in accordance with its morphophonemic representation /śaci+ā/.

We show schematically in (15) the linguistic input to the metrical constraints:

(15)

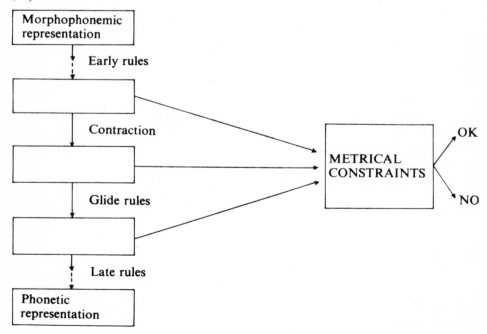

On the basis of evidence presently available, one of the generalizations which can be made about metrical systems of this sort is that the set of input representations must form a consecutive block of rules. Two metrically relevant stages in the derivation do not seem to be separable by a stage which is not a permissible input to the meter. This seems a rather plausible restriction on the psychological availability of intermediate stages in a derivation. Let us now see whether this restriction can be maintained in Sanskrit.

In Kiparsky (1972), it is argued that when the *Rigveda* was composed, glides [y,v] and high vowels [ǐ,ǔ] were in complementary distribution, but because of various other phenomena underlying glides had to be kept distinct from underlying high vowels. The surface distribution appears to have been in agreement with Sievers' Law, a rule which is widely thought to have operated in the Indo-European proto-language. Thus we have the distribution of glides and vowels shown in (16); we shall refer to these environments as G and V, respectively:

(16)　GLIDES (y,v)　　　VOWELS (i,u)

$$\text{V\_\_\_V} \qquad\qquad \text{\_\_\_C}$$

$$\left\{\begin{matrix} \breve{\text{V}} \\ \# \end{matrix}\right\}(\text{C})\text{\_\_\_V} \qquad \begin{matrix} \bar{\text{V}}\text{C}_1\text{\_\_\_V} \\ \text{CC\_\_\_V} \end{matrix}$$

In the present theory of generative phonology, the distribution of glides and vowels in (16) would have to be given by two conjunctively ordered rules. There are two different ways in which this could be done. One way is to have all [+high, −consonantal] segments become syllabic everywhere and then turn nonsyllabic in the environment G of (16). The rules and sample derivations are given in (17):

(17)　$\begin{bmatrix} +\text{high} \\ -\text{consonantal} \end{bmatrix} \rightarrow \left\{\begin{matrix} [+\text{syllabic}] \\ [-\text{syllabic}] \text{ in environment G} \end{matrix}\right.$　(a)　(b)

/ūti + ā/	/śacī + ā/	/adug + dhvam/	/ajuṣa + dhvam/	
		adugdhuam	ajuṣadhuam	(a)
	śacyā		ajuṣadhvam	(b)
ūtiā	*śacyā*	*adugdhuam*	*ajuṣadhvam*	

The other way to account for the distribution of glides and vowels is simply the reverse of that shown in (17), with everything becoming nonsyllabic first and then syllabic in the environment V of (16).

Given the Elsewhere Condition, we have the same two rules and, of course, the same output. The only difference is that, because of the disjunctive relationship between the two rules, each form is derived in a single step. That is, rule (18b) applies if and only if rule (18a) does not apply:

(18)　$\begin{bmatrix} +\text{high} \\ -\text{consonantal} \end{bmatrix} \rightarrow \left\{\begin{matrix} [+\text{syllabic}] \\ [-\text{syllabic}] \text{ in environment G} \end{matrix}\right.$　(a)　(b)

/ūti + ā/	/śacīa + ā/	/adug + dhvam/	/ajuṣa + dhvam/	
ūtiā	śacyā	adugdhuam	ajuṣadhvam	(a)/(b)
ūtiā	*śacyā*	*adugdhuam*	*ajuṣadhvam*	

In spite of the fact that the rules and the output are the same in the two theories, the metrical reflection of these rules allows us to investigate the actual derivations, thereby enabling us to determine which of the theories is correct.

We know that the metrical range includes a level before the application of the glide rules (since, for example, [śacyā] can be scanned as *śaciā*, its form before the glide rules apply) and also a level after the application of these rules (since, for example, [adugdhuam] can be scanned as *adugdhuam*, its form after the glide rules apply). But the derivation required in the conjunctive solution contradicts the hypothesis that the metrically relevant stages form a consecutive block in the derivation. Since the theory of Chomsky and Halle (1968) forces us to have conjunctively ordered rules, we have an intermediate stage, that is, when only the first rule has applied, which *ex hypothesi* should also be in the metrical range. But it cannot be there. The critical type of case is represented by *ajuṣadhvam*, with an underlying and phonetic glide which is also regularly a metrical glide. As shown in (17), under the present theory our rules send this form through the "fake" intermediate stage *ajuṣadhuam* which cannot serve as input to the metrics. And we encounter the same type of problem if we reformulate the rules taking glide formation as the general case.

In a theory that includes the Elsewhere Condition, on the other hand, the application of these rules is disjunctive, thereby eliminating the "fake" intermediate stage in the derivation which causes the problem in the conjunctive mode of application. We have, then, additional evidence in favor of the Elsewhere Condition.

A noteworthy feature of this example is that the rejected solutions do not "miss a generalization" of any kind insofar as the formal regularities of the system are concerned; both conjunctive and disjunctive ordering are fully adequate to "capture the regularities" inherent in the data. This simply shows that the choice between alternative theories in linguistics turns on considerations other than language-internal "descriptive adequacy" and "explanatory adequacy." Conjunctive ordering is wrong here not because it fails to "capture" a generalization but because it represents the generalization in the wrong way, namely, by requiring a stage in phonological derivations which, as the metrical evidence shows, has no psychological reality.

Consider now expressions like C_0 which are used to abbreviate an infinite set of strings. How should rule schemata containing such expressions be applied? The question was given a somewhat tentative answer by Chomsky and Halle (1968, pp. 313–314): they proposed that each rule in the infinite set of rules given by the schema applies simultaneously. For example, the rule (19) is a schema which stands for the rules in (20):

(19) $C \rightarrow \phi \;/\; \underline{\quad} C_0 \#$

(20) (a) $C \rightarrow \phi \;/\; \underline{\quad} \#$
     (b) $C \rightarrow \phi \;/\; \underline{\quad} C \#$
     (c) $C \rightarrow \phi \;/\; \underline{\quad} CC \#$
     (d) $C \rightarrow \phi \;/\; \underline{\quad} CCC \#$
        ⋮

These rules would apply simultaneously to a string of the form XVCCC$\#$ to give the output XV$\#$. On the other hand, the rule in (21) would drop only the last C in such a string since Chomsky and Halle assume that rules do not apply to their output:

(21) $C \rightarrow \phi \;/\; \underline{\quad} \#$

Such rule schemata also figure in many prosodic rules. A rule such as the Southern Paiute Alternating Stress Rule, which stresses the second, fourth, sixth, and so on mora of each word, would be formulated as in (22):[5]

(22) $V \rightarrow [+\text{stress}] / \#C_0V(C_0VC_0V)^*C_0\_\_\_$

Anderson (1969), Johnson (1970), and Howard (1972) have argued—convincingly, I think—that simultaneous application of rules is not the appropriate convention; rather, rules apply iteratively to their own output. Johnson shows that this iterative application must be constrained in a left-to-right or right-to-left direction so that a rule "eats" its way rightward or leftward in a word; he terms this the "left-linear" or "right-linear" mode of application. This eliminates many of the schemata. For example, rule (19), which converts XVCCC$\#$ to XV$\#$ can now be stated as rule (23), operating leftward:

(23) $C \rightarrow \phi / \_\_\_ \#$

The same rule operating rightward drops just the last C, giving XVCC$\#$. And the Southern Paiute Alternating Stress Rule (22) can now be stated simply as rule (24), operating from left to right:

(24) $V \rightarrow [+\text{stress}] / \begin{bmatrix} V \\ -\text{stress} \end{bmatrix} C_0\_\_\_$

Let us now consider the question of disjunctive versus conjunctive application of rules represented by schemata in the cases where they cannot be reformulated as rules applying to their own output. It is clear that disjunctive ordering is sometimes required. According to Itkonen (1966, p. 156), certain dialects of Eastern Cheremis have the rule for word accentuation in (25):

(25) (a) The accent falls on the syllable containing the last full vowel of the word
    (b) If the word has only reduced vowels, the accent is usually on the first syllable

The corresponding formal rule can be stated as (26), where $\check{V}$ represents a reduced vowel:

(26) $V \rightarrow [+\text{stress}] / \_\_\_[C_0\check{V}C_0]_0\#$

Itkonen (1966) also notes that the Eastern Permyak dialects of Komi, in which there is a similar division of vowels into light and heavy, have stress governed by the rule in (27):

(27) (a) The accent normally falls on the syllable containing the first heavy vowel of the word
    (b) If the word has only light vowels, the accent is on the last syllable

Rule (27) is exactly the mirror image of the Eastern Cheremis rule (25), as is immediately obvious from the formal version in (28), where $\check{V}$ stands for what Itkonen terms a "light" vowel:

(28) $V \rightarrow [+\text{stress}] / \#[C_0\check{V}C_0]_0\_\_\_$

[5] Chomsky and Halle's formulation of this rule (1968, p. 347) incorporates a few complications which are probably best taken care of by separate rules. For example, the fact that final morae are not stressed presumably does not require a special restriction on the Alternating Stress Rule but is a consequence of the devoicing of final morae.

Now note that the success of these rules depends on the *disjunctive* application of the infinite set of cases represented by the environment $[C_0 \breve{V} C_0]_0$. We require that the *longest* applicable expansion, and *only* this, should apply to each input. Conjunctive application in Cheremis (rule (25)) would stress not only the last full vowel but all the reduced vowels to its right; and words containing only reduced vowels would be stressed not only on the first syllable but on every syllable. As this would be a very peculiar sort of stress situation, we might look for a general principle that would predict the disjunctive ordering of rules like (26) and (28).

We cannot say that disjunctive ordering is associated with *all* schemata that stand for infinite sets of rules. One example in which the ordering appears to be conjunctive is the Umlaut Rule in its original form in the old Germanic languages. The rule, stated in (29), fronts vowels and diphthongs which are followed by *i* or *j* with only consonants intervening:

(29)

$$[-\text{consonantal}] \;\rightarrow\; [-\text{back}] \;/\; \underline{\hspace{1.5em}}[-\text{syllabic}]_0 \begin{bmatrix} +\text{high} \\ -\text{back} \\ -\text{consonantal} \end{bmatrix}$$

I will assume that the raising phenomena in short vowels that tend to be associated with umlauting ($\ae > e, e > i$) are due to a separate process (or several separate processes) which, even if collapsible with the Umlaut Rule, will not affect the point to be made.

In Old Norse the rule applies as shown in (30) (Noreen (1923, pp. 57 ff.)):

(30) $aC_0i > \ae C_0i$ *saljan > ONorw *sælia*
      ($> $ OIcel *eCi*) $>$ OIcel *selia* 'sell'
                       (NB the special case *ai
                          $>$ ONorw *æi* > OIcel *ei*)
    $a C_0 i > \ae C_0 i$ *lātiz > *lætr* 'let (2sg)'
    $o C_0 i > \ddot{o} C_0 i$ *norþire > *nørþre* 'more northerly'
    $o C_0 i > \bar{\ddot{o}} C_0 i$ *blōtiz > *blǿtr* 'sacrifice to someone (2sg)'
    $u C_0 i > \ddot{u} C_0 i$ *fulljan > *fylla* 'fill'
    $\bar{u} C_0 i > \ddot{u} C_0 i$ *lūkiz > *lýkr* 'close (2sg)'

Before $C_0 u,w$, *a* turns to o ($aCu > \mathit{o}Cu$, $au > \mathit{o}u$). If *i* or *j* also follows, the result is $\bar{\mathit{o}}$.

Now consider the underlying back diphthong /au/. We get $au > \mathit{o}u$ by *u*-umlaut and, where *i*, *j* follows, *i*-umlaut to $\ddot{o}\ddot{u}$: [drɔwmr], *droumr*, *draumr* 'dream', [drɔ̈ẅmi], *drøymi* 'dream'. That is, we get umlauting of *both* components of the diphthong. In Old High German, too, back diphthongs have both components fronted ($ou > \ddot{o}\ddot{u}$). The umlauted diphthong is written $\ddot{o}u$, with the second part then unrounded to give $\ddot{o}i$, which is still the pronunciation in some dialects (for example, Baltic German). Standard German turns $\ddot{o}i$ to *oi*.

Now (29) will front both components only if it is interpreted as a *conjunctively* ordered set of rules. Given the input [drɔwmi], we want both applicable subrules of (29) to take effect, that is, the case (31a) of (29), to give [drɔ̈wmi], and the case (31b), to give [drɔ̈ẅmi] = *drøymi*:

(31)

(a) $[-\text{consonantal}] \;\rightarrow\; [-\text{back}] \;/\; \underline{\hspace{1.5em}}[-\text{syllabic}][-\text{syllabic}] \begin{bmatrix} +\text{high} \\ -\text{back} \\ -\text{consonantal} \end{bmatrix}$

(b) $[-\text{consonantal}] \rightarrow [-\text{back}] / \_\_\_[-\text{syllabic}]\begin{bmatrix} +\text{high} \\ -\text{back} \\ -\text{consonantal} \end{bmatrix}$

Why are the rule schemata interpreted disjunctively in the Cheremis and Komi stress examples but conjunctively in the Germanic umlaut examples? In these cases at least, the correct interpretation follows directly from the Elsewhere Condition. To see this, consider the relationship of the subrules in each case. Let S stand for any syllable and R a syllable with a reduced vowel. Then the subrules of the Cheremis rule (25)–(26) are as shown in (32):

(32)
$$S \rightarrow [+\text{stress}] / \begin{Bmatrix} \_\_\_\# \\ \_\_\_R\# \\ \_\_\_RR\# \\ \_\_\_RRR\# \\ \vdots \end{Bmatrix} \begin{matrix} (a) \\ (b) \\ (c) \\ (d) \\ \vdots \end{matrix}$$

Now note that an input subject to any one rule in the infinite list in (32) will necessarily also be subject to all the earlier rules. That is, a subset relationship holds between the inputs of each pair of rules. The Elsewhere Condition therefore establishes disjunctive ordering within the entire set of rules.

Now compare the umlaut example. The subrules of rule (29) are as shown in (33):

(33) $[-\text{consonantal}] \rightarrow [-\text{back}] /$

$$\begin{Bmatrix} \_\_\_\begin{bmatrix} +\text{high} \\ -\text{back} \\ -\text{consonantal} \end{bmatrix} & (a) \\ \_\_\_[-\text{syllabic}]\begin{bmatrix} +\text{high} \\ -\text{back} \\ -\text{consonantal} \end{bmatrix} & (b) \\ \_\_\_[-\text{syllabic}][-\text{syllabic}]\begin{bmatrix} +\text{high} \\ -\text{back} \\ -\text{consonantal} \end{bmatrix} & (c) \\ \_\_\_[-\text{syllabic}][-\text{syllabic}][-\text{syllabic}]\begin{bmatrix} +\text{high} \\ -\text{back} \\ -\text{consonantal} \end{bmatrix} & (d) \\ \vdots & \vdots \end{Bmatrix}$$

Unlike the case in (32), an input subject to a rule in (33) is not necessarily subject to all the earlier rules; no subset relationship holds between the inputs of the subrules. For example, [namnian] > [nemnian] (OIcel *nefna* 'name') is subject to case (c) but not (a) or (b). Hence the Elsewhere Condition is inapplicable, and a word like [drɔwmi] will be subject to cases (b) and (c), giving *drøymi*. The Elsewhere Condition, then, makes exactly the correct predictions in these two cases.

Of course one cannot put too much stock in this argument until more examples are found. I must also say that the applicability of the Elsewhere Condition in the case of infinite sets of rules is intuitively less clear to me than where a simple pair of rules is involved. Nevertheless, the examples with infinite sets of rules do appear to be consistent with what is predicted by the Elsewhere Condition.

Let us now briefly consider some ways in which the Elsewhere Condition might be generalized. The first possibility is that this condition might be applicable not just to rules which are adjacent in the ordering, but also to rules which are separated by other rules. Another possibility is that a subset relationship in the external context— namely, P____Q, R____S in (4)—rather than the whole structural analysis—PAQ, RCS—might suffice to establish disjunctivity.

The possibility of disjunction between nonadjacent rules on the basis of the Elsewhere Condition is suggested, for example, by Halle's analyses of Slavic accent (Halle (1971)). In Halle's system, a number of early accent rules place accent marks on stems and endings of words, depending on morphological features of these stems and endings. Close to the end of the phonology, another accent rule (the "circumflex" rule) puts an initial accent on any word which has not been accented by the earlier rules. As Halle remarks (p. 14, note 8), the circumflex rule is *disjunctive* with respect to earlier accent rules. However, there can be no question of getting this disjunctivity from any parentheses or angled brackets since *other rules intervene* between the early accent placement rules and the circumflex rule. Therefore, in the present theory we must add to the circumflex rule an unsightly annotation which says that the rule only applies to words which as yet carry no accent. In general, such annotated rules must be regarded as indications that something is wrong with the theory. In this case such a conclusion might be supported by the following consideration. Let us imagine a hypothetical Slavic language which differs from the actual languages only in that its circumflex rule lacks the annotation. We might expect this to be the normal case. However, not only is such a Slavic language unattested, but it seems reasonable to assume that it could not exist at all.

The subset relation holds between the early accent rules, which apply to words whose morphemes belong to certain specified categories, and the circumflex rule, which (as Halle states it) applies to any word at all. If, then, we allow the Elsewhere Condition to hold for nonadjacent rules, we obtain the desired interpretation. This again restricts the class of possible grammars.

A second problematic extension of the Elsewhere Condition is indicated by an example that involves external sandhi in Sanskrit. A final dental (including -*s*) assimilates obligatorily in place of articulation to a following coronal stop. In addition, -*s* assimilates optionally to any following segment (in practice, to any following voiceless segment—I assume that *s* before voiced segments has been eliminated by earlier rules). Elsewhere (when a pause follows, or when the optional assimilation rule has not been applied), *s* turns to *ḥ*. I illustrate in (34):

(34) $t \# ṭ \rightarrow ṭ \# ṭ$
$\quad t \# c \rightarrow c \# c$
$\quad s \# ṭ \rightarrow ṣ \# ṭ$
$\quad s \# c \rightarrow ś \# c$
$\quad t \# p = t \# p$
$\quad t \# ṣ = t \# ṣ$
$\quad s \# p \rightarrow \varphi \# p \quad$ or $\quad ḥ \# p$
$\quad s \# k \rightarrow x \# k \quad$ or $\quad ḥ \# k$
$\quad s \# ś \rightarrow ś \# ś \quad$ or $\quad ḥ \# ś$
$\quad s \# ṣ \rightarrow ṣ \# ṣ \quad$ or $\quad ḥ \# ṣ$
$\quad s \# \rightarrow ḥ \#$

We have, therefore, the Assimilation Rules in (35) and (36):

(35) $[+\text{coronal}] \rightarrow [\alpha\text{place}] \ / \ \underline{\hspace{1cm}} \# \begin{bmatrix} \alpha\text{place} \\ +\text{coronal} \\ -\text{continuant} \end{bmatrix}$ *Obligatory*

(36) $\begin{bmatrix} +\text{coronal} \\ +\text{continuant} \end{bmatrix} \rightarrow [\alpha\text{place}] \ / \ \underline{\hspace{1cm}} \# [\alpha\text{place}]$ *Optional*

The present theory does not allow us to write the "elsewhere" case simply as (37):

(37) $\begin{bmatrix} +\text{coronal} \\ +\text{continuant} \end{bmatrix} \rightarrow \d{h} \ / \ \underline{\hspace{1cm}} \#$

This rule would apply incorrectly to *devas* # *tiṣṭhati* to produce *devaḥ tiṣṭhati. To prevent this, we must restrict rule (37) as in (38):

(38) $\begin{bmatrix} +\text{coronal} \\ +\text{continuant} \end{bmatrix} \rightarrow \d{h} \ / \ \underline{\hspace{1cm}} \# \left\{ \begin{matrix} \left\{ \begin{matrix} [-\text{coronal}] \\ [+\text{continuant}] \end{matrix} \right\} \\ \text{pause} \end{matrix} \right\}$

But this restriction merely serves to exclude the case in which the first Assimilation Rule (35) is obligatory, namely, the environment before coronal stops.

It would be desirable to be able to extend disjunctivity to cover a relation like that between rules (35) and (37). The Elsewhere Condition, as formulated in (4), is not sufficient to do this because the requisite subset relation does not hold between the inputs. One possibility is that (4) be extended to the case where $P\underline{\hspace{0.5cm}}Q$ is a subset of $R\underline{\hspace{0.5cm}}S$, that is, where the external context only is taken into consideration.

At this point such extensions of (4) are hardly more than speculation. The Elsewhere Condition itself, however, seems to work right in a sufficiently wide range of examples to be taken as a serious candidate for a general principle of phonological theory.

REFERENCES

Anderson, S. (1969), *West Scandinavian Vowel Systems and the Ordering of Phonological Rules*, unpublished Ph.D. dissertation, M.I.T.

Bright, W. (1957), *The Karok Language*, University of California Publications in Linguistics, 13.

Chomsky, N., and M. Halle (1968), *The Sound Pattern of English*, New York: Harper & Row.

Halle, M. (1971), "Remarks on Slavic accentology," *Linguistic Inquiry*, 2, 1–20.

Howard, I. (1972), *A Directional Theory of Rule Application in Phonology*, unpublished Ph.D. dissertation, M.I.T.

Itkonen, E. (1966), *Kieli ja sen tutkimus*, Helsinki: WSOY.

Itkonen, T. (1964), *Proto-Finnic Final Consonants*, Helsinki.

Johnson, C. D. (1970), *Formal Aspects of Phonological Description*, POLA Reports, 11, Berkeley.

Kielhorn, F. (1880), *The Vyākaraṇa-Mahābhaṣya of Patañjali*, I–III, Poona.

Kielhorn, F. (1960²), *The Paribhāśenduśekhara of Nāgojībhaṭṭa*, 2nd ed., K. V. Abhyankar, ed., Poona: Bhandarkar Institute.

Kiparsky, P. (1972), "Metrics and Morphophonemics in the *Rigveda*," in M. Brame, ed.,
    Contributions to Generative Phonology, Austin: University of Texas Press.
Koutsoudas, A., J. Sanders, and G. Noll (1971), "On the Application of Phonological
    Rules," reproduced by the Indiana University Linguistics Club.
Noreen, A. (1923), *Altisländische Grammitik*, Halle: Niemeyer.
Sapir, D. (1965), *A Grammar of Diola-Fogny*, Cambridge: University Press.
Wiik, K. (1969), *Suomen kielen morfofonemiikkaa*, Turun yliopiston fonetiikan laitoksen
    julkaisuja.

on the evolution of human language[1]

Philip Lieberman

University of Connecticut
and
Haskins Laboratories

1. INTRODUCTION

The uniqueness of human language has been viewed as one of the defining characteristics of *Homo sapiens* at least since the time of Descartes. To Descartes, human
linguistic ability was essentially a manifestation of the intercession of divine will.
He believed that human language reflected the presence of a soul. It was God's gift
to man, a gift which made him distinct from the animals.

More recently, in the light of the fossil evidence of hominid evolution, the
"uniqueness" of human language has come to present certain problems. Human
language is unique insofar as no other living animal has modern man's linguistic
ability. The fossil evidence, however, demonstrates that man is related to animals that
clearly do not possess this ability. The living nonhuman primates, the apes and
monkeys, cannot produce "articulate" human speech and they do not appear to
communicate by means of a linguistic "code." Present-day apes and monkeys therefore must lack the particular species-specific physical attributes that underlie human
language.

Many other aspects of human behavior also involve "unique" species-specific
physical attributes. Modern man's upright posture, for example, has to do with his
particular spinal flexture, pelvis, and foot, as well as with the foramen magnum,
occipital condoyles and such of the human skull. No other living animal has these

[1] This work would not have been possible without the anatomical insights of E. S. Crelin of the
Yale University School of Medicine. I would also like to note the contribution of D. H. Klatt of
M.I.T., as well as the comments of A. M. Liberman, C. Darwin, and T. Rand of Haskins Laboratories,
which have been incorporated in the discussion of speech encoding.

physical attributes, which are necessary conditions for an upright human posture. It is, however, possible to reconstruct the gradual development of these attributes through the study of extinct hominid species. The Darwinian theory of evolution is credible since the evolution of these "unique" physical characteristics of modern man can be traced to creatures that ultimately resemble, in many ways, present-day non-human primates. The "unique" physical attributes that underlie modern man's upright posture are thus unique only in a synchronic sense.

Human language presents a similar case. It is "unique" only insofar as no living animal possesses even a degree of linguistic ability that approximates man's. The "uniqueness" of human language is superficially more striking than the "uniqueness" of an upright human posture: whereas some living animals can assume a semiupright humanlike posture for short periods of time, no living animal can speak at all.[2] Nevertheless, we will demonstrate that it is possible to trace the evolution of human language once we have identified some of the relevant species-specific mechanisms that underlie language in modern man.

Human language undoubtedly involves the presence of the human brain. The fossil evidence convincingly shows that hominid brains have gradually tended to increase in size over the past three million years, both absolutely and relatively. The special role of the human brain was, in fact, recognized by Descartes, who based the distinction between human language and animal communication solely on its presence. Descartes believed that animals like apes had the physical mechanism that is necessary for the production of human speech. Studies like Perrault's (1676) and Tyson's (1699) comparative anatomies of the chimpanzee showed that the larynx, lips, teeth, and jaws of the nonhuman primates are similar to those of man. Descartes and his successors thus believed that apes could learn to talk if they had the necessary mental ability. La Mettrie (1747) said that apes are, in effect, mentally retarded people. Since apes supposedly have the necessary mechanism for the production of human speech, La Mettrie believed that if they were carefully tutored, as though they were deaf children, for example, they could be taught to speak. The ape would then, in La Mettrie's terms, "be a perfect little gentleman."

The belief that apes have a speech output mechanism that would be adequate for the production of human speech has persisted to the present time. Osgood (1953), for example, states that "the chimpanzee is capable of vocalizations almost as elaborate as man's." Yerkes and Learned (1925) identify more than thirty-two speech sounds for the chimpanzee. Accordingly, attempts to teach chimpanzees to talk continue to be made. A study by Hayes (1952), for example, centered about an attempt to teach a chimpanzee to talk by raising it as though it were a retarded child. No one, however, has ever succeeded at this task (Kellogg (1968)).

The failure of all such attempts has a simple explanation. The assumption that apes have the anatomical mechanism that is necessary for the production of human speech is false (Lieberman (1968), Lieberman *et al.* (1969)). Without this mechanism, apes would not be able to produce "articulate" human speech even if they had the necessary mental ability.[3]

[2] The "speech" of "talking birds" is not similar to human speech either at the acoustic or anatomic level (Greenewalt (1967)). A parrot's imitation of speech resembles a human's imitation of a siren. The signal is accepted as mimicry. It has different acoustic properties and it is produced by means of a different apparatus.

[3] We shall define "articulate" speech, for the purposes of this discussion, as speech that encompasses the full range of sounds that are used in human language. Although adult humans generally lose the ability to produce this entire range of sounds, all normal human speakers possess the necessary anatomical and neural mechanisms. Any normal adult could have learned to speak any language if he or she had been exposed to the proper linguistic environment as a child.

We have been able to trace the evolution of the species-specific anatomical mechanism that is needed in order to produce human speech (Lieberman and Crelin (1971), Lieberman *et al.* (1972)). The anatomical mechanism that is a necessary condition for the production of human speech is obviously not a sufficient condition for the possession of human linguistic ability. Certain neural mechanisms, probably specialized species-specific ones, must also be present (Lenneburg (1967)). It is difficult to make any substantive inferences about the presence of particular neural mechanisms in the brains of extinct fossil hominids since we can deduce only the external shape and size of the brain from a fossil skull. Also, we lack a detailed knowledge of how the human brain functions. We could not really assess the linguistic abilities of even a modern man simply by examining his brain. We can, however, form some substantive hypotheses concerning the perceptual and linguistic "encoding" abilities of extinct hominid species, as well as living nonhuman primates, by means of recent theoretical and experimental advances relating to the production and the perception of speech.

2. ACOUSTIC THEORY OF SPEECH PRODUCTION

Some knowledge of the acoustic and anatomical basis of human speech is necessary in order to understand the significance of the evolution of the human speech-producing mechanism. Human speech essentially involves the generation of sound by the mechanism of vocal cord vibration and/or air turbulence and the acoustic shaping of these sound sources by the resonances of the supralaryngeal vocal tract. During the production of speech, the shape of the human supralaryngeal vocal tract changes continually, producing corresponding changes in its resonant properties.

A useful mechanical analog to the aspect of speech production that is of concern here is a pipe organ. The musical function of each pipe is determined by its length and shape. (The pipes are of different lengths and may be open at one end or closed at both ends.) The pipes are all excited by the same source. It is the resonant modes of each pipe that determine the note's acoustic character. In human speech the phonetic properties that differentiate vowels like [i] and [a] are determined by the resonant modes of the supralaryngeal vocal tract. The frequencies at which resonances occur are called "formant" frequencies.

The acoustic theory of speech production thus relates an acoustic signal to a supralaryngeal vocal tract configuration and a source. It is therefore possible to determine some of the constraints on an animal's phonetic range if the range of its supralaryngeal vocal tract variation is known. The phonetic repertoire of an animal can obviously be expanded if different sources are used with similar supralaryngeal vocal tract configurations. We can, however, isolate the constraints that the range of supralaryngeal vocal tract variation will impose on the phonetic repertoire.

3. VOCAL TRACT ANATOMY

The anatomic specializations that are necessary for human speech become evident when we compare the supralaryngeal vocal tract of adult modern man with that of creatures who lack human speech.

In Figures 1–4 we show lateral views of the skulls of newborn man, adult chimpanzee, the La Chapelle-aux-Saints Neanderthal man, and adult modern man. The

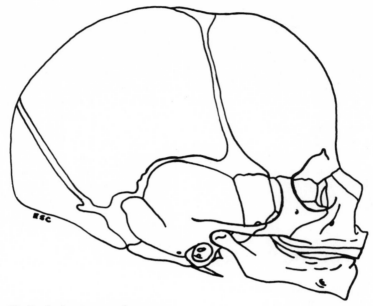

Figure 1. Skull of a human newborn.

skulls have all been drawn to appear nearly equal in size. The newborn skull is obviously much smaller than any of the other skulls and would superficially appear to be quite different from the others if the skulls were presented in their natural scale.

We shall give a brief account of the skeletal similarities in newborn modern man, adult chimpanzee, and Neanderthal man that make it possible to reconstruct

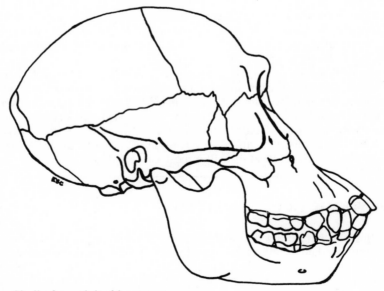

Figure 2. Skull of an adult chimpanzee.

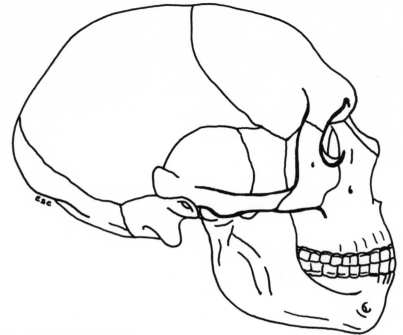

Figure 3.   Skull of fossil Neanderthal man.

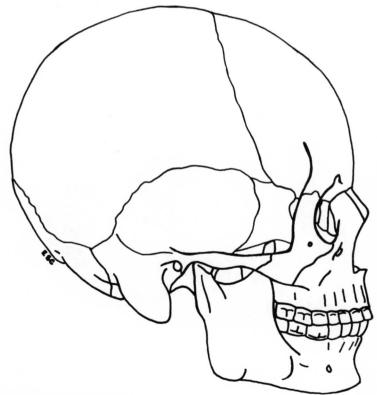

Figure 4.   Skull of an adult human.

the supralaryngeal vocal tract of Neanderthal man. To begin with, note the similar "flattened-out" skull bases in the newborn, chimpanzee, and Neanderthal skulls (Figures 1–3). Other features that make the newborn, chimpanzee, and Neanderthal skulls similar to one another, but different from the adult modern man's skull (Figure 4) are as follows: (*a*) there is no mastoid process, (*b*) there is no chin, (*c*) the body of the mandible is much longer than the ramus, (*d*) the posterior border of the mandibular ramus is slanted away from the vertical plane, (*e*) there is a more horizontal inclination of the mandibular foramen leading to the mandibular canal, (*f*) the pterygoid process of the sphenoid bone is relatively short and its lateral lamina is more inclined away from the vertical plane, (*g*) the styloid process is more inclined away from the vertical plane, (*h*) the dental arch of the maxilla is U-shaped instead of V-shaped, (*i*) the basilar part of the occipital bone between the foramen magnum and the sphenoid bone is only slightly inclined away from the horizontal toward the vertical plane, (*j*) the roof of the nasopharynx is a relatively shallow elongated arch, (*k*) the vomer bone is relatively short in its vertical height and its posterior border is inclined away from the vertical plane, (*l*) the vomer bone is relatively far removed from the junction of the sphenoid bone and the basilar part of the occipital bone, (*m*) the occipital condoyles are relatively small and elongated.

The chimpanzee (Figure 2) differs from newborn and adult modern man and Neanderthal man insofar as its mandible has a "simian shelf," that is, internal buttressing of the anterior portion of the mandible. The simian shelf inhibits the formation of a large air cavity behind the teeth. In adult man a large cavity behind the teeth can be formed by pulling the tongue back in the mouth.

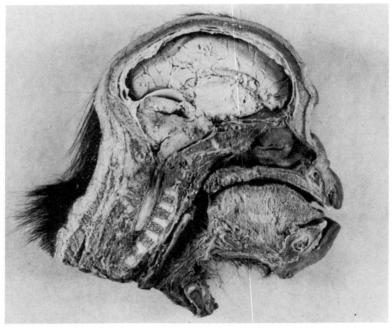

Figure 5.   Left half of the head and neck of a young adult male chimpanzee sectioned in the midsagittal plane.

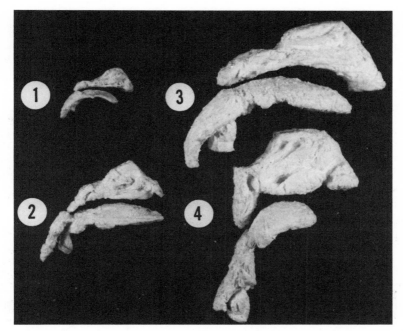

Figure 6.   Casts of the nasal, oral, pharyngeal, and laryngeal cavities of (1) newborn human, (2) adult chimpanzee, (3) Neanderthal reconstruction, and (4) adult human.

The significance of these skeletal features can be seen when the supralaryngeal vocal tracts that correspond to these skulls are examined. In Figure 5 a photograph of the head and neck of a chimpanzee sectioned in the midsagittal plane is presented (see Lieberman *et al.* (1972)). A silicone rubber cast was made of the air passages, including the nasal cavity, by filling each side of the split air passages separately in the sectioned head and neck to insure perfect filling of the cavities. The casts from each side of the head and neck were then fused together to make a complete cast of the air passage. Similar casts were made using the same technique for specimens of newborn and adult man (Lieberman and Crelin (1971)). These casts are shown in Figure 6, together with a cast of the reconstructed supralaryngeal air passages of Neanderthal man. Because of the many similarities among newborn, chimpanzee, and Neanderthal with regard to the base of the skull and the mandible, along with the known detailed anatomy of newborn, adult man, and apes, it was possible to locate the larynx of Neanderthal man in relation to his skull and to reconstruct his tongue and pharyngeal musculature.[4]

Even though the cast of the newborn air passages is much smaller than the other casts, the similarity between the newborn and the chimpanzee is quite apparent. When outlines of the air passages from all four are made nearly equal in size in

[4] A detailed discussion of the reconstruction and phonetic ability of Neanderthal man is presented in Lieberman and Crelin (1971). The evolutionary status of Neanderthal man and Haeckel's Law of Recapitulation are also discussed.

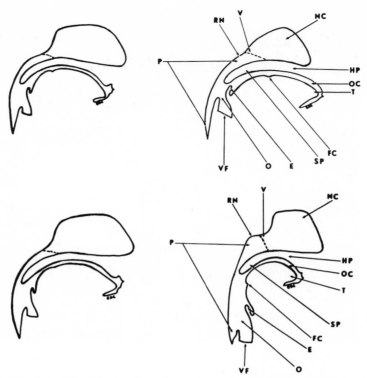

Figure 7.   Diagrams of the air passages of newborn human, adult chimpanzee, Neanderthal man, and adult human. The anatomical details that are keyed on the chimpanzee and adult man are as follows: P—pharynx, RN—roof of nasopharynx, V—vomer bone, NC—nasal cavity, HP—hard palate, OC—oral cavity, T—tongue, FC—foramen cecum, SP—soft palate, E—epiglottis, O—opening of larynx into pharynx, VF—level of vocal folds.

Figure 7, one can more readily recognize what the basic differences and similarities are:

(*a*) In the chimpanzee, Neanderthal man, and newborn human, the tongue at rest is completely within the oral cavity, whereas in adult man the posterior third of the tongue is in a vertical position forming the anterior wall of the supralaryngeal pharyngeal cavity. The foramen cecum of the tongue is thus located at a far more anterior point in the oral cavity in the chimpanzee and newborn than it is in adult man.

(*b*) In the chimpanzee, Neanderthal, and newborn, the soft palate and epiglottis can be approximated, whereas they are widely separated in adult man and cannot approximate.

(*c*) There is practically no supralaryngeal portion of the pharynx in the direct airway out from the larynx when the soft palate shuts off the nasal cavity in the chimpanzee, Neanderthal, and newborn; in adult man half of the supralaryngeal vocal tract is formed by the pharyngeal cavity. This difference is a consequence of the opening of the larynx into the pharynx, which is immediately behind the oral cavity in the chimpanzee, Neanderthal, and newborn; in adult man this opening occurs farther down in the pharynx. Note that the supralaryngeal pharynx in adult man serves both as a pathway for the ingestion of food and liquids and as an airway to the larynx. In the chimpanzee, Neanderthal, and newborn, the section of the pharynx that is behind the oral cavity is reserved for deglutition. The high epiglottis can, moreover, close the oral cavity to retain solids and liquids and allow unhampered respiration through the nose.

(*d*) The level of the vocal folds (cords) at rest in the chimpanzee is at the upper border of the fourth cervical vertebra, whereas in adult man it is between the fifth and sixth in a relatively longer neck. The position of the hyoid bone is high in the chimpanzee, Neanderthal, and newborn, concomitant with the high position of the larynx.

4. SUPRALARYNGEAL VOCAL TRACT CONSTRAINTS ON PHONETIC REPERTOIRES

We have noted that human speech production involves a source of sound and a supralaryngeal vocal tract that acts as an acoustic "filter" or modulator. Man uses his articulators (the tongue, lips, mandible, velum, pharyngeal constrictors, and so on) to modify dynamically in time the resonant structure that the supralaryngeal vocal tract imposes on the acoustic sound pressure radiated at the speaker's lips and nares.

The phonetic inventory of a human language is therefore limited by (*a*) the number of acoustically distinct sound sources that man is capable of controlling during speech communication, and (*b*) the number of distinct resonant patterns available through the positioning and dynamic manipulation of the articulators. In most human languages a phonetic analysis will reveal a phonemic inventory on the order of twenty to forty distinct sound types (Trubetzkoy (1939), Jakobson *et al.* (1952)). Most of the segment proliferations are achieved through the varied use of the articulators. For example, in English there are ten vowels that differ only in the articulatory configuration of the supralaryngeal vocal tract and concomitantly in the resonant structure, that is, the formant structure, of the acoustic output (Peterson and Barney (1952)).

There is a direct relationship between the articulatory configuration of the supralaryngeal vocal tract and the formant structure (Fant (1960)). The relationship depends exclusively on the area function or cross-sectional area of the vocal tract as a function of the distance from the vocal cords to the lips. The availability of digital computers makes it possible to determine the range of formant frequency patterns that a supralaryngeal vocal tract can produce. If the supralaryngeal vocal tract area function is systematically manipulated in accord with the muscular and anatomical constraints of the head and neck, a computer can be programmed to compute the formant frequencies that correspond to the total range of supralaryngeal vocal tract variation (Henke (1966)). In other words, a computer-implemented model of a supralaryngeal vocal tract can be used to determine its possible contribution to the phonetic repertoire.

We can conveniently begin to determine whether a nonhuman supralaryngeal vocal tract can produce the range of sounds that occurs in human language by exploring its vowel-producing ability. Consonantal vocal tract configurations can also be modeled; however, it is reasonable to start with vowels since the production of consonants may also involve rapid, coordinated articulatory maneuvers which we can only speculate about with regard to the abilities of fossil hominids.

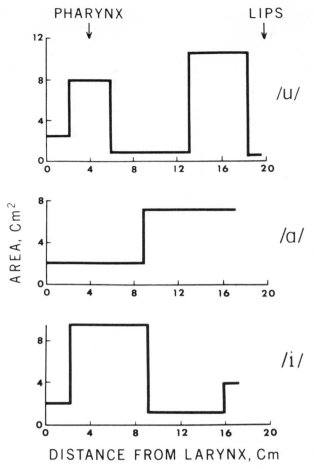

Figure 8. Stylized supralaryngeal vocal tract area functions that characterize the human vowels [a], [i], and [u].

5. THE VOWEL TRIANGLE

5.1. Adult Human

Articulatory and acoustic analyses have shown that the three vowels [a], [i], and [u] are the limiting articulations of a vowel triangle that is language-universal (Trubetzkoy (1939)). The body of the tongue is high and fronted to form a constricted oral cavity in [i], whereas it is low to form a large oral cavity in [a] and [u]. The tongue body forms a large pharyngeal cavity in [i] and [u] and a constricted pharyngeal cavity in [a]. If the tongue body moves to form any greater constrictions, turbulent friction noise is generated at the vocal tract constriction and the articulation produces a consonant, not a vowel. Other English vowels are produced by means of supralaryngeal vocal tract configurations within the articulatory triangle defined by [a], [i], and [u].[5]

---

[5] It can be argued that [ɔ] forms a fourth position on a vowel "quadrangle," but this modification will not affect our arguments in any essential way.

The universality and special nature of [a], [i], and [u] can be argued from theoretical grounds as well. Employing the simplified and idealized area functions shown in Figure 8, Stevens (1969) has shown that these articulatory configurations (*a*) are acoustically stable for small changes in articulation and therefore require less precision in articulatory control than similar adjacent articulations, and (*b*) contain a prominent acoustic feature, that is, two formants that are in close proximity to form a distinct energy concentration.

The vowels [a], [i], and [u] have another unique property: they are the only vowels in which an acoustic pattern can be related to a unique vocal tract area function (Lindblom and Sundberg (1969), Stevens (1969)). Other vowels, such as [e], [ɪ], [ʊ], can be produced by means of several alternate area functions (Stevens and House (1955)).

A human listener, when he hears a syllable that contains a token of [a], [i], or [u] can calculate the size of the supralaryngeal vocal tract that was used to produce the syllable. The listener, in other words, can tell whether a speaker has a large or small vocal tract. This is not possible with other vowels since a speaker with a small vocal tract can, for example, by increasing the degree of lip rounding, produce a token of /ʊ/ that would be consistent with a larger vocal tract with less lip rounding. These uncertainties do not exist for [a], [i], and [u] since the required discontinuities in the supralaryngeal vocal tract area functions (Figure 8) produce acoustic patterns that are beyond the range of compensatory maneuvers. The degree of lip rounding for the [u] in Figure 8, for example, is so extreme that it is impossible to constrict the lip opening any more and still produce a vowel.[6] The vowels [a], [i], and [u] are therefore different in kind from the remaining "central" vowels. These "vocal-tract size calibrating" properties of [a], [i], and [u] play a crucial role in the perception of speech, and we will have more to say on this matter.

We can conclude from these considerations that the vowel space reserved for human language is delimited by the vowels [a], [i], and [u]. A study of the theoretical limitations on vowels produced by a related species can therefore proceed by determining the largest vowel triangle that its articulatory system is capable of generating.

5.2. Chimpanzee and Newborn Human

In Figure 9 we have plotted the vowel range of the chimpanzee relative to that of modern man. This is done on a plot of first formant frequency versus second formant frequency. The chimpanzee supralaryngeal vocal tract shown in Figures 5, 6, and 7 was modeled on the digital computer in an attempt to produce vowels that were as close as possible to the human vowels [a], [i], and [u] (see Lieberman *et al.* (1972)). This was done by generating area functions that were as close to those of the adult human as the chimpanzee's anatomy would permit. Articulatory maneuvers that were not exactly equivalent to those of adult humans were also admissible when they produced the appropriate acoustic results. The formant frequencies produced by the most "successful" chimpanzee vocal tract configurations were scaled down in frequency by a factor proportional to the ratio of a chimpanzee vocal tract of 10 cm to the mean vocal tract length of 17 cm of adult man so that they could be compared directly with comparable data in adult man. The data points labeled "C" in Figure 9 show these formant frequencies, which delimit the chimpanzee vowel triangle. The

---

[6] If the constriction becomes too small, turbulent noise will be generated at the constriction and the sound will no longer be a vowel.

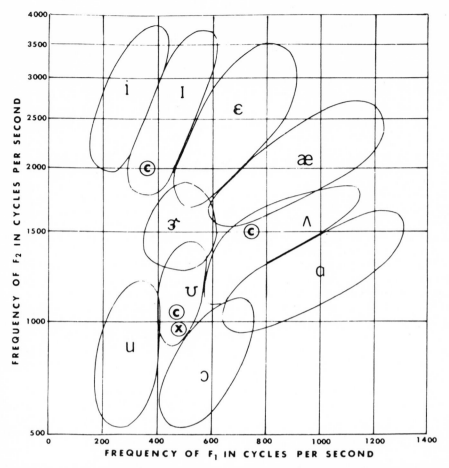

Figure 9.   Plot of first and second formant frequencies for chimpanzee (C) and newborn (X) "extreme" vowels. The closed loops enclose 90 percent of the data points derived from a sample of 76 adult men, women, and children producing American–English vowels. Note that the chimpanzee and newborn vocal tracts cannot produce the vowels [a], [i], and [u].

chimpanzee vocalizations are compared to normative data for modern man, derived from a sample of 76 men, women, and children (Peterson and Barney (1952)).[7] The labeled loops enclose the data points that accounted for 90 percent of the samples in each vowel category. Note that the chimpanzee vowel formant frequencies do not fall within the regions that specify the formant frequency patterns that are necessary for the human vowels [a], [i], [u].

The supralaryngeal vocal tract of the newborn human does not differ substantially from that of the chimpanzee (Figures 5–7). The absence of a simian shelf in the mandible, however, allows the formation of a larger front cavity in the production of vowels that approximate the adult human [u]. In Figure 9 the formant locations of this area function, which resemble that of the chimpanzee with a larger front cavity, are computed, scaled, and plotted as data point "X." The resulting vowel

[7] The children in the Peterson and Barney study all had vocal tracts that conformed to that typical of adult morphology (Lieberman *et al.* (1968)).

sound is comparable to the English vowel /ʊ/, not /u/, but it is a closer acoustic approximation to /u/. The acoustic output of the newborn vocal tract does not otherwise differ substantially from that of the chimpanzee. Perceptual and acoustic studies of the vocalizations of human newborns (Irwin (1948), Lieberman *et al.* (1968)) show that all and only the vowels that can be produced are indeed produced.

5.3. Neanderthal Man

The vowel-producing abilities of the reconstructed supralaryngeal vocal tract of the La Chapelle-aux-Saints Neanderthal fossil are represented in Figure 10. The formant frequencies of the Neanderthal supralaryngeal vocal tract configurations that best approximated the human vowels [a], [i], and [u] were computed, scaled, and plotted with respect to adult modern man (Lieberman and Crelin (1971)). Note that the Neanderthal vowels which are each labeled "N" do not fall in the human ranges for [a], [i], or [u].

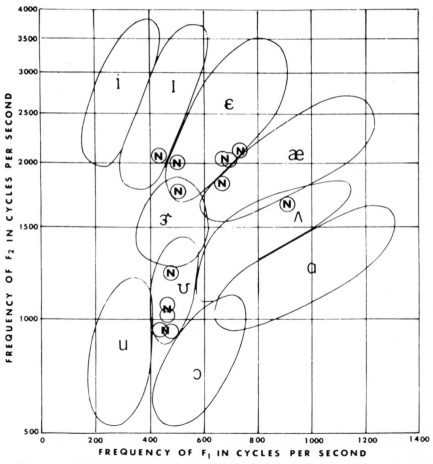

Figure 10. Plot of first and second formant frequencies for "extreme" vowels of reconstructed Neanderthal vocal tract.

The Neanderthal vocal tract was given the benefit of all possible doubts in the computer modeling. For example, the maximum range of laryngeal cavity variation typical of modern man (Fant (1960)) was used in a manner that would enhance the phonetic ability of the Neanderthal vocal tract. Articulatory maneuvers that would be somewhat acrobatic in modern man were also used to enhance Neanderthal phonetic ability. Our computer modeling was guided by the results of x-ray motion pictures of speech production, vocalization, swallowing, and respiration in adult man (Perkell (1969), Haskins Laboratories (1962)) and in the newborn (Truby *et al.* (1965)). This information, plus the known comparative anatomy of the living primates, allowed a fairly "conservative" simulation of the vowel-producing ability of this fossil specimen who is typical of the range of "classic" Neanderthal man.[8] We may have permitted a greater vowel-producing range for Neanderthal man since we consistently generated area functions that were more humanlike than apelike whenever we were in doubt. Despite these compensations, the Neanderthal vocal tract still cannot produce [a], [i], or [u].

Our modeling of the newborn vocal tract served as a control procedure since we were able to produce the vowels that newborn humans actually produce. We produced, however, a greater vowel range than has been observed in the acoustic analysis of chimpanzee vocalizations (Lieberman (1968)). We will return to this point later in the discussion since it may reflect the absence of neural mechanisms in the nonhuman primates.

5.4. General Observations

Some general observations on the anatomical basis of the absence of the vowels [a], [i], and [u] from the phonetic repertoires of the chimpanzee, newborn human, and Neanderthal man are appropriate before we go on to discuss consonant-producing abilities. The idealized vocal tract area functions that specify these vowels (Figure 8) require a large ratio of the areas of the small and large sections. In addition they require rather abrupt boundaries between sections. These conditions are satisfied when adult humans produce these vowels (Fant (1960), Perkell (1969)). The low position of the adult human larynx, together with the presence of a supralaryngeal pharyngeal region that can change its cross-sectional area independent of the area of the oral region, allows the production of the vowels.

Abrupt area function changes at the midpoint of the vocal tract can be achieved in adult man at the junction of the pharyngeal and oral cavities where the styloglossus muscle can be effective in pulling the body of the tongue upward and backward in the direction of the nasopharynx (Sobotta-Figge (1965), Perkell (1969), Lieberman (1970)). The cross-sectional area of the oral and pharyngeal cavities can be independently manipulated in adult man while a midpoint constriction is maintained. The supralaryngeal vocal tract of adult man can thus, in effect, function as a "two tube" system. The lack of a supralaryngeal pharyngeal region prevents the chimpanzee and newborn human from employing these mechanisms. There can only be an attempt to distort the tongue body in the oral cavity to obtain changes in cross-sectional area. The intrinsic musculature of the tongue severely limits the range of deformations that the

---

[8] It has been noted (Lieberman and Crelin (1971)) that a number of fossils that differ slightly in other ways all have a "flattened-out" skull base and other anatomical features that indicate the absence of a supralaryngeal vocal tract like that of adult modern man. There is, in other words, a class of "Neanderthaloid" fossils who lack the ability to produce the full range of human speech.

tongue body can be expected to employ. The chimpanzee and newborn human, in effect, have "single tube" resonant systems.

The absence of the vowels [a], [i], and [u] from the vowel systems of chimpanzee, newborn human, and Neanderthal man in Figures 9 and 10 is thus an indirect way of showing that the vocal tracts of these creatures cannot form the abrupt area functions that are necessary for these vowels.

6. SPEECH PRODUCTION AND SPEECH PERCEPTION

Supralaryngeal vocal tract area functions that approximated typical consonantal configurations for adult man (Fant (1960), Perkell (1969)) were also modeled on the digital computer (Lieberman and Crelin (1971), Lieberman *et al.* (1972)). The chimpanzee, newborn human, and Neanderthal man all appeared to have anatomical mechanisms that would allow the production of both labial and dental consonants such as [b], [p], [t], [s] if other muscular and neural factors were present.

It is obvious that some of these other factors are not present in newborn humans since dental consonants do not occur, although labial consonants are fairly common (Irwin (1948)). X-ray motion pictures of the swallowing maneuvers of newborn humans (Truby *et al.* (1965)) show that the newborn infant's tongue can execute maneuvers that are similar to those that would be necessary for the production of dental consonants during vocal activity. The nonoccurrence of dental consonants in the utterances of newborn humans therefore cannot be due simply to deficiencies involving the musculature of the tongue. The occurrence of labial consonants likewise suggests that the nonoccurrence of dental consonants is probably not a consequence of a general inability to produce rapid, controlled articulatory maneuvers.

A similar discrepancy between the constraints that the supralaryngeal vocal tract imposes on the phonetic repertoire and actual performance also appears to exist in chimpanzees. Chimpanzees do not appear to produce dental consonants even though they have the anatomical "machinery" that would permit them to do so. For example, observations of captive chimpanzees have not revealed patterns of vocal communication that utilize contrasts between labial and dental consonants (Lieberman (1968)).

It is unlikely that the failure to observe dental consonants in chimpanzee vocalizations is due to a limited data sample since attempts to train chimpanzees to mimic human speech have not succeeded in teaching them to produce dental consonants. At least one chimpanzee has been taught to produce labial consonants like [p] (Hayes (1952)).

Our computer modeling of the chimpanzee vocal tract shows that these animals have the anatomic ability to produce a number of vowels that in human speech are "phonemic" elements, that is, sound contrasts that convey linguistically meaningful information. Chimpanzees, however, do not appear to make use of these vowel possibilities. Instead, they seem to make maximum use of the "neutral" uniform cross-section supralaryngeal vocal tract shape (Jakobson *et al.* (1952), Lieberman (1968)) with source variations. Chimpanzees, for example, will make calls that are different insofar as the glottal excitation is weak, breathy, has a high fundamental frequency, and so on.[9]

The absence of sounds that are anatomically possible may reflect perceptual limitations. In other words, chimpanzees and newborn humans may not use dental

[9] Meaningful chimpanzee calls can be "seen" in context in the recent sound motion pictures taken by P. Marler at the Gombe Stream Reserve chimpanzee project of J. Goodall (1965).

consonants in contrast with labial consonants because they cannot perceptually differentiate these sounds. Differences in vowel quality, such as between /ɪ/ and /e/, for example, may also be irrelevant for chimpanzees. The absence of the vowels [a], [i], and [u] from the chimpanzee's phonetic abilities is consistent with this hypothesis, which has wider implications concerning the general phonetic and linguistic abilities of the living nonhuman primates and hominid fossils like Neanderthal man.

7. SPEECH AND LANGUAGE

Linguists have, in general, tended to ignore the phonetic level of language and speech production. The prevailing assumption is that the interesting action is at the syntactic and semantic levels and that just about any sequence of arbitrary sounds would do for the transfer of linguistic information. Some linguists might point out, for example, that even simple binary codes, such as Morse code, can be used to transmit linguistic information. Neanderthal man, in this view, would therefore need only one sound contrast to communicate. After all, modern man can communicate by this means; why not Neanderthal man?

The answer to this question is quite simple. Human speech is a special mode of communication that allows modern man to communicate at least ten times faster than any other known method. Sounds other than speech cannot be made to convey language well.[10]

For 55 years attempts have been made to produce nonspeech sounds for use in reading machines for the blind, that is, devices that scan the print and convert it into meaningful sounds. In spite of the most diligent efforts in connection with the development of these machines, no nonspeech acoustic alphabet has yet been contrived that can be made to work more than one tenth as well as speech (Liberman *et al.* (1967)). Nor has any success attended efforts toward the use of visual displays in the development of "hearing" machines for the deaf.

The problem is quite clear when one considers the rate at which information is transferred in human speech. Human listeners can perceive as many as 25 to 30 phonetic segments per second in normal speech. This information rate far exceeds the resolving power of the human auditory system. It is, for example, impossible even to count simple pulses at rates of 20 pulses per second; the pulses simply merge into a continuous tone. Communication by means of Morse code would be possible, but it would be very slow. Human speech achieves its high information rate by means of an "encoding" process that is structured in terms of the anatomic and articulatory constraints of speech production. The presence of vowels like [a], [i], and [u] appears to be one of the anatomic factors that makes this encoding process possible.

8. SPEECH ENCODING AND THE "MOTOR THEORY" OF SPEECH PERCEPTION

In human speech a high rate of information transfer is achieved by "encoding" phonetic segments into syllable-sized units. The phonetic representation of a syllable like [du] essentially states that two independent elements are being transmitted. This

---

[10] I am essentially paraphrasing the discussion presented by A. M. Liberman (1970) with regard to the linguistic status of human speech and the process of speech encoding. Liberman's logic is clear, correct, and succinct.

syllable can be segmented at the phonetic level into two segments, [d] and [u], which can combine independently with other phonetic segments to form syllables like [di] and [gu]. Phonetic segments like [d], [g], [u], and [i] are also independent at the articulatory level insofar as they can each be specified in terms of an articulatory configuration. The phonetic element [u] thus involves a particular vocal tract configuration which approximates that in Figure 8. The phonetic element [d] likewise involves a particular vocal tract configuration in which the tongue blade momentarily occludes the oral cavity. It is possible to effect a segmentation of the syllable [du] at the articulatory level. If an x-ray motion picture of a speaker producing the syllable were viewed, it would be possible to see, for example, the articulatory gesture that produces the [d] in the syllable [du]. It is not, however, possible to segment the acoustic correlates of [d] from the speech signal.

In Figure 11 we have reproduced two simplified spectrographic patterns that will, when converted to sound, produce approximations to the syllables [di] and [du] (Liberman (1970)). The dark bands on these patterns represent the first and second formant frequencies of the supralaryngeal vocal tract as functions of time. Note that the formants move rapidly through a range of frequencies at the left of each pattern. These rapid movements, which occur in about 50 msec, are called transitions. The transition in the second formant, which is encircled, conveys the acoustic information that human listeners interpret as a token of a [d] *in the syllables* [di] *and* [du]. It is, however, impossible to isolate the acoustic pattern of [d] in these syllables. If tape recordings of these two syllables are "sliced" with the electronic equivalent of a pair of scissors (Lieberman (1963)), it is impossible to find a segment that contains only [d]. There is no way to cut the tape so as to obtain a piece that will produce [d] without also producing the next vowel or some reduced approximation to it.

Note that the encircled transitions are different for the two syllables. If these encircled transitions are isolated, listeners report that they hear either an upgoing or a falling frequency modulation. In context, with the acoustic correlates of the entire syllable, these transitions cause listeners to hear an "identical"-sounding [d] in both syllables. How does a human listener effect this perceptual response?

We have noted that the formant frequency patterns of speech reflect the resonances of the supralaryngeal vocal tract. The formant patterns that define the syllable [di] in Figure 11 thus reflect the changing resonant pattern of the supralaryngeal vocal tract as the speaker moves his articulators from the occlusion of the

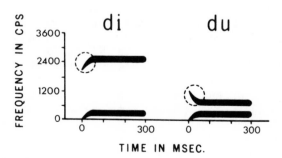

Figure 11. Simplified spectrographic patterns sufficient to produce the syllables [di] and [du]. The circles enclose the second formant frequency transitions. (After Liberman (1970).)

tongue tip against the palate that is involved in the production of [d] to the vocal tract configuration of the [i]. A different acoustic pattern defines the [d] in the syllable [du]. The resonances of the vocal tract are similar as the speaker forms the initial occlusion of the [d] in both syllables; however, the resonances of the vocal tract are quite different for the final configurations of the vocal tract for [i] and [u]. The formant patterns that convey the [d] in both syllables are thus quite different since they involve transitions from the same starting point to different end points. Human listeners "hear" an identical initial [d] segment in both of these signals because they "decode" the acoustic pattern in terms of the articulatory gestures and the anatomical apparatus that are involved in the production of speech. In this process, which has been termed the "motor theory of speech perception" (Liberman *et al.* (1967)), the listener operates in terms of the acoustic pattern of the entire syllable. The acoustic cues for the individual "phonetic segments" are fused into a syllabic pattern. The high rate of information transfer of human speech is thus due to the transmission of acoustic information in syllable-sized units. The phonetic elements of each syllable are "encoded" into a single acoustic pattern which is then "decoded" by the listener to yield the phonetic representation.

In order for the process of "motor theory perception" to work, the listener must be able to determine the absolute size of the speaker's vocal tract. Similar articulatory gestures will have different acoustic correlates in different sized vocal tracts. The frequency of the first formant of [a], for example, varies from 730 to 1030 Hz in the data of Peterson and Barney (1952) for men and children. The frequencies of the resonances that occur for various consonants likewise are a function of the size of the speakers' vocal tract. The resonant pattern that is the correlate of the consonant [g] for a speaker with a large vocal tract may overlap with the resonant pattern of the consonant [d] for a speaker with a small vocal tract (Rand (1971)). The listener therefore must be able to deduce the size of the speaker's vocal tract before he can assign an acoustic signal to the correct consonantal or vocalic class.

There are a number of ways in which a human listener can infer the size of a speaker's supralaryngeal vocal tract. He can, for example, note the fundamental frequency of phonation. Children, who have smaller vocal tracts, usually have higher fundamental frequencies than adult men or adult women. Adult men, however, have disproportionately lower fundamental frequencies than adult women (Peterson and Barney (1952)); thus, fundamental frequency is not an infallible cue to vocal tract size. Perceptual experiments (Ladefoged and Broadbent (1957)) have shown that human listeners can make use of the formant frequency range of a short passage of speech to arrive at an estimate of the size of a speaker's vocal tract. Recent experiments, however, show that human listeners do not have to defer their "motor theory" decoding of speech until they hear a two- or three-second interval of speech. Instead, they use the vocalic information encoded in a syllable to decode the syllable (Darwin (1971), Rand (1971)). This may appear to be paradoxical, but it is not. The listener makes use of the formant frequencies and fundamental frequency of the syllable's vowel to assess the size of the vocal tract that produced the syllable. We have noted throughout this paper that the vowels [a], [i], and [u] have a unique acoustical property. The formant frequency pattern for these vowels can always be related to a unique vocal tract size and shape. A listener, when he hears one of these vowels, can thus instantly determine the size of the speaker's vocal tract. The vowels [a], [i], and [u] (and the glides [y] and [w]) thereby serve as primary acoustic calibration signals in human speech.

The anatomical impossibility of the chimpanzee's producing these vowels is thus consistent with the absence of meaningful changes in vowel quality in the vocal communications of these animals. Chimpanzees probably cannot perceive these differences in vowel quality because they cannot "decode" specific vowels and consonants in terms of the articulatory gestures that speakers use to produce these signals. A chimpanzee, on hearing a particular formant frequency pattern, would not be able to tell, for example, whether it was produced by a large chimpanzee who was using an [ɪ]-like vocal tract configuration or a smaller chimpanzee who was using an [e]-like vocal tract configuration. Chimpanzees simply may not have the neural mechanism that is used by modern man to decode speech signals in terms of the underlying articulatory maneuvers.

The absence of a humanlike pharyngeal region in chimpanzees is thus quite reasonable. The only function that the human supralaryngeal vocal tract is better adapted to is speech production, in particular the production of vowels like [a], [i], and [u]. The human supralaryngeal vocal tract is less well adapted for the primary vegetative functions of respiration and swallowing (Negus (1949)). It is quite easy for food to be caught in the human larynx, with fatal consequences, whereas chimpanzees and other nonhuman primates cannot choke on their food. The nonhuman primates, moreover, can breathe while liquids are in the oral cavity, which man cannot do.

This suggests that the evolution of the human vocal tract to allow vowels like [a], [i], and [u] to be produced and the universal occurrence of these vowels in human languages reflect a parallel development of the neural and anatomic abilities that are necessary for language. This parallel development would be consistent with the evolution of other human abilities. The ability to use tools depends, for example, on upright posture and an opposable thumb and on neural ability as well.

Neanderthal man lacked the vocal tract that is necessary to produce the human "vocal-tract size calibrating" vowels [a], [i], and [u]. This suggests that the speech of Neanderthal man did not make use of syllabic encoding. While communication is obviously possible without syllabic encoding, studies of alternate methods of communication in modern man show, as noted before, that the rate at which information can be transferred is about one tenth that of normal human speech.

The principle of encoding extends throughout the grammar of human languages. The process wherein a deep phrase marker with many elementary S's is collapsed into a derived surface structure may be viewed as an encoding process that is similar to the encoding that occurs between the phonetic level and speech (Liberman (1970)). A transformational grammar may be viewed as a mechanism that encodes strings of semantic units into a surface structure. The derived surface string can be readily transmitted by a speaker and perceived and stored in short-time-span memory by a listener. There is no other reason why adult humans do not speak in short sentences like *I saw the boy*, *The boy is fat*, *The boy fell down* instead of the "encoded" sentence *I saw the fat boy who fell down*. The "encoded" sentence can be transmitted more rapidly and it transmits the unitary reference of the single *boy* within the single breath group (Lieberman (1967)).

Neanderthal man would have had a rather primitive linguistic ability compared to modern man insofar as encoding was absent. The evolution of modern man thus may be viewed as the evolution of an integrated system. Neural mechanisms, like those that are necessary for the perception of encoded phonetic elements at high data rates, and anatomic mechanisms, like those involved in the production of vowels like [a], [i], and [u], must have evolved in a complementary manner. Human linguistic ability thus must be seen as the result of a long evolutionary process that involved changes in anatomical structure through a process of mutation and natural selection which enhanced speech communication. Modern man's linguistic ability is necessarily tied to his phonetic ability. Rapid information transfer through the medium of human speech must be viewed as a central property of human linguistic ability. It makes human language and human thought possible. The occurrence of extinct fossil hominids like Neanderthal man who, at the very least, lacked the anatomical mechanism that is a necessary condition for human language, is surely not surprising. The surprising thing is that the necessary evolutionary development occurred so that we are as we are.

REfERENCES

Darwin, C. (1971), "Ear differences in the recall of fricatives and vowels," *Quarterly Journal of Experimental Psychology, 23,* 386–392.

Fant, C. G. M. (1960), *Acoustic Theory of Speech Production,* The Hague: Mouton.

Goodall, J. (1965), "Chimpanzees of the Gombe Stream Reserve," in I. DeVore, ed., *Primate Behavior,* New York: Holt, Rinehart and Winston.

Greenewalt, C. A. (1967), *Bird Song: Acoustics and Physiology,* Washington, D.C.: Smithsonian.

Haskins Laboratories (1962), *X-ray Motion Pictures of Speech,* New York: Haskins Laboratories.

Hayes, C. (1952), *The Ape in Our House,* New York: Harper & Row.

Henke, W. L. (1966), *Dynamic Articulatory Model of Speech Production Using Computer Simulation,* unpublished Ph.D. dissertation, M.I.T.

Irwin, O. C. (1948), "Infant speech: development of vowel sounds," *Journal of Speech and Hearing Disorders, 13,* 31–34.

Jakobson, R., C. G. M. Fant, and M. Halle (1952), *Preliminaries to Speech Analysis,* Cambridge, Mass.: M.I.T. Press.

Kellogg, W. N. (1968), "Communication and language in the home-raised chimpanzee," *Science, 162,* 423–427.

Ladefoged, P., and D. E. Broadbent (1957), "Information conveyed by vowels," *Journal of the Acoustical Society of America, 29,* 98–104.

La Mettrie, J. O. (1747), *De l'Homme-machine,* A. Vartanian, ed. (1960 critical edition), Princeton, N.J.: Princeton University Press.

Lenneberg, E. H. (1967), *Biological Foundations of Language,* New York: Wiley.

Liberman, A. M. (1970), "The grammars of speech and language," *Cognitive Psychology, 1,* 301–323.

Liberman, A. M., D. P. Shankweiler, and M. Studdert-Kennedy (1967), "Perception of the speech code," *Psychology Review, 74,* 431–461.

Lieberman, P. (1963), "Some effects of semantic and grammatical context on the production and perception of speech," *Language and Speech, 6,* 172–187.

Lieberman, P. (1967), *Intonation, Perception and Language,* Cambridge, Mass.: M.I.T. Press.

Lieberman, P. (1968), "Primate vocalizations and human linguistic ability," *Journal of the Acoustical Society of America, 44,* 1574–1584.

Lieberman, P. (1970), Review of J. S. Perkell (1969), *Physiology of Speech Production,* in *Language Sciences, 13,* 25–28.

Lieberman, P., K. S. Harris, P. Wolff, and L. H. Russell (1968), "Newborn Infant Cry and Nonhuman Primate Vocalizations," Status Report 17/18, New York: Haskins Laboratories.

Lieberman, P., K. H. Klatt, and W. A. Wilson (1969), "Vocal tract limitations of the vocal repertoires of rhesus monkey and other nonhuman primates," *Science, 164,* 1185–1187.

Lieberman, P., and E. S. Crelin (1971), "On the speech of Neanderthal man," *Linguistic Inquiry, 2,* 203–222.

Lieberman, P., E. S. Crelin, and D. H. Klatt (1972), "Phonetic ability and related anatomy of newborn and adult human, Neanderthal man, and chimpanzee," *American Anthropologist, 74,* 287–307.

Lindblom, B., and J. Sundberg (1969), "A Quantitative Model of Vowel Production and the Distinctive Features of Swedish Vowels," Speech Transmission Laboratory Report 1, Stockholm: Royal Institute of Technology.

Negus, V. E. (1949), *The Comparative Anatomy and Physiology of the Larynx,* New York: Hafner.

Osgood, C. E. (1953), *Method and Theory in Experimental Psychology,* New York: Oxford.

Perkell, J. S. (1969), *Physiology of Speech Production: Results and Implications of a Quantitative Cineradiographic Study,* Cambridge, Mass.: M.I.T. Press.

Perrault, C. (1676), *Mémoires pour servir à l'histoire naturelle des animaux,* Paris: l'Imprimerie Royale.

Peterson, G. E., and H. L. Barney (1952), "Control methods used in a study of the vowels," *Journal of the Acoustical Society of America, 24,* 175–184.

Rand, T. C. (1971), "Vocal Tract Size Normalization in the Perception of Stop Consonants," Status Report, New Haven, Conn.: Haskins Laboratories.

Sobotta-Figge (1965) (J. Sobotta and F. H. J. Figge), *Atlas of Human Anatomy,* Vol. 2, New York: Hafner.

Stevens, K. N. (1969), "The Quantal Nature of Speech: Evidence from Articulatory-Acoustic Data," in E. E. David, Jr., and P. B. Denes, eds., *Human Communication: A Unified View,* New York: McGraw-Hill.

Stevens, K. N., and A. S. House (1955), "Development of a Quantitative Description of Vowel Articulation," *Journal of the Acoustical Society of America, 27,* 484–493.

Trubetzkoy, N. S. (1939), *Principes de phonologie,* Paris: Klincksiek.

Truby, H. M., J. F. Bosma, and J. Lind (1965), *Newborn Infant Cry,* Uppsala: Almqvist and Wiksells.

Tyson, E. (1699), *Orang-outang, Sive Homo Sylvestris: or, the Anatomy of a Pygmie Compared with That of a Monkey, an Ape, and a Man,* London: Thomas Bennet and Daniel Brown.

Yerkes, R. M., and D. W. Learned (1925), *Chimpanzee Intelligence and Its Vocal Expressions,* Baltimore: Williams & Wilkins.

on the formulation
of grassmann's law in greek

Theodore M. Lightner

University of Texas

Reduplicated forms such as *ti-t^{h}ēmi, pe-p^{h}euga, ki-k^{h}rēmi* show that consonants are deaspirated before a syllable containing an aspirate: this phenomenon is called "Grassmann's Law."[1]

If the second aspirate loses its aspiration in combination, then the first retains it: *t^{h}riks* (nom), *trik^{h}os* (gen); *trep^{h}ō* (pres), *t^{h}repsō* (fut); and so on.

The two ordered rules (1) and (2) account for these data:

(1) $C \rightarrow [-\text{aspirated}] \ / \ \underline{\hspace{1em}} \begin{bmatrix} C \\ -\text{aspirated} \end{bmatrix}$

(2) $C \rightarrow [-\text{aspirated}] \ / \ \underline{\hspace{1em}} C_0 V C_0 C^h$

The derivations of *t^{h}riks* (nom sg) and *trik^{h}os* (gen sg) are as shown in (3):

(3)
t^{h}rik^h+s	t^{h}rik^h+os	
t^{h}riks		(1)
	trik^{h}os	(2)
t^{h}riks	*trik^{h}os*	

Forms of the verb 'have' show that Grassmann's Law must be revised to drop *h* as well as to deaspirate consonants: *ek^{h}ō* (pres), *heksō* (fut), *esk^{h}on* (aor).

The aorist form has weak grade of the root (see also *leipō* (pres), *elipon* (aor)).

---

[1] Although Grassmann is generally given credit for this proposal, it seems that von Raumer (1837) was actually the first to make the observation.

Thus from $e + sek^h + on$, the aorist $esk^h on$ is immediately derived by application of the regular vowel gradation rule.

The future form $heks\bar{o}$, from $sek^h + s + \bar{o}$, shows not only the deaspiration of k^h before s (as in $t^h riks$), but also the shift of initial s to h before a sonorant.

For the present form, from $sek^h + \bar{o}$, therefore, we expect $*hek^h\bar{o}$. The attested form $ek^h\bar{o}$ shows that h must have been dropped before the aspirate in the following syllable (initial $h < s$ does not drop in forms with no following aspirate: $hre\bar{o}$, compare Sanskrit sru-; $hepta$, compare Latin *septem*).

The revision in (4) of rule (2) thus seems necessary to account for the present form $ek^h\bar{o}$:

(4) $\begin{cases} C \rightarrow [-\text{aspirated}] \\ h \rightarrow \phi \end{cases} / \underline{\quad} C_0 V C_0 C^h$

Two things are suspicious about this formulation of Grassmann's Law. First, rule (4) claims that there is no relation (other than the environment condition) between deaspiration and h-truncation, that these are two disparate phenomena. Intuitively, however, one feels that deaspiration and h-truncation are really two aspects of the same dissimilation process; the fact that they take place in the same environment strengthens this feeling. Second, there are very few forms subject to this kind of h-truncation. Szemerényi (1964) suggests one, but it is not proven. Thus, it looks almost as if the special h-truncation part of Grassmann's Law has been formulated solely to account for the one form $ek^h\bar{o}$.

Let us return to the first formulation of Grassmann's Law, rule (2). The segment h represents the bundle of feature specifications in (5):

(5) $\begin{bmatrix} +\text{aspirated} \\ +\text{continuant} \\ -\text{round} \\ -\text{nasal} \\ -\text{strident} \\ \vdots \end{bmatrix}$

Rule (2) applies to this feature matrix and simply changes the feature specification [+aspirated] to [−aspirated].

Changing the feature matrix of h from [+aspirated] to [−aspirated] does not seem to be equivalent to dropping h. But, one may ask, what is h other than pure aspiration? Certainly one can superimpose various features on this aspiration, but such features all seem to be assimilated from neighboring segments.[2] Since the essence of h is aspiration, I suggest that the first formulation of Grassmann's Law in (2) be accepted as correct. Linguistic theory must then supply an interpretive convention such that when h is specified as [−aspirated], the effect is not merely deaspiration of h but its complete elimination, on the basis of the fact that nonaspiration is incompatible with h, the aspirate *par excellence*.

---

[2] Jakobson (1962), in his strikingly original discussion of Arabic *mufaxxama*, makes the same remark: "The extra-buccal phonemes are obviously deprived of any features generated in the mouth resonator, and in particular of the features grave *vs* acute and compact *vs* diffuse. They are both non-vocalic and non-consonantal phonemes (glides). *Hamza* /ʔ/ is entirely unmarked: neither fortis nor flat; /h/ is not flat but fortis; *ayn* /ʕ/ is not fortis but flat; /ḥ/ is doubly marked: both flat and fortis."

REFERENCES

Jakobson, R. (1962), "Mufaxxama: the 'Emphatic' Phonemes in Arabic," *Selected Writings, I,*
    The Hague: Mouton.
von Raumer, R. (1837), *Die Aspiration und die Lautverschiebung,* Leipzig.
Szemerényi, O. (1964), *Syncope in Greek and Indo-European and the Nature of Indo-European
    Accent,* Naples.

Remarks on nasality: the case of Guaraní

Horace G. Lunt
Harvard University

Nasalized vowels that are clearly opposed to nonnasal vowels have been noted in descriptions of the surface structures of languages in all parts of the world. Generativists ordinarily see this sort of distinctive nasalized vowel as the result of rules applied to an underlying sequence of vowel plus nasal consonant (VN). More traditional analysts may abstract the nasality in much the same way, but with quite different assumptions and conventions, or they may operate with some sort of "additive component" of nasality. Some assume a nasal prosody or accent, though it is not always easy to discern precisely how these different labels relate to specific facts and theories.[1]

For European languages (Polish, French, Portuguese), there seems to be little difficulty in finding considerable synchronic justification for generating the surface nasal vowels (with all "allophones") from sequences of vowel plus nasal sonorant.[2] The domain of rules affecting the VN groups is the single syllable, and the distinctive feature [nasal] applies primarily to individual segments.

Things are quite different in certain South American languages, as can be seen from the somewhat skimpy information provided about Desano by Kaye (1971) and implied in descriptions of several other languages. Here there is no obvious justification for deriving the distinctive nasalized vowels of surface structure from underlying VN sequences, but it is clear that there is a deep opposition between two underlying types

---

[1] Trubetzkoy (1939, pp. 110–114, 160–166 = 1949, pp.130–134, 189–196) provided a detailed survey of the role of nasality in numerous languages. For a series of general observations and further instructive literature, see Ferguson (1966), and for discussion of the generative point of view, see Lightner (1970).

[2] For Polish, see Gladney (1968) and Lightner (1970); for French, Schane (1968). I am not aware of a generative treatment of Portuguese, but the information provided in Morais-Barbosa (1965) and the literature he and Lacerda and Head (1963) cite offer ample hints as to how such an analysis might be made.

of *morphemes*, which need not be monosyllabic. I should like to comment briefly on a similar but more complicated situation in Guaraní, the home language of most Paraguayans.

A competent description of Guaraní within Hockett's theoretical framework has been provided by Gregores and Suárez (1967). Their corpus is somewhat artificially restricted, but they provide good information about the general processes of morphology and syntax. It is obvious that they know the language and that they have thought deeply about phonology, but they furnish very little phonetic data. The "strictly phonemic transcription" in which they write all their texts is useful for some distinctions, but it obscures certain important details that appear in traditional spelling.

I do not claim to know Guaraní; my observations are based on Gregores and Suárez (hereafter GS), amplified by Guasch (1948; 1956; 1961) and other printed sources, and checked briefly with informants.[3] I shall raise a number of questions but shall try to suggest answers for only a few.

Guaraní has the phones listed in (1) and (2) at a surface level that some years ago I would have called phonemic: they are on the whole well represented in ordinary spelling and manipulable by informants.

(1) p   t   k   k^w ʔ
         s   ś   x
    v r   l   γ   γ^w
    m n   ñ   ŋ   ŋ^w
   mb nd ǵ ŋg ŋg^w

(2) (a) i   ɨ   u
       e   a   o
  (b) ĩ   ɨ̃   ũ
       ẽ   ã   õ

The voiceless stops and fricatives and the ʔ are not audibly affected by a neighboring nasal vowel or vowels, while *v, r, l, γ, γ^w* become nasalized.[4] The prenasalized voiced stops and voiced palatal *ǵ* occur only before nonnasal vowels; the five nasal sonorants never occur before stressed nonnasal vowels. On grounds of complementary distribution, GS, leaving *ñ* and *ǵ* aside, lump the two series together: with nasality as the basic feature, *m, n, ŋ,* and *ŋ^w* are normal and *mb, nd, ŋg, ŋg^w* are their predictable variants. In Trubetzkoy's terminology, then, we have continuous versus instantaneous (Dauerlaut versus Momentanlaut).

Morphophonemic alternations make it clear that there is indeed a very close relationship here, but it is not immediately obvious which series, if either, is primary. The first line and the last two lines of (1) must contrast in underlying forms. I shall label this contrast *tenuis* versus *media*.[5] Thus labial tenuis /p/ is opposed to labial

---

[3] I am deeply grateful to Mrs. L. B. of West Roxbury, Massachusetts, and her relatives and friends for their enthusiastic cooperation.

[4] GS write *ṽ, γ̃, γ̃^{w}*, and I am inclined to agree, yet it may well be that important signals of nasalization for *ṽ* and *γ̃* are provided by the vocalic context. The offglide in *γ̃^{w}* is unmistakably nasalized, as are *r̃* (phonetically an alveolar tongue-flap, distinct from *n* and *ñ* both in articulation and, I believe, duration) and the rare *l̃*.

[5] I am purposely using the old, neutral cover terms in order to avoid a speculative assignment of the unsatisfactory terms "voiceless/voiced" and "tense/lax" or the newly proposed features combining spread versus constricted glottis and stiff versus slack vocal cords (Halle and Stevens (1971)).

media /B/, which under appropriate conditions appears in surface forms as the sonorant *m* or the prenasalized voiced stop *mb*.[6]

The palatal *ñ* seems appropriately in place, but the *ǵ* is not prenasalized. Postponing discussion, I accept for the moment GS's position that *ǵ* and *ñ* derive from an underlying palatal glide. I further hypothesize that surface *v* represents underlying /w/ and suggest that *γ* and *γ*ʷ are also to be interpreted as glides.

The nonvocalic system underlying (1) then becomes (3):

(3) p   t   k   kʷ
   B   D   G   Gʷ
      s   ś   x
  w   y   γ   γʷ   ʔ
    r   l

All informants and analysts affirm the distinctive contrast of nasal versus oral vowels, yet the distinction is often unclear in the stream of speech. Both the Spanish and the Guaraní of my informants is characterized by rather lax articulation, which includes a somewhat relaxed velum and therefore a slight nasalization of the whole utterance.[7] In emphatic or careful speech, "nasal" high vowels become very strongly nasalized, and in some instances a homorganic nasal consonant may appear before a following fricative.[8]

GS account for nasalized vowels in two ways: (*a*) as automatic when preceding the inherently nasal consonants (*m/mb*, and so on), and (*b*) as the result of a "long component phoneme of nasality" having as its domain a span which may contain several syllables. The nasal peak of a span coincides with the stress peak (usually but not always the last syllable) and contains the most strongly nasalized vowel. Now, the ordinary noninterrupted nasal consonants occur in nasal spans, so that the GS conventions tell us that phonemic *aní* 'don't' is to be read with *n* (not *nd*) and *amã́* 'rain' with *m* (not *mb*). In both, the initial vowel is nasalized (*a*) "phonemically" because of the "long component /˜/" and (*b*) "nonphonemically" because of the following *n/m*: [ãní], [ãmã́]. But, in the apparent compound *amanáu* 'hail', the *n* is to be read with oral release because it is not marked as being in a nasal span; the preceding *a* is "nonphonemically" nasalized and in turn assures the nasal release of the *m* which causes nasalization of the initial *a*: [ãmãndáu]. Further, a *y* in a nasal span is automatically converted to *ñ*: GS cite *omayã́* 'he looks' > [õmãñã́], where the nasal quality of the first two vowels is both "phonemic" and "conditioned."

The elusive value of nasality in Guaraní vowels is partially reflected by the extreme variation in domestic orthographic proposals and chaos in practice. Like matters of accent and vowel length in many languages, nasalization here seems to be

---

[6] The phonetic facts on variants of *mb*, *nd*, *ŋg*, *ŋg*ʷ are carefully recorded by GS, albeit with far too few examples.

[7] Dahl (1953) indicated very few nasal vowels in his phonetic transcription, presumably a "broad" one; indeed, he missed some distinctive cases.

[8] High vowels universally tend to resist nasalization, but Guaraní speakers obviously compensate in order to emphasize nasality. From the Portuguese or Polish point of view, it is striking that no consonant develops before tenuis stops—for example, [pĕtĕí] 'one', [tũpã́] 'God'. GS's two examples [tămõraʔé] 'would that, *ojalá*' and [nĩŋkó] (also [nĩkó]) 'indeed, certainly' were firmly rejected by my informants in favor of [tãmõraʔé] or [tãmburaʔé] and [nikó] with weakly nasalized *i*.

The common *-nte* 'only' (as in [šĕn.te] 'only I') remains a problem. The *-n-* forms a syllabic coda with the preceding vowel and provides the only examples of closed syllables in [+native] words. Such sequences are common in the Spanish morphemes pervasively scattered throughout most utterances, for example, [ĕntéro] 'all, every', [ĕntĕndé] 'to understand'.

regarded as a self-evident feature, to be marked only in cases of possible ambiguity. Yet GS's nasal spans do correspond to a kind of reality, and the final rules worked out by Father Guasch (1956; 1961) agree by marking only the stressed vowel in such a span (for example, *kiriri* 'silence' for earlier *kîrîrî* [kĩrĩrĩ].

However, I submit that these spans cannot be discovered on the basis of phonetics alone, and the achievement of GS is to be attributed to their knowledge of the language. Some weaknesses and inconsistencies result, one feels, from their honest effort to ignore their acquired competence in Guaraní and follow rigorously the methodology they had chosen.

In fact, the initial vowels of a long nasal span which contains no nasal consonants are so neutral phonetically that informants are quite unsure as to how to class them. The velum may be fully raised at the outset and be gradually lowered toward the peak syllable, which contains the strongest nasalization. Using a subscript hook to indicate weak nasalization and the tilde to indicate strong nasalization, the nasal stem *pitivõ* 'help' is then [pi̜ti̜vṍ]. An object prefix like *ro* 'you' assimilates nasality, but *śe ro-i-pitivõ̜-kʷaá* 'I you-help-know = I can help you' is approximately [roipi̜ti̜vṍ], with no audible nasal quality in [ro-i-] (or *śe*, which is also within the domain of the nasalization rule). Negation in this case entails the addition of "nonnasal" *ndo* or "nasal" *no* (plus suffixed *i/ĩ*). Here *no* appears, a selection that cannot be justified in terms of surface phonetics: it is the underlying theoretical nasality of the conditioning major class morpheme *pitivõ* that produces *śe noroipitivõkʷaái* 'I can't help you'. And then the specification of the full nasality in the nonabrupt sonorant initial consonant produces something like [śẽnõ̜ṟo̜ipi̜ti̜võ̜̀kʷaái].[9]

In a generative description, underlying major class morphemes must be specified as nasal,[10] and affixes may acquire their marking by the sort of assimilation rules discussed by Kaye (1971) for Desano. Thus the object prefix *roi-* falls within the domain of the verb and by a very early rule assimilates the nasality of /ɴpitiwoᴺ/. The negative affix /Do . . . i/ is assimilated in turn: /ɴDo + roi + pitiwoᴺ + kʷaa + i/.[11] A somewhat later rule turns *D* into the continuant *n*, and a series of further rules, some optional, spell out the exact degree of nasalization in the vowels.

This is fully comparable to Desano thus far, but there are complications in Guaraní. The underlying mediae *B, D, G, Gʷ* *always* appear in the surface forms with [+nasal], even in nonnasal segments: a vowel preceding such a segment in nasal, as in /kaGʷe/ 'bone' > [kãŋgʷé], /śe-Baʔe/ 'my thing' > [śẽmbaʔé].[12] Furthermore, before an "oral" segment containing a media, the "nasal" variant of a prefix is selected: /De-Baʔe/ 'your thing' > [nẽmbaʔé], /De-kaGʷe/ 'your bone' > [nẽkãŋgʷé], /Da-a-Baʔapo-i/ (neg+I+work+neg) 'I don't work' > [nãmbaʔapói]. Therefore the mediae must be specified as [+nasal] from a very early stage of generation.

Two treatments suggest themselves. Either the feature [nasal] is pertinent for segments of morphemes in the lexicon or it is not. Inasmuch as whole major class

---

[9] The underlying nasality of the initial morpheme has been spelled out as full continuant sonorant nasality in the *n* because of the nasality of the dominant major class morpheme. The nasal release is then a strong marking signal that the following vowel *cannot* represent an underlying [−nasal] segment. In this situation, the [+nasal] mark of the vowel no longer requires phonetic nasalization: [no̜] or even [no] is possible.

[10] I shall use a subscript and a superscript N to mark the beginning and end, respectively.

[11] Note that the *-i* of the negation remains oral because it follows a nonnasal segment.

I am ignoring a series of problems—the underlying form of *roi-* (or *ro-i*) which must somehow be related to the more usual shape /De/, the vowel in the negation (surely /Da/), assignment of degrees of stress, and the likelihood of different kinds of boundaries.

[12] An oral vowel is a signal that a boundary intervenes: [mbaʔèmbiasi̜] 'sadness' < /Baʔe + Biasi/. In compounds of major class morphemes, no deep nasal assimilation takes place.

morphemes like /pitiwo/, /kiriri/, and /aBa/ 'rain' must be lexically marked [+nasal], while others like /kʷaa/ and /kaGʷe/ must be [−nasal], I prefer to regard all individual segments as unmarked for nasality. An early and general phonological rule then assigns [+nasal] (*a*) to every segment in [+nasal] morphemes, probably excepting [+tenuis], and (*b*) to every [−tenuis, −continuant] segment in [−nasal] morphemes. It is the second part of this rule, with its lower-level consequences, that distinguishes the morphophonemic type of Guaraní from that of Desano.

The oral-release, obstruent quality of *B, D, G, Gʷ* could be characterized as "basic" in the GS framework by calling *mb, nd, ŋg, ŋgʷ* the "phonemes" (as suggested in (3)) and calling the ordinary nasal sonorants the "allophones" determined by the more abstract long component /˜/. This is clearly consistent with the instinctive reaction of informants that the prenasalized stops are normal, as well as with Guasch's efforts (1948, pp. 14–15) to deny nasality to the true nasal consonants. All sources speak first of various auxiliary morphemes in "nonnasal" shape (such as *mbo, nda*), and they do not always remember to note the automatic "nasal" shape (such as (*mo, na*).

The association of the tenuis stops with the mediae is assured by a series of morphophonemic alternations. One common example is suffixed elements, wherein tenuis is added to nonnasal morphemes, but media to nasal ones: *pe-i-ke-pa* (you+enter+all) 'all of you come in' versus *pe-sẽ-mba* 'all of you go out'. The processes are not fully automatic, and I am in no way prepared to guess at the conditioning factors. Furthermore, there is not full agreement. For example, there is the form *avati* 'corn' + *ti* > *avatiti* 'cornfield'. *Petĩ* 'tobacco' should, according to GS and Guasch, take *-ndi*: *petĩndi* 'tobacco field'. But my informants insist that it must be *petĩtĩ*. Stems taking the widely productive factitive prefix /Bo/ give rise to a similar uncertainty. From *ke* 'sleep', /Bo+ke/ 'cause to sleep' produces either *-mongé* (Guasch) or *-mboké* (a variant accepted by my informants). Guasch (1956, pp. 29–30) gives a brief discussion of some examples of this sort of dialect, and many more can be found in dictionaries and quickly elicited from informants.

The low-level rules for assigning degrees of phonetic nasalization in vowels may operate across a nasal-oral boundary to affect an unstressed vowel following a nasal vowel with potential secondary stress: /ₙaBaᴺ+sapiʔa/ (rain+sudden) 'downpour' > ãmã̀sapiʔá, with [-sạ-] or [-sã-] in rapid speech. Such leakage is prevented by the prenasalized stops: /ₙaBaᴺ+Daiwi/ 'drizzle' > [ãmã̀ndaiví]. Perhaps the media-initial shape of some morphemes serves precisely to mark the boundary separating a nasal from an oral span. There seem to be a number of cases of uncertainty between tenuis and media word-initially (*puruʔá* or *mburuʔá* 'pregnant' versus nasal *puruʔã̀* 'navel'), but I can at present only confirm that such variants are accepted by informants.

The early rules of nasal assimilation to the left are matched by (or include) assimilation to the right from major class morphemes, but they affect relatively few suffixes, which are by definition unstressed. One of the most important is *-pe* 'at, in, on, to, for', which then assumes the shape /ₙBeᴺ/ > [mẽ]; hence, [avatípe] but [petĩ̀mẽ].

All of this evidence points to a close tie between the two series of underlying stops, tenues and mediae, and at the same time demonstrates that the mediae are essentially nasal. The loss of the feature [−continuant] in the environment ₙ＿＿＿ᴺ automatically produces the sonorant nasal consonants.

A sketch of major rules can now be outlined informally as in (4)–(9). It is assumed that the input from the syntax and lexicon is strings of morphemes with the necessary boundaries to insure correct working of assimilation rules and accent assignment. Prefixes and certain suffixes are unmarked for nasality.

(4) Unmarked affixes become [+nasal] when they are in the domain of a [+nasal] major class morpheme; otherwise they are [−nasal]

(5) Every media becomes [+nasal]

(6) Every [+sonorant] within a nasal span (that is, a nasal major class morpheme plus affixes assimilated on the basis of (4)) becomes [+nasal]

(7) (a) A media within a nasal span becomes [+continuant]
    (b) A media which precedes a media within a phonological word becomes [+continuant]
    (c) A media becomes a prenasalized voiced stop

(8) Pretonic nasalized sonorants (excluding *m, n, ñ*) are assigned descending degrees of nasality or become [−nasal]

(9) (a) A vowel becomes [+nasal] if it is adjacent to a nasal consonant
    (b) A [+sonorant] segment becomes nasalized if the vowel of an adjacent syllable is nasal

Rules (4)–(7) are obligatory and relatively deep. Note that (6) specifies nasalization for vowels and for *w, r, l* (hence surface ṽ, r̃, l̃); we will deal with the other sonorants shortly. Rules (8) and (9) are close to the surface and operate with *n*-ary distinctions. Apparently (9a) operates ordinarily to produce at least a slight nasalization, but all of (8) and (9) must include a variety of constraints that I am not prepared to state (see also footnote 9).

Sample derivations are given in (10) and (11):

(10) śe-ro-i-$_N$pitiwo^N-k^{w}aa   śe-Do-ro-i-$_N$pitiwo^N-k^{w}aa-i

    $_N$śe-ro-i- pitiwo^N-k^{w}aa $_N$śe-Do-ro-i- pitiwo^N-k^{w}aa-i   (4)

     ẽ r̃õ ĩ   ĩ ĩw̃õ   ẽ   õ r̃õ ĩ   ĩ ĩw̃õ   (6)

                           n   (7a)

     e ro i   i̧   e   o ro i   i̧   (8)

                   ẽ   õ r̦o̧   (9)

   śeroipi̧tĩṽo̊k^{w}aá   śẽnõr̦o̧ipi̧tĩṽo̊k^{w}aái

(11) De-Baʔe De-kaG^{w}e Da-a-Baʔapo-i   De-$_N$peti^N

                               $_N$De- peti^N (4)

                               ẽ   ẽ ĩ   (6)

                                 n   (7a)

   n   n   n   (7b)

    mb   ŋg^w mb   (7c)

                              ȩ   ȩ   (8)

   ẽ   ẽ ã   ã   ẽ   (9)

   nẽmbaʔé nẽkãŋg^{w}é nãmbaʔapói   nẽpȩti̧

Let us return now to the *ǵ* and *ñ* listed in (1). As a pair, they fit in plausibly with the voiced stop and nasal series, and it might be an insignificant idiosyncracy that *ǵ* is not prenasalized. Nasal versus nonnasal parallelism can be found: [ǵa-puká] 'we laugh' versus [ñã-kīrīrí] 'we are silent'. Underlying ḱ might be called upon to explain *ś*, for Spanish *č* ordinarily turns up in Guaraní as *ś* (*víśo* 'insect' < *bicho*). But this symmetrical schema cannot stand up against other facts. It is crucial that the media are prenasalized, for they affect preceding segments; *ǵ* does not: [ǵaǵeǵohéi] 'we wash ourselves', [nda-ǵa-puká-i] 'we aren't laughing', [nde-ǵaɣ^{w}á] 'your dog'.[13] Moreover, there is not the slightest evidence that *ś*—presumably from ḱ—alternates with either *ǵ* or *ñ* (as *p* alternates with both *mb* and *m*).[14] A /w/ is surely the source of the weak labiodental surface *v*, and a system with no palatal glide seems unlikely on general grounds. Assigning *ǵ* and *ñ* to underlying /y/ is, then, justified. Therefore we have the following underlying forms for the examples cited in this paragraph: /ya+puka/, /ya+$_N$kiriri^N/, /ya+ye+yoxei/, /Da-ya-puka-i/, /De-yaɣ^{w}a/.

Rule (4) will produce $_N$*ya-kiriri*^{N} and the like, and (6) will convert the *y* of the affix to *ñ* in this case, as required. But in the prefix 'we (inclusive)', as in /yaDe-yaɣ^{w}a/ 'our dog', the *y* remains until (7c) and (9a) have produced *yãnde*; (9b) then yields *ñãnde*. Here we see the crucial importance of phonological rule (5) and its sequels (7b,c) and (9) in determining many of the phonetically nasal or nasalized surface segments. In /Da-yaDe-BaDuʔa-i/ 'we don't remember', there is no nasality in the lexical forms for the major class morpheme is nonnasal. The four mediae acquire [+ nasal] by (5); (7b) turns the first three into continuants, and (7c) turns the last into a prenasalized stop—*na-yane-manduʔái*; (9a) nasalizes the first four vowels, and finally (9b) produces *ñ*—*nãñãnẽmãnduʔái*. (GS see nasality here as an inherent "phonemic" property of the four consonantal segments I call mediae: they would write /na yane-manuʔá i/. The nasality of the vowels and *ñ* is for them "non-phonemic.")

A *y* which is not affected by any of the rules I have given must finally be specified as an obstruent. My informants insisted on the palatal stop *ǵ*, firmly rejecting the *ź* variant of GS and other sources.

The status of *ɣ* and *ɣ^w* is debatable; I am simply making what I hope is an educated guess that they are glides. Except in the ubiquitous Spanish loans (a large number of which must be marked [−native] and treated in special ways, as GS are well aware—see pp. 88–93), *ɣ* is rare and, in intervocalic position, not altogether stable.[15] There is some alternation (or simply confusion) between *ɣ* and *ɣ^w*, and the velar element is often weak or even absent. Full nasalization would result in *ŋ* and *ŋg*; GS make no mention of this happening. But they do cite sporadic cases where a prenasalized labiovelar media appears optionally: *ɣ^{w}ivé* 'since' ∼ *ŋg^{w}ivé* (p. 104) ∼ *ɣivé* ∼ *ɣié* (§10.41); *raɣ^{w}é* 'hair' ∼ *raŋg^{w}é* (§10.46). In the compound /$_N$aka^N+ɣ^{w}asu/ 'head + big' the low-level nasal assimilation to the right (9b) may be blocked by

---

[13] To simply point out a further problem, the negational suffix *-i* appears as zero in [nda-ǵaǵeǵohéi] 'we don't wash ourselves' and as final *-ri* with assimilated nasalization in *na-ñakiriri-ri* (the whole thing fully nasalized) 'we are not silent'. GS say the variation is optional.

[14] My only example of nasal vowel + *ǵ* is one cited by GS (p. 83) in which an optional nasal consonant appears before spirant [ʔiñãkånyeká] 'he broke his head' < /i+$_N$aka^N+yeka/. My informants have clear *ǵ* here, and the *n* did appear once in an unguarded moment during a series of contemplative repetitions. But this is precisely the position where *k* is frequently replaced by *ŋg*. (The *ñ* comes from a variant /iy/ of the very irregular third person pronominal element /i/ in position before vowels.)

[15] It is plausible enough to assume a glide that parallels the high unrounded *i*: Spanish *doctor*, *consigna* > *doitór*, *kõsíínã*. Perhaps, indeed, unstressed final *i* and *i* after vowel represent underlying glides /y/ and /ɣ/.

substituting the media—[ãkãŋ^{w}asú] for ordinary [ãkãỹ̃^{w}ạsú] (GS, p. 104, note 2). Careful work with informants is required to clarify these issues.[16]

Thus there are two sources for the nasal vowels of Guaraní (see (2b)): they result from early rules applying to morphemes that are lexically specified $_N$____^{N}, and they arise from one or more low-level rules of assimilation (like (9)) to nasal consonantal segments which derive from underlying mediae that are not specified in the lexicon as nasal. This contrasts with Desano, where, it appears, the surface nasalization in both vowel and consonant segments derives exclusively from $_N$____^{N} morphemes. The exact nature of this kind of lexical marking in generative theory remains to be explored.

The Guaraní data are typologically close to what Kaye (1971) reports for Desano but significantly different in detail. At the same time it is clear that typological comparisons between these native languages and the neighboring Portuguese of Brazil must be on a very different level from comparisons that have thus far been attempted.[17]

---

[16] There are a few instances where there is some doubt as to the nasal status of a morpheme. Let me offer one anecdotal observation. *Tupã* 'God' is fully nasal (versus nonnasal *tupá* 'bed'); *si* 'mother' is nonnasal. GS write fully oral *tupasí* for 'Mother of God, Mary', while the Jesuit professor Guasch specifies all three syllables as nasal. My informants were split and argued spiritedly among themselves. Finally, under my prompting, an informant who advocated nonnasality undertook to utter a fervent prayer to the Virgin: *t̃ũp̃ãsĩ* came out, fully nasal! This suggests that the nasalization of morphemes may be called on to play a secondary, emotional role (whose domain should be investigated), comparable to the stylistic use of pharyngealization in Arabic dialects. (See Harrell's (1957) similarly anecdotal commentary, pp. 80–82. He suggests treating pharyngealization as a "long component.")

[17] The surface nasal vowels of Portuguese are chiefly the historical result of (*a*) vowel + tautosyllabic *m/n*, or (*b*) vowel following nasal consonant; underlying forms for a generative description surely need only consonantal *m/n* and rules that are not particularly deep. But European Portuguese has partial nasalization spreading over several syllables or whole words: see, for example, the nasalization in the *r*, *l*, *ð*, and the coda of the final syllable of the word *marmelada* in Lacerda and Head's (1963) chromographic analysis. Very late rules must be required to produce these phonetic nuances. One can speculate that in time this sort of rule might, in conjunction with other structural changes, acquire progressively deeper status as the system develops, perhaps finally resulting in required [+ nasal] marking of whole morphemes in the lexicon.

REfERENCES

Dahl, I. (1953), [Guaraní text] *Le maître phonétique*, 99, 7–8.

Ferguson, C. A. (1966), "Assumptions about Nasals: a Sample Study in Phonological Universals," in J. Greenberg, ed., *Universals of Language*, Cambridge, Mass.: M.I.T. Press.

Gladney, F. Y. (1968), "Some Rules for Nasals in Polish," *Studies Presented to Professor Roman Jakobson by His Students*, Cambridge: Slavica.

Gregores, E., and J. A. Suárez (1967), *A Description of Colloquial Guaraní*, The Hague: Mouton.

Guasch, P. Antonio, S.J. (1948), *El idioma Guaraní: gramática, lecturas, vocabulario doble*, 2nd ed., Buenos Aires.

Guasch, P. Antonio, S.J. (1956), *El idioma Guaraní: gramática y antología de prosa y verso*, 3rd ed., Asuncion: Casa América, Moreno Hermanos.

Guasch, P. Antonio, S.J. (1961), *Diccionario Castellano-Guaraní y Guaraní-Castellano*, 4th ed., Sevilla.

Halle, M., and K. N. Stevens (1971), "A note on laryngeal features," *Quarterly Progress Report of the Research Laboratory of Electronics*, *101*, M.I.T., 198–213.

Harrell, R. S. (1957), *The Phonology of Colloquial Egyptian Arabic*, New York: American Council of Learned Societies.

Kaye, J. D. (1971), "Nasal harmony in Desano" *Linguistic Inquiry*, *2*, 37–56.

Lacerda, A. de, and B. F. Head (1963), *Análise de sons nasais e sons nasalizados do português*, Laboratório de Fonética Experimental da Faculdade de Letras da Universidade de Coimbra.

Lightner, T. M. (1970), "Why and how does vowel nasalization take place?" *Papers in Linguistics*, *2*, 179–226.

Morais-Barbosa, J. (1965), *Etudes de phonologie portugaise*, Estudos de Ciências Políticas e Sociais, 77, Lisbon: Junta de Investigações do Ultramar.

Schane, S. A. (1968), *French Phonology and Morphology*, Cambridge, Mass.: M.I.T. Press.

Trubetzkoy, N. S. (1939), *Grundzüge der Phonologie, Travaux du Cercle Linguistique de Prague*, 7.

Trubetzkoy, N. S. (1949), *Principes de phonologie*, J. Cantineau, trsl., Paris: Klincksieck.

some tonga tone rules

James D. McCawley

University of Chicago

Many Bantu languages have a surface contrast between high and low tones which exactly matches an underlying high/low tone contrast, but there are others in which the relationship between surface and underlying tones is far from obvious. In Tonga, Bangubangu, and Sukuma, for example, underlying tone contrasts are manifested not on the syllable that bears them but elsewhere in the phrase: for example, in Bangubangu an underlying high tone is generally manifested as a high tone on the following syllable (Meeussen (1954), McCawley (1971)), and in Sukuma an underlying high tone is manifested as a high tone one, two, or three syllables later (Richardson (1959)). In these languages it is often far from obvious which member of an underlying tone contrast should be designated "underlying high" and "underlying low." Thus, many scholars (Meeussen (1954; 1963), Stevick (1969)) have avoided such terms, preferring DETERMINANT and NEUTRAL, where determinant is that underlying tone which (under at least some conditions) causes deviations from the "least marked" tonal contour (which generally is level low pitch).

The Tonga paradigm in (1), representing the present tense affirmative, shows that in at least some forms the interchange of *tu-* 'we' and *ba-* 'they', or of *-mu-* 'him' and *-ba-* 'them', or of *-lang-* 'look at' and *-bon-* 'see' may result in a difference in tone on an adjacent syllable, even though none of these morphemes has a constant tonal effect throughout the whole paradigm:

(1) 'we/they V'   'we/they V him'   'we/they V them'

'we/they V'	'we/they V him'	'we/they V them'
tu-la-lang-a	*tu-la-mu-lang-a*	*tu-la-ba-lang-a*
ba-la-lang-a	*ba-la-mu-lang-a*	*ba-lá-ba-lang-a*
tu-la-bon-a	*tu-la-mu-bon-a*	*tu-la-ba-bon-a*
ba-lá-bon-a	*ba-lá-mú-bon-a*	*ba-lá-ba-bon-a*

Meeussen noted that these morphemes can be assigned to two groups, DETERMINANT and NEUTRAL, in such a way that the high tones which appear in the paradigm are on those neutral syllables which are between determinants. Examples are given in (2), where determinants appear in boldface type:

(2) *tu-la-lang-a*   *tu-la-mu-lang-a*   *tu-la-ba-lang-a*
    ba-la-lang-a   *ba-la-mu-lang-a*   *ba-lá-ba-lang-a*
    tu-la-bon-a   *tu-la-mu-bon-a*   *tu-la-ba-bon-a*
    ba-lá-bon-a   *ba-lá-mú-bon-a*   *ba-lá-ba-bon-a*

Under the assumption that all "neutrals" correspond to one underlying tone and all "determinants" to another and that the underlying tones in an underlying two-tone system must be "high" and "low," the question arises whether "determinant" is underlying high or underlying low. If it is underlying low, then rather than a rule being necessary to do something to neutrals that are between determinants (they will simply retain their underlying high tone), a rule will be needed to lower neutrals that are not between determinants. We can formulate this rule, which we call Terminal Lowering, as in (3) (where ‖ denotes phrase boundary):[1]

(3) Terminal Lowering $H^n \rightarrow L^n \, / \, \left\{ \begin{array}{c} \| \underline{\quad\quad} \\ \underline{\quad\quad} \| \end{array} \right\}$

On the other hand, if "determinant" is underlying high, it will be necessary to change the tone not only on neutrals that are between determinants but also on the determinants that they are between. This would all have to be done by a single rule such as (4):[2]

(4) $H(L^n H) \rightarrow L(H^n L)$

Otherwise, global rules will be necessary: if the lows between the highs are made high before the highs are made low, the rule that makes the highs (determinants) low will have to distinguish underlying highs from derived highs, that is, it will have to make reference to a stage of the derivation earlier than its input.

Though the choice between DETERMINANT = HIGH and DETERMINANT = LOW is far from clear, I will adopt the alternative that lets one do without global rules, that is, I will take the position that determinants are underlying lows.[3]

There are a number of phonological rules which will have to be discussed before taking up the more complicated tonal phenomena to be treated here. The negative form *tabalángi* 'they do not look at' provides reason for taking the suffix *-i* to be a determinant. Thus, we can now assign tone correctly to all but one of the negative forms in (5):

(5) 'they do not V'   'they do not V him'   'they do not V them'
    ta-ba-láng-i   *ta-ba-mú-láng-i*   *ta-ba-bá-láng-i*
    ta-ba-bon-i   *ta-ba-mú-bon-i*   *ta-ba-ba-bon-i*

The one form whose tone is not accounted for is *tababálángi* 'they do not look at them', where the incorporated object *-ba-* is pronounced high even though it is known to be determinant. Such forms as this led Meeussen to posit a Dissimilation Rule

---

[1] The reason for taking phrase boundary to be the relevant environment rather than word boundary will be given at a later point.
[2] Parentheses have been added so that the rule will cover isolated determinants, as in *balamulanga*.
[3] I note in passing that *determinant* corresponds to proto-Bantu high, not low.
  The possibility of global rules should not be dismissed lightly. See McCawley (to appear) for a demonstration that global rules rather similar to those just mentioned here are necessary in a description of tone in Bangubangu.

which makes a determinant neutral after another determinant. In the framework adopted here, this rule would appear as in (6):

(6) Dissimilation   L → H / L ____

As formulated, this rule would be applicable not only to *tababálángi* but also to *tabababoni* (which ends with four consecutive determinants) and *tulababona* 'we see them' (in which the third and fourth syllables are determinant). However, if Dissimilation is ordered before Terminal Lowering (3), the correct forms will result, as shown in (7):

(7) tá-bà-bà-láng-ì   tá-bà-bà-bòn-ì   tú-lá-bà-bòn-á
            bá   bá-bón-í   bón   Dissim
    tà   tà   bà-bòn-ì   tù-là   bòn-à   TL
    tà-bà-bá-láng-ì   *tà-bà-bà-bòn-ì*   *tù-là-bà-bòn-à*

A second phenomenon illustrated by present negative forms is that in many tenses[4] the underlying tone contrast on the agreement marker is neutralized. With the agreement marker *tu-* 'we' the tones in the negative present tense are exactly the same as with *ba-* 'they': *tatubálángi* 'we do not look at'. There is thus some rule which, prior to Dissimilation, imposes a tone (in this case a low tone) on the agreement marker in various tenses. Details of this rule will be given later.

A further phenomenon which appears in various forms is DOWNSTEP, as in the present perfect affirmative form *balí'bálángide* 'they have looked at them'. Downstep (indicated by ') consists of a lowering of the pitch of subsequent highs relative to the pitch of preceding highs: *-balang-* in the last example is on a slightly lower pitch than *-li-*; by contrast, in *balímúlángide* 'they have looked at him', *-li-*, *-mu-*, and *-lang-* are all on the same pitch. Tonga seems amenable to the analysis originally proposed by Stewart (1964, cited in Schachter and Fromkin (1968, p. 110)) for downstep in Twi. According to this, downstep arises from HLH sequences via (*a*) pitch assignment rules which make H after L lower in pitch than H before L (that is, the drop in pitch from H to a following L exceeds the rise in pitch from L to a following H) followed by (*b*) rules which either eliminate L between H's or assimilate L between H's to the pitch of one of the surrounding H's. The form in question appears to be a case of assimilation, and, indeed, all forms in which the tone rules given so far would yield ...HLH... in fact exhibit ...H'HH.... Thus *balí'bálángide* appears to demand the derivation in (8), where the interval between *li*[5] and *ba*[4] constitutes downstep (with lower numbers standing for lower pitch):

(8) bà-lí-bà-láng-ìdé
          −   Dissim
                    è   TL
    ba³li⁵ba²la⁴ngi¹de¹   Pitch Assgnmt
    ba⁴   Assim
    ba³li⁵ba⁴la⁴ngi¹de¹

The major portion of this paper will be devoted to the topic of initial and final high pitches, which according to the rules given so far ought not to be possible. In the course of discussing this question, it will be necessary to take up in detail the relationship of PREINITIAL morphemes (morphemes which precede the agreement marker) to the neutralization of tonal contrasts in agreement markers.

---

[4] Bantuists use *tense* to refer to a combination of mood, tense proper, positive/negative, strong/weak, predicative/attributive, and so on and thus do not hesitate to speak of "tense number 65," for example. Since I know of no standard term which corresponds to the Bantuists' *tense* I have adopted their usage within this paper.

I am aware of four classes of circumstances in which an initial syllable in Tonga is on a high pitch. The first of these apparently corresponds to a minor restriction on Terminal Lowering. Consider the full paradigm for the present perfect affirmative in (9) (where *-siy-* is 'leave behind'):

(9) 'we/they have V-ed' 'we/they have V-ed him' 'we/they have V-ed them'

tú-lí-láng-ide	tú-lí-mú-láng-ide	tu-li-ba-láng-ide
ba-lí-láng-ide	ba-lí-mú-láng-ide	ba-lí-'bá-láng-ide
tu-li-siy-ide	tu-li-mu-siy-ide	tu-li-ba-siy-ide
ba-lí-siy-ide	ba-lí-mú-siy-ide	ba-lí-ba-siy-ide

The first two forms of the first line have an initial sequence of high syllables, rather than being entirely low pitched as the rules given so far would predict them to be. This phenomenon occurs only when a neutral verb root is preceded by only neutral elements. Some further examples are given in (10):

(10) *ndí-lí-mú-tóbel-ide*   'I have followed him'
ndí-lí-mú-yándaul-ide   'I have looked for him'

Since the perfect morpheme *-ide* has the property of making determinant the EXTENSION, that is, the part of the verb stem after its first syllable, the class of forms under discussion here can be characterized as those in which a sequence of underlying high pitches terminates in a high-pitched verb-root syllable followed by a low tone. The clause of Meeussen's pitch assignment rules which covers this case is equivalent to the restriction on Terminal Lowering that is built into the revised statement of the rule in (11):

(11) Terminal Lowering$_2$ $H^n \rightarrow L^n / \begin{Bmatrix} \| \underline{\quad} & \text{except} / \underline{\quad} & \text{Root L} \\ \underline{\quad} \| \end{Bmatrix}$

The second case of initial high pitches is the imperative. An imperative consists of a bare verb stem followed by the suffix *-a*, the former pronounced on a high pitch and the latter on a low pitch, as illustrated in (12):

(12) *láng-a* 'look at!'   *tóbél-a* 'follow!'   *yándáúl-a* 'look for!'
bón-a 'see!'   *sílík-a* 'treat!   *swíílíl-a* 'listen to!'
                          (medically)'

The verbs in the first line are neutral, those in the second line determinant. Meeussen analyzed imperatives as having an initial segmentless determinant. This would neutralize tonal contrasts in the verb since dissimilation would make the first syllable of a determinant verb neutral. To get this proposal to work, Meeussen had to treat the suffix not as a single vowel but as an underlying geminate, the first element of which is neutral and the second determinant: a determinant is needed so that neutral *-lang-*, for example, can be between two determinants and thus pronounced high, but that determinant cannot immediately follow the verb stem since Dissimilation would then apply to the suffix of determinant *-bon-a*, for example, and the whole word would end up on a low tone. Meeussen's proposal thus corresponds to the derivations in (13):

(13)
ɸ-bòn-áà	ɸ-láng-áà	
bón	–	Dissim
–	–	TL
à	à	Contr
bón-à	láng-à	

The correct formulation of the contraction rule(s) is a major problem which will come up again later in this paper.

Since the hortative (which may be used as an imperative and which is indeed the only way of expressing an imperative when there is an incorporated object) causes the agreement marker to be made determinant, the proposal of an initial segmentless determinant is fairly plausible: it posits the tone which would be there if an agreement marker were overtly present.

A third case of initial high pitches involves preinitial morphemes. All preinitials have fixed tone. Meeussen (1963) calls high-pitched preinitials determinant and low-pitched preinitials neutral on the grounds that "a low preinitial never [is] followed by a high . . . ; a high preinitial should be viewed as a determinant . . . since the following syllables are high before a primary[5] determinant" (p. 75). This is illustrated by the data in (14), in which = marks the boundary between preinitial and agreement marker and boldface type indicates what Meeussen takes to be determinant (in both tenses neutral tone is imposed on the agreement marker):

(14) *i*=*bá-bon-ide* 'they who have seen'
    ni=*nd-a-mú-bon-a* (< *ni*=*ndi-a-* . . .)   'if I had seen him (today)'

If *i*= were neutral, the result should be **ibabonide*; if *ni*= were determinant, the result should be **nindámúbona* or **nindá'múbona*, depending on certain details in the Contraction Rule. Attempting to recast this proposal of Meeussen's in terms of "high" and "low" rather than "determinant" and "neutral" puts one in something of a quandary. On the one hand, we can propose that determinant preinitials have the same underlying tone as other determinants, namely, low, in which case a rule will be needed to reverse the pitch of preinitials. On the other hand, we can say that the Dissimilation Rule, assuming that it operates in the examples in (15) in the way that Meeussen indicates, has to turn a low into high after a low non-preinitial or a high preinitial but not after a low preinitial, so that *tu-*, *-a-*, and *-bon-* or *-silik-* all become high pitched:

(15) *ni*=*tu-a-bon-aa* (/ní=tù-à-bòn-áà/) → *nítwábóna* 'when we saw (today)'
    tiyi=*tu-a-silik-aa* (/tìyí=tù-à-sìlík-áà/) → *tiyítwásílíka* 'we did not treat (today)'

Either way, Terminal Lowering would have to be inhibited from making a preinitial low.

One is hoisted firmly onto one horn of this dilemma by a consideration of the one morpheme in Tonga which is a preinitial in some tenses but not in others, namely, the negative marker *ta*. *Ta* is preinitial except in the following tenses, where it follows the agreement marker—tenses that have another preinitial, subjunctive tenses, and past participles. Preinitials always impose a tone on the agreement marker (which immediately follows the preinitial). The subjunctive tenses and the past participles are the only tenses in which there is no preinitial but a tone is imposed on the agreement marker anyway. Thus, there is reason to posit a segmentally zero preinitial in the subjunctive and the past participles. Then a tone is imposed on the agreement marker if and only if there is a preinitial (and the preinitial determines *which* tone is imposed on the agreement marker), and, furthermore, *ta-* will appear after the agreement marker if and only if there is some preinitial other than *ta-* present.

Meeussen attributes three different tonal behaviors to *ta* in various tenses: he treats it as neutral when preinitial and determinant when it follows the agreement marker, except in the present subjunctive, where he says that it is given the opposite

---

[5] By "primary" determinant, Meeussen means a determinant which has not become neutral through the Dissimilation Rule.

underlying tone from the root (that is, it is determinant with a neutral root and vice versa). However, an alternative analysis is available which eliminates this third case. The forms in the present subjunctive are given in (16):

(16) 'that we not V'   'that we not V him'   'that we not V them'
     tu-tá-tóbel-i   *tu-tá-mú-tóbel-i*   *tu-tá-bá-tóbel-i*
     tu-tá-silik-i   *tu-tá-mú-silik-i*   *tu-tá-ba-silik-i*

If present subjunctive negatives are derived from underlying forms in which *ta* is determinant (as it normally is when it follows the agreement marker), the agreement marker is determinant (as in other subjunctive tenses), and the suffix *-i* is determinant (as in other negative present tenses), then the resulting output would differ from the forms in (16) only to the extent that *tutásiliki* and *tutábasiliki* would all be low, rather than having *ta* high. *Ta* in fact has surface high pitch not only in all present subjunctive negative forms but in all subjunctive negative forms. Thus the correct pitches result if *ta* is taken to be a determinant and there is a rule ordered after Terminal Lowering which makes *ta* high pitched in the subjunctive. Under this proposal *ta* is neutral if preinitial and determinant otherwise. Under the assumption that *ta* has the same underlying tone regardless of where it occurs and that the earlier decision to treat non-preinitial determinants as underlying lows is correct, we arrive at the conclusion that the underlying tones of preinitials are identical to their surface tones. That is, [í=], which Meeussen called "determinant," is an underlying high tone, and [tà=] and the conditional [nì=], which Meeussen called "neutral," are underlying low tones.

The most reasonable approach to getting off the horn of the dilemma is to see if an alternative analysis is possible in which the Dissimilation Rule does not apply to examples such as those of (15). To investigate this possibility, I will have to examine the various preinitials and the tones which they impose on the agreement marker. In (17) the preinitials have been arranged in three groups according to the tonal sequence across the = boundary given Meeussen's analysis:

(17) (a) D=N   *i* 'direct relative'   *í=bá-láng-a* 'they who looked at'
                ni 'potential'   *ní=nd-a-lang-a* 'I would have looked at'
    (b) N=D   *ka* 'hortative'   *ka=mu-láng-a* 'let him look at'
                aa 'hortative'   *á='tú-láng-e* 'let him look at'
                φ 'subjunctive'   *tu-láng-e* 'that we look at'
                ta 'negative'   *ta=tu-láng-i* 'we do not look at'
                kaa 'present participle'   *ká='tú-láng-a* 'we looking at'
                φ 'past participle'   *tw-á-láng-a* 'we having looked at'
                ni 'conditional'[6]   *ni=nd-a-lang-a* 'if I had looked at'
    (c) D=D   *tiyi* 'negative'   *tiyí=tw-á-sílík-a* 'we did not treat'
                ni 'temporal'   *ní=tw-á-láng-a* 'when we looked at'
                n . . . 'indirect relative'[7] *n-cí=tw-á-láng-a* 'which we looked at'

[6] Meeussen notes that the same tones result in this tense regardless of what underlying tone one assumes for the agreement marker. It is put into the (b) category here because all other preinitials impose a tone on the agreement marker and because there are otherwise no examples of N=N.

[7] The indirect relative contains a concord marker (determined by the noun that it modifies) followed by a (subject-)agreement marker (determined by the verb's own subject). Both morphemes come out on a high tone except in the present tense, where an *-o-* appears between the concord marker and the subject-agreement marker and the latter has low tone (or downstep arising from low tone on it): *n-c-ó='tú-láng-a* (< *n-c-ó=tù-láng-à*) 'which we do not look at', *n-c-ó=tu-ta-bon-i* 'which we do not see'. Meeussen treats *n-c-ó* as arising from *n-cí-ò*, in which case *-o-* would belong to group (c).

It is only with the three morphemes of group (c) that Meeussen has occasion to treat the preinitial as conditioning Dissimilation. Note that more is involved than just the surface tone of the agreement marker. In *tiyí=twásílíka*, *-a-* must be determinant if Dissimilation is to make *-sil-* of *-silik-* high, and *-tu-* (which is neutral in tenses without a preinitial) must be determinant if *-a-*, which has just been shown to be determinant, is to be pronounced on a high pitch; and if something such as Dissimilation does not apply to make *-tu-* high, the result will involve downstep: **tiyí='twásílíka*. The only alternative that I can see to the peculiar formulation of Dissimilation which this would require is to say that an extra rule is involved in the cases where Meeussen has a preinitial conditioning Dissimilation, for example, a rule ordered after Dissimilation (and before Terminal Lowering) which would make the agreement marker high after the morphemes of group (c). One peculiarity here is that the extra rule would cause the three morphemes to impose on the agreement marker the opposite of the tone that they had imposed on it by an earlier rule. For a slightly improved approach, suppose for the moment that groups (a) and (b) are all the preinitials that there are. Then the rule by which preinitials impose a tone on the agreement marker can be taken to be a simple assimilation rule as in (18):

(18) Preinitial Assimilation   Syllable → αH/αH=____

This rule would not suffice to handle group (c): the obvious proposal of treating the morphemes of group (c) as having an extra tone which is assimilated onto the agreement marker (*tìyîi=*, *nîi=*) will not work, since precisely that kind of underlying form is needed for the tonal behavior of [á=] and [ká=] of group (b), which are followed by downstep, whereas the items of group (c) are not.

Rather than treating the preinitials of group (c) as exceptional to two different rules that impose a tone on the following syllable (one rule coming before Dissimilation and one after it), it is possible to incorporate all of the irregularity into a single rule by saying that these preinitials in fact make the agreement marker "neutral" (that is, behave like group (a) with respect to assimilation) but are subject to a later rule (ordered after Dissimilation) which makes the morpheme after the agreement marker (always the infix *-a-* in the cases in question) high pitched. We would then have the derivations in (19):

(19) í=bà-láng-áà   kà=mú-láng-áà   ní=tú-à-bòn-áà
    bá   mù   (tú)   PAssim
    −   −   bón   Dissim
                                              á   Minor Raising
       à   à   à   Contr
  í=bálángà   kà=mùlángà   ní=twábónà

The fourth case in which an initial syllable in Tonga may be high pitched involves noun prefixes. There are no underlying tone contrasts in noun prefixes, the tone on the prefix being determined by the noun to which it is attached. Consider the forms in (20):

(20) *i-ma-tongo*   'ruins'
    í-má-kani   'news'
    í-mú-súne   'ox'

These examples consist of *i-*, which begins the so-called "double prefix," followed by the prefix proper, followed by the noun. Since infinitives in Bantu languages are morphologically nouns, they provide material that is essential for making the analysis of nouns consistent with that of verbs. The prefix of an infinitive is low before a neutral verb and high before a determinant verb, as illustrated in (21):

(21) *i-ku-lang-a*   'to look at'
      i-kú-bon-a   'to see'

Of the devices that have been used to derive word-initial tones in previous examples, the only one which would work here is that of positing a segmentless low tone at the beginning of the word: since the prefix is not high before all verbs, it cannot be exempted from Terminal Lowering in the way that preinitials are, and since the prefix is high before determinant and not neutral verbs, the initial high cannot be ascribed to the restriction which exempts from the first clause of Terminal Lowering sequences of neutrals terminating in a neutral verb root followed by a determinant. I thus tentatively assign to the nouns in (20) the underlying forms and derivations in (22):[8]

(22) φ̀-í-má-tóngó   φ̀-í-má-kàní   φ̀-í-mú-súnè
      ì-mà-tòngò   ì   —   TL
      ì-mà-tòngò   *í-má-kàní* *í-mú-súnè*

Such underlying forms yield correct results for the genitive construction, which is made up of the head noun followed by a word that consists of an agreement marker of the class of the head noun, a linking element -*a*-, and the dependent noun with its own single prefix. In the examples in (23), each of the two nouns is given in its isolation form, and then a genitive construction is given with the first noun as head:

(23)   *í-kú-boko*   'arm'
       í-mú-kaintu   'woman'
       í-kú-'bókó kw-á-'mú-kaintu   'woman's arm'
     < φ̀-í-kú-bòkó kú-à-mú-kàíntú

       í-bú-lwazi   'disease'
       í-n-kuku   'fowl'
       í-bú-'lwázi bw-á-n-kuku   'disease of fowl'
     < φ̀-í-bú-lwàzí bú-à-ń-kùkú[9]

       í-kú-boko   'arm'
       i-mu-sankwa   'boy'
       i-kú-'bókó kw-á-mu-sankwa   'boy's arm'
     < φ̀-í-kú-bòkó kú-à-mú-sánkwá   *(Continued)*

---

[8] I have treated *i-má-kani* as underlying LH rather than LL since in the one case I have found where a noun of this tonal shape is directly followed by a determinant, its final syllable fails to cause dissimilation: *i-ci-'fúmó-fumo* 'morning', compare *i-ci-fumo* 'tomorrow'. Assuming that 'morning' is a case of simple reduplication, /fùmò/ would yield *i-ci-fumo-fumo.

I have been unable to formulate underlying forms for infinitives which adequately cover infinitives with incorporated object and negative infinitives. The interested reader may attempt to grapple with the following data:

'to V'	'to V him'	'to V them'
i-ku-lang-a	*i-kú-mu-lang-a*	*i-kú-ba-lang-a*
i-kú-bon-a	*i-kú-mu-bon-a*	*i-kú-ba-bon-a*
'not to V'	'not to V him'	'not to V them'
i-kú-ta-lang-a	*i-kú-tá-mu-lang-a*	*i-kú-tá-ba-lang-a*
i-kú-ta-bon-a	*i-kú-tá-mú-bon-a*	*i-kú-tá-ba-bon-a*

[9] There is no downstep in the second word because the HLH sequence is within a single syllable; compare the preceding example.

í-mú-súne	'ox'
í-mú-nene	'old man'
í-mú-sú'né w-á-'mú-nene	'old man's ox'
< `ɸ-í-mú-súnè ú-à-mú-nèné`	
í-cí-sálu	'hide'
í-mú-súne	'ox'
í-cí-sá'lú c-á-'mú-súne	'hide of ox'
< `ɸ-í-cí-sálù cí-à-mú-súnè`	
i-mu-limo	'work'
í-mú-límó 'w-á-mú-kaintu	'woman's work'
< `ɸ-í-mú-límó ú-à-mú-kàíntú`	
í-mú-límó w-a-mu-sankwa	'boy's work'
< `ɸ-í-mú-límó ú-à-mú-sánkwá`	

Note that Terminal Lowering does not apply to *i-mu-limo* when a genitive follows, which shows that phrase boundary rather than word boundary is indeed the environment for this rule.

I turn now to cases where a phrase-final high pitch occurs in Tonga. Aside from two enclitics (Carter (1962, p. 15)) about which I have nothing to say, I know of three classes of cases where this occurs, all of which involve relatively short nouns and verbs. In a large number of tenses, forms occur in which a monosyllabic determinant verb stem is preceded by downstep and followed by a high-pitched suffix, as in *tiyí=bá-ká-'bón-á* 'they did not see (yesterday)'. Before pitch assignment, these forms of course have the verb stem low and the suffix high. In all of the tenses in question, Meeussen's analysis involves an underlying geminate suffix whose first component is neutral and whose second is determinant. Forms with a determinant incorporated object show it to be necessary to treat the suffix as *-áà* in the tense just cited, the hesternal negative, as illustrated in (24):

(24) *tiyí=bá-ká-'bá-láng-a < tìyí=bà-ká-bà-láng-áà*
     tiyí=bá-ká-'bá-bón-a < tìyí=bà-ká-bà-bòn-áà

There must be a determinant after *-lang-* for it to end up on a high pitch. However, the determinant cannot come directly after the verb stem since it would then be subject to Dissimilation in the forms with *-bon-*, and the resulting -HH sequence would become -LL by Terminal Lowering, yielding **tiyí=bá-ká-ba-bon-a*. The final high pitch on *tiyí=bá-ká-'bón-á* (and the other forms alluded to) can thus be accounted for by appropriate formulation of the contraction rules: rather than a V́V̀ suffix always yielding a low output (as it has in all the examples up to now), it yields a low output after a high pitch and a high output after a low pitch, as in (25):[10]

(25) tìyí=bà-ká-bòn-áà   tìyí=bà-ká-bà-bòn-áà
          bá   bá   PAssim
          –   bón   Dissim
                  á   à   Contr
     tìyí=bá-ká-bòn-á   tìyí=bá-ká-bà-bón-à

Contraction, or at least the case of it which applies to V́V̀ after V̀, must then apply later than Terminal Lowering so that the high pitch which it leaves will not yet be final when Terminal Lowering applies.

[10] The output of (25) must still undergo the "downstep" rules discussed previously with regard to (8) in order for the appropriate representations to be achieved.

The second case where a final high pitch occurs involves what I will refer to as "nonsyllabic verbs," that is, verbs whose stem has the surface form of a single consonant, as in (26):

(26) *tu-la-ty-a* 'we pour'
      tu-la-p-a 'we give'

The fragmentary data that I have seen on the perfect tenses of these verbs (Carter (1962, pp. 51–52)) suggest that, just as in Ganda (Tucker (1967, p. *xxiv*)), the verbs have underlying CV forms whose vowel is lost everywhere except in the perfect tenses. One reason for wanting to set up underlying forms with vowels is that these verbs bear underlying tonal contrasts and thus would otherwise conflict with the apparently valid claim that tones in underlying forms can be borne only by syllables or moras. The tonal contrast between *-ty-* and *-p-* is illustrated by the forms in (27), in which the tonal behavior of the present tense marker *-la-* is exactly the same as with neutral and determinant verbs that have a CVC shape:

(27) *ba-la-ty-a* 'they pour'   (cf. *ba-la-lang-a* 'they look at')
      ba-lá-p-a 'they give'   (cf. *ba-lá-bon-a* 'they see')

There are a rather large number of forms in which nonsyllabic verbs may end on a high pitch. Some examples are given in (28):

(28) *ty-á* 'pour!'   *ka-mu-ty-á* 'let him pour'
      p-á 'give!'   *ka-mu-p-á* 'let him give'

As shown in the derivations in (29), such forms require extra clauses of the contraction rule(s) to cover three-tone sequences but otherwise cause no problems:

(29) ɸ-tí-áà   ɸ-pè-áà   kà=mú-tí-áà   kà=mú-pè-áà
                                  mù   mù   PAssim
                                                pé   Dissim
        tyá   pá   tyá   pá   Contr
      ty-á   *p-á*   *kà-mù-ty-á*   *kà-mù-p-á*

Evidently, V́V́V̀ yields V́ and, as the contrasting examples in (30) indicate, V̀V́V̀ (the left-hand form) yields V̀:

(30) 'let him give me'   'let him give them'
      kà=mú-ndí-pà-áà   kà=mú-bà-pè-áà
              mù   mù   PAssim
                            bá-pé   Dissim
                pà   pá   Contr
      kà-mù-ndí-p-à   *kà-mù-bá-p-á*

I wish I could report here that these proposals correctly predict all final high tones after nonsyllabic verb stems. However, there remain a large number of forms which I am unable to account for without, for example, taking certain suffixes to have a different form after a nonsyllabic stem. The subjunctive form *tu-tá-bá-p-í* 'that we not give them', for instance, remains a mystery: the expected underlying form ɸ=*tú-tà-bà-pè-ì* should yield *tu-tá-ba-p-i (by, among other rules, the one that makes *ta* high in subjunctives).

The last case of final high pitch which I know of involves monosyllabic nouns. Just like two-syllable nouns, one-syllable nouns exhibit a three-way tonal contrast, as illustrated in (31):

(31) *i-bu-su*   'flour'
      i-bú-si   'smoke'
      i-má-lí   'money'

The first and second of these examples can obviously be derived from ɸ-*i-bú-sú* and ɸ-*i-bú-sì*, respectively. However, there is no obvious underlying form for 'money' which would make it tonally distinct from 'flour'. One possibility is to treat the final vowel as a geminate, -*lìì*; but this would force a revision of the contraction rules since in their present formulation they would make -*lìì* low-pitched after the high-pitched -*má*-. Moreover, such a proposal would involve setting up a combination of segments which otherwise does not occur in nouns and indeed is required only in verb suffixes and preinitials.[11]

While both one- and two-syllable nouns fall into three tonal types, the number of tonal distinctions for nouns in general increases with the number of syllables. For example, as illustrated in (32), there are five possibilities for three-syllable nouns:[12]

(32)   PRESUMED
         PRONUNCIATION   UNDERLYING FORM
      i-mú-cáyíli   'driver'   *cáyìlì*
      i-n-'káláya   'rust'   *kàláya*
      i-n-gówani   'hat'   *gówànì*
      i-m-bilila   'incense'   *bílílá*
      i-cí-jatizyo   'handle'   *jàtizyo*

Since the rules of Tonga are such that the eight logical possibilities for tones on three syllables can yield only five surface distinctions (LHH, LLH, and LLL would all yield the pitch of *icí-jatizyo*, and HLH and HLL would both yield the pitch o *i-n-gówani*),[13] it would appear as if pitches were freely combinable in underlying forms of nouns. However, if the possible tonal underlying forms for nouns were simply the different assignments of H or L to each syllable, there would be only two tonal possibilities for monosyllabic nouns rather than the three that actually occur. The only alternative that I can think of which might avoid this problem would involve a rather drastic change in the underlying forms for Tonga, namely, representing the tonal behavior of morphemes not in terms of high and low pitches on the various syllables but in terms of places where pitch falls, as in my treatment of Japanese (McCawley (1968)), especially the dialects of the Kansai area (Kyōto, Kōchi, Hyōgo, and so on). In these dialects, nouns differ as to whether they begin on a high or a low pitch and as to where, if anywhere, there is a fall in pitch. Using ' to represent fall in pitch and also using a preposed ' to represent initial low pitch (which is reasonable in that there is in fact a fall in pitch at the boundary between a high pitched item, a demonstrative, for example, and a following initial low pitch), the accentual possibilities for three-syllable nouns in Hyōgo Japanese are illustrated in (33):[14]

---

[11] Meeussen's analysis has an infix -*àà*- in the indicative affirmative hodiernal past tense (tense number 15). However, since all other past tenses (all 35 of them) have an infix -*à*- instead, it seems preferable to treat the peculiar tonal behavior of this tense by means of some minor rule(s) rather than a difference in underlying form.

[12] The unmarked vowels in the underlying forms are those whose underlying tone I have been unable to determine.

[13] Data on compounds might force one to distinguish between these possibilities; see also note 8.

[14] The data are from Hirayama (1960).

(33) PRONUNCIATION[15]   UNDERLYING FORM
    kúrúmá; kúrúmá gá   'vehicle'   *kuruma*
    ùsàgí; ùsàgì gá   'rabbit'   *'usagi*
    ábùrà; ábùrà gà   'oil'   *a'bura*
    ázúkì; ázúkì gà   'red bean'   *azu'ki*
    ùsírò; ùsírò gà   'rear'   *'usi'ro*

Any Hyōgo noun contains at most two "accents," one before it and one within it. There are no three-syllable or longer nouns in Hyōgo Japanese which have a final accent. However, this possibility does occur in one- and two-syllable nouns, as shown in (34):

(34) PRONUNCIATION   UNDERLYING FORM
    é; é gá   'picture'   *e*
    hî; hí gà   'day'   *hi'*
    hǐ; hì gá   'fire'   *'hi*

    úsí; úsí gá   'cow'   *usi*
    ìtó; ìtò gá   'thread'   *'ito*
    ótò; ótò gà   'sound'   *o'to*
    àmê; àmé gà   'rain'   *'ame'*

If Tonga nouns are represented using ' to indicate fall in pitch, the possibilities for one- and three-syllable nouns exactly match those for Hyōgo Japanese, and the possibilities for two-syllable nouns differ only to the extent of there being no Tonga counterpart to words such as *àmê* which are both preaccented and final-accented. I illustrate in (35):

(35) *su*   'flour'
    'si   'smoke'
    li'   'money'

    tongo   'ruins'
    'kani   'news'
    su'ne   'ox'

    bilila   'incense'
    'jatizyo   'handle'
    go'wani   'hat'
    cayi'li   'driver'
    'kala'ya 'rust'

I will not redo all the rules in accordance with this proposal since my principal reason for suggesting it relates to the underlying representations of nouns, and the information which I have about nouns in Tonga, particularly nouns of more than three syllables, is too fragmentary to serve as a basis for anything. There seem to be no major problems in recasting the rules presented earlier in terms of "accents"; for example, the Dissimilation Rule would delete an accent that is one syllable after an accent. One attractive feature of this proposal is that, since it allows the possibility of a three-way contrast in suffixes containing a single vowel (-a, -'a, -a'), it appears to make unnecessary the underlying geminates which Meeussen set up for suffixes such as that of the imperative (which can be represented as *-a'* rather than *-áà*) and for

---

[15] Both the isolation form and the form with nominative case marker *ga* are given.

certain preinitials. The low tone on these morphemes could be attributed to a rule which retracts final accent by one syllable except when either (*a*) the retraction would cause there to be accents on two consecutive syllables[16] or (*b*) the retraction would move the accent off a monosyllabic noun (or verb?). There would thus be derivations such as those in (36):

(36) 'see!'   'they did not see'   'they did not see them'
     'ɸ-'bon-a'   'tiyi='ba-ka-bon-a'   'tiyi='ba-ka-'ba-'bon-a'
     'ɸ-bon-a'   –   bon-a'   Dissim
     'ɸ-bo'n-a   –   bo'n-a   Retrac
     bónà   *tìyí=bákáʼbónà*   *tìyí=bákáʼbábónà*

Morphemes other than nouns, suffixes, and preinitials would come in only two underlying tonal types, namely, preaccented and unaccented.

REFERENCES

Carter, H. (1962), *Notes on the Tonal System of Northern Rhodesian Plateau Tonga*, Colonial Research Study 35, London: Her Majesty's Stationery Office.

Hirayama T. (1960), *Zenkoku akusento ziten*, Tōkyō: Tōkyōdō.

McCawley, J. D. (1968), *The Phonological Component of a Grammar of Japanese*, The Hague: Mouton.

McCawley, J. D. (to appear), "Global Rules and Bangubangu Tone," in C. Kisseberth, ed., *Studies in Generative Phonology*.

Meeussen, A. E. (1954), *Linguistische Schets van het Bangubangu*, Linguistische uitgaven van het Koninklijk Museum voor Midden-Afrika, Tervuren, Belgium.

Meeussen, A. E. (1963), "Morphotonology of the Tonga verb," *Journal of African Languages*, 2, 72–92.

Richardson, I. (1959), *The Role of Tone in the Structure of Sukuma*, London: School of Oriental and African Studies.

Schachter, P., and V. Fromkin (1968), *A Phonology of Akan*, UCLA Working Papers in Phonetics, 8.

Stevick, E. (1969), "Tone in Bantu," *IJAL*, *35*, 330–341.

Stewart, J. M. (1964), *The Typology of the Twi Tonal System*, Legon: Institute of African Studies.

Tucker, A. N. (1967), Introduction to R. A. Snoxall, *Luganda-English Dictionary*, Oxford: Clarendon Press.

[16] This restriction has the same effect as the extra clause of contraction which made V̂V high if the preceding syllable was low.

thoughts
on k-fronting in Crow

G. Hubert Matthews

Massachusetts Institute of Technology

Kaschube (1960, pp. 5–6) describes the velar stop /k/ in Crow as having four allophones which can be described by the interaction of two phonological rules, one that voices the segment in intervocalic position and one that palatalizes and slightly fronts it when it immediately follows /š/, /č/, /i/, /i:/, /e/, /e:/, or one of these vowels (the only front vowels in the language) plus /h/. The second of these rules, in conjunction with various distributional properties of phonological segments in Crow, has some interesting implications for the general theory of phonology. The most straightforward way of stating this rule is as in (1):

(1)

$$\begin{bmatrix} +\text{high} \\ +\text{interrupted} \end{bmatrix} \rightarrow [-\text{back}] \; / \; \left\{ \begin{matrix} \begin{bmatrix} -\text{anterior} \\ -\text{back} \end{bmatrix} \\ \begin{bmatrix} -\text{back} \\ +\text{syllabic} \end{bmatrix} \left(\begin{bmatrix} -\text{consonantal} \\ -\text{voice} \\ -\text{syllabic} \end{bmatrix} \right) \end{matrix} \right\} \underline{\quad}$$

If we now examine the distribution of /k/ in Crow, we find that this rule can be somewhat simplified. Clusters of the type /Chk/ do not occur in Crow; hence, it is not necessary to specify the segment that precedes the /h/ in the environment as [+syllabic]. Therefore, we can replace rule (1) by rule (2):

(2)

$$\begin{bmatrix} +\text{high} \\ +\text{inter} \end{bmatrix} \rightarrow [-\text{back}] \; / \; \begin{bmatrix} -\text{ant} \\ -\text{back} \end{bmatrix} \left(\begin{bmatrix} -\text{cons} \\ -\text{voice} \\ -\text{syll} \end{bmatrix} \right) \underline{\quad}$$

That is, if /k/ is preceded by a [−anterior, −back] segment either immediately or with an intervening /h/, it becomes a palatal stop.

Finally, since the only other [+ back] consonant in the language is /x/, and since this never occurs in the environment expressed in rule (2), it is not necessary to specify that only velar stops undergo the rule.[1] We therefore restate the rule as (3):

(3)
$$[+\text{cons}] \rightarrow [-\text{back}] \;/\; \begin{bmatrix} -\text{ant} \\ -\text{back} \end{bmatrix} \left(\begin{bmatrix} -\text{cons} \\ -\text{voice} \\ -\text{syll} \end{bmatrix} \right) \underline{\qquad}$$

Now let us look more closely at just what is involved in this rule. Clearly it is a case of assimilation of the velar stop to the preceding [− back] segment. But how is it that this assimilation can operate across /h/, which is a [+ back] segment?[2] And if it can operate across /h/, then why does it not operate across other segments as well? For example, the /k/ in such forms as *ríxkak* 'he asked for something' and *xawí:ak* 'he did wrong' is not fronted. The obvious answer to these questions is that an /h/ which is preceded by a front vowel and followed by a consonant is phonetically [− anterior, − back]—that is, it has assimilated to the preceding vowel; hence, it has the same effect on a following /k/ as do /š/ and /č/.

Rule (4) is the rule that assimilates /h/, and rule (5) now replaces rule (3) for the assimilation of /k/:

(4)
$$\begin{bmatrix} -\text{cons} \\ -\text{syll} \end{bmatrix} \rightarrow [-\text{back}] \;/\; \begin{bmatrix} -\text{ant} \\ -\text{back} \end{bmatrix} \underline{\qquad}$$

(5)
$$[+\text{cons}] \rightarrow [-\text{back}] \;/\; \begin{bmatrix} -\text{ant} \\ -\text{back} \end{bmatrix} \underline{\qquad}$$

But, since any [+ consonantal] segment is [− syllabic], rules (4) and (5) can be collapsed into rule (6):

(6)
$$[-\text{syll}] \rightarrow [-\text{back}] \;/\; \begin{bmatrix} -\text{ant} \\ -\text{back} \end{bmatrix} \underline{\qquad}$$

Chomsky (1967, p. 121) has conjectured that whenever a set of rules can be collapsed by the use of parentheses, the rules are disjunctively ordered, that is, they *must* be collapsed. It seems quite natural that this same conjecture should apply to sets of rules such as (4) and (5), even though the use of parentheses is not involved. This means, however, that rule (6) *must* be the rule in Crow. It applies to /h/ and to /k/, it does not apply to /x/, which does not occur in this environment, and it applies vacuously to the other [− syllabic] segments in the language.

However, whereas rules (4) and (5) produce the desired results, rule (6) does not. Consider, for example, the word *i:hka* 'his chin'. Rule (4) fronts the /h/, and rule (5) fronts the /k/. However, rule (6) accomplishes only the fronting of the /h/: the /k/ cannot be fronted by rule (6) in accordance with the general principle that a rule does not apply to its own ouput. Hence, if we accept both this principle and Chomsky's

---

[1] Within morphemes I have found two exceptions to this statement in the literature—*ríxka* 'to request' (Kaschube (1960, p. 118)) and *wixxúa* 'to spill' (Lowie (1960, p. 66))—and there is no indication in the literature that the /x/ here is fronted. One way of treating these forms is to say that they are exceptions to rule (3). Alternatively, we might say that they undergo rule (3) but by a later rule assimilate to the following velar. However, my Crow consultants consistently replace the high front vowel in these stems by a diphthong, that is (following the orthography that appears in the literature), they would spell these stems *ríaxka* and *wiaxxúa*. In any case, I do not find the existence of these stems reason enough for choosing rule (2) over rule (3).

[2] Note that although /h/ is characterized as [− back] in Chomsky and Halle (1968) on pages 177 and 307, the correct [+ back] specification is clearly implied on pages 407 and 414.

conjecture about disjunctive ordering, we must conclude that the fronting of /h/ after a front vowel takes place before the fronting of /k/ and that these two processes are in no way related—and this in spite of the fact that the general formalism by which phonological processes are expressed forces us to state that they are related in accordance with rule (6).

If we look again at the phonetic characteristics of the /h/ in *i:hka*, we see that not only is it a [−anterior, −back] segment, but it is also [+high, −low, −coronal, −round, −voice, −syllabic]. In other words it has all of the phonetic features of the preceding vowel except that it is [−voice, −syllabic]. In fact, every occurrence of /h/ in Crow is assimilated to the neighboring vowel in all of its features save voicing and syllabicity. This, of course, is not surprising: /h/ assimilates in many languages in just this manner, usually to a following vowel if there is one, otherwise to a preceding vowel, although the direction of assimilation might very well be language-specific. Accordingly, I would like to suggest that the most unmarked /h/ is that which is assimilated to the neighboring vowel in all its features other than voicing and syllabicity, and if an /h/ is marked for a given feature, then the value thereof is opposite that which the neighboring vowel has. I propose the marking conventions (7) for glides as alternatives to those given by Chomsky and Halle (1968, p. 407):

(7)

(xxxv)
$$\begin{bmatrix} -\text{syll} \\ -\text{cons} \end{bmatrix} \rightarrow \begin{bmatrix} +\text{son} \\ -\text{cor} \\ -\text{ant} \end{bmatrix}$$

(xxxvi)   [Uvoice] → [+voice]

(xxxvii)   [UF] → [αF] / $\begin{bmatrix} \underline{} \\ -\text{voice} \end{bmatrix}$ // $\begin{bmatrix} -\text{cons} \\ \alpha\text{F} \end{bmatrix}$

F = {high, low, back, round, nasal}

(xxxviii)   [Uhigh] → [+high]

(xxxix)   [Ulow] → [−low]

(xl)   [Uround] → [αround] / $\begin{bmatrix} \underline{} \\ \alpha\text{back} \end{bmatrix}$

(xli)   [Unasal] → [−nasal]

The double slash in convention (xxxvii) is to be read "in the neighborhood of." This convention is actually a schema for five conventions, which collectively state that when a glide is voiceless, the unmarked value for each of the features [high], [low], [back], [round], and [nasal] is the same as the value for each of these features in the neighboring vowel.

With these marking conventions we are able to present rule (6) as an intuitively more natural description of *k*-fronting in Crow than is rule (3). And there are certain other advantages as well. For example, the Crow stems *rù:hkapi* 'to scratch by hand' and *rà:hkapi* 'to scratch with the teeth' both contain the basic stem *hkapi* 'to scratch' and a prefix indicating manner. In these stems the /h/ assimilates to the preceding vowel; hence, /h/ appears the same way in the underlying representation in both forms, which is what we want since it is in fact the same segment in the same morpheme in both cases. In addition, there is no need to formulate rules to account for the different pronunciations of the /h/ in these forms since this is accomplished by means of the marking conventions.

Given such marking conventions as (xxxvii), that is, conventions which refer to a preceding or following environment, it is necessary to re-examine the linking of markedness conventions and phonological rules (see Chomsky and Halle (1968, p. 419). Consider, for example, the initial sounds in German *Huhn* 'hen' and *Hühner* 'hens'. They differ in that the first is [+back] whereas the second is [−back]. Hence, if the phonology of German has a rule for fronting the stem vowel in the plural form, then the initial /h/ as well must be fronted following the application of this rule. However, given our marking conventions for /h/, the fronting is automatic. To accomplish this, the conditions for linking need be only slightly extended over those given in Chomsky and Halle (1968, p. 420), as shown in (8) and (9):

(8) $X \rightarrow G \, / \, Y$

(9) $[UH] \rightarrow [\alpha H] \, / \, \begin{bmatrix} \overline{} \\ Z \end{bmatrix} W$

If the segment to which rule (8) applied is, after the application of (8), a supersegment of *W*, and if the preceding segment meets the conditions subsumed under *Z*, then the feature specification [αH] is assigned to this preceding segment.

The rule for umlauting in German is presumably something like (10), where E stands for the environment in which this rule applies:

(10) $[+syll] \rightarrow \begin{bmatrix} -back \\ -low \end{bmatrix} \, / \, E$

Hence the fronting of the initial /h/ in *Hühner* is brought about by the fact that this rule is linked with convention (xxxvii), where F = [back]. In (8) and (9), for this case, X = [+syllabic], G = [−back, −low], Y = E, H = [back], α = −, Z = [−voice], and W = [−consonantal, −back].

Chomsky and Halle (1968, pp. 192 ff.) argue for a rule that inserts a *y*-glide before the stressed vowel in such words as *cure, pure, use*. This rule applies also to words in which the stressed vowel is preceded by /h/, as in *humor, huge, human*, and, last but not least, *Hugh*. The underlying representation for *hue* is /huɛ/, where /u/ is a lax high back rounded vowel and /ɛ/ is a mid front glide. From this, the rules given in Chomsky and Halle yield [hyúw]. Given the marking conventions in (7) and starting with an unmarked /h/ in the underlying representation, the /h/ in the derived form is [−back, +high, −round]. However, in some dialects—my own included— the phonetic form of these words does not have a *y*-glide following the initial /h/; thus, there must be a rule which deletes it, just as it is deleted when it follows a [+coronal] segment. Note that when this *y*-glide is deleted, the initial /h/ remains front and unrounded, even though it now precedes a back rounded stressed vowel. But this is just as we should expect given (8) and (9): the segment which follows the /h/ after the application of the rule is not the segment to which the rule applied; hence, linking is blocked. Note that linking is not blocked in the converse case, namely, when a segment is added to a phonological matrix. Thus, when the *y*-glide is inserted in front of the stressed vowel in *hue*, it is the segment to which the rule applied, and hence this rule is linked to convention (xxxvii).

While we are on the subject of /h/ in English, it should be noted that in some dialects the initial sounds of *heel* and *wheel* are distinct in that *heel* begins with an /h/ which is fully assimilated to the following vowel, whereas *wheel* begins with a back rounded /h/. In the lexicon, both of these initial sounds are specified as [−syllabic, −consonantal, Mvoice], but the initial of *wheel* is also [Mback, Mround]. In addition, the initial segment of *who*, although its feature specification is identical to that of *wheel*, is listed in the lexicon as identical to that of *heel*.

The analysis of underlying /h/ in the neighborhood of vowels can easily be extended to cases where it is adjacent to other sonorants. Consider, for example, Old English *hlāford* 'lord'. We do not know the details of the pronunciation of Old English, of course, but it would seem most natural—and least marked—if during the pronunciation of the initial /h/ of *hlāford* the tongue was already positioned for the pronunciation of the /l/. This means that the /h/ assimilates to the adjacent sonorant with respect to the feature [lateral]. If this is in fact the case, we see that the only difference between the /h/ and the /l/ on the phonetic level is in the value of the feature [voice]. The /h/ is marked in this lexical item to the extent that the /h/ and /l/ in *hlāford* differ in the values of any other feature.

REferences

Chomsky, N. (1967), "Some general properties of phonological rules," *Language*, *43*, 102–128.
Chomsky, N., and M. Halle (1968), *The Sound Pattern of English*, New York: Harper & Row.
Kaschube, D. V. (1960), *Structural Elements of Crow*, unpublished dissertation, Indiana University.
Lowie, R. H. (1960), *Crow Word Lists: Crow-English and English-Crow Vocabularies*, University of California Press.

some Remarks on old and middle english stress[1]

Wayne O'Neil

Massachusetts Institute of Technology

1. ON ADDING THE LATIN STRESS RULE TO OLD ENGLISH GRAMMAR

Halle and Keyser (1971) have argued that in Old English

> the assignment of stress to the initial syllable of the stem was a productive process . . . , as shown by the fact that words borrowed from the classical languages received initial stress regardless of their original accentuation (p. 88).

In this way Halle and Keyser defer the entrance of the Latin Stress Rule (LSR) into English until the Middle English period and capture the facts of Old English word-level stress, as they see them, quite simply in the set of rules in (1)–(2):[2]

(1) $\text{V} \rightarrow [1\text{stress}] \ / \ [(X\#)\text{C}_0\underline{\quad}Y]$

(2) $\text{V} \rightarrow [1\text{stress}] \ / \ [\text{C}_0\underline{\quad}Z\#\text{C}_0\overset{1}{\text{V}}\text{C}_0]_N$

Rule (1) is the Initial or Germanic Stress Rule (GSR); rule (2) is the Stress

[1] This work was supported in part by National Institute of Mental Health, Grant No. MH-13390-04.

[2] Halle and Keyser (1971, p. 90). Rule (2) is further complicated in their exposition, but since the complication is not at issue here, I leave (2) in its first and simpler form. Halle and Keyser argue that the rules are unordered or, rather, that there is no principled way of deciding their relative order. But since the form of (2) implies that a stress assignment rule has already applied, it seems impossible not to accept the ordering (1), (2).

I assume throughout that [2stress] will be weakened to [3stress] by some later rule that applies within the limits of word boundaries when [2stress] is preceded by [1stress].

Retraction Rule (SRR). GSR, forgiving a possible prefix—$(X\#)$—assigns [1stress] to the initial vowel of the stem, yielding forms such as those in (3):

(3) (a) *wórd*   'word(s)'

   (b) *stánas*   'stones'

   (c) *and#gíet* 'understand(ing)'

SRR, rule (2), then assigns [1stress] to the initial syllable of prefixed substantives (= N), provided that the prefix belongs to the class "stressable." A consequence of SRR is the automatic weakening of the [1stress] assigned by GSR to [2stress], thus accounting for noun/verb contrasts such as those in (4):[3]

(4) (a) *ànd#gíet*ₙ   'understanding'

      *on#gíetan*ᵥ   'to understand'

   (b) *wìþer#sáca*ₙ 'adversary'

      *wiþ#sácan*ᵥ 'to oppose'

In Old English alliterative poetry, alliterating syllables must bear [1stress]. Thus Latin loans, since they alliterate on their initial syllable, have initial stress and clearly are subject to GSR, as illustrated in (5):

(5) (a) *sǽðerìe* 'savory (plant)' (cf. Latin *satureìa*)

   (b) *Hólofernùs* (cf. Latin, from Hebrew, *Holofernùs*)

About this primary stress there is no question. What is open to argument is the matter of antepenultimate or penultimate [2stress] on Latin loans, at least on later borrowings. Campbell (1959), for one, states flatly:

> §548. Late loan-words, like early ones, transferred the main stress to the first syllable, but a strong half-stress remained on the syllable which had borne the main stress in Lat[in]. . . (p. 216).

If it can be demonstrated that Old English *Holofernus*, for example, is stressed *Hólòfernùs*, not *Hólofernùs*, then Halle and Keyser must either admit LSR to Old English or they must give Nebuchadnezzar's general, Judith's victim, and their ilk unlikely lexical representations like /Holo#fernus/, this being, of course, simply a notational way of admitting LSR. Halle and Keyser have no other way of getting [2stress] on the penultimate syllable: in their system secondary stress results only from primary stress weakened by SRR (or by the Compound Rule—an even less likely explanation of *Hólofèrnùs* being /Holo# #fernus/).

What are the facts to support the opposing claims of Halle and Keyser, on the one hand, and Campbell, representing the traditional view, on the other? The strongest evidence that the traditional approach can muster is metrical evidence, for

---

[3] The fact that the prefix is unstressed in nonsubstantives accounts for its phonological reduction, among other things.

the ordinary notions of Old English metrics and scansion depend now and again on [2stress] here, there, and everywhere:

> §87. *The Old English metrical system shows* [emphasis mine] that many words had both a stressed and a half-stressed syllable. A half-stress always fell on the second element of a compound when both elements retained full semantic force. . . .
>
> §88. . . . *The verse shows* [emphasis mine] that the general rule is that [the second elements which did not retain their original semantic force fully] retain a half-stress only when they are themselves disyllabic . . . or have an inflexional syllable added. . . .
>
> §89. Similarly, heavy derivative suffixes have a half-stress after a long syllable . . . or its equivalent . . ., when followed by an unaccented syllable. . . .
>
> §90. As well as these suffixes, any long final syllable, after another long syllable or its equivalent, acquires half-stress when it becomes internal by the addition of an inflexion . . . (Campbell (1959), pp. 34–35).

Halle and Keyser, however, have argued convincingly that traditional theories of Old English metrics, particularly in their dependence on [2stress], are untenable and that if the metrics is organized solely around [1stress], there is no need to worry secondary stress so: the general will be as acceptable metrically whether we have penultimate secondary stress or no.

There is, however, other (weaker) evidence for the traditional view which comes from Old English orthography, a quite sensitive indicator of phonological change and weakening. Thus, in the native vocabulary, unstressed syllables, as opposed to their stressed counterparts, undergo profound changes in spelling and, we can presume, pronunciation. This can be seen, for example, in the prefixes cited in (4), as well as others—$\overset{1}{and}\#/on\#$, $\overset{1}{wiþer}\#/wiþ\#$, $\overset{1}{æ}\#/a\#$—and also in the second elements of original compounds (which, I suppose, "did not retain their original semantic force fully")—$\overset{1}{full}\#\#\overset{1}{team} > \overset{1}{fultum}$ 'army', $\overset{1}{hlaf}\#\#\overset{1}{weard} > \overset{1}{hlaford}$ 'lord' versus $\overset{1}{team}$ 'band', $\overset{1}{weard}$ 'guard' (Campbell (1959, p. 34)).[4] For early Latin loans the evidence is much the same: unstressed syllables are spelled—and presumably modified and pronounced—without regard for whether they were stressed or unstressed in Latin. But later Latin borrowings, which were mainly of a literary nature, "generally reproduce the Latin vowels and consonants in writing without change" (Campbell (1959, p. 215)).

There are two possible explanations for this: the later loan words were spelled more like Latin either because their spellers knew more Latin or because the vowels stressed in Latin maintained [2stress] in Old English; the latter alternative implies that LSR did operate in Old English. Both explanations seem right and not necessarily in contradiction. If an Old English speaker knew many Latin words, it is likely that he would spell and pronounce them as if he knew them, while at the same time adapting the pronunciation (partially) and the inflections (certainly) to English as he went about making Old English poems, prayers, sermons, and conversation, and adapting them in some principled way. On balance, the principled way that suggests itself is for Old English grammar to contain two stress assignment rules, namely, GSR for native,

---

[4] Old English orthography can thus be seen to be not phonological but, rather, broadly phonetic. The reason for this would seem to lie in the fact that the orthography was created and wielded by men who were working like foreigners in their own language or who were in fact foreigners (Irish and Latin churchmen). In the same way and for the same reasons, the orthographies of many modern, previously unwritten languages are phonetic rather than phonological, thereby serving the nonnative speaker better than the native, as exploited peoples and their nations must in general do.

Germanic words and LSR for the later Latin loan words, SRR then being appropriately modified in order to get the [1stress] of the latter onto the initial syllable:[5]

(6) (a) Latin Stress Rule

$$V \rightarrow [1\text{stress}] \ / \ [X\underline{\quad}C_0(\begin{bmatrix} -\text{tense} \\ V \end{bmatrix}C_0^1)\begin{bmatrix} -\text{tense} \\ V \end{bmatrix}C_0]$$

(b) Germanic Stress Rule (= (1))

$$V \rightarrow [1\text{stress}] \ / \ [(X\#)C_0\underline{\quad}Y]$$

(7) Stress Retraction Rule[6]

$$V \rightarrow [1\text{stress}] \ / \ [C_0\underline{\quad}Z(\#)C_0\overset{1}{V}W]_N$$

By (6a) we get forms such as those in (8):

(8) (a) *Holof$\overset{1}{e}$rnus*

  (b) *m$\overset{1}{a}$gister*

  (c) *Greg$\overset{1}{o}$rius*

By (6b) we get forms such as those in (9):

(9) (a) *w$\overset{1}{o}$rd, st$\overset{1}{a}$nas*

  (b) *and#g$\overset{1}{i}$et*

Then by (7) we get the forms in (10):

(10) (a) *H$\overset{1}{o}$lof$\overset{2}{e}$rnus, m$\overset{1}{a}$g$\overset{2}{i}$ster, Gr$\overset{1}{e}$g$\overset{2}{o}$rius*

  (b) *$\overset{1}{a}$nd#g$\overset{2}{i}$et$_N$, $\overset{1}{a}$nd#gi$\overset{1}{e}$t$_V$*

Adding LSR (6a) to Old English grammar entails no great consequences for the history of the language. It means simply that a subpart of the Middle English Romance Stress Rule was introduced into the language earlier than Halle and Keyser have claimed and that SRR was modified much earlier than the late sixteenth century (Halle and Keyser (1971, pp. 109 ff.)), a matter to which we shall return.

2. ON SUBTRACTING THE GERMANIC STRESS RULE FROM MIDDLE ENGLISH GRAMMAR

Halle and Keyser (1971) have argued convincingly that GSR and SRR, (1) and (2), are clearly insufficient to explain the facts of late Middle English stress. Nor is LSR sufficient to the task, for in Middle English the loans come in from Old French and

---

[5] I wish to leave open the question, finally, of whether or not SRR is to be reformulated as in (7), plus a further restriction we come to later, or left as in (2), with (2) then applying poetically to [+Latin] words. See Section 3. Sometimes Latin loans accommodated themselves to the "genius" of the English language by apocope: *stær* 'history', *renge* 'spider', *Commedia* 'Nicomedia', from Latin *historia, aranea, Nicomedia*, respectively (Campbell (1959, pp. 208, 215)).

[6] The "N" subscript of (2) can apparently be left to stand on (7) since there seem to be no Old English verbs out of Latin to be accounted for by (7).

Norman French as well as from Medieval Latin. The stress data to be accounted for in a Middle English grammar are illustrated in (11):

(11) (a) *forsée*

    (b) *fórsíght*

    (c) *Cappáneus*

    (d) *Satúrnus, solémpne*

    (e) *Neptúnus*

    (f) *hónour, degrée*

Halle and Keyser explain (11a,b) with GSR and SRR, (1) and (2). But the Romance Stress Rule (RSR), an amalgam of LSR and the Old French Stress Rule, is brought to bear on (11c–f). This rule lays [1stress] on the antepenultimate vowel if the penultimate syllable is weak and the final vowel is lax, on the penultimate vowel if that syllable is strong and the final vowel lax, and on the final vowel otherwise, that is, when it is tense. Formally, then, the three subrules of RSR are (a)–(c) of (12), and the abbreviated form of the rule is (13):

(12) (a) $V \rightarrow [1stress] / [X\_\_\_\_C_0 \begin{bmatrix} -tense \\ V \end{bmatrix} C_0^1 \begin{bmatrix} -tense \\ V \end{bmatrix} C_0]$

    (b) $V \rightarrow [1stress] / [X\_\_\_\_C_0 \begin{bmatrix} -tense \\ V \end{bmatrix} C_0]$

    (c) $V \rightarrow [1stress] / [X\_\_\_\_C_0]$

(13) $V \rightarrow [1stress] / [X\_\_\_\_C_0 ((\begin{bmatrix} -tense \\ V \end{bmatrix} C_0^1) \begin{bmatrix} -tense \\ V \end{bmatrix} C_0)]$

We then get forms such as (11c) by rule (12a), forms such as (11d,e) by (12b), and forms such as (11f) by (12c). There are, further, some disyllabic words like *Jesús, abbót, Judíth, Oréb, tempést*, many of which also appear in Chaucer with initial stress (Halle and Keyser (1971, p. 101)), whose stress when final cannot be accounted for by (12) since (12b) yields *Jésus, ábbot*, and so on. Halle and Keyser propose that these words be marked [−rule (12b)], which then allows them to be stressed according to (12c); this result, of course, is right only some of the time, that is, when the words are to receive final rather than initial stress. Halle and Keyser then account for other minor complications in a similar fashion.

    The question to be raised here is the following: what and how much work is GSR doing? Since native words are nearly all monosyllabic or disyllabic (not counting prefixes) and the disyllabic ones end in a lax vowel, they could just as well be handled by rule (12b), provided that a condition is put on X to the effect that it contain no instance of #, a necessary condition in any case. In this way we could do away with GSR.

    What are the consequences? Strangely enough, with the exception of one class of native words (to which we will return), GSR is necessary only to explain stress doublets in the *Romance* part of the lexicon, such as the doublets in (14):

(14) (a) *Custance/Custance*

    (b) *service/service*

    (c) *Criseyde/Criseyde*

In each of the pairs in (14), the first member is accounted for in the regular way, namely, by (12b). But the second member of the pair, Halle and Keyser argue, can be accounted for only by GSR; thus this rule must be available to the speaker of Middle English if there is to be a principled way of accounting for these and several other kinds of stress doublets.

There is, however, another principled way. Let us assume along with Halle and Keyser that the lexicon is bifurcated, that is, that there is an unmarked category of lexical items ([URomance] → [+Germanic, −Romance]) and a marked category ([MRomance] → [−Germanic, +Romance]). Rule (12), then, applies unconstrained by these lexical features, while rule (7), the modified version of SRR, applies only to the unmarked, [+Germanic] category. Notice that (7) is now restricted in a way that it was not in Old English,[7] but this is not unreasonable given the marginal role of Latin loans in Old English and the dominant role of Romance loans in Middle English. We can now account for *Custance, service, Criseyde*, and so on by extending (7) poetically to [−Germanic] words. We are, then, still saying that the explanation of stress doublets lies in there being a rule available to explain the doublets, but our rules are fewer.

There is a further virtue in this proposal. Consider the case of native doublets like *ridynge/ridynge*. The first form now follows quite naturally from the explanation of the irregular or poetic *Custance* and so on. *Ridynge*, however, is an unnatural, poetic interruption of the normal application of the rules. A consequence of understanding Middle English word level stress as simply a function of rule (12) plus rule (7) is that [2stress] is left strewn all over the place, that is, it results whenever (7) applies nonvacuously to the output of (12). Thus these rules will turn out *Custance, ridynge*, and so on. The nice thing about these secondary stresses is that they can be neither proved nor disproved.

What I am arguing, then, is not so much that the suggestions made here for explaining Middle English (and Old English) stress are right and Halle and Keyser's wrong, but rather that the dearth of data allows both explanations to be supported. And at least for Middle English, the explanation just given here is simpler and results in no evil or metrically wrong answers, which is no mean achievement.

3. ON GRANTING POETS THEIR LICENSE

It is a fact that poets violate rules of grammar:

> Sentences that break selectional rules can often be interpreted metaphorically (particularly, as personification—cf. [M.] Bloomfield, 1963) or allusively in one way or another, if an appropriate context of greater or lesser complexity is supplied (Chomsky (1965, p. 149)).[8]

[7] But not necessarily; see note 6 and Section 3 here.
[8] See also Chomsky (1971).

Poets often also relax constraints on grammatical transformations, as illustrated in (15)–(17):[9]

(15) Relativization
> . . . *in thy book record* their *groans*
> Who *were thy sheep* . . .

(16) Pronominalization and Pronoun Deletion
> *Their moans*
> *The vales redoubled to the hills, and* they
> *To Heaven.*

(17) *be*-Deletion under conjunction
> *Who were thy sheep and in their ancient fold*
> *Slain by the bloody Piedmontese* . . .

In general, semantic and syntactic constraints are relaxed in poetry while phonological constraints are increased. On the one hand, poetry is semantically and syntactically figurative and ambiguous (as in (16)) or simply ungrammatical (as in (15), (17)) without attendant figures of speech or ambiguity. On the other hand, poets must rime, alliterate, and be metrical; they must obey phonological constraints which are not a part of ordinary grammar or of grammar at all but which are added onto and built out of the stuff of the language, its grammar.

There are, then, obvious difficulties involved in trying to pull a systematic account of Middle English stress, for example, out of metrical data alone, without any orthoepic evidence. Thus Halle and Keyser's explanation of sixteenth- to eighteenth-century English stress, as opposed to their account of the earlier periods, is much enriched by the availability of orthoepic data. It appears to me, furthermore, that Halle and Keyser, in their account of Old English and Middle English, have not conquered the difficulties inherent in working solely out of metrical material. For example, it is correct to say

> The existence of rules that provided a number of alternatives for stressing a given word was put to poetic use by Chaucer and his contemporaries (Halle and Keyser (1971, p. 106)).

But quite another thing to say

> Since words of this type [*Jesus, abbot, Judith, Oreb, tempest*—many of which are also found in Chaucer with initial stress] would receive nonfinal stress by rule [(12b)], we suggest that they are marked as exceptions to this rule (p. 101).[10]

---

[9] The lines are from Milton's sonnet "On the Late Massacre at Piedmont." I have quite consciously chosen a nonmodern poem to show that poetic violation is not simply a modern thing, found only in the poems of e. e. cummings and Dylan Thomas, an impression that might well follow from many of the linguistic discussions of poetry.

In (15) the ungrammatical relativization on *their* is at issue, the referent of *who*. In (16) the referent of *they* is ambiguous. Presumably "and they/To Heaven" is to be taken as a deletion from "and the hills redoubled their moans to Heaven," with "redoubled" and "their moans" deleted and "the hills" pronominalized to "they." In (17) there is deletion of *be*, the passive *be* of underlying "were slain by NP" being identified with the copulative *be* of "were NP" and (ungrammatically) deleted in the conjunction of the two VPs.

[10] In cases of this sort the rules of phonology are neither being added to nor, as in syntax and semantics, relaxed; instead, there is simply a shifting of lexical items into categories to which they do not ordinarily belong. It is possible, of course, for there to be a relaxation of phonological rules, as, for example, in ballad rimes which allow (*inter alia*) rimes like *Sam/ran, bib/tip* and like *had/blade, side/did.* Halle and Keyser, unfortunately, use such evidence at one point to argue against "ad hoc tensing" and in favor of the laxness of the final vowel of *Kaukascus* (riming with *hous* 'house') and at another point in favor of the laxness of the final vowel of *pulpet* 'pulpit' because of its rime with *yset* (pp. 104–105).

Why in one case is the poet using the rules poetically and creatively but in the other simply following the grammar? The distinction is a dubious one at best, as well as a complicating one. If, on the other hand, such a distinction is not made, if one relies solely on the former explanation, the grammar is considerably less complicated since there is then no need for a subcategory of Romance words marked [−rule (12b)] and so on. This seems to me to be the right approach, namely, to enrich the grammar in the case of Middle English stress so as to have available a rule to which to refer "poetic use" but not to incorporate "poetic use" into the grammar.

REFERENCES

Campbell, A. (1959), *Old English Grammar*, Oxford: Oxford University Press.
Chomsky, N. (1965), *Aspects of the Theory of Syntax*, Cambridge, Mass.: M.I.T. Press.
Chomsky, N. (1971), *Problems of Knowledge and Freedom—The Russell Memorial Lectures*, New York: Pantheon.
Halle, M., and S. J. Keyser (1971), *English Stress: Its Form, Its Growth, and Its Role in Verse*, New York: Harper & Row.

Leftward, ho![1]

John Robert Ross
Massachusetts Institute of Technology

This paper derives from an important generalization about English stress. It has traditionally been observed that, while noun-verb pairs can be found in which both members exhibit final stress, as in (1a), or in which both exhibit stress retraction, as in (1b), or in which the noun exhibits stress retraction but not the verb, as in (1c), there are no pairs in which only the verb exhibits retraction: real words like the hypothetical examples in (1d) cannot be found:

(1) (a) $\overset{1}{arrest}_{V,N}$, $\overset{1}{return}_{V,N}$, $\overset{1}{lament}_{V,N}$, $\overset{1}{delay}_{V,N}$, $\overset{1}{desire}_{V,N}$, $\overset{1}{resort}_{V,N}$

    (b) $\overset{1\ \ 3}{comment}_{V,N}$, $\overset{13}{triumph}_{V,N}$, $\overset{1\ \ 3}{ambush}_{V,N}$, $\overset{1\ 3}{boycott}_{V,N}$, $\overset{1\ 3}{relay}_{V,N}$

    (c) $\overset{3\ \ 1}{torment}_V$–$\overset{1\ \ 3}{torment}_N$, $\overset{3\ \ 1}{import}_V$–$\overset{1\ 3}{import}_N$, $\overset{3\ 1}{ally}_V$–$\overset{1\ 3}{ally}_N$

    (d) $\overset{1}{police}_N$–$\overset{1\ 3}{*police}_V$, $\overset{1}{repair}_N$–$\overset{1\ 3}{*repair}_V$, $\overset{1}{delight}_N$–$\overset{1\ 3}{*delight}_V$

From such facts, the generalization in (2) follows directly:

(2) In English, stress is never retracted farther in the verb in a noun-verb pair than it is in the noun

[1] A version of this paper was presented at the Winter 1969 meeting of the Linguistic Society of America.

This work was supported in part by a grant from the National Institute of Mental Health (Grant No. 5-P01-MH 13390-04) and a grant from the National Science Foundation (No. GS-3202) to the Language Research Foundation.

I would like to acknowledge the kindness of several friends whose suggestions and criticisms have considerably sharpened and broadened the argumentation in this paper: Michael Brame, Morris Halle, Jay Keyser, Paul Kiparsky, and Charles Kisseberth.

Kiparsky[2] noted that (2) would cover the facts not only in (1), where stress retraction is effected by rules that appear to be well motivated in English phonology, but also in such cases as (3), where no satisfactory analysis of the stress alternations exists:

(3) $\overset{1\ 3}{attribute_V}-\overset{1\ \ 3}{attribute_N}$

It was also suggested by Kiparsky that some extension of (2) might be able to account for the forms in (4), which do not undergo retraction but which seem to exhibit the type of phenomenon under discussion:

(4) $\overset{1}{arithmetic_A}-\overset{1}{arithmetic_N}$

This paper is devoted to showing how this latter conjecture can be extended to a number of new cases.

English stress phenomena are incredibly complex superficially, but I believe that they can be optimally described by the set of three basic ordered processes described in (5):[3]

(5) (a) Main Stress Rule $\quad$ V → [1stress] / ___$C_0((W)\check{V}(C_b))$]

Primary stress is assigned finally or nonfinally. If nonfinally, the stress will fall on the antepenult of words whose penult contains a weak cluster and on the penult of all other words

(b) Retraction Rule

Main stress is moved from one to five syllables leftward from a word-final main-stressed syllable under complicated conditions which need not concern us here[4]

(c) Destressing

Certain vowels bearing [2stress] are made stressless

It is far too cumbersome a task for the present paper to show how the three rules of (5), properly formulated, can account for all the stress contours and alterations in English, up to unpredictable, lexically governed exceptions to various of the rules. Therefore, I will presuppose the correctness of this skeletal system and will not go into a more detailed explanation of these rules unless it is directly relevant to the purpose here.

A generalized version of (2) which I would now like to provide evidence for is given in (6):

(6) The Leftward Ho! Conspiracy

In English primary stress in nouns may be followed by a larger number of unstressed syllables than is the case for primary stress in verbs, and, similarly,

---

[2] In class lectures at M.I.T. in the spring of 1968.

[3] These rules derive from a larger work of mine (Ross (1972)) and borrow heavily from Chomsky and Halle's (1968) analysis. In particular, the symbol "W" abbreviates the sequence [+vocalic, −consonantal, −tense]$C^1(\{r,w\})$ from Chomsky and Halle. The symbol "C_b" is explained later, in connection with (8) and (9).

[4] See Ross (1972) for details.

stress may be retracted farther leftward in nouns than is possible in verbs;[5] in other words, primary stress in English nouns is farther to the left than primary stress in English verbs[6]

I will try to show that (6) operates in English in a way quite similar to the way a derivational constraint, in the sense of Lakoff (1970), operates in syntax: many special conditions on the rules in (5) can be seen to be consequences of the general tendency stated in (6). That is, one might speak of the various conditions to be described here as "conspiring" to produce the effect of (6).

The first of the conditions I will discuss has to do with rule (5a), the Main Stress Rule (MSR). It concerns the question of the predictability of final versus nonfinal stress assignment by this rule. Note first that (almost[7]) all words whose final vocalic nucleus is long or complex receive final stress by the MSR. Some examples are given in (7):

$$
\overset{1}{\text{cocaine}}, \quad \overset{1}{\text{maroon}}, \quad \overset{1}{\text{appear}}, \quad \overset{1}{\text{cajole}}, \quad \overset{1}{\text{supreme}}
$$

(7) *cocaine, maroon, appear, cajole, supreme*

If the last syllable of a word contains a lax vowel, whether or not stress can be nonfinal depends on phonological properties of the consonants at the end of the word and *on the category of the word*. For nouns, nonfinal stress is possible only if the final consonant is a single sonorant, a single dental, or one of the clusters /nt/, /st/, /ts/, and a few more. This class of segments I abbreviate as C_b *for nouns* in the rule in (5a). Some examples appear in (8):

(8) *m*   amalgam   modicum

 n   phlogiston   venison

 r   October   integer

 l   utensil   arsenal

 t   Narragansett   Titicut

 d   bicuspid   pyramid

 s   meniscus   abacus

 z   Ramirez   ————[8]

[5] I am aware that the assertion that stress retraction is similar to primary stress assignment is not a trivial one. The basis for my use of the word "similar" here is the strong intuition that the evidence I will present for (6), while it could be broken down into two conspiracies, one for primary stress assignment and one for stress retraction, is really a reflection of only one phonological process. For an analysis of English stress that attempts a total unification of primary and retracted stress, see G. Lee's important paper (Lee (1969)).

[6] It is possible to argue that primary stress in adjectives is "between" primary stress for verbs and primary stress for nouns, but I will not attempt to demonstrate this fact here.

[7] I exclude here such words as *Pulaski* and *fiasco*, whose final strong clusters derive from underlying lax vowels which are subsequently tensed, as proposed by Chomsky and Halle (1968).

[8] Such dashes in (8) and elsewhere indicate cases for which I can find no occurring examples but which are, to the best of my knowledge, accidental rather than systematic gaps.

θ ——————— Elizabeth
$\overset{1\ \ 0}{}$

$\overset{1\quad 0}{}$ $\overset{1\quad 0}{}$
nt   disinfectant   elephant

st   ——————— Everest
$\overset{1\quad 0}{}$

$\overset{1\ 0}{}$ $\overset{1\quad 0}{}$
ts   Massachusetts   Horowitz

With regard to verbs, on the other hand, only those ending in a single sonorant can be nonfinally stressed: verbs ending in any obstruent or in any cluster must receive final stress by the MSR. In (9) I list some examples:

(9) *t*   abut, regret, boycott
$\overset{1}{}$ $\overset{1}{}$ $\overset{1\ \ 3}{}$

s   caress, harass, dehisce
$\overset{1}{}$ $\overset{1}{}$ $\overset{1}{}$

nt   torment, lament, comment, fragment
$\overset{1}{}$ $\overset{\cdot}{}$ $\overset{1}{}$ $\overset{1\ \ 3}{}$ $\overset{1\ \ 3}{}$

st   arrest, attest, accost, flabbergast
$\overset{1}{}$ $\overset{1}{}$ $\overset{1}{}$ $\overset{1}{}$ $\overset{3}{}$

ts   ———————

Thus C_b for verbs is a subset of C_b for nouns.

It can be shown, I believe, that such apparent counterexamples to this claim as verbs like *warrant* and *scavenge* are assigned final stress by the MSR; this stress is retracted and then removed by a branch of (5c), Destressing, which destresses a lax vowel after a weak cluster with higher stress (such phonetic sequences as *[skævenǰ] are in general impossible). I will not argue in detail for this analysis here, however.[9]

Another class of verbs which end in an obstruent not preceded by primary stress is that illustrated in (10):

(10) *credit, diminish, deposit, finish, develop, inhabit*

Briefly, I believe that it can be shown that even these verbs do not constitute counterevidence to my claim that verbs ending in obstruents get final stress by the MSR, for the verbs in (10) must end in a lax /æ/ in underlying representations. This underlying final lax vowel will cause the MSR to assign stress to the deep antepenultimate syllable and then will delete by a generalized version of the rule of *e*-Elision proposed by Chomsky and Halle (1968, pp. 45–50). The generalized rule is given in (11):

(11) $\begin{bmatrix} +\text{vocalic} \\ -\text{back} \\ -\text{high} \\ \langle -\text{low} \rangle \end{bmatrix} \rightarrow \phi \ / \ \begin{bmatrix} \underline{\quad\quad} \\ \langle +\text{noun} \rangle \end{bmatrix} \#$

This final /æ/ explains the laxing of the tense underlying vowels of *crĕdit* (cf. *crēdence*), *dimĭnish* (cf. *mīnor, mīnute*), *depŏsit* (cf. *-pōse*), and so on.[10] And its deletion

---

[9] Evidence for this claim can be found in Ross (1972).

[10] That is, if *credit* and *deposit* derive from underlying /krēd+itæ/ and /de+pōz+itæ/, their long vowels can be laxed by the Trisyllabic Laxing Rule (which is motivated on pp. 180–181 of Chomsky and Halle (1968)).

accounts for the fact that no nondenominal verbs end in [ə], that is, there are no verbs like **to sofa*, **to basilica*, **to india*. This phonetic gap is explained by rule (11): although lax unstressed final /æ/ normally becomes [ə], in verbs all such final underlying segments get deleted by (11).

Notice how the angled bracket condition on (11) is part of the conspiracy to effect (6). While there are nouns whose main stress is followed by two unstressed syllables of the form [əC₀ə#] (*America*, *Pamela*, *taffeta*, and so on), there can be no such verbs: rule (11) will delete the final vowel. Thus verbs will *appear* to be stressed only penultimately or finally, in contrast to nouns, which show up phonetically with stress on any of the last three syllables (*Titicut*, *Narragansett*, *Tibet*). The fact that rule (11) is more general for verbs thus conspires with the fact, noted in connection with the MSR, that a larger class of consonants can be "disregarded" in assigning nonfinal stress to nouns than can be disregarded in assigning stress to verbs, that is, that C_b for verbs is a subset of C_b for nouns.

Proceeding now from primary stress placement to stress retraction, we find several independent facts which are instances of (6). Consider, for example, the contrast between (a) and (b) of (12):

(12) (a) *to intercept*ᵥ–*an intercept*ₙ

        *to import*ᵥ–*an import*ₙ

    (b) *to telephone*ᵥ–*a telephone*ₙ

        *to biplane*ᵥ–*a biplane*ₙ

These examples are representative of huge numbers of Latin- and Greek-derived prefix-stem combinations in which stress is unretracted only in Latin-derived *verbs*. This suggests a redundancy rule like (13):

(13)
$$\begin{bmatrix} +V \\ +\text{Latin} \\ +\text{stem} \\ +\text{verb} \end{bmatrix} \rightarrow [-\text{Retraction}]$$

Once again, the fact that it is the Latin *verbs* that do not exhibit retraction is a manifestation of (6).[11]

By and large, stress retraction is obligatory in words of three syllables or more: we say *hurricane*, *anecdote*, *operate*, not **hurricane*, **anecdote*, **operate*. But what

[11] The retraction contrast between (12a) and (12b) is accounted for by Chomsky and Halle (1968) by postulating an extra cycle (on stems) for Greek words, nouns or verbs. Whether or not this is correct (in Ross (1972) I argue that it is not), note that within Chomsky and Halle's framework, there is still no reason why underlying, intuitively plausible pairs like [*police*]ₙ–[[*police*]ₙ]ᵥ (paralleling [*intercept*]ᵥ–[[*intercept*]ᵥ]ₙ) should not be possible. The latter pair produces, by Chomsky and Halle's rules, stress retraction in deverbal nouns. The former, impossible (see (1d)) pair would produce stress retraction in denominal verbs. Thus in any revision of Chomsky and Halle's rules which did not incorporate (13), whatever restriction was formulated to exclude underlying forms such as the one for [[*police*]ₙ]ᵥ would be part of the conspiracy instead of the feature [+verb] in (13).

about stress retraction in disyllables? For disyllabic verbs and adjectives, it appears to be the case that stress retraction normally does not take place: words such as those in (14a) are more common than words such as those in (14b):

(14) (a) *cavort, torment, arrest, avoid, carouse, deprive*

   supreme, bizarre, aware, devoid, devout

   (b) *ambush, kidnap, comment, senile*

For disyllabic nouns, on the other hand, stress retraction is unpredictable: there are as many words like (15a) as there are words like (15b):

(15) (a) *cocaine, monsoon, elite, rattan, Quebec*

   (b) *envoy, carboy, migraine, Esau*

To describe these facts, we need a redundancy rule like (16), which states that verbs (and adjectives) conspire in yet another way with respect to stress retraction:

(16) $V \rightarrow [-\text{Retraction}] \ / \ \#C_0VC_0\underline{\quad}C_0]\#_{V,A}$

Another fact about stress retraction which provides further support for (16) is the following. Kiparsky has observed (see note 2) that while words ending in most phonological sequences can be exceptions to stress retraction (compare *Tennessee* with the normal, retracted *chickadee*; *attaché* with *Fotheringay*; *Mattapan* with *caravan*; *promenade* with *marmalade*, and so on), words ending in /īn/ (phonetic [āyn]) always retract stress, as shown in (17):[12]

(17) *Palestine, turpentine, porcupine, anodyne*

   carbine, quinine, feline

Actually, Kiparsky's observation is part of the larger regularity stated in (18):

(18) Words which end in /iC₀/ always undergo stress retraction *unless they are disyllabic verbs*

There are possibly twenty valid counterexamples to (18), some of which I have listed in (19):

(19) *July, assai, attire, assize(s), contrite, sublime, entire, Havasupai*

The fact that (18) expresses an important generalization about English stress retraction can be seen from the size of the list of corroborating examples in (20), a list which can easily be extended almost indefinitely:

---

[12] The one counterexample to Kiparsky's observation that I know of is *divine*. Words like *benign* and *malign, design, assign* presumably derive from /ign/ (cf. *malignant, benignant, designate, assignation*). Verbs like *recline, refine* are covered by the last clause of (18).

(20) (a) *Mordecai, samurai, Gemini, alkali, alumni, Eli, Levi, dynamite, troglodyte,*
  stalactite, Ozite, Lucite, parasite, bromide, sulfide, paradise, camomile,
  projectile, crocodile, diatribe, porcine, vulpine, supine, satire, sapphire, empire,
  umpire .

  (b) *excite, desire, rely, reply, delight, ignite, devise, recline, repine, define, apprise,*
  surprise, invite, divide, imbibe

The fact that it is for disyllabic *verbs* that the extension of Kiparsky's observation does not hold is again part of the conspiracy in (6).

One final fact with reference to stress retraction. I believe it to be demonstrable that the stress on such words as *resell, mismatch, crossclassify* is assigned by an extension of the Nuclear Stress Rule of Chomsky and Halle (1968). This rule will restress the final primary stress in verbs which are preceded by a prefix followed by a word boundary, but not in nouns, as shown by the examples in (21):

(21) *resale*$_N$, *mismatch*$_N$, *presale*$_N$

Thus, once again, there must be a condition on whatever rule effects stress retraction in these compounds, whether it is an extension of the Compound Rule or some entirely different rule, a condition which will insure that stress is retracted in accordance with (6).

The last stress phenomenon I will examine in connection with (6) has to do with destressing. Consider such pairs as *delegate*$_V$–*delegate*$_N$, *alternate*$_V$–*alternate*$_N$, *appropriate*$_V$–*appropriate*$_A$. The reduction of the final vowel occurs only in words of three or more syllables (compare *castrate*$_{N,V}$, *rebate*$_{N,V}$, *probate*$_{N,V}$), and it never affects any phonological sequences other than *-ate* (*a prostitute*$_N$–*to prostitute*$_V$, not *to prostitute*, and similarly for *dynamite*$_{N,V}$, *merchandise*$_{N,V}$, and so on). This suggests that the cyclical account of the stress alternations of *delegate, alternate* proposed by Chomsky and Halle (1968) is incorrect and that instead some destressing rule like (22) is necessary:[13]

$$(22) \quad [2\text{stress}] \rightarrow [-\text{stress}] \ / \ \overset{1}{V}C_0VC_0 \left[\overline{\overline{æ}} \right] t]_{N,A} \#$$

The fact that it is nouns and not verbs whose final *-ate* is destressed again results in phonetic forms which are consistent with the "Leftward Ho!" stress tendency for nouns stated in (6).

We have seen that the conditions on the rules of English word stress in (23) conspire in the Leftward Ho! noun stress effect:

[13] For a fuller justification of these remarks, see Ross (1972).

(23) (a) C_b for nouns is a superset of C_b for verbs: thus more final-syllable types can be disregarded in assigning nonfinal stress to nouns than to verbs (compare (8) and (9))

(b) More vowels get deleted at the end of verbs than at the end of nouns, thus producing the impression that verbs cannot be stressed antepenultimately while nouns can (see the condition on (11))

(c) Of all prefix-stem nouns and verbs, only Latin verbs do not retract stress (see (12))

(d) In disyllabic nouns, stress may or may not retract, that is, retraction must be lexically marked; however, in disyllabic verbs, stress generally does not retract (compare (14) and (15))

(e) Stress retraction is normally obligatory for all words ending in $/\bar{\imath}C_0/$, but stress is not retracted in disyllabic verbs (see (20))

(f) In words composed of a prefix followed by a word boundary and a stem, stress retracts in nouns (see (21)) but not in verbs

(g) Secondary stress on final *-ate* is removed in nouns (and adjectives) with more than two syllables (see (22))

All of these different conditions, most of them on different rules, produce the same phonetic effect, namely, that described in (6). This same kind of phenomenon, a conspiracy, has been insightfully described in Yawelmani by Kisseberth (1970), and other examples of conspiracies in phonology are turning up.

At present, it seems premature to attempt any formal modification in phonological theory to distinguish phonologies with conspiracies from phonologies without such functional similarities. Far too many questions remain to be answered. For example, what types of rules can conspire? Can syntactic rules conspire with phonological rules? What can be conspired to, that is, what is the set of possible "targets" of conspiracies? These lesser questions, and the larger task, too, must be deferred at least until a greater number of descriptions of conspiracies becomes available.

REFERENCES

Chomsky, N., and M. Halle (1968), *The Sound Pattern of English*, New York: Harper & Row.

Kisseberth, C. (1970), "On the functional unity of phonological rules," *Linguistic Inquiry*, *1*, 291–306.

Lakoff, G. (1970), "Global rules," *Language*, *46*, 627–639.

Lee, G. (1969), "English Word Stress," *Papers from the Fifth Regional Meeting of the Chicago Linguistic Society*, University of Chicago.

Ross, J. R. (1972), "A Reanalysis of English Word Stress," in M. Brame, ed., *Contributions to Generative Phonology*, Austin: University of Texas Press.

[ʙᴀᴄᴋ] ᴀɴᴅ [ʀᴏᴜɴᴅ]

Sanford A. Schane

University of California at San Diego

1. INTRODUCTION

The phonetic parameters relating to the position of the tongue in the horizontal dimension and to the shape of the lips are traditional for classifying vowels into four series—front unrounded, back rounded, front rounded, and back (or central) unrounded. For Trubetzkoy frontness or backness and rounding or unrounding are intimately related as *localization* or *timbre* features, which are jointly opposed to his *aperture* or *saturation* features used for characterizing vowel height. Jakobson's grave/acute and flat/plain specify the four series of vowels and along with sharp/plain constitute a set of *tonality* features. For Chomsky and Halle it is the *cavity* features [back] and [round] which jointly specify these four series.

We shall examine the relationship between frontness/backness and rounding/unrounding and shall show that (*a*) tongue position (*frontness*) is primary for vowels such as *i, e, æ*, whereas lip shape (*rounding*) is primary for vowels such as *u, o, ɔ*, and (*b*) where these two parameters form a hierarchy, tongue position takes precedence over lip shape.

Consider the common vowel pattern *i, e, a, o, u*—what Trubetzkoy (1957) called a five-vowel triangular system. For the nonlow vowels Trubetzkoy allowed the particular language system to decide which of his localization features was the primary one. Three situations are possible:

(*a*) Tongue position is primary and lip shape is redundant. In Japanese, plain and palatalized consonants contrast before *u, o, a* but are neutralized before *i, e*. Because of this neutralization there is a class of front vowels opposed to a class of back ones, and lip shape becomes subordinate.

(*b*) Lip shape is primary and tongue position is redundant. In Russian, vowels have fronted variants between palatalized consonants and backed variants after plain (phonetically velarized) consonants. Since what is constant for Russian vowels is the shape of the lips, this is primary and tongue position is subordinate.

(*c*) Neither feature has precedence over the other. In Spanish, there are no neutralizations involving the vowels nor are there allophones characterized by different degrees of backness or rounding: *i, e* are always realized as front unrounded, and *u, o* as back rounded. Hence, neither localization feature can be extracted as primary. Rather, both features combine to form two maximally opposed series— what Trubetzkoy impressionistically called *light* and *dark*, an equipollent opposition. For triangular vowel systems (where there is one low vowel), Trubetzkoy considered the equipollent cases to be the most frequent.[1]

For Trubetzkoy there is no "inherent" hierarchy between his localization features. The relative importance of each feature is language-specific, and depending on the system either feature can be the primary one.

At first it appears that Jakobson allows the same three situations as Trubetzkoy:

> In vowel patterns with only one tonality feature the following three cases are found: (a) the opposition grave vs. acute alone [e.g., Wichita, Slovak, Japanese]; (b) rarely, the opposition flat vs. plain alone [e.g., Russian]; (c) quite frequently a fusion of the two oppositions [e.g., Spanish, Italian] (Jakobson, Fant, and Halle, (1965, p. 33)).

But, further on, one gets the impression that flat/plain is viewed as subordinate to grave/acute:

> The opposition flat vs. plain as a *secondary tonality feature* [emphasis mine] of vowels supplements the optimal grave vs. acute opposition by an attenuated grave and/or acute: for instance /u/ and /i/ by /ɨ/ and/or /y/ (p. 36).

This "inherent" hierarchy is corroborated by the redundancy-free matrices given in the appendix to Jakobson, Fant, and Halle, where grave/acute is the nonredundant specification for the English vowels (p. 44) and, surprisingly, even for the Russian vowels (p. 45). For Jakobson, then, flat/plain as a tonality feature seems to be "universally" subordinate to grave/acute.

What may have been implicit in Jakobson becomes explicit within generative phonology. Where an inventory of segments is given, one frequently finds "distinctive" matrices such as in (1) (where redundant specifications appear in parentheses):[2]

(1)

	i	e	a	o	u
high	+	−	−	−	+
low	(−)	−	+	−	(−)
back	−	−	(+)	+	+
round	(−)	(−)	(−)	(+)	(+)

In this matrix the nonlow vowels are *nonredundantly* specified for the feature [back].[3] Values for [round] can be predicted for these vowels through a morpheme structure rule such as (2):

(2) $\begin{bmatrix} -\text{low} \\ \alpha\text{back} \end{bmatrix} \rightarrow [\alpha\text{round}]$

[1] Had Trubetzkoy allowed morphological criteria, equipollent systems might have been less common. For example, in Spanish *i, e, a* function as thematic vowels in the verb conjugation.

[2] In pre-1968 generative studies, the features [grave] and [flat] are used for specifying vowels instead of [back] and [round]. For the sake of consistency, when discussing generative phonology we shall use only [back] and [round]. However, anything said about these features applies *mutatis mutandis* to [grave] and [flat].

[3] One notable exception to the setting up of [back] as the nonredundant feature is found in Halle's (1959) treatment of the Russian vowels. Following Trubetzkoy and Jakobson, Halle considers [round] (his "low tonality") to be the nonredundant specification.

However, the choice of [back] as the nonredundant feature is totally arbitrary since a matrix of equal complexity will result if the nonlow vowels are *nonredundantly* specified for [round]. Then the values for [back] become redundant and we have the morpheme structure rule (3):

(3) $\begin{bmatrix} -\text{low} \\ \alpha\text{round} \end{bmatrix} \rightarrow [\alpha\text{back}]$

From a purely formal point of view, there is no reason for selecting either partially specified matrix over the other.

With the advent of "markedness," the role of partially specified matrices and morpheme structure rules has taken on less importance. But the relative ranking of [back] and [round] remains unchanged. As shown in (4), within Chomsky and Halle's (1968) system of markedness, [back] is the primary feature for the vowels *i, e, u, o* as each of these vowels must be specified for it; values for [round] are redundant in that these four vowels are all unmarked for it:

(4)

	i	e	æ	u	o	ɔ	ü	ö	œ	ɨ	ʌ	a
high	U	M	U	U	M	U	U	M	U	U	M	U
low	U	U	M	U	U	M	U	U	M	U	U	U
back	−	−	M	+	+	U	−	−	M	+	+	U
round	U	U	U	U	U	M	M	M	M	M	M	U

Furthermore, to insure the selection of the optimal five-vowel pattern, Chomsky and Halle propose as conditions on vowel systems that "no vowel segment can be marked for the feature 'round' unless some vowel segment in the system is marked for the feature 'high'" and "the availability for marking of the features 'high' and 'low' depends on the prior marking of the feature 'back', resulting in the hierarchical structure shown in [5]:" (p. 410):

(5)

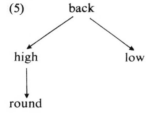

With regard to the features [back] and [round] in Chomsky and Halle's system, the former is both the "primary feature" for distinguishing certain vowels and the "higher feature" on the hierarchy. However, "primary feature" and "higher feature" are not necessarily coextensive notions. The concept of "primary feature" applies to the intrinsic content of segments. We shall show that for certain vowels [back] is the primary or distinguishing feature while for other vowels [round] is primary. On the other hand, the notion of "higher feature" is extrinsic to segments. It characterizes properties of phonological systems—for example, the availability of features for marking or the conditions under which feature specifications can be modified.

2. [BACK] AND [ROUND] AS PRIMARY FEATURES

Assimilation often reveals which feature is primary. Palatalization and labialization are processes where consonants acquire vowel-like features. In Nupe (Hyman (1970)), which has an underlying seven-vowel system, consonants are palatalized before *i, e, æ* and they are labialized before *u, o, ɔ*. What is significant about these assimilations is that the palatalized consonant acquires the *tongue position* characteristic of *front* vowels while the labialized consonant acquires the *lip shape* characteristic of *rounded* vowels. Before *a* neither assimilation occurs: *a* has neither the tongue position of front vowels nor the lip shape of rounded ones.[4]

In Menomini (Bloomfield (1964)), "nonsyllabics are often strongly palatalized or labiovelarized by the preceding vowel, initial nonsyllabics by the following vowel: *mip* 'early in the morning' (both consonants palatalized), *mwāk* 'loon' (both consonants labiovelarized)" (p. 107). The vowel *a* is phonetically rounded: "*a* [ranges] from French *pâte* to English *saw*".

In Nupe and Menomini the palatalized and labialized consonants are frequently allophonic variants of the plain ones. Where these consonant articulations have become contrastive a different situation presents itself. The Russian palatalized consonants historically had their origin as palatalizations due to a following front vowel or glide. Subsequently palatalization became contrastive. As Trubetzkoy pointed out, to insure maximal differentiation between contrasting palatalized and plain consonants, the latter often become velarized. In this way the palatalized and plain consonants are phonetically opposed as high tonality versus low tonality. Once front tongue position becomes a contrastive consonant feature, at the surface level it loses its distinguishing force as a vowel feature. In such systems lip shape then becomes the constant phonetic trait for identifying the vowels and the tongue position of the vowel is free to assimilate to that of the consonant. This assimilation is merely another way of insuring the optimal contrast between palatalized and plain consonants: the vowel allophones provide further information concerning the tonality of the adjacent consonants. It is this phonetic aspect of the Russian vowels which led Trubetzkoy, Jakobson, and Halle to consider lip shape as the primary feature. We would claim, rather, that this constant lip shape of vowels is simply a superficial aspect of systems containing contrastive palatalized consonants. At a deeper level, front tongue position *still* has to be the primary feature for characterizing Russian *i, e*. Synchronically, there are morphophonemic processes where underlying plain consonants become palatalized when followed by these vowels. (See Lightner (1965b)).

Umlauting can be viewed as assimilation between vowels. In Germanic, back vowels were influenced by a following *i*: in the case of the nonlow vowels, *u* became *ü* (not *i*), and *o* became *ö* (not ʌ). Icelandic is particularly interesting since, in addition to *i*-umlaut, there is also *u*-umlaut due to a following *u*: *i* becomes *ü* (not *i*), and *e* becomes *ö* (not ʌ). For both kinds of umlaut, the vowel which undergoes umlaut assimilates the *primary feature* of the *conditioning vowel* without losing its own primary feature. Thus, when *u, o* become *ü, ö* by *i*-umlaut, they acquire the tongue position of *i* while retaining their original lip shape, and when *i, e* become *ü, ö* by *u*-umlaut they acquire the lip shape of *u* and keep their original tongue position. Since *a* is "negative" in the sense that it has neither the tongue position characteristic of front vowels nor the lip shape characteristic of rounded vowels, it can partake equally of *i*-umlaut and *u*-umlaut, yielding *æ* and *ɔ*, respectively.

[4] Hyman (1970) has claimed that the labialized consonants of Nupe are also velarized—that is, they have the tongue position as well as the lip shape of back rounded vowels. This coarticulation is to be expected whenever the consonant articulation anticipates that of the following vowel. In fact, it would not surprise us if in languages with autonomous labialized consonants, these consonants were also velarized. Such coarticulation would have the further advantage of accentuating the tonality difference between the labialized and the plain consonants. In any case, whether or not labialization is accompanied by velarization, there is no question that lip shape is the important distinguishing trait for these consonants.

The French front rounded vowels did not arise from umlauting, but they still had their origin in back rounded vowels. For example, Latin $\bar{u}$ spontaneously shifted to $\ddot{u}$ everywhere. Why $\ddot{u}$ and not i? If rounding is the primary feature for back rounded vowels, then in a change from u to $\ddot{u}$ the *primary* feature is preserved while the subordinate feature, tongue position, is affected. Synchronically, within French, one can still demonstrate that the front rounded vowels belong structurally with rounded and not with front vowels (Schane (1968)).

Neutralization provides further evidence that front tongue position is primary for i, e, and lip rounding for u, o. We already noted that in Japanese plain and palatalized consonants contrast before u, o, a, but are neutralized before i, e. Conversely, Trubetzkoy observes that in Artshi, spoken in the East Caucasus, plain and labialized consonants contrast before i, e, a, but are neutralized before u, o. Classical Latin had contrasts between k and k^w. In the development of several of the Romance languages the loss of this contrast before u, o preceded its loss before other vowels.

Trubetzkoy noted that languages with "mixed" series of vowels—front rounded and/or back unrounded—also have the "basic" series—front unrounded and back rounded. He further observed that of the two mixed series front rounded is the more common. This observation has a natural explanation within a system where tongue position is primary for front vowels and lip shape is primary for rounded vowels. Within such a framework the unmarked situation for front vowels is to be unrounded (i, e, $æ$), and the unmarked situation for rounded vowels is to be back (u, o, $ɔ$). A marked front vowel would be rounded ($\ddot{u}$, $\ddot{o}$, $æ$); a marked rounded vowel would be front ($\ddot{u}$, $\ddot{o}$, $æ$). Consequently, marking either "basic" series produces front rounded vowels. Further on we shall consider the status of back unrounded vowels.

Let us return to the matrix of the standard five-vowel system as shown in (6) (where redundant values appear in parentheses):

(6)
	i	e	a	o	u
high	+	−	(−)	−	+
low	(−)	(−)	+	(−)	(−)
back	−	−	(+)	(+)	(+)
round	(−)	(−)	(−)	+	+

The redundancies in (7) hold:

(7) (a) (i) $[+\text{high}] \rightarrow [-\text{low}]$
        (ii) $[+\text{low}] \rightarrow [-\text{high}]$

   (b) (i) $[-\text{back}] \rightarrow [-\text{round}]$
        (ii) $[+\text{round}] \rightarrow [+\text{back}]$

   (c) (i) $[+\text{low}] \rightarrow \begin{bmatrix} +\text{back} \\ -\text{round} \end{bmatrix}$

        (ii) $\left.\begin{cases} [-\text{back}] \\ [+\text{round}] \end{cases}\right\} \rightarrow [-\text{low}]$

Each (i)-(ii) pair is inversely symmetrical. Given either member one can predict the other by interchanging the features on each side of the arrow and switching their values, and in the case of (c) a conjunction on the right is replaced by a disjunction on the left. The redundant-free matrix (unparenthesized values) does not meet the "distinctiveness" criterion but the segments are still "distinguishable" in the sense discussed by Stanley (1967). If one fully extracts all observable redundancies, an operation which entails replacing a strong condition of "distinctness" by a weaker condition of "distinguishability," the resulting redundant-free matrix reveals that *frontness*

([−back]) is the nonredundant specification for *i*, *e*, whereas *rounding* ([+round]) is the nonredundant specification for *u*, *o*. Furthermore, this fully reduced matrix is nonarbitrary, unlike the matrices presented previously (see (1)–(3) and the discussion there) where either [back] or [round], but not both, served as the nonredundant feature.

3. THE HIERARCHY FOR [BACK] AND [ROUND]

Jakobson (1968) has observed that, during acquisition, where there are corresponding pairs of front unrounded and back rounded vowels, the former frequently emerge first. He noted further that for language systems with unequal numbers of vowels in the two basic series it is not unusual for there to be more front unrounded vowels than back rounded ones. Martinet (1955) has expressed a corresponding view for the diachronic picture: of the two basic series, front unrounded vowels are the more stable.[5] For example, he has claimed that Latin *ū* became French *ü* because of the instability of a vowel system containing too many back rounded vowels.

If tongue position is primary for the front unrounded vowels and lip shape for the back rounded ones, then from these initial observations it appears that tongue position is higher-ordered than lip shape.

The spontaneous shift of "mixed" vowels to one of the "basic" series provides further support for this hierarchy. In the history of English, *ü*, *ö* (resulting from umlaut) eventually became *i*, *e*, and in Hungarian *i* shifted to *i*. It is understandable that a *more marked* "mixed" vowel should spontaneously become a *less marked* "basic" vowel. But for both series of mixed vowels the preference was a change to front unrounded rather than to back rounded, that is, the resulting vowel is marked for tongue position and unmarked for lip shape, rather than marked for lip shape and unmarked for tongue position.

Finno-Ugric vowel harmony further suggests that [back] is higher-ordered than [round]. In some of these languages vowels can harmonize for [back] alone and for both [back] and [round], but not for [round] alone. In Classical Mongolian, only the feature [back] harmonizes—that is, within the word vowels agree in *backness* but there can be mixed rounding (Lightner (1965a)).

In Turkish, suffixes with high vowels harmonize for [back] and [round], whereas suffixes containing nonhigh vowels harmonize only for [back], as shown in (8):[6]

(8)

			First Singular
	Singular	Plural	Possessive
'tooth'	*diš*	*dišler*	*dišim*
'arm'	*kol*	*kollar*	*kolum*
'heart'	*gönül*	*gönüller*	*gönülüm*
'head'	*baš*	*bašlar*	*bašim*

This restriction for nonhigh vowels is tied up with the fact that *ö*, *o* in Turkish do not appear in noninitial syllables. That is, in such positions the feature [round]

---

[5] Martinet's explanation for the stability of front vowels is a physiological one. Where there are equal numbers of front and back vowels, since there is more "space" toward the front of the oral cavity than farther back, the articulatory distance between vowels of the same series is more compressed for back vowels than for front ones.

[6] Data from Gleason (1955).

is not available for marking. Thus, for noninitial nonhigh vowels there can be an opposition in tongue position but not in lip shape.

Hungarian has two-way (e.g., *val* ∼ *vel*), three-way (e.g., *hoz* ∼ *höz* ∼ *hez*), and four-way (e.g., *ok* ∼ *ök* ∼ *ak* ∼ *ek*) harmonizing suffixes. Two-way suffixes harmonize only for backness; three-way suffixes for backness and, for front vowels only, for rounding; and four-way suffixes for both features. This is schematized in (9):

(9)

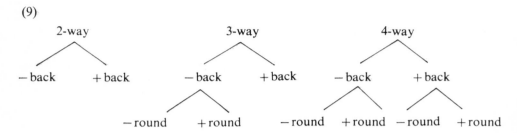

The Hungarian data show not only that rounding harmony presupposes backness harmony, but also that rounding for back vowels presupposes such harmony for *front* vowels.

Similar relationships between tongue position and lip shape appear to hold for Germanic umlauting. For most languages there is only *i*-umlaut, but Icelandic has both *i*-umlaut and *u*-umlaut. Hence, for this family of languages, *u*-umlaut presupposes *i*-umlaut. These implications do not seem to hold for palatalization and labialization. Trubetzkoy cites quite a few languages with labialized consonants which do not also have a palatalized series. However, Martinet (1955) has noted that, if a language has both palatalized and labialized consonants and subsequently one of these series is lost, it will be the labialized one. A similar phenomenon occurs in the Old Irish "infected" consonants. Sequences of "palatalized" consonants can occur before rounded vowels, but sequences of "labialized" consonants are replaced by "palatalized" ones before front vowels.

If it is the case that tongue position is primary for front vowels whereas lip shape is primary for rounded ones and, furthermore, that tongue position is higher on the hierarchy, these observations ought to be reflected in a system of markedness. In particular, all front unrounded vowels would be marked for frontness (i.e., for [−back]) but unmarked for rounding, whereas all back rounded vowels would be marked for rounding (i.e., for [+round]) but unmarked for backness. Front rounded vowels, with the tongue position of *i, e, æ* and the lip shape of *u, o, ɔ*, would be marked for both backness and rounding. Since *a* has neither the tongue position of front vowels nor the lip shape of rounded ones, it would be unmarked for these features. The resulting specifications are shown in (10):

(10)	i	e	æ		u	o	ɔ		ü	ö	œ		a
back	M	M	M		U	U	U		M	M	M		U
round	U	U	U		M	M	M		M	M	M		U
high	U	M	U		U	M	U		U	M	U		U
low	U	U	M		U	U	M		U	U	M		U

For vowels which are marked for [back] and/or [round], the preferred vowel height is *high* (i.e., maximally opposed to low *a*). High vowels, then, are unmarked for [high] and [low], mid vowels are marked for being nonhigh, and low vowels are marked for being low.

For the vowels in (10), our markings for the features [high] and [low] are identical to those of Chomsky and Halle (1968). Similarly, our markings for [back] and [round] for the low vowels coincide with theirs. The difference resides in the nonlow vowels. Chomsky and Halle specify these as [−back] or [+back]. The "basic" vowels are then unmarked for rounding, whereas the "mixed" vowels are marked for this feature. In our system, on the other hand, all front vowels are marked for the feature [back], whereas all back vowels are unmarked for this feature, and all rounded vowels are marked for the feature [round] whereas all unrounded vowels are unmarked for this feature. Actually, our treatment is not so radically different from Chomsky and Halle's. They specify *æ* as [Mback, Uround], *ɔ* as [Uback, Mround], and *œ* as [Mback, Mround]. We have merely extended these specifications to the nonlow vowels of the same series.

This revised system seems to us to have several advantages:

(*a*) Only M's and U's appear in matrices, rather than M's, U's, +'s, and −'s.

(*b*) All vowels of the same series are marked identically, rather than nonlow vowels being marked differently from low ones. For example, in our system *u, o, ɔ* are all [Uback, Mround], whereas for Chomsky and Halle *u, o* are [+back, Uround] but *ɔ* is [Uback, Mround].

(*c*) As a consequence of (*b*), the marking conventions for replacing U's and M's by +'s and −'s are simpler for the features [back] and [round], as shown in (11):

(11) [Uback] → [+back]
      [Uround] → [−round]

(*d*) Given that there is a hierarchy for [back] and [round], no two vowels need have the same complexity. Although *i* and *u* each have one M, *i* would be more highly valued since the M is for a higher-ordered feature. Of course, both *i* and *u* are more highly valued than *ü*, which has two M's. Thus we can capture Jakobson's observation that front unrounded vowels are preferred to back rounded ones and that both of these series are preferred to front rounded.

If all vowels can be ordered, it is our belief that the following ordering is appropriate: *a, i, u, e, o, ü, ö, æ, ɔ, œ*.[7] Note that [high] and [low] also constitute a hierarchy, where [high] precedes [low]. Consequently, mid vowels are more highly valued than low ones since their M is for a higher-ordered feature. However, the high-low hierarchy does not follow the back-round one; rather, the two hierarchies intersect, as shown in (12):

(12)

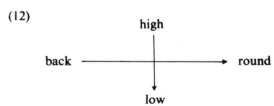

[7] Our reasons for ordering *ü, ö* before *æ, ɔ* are twofold: (*a*) both Trubetzkoy and Hockett (1955) cite more languages having seven-vowel systems of the type *i, e, ü, ö, a, u, o* than *i, e, æ, a, ɔ, o, u*; (*b*) Martinet observes that vowel systems containing *u, o, ɔ* may shift to *ü, u, o* (e.g., Latin to French). The relative ordering of vowels is, in any case, an empirical question. A different ordering would not change the feature hierarchy but only the conditions governing which features can be marked first.

The following conditions determine the order in which features are available for marking:[8]

(a) Each tonality feature (but not both together) is separately available for marking before any height feature

(b) [high] is available for marking before both tonality features can be simultaneously marked

(c) Both tonality features are simultaneously marked in preference to [low]

The diagram in (13) illustrates the relevant ordering:

(13)

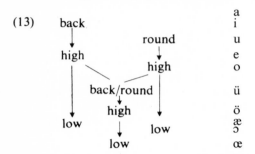

a
i
u
e
o

ü

ö
æ
ɔ
œ

We have not yet considered the unrounded central vowels *i* and *ʌ*. It is evident that, if front unrounded vowels are specified as [Mback, Uround], back rounded vowels as [Uback, Mround], and front rounded vowels as [Mback, Mround], the central vowels in question can only be [Uback, Uround]. These specifications are, of course, shared with *a*, so that *i* and *ʌ* must be differentiated from *a* through the height features. To the matrix in (10) we now add the columns in (14) for *i* and *ʌ*:

(14)

	i	ʌ
back	U	U
round	U	U
high	M	U
low	U	M

It would appear that *i* and *ʌ* have simpler specifications than several of the more common vowels. For example, both *i* and *e* are marked for the feature [high]; but, while *e* is also marked for [back], *i* is marked for no other feature. How, then, can it be claimed that the specifications we have given are appropriate for these central vowels?

According to Jakobson (1968), in the acquisition of vowels there are two possible progressions: the two vowels which appear after *a* may differ in tonality (*i* and *u*) or they may differ in height (*i* and *e*). He further notes that within the languages of the world a minimal vowel system can be based either on distinctions in tonality (*i, a, u*) or, as in some Caucasian languages, on distinctions in height (*i, ʌ, a*). In either case, the three vowels should minimally differ by the same number of specifications. This is just what happens under the system presented here, as shown in (15):

(15)

	i	u	a		i	ʌ	a
back	M	U	U	high	M	U	U
round	U	M	U	low	U	M	U

[8] See Chomsky and Halle's conditions on vowel patterns cited previously.

Where the three vowels differ in tonality, the vowels other than *a* are marked for either [back] or [round], and all three vowels are unmarked for height features. Where the three vowels differ in height, the vowels other than *a* are marked for either [high] or [low], and all three vowels are unmarked for tonality features. Thus there is a type of symmetry between the two different three-vowel patterns.

Having shown that the distribution of M's and U's for the central vowels is appropriate, we must now show how these vowels are evaluated properly. If a vowel system has more than three vowels, then it must make distinctions in both tonality and height. For such systems the expected situation is that distinctions in vowel height will be restricted to noncentral vowels. In these cases vowels which are marked for either the feature [high] or [low] are *always* marked for at least one of the features [back] and [round]. Consider what happens if a vowel system contains more than three vowels, among which are the nonlow central vowels. The vowels *i* and *ʌ* would be marked for height *without* also being marked for any of the tonality features. Consequently, they would not conform to the expected conditions on vowel systems— in particular, our condition (*a*). Notice that *a* never violates these conditions. Although it is unmarked for tonality features, it is never marked for height features.

The marking conventions for the height features cannot apply to *i* and *ʌ*. These conventions are as in (16), for vowels other than *a*:[9]

(16) [Ulow] → [−low]
     [+low] → [−high]
     [Uhigh] → [+high]

For central vowels, on the other hand, the marking conventions for the height features are those in (17):

(17) [Uhigh] → [−high]
     [+high] → [−low]
     [Ulow] → [+low]

The complexity of nonlow central vowels, then, arises from the following: (*a*) they are marked for height features without also being marked for tonality features, and (*b*) the marking conventions for the height features and the order in which they apply are not the same as for the noncentral vowels.

4. EPILOGUE

Although we have used the feature [back] for characterizing the front/back dimension, it appears that the proper feature should instead be [front]. First, if frontness is primary for vowels such as *i*, *e*, *æ*, then it is natural that such vowels should be marked for being *front* rather than for being *nonback*. And, whereas the vowels *ü*, *ö*, *œ* are front vowels, the vowels *i*, *ʌ*, *a* are not usually "back" in the traditional sense but

---

[9] We assume that the first marking convention is [Ueverything] → *a*. All following marking conventions, then, apply to vowels which are marked for at least one feature. This constraint captures the observation that within a markedness system *a*, as the unmarked vowel, behaves differently from the other vowels. Any set of marking conventions which attempts to interpret *all* the U markings of *a* along with the U's and M's of the other vowels becomes excessively complex. For noncentral vowels, values are assigned to [low] before being assigned to [high] because of the rule [+low] → [−high]. The order in which the marking conventions apply has nothing to do with the feature hierarchy: the particular order allows the simplest set of marking conventions.

most often "central"; hence, [−front] is a more appropriate designation for central and back vowels than is [+back]. Second, since consonants can be palatalized not just before *i* but before any front vowel, palatalized consonants could be characterized as [+front], as assimilation to the front tongue position, rather than as [+high] as in Chomsky and Halle. We could then impose as a condition on consonant systems that whenever [+front] is used as a contrastive feature, as in Russian, all consonants, both palatalized and plain, automatically become [+high]. As a consequence, plain consonants which are [−front] would become velarized, i.e., [−front, +high].

With this system, consonants which are *not* [−anterior, −coronal] (and neither palatalized nor velarized) would be specified as [−front, −high, −low], palatal or palatalized consonants would be [+front, +high], velar or velarized consonants would be [−front, +high], and pharyngeal or pharyngealized consonants would be [−front, +low]. Uvulars would be distinguished from velars through the feature [distributed], which would fill a gap in the Chomsky and Halle system, where [distributed] does not play a role for [−anterior, −coronal] consonants. Furthermore, this treatment would eliminate the potential, but apparently never realized, series of uvularized consonants which Chomsky and Halle cite.

REFERENCES

Bloomfield, L. (1964), "Menomini morphophonemics," *Études phonologiques dédiées à la mémoire de M. le Prince N. S. Trubetzkoy*, University, Alabama: University of Alabama Press.

Chomsky, N., and M. Halle (1968), *The Sound Pattern of English*, New York: Harper & Row.

Gleason, H. A. (1955), *Workbook in Descriptive Linguistics*, New York: Holt, Rinehart and Winston.

Halle, M. (1959), *The Sound Pattern of Russian*, The Hague: Mouton.

Hockett, C. F. (1955), *A Manual of Phonology, International Journal of American Linguistics*, Memoir 11, Baltimore: Waverly Press.

Hyman, L. (1970), "How concrete is phonology?" *Language*, 46, 58–76.

Jakobson, R. (1968), *Child Language, Aphasia, and Phonological Universals*, The Hague: Mouton.

Jakobson, R., C. G. M. Fant, and M. Halle (1965), *Preliminaries to Speech Analysis*, Cambridge, Mass.: M.I.T. Press.

Lightner, T. (1965a), "On the description of vowel and consonant harmony," *Word*, 21, 244–250.

Lightner, T. (1965b), *Segmental Phonology of Modern Standard Russian*, unpublished Ph.D. dissertation, M.I.T.

Martinet, A. (1955), *Economie des changements phonétiques*, Berne: Francke.

Schane, S. A. (1968), *French Phonology and Morphology*, Cambridge, Mass.: M.I.T. Press.

Stanley, R. (1967), "Redundancy rules in phonology," *Language*, 43, 393–436.

Trubetzkoy, N. S. (1957), *Principes de phonologie*, Paris: Klincksiek.

BOUNÒARIES
IN PhONOLOGY
Richard Stanley

Addison, Maine

1. INTRODUCTORY REMARKS

It has long been observed that phonological segments behave differently at morphological and syntactic boundaries than when no boundaries are present. This is shown, for instance, by the familiar examples *nitrate, Nye-trait, night rate*: *t* has three different phonetic realizations here depending on whether it is next to no boundary, after a boundary, or before a boundary, even though it is in the same segmental environment (ay____r) in each case (where by segmental environment I mean the environment exclusive of boundaries).

A common approach to such phenomena among American structuralists was to postulate two or three "junctures" for use in phonemic representations, where the presence of a particular juncture in the environment of a phoneme would give rise to a different allophone of that phoneme than would appear if no juncture was present. It was insisted that no juncture could be put in phonemic representations unless its presence was directly reflected in some unambiguous way in phonetic representations.

The type of approach to boundary phenomena that has been adopted in generative phonology is in some ways roughly similar. Various boundary elements (such as +, =, and # in Chomsky and Halle (1968)) appear in underlying phonological representations between morphemes, between words, between phrases, and so forth. The phonological rules are sensitive to the presence of these boundaries and can affect a segment differently depending on what (if any) boundaries are in its environment. Thus, the ultimate output of the phonological rules, the phonetic representations, reflect indirectly the presence of the underlying boundaries. The boundaries themselves have no direct phonetic manifestation (except, perhaps, in the case of word boundary, as potential pause) and are signaled phonetically only by their effect via the phonological rules on the surrounding segments (see Chomsky and Halle (1968, p. 364)).

Still there is a crucial difference in orientation between the structural and the generative approach. Structuralists attempted to work out the phonology before moving to the morphology and syntax and thus required that all junctures in phonemic representations be directly predictable from phonetic considerations. Generativists, on the other hand, have said that the boundaries present in underlying phonological representations are determined by syntactic and morphological considerations (in particular, they have let the boundaries be determined by the full surface structure of the sentence). The structural approach is based on a discovery procedure program for grammars, a program that is too complex for our present knowledge. The generative approach involves an intermediate goal that can be more fruitfully worked on now, a goal which, moreover, is logically prior to any discovery procedure.

This paper is an exploration of the role of boundaries in phonology considered from a generative point of view. The problems to be investigated fall into two main categories, involving (*a*) the nature of the principles that assign boundaries to the underlying phonological representation on the basis of the surface structure, and (*b*) the ways in which phonological rules are sensitive to these boundaries.

I should note that several crucially important specific issues relating to boundary phenomena do not receive explicit discussion until later in the paper and even then are not dealt with thoroughly. For example, the definition of words and the role of word boundary, on the one hand, and the special status of the weakest boundary ("formative boundary" in Chomsky and Halle (1968)), on the other, fall into this category. In the earlier part of the paper I try to deal with more general questions than these and to sort out the basic sorts of issues that must be dealt with before more specific phenomena can be effectively approached. The range of boundary phenomena is bewilderingly complex, and this paper for the most part does no more than offer a framework within which such phenomena can be profitably investigated and suggest the kind of data that are relevant.

2. INFORMAL EXAMPLES ILLUSTRATING THE TYPES OF BOUNDARY PHENOMENA

Not all boundaries have the same type of phonological effect on surrounding segments. In fact, three formally quite distinct sorts of interaction between boundaries and phonological rules can be distinguished: (*a*) a rule may apply generally except when blocked by a strong boundary in the interior of its environment; (*b*) a rule may apply only when a particular boundary type is present; and (*c*) a rule may apply only when a boundary of a certain type or stronger appears at the (right or left) end point of the environment of the rule. These three sorts of boundary phenomena will be discussed and illustrated informally in the present section. Most of the section is simply a collection of relevant sorts of examples, and no attempt is made to formulate and defend a theory of boundaries until later sections. Still, the examples clearly illustrate the need for (and will be discussed in terms of) a hierarchy of boundary types from weak to strong.[1] Frequently, some familiarity with Chomsky and Halle's (1968) use of boundaries will be assumed in the examples. A discussion of their boundary theory is given in Section 6.

---

[1] The notion of "strength" of boundaries will be given full discussion in later sections; roughly, the boundaries associated with unproductive affixes are weaker than the boundaries associated with productive affixes, which in turn are weaker than word boundaries.

2.1. Rules Ranked by a Boundary

I will apply the term "ranking" to those cases where a phonological rule is blocked by a strong boundary but applies whenever weaker boundaries are present. This is the situation that obtains where a phonological rule will affect a segment A in the environment $B\_\_\_\_C$ just in case the string BAC does not contain boundaries stronger than a certain type. A rule can be said to be ranked by the weakest boundary that biocks its application (see McCawley (1968) and Section 6 here).

As an example consider the Trisyllabic Laxing Rule in English, formulated roughly in (1) (see rule (20IV) of Chomsky and Halle (1968, Chapter 5)):

$$(1) \quad \begin{bmatrix} V \\ \alpha\text{round} \\ \alpha\text{back} \end{bmatrix} C \begin{bmatrix} V \\ -\text{stress} \end{bmatrix} C_0[-\text{consonantal}]$$
$$\downarrow$$
$$[-\text{tense}]$$

This rule applies to lax the boldfaced vowels in words such as *profanity, derivative, linear, explanatory, gratitude* (compare *profane, derive, line, explain, grateful*, with tense vowels). However, rule (1) does not apply in words such as *privateer, focusing, lowlier*, even though the phonological shape of these words is perfectly parallel to those words where the rule does apply. It is clear that the difference lies in the suffixes involved. The boundary that occurs between the stem and suffixes such as *-ity, -ative, -ar, -atory, -itude* is weaker than the boundary associated with suffixes such as *-eer, -ing, -er* in the sense that the latter but not the former blocks the application of rule (1). This example shows that phonological rules must be sensitive to at least two different types of word-internal boundaries.

A similar situation is revealed by rule (2) (see Chomsky and Halle (1968, Chapter 5, rule (20III))):

$$(2) \quad VCC$$
$$\downarrow$$
$$[-\text{tense}]$$

This rule applies to lax the boldfaced vowel in words such as *left, kept, deduction, perception, description, content* (compare *leave, keep, deduce, perceive, describe, contain*, with tense vowels). However, words such as *grieved, peeped, reduced, perceived, described, restraint*, which are phonologically perfectly parallel, do not show the laxing. Again this can be taken as indicating two different strengths of boundaries, a stronger one that blocks (2) and a weaker one that does not. An additional point to notice here is that the same suffix morpheme may be associated with different strengths of boundaries, depending on the stem. Thus, *left* and *kept* have weaker boundaries, in this terminology, than do *grieved* and *peeped*. That is, what is irregular about *leave* and *keep* is that they take a weaker past tense boundary than normal; they are completely regular with respect to the phonological rules.

Similar examples showing the existense of boundaries of different strengths can be given from among the stress rules for English. One part of the principle for assigning stress is given in (3) (see rule (15) of Chomsky and Halle (1968, Chapter 5)):

$$(3) \quad VC_0 \begin{bmatrix} V \\ -\text{tense} \end{bmatrix} C_0^1$$
$$\downarrow$$
$$[1\text{stress}]$$

This rule assigns stress to the penultimate syllable in words like *astonish, solid,* but does not stress the penultimate syllable in words like *astonishing, solider, commonish, yellowish.* Again, roughly and intuitively, this seems to indicate that the boundary associated with suffixes like *-ing, -er, -ish* is what is blocking the application of the rule to the full strings; instead, rule (3) applies to the substring that precedes the boundary.

A large category of boundary phenomena falling under the heading of what we are calling rule ranking involves the many examples where a phonological rule applies generally within a word but not across word boundaries. That is, word boundaries in many languages quite clearly rank the phonological rules into those that apply across word boundaries and those that do not.

The phonology of Navaho, as will become quite clear in later sections, shows a range of boundary phenomena much more complex than that of English. Here I will confine myself to a few examples of rule-ranking boundaries.[2]

First, consider rule (4) (see rule (8a) of Stanley (1969, Chapter 3)):

(4) V[+continuant]V
$$\downarrow$$
[+voice]

This rule applies to voice the final consonant in the perfective of verb stems, giving rise to forms such as (phonetic) *-gǫẓ,* (perfective of 'to make sausage'). (The final vowel in this form, the perfective suffix, is dropped by a later rule.) Compare the progressive form *-gǫš,* where (4) does not apply because no vowel ever followed the *š.* More important, compare such forms as *-gǫší,* which have the relative suffix *-í.* The boundary associated with this suffix blocks the application of (4), whereas the weaker boundary associated with the much more closely attached perfective suffix does not.

Similarly, the Vowel Lengthening Rule (5) (rule (5) of Stanley (1969, Chapter 3)) applies to eliminate stem shapes of the form -CV̆[−sonorant], with a short high vowel followed by an obstruent, in favor of stem shapes of the form -CV̄[−sonorant], with a long vowel:

(5) $\begin{bmatrix} +\text{vocalic} \\ +\text{high tone} \end{bmatrix}$[−sonorant]
$$\downarrow$$
[+long]

Still, the rule is blocked by the presence of certain boundaries, for example, stem-initial boundaries; thus, in the optative we get forms of the shape γóš+stem, where the *ó* remains short.

In particular cases of what I have called rule ranking, it is tempting to find some purely phonological difference between the cases that undergo the rule and those that do not, where by purely phonological I mean a difference unrelated to differences in boundary strength. Wherever such a purely phonological difference can be found and justified as being the relevant difference, the rule should of course be formulated on the basis of this difference and the boundaries forgotten. However it is quite clear, especially in Navaho, where the great morphological complexity of the verb provides situations not so easily found in languages like English, that there are many cases of rule-ranking phenomena that cannot possibly be described adequately in purely phonological terms (that is, without referring to a hierarchy of boundary strengths).

---

[2] For fuller discussion of Navaho see Stanley (1969).

It is also clear that rule ranking may have to distinguish among different types of word boundaries that are outside words (as they are normally thought of): in Welsh, for example, preposition plus noun sequences are closer phonologically than are other two-word sequences. See also the remark in Chomsky and Halle (1968, p. 368) about Russian prepositions.

2.2. Rules Requiring a Particular Boundary

In some cases, a rule seems to require the presence of a particular type of boundary at a particular place in its environment if it is to apply. This is the situation where a rule affects a string XY only if the particular boundary b appears between the two strings: XbY. If a weaker or stronger boundary appears in the place of b, the rule will not apply.

To illustrate from English, consider rule (6) (see rule (20IV) of Chomsky and Halle (1968, Chapter 5)):

(6)
$$VCC + \begin{bmatrix} V \\ -stress \end{bmatrix} C_0 V$$
$$\downarrow$$
$$[-tense]$$

This rule applies to lax the underlined vowel in *profundity, pronunciation, wilderness*, but it does not apply either when there is no boundary present in the relevant place, as in *mountainous, countenance, counterfeit, bountiful*, or when there is a boundary that is too strong in the position of the $+$, as in *blindingly, childishness, binderlike* ('like a binder'). The fact that rule (6) does not apply in the cases where there is no boundary present in the relevant position indicates that the $+$ boundary in the environment is playing quite a different role than the rule-ranking boundaries discussed previously.

Another example is rule (7) (see rule (26) of Chomsky and Halle (1968, Chapter 5)):

(7) $t + i$
$\downarrow$
s

This rule spirantizes t when t is followed by a certain type of boundary which in turn is followed by i, as is shown in *legitimacy* as compared with *legitimate*. However, notice that the rule does not apply when no boundary follows the t, as in *faculty, advertise*, nor does it apply when too strong a boundary follows the t, as in *advocating, agenty* ('like an agent'). In their solution, Chomsky and Halle are able to avoid this type of use of boundaries since they have the rule applying in the environment of the glide y instead of the vowel i, and they use y in the representation of the suffix in *legitimacy*. Still, this use of y is not without its problems and can be avoided, at least in this case, by distinguishing different types of boundaries. Moreover, these different types of boundaries have to be distinguished anyway, as is clear from many of the examples that have been or will be pointed out in this paper.

For another example, consider the rule in (8), which provides penultimate stress before certain suffixes (see rule (15) of Chomsky and Halle (1968, Chapter 5)):

(8)
$$VC_0 + C_0 \begin{bmatrix} V \\ -tense \end{bmatrix} C_0$$
$$\downarrow$$
$$[+stress]$$

This rule assigns the stress in words such as *anecdótal, dialéctal*, where the appropriate boundary is present, but does not apply in *abstract, immense, absurd*, which meet the environment except for having no boundary, nor in *anecdoteless*, which meets the environment except for having too strong a boundary before the suffix *-less*.

As another example, consider rule (9) (see rule (10) of Chomsky and Halle (1968, Chapter 5)):

(9) +i#
     ↓
     φ

Here I am interested only in the + boundary in (9). (The # boundary serves a different function, discussed in Section 2.3.) This rule drops an *i* augment in word-final position in such words as *reptile* (see *reptilian*), *professor* (see *professorial*). But the rule does not apply when there is no boundary present, as in *city*, or when the boundary present is too strong, as in *windy*. Rule (9) is worthy of note in that the boundary + is actually at the end point of the environment and not in the interior as in the previous examples. Nevertheless, this boundary does behave like the boundaries discussed in this section rather than like those discussed in the next section, which also occur at the end point of the environment; the rules discussed in 2.3 apply when the boundary in question *or a stronger one* is in the relevant position.

One final example of internal boundaries, this time from Navaho, is provided by rule (10) (see rule (7d) of Stanley (1969, Chapter 3)):

(10) ⎡ +vocalic   ⎤
      ⎢ +high tone ⎥ = C
      ⎣ −long   ⎦   ↓
                       φ

Here the boundary = is the stem-final boundary. The rule drops a certain consonantal suffix (continuative aspect) after a stem ending in a short high-tone vowel; it does not apply when there is no boundary present (compare the reflexive morpheme *ʔádi* where the *d* does not drop since no boundary precedes) nor does it apply when there is a boundary stronger than = present (the adverbializing suffix *-go* added to a stem ending in a short high tone vowel does not lose the *g*). Here again, an initially plausible way of looking at this example is via the assumption that one suffix, the continuative aspect *-ʔ*, is much more tightly bound to the stem and thus separated by a weaker boundary (=) than is the adverbializing suffix *-go*, together with the convention that a boundary mentioned in the environment of a rule (as = is mentioned in (10)) must itself be explicitly present in the forms to which the rule applies.

2.3. Rules Delineated by a Boundary

A very commonly referred-to rule that falls into neither of the categories 2.1 nor 2.2 is rule (11), the final devoicing rule of German:

(11) [−sonorant]#
           ↓
      [−voice]

This rule very clearly depends on the word boundary # ; in fact the rule applies whenever word boundary or any stronger boundary (such as phrase boundary, sentence boundary) follows. The general situation is where a rule applies to a string X whenever X is before (or after) a certain boundary b or a boundary stronger than b.

As another example, consider rule (12) (see rule (23IV) of Chomsky and Halle (1968, Chapter 5)):

(12) $\begin{bmatrix} V \\ -\text{low} \end{bmatrix} =$
$\downarrow$
[+tense]

This rule tenses vowels before the boundary = (*pretend, resist*) and before stronger boundaries (*clumsiness, clumsy,* but compare *clumsily, citify,* where the vowel is laxed by a different principle). The rule does not tense vowels before boundaries like +, which are weaker than = (compare *pitiful, beautiful*). Nor, of course, does the rule apply when no boundary follows.

Another example is rule (13) for English:

(13) ng#
$\downarrow$
φ

This rule drops *g* before the boundary #, as in *singer* (which Chomsky and Halle represent as *sing#er*), as well as before the stronger ## appearing at full word boundaries, as in *sing*. The rule does not apply before the weaker +, as in *longer* (which Chomsky and Halle represent as *long+er*), nor, of course, does it apply before no boundary (*finger*).

It is quite clear that there are a great many rules among the world's languages that apply in an environment of the form X____#, where # is a word boundary which, in the terminology of this section, functions to delineate the domain of the rule. Still, it is much harder to find examples of this phenomenon with boundaries weaker than #, and it may be that with a slightly different way of looking at the special boundary status of word boundary, the cases of this section will fall together with those of the two preceding ones.[3]

The principal point of the three types of examples discussed is that phonological rules must be sensitive to boundaries in their application, as well as to phonological segments. Moreover, the examples show that more than one type of boundary is necessary and that it makes initial sense to consider boundaries as ranked from strong to weak; it can be seen also that there is a general correlation between the strength of the boundary associated with an affix and the degree of morphological productivity of that affix, and this goes along with the well-known fact that productive affixes do not undergo as much collapsing with the stem as do less productive affixes. None of this, of course, is new. But another point brought out by the examples we have given is not so well-known. That is, there are three formally quite distinct ways that boundaries can interact with the phonological rules, as detailed in Sections 2.1, 2.2, and 2.3.[4]

---

[3] See Section 5.

[4] It should be clear that a particular occurrence of a boundary might function in one way with respect to one rule and in another way with respect to another rule.

Having seen informally the need for some sort of nontrivial boundary theory, we must proceed with questions such as how many different types of boundaries are needed, how they are to be assigned to the proper place in the representation of utterances, and how precisely we are to indicate in each phonological rule how it interacts with boundaries in the representations to which it applies.

3. THE NUMBER OF DIFFERENT BOUNDARY TYPES

From a morphological or syntactic point of view there are many readily distinguishable types of boundaries—boundaries associated with derivational affixes, boundaries associated with inflectional affixes, word boundaries, phrase boundaries, sentence boundaries, and so forth. The question I would like to consider here, however, is how many boundary types must be distinguished for purely phonological purposes. That some boundaries are required is obvious to any linguist; that is, any theory that has phonological rules applying to boundaryless underlying phonological representations can easily be seen to be incapable of producing descriptively adequate grammars. A theory that has just one type of boundary, morpheme boundary, occurring indiscriminately between every pair of adjacent morphemes in underlying phonological representations will also fail, as can be seen by the examples of Section 2, many of which point to cases where a phonological rule must be sensitive to boundaries of at least two different "strengths." According to Chomsky and Halle (1968), two boundary types are not enough; they operate tentatively (for English) with a system of three boundaries, $+$, $=$, and $\#$, all of which occur internal to words. (Word boundary and higher boundaries are signaled by sequences of the boundary $\#$.)

Ideally, to prove that n different types of boundaries are phonologically necessary, we would have to find a sequence of underlying phonological segments XY that showed up in n different ways phonetically, depending on what kind of morphological break occurred between X and Y. For example, in English the underlying sequence *long er* shows up phonetically as *longer* or as *loŋer*, depending on whether the *er* is the comparative or the agentive suffix, respectively, and this demonstrates that at least two different boundary types are required. Unfortunately, such "minimal pairs" for boundary phenomena are difficult to find, in general, and less direct methods of justifying new boundary types must be used.

It is useful at this point to take a closer look at boundary phenomena in Navaho, where the need for several phonologically different boundary types is intuitively fairly obvious. The morphological structure of the Navaho verb can be indicated schematically as in (14):

(14) $\#$1-2-3-4-5-6-7-8-9-10-11-12-ROOT-I_1-I_2-13-14-15$\#$

Thus, there are twelve prefix positions and three suffix positions, each of which can be filled by a single morpheme (in some cases by a sequence of morphemes). Some positions are mutually exclusive, but it is not uncommon to find a verb with, say, ten of the prefix and suffix positions filled. Every verb must have at least one prefix position filled. The stem of a verb consists of a root (ROOT) plus zero, one, or two of the "increments" I_1 and I_2; these increments are required for phonological reasons only since the root-plus-increment complex always forms an indivisible unit syntactically and semantically.

As can be seen from (14), a total of seventeen morphologically different types of boundaries exists in the Navaho verb. The question to be answered is how many of these boundary types are different phonologically. It is clear that at least two distinct types are necessary since relevant "minimal pairs" can be found. For example, an underlying phonological representation of the form . . . *ni-X* . . . (where *X* indicates a certain prefix from position 9) will show up differently phonetically depending on whether the *ni-* is from position 2 or from position 7, even though the prefix *X* from position 9 is the same in both cases. In particular, the *ni-* from position 2 remains unchanged before *X*, while the *ni-* from position 7 collapses with the following *X*. This is best taken to be an indication that the boundary after prefix position 2 is stronger than the boundary after prefix position 7 and that the collapsing rule can apply across the latter but not across the former.

At this point we might attempt to divide the seventeen boundaries of (14) into two different types, stronger and weaker, depending on the extent to which the associated affixes interact phonologically with surrounding segments. But no adequate way of doing this with just two boundary types exists, as becomes fairly clear with just a little bit of work with the data. That is, after considering all the boundaries of one type (say the weaker), it will soon be found that some are actually weaker than others in the sense that certain phonological rules will apply across some and not others. In Stanley (1969) I arrive at reasonable phonological rules utilizing a system of six different word-internal boundary types, but my present guess is that even more are needed for full adequacy.

The great difficulty in deciding how many boundary types are needed is that phonologically parallel contexts can seldom be found to distinguish more than two or three types. For example, I am fairly convinced that the phonological rules should be able to tell the difference between stem-initial boundary and stem-final boundary (that is, that stem-initial and stem-final boundary are of different types). However, every example I can construct of different phonological behavior of segments across stem-initial and stem-final boundaries is ambiguous: the different behavior might be due to a difference in boundary type, but it might also be due to the fact that a stressed vowel (the stem vowel) *follows* in the case of the stem-initial case and *precedes* in the stem-final case (in which event one would need only one boundary type for stem-initial and stem-final position). Intuitively, in many of these cases, it seems quite clear that the relevant difference is indeed in the type of boundary and not in some purely phonological aspect (such as the position of the stressed vowel), but this is a difficult thing to prove.

In short, it is intuitively clear that languages like Navaho with complex morphologies must have several phonologically distinguishable boundary types, but deciding precisely how many types are needed and how they are distributed is exceedingly difficult.

4. ASSIGNMENT OF BOUNDARIES: SOME UNSATISFACTORY APPROACHES

So far we have informally considered the phonological effect of boundaries and have seen that several different types of boundaries (perhaps ranked from strongest to weakest) are needed. We must now determine what principles are needed to assign these boundaries to underlying phonological representations. The input to the phonological component of a grammar is the output of the syntactic component and in each case consists of a string of morphemes in underlying phonological representation together with a labeled bracketing (the surface structure) of this string. No phonological boundaries are present at this stage. The goal is to formulate principles for inserting the phonological boundaries, principles which depend only on the surface structure of the sentence for their operation.[5] These principles will be adequate only if they define enough different types of phonological boundaries (and put them in the right places) to account for the kinds of boundary phenomena discussed from a purely phonological point of view in the previous sections of this paper.

The difference of orientation of this approach (the generative approach) from the structural approach should be clear. The structuralists wanted to postulate boundaries (in phonemic representations) only when they could be unambiguously predicted from the phonetic representation of the sentence. The assumption behind the generative goal is that it is possible to predict from the syntactic (surface) structure of the sentence the phonologically relevant boundaries for that sentence in a relatively straightforward way. This is only an assumption, of course, but it is fairly difficult to see how a language would be learnable if this were not the case.

In the present section I will outline three particularly simple ways of approaching the problem of assigning boundaries on the basis of the surface structure and will show that each of them is *too* simple and fails in fairly basic ways to form an adequate boundary theory.

4.1. Pure Immediate Constituent Approach

It is clear that very frequently the strength (from a phonological point of view) of a boundary is directly proportional to the depth of the immediate constituent break associated with that boundary. For example, boundaries between words are phonologically stronger as well as deeper from an IC point of view than are boundaries within words, generally speaking. Thus one could imagine a principle for assigning phonological boundaries which simply assigned a boundary at every IC break and which let the strength of the boundary be equal to the depth of the IC break. However, as it stands, this principle is wholly inadequate. For example, words like *womanhood* and *presidency* would be assigned the same phonological boundary, while it is clear that the former requires a stronger boundary than the latter. Further, such a theory would imply that the strength of the phonological boundary before the *-ing* in *hitting* would be different from the strength of the boundary in the same position in *solidifying* due to the difference in depth of the IC structure; but it seems correct to say that the strength should be the same since the same suffix *-ing* is involved in each case.

Such a pure IC approach to the assignment of boundaries fails, of course, because the principles can refer only to the geometry of the surface structure tree. Any successful approach will have to be capable of referring explicitly to the varous categories that label the surface structure tree.

4.2. Pure Lexical Approach

Perhaps the opposite extreme to a pure IC approach would be to provide each lexical entry with a pair of boundaries that are explicitly present in the lexicon. That is, the phonological part of each lexical entry would have the general form $b_i m b_j$, where b_i

---

[5] It should be clear why the principles for *assigning* phonological boundaries must not be based on phonological criteria but rather on information present in the surface structure. The purpose of the boundaries is precisely to account for phonological boundary phenomena; it would be vacuous to assume that phonological boundaries were assigned simply on the basis of the phonological phenomena they are designed to account for.

and b_j are (possibly different) phonological boundaries and m is the underlying distinctive feature matrix. It is possible that general principles could be found governing the type of boundaries associated with various types of lexical entries: for example, perhaps all noun stems would be found to take the same pair of boundaries. In this sort of theory, whenever an entry from the lexicon is used in a sentence, its boundaries are brought along with it. Thus two boundaries would appear between each pair of morphemes in a sentence. (Perhaps some convention collapsing such a sequence of boundaries to the stronger one would be in order.)

This approach, however, is also inadequate for fairly basic reasons. For example, consider the sequence *is not* in *John is not here* and in *What John is, not what he was, is the question*. Clearly, the boundary must be stronger, for phonological reasons, in the second case. But this simple fact will not arise from the pure lexical boundary theory just described.

In fact, it is easy to see that the pure lexical approach to boundaries suffers from lack of *any* reference to IC structure, just as the pure IC approach of the last section suffered from lack of reference to anything but IC structure. The correct approach must obviously lie somewhere between these two.

4.3. Positional Boundary Approach

In Stanley (1969) a different approach to boundary phenomena was introduced, one that makes use of "positional boundaries." The system was devised explicitly to deal with the complex boundary-related problems that arise in the Navaho verb. At the time it seemed to me that this approach provided a rather natural framework for treating boundary phenomena, and indeed the resulting phonological rules appeared to be quite reasonable. Since then, however, I have come to believe that the positional boundary approach was able to succeed by brute force only and that many crucial problems were left untouched. It will be instructive, perhaps, to review briefly that approach and to point out some flaws.

A rough outline of the morphological structure of the Navaho verb was given in (14). Note in particular that there can be up to seventeen boundaries internal to a verb. Suppose that we determine on phonological grounds how many different boundary types these seventeen tokens encompass (see Sections 2 and 3). The decision reached in Stanley (1969) was that seven different boundary types varying linearly from strong to weak were motivated phonologically.[6] These seven boundaries were distributed as shown in (15) (a refined version of (14)):

(15) $\#$1-2-3*4-5-6!7''8$+$9-10-11-12$=$ROOT-I_1-$I_2$$=$13-14*15$\#$

Here the seven boundaries are, from strong to weak, $\#$, $=$, *, !, '', $+$, and -. Suppose, then, that we imagine each (verb) root as being entered in the lexicon with the full boundary structure as given in (15) intact, except with empty slots for each of the affix positions 1, 2, and so on. During the transformational derivation of any sentence, the various affixes of the verb are put in place one by one; that is, all affix-attaching transformations are formulated in such a way that they place the affix they are moving in the correct place with respect to the boundary configuration of (15). The result is that each verb, when the sentence leaves the syntax and enters the phonology, has the general form of (15), with the root and various of the numbered affix

---

[6] I am omitting in this brief outline several details of the earlier presentation.

positions filled with distinctive feature matrices and with other affix positions empty.[7]

The approach just outlined was successful in the case of Navaho in that the seven boundary types distributed as in (15) allowed relatively simple and natural phonological rules to be formulated, whereas with an undifferentiated system of boundaries as in (14) there was no hope for rules with any appreciable degree of generality.

As mentioned, however, there are serious problems with a positional boundary approach. Consider first an example from English. From a phonological point of view it seems clear that the boundary before the *-hood* of *childhood* is stronger than the boundary before the *s* of *child's*: *-hood* is a suffix showing little phonological interaction with stems, whereas the possessive *s* combines phonologically in well-known ways with what precedes. But given a positional boundary theory as outlined in this section, it is inevitable that there are more and stronger boundaries in *child's* than in *childhood* since, as is shown by the occurrence of *childhood's* in *The girl with the unhappy childhood's sister is pregnant*, the possessive *s* is affixed farther out than the *-hood* suffix.

In fact, regardless of the details of this particular example, it is clear that whenever a cliticlike element is attached by syntactic principles to the outside of a word in a way independent of the morphology of the word, we will have a similar case, provided that the clitic happens to phonologically interact closely with what it attaches itself to. Thus, at best, a theory of positional boundaries will have to assign clitic boundaries by a different principle.

But there are further problems of a more basic sort. The positional boundary system gives the appearance of working only when a single word type is considered. When derivational affixes that change nouns to verbs, adjectives to nouns, and so on are considered, this approach becomes impossible even to formulate.

Finally, and perhaps most seriously, it seems difficult to imagine how assigning boundaries via a positional boundary approach can make fruitful use of the syntactic (surface) IC structure of words and sentences, even though this structure is provided automatically by the syntactic component of the grammar anyway. In other words, in the positional boundary approach the surface IC structure of sentences and the boundary systems (such as in (15)) are treated as wholly separate problems, thus in effect denying the obvious fact that phonological boundaries are related in *some* way to the surface IC structure (though precisely *how* they are related is one of the main questions to be answered by a boundary theory).

In short, it is clear that none of the approaches to the problem of boundary assignment outlined here is satisfactory. In Section 7 I will sketch another approach that manages to avoid most of the pitfalls encountered so far. In the meantime, the kinds of questions left unanswered include: (*a*) Precisely how does boundary assignment depend on surface IC structure? (*b*) Is there a *single* boundary for each morpheme *division* or a *pair* of boundaries surrounding the material dominated by each *node* of the IC structure? (*c*) Do sequences of boundaries (if they arise) collapse

---

[7] It is conceivable that at this stage the situations where two or more boundaries appear adjacent to each other in a verb (due to one or more adjacent affix positions being empty in that particular verb) could be governed by a convention that would collapse the sequence of boundaries into a single boundary (perhaps the strongest boundary of the sequence). As it turns out, I found good reason not to collapse sequences of boundaries; that is, I found reason to let the phonological rules have access to the full boundary structure of (15) for each verb, regardless of how many affixes the verb happened to have. But I now see this question as relatively unimportant in light of more basic failings of this whole approach to boundaries.

to a single boundary? (*d*) Are boundary types linearly ordered in strength? (*e*) Is it necessary to actually assign specifically phonological boundaries at all, or can phonological rules simply be made directly sensitive to the relevant properties of the surface structures?

5. THE ROLE OF BOUNDARIES IN THE FORMULATION AND APPLICATION OF PHONOLOGICAL RULES

In the last section we considered the question of assigning phonological boundaries on the basis of the surface structure of the sentence. Even though no satisfactory theory of boundary assignment resulted from the discussion, it will be useful to proceed in this section with a logically subsidiary problem, namely, the precise nature of the interaction of phonological rules with boundaries. That is, we will assume for the moment that some way of assigning phonological boundaries has been devised, and we will go on to consider in precisely what ways phonological rules must be sensitive to the presence of these boundaries. In Section 7 we will return to the question of boundary assignment.

In Section 2, three different types of boundary phenomena were illustrated. The first type, discussed under 2.1, "Rules Ranked by a Boundary," involves the situation where a particular phonological rule is blocked by the presence of boundaries of a certain strength (or stronger) but applies across all weaker boundaries. In such a case we can say that the weakest boundary that blocks the application of the rule ranks that rule (or is the rank of that rule). When a phonological rule is ranked by a boundary, that boundary is associated with the rule as a whole and determines the domain of application of the rule (in a way we shall make precise). It is important to notice that the boundary that ranks the rule does not appear at any particular point in the environmental statement (structural description) of the rule.

The second type of boundary situation, discussed under 2.2, "Rules Requiring a Particular Boundary," involves the case where a particular phonological rule requires a certain boundary (no weaker or stronger boundary will do) at a definite point in its structural description. Here, of course, the boundary in question will be part of the structural description of the rule. The relevant examples show that such a boundary can appear in the interior of the structural description or at one of the end points.

The third type of boundary phenomenon, discussed under 2.3, "Rules Delineated by a Boundary," involves the situation where a particular phonological rule requires a certain boundary (or a stronger one) at the (right or left) end point of its structural description.

It will be noticed that these three types of boundary phenomena form only a small and quite "asymmetrical" subset of all the logically possible ways that phonological rules might interact with boundaries, though it nevertheless seems to me that it is an empirical fact that these are the types that exist. However, it also seems to me that there are really only two thoroughly distinct types of boundary situations, namely, the first two. The third type can be viewed as an instance of the first type if things are looked at one way, and as an instance of the second type if things are looked at in another way. My reason for separating out the third type is that I do not know the correct way of viewing the situation; the issues involved will be raised later in this section. Meanwhile, it should be kept in mind that a single phonological rule may exhibit boundary phenomena of more than one type; for example, a rule might require a particular boundary in its structural description yet might also be ranked by either the same or a different boundary.

Let us consider in somewhat more detail how phonological rules interact with boundaries in their application. Suppose we have a rule of rank b_i which has the form $Y \rightarrow Y' \mid W\_\_\_\_Z$. To apply such a rule to a sentence, we break up the representation of the sentence into a partitioned version with the general shape $b_{j_0}X_1b_{j_1}X_2\ldots$ $X_nb_{j_n}$, where each $b_{j_0}, b_{j_1}, \ldots, b_{j_n}$ is a boundary equal to or stronger than the boundary b_i (which is the rank of the rule), and where each $X_1, X_2, \ldots, X_n$ is a string of phonological segments and boundaries that contains *no* boundaries equal to or stronger than the boundary b_i. Then the rule applies to each of the sections $X_1, X_2, \ldots, X_n$ *separately*. For example, if the rule had word boundary as its rank (if it applied freely within words but not across word boundary), then the sections X_i would be exactly the words of the sentence, and the rule would apply to each of the words separately.[8]

We have left unsaid exactly how the rank b_i rule $Y \rightarrow Y' \mid W\_\_\_\_Z$ applies to each of the sections of the representation X_j that have been marked off. In the case where W and Z contain only phonological segments (no boundaries), we attempt to match the string WYZ with some continuous substring of X_j, *ignoring for the purpose of this match any boundaries that* X_j *might contain*. If a match is found, then the rule applies according to the usual conventions. In the case where W and/or Z contains boundaries (these will, of course, always be weaker than b_i, the rank of the rule), we again attempt to match the string WYZ with some continuous substring of X_j; but in this case we require that for a match any boundary present in WYZ must also be present explicitly (in the appropriate place) in the string X_j, though all other boundaries that happen to be in X_j may be ignored.

Notice that the phonological rules make use of the phonological boundaries present in the representations to which they apply, but the rules do not insert boundaries or delete them. We do assume, with Chomsky and Halle (1968), that a general convention deletes all traces of boundaries in phonetic representations after all the phonological rules have applied. This reflects the fact that boundaries affect the realization of phonological segments in their environment but have no direct phonetic manifestation themselves. It is also possible that, before the phonological rules apply, certain principles operate to reduce or eliminate boundaries. (Chomsky and Halle discuss some such principles in connection with readjustment rules.) But the phonological rules themselves utilize boundaries without adding or deleting any of them.

This discussion covers the use of boundaries illustrated under Sections 2.1 and 2.2; it remains to be seen how 2.3 is to be handled. The 2.3 case, "Rules Delineated by a Boundary" is like the 2.1 case in that in applying the rule one looks for either the boundary associated with the rule *or a stronger boundary*. The 2.3 case is like the 2.2 case in that the boundary associated with the rule must be mentioned in the structural description of the rule.

Reference to the opening paragraphs of the section will clarify these statements. To illustrate, take a typical 2.3 type of case, as illustrated in (16) (which is the same as (13)):

(16) $ng\#$
    $\downarrow$
    ϕ

This is a rough formulation of the rule in English that drops final g before certain word-internal boundaries, here symbolized by $\#$ (for example, *singer*), as well as

---

[8] Chomsky and Halle (1968) have a special way of looking at the status of word boundary that is more complex than this suggests. There will be some discussion later.

before stronger boundaries, such as word boundary (for example, *sing*). Here we are supposing that the boundary internal to *singer* is $\#$ and that whatever boundary symbolizes word boundary is stronger than $\#$. Now, according to the way we have been working with boundaries thus far, rule (16) unquestionably involves a 2.3 type of boundary situation. It cannot be 2.1 as it stands because the relevant boundary appears in the structural description of the rule explicitly. It cannot be 2.2 because the rule does not require only the word-internal boundary $\#$ and nothing else; rather, it requires $\#$ or a stronger boundary.

Actually, according to the special use that Chomsky and Halle (1968) make of the boundary $\#$, (16) *can* be regarded as a 2.2 type of boundary situation: a *single* occurrence of $\#$ appears internally in words like *singer*, while the stronger word boundary is attended by (at least) *two* occurrences of $\#$ in sequence. Thus, wherever we want rule (16) to apply, we actually have the boundary $\#$ present and thus can let (16) apply fully according to the 2.2 type of conventions.

All I want to do at this time is simply indicate that with the conventions on use of sequences of $\#$ in Chomsky and Halle (1968), rule (16) is not a distinct 2.3 type of boundary situation, but a normal 2.2 type. I do not want to argue for or against these conventions on sequences of $\#$. In fact the whole question of whether or not boundaries should be assigned in such a way as to allow sequences of boundaries is a rather difficult one. One approach to the problem will be offered in Section 7.

There is a different way of looking at things whereby rule (16) turns out to involve a 2.1 type of use of boundaries. Suppose that in writing the structural description of any rule we enclose the whole string with variables. For example, consider rule (2), the rule in English that laxes vowels before consonant clusters. Instead of formulating this in the usual way as (17a), suppose we formulate it with variables surrounding the structural description, as in (17b):

(17) (a)   VCC
              ↓
            [−tense]

(b)   *W*VCC*Y*
              ↓
            [−tense]

Interpreting the variables *W* and *Y* as arbitrary strings of (zero or more) elements, it is clear that this reformulation will not change the outcome. That is, in applying (17b) to a chunk of a representation X_j (given the notation we used earlier in the section), we interpret the variables *W* and *Y* in such a way that the string *W*VCC*Y* must fit exactly over the *whole* string X_j (and not just some continuous substring of X_j as before).

Suppose now we return to rule (16) to see how it might be formulated as a type 2.1 rule. The first thing we might try is to call it a rank $\#$ rule and formulate it as $g \rightarrow \phi / n$____. But this would drop any segment *g* following an *n* so long as no boundary $\#$ or stronger appears between the *n* and the *g*, and this is clearly wrong. However, using variables, we can correctly reformulate (16) as a rank $\#$ rule as in (18):

(18) *W*ng
        ↓
        φ

Here, the fact that no variable appears to the right of the structural description will automatically be interpreted as requiring that the *Xng* sequence to which that rule applies must be followed immediately by the boundary # *or stronger*.

In short, it appears that rules exhibiting type 2.3 boundary situations really belong under type 2.1 or 2.2, but deciding which one depends on relatively detailed questions such as the status of boundary sequences and the role of variables in rule formulation. Further, it is hard to decide about rules of type 2.3 that have a weaker boundary than # at the (right or left) end of the structural description. Such rules seem to be rare.

It seems that almost every phonological rule will be of rank b_i for some boundary b_i. Thus, it is generally assumed that rules are rarely if ever blocked by the weakest boundary (formative boundary + in Chomsky and Halle (1968, p. 364)) so that every (or almost every) rule has rank greater than +. On the other hand, every rule must be blocked by some boundary (though it may be a relatively strong boundary) and so will have that boundary as its rank. In fact, the only sort of case that I can imagine where a rule would not be ranked by some boundary would be one with a structural description of the form XYZ where the rule applies across boundaries of the type b_i or weaker if they occur between X and Y but only across boundaries of the type b_j or weaker if they occur between Y and Z, where, say, b_j is weaker than b_i.

The Alternating Stress Rule in English (Chomsky and Halle (1968, p. 240)) is a case in point. Here the rule will apply across = in some positions but not others so that the = must be in the structural description to indicate the place where the domain can span = . But then the rule cannot have rank higher than = since it would apply across = in all positions, nor can it have rank equal to (or lower than) = since it would not apply to long enough stretches to ever span =. The only solution that preserves the notion of ranking is to let the rule be ranked by = and to indicate = in the structural description as well. This would require a slightly different set of conventions for rule applications.[9]

There are many unanswered questions concerning the interaction of phonological rules and boundaries. In particular, the discussion up to this point has been overly formal because of the assumption that all boundaries have a parallel status in the theory, differing only in their position along the "strength" hierarchy. It is much more natural to expect that, for example, word boundary has a special status in the theory attended by special characteristics unrelated to its relative strength and that phonological rules treat word boundary as different in kind as well as different in strength from the other boundaries. However, these difficult questions must be left until another time.

6. SOME PREVIOUS BOUNDARY THEORIES

In this section I will discuss, quite briefly, two previous boundary theories, those of Chomsky and Halle (1968) and McCawley (1968). Chomsky and Halle make use of just three boundary types, +, =, and #. These boundaries are assigned their proper place in underlying phonological representations according to very simple principles. The boundary = is simply present in the lexical entry of certain phonologically complex words such as *per=mit*, *com=pre=hend*, *de=signate* and is carried along when these words enter into derivations. The boundary + (formative boundary)

---

[9] See also McCawley (1968, p. 123, rule (2)).

is viewed as being present in the lexicon in the case of all other phonologically complex words that have a single lexical entry, such as *para + site*. But more generally, + is assumed to be present in the lexicon before and after every (simple or complex) lexical entry. Thus, when two lexical entries come together in a sentence they will always be separated by + (in fact, by two occurrences of +—supposedly the sequence of two +'s is later reduced by convention to a single occurrence of +). The boundary # is not present in the lexicon at all but is assigned by a principle that refers to the surface structure and its labeling. Specifically, # is placed before and after any string dominated by N, V, or ADJ and before and after any string dominated by a node that dominates N, V, or ADJ. (Supposedly the assignment of # replaces or supersedes any + that might already be in that position.) This principle, it is clear, will frequently give rise to sequences of two or more occurrences of #.

Once these boundaries have been assigned, certain occurrences of # are deleted (or, perhaps more precisely, reduced to +). Thus, for example, *adjectival* would originally have # surrounding both *adjective* (because it is an N) and the whole word *adjectival* (because it is an ADJ): # # *adjectiv* # *al* #. But a special rule (a type of "readjustment rule") will reduce this to # *adjectiv + al* # (that is, it will remove the occurrences of # around *adjectiv*) in order to capture the relatively close phonological union of stem and suffix in this case.

The role of the boundary # and the status of the word are very important in Chomsky and Halle (1968), and, although there is much to say about this, only the most general aspects can be treated here. Words are defined in terms of the surface structure and the distribution of #; words frequently contain internal occurrences of # (as in # # *sing* # *ing* #) and even internal occurrences of # # (as in # # # *transfer* # # *less* # 'without a transfer').

Having discussed how boundaries are assigned, we must now turn to the question of how precisely the phonological rules make use of boundaries. The situation is perhaps clearest with respect to the formative boundary, +. Chomsky and Halle explicitly state (p. 364) that any rule that does not mention + in its structural description may still apply across +; this is like saying, in our terms, that all rules are ranked by some boundary stronger than +. It is also said that a rule that actually mentions + in its structural description must find an explicit + in the stated position in any string to which it applies. But a question that arises here is whether a rule with the structural description $X + Y$ will apply to the configurations $X = Y$ or $X \# Y$. The answer would quite probably be no in the case of the configuration $X \# Y$; the only rules that apply across # at all are the cyclical rules of Compound Stress, Nuclear Stress, and Stress Adjustment, and these all mention # explicitly in the structural description wherever the domain of the rule is to span a #. But Chomsky and Halle find reason to state explicitly for two rules with a variable X in the structural description (rules (15) and (16) of Chapter 5) that X is to contain no occurrence of # in the strings to which the rule applies. Whether a rule with the structural description $X + Y$ would apply to $X = Y$ is less clear; it seems intuitively that it would, but I cannot find relevant examples or discussion in Chomsky and Halle.

Turning now to the boundary =, it is not at all clear to me whether a rule that has no boundaries in its structural description is to apply across occurrences of =. When = is mentioned in the structural description it seems to be the convention that an explicit = (and not a + or a #) must be found for the rule to apply (so that this is like our 2.2 type of case). The appearance of = in parentheses (that is, optionally) in the structural description of the Alternating Stress Rule would seem to indicate that it would be better to let such a rule be a ranked rule (in our sense) with rank stronger than $=$ so that it would be automatic that the rule applied across $=$. But the impossibility of this is demonstrated in Chapter 8 (p. 371) when Chomsky and Halle discuss a proposal of McCawley's.[10]

Turning finally to the boundary #, it seems quite clear from Chomsky and Halle (1968) that a rule not mentioning # in its structural description would not apply across # and that a rule mentioning # must find an explicit # (or a sequence of occurrences of #) and not a mere + or $=$.[11]

As we have implied, there are aspects of what we have called ranking of rules implicit in Chomsky and Halle (1968), especially with respect to rules automatically applying across +. Moreover, Chomsky and Halle explicitly state that all the non-cyclic rules apply to words separately. (There are only five cyclic rules, (15) to (19) in Chapter 5.) This is like saying that all noncyclic rules are ranked by word boundary.[12] However, it seems that in point of fact a stronger statement about ranking can be made. That is, since no rules apply across # without mentioning it, all rules are actually ranked by #.

McCawley (1968) tentatively suggests a system of six boundaries which he wants to arrange in a hierarchy from strong to weak: starting with the strongest, they are: $, phrase boundary; #, word boundary; #$_i$, used in compounds formed from two words (pp. 58, 117–118); :, used in compounds neither of whose constituents is a word (p. 79); &, morpheme boundary, the weakest boundary, corresponding to Chomsky and Halle's +. The sixth boundary is *, and is used to keep g from dropping after certain prefixes (p. 87). For reasons that McCawley is "not prepared to discuss" in his monograph, this * cannot be part of the linear ordering of the other five boundaries. McCawley develops a system of ranking of rules, whereby each rule is ranked by one of the six boundaries, meaning (as in this paper) that it will apply across all weaker boundaries. He explicitly says that between every pair of morphemes in a sentence there will be exactly one boundary (pp. 57–58), thus contrasting sharply with Chomsky and Halle.

In addition to a ranking function, boundaries may appear explicitly in the structural description of a rule, a situation which is treated similarly to the cases of our type 2.2.

7. A NEW APPROACH

I will now attempt to pull together much of what has been dealt with throughout the previous sections by outlining an approach to boundary theory that manages to avoid most of the problems already encountered. This "new" approach is not wholly new, of course (it incorporates many of the features of Chomsky and Halle (1968), McCawley (1968), and Stanley (1969)). Further, it involves various decisions that I cannot, in all cases, justify in detail since I lack supporting data from a variety of languages (and since the data in the languages I have looked at closely for boundary

[10] See the discussion at the end of Section 5 of this paper.

[11] A confusing aspect of the work under discussion, however, concerns the role of boundaries in rules that refer to constituent structure. A rule $X \rightarrow Y \mid W\_\_\_\_Z]$ may sometimes apply to a configuration $WXZ\#]$ (p. 14), as well as, supposedly, to a configuration $WXZ]$, and perhaps even to $WXZ\#\#]$, and so on.

[12] By word boundary here we mean the configuration of boundary elements that appears between words, not #, which is often referred to informally as word boundary. In Chomsky and Halle (1968) there is no constant configuration between each pair of words because of the way in which words are defined.

phenomena, namely, English and Navaho, are so complex in many respects that no clear direction is indicated). Still, I think that the approach involves a reasonably coherent framework in which many of the relevant issues have been sorted out and within which further research on boundary phenomena may be profitably carried out.

Consider, first, boundary assignment. For lexical entries with complex internal structure (that is, where a complex unit must be listed in the lexicon as a whole and not assembled by transformational rules), the internal boundaries will simply be present in the lexical entry as it is listed in the lexicon. Different strengths of boundaries will surely be required, analogous to Chomsky and Halle's treatment of *person+al*, *para+site*, and so on, with +, and *com=pre=hend*, *per=mit*, and so on, with =. The situation is not without complication, for in Navaho there are cases where we want to list certain prefix-plus-stem combinations as a unit in the lexicon (since the combination is semantically indivisible) but where various transformational rules will have to insert other prefixes between this prefix and the stem. In such forms the boundary entered in the lexicon between the prefix and the stem will stay with the prefix when additional material is inserted. Relevant here too, of course, is the current controversy between "lexicalists," who want to list as units in the lexicon many not fully productive complex forms (such as *arrival*) and "transformationalists," who want to derive such complex forms by transformational rules.

All boundaries not present in the lexicon will be inserted by rule on the basis of the surface structure of the sentence. Here I would adopt a system similar to (but not identical with) that of Chomsky and Halle (1968). Let each lexical category (N, V, ADJ, ADV, and perhaps others) in the surface IC structure govern the placement of a boundary # before and after the string dominated by the category (placed just inside the brackets associated with the category). It is not necessary to associate # in this way with higher categories such as NP as long as rules are given for adjusting the IC structure so as to attach various elements such as articles and conjunctions to adjacent lexical categories under certain conditions. These rules would be analogous to the rules in Chomsky and Halle (p. 368) for altering the constituent structure so that every word (as there defined) is a constituent of the surface structure. The problem of what these rules look like in detail is an extremely difficult one that goes far beyond the scope of the present discussion.

It is possible that a stronger theory is required, a theory that does not associate the same boundary # with all categories but which associates different boundaries with different categories. However, I have no positive evidence pointing in this direction.

The principles for assigning # as discussed so far would produce representations such as those in (19):

(19) $[_{NP} [_A \# [_N \# \text{person} \#]_N \text{al} \#]_A [_N \# [_N \# \text{loss} \#]_N \text{es} \#]_N]_{NP}$

And in general every suffix would be separated from what precedes (and every prefix from what follows) by a single occurrence of #, or a double occurrence in those case where a derivational process is marked with a zero affix, as in $[_N \# [_N \# [_V \# \text{survey} \#]_V \#]_N \text{s} \#]_N$.

At this point I would suggest that an elaborate set of principles apply to weaken various occurrences of the boundary #. These principles would first involve setting up a hierarchy of classes of affixes, where class membership is determined by how closely the affix combines phonologically with adjacent material. For English there would be at least two classes, as can be seen from the examples in Section 2.1, but more than two would be required in general. The principles for weakening # would depend on the class of associated affixes, and there would be as many different weakened versions of # (each of which would be regarded as a distinct boundary type) as there are affix classes. Further, I would suggest that each time # between a prefix and what follows (or between a suffix and what precedes) is weakened in this way, the occurrence of # on the other side of the stem that is paired with this (weakened) # is simply eliminated. This convention is reasonable since, for example, the addition of a *suffix* to a stem does not affect how closely this stem combines phonologically with what *precedes* it (the stem). But this is, of course, an empirical question.

If, for the purposes of the example, we suppose that the two suffixes of (19) are in different affix classes, these principles would yield (20) from (19):

(20) $[_{NP} [_A \# [_N person^*]_N al \#]_A [_N \# [_N loss!]_N es \#]_N]_{NP}$

Without the brackets (which serve simply to indicate the domain of cyclical rules), we have just $\# person^* al \# \# loss! es \#$. Here we are assuming that the weakened version of # associated with the *-al* class is * and that for the plural class is !. In such a system every word would be surrounded by # . . . #, and a single boundary weaker than # would occur at every word-internal juncture. A case of zero affixation as in the case of *survey* cited earlier would entail deletion of both boundaries, rather than weakening of one and deletion of the other, so that we would have $[_N \# [_V survey]_V \#]_N$ for the noun *survey*, $[_N \# [_N [_V survey]_V !]_N es \#]_N$ for its plural. In short, every addition of an affix causes weakening and/or deletion of the pair of boundaries associated with the constituent it is affixed to.

In certain cases different instances of the same affix morpheme will fall into different affix classes, depending on the stem. Thus the past tense *d* for the verb *weep* falls into a class associated with a weaker boundary than does the past tense *d* for the verb *peep* since we have more collapsing in *wept* than in *peeped*.

It seems likely that some of the weakened versions of # will turn out to be identical with the formative boundary + present in the lexicon (and perhaps other weakened versions of # will be identical with other boundaries present in the lexicon), but this is difficult to decide.

For a language like Navaho, with its more complicated verbal morphology, the surface structure of the verb will look something like (21). The affix positions in (21) are numbered as in (15) (although the arrangement of positions 8–12 is different in (21) from that implied in (15), a reflection of certain changes in my thinking since Stanley (1969) from which (15) is drawn):

(21)

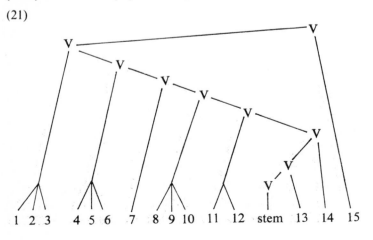

1 2 3   4 5 6   7   8 9 10   11   12   stem   13   14   15

Each node V in (21) will determine a pair of occurrences of # around the string dominated by that V, and then those occurrences of # that are internal to the word will be weakened or deleted according to the sort of principles discussed earlier. For the purposes of these principles, affixes are grouped into the following eight classes (listed in decreasing order according to the strength of the weakened version of # they determine): 15; 1, 2, 3; 4, 5, 6; 7; 8, 9, 10; 11, 12; 14; 13. When more than one prefix of the same class, for example the class 1, 2, 3, occurs in a verb, the prefixes will be separated by the weakest boundary, formative boundary.

Having assigned the boundaries as just described, we will assume that each rule is ranked by one of the boundaries. Some such assumption is needed to avoid having to specify in an ad hoc way for each rule what boundaries it can and cannot apply across. However, this assumption does not fully account for such cases as mentioned in Section 5, and I do not know how to deal with them.

In addition to performing a ranking function, boundaries can be mentioned at a particular point in the structural description of a rule (either in the interior or at one end). We will assume that such a rule must find exactly the mentioned boundary in representations to which it applies. This is just the 2.1 situation discussed earlier. It is possible that there are cases where a particular point in the structural description of a rule requires not one particular boundary type but any of a range of boundary types. In such a case it would seem that a feature system for the boundaries would be required.

Finally, we will assume that the sorts of cases with a boundary at the (right or left) end of the structural description which we originally classed under type 2.3 will be subsumed under the ranking function of boundaries, using the sort of variables in setting up the structural descriptions as discussed in Section 5. This leaves us with just two uses of boundaries: they may be used to rank rules or to form part of the structural description of rules.

In closing, I will mention a potentially quite interesting consequence of rule ranking. In any grammar, rules of low rank will apply to relatively short chunks of representations. The lowest ranked rules will apply only within single morphemes and within stem plus affix (or affix plus affix) combinations that are considerably fused together phonologically (and, supposedly, rather nonproductive semantically). Higher ranked rules will become progressively more general until we reach word-level rules, where the bulk of the most widespread and regular rules of the language will lie. When we consider the problem of language acquisition, it seems clear that the first rules to be incorporated actively and productively in the child's grammar are the high ranking rules. The morpheme combinations that are related by the low ranking rules are probably simply learned as indivisible units. As his knowledge of the language grows, the child will learn rules of lower and lower rank and will thus learn how to analyze some of these formerly indivisible units. But when he reaches a certain point, he might find it easier to simply memorize certain paradigms of morpheme combinations than to incorporate rules of still lower rank. Thus, perhaps, the competence grammar of adults is not fully in terms of rules but partially in terms of memorized paradigms.

As a case in point, let me mention certain aspects of prefix behavior in Navaho. Every verb has an affix in prefix position 8 (see (14)) that indicates the "mode" of the verb. The following position, position 9, is occupied by pronominal prefixes that indicate the subject of the verb if it is other than third person. Now these position 8 and position 9 prefixes fuse phonologically to a considerable extent, and even more fusion occurs when position 10, marking perfective aspect, is filled. The (phonetic) results of certain of these combinations are given in the paradigms of (22), where "1" is first person, "2" is second person, "sg" is singular, "pl" is plural, "*y*," "*n*," "*p*," and "*o*" are indications of different mood prefixes in position 8, and the "*p*" in parentheses indicates when the perfective prefix of position 10 is present:

(22)		1 sg	2 sg	1 pl	2 pl
	y	*yiš*	*ni*	*yiid*	*γoh*
	n	*niš*	*ní*	*niid*	*noh*
	p	*yiš*	*yí*	*yiid*	*γoh*
	o	*γós*	*γóó*	*γood*	*γooh*
	y(p)	*yí*	*yíní*	*yiid*	*γoo*
	n(p)	*ní*	*yíní*	*niid*	*noo*

Now it is possible to find underlying phonological representations for each of the four modal (position 8), four pronominal (position 9), and one aspectual (position 10) prefixes involved in (22) and to give corresponding phonological rules that yield the phonetic results of (22) (see Stanley (1969, Chapter 5)). In the terms of this paper, the boundaries that separate the prefix positions 8, 9, and 10 are relatively weak, and the rules that apply across them are of low rank; these rules do not apply elsewhere in the verb, in general, being blocked by stronger boundaries. Still, more than a few rules are needed to account for the phenomena of (22), and, as just implied, many of them are not very general. What I am suggesting is that in this case the paradigms of (22) are simply memorized (incorporated intact in the competence grammar) and that the low ranking rules just referred to are never learned at all.

REFERENCES

Chomsky, N., and M. Halle (1968), *The Sound Pattern of English*, New York: Harper & Row.

McCawley, J. D. (1968), *The Phonological Component of a Grammar of Japanese*, The Hague: Mouton.

Stanley, R. (1969), *The Phonology of the Navaho Verb*, unpublished Ph.D. dissertation, M.I.T. (a revised and expanded version is to be published as *Navaho Phonology* in the series Language Science Monographs).

latvian folk meters and styles[1]

Valdis J. Zeps

University of Wisconsin

Latvian folk singers make use of three meters—the so-called *trochee*, the so-called *dactyl*, and a third meter in which the so-called *asymmetric verse* is composed. An example of verse composed in each of the three meters is given in (1), (2), and (3), respectively:[2]

(1) *Mẹ́lna čúska míltus mala*   'A black snake grinds flour
    vídū jūṛas úz akmens;   on a rock in mid-sea;
    túos būs ēst tíem kungiem,   to be fed to the masters
    kás bez saules strádināja.   who work you past sunset'.

(2) *Zílīte žúbīte*   'The titmouse and the finch
    áudeklu méta;   were arranging the warp;
    átskrēja vánags,   by came the hawk
    sámudžināja.   and tangled it up'.

(3) *Ápkārt kalnu gájú,*   'I walked around the hill,
    kálniņā uzkápu,   I climbed to the hilltop,
    iéraudzīju lígaviņu   I saw my betrothed
    gáuži raudājám.   bitterly crying'.

The trochee (1), a binary meter, forms the basis for the great majority of all folk songs collected, and songs which have become a permanent part of the folk song inventory are typically in this meter. By way of contrast, the so-called dactyl (2),

---

[1] Some of the formulations presented in this paper arose during a discussion with Paul Kiparsky.
[2] Reciting or singing stress has been marked by an acute accent for the reader's convenience. This is *not* normal word stress nor does it constitute part of the meter.

a ternary meter, is strongly associated with musical rendition (dance, wedding songs) and is more open to improvisation. The asymmetric verse (3) is often omitted from scholarly consideration and said to be "inferior," borrowed from Lithuanians or Belorussians, or "mere doggerel" or is adduced as "violating or relaxing" the folk meter.

In two previous articles (Zeps (1963; 1969)) I tried to show that both the binary and the ternary meters are syllable-counting meters, with obligatory word breaks (caesuras) and obligatory absences of such word breaks (bridges) being the only other terms that enter into the metric design. In the syllable counting, however, there is a complication that provides for a fair amount of variety in the verse, so much so that it has in the past misled researchers (notably Bērziņš (1940, pp. 57–80) and Rudzītis (1954)) into thinking that Latvian folk verse was not composed in a syllable-counting meter. The principle has been spelled out in detail elsewhere (Zeps (1963; 1969) and Halle (1970, pp. 68–69)). It suffices to say here that in certain positions metric syllables may be or must be counted prior to the application of a morphophonemic rule that truncates the final vowel. As a result, even though the meter may provide for a fixed number of syllables, the actualization rules can produce considerable variety in the count of phonetic syllables.

To illustrate briefly how the syllable-counting operates, consider a trochaic half-line (colon) which is composed on the pattern shown in (4), where X is a metric syllable, = a bridge, and | a caesura:

(4) X X X = X |

The first colon from line 3 in (1) is repeated in (5)—in phonetic transcription in (5a) and morphophonemic transcription in (5b):

(5) (a) *tuos būs ēst*
    (b) *tuos būsi ēsti*

As can be seen, (5b) is two syllables longer than (5a). The composition principles of the trochee require that the morphophonemic syllable at the end of the colon (*ti* in (5b)) always be counted as a metric syllable. Medial syllables, however, can be counted either before or after the truncation rule. In (5a) we must truncate the *i* in *si* before counting the syllables. But the final syllable, though deleted phonetically, is crucial for the meter, being one of the two final syllables joined by the bridge.

The five morphophonemic syllables of (5b) correspond to four metric syllables in (4) and to three phonetic syllables in (5a). Such variation among levels, of course, is not a necessary occurrence, as the initial colon of (1) illustrates: it is derived from underlying *mȩlnaa čuskaa*, which is also a four-syllable entity.

While the trochaic stanza is a straightforward multiple of the half-line by successive factors of two (that is, two cola make a line, two lines a distich, two distiches a stanza), the cola of the folk dactyl vary somewhat. Only the bridge is obligatory throughout. The basic pattern is shown in (6):

(6) X X = X |

This pattern can be expanded by an extra phonetic syllable in all but the last colon of a distich or decreased by one syllable in a line-final colon, giving the pattern in (7):

(7) (X) X X = X | (X) (X) X = X |
    (X) X X = X | (X) X = X |

The second line of a dactylic distich has a variant, namely, a line without a caesura but with three bridges, as shown in (8):

(8) (X) (X) X = X = X = X |

The precise metric subscheme that underlies example (2) is given in (9):

(9) X X = X | X X = X |
     X X = X | X = X |
     X X = X | X X = X |
     X X = X = X = X |

In addition to the binary versus ternary character of the meters just discussed, variety in the pre-bridge syllables is provided for by two different means. In the trochee, variety results from the truncation rule. This rule is of no interest for the pre-bridge syllables of the dactyl, however, where variety is instead produced by the optional phonetic syllables provided for in the meter.

In the asymmetric verse, six-syllable sequences alternate with eight-syllable sequences, as illustrated in (10):

(10) *Ja es duošu tēvam guodu*   'If I make the proper representations to your father,
     vai tu būsi mana?   will you be mine?'

The six-syllable line has no caesura, and the eight-syllable line has one after the fourth syllable. This much is obvious and has been noted in the literature (Rudzītis (1960, p. 122)). It has not been previously noted, however, that the asymmetric verse also requires the colon-final bridge; that is, the meter that underlies (10) is as shown in (11):

(11)   X X X = X | X X X = X |
      X X X X X = X |

The long lines and the short lines occur in various arrangements, with the 6-6-8-6 stanza illustrated in (3) being the most popular.

The asymmetric verse differs from the trochee and the dactyl in yet another respect. In the trochee and the dactyl, a morphophonemically truncated colon-final syllable *must* be counted among the metric syllables; in asymmetric verse such "extra" syllables *may* be counted among the metric. Thus *gauži raudājam* (the last line in (3)) is a correct six-syllable line, as it derives from *gaužiV raudājami*. But consider (12):

(12) *Puiši stāvat riņķī*   'Stand ye lads in a circle'

This is also a correct six-syllable line, even though it derives from a sequence overlong from the point of view of the trochee/dactyl scheme.[3] The effect of the relaxation of the requirement that the line-final "extra" morphophonemic syllable has to be counted is the impression that the song has been composed on a near-phonetic level, hence its "doggerel"-like quality.

To summarize the shared and differential features of the three meters, they are all syllable-counting meters and all use the bridge and caesura as organizing principles. They all involve, though to a varying degree, reference to a morphophonemic level: for trochaic songs this reference is obligatory in colon-final position and optional

---

[3] The underlying form of the last word should be *riņķīji*.

elsewhere; for dactylic verse this reference is obligatory in colon-final position only; for asymmetric verse, the reference is optional in colon-final position only. The degree of morphophonemic reference correlates with the "message" conveyed by the meter—"neutral" by the trochee, "frivolous" by the dactyl, and "trashy" by the asymmetric.

All three meters form an integral part of the folk repertoire; in particular, the asymmetric verse cannot be brushed aside as alien or degraded.

Some further generalities concerning the Latvian meter are revealed when we pursue the formalism utilized by Halle (1970) and Halle and Keyser (1971). They postulate strongly constrained (S) and weakly constrained (W) metric entities which are mapped onto actual phonetic matter. The S of any colon in Latvian corresponds, of course, to the bridged syllables followed by the caesura; W can then stand for any syllable preceding S. Halle (1970, pp. 68–69), in fact, handles the Latvian trochee and provides the abstract pattern in (13) for the trochaic line:

(13) WWS WWS

His mapping rules (somewhat abbreviated) are as follows:

> The W's of the meter must correspond one:one to the syllables of the line of verse either in their surface or in their underlying [i.e., morphophonemic] representation . . . The S's of the meter must correspond to a word-final sequence of two syllables in the underlying representation.

Extending the argument to the dactyl, we can now define the dactylic distich as in (14):

(14) WS WS WS (W)S

The mapping rules for (14) are as follows. The W's of the meter typically correspond one:one to syllables in lines of verse; the first three W's may be mapped into two syllables each; the second and the final W (i.e., the fourth; or the third, if there is no fourth) may be mapped into zero syllables each. The S's of the meter must correspond to a word-final sequence of two syllables in the underlying representation. Two successive S's must be mapped as a word-final sequence of four syllables in the underlying representation.

In the case of the asymmetric verse, the six-syllable line will be represented as in (15) and the eight-syllable line as in (16):

(15) WWWWS
(16) WWS WWS

That is, the number of W's remains constant; the asymmetric character of the verse is due to the number of S's per line. The mapping rules are as follows. The W's of the meter correspond one:one to syllables in lines of verse. The S's of the meter correspond to a word-final sequence of two syllables in either the surface or in the underlying representation.

Unlike the trochee or the dactyl, which provided for phonetic variety in their W sections, the asymmetric verse provides for variety in the S section, in part by admitting "overruns" of the type illustrated in (12). The artistic effect of such overruns is dubious.

REFERENCES

Bērziņš, L. (1940), *Ievads latviešu tautas dzejā*, Rīga.

Halle, M. (1970), "On Meter and Prosody," in M. Bierwisch and K. H. Heidolph, eds., *Progress in Linguistics*, The Hague: Mouton.

Halle, M., and S. J. Keyser (1971), *English Stress: Its Form, Its Growth, and Its Role in Verse*, New York: Harper & Row.

Halle, M., and V. J. Zeps (1966), "A survey of Latvian morphophonemics," *Quarterly Progress Report of the Research Laboratory of Electronics, 83*, M.I T., 105–113.

Rudzītis, J. (1954), "Tautas dziesmu metrika," in A. Švābe, K. Straubergs, and E. Hauzenberga-Šturma, eds., *Latviešu tautas dziesmas*, vol. 5, Copenhagen.

Rudzītis, J. (1960), "Asimmetriskās strofas latviešu trochaju dziesmās," *In Honorem Endzelini*, Chicago.

Zeps, V. J. (1963), "The meter of the so-called trochaic Latvian folksongs," *International Journal of Slavic Linguistics and Poetics, 7*, 123–128.

Zeps, V. J. (1969), "The meter of the Latvian folk dactyl," *Ceļi, 14*, 45–47.

PART
2

the ROLe of focus
in the inteRpRetation
of anaphoRic expRessions[1]

Adrian Akmajian
University of Massachusetts at Amherst

1. In this paper we are concerned with certain problems in the semantic inter-pretation of anaphoric expressions such as those illustrated in (1):

(1) (a) Pratt roasted a pig in the fireplace last year, but none of his friends realize *it*
   (b) Pratt roasted a pig in the fireplace last year, and Whitney did *it* too
   (c) Pratt roasted a pig in the fireplace last year, and Whitney tried *it* with a game hen

In (1a) the anaphoric expression *it* refers back to ("stands for") the entire antecedent clause.[2] Thus, the anaphoric clause[2] of (1a) is interpreted to mean that none of Pratt's friends realizes that he roasted a pig in the fireplace last year. In (1b), however, the anaphoric expression does not refer to the entire antecedent clause. Its inter-pretation in fact excludes a certain portion of the antecedent clause, namely, *Pratt*. We do not assert of Whitney that *Pratt* roasted a pig; rather, the interpretation of the anaphoric clause is that *Whitney* roasted a pig in the fireplace last year. Finally, in (1c), the interpretation of the anaphoric expression excludes the antecedent items *Pratt* and *a pig*, and thus the anaphoric clause is interpreted to mean that *Whitney* tried

[1] I am grateful to Noam Chomsky, Morris Halle, Ray Jackendoff, Will Leben, and John R. Ross for valuable comments on the material presented in this paper. To Morris Halle I owe a special debt of gratitude, not only for insightful criticism of the work contained in this paper, but also for providing generous encouragement and invaluable stimulation as both a teacher and an adviser. It is to his spirit of teaching that this paper is dedicated.

The research contained in this paper is based on Akmajian (1968) and is also reported on in a section of Akmajian (1970).

[2] We use the term *anaphoric clause* to refer to that clause containing the anaphoric expression. The term *antecedent clause* refers to the more fully specified clause, that is, the one to which the anaphoric expression refers.

roasting *a game hen* in the fireplace last year.[3] In sum, the portion of the antecedent clause referred to in each case is as in (2a,b,c), respectively:

(2) (a) [Pratt roasted a pig in the fireplace last year]
    (b) [. . . roasted a pig in the fireplace last year]
    (c) [. . . roasted . . . in the fireplace last year]

Our task here is to determine the principles which govern the interpretation of anaphoric expressions such as *it*. Why, for example, is *it* interpreted to refer to the entire antecedent clause in (1a), but only to a portion of the antecedent clause in (1b) and (1c)? We assume that the most critical task of any theory is to determine the constraints on possible interpretations of anaphoric expressions such as those in (1).

    2. Sentences such as (1b) and (1c) differ from (1a) in an intuitively clear way: in such sentences the speaker has set up a contrast between some specific item(s) within the first clause and some item(s) within the second clause. For example, in (1b) two persons, Pratt and Whitney, are compared and contrasted with respect to one given action, namely, roasting a pig in the fireplace last year. Note, in particular, that the contrasted items in (1b) and (1c) must bear prominent stress:

    (b) Prátt roasted a pig in the fireplace last year and Whítney did it too
    (c) Prátt roasted a píg in the fireplace last year and Whítney tried it with a gáme
        hen

In sentences such as (1a), on the other hand, no portion of the first clause is placed in contrast with any given portion of the second clause. The speaker simply presents the first clause and then goes on to comment on the entire proposition expressed in it. As we would expect, both clauses of (1a) receive neutral intonation, that is, no given portions of either clause are emphatically or contrastively stressed.

    On the basis of such observations, we might posit the informal principle in (3):

(3) The interpretation of anaphoric *it* excludes only those portions of the antecedent clause which have been placed in contrast with given portions of the anaphoric clause

Assuming that we have a well-defined notion of contrast, principle (3) predicts that the anaphoric expression in (1a) should refer to the entire antecedent clause. In (1b), where a contrast has been set up between *Pratt* and *Whitney*, the principle predicts that the interpretation of *it* excludes the antecedent subject, *Pratt*. Finally, in (1c), where the subjects of both clauses (*Pratt*, *Whitney*) as well as the objects of both clauses (*a pig*, *a game hen*) are in contrast, the prediction is that the interpretation of *it* excludes both *Pratt* and *a pig*. Intuitively speaking, then, specific items can be contrasted across two clauses, and the contrasted items of the antecedent clause are "canceled out" of the interpretation of the anaphoric expression of the anaphoric clause. The claim here is that one of the constraints on possible interpretations of an anaphoric expression such as *it* must involve reference to contrast relations holding between clauses.

    The question we must ask at this point is whether an intuitive notion such as "contrast" can be made precise enough to be of value in explaining the data before us. In other words, is it possible to incorporate some such notion into a generative

---

[3] Other anaphoric expressions which function in a similar manner are as follows:

Pratt roasted a pig in the fireplace last year, and Whitney tried $\begin{Bmatrix} that \\ the\ same\ (thing) \end{Bmatrix}$ with a game hen

grammar? A useful beginning in finding the answer to such questions can be made by taking into account the notions of "focus" and "presupposition" as outlined in Chomsky (1971).

3. Chomsky (1971) uses *focus* as a technical term referring to a constituent of a sentence (where "constituent" is taken in such a way that the entire sentence may be a constituent) which contains the intonation center, that is, the position of highest pitch and stress. The *presupposition* of a sentence, in Chomsky's sense, is defined in terms of the notion of focus: the presupposition is an expression derived by replacing the focus of a sentence with an appropriate variable.[4]

Consider the sentences in (4):

(4) (a) Mítchell urged Nixon to appoint Carswell
    (b) Mitchell urged Níxon to appoint Carswell
    (c) Mitchell urged Nixon to appoint Cárswell

The differences we intuit among such sentences are a function of the shifting focus-presupposition relations. According to our definitions, these would be as in (a), (b), and (c) of (5), respectively:[5]

(5) (a) FOCUS: Mitchell
    PRESUPPOSITION: x urged Nixon to appoint Carswell
    (b) FOCUS: Nixon
    PRESUPPOSITION: Mitchell urged x to appoint Carswell
    (c) FOCUS: Carswell
    PRESUPPOSITION: Mitchell urged Nixon to appoint x

In each case, the presupposition of the sentence represents information which is shared by both speaker and hearer within a given universe of discourse. The focus of the sentence, on the other hand, represents information which the speaker assumes to be novel to the hearer. Thus, to say that the sentences of (4) have different focus-presupposition relations is to say that in each case the speaker makes different assumptions as to what information is novel and what is already known to the hearer.

This can be seen clearly by noting that the three sentences of (4) would be used in different contexts of discourse and, in particular, they answer different questions, namely, the three questions in (6), respectively:

(6) (a) Who urged Nixon to appoint Carswell?
    (b) Who did Mitchell urge to appoint Carswell?
    (c) Who did Mitchell urge Nixon to appoint?

Thus, in (6a) it is presupposed by the speaker that *someone* urged Nixon to appoint Carswell, and he requests information as to the identity of that person. Only sentence (4a) is an appropriate response to this question since it shares the presupposition and in addition provides the required new information. An analogous situation holds for questions (6b) and (6c) and responses (4b) and (4c), respectively.

---

[4] Throughout this paper, the term *presupposition* is used only in this sense.

[5] We assume that the phonological component can assign emphatic stress to any independent lexical item in a given surface structure. If an emphatically stressed lexical item is phrase-final, then the entire containing phrase may be taken as a focus constituent. Thus, as discussed in Chomsky (1971), a sentence such as (4c) can be bracketed as follows:

[Mitchell[urged Nixon[to appoint[Cárswell]]]]

Any constituent enclosed by brackets can serve as the focus of this sentence. In a sentence such as (4a), on the other hand, the constituent *Mitchell* is the exclusive focus since it is not part of a larger phrase in which it is phrase-final.

3.1. We will represent the focus-presupposition relations of a sentence as a two-part expression, as in (7) (where (4a) is used as an illustration):

(7) [x urged Nixon to appoint Carswell], [x = Mitchell]

A bipartite expression such as (7) is intended to represent the focus and presupposition components of the semantic reading of a sentence. Note that (7) is represented in a semi-formal notation which is just precise enough to illustrate the general interpretive principles to be discussed. Although we will speak of such expressions as representing relevant aspects of the meaning of a sentence, we will leave it open as to exactly how expressions like (7) are to be derived formally.[6] However, it is relevant to note that in order to construct a representation with the essential properties of (7) it is apparently necessary to follow the steps outlined in (8) or some analogous procedures with equivalent results:

(8) (a) Locate the focus constituent of the (phonetically interpreted) surface structure and mark that portion of the semantic reading which corresponds to it
   (b) Replace the marked portion of the semantic reading by a variable, and form the expression which specifies the variable

The term *focus* is, thus, ambiguous: when applied to a surface phrase marker it refers to a syntactic constituent which forms an intonation center; when applied to a semantic reading it refers to that component of the reading which consists of a specification of a variable, as in (7).

The procedure just outlined presupposes that the semantic reading of a sentence is determined by factors of surface structure as well as deep structure. In particular, it presupposes that the syntactic deep structure of a sentence is assigned a semantic reading representing grammatical relations, given in a universal semantic notation, and, in addition, that the semantic reading assigned to a deep structure may be further modified by semantic interpretive principles which utilize information of surface structure phrase markers. Hence, our hypothesis falls within the framework of the so-called revised standard theory discussed in Chomsky (1971).[7]

3.2. Note that in the representation in (7) the focus component of the semantic reading is given as a semantic *relation*, not a single term. This reflects the fact that the focus constituent of a sentence represents novel information not because the constituent itself is necessarily novel, but rather because the semantic relation which the constituent enters into is novel with respect to a given universe of discourse. For

---

[6] See Jackendoff (1972, Chapter 6) for one proposal for representing focus-presupposition relations formally within the framework of a specific semantic theory.

[7] So far we have made the following assumptions concerning focus-presupposition relations:

(a) (i) that such relations form part of the semantic reading of sentences, and
   (ii) that such relations are determined according to generalizations on surface syntactic structure

We base both of these assumptions on arguments presented in Chomsky (1971), Jackendoff (1969), Jackendoff (1972), and Anderson (1970). A detailed justification of these assumptions would be beyond the scope of this paper. However, it will be useful to keep in mind the sort of arguments which are used to justify assumption (i), in particular. A typical argument involves the properties of "logical scope" (see Jackendoff (1969; 1972)). For example, consider the sentence (b):

(b) Pratt didn't make the claim that Whitney was fired for *insubordinátion*

Assume that the constituent *insubordination* bears emphatic stress. In uttering such a sentence, the speaker does not deny that Pratt made the claim that Whitney was fired. Rather, he denies only that Pratt ascribed Whitney's being fired to insubordination. Thus, it is presupposed in (b) that Pratt did

example, a sentence such as (4a) could be used in a discourse context in which Mitchell has been mentioned repeatedly. Hence, the novelty associated with this constituent is not necessarily the novelty of "first mention"; rather, it is the specification of Mitchell as the one who urged Nixon that represents novel information. The entire expression "[x = Mitchell]," then, is taken to be what the speaker assumes to represent novel information to the hearer.

4. Let us now return to the sentences of (1) in order to see how we might utilize the representation of focus-presupposition relations in determining the semantic interpretation of anaphoric expressions such as *it*. First of all, we adopt the position that the anaphoric clauses of the sentences of (1) are generated by the base component in essentially their surface forms. In particular, the expression *it* is generated as a basic noun phrase. Thus, the anaphoric clause of (1c), for example, would be generated as in (9):

(9)

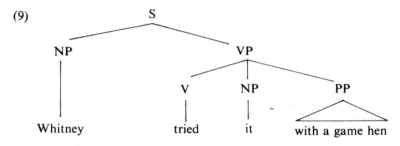

make the claim that Whitney was fired for some reason, and the scope of negation is associated strictly with the constituent *for insubordination*.

The problem in assigning a semantic interpretation to such a sentence resides in the fact that the negative morpheme is generated syntactically in the matrix sentence; however, its semantic scope includes only a single constituent in the embedded complement. Note that there are several reasons to assume that the negative morpheme is generated within the matrix sentence. Suppose that one were to claim for such cases that the negative originates within the complement sentence, to be transformationally shifted later into the matrix sentence. First of all, a general hypothesis of this sort would be possible only within a framework in which transformations were not necessarily meaning-preserving, since the expressions *to make the claim that not X* and *to not make the claim that X* are not synonymous. More importantly, there is no *syntactically* motivated deep structure in which the negation in sentence (b) could be generated as part of the constituent which forms its scope. To take just one example, (b) has no "clefted" form which could serve as its syntactic source; that is, (c) is ungrammatical:

(c) *It wasn't for insubordination that Pratt made the claim that Whitney was fired

Finally, as Anderson (1970) points out for analogous cases involving the scope of *even*, the hypothesis under consideration would allow violation of Ross's Complex NP Constraint (see Ross (1967)) since the negative morpheme would have to be moved out of the complex NP "*the claim that. . .*".

We can account for the interpretation of such sentences by assuming that, semantically, the negation must be associated with the focus component of the semantic reading. Thus, if we partition the semantic reading of sentence (b) as in (8) and we further require that in the semantic reading the negation be placed on the focus component, we arrive at a representation such as (d):

(d) [Pratt made the claim that Whitney was fired for x], [NEG[x = insubordination]]

Thus, we account for the syntactic distribution of the negative morpheme by allowing it to be generated in the matrix sentence. We account for its semantic scope by requiring that the negation be associated with the focus component of the semantic reading. Assumption (a(i)) is justified insofar as the notion of focus plays a crucial role in describing the logical properties of sentences, in this case the scope of negation.

It is reasonable to generate *it* as a noun phrase object of *try* since sentences like (1c) can appear in passivized form, as illustrated in (10):

(10) Pratt roasted a pig in the fireplace last year, but it hasn't been tried by many people since then

Given this hypothesis, we must assume that *it* is marked as a pro-form, with a minimal set of semantic features to distinguish it from other pro-forms. Such a pro-form in itself contains no further semantic information. Thus, if sentences such as (9) happen to be generated independently (as single sentences), their semantic representation will indicate a semantic "gap": the reference of *it* will not be specified.

4.1. Let us consider first how we would derive the semantic interpretation of the anaphoric clause of (1b). We begin by examining the antecedent clause, and, as has already been noted, the constituent *Pratt*, since it is emphatically stressed, forms the focus constituent of that clause. We would thus assign the focus-presupposition relations in (11) to the antecedent clause of (1b):

(11) [x roasted a pig in the fireplace last year], [x = Pratt]

Notice now that the presupposition component of (11) represents just that portion of the semantic reading of the antecedent clause which is carried over into the reading of the anaphoric clause (see (2b)). Thus, let us suppose that the presupposition of the antecedent clause is assigned to the semantic reading of the anaphoric clause in some manner. The clause *Whitney did it too* will now have as part of its semantic reading the presupposition in (11).

We note that the presupposition in question has a variable within it, and we now ask how this variable is to be specified. Within the anaphoric clause, the constituent *Whitney* is emphatically stressed and thus forms the focus constituent of that clause. Let us now suppose that the focus of the anaphoric clause specifies the variable of the presupposition assigned to it from the antecedent clause. This would give the representation in (12):[8]

(12) [x roasted a pig in the fireplace last year], [x = Whitney]

The expression (12) now forms part of the semantic reading of the anaphoric clause of (1b), and we correctly predict that part of the meaning of that clause is that Whitney roasted a pig in the fireplace last year.

Turning now to sentence (1c), we arrive at representation (13) for the focus-presupposition relations of the antecedent clause (given the stress pattern indicated):

(13) [x roasted y in the fireplace last year], [[x = Pratt], [y = a pig]]

As with (1b), let us now assign the presupposition of the antecedent clause to the semantic reading of the anaphoric clause. Furthermore, we will utilize the foci of the anaphoric clause (*Whítney, a gáme hen*) as new specifications of the variables of the assigned presupposition. The result is (14):

(14) [x roasted y in the fireplace last year], [[x = Whitney], [y = a game hen]]

Once again, part of the interpretation of the anaphoric clause will thus consist of the presupposition assigned from the antecedent clause, and the variables within this presupposition will be specified by the foci of the anaphoric clause.

---

[8] This expression represents only a *partial* semantic reading for the anaphoric clause. We discuss shortly the derivation of the total reading.

4.2. If what we have said so far is true, we would predict that a shift in the intonation center(s) of the antecedent clause (and thus a shift in its focus-presupposition relations) should cause an analogous shift in the interpretation of the anaphoric clause. This is in fact the case, as we can see from examples such as those in (15):

(15) (a) Prátt scolded Carmen for failing to turn in the homework, but it wouldn't
          have happened with Whítney
     (b) Pratt scolded Cármen for failing to turn in the homework, but it wouldn't
          have happened with Whítney

The anaphoric clause of (15a) has the interpretation that Whitney wouldn't have scolded Carmen for failing to turn in the homework. The interpretation of the anaphoric clause in (15b), however, is that Pratt wouldn't have scolded Whitney for failing to turn in the homework. We predict this result since we assign the presupposition components (16a) and (16b) to the semantic reading of the antecedent clauses of (15a) and (15b), respectively:

(16) (a) [x scolded Carmen for failing to turn in the homework]
     (b) [Pratt scolded x for failing to turn in the homework]

If these expressions are assigned to the semantic reading of the anaphoric clauses, then the focus of the anaphoric clauses, *Whítney*, will specify the variable of (16a) in sentence (15a) but the variable of (16b) in sentence (15b). Hence, we can account for the shift in meaning.

We must now ask just how the presuppositions of antecedent clauses are to be assigned to the semantic reading of anaphoric clauses. We first note that the anaphoric clauses of (15), as independent clauses, must be assigned semantic readings. Further, given the hypothesis we have established, such clauses have their own focus-presupposition relations. For example, the anaphoric clauses of (15) would have the representation in (17):

(17) [it wouldn't have happened with x], [x = Whitney]

Such an expression is produced, as before, by replacing the focus, *Whitney*, with a semantic variable. When we assign the presupposition of an antecedent clause to an anaphoric clause, we in fact *combine* the antecedent presupposition with the presupposition obtained for the anaphoric clause. In effect, the presupposition of the antecedent clause replaces the term *it* in the semantic reading of the anaphoric clause. If we take the expressions in (16) and insert these into (17) to replace *it*, we arrive at (18):

(18) (a) [[x scolded Carmen for failing to turn in the homework]
          wouldn't have happened with x], [x = Whitney]
     (b) [[Pratt scolded x for failing to turn in the homework]
          wouldn't have happened with x], [x = Whitney]

Here the focus of the anaphoric clause, *Whitney*, specifies both the variable of the antecedent presupposition and the variable within its own presupposition (17). In this way we derive the total semantic interpretation of the anaphoric clauses of (15).

4.3. The essence of our hypothesis, then, is that the presupposition derived from the antecedent clause is assigned to all following anaphoric clauses in sentences such as (1b) and (1c). In effect, all clauses "share" the same presupposition expression, but the variables within this expression are respecified for each new clause by the particular foci of that clause. Returning to our original comments on contrast, to say that the contrasted portions of the antecedent clause are excluded from the interpretation of the anaphoric clause is to say that the *foci* of the antecedent clause are excluded from the interpretation of the anaphoric clause. We attempt, then, to formulate the notion of contrast as a notion of "pairing of foci": a focus *x* of the antecedent clause and a focus *y* of an anaphoric clause are *paired* just in case *x* and *y* are interchangeable as specifications for the same variable in a given presupposition. When foci of an antecedent clause and an anaphoric clause are paired, only the presupposition of the antecedent clause is assigned to the anaphoric clause; the foci of the antecedent clause are excluded from the reading of the anaphoric clause.

4.4. We must now consider cases in which foci of an anaphoric clause cannot specify the variable(s) of the presupposition of an antecedent clause. We refer in particular to cases in which the foci of two clauses do not have the same semantic function within their respective clauses. In this regard, consider an ill-formed sentence such as (19):

(19) *Prátt knew the answer and Whítney did it too

The anaphoric clause, by itself, has the interpretation that Whitney carried out some action, that is, *Whitney* has the semantic function of volitional agent. On the other hand, *Pratt*, in the antecedent clause, is not assigned an agentive function since the phrase *knew the answer* does not denote a volitional act.

According to the procedure we have established, we would assign the presupposition (20) to the antecedent clause of (19):

(20) [*x* knew the answer]

However, this expression cannot be associated with the reading of the anaphoric clause since a semantic contradiction would result. Let us suppose, then, that foci can be paired only if they fulfill the same semantic function within their containing clauses. In a sentence such as (19), where the foci do not have the same semantic function, they cannot function as interchangeable specifications of the same variable (namely, that in (20)). In general, then, deviant sentences such as (19) are to be filtered out on the basis of conflicts in semantic interpretation between the clauses in question.

4.5. Turning our attention now to sentences such as (1a), we have already noted that the clauses of (1a) contain no contrasted elements, and both clauses receive neutral intonation. In fact, in such sentences it appears that foci cannot be paired. That is, for sentences such as (1a) we cannot form a presupposition for the antecedent clause such that its variables can be specified by foci of the anaphoric clause. With respect to sentences in which there are no paired foci, then, a reasonable hypothesis at this stage is that the anaphoric clause is assigned the entire semantic reading of the antecedent clause. In the case of (1a) the entire reading of the antecedent clause replaces *it* in the reading for the anaphoric clause, as shown in (21):

(21) [none of his friends realize
     [Pratt roasted a pig in the fireplace last year]]

The difference between sentences such as (1a) and sentences such as (1b) and (1c) can be illustrated in an interesting way by pairs of sentences such as (22a,b):

(22) (a) Prátt believes that there are unicorns, but Whítney doesn't believe it
     (b) Pratt believes that there are únicorns, but Whitney doesn't believe it

In (22a), where contrastive stress is placed on the two clause subjects, the interpretation of the second clause is that Whitney does not believe that there are unicorns. In (22b), on the other hand, where both clauses have neutral clause-final intonation centers, the interpretation of the anaphoric clause is that Whitney does not believe that Pratt believes that there are unicorns. This difference in interpretation can be accounted for on our hypothesis. We would predict that in (22a) the focus *Prátt* does not carry over into the interpretation of the anaphoric clause.[9] In (22b), on the other hand, where there are no paired foci,[10] the entire reading of the antecedent clause must be associated with the anaphoric clause.

With regard to the interpretation of anaphoric expressions, then, we must be able to recognize the difference between sentences in which antecedent and anaphoric clauses receive neutral intonation and sentences in which emphatic or contrastive stress is placed on given items within clauses. In sentences such as (1b), (1c), and (22a), the items *Pratt* and *Whitney* are emphatically stressed and are also inter-changeable as specifications for the same variable of the same presupposition. In such cases, only the presupposition of the antecedent clause is assigned to the reading of the anaphoric clause. In sentences such as (1a) and (22b), where neutral intonation is assigned to both clauses, the entire reading of the antecedent clause is assigned to the reading of the anaphoric clause. Thus, one of the constraints on possible interpretations of an anaphoric expression such as *it* is that foci of an antecedent clause will be excluded from its interpretation just in case these foci are paired with foci of the anaphoric clause, in the sense defined previously.

5. J. R. Ross (1969) considers data of the general sort we have examined here and proposes that sentences such as those we have discussed are to be derived by syntactic deletion. For example, a sentence such as (1b) would derive from a deep structure source such as that shown in (23):

(23)

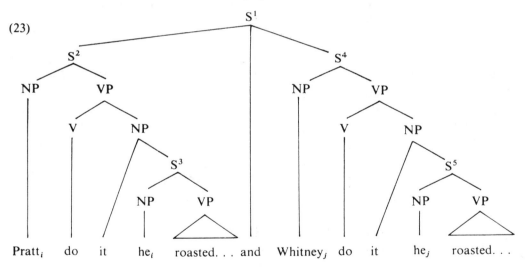

On Ross's hypothesis, a rule of S-deletion would operate to delete S^5 in (23), and various other processes would take place to ultimately yield the desired output.

[9] A further comment must be made concerning (22a). The antecedent clause and the anaphoric clause have the presuppositions (a) and (b), respectively:

    (a) [*x* believes that there are unicorns]
    (b) [*x* doesn't believe it]

Note that these are partially identical in that *x believes* occurs in both. We must stipulate that only the nonidentical portion of the presupposition of the antecedent clause is assigned to the reading of the anaphoric clause. Hence, only the portion of (a) including *that there are unicorns* will replace *it* in (b).

[10] Even if *unicorns* and *believe* are taken as the intonation centers of their respective clauses, these would not form paired foci since they would not be interchangeable as specifications for the same variable in the same given presupposition.

Given the general conventions on recoverability of deletion, however, we know that S^5 must be deleted under identity with some other S in the given structure. In cases such as (23), Ross's theory would allow S^5 to delete under identity with S^3, given the definition (24) of "sloppy identity":

(24) Constituents are identical if they have the same constituent structure and are identical morpheme for morpheme, or if they differ only as to pronouns, where the pronouns in each of the identical constituents are commanded by antecedents in the nonidentical portions of the phrase marker (Ross (1967, §5.2.3.1))

Thus, even though S^5 and S^3 have nonidentical pronoun subjects in (23), since these pronouns are each commanded by NPs in higher sentences, S^5 and S^3 are allowed to be considered identical.

In presenting the notion of sloppy identity, Ross argues that it is necessary in order to account for ambiguities of the sort found in sentences such as (25):

(25) Harold scratched his arm and so did I

This sentence, as Ross notes, can have either of the interpretations in (26):

(26) (a) Harold$_i$ scratched his$_i$ arm and I$_j$ scratched his$_i$ arm too
    (b) Harold$_i$ scratched his$_i$ arm and I$_j$ scratched my$_j$ arm too

Ross argues that a sentence such as (25) can be derived from either of the sentences of (26) by a rule of VP-deletion. If (25) derives from (26a), there is no problem, since the verb phrases of both clauses are identical (that is, *scratched his$_i$ arm*). In order to derive (25) from (26b), however, it is necessary to invoke the notion of sloppy identity since the two verb phrases are not identical (*scratched his$_i$ arm* and *scratched my$_j$ arm*).

5.1. Ambiguities such as those found in sentences such as (25) can be accounted for within the theory we have outlined here by adding the general principle (27):

(27) If some item is chosen as focus and is replaced by a variable in the semantic reading, then all following pronominal coreferents to that item may also be replaced by variables

To see how such a principle would be used, consider an example such as (28):

(28) Prátt$_i$ always makes fun of his$_i$ little brother, and Whítney$_j$ does it too

The anaphoric clause in (28) can be interpreted to mean either that Whitney makes fun of Pratt's little brother or that he makes fun of his own little brother. Taking *Prátt* as the focus of the antecedent clause, we can establish the two presuppositions in (29) for that clause, given principle (27):

(29) (a) [x always makes fun of his$_i$ little brother]
    (b) [x always makes fun of x's little brother]

We can now assign either of these presuppositions to the anaphoric clause, and the focus item *Whitney$_j$* specifies the variables of either (29a) or (29b). In this way, both readings can be associated with the anaphoric clause.[11]

---

[11] Note, in addition, that pronominal coreferents may also be emphatically stressed. Consider sentence (a):

    (a) Prátt$_i$ always makes fun of hís$_i$ little brother, and Whítney$_j$ does it too

A sentence such as (a) is unambiguous: the anaphoric clause is interpreted to mean only that Whitney makes fun of Whitney's little brother. This is predicted on our hypothesis since, in this particular case, both *Prátt$_i$* and *hís$_i$* in the antecedent clause are foci and thus must be replaced by variables. Only one presupposition could be derived for the antecedent clause of (a), namely (29b), and hence the anaphoric clause of (a) could have only the reading associated with (29b).

5.2. An interesting confirmation of our approach is found when more than one anaphoric clause is present. Consider, for example, sentence (30):[12]

(30) Pratt always makes fun of his little brother, and although Whitney does it also, Carmen doesn't do it

The interpretation of the two anaphoric clauses is that (*a*) although Whitney makes fun of Pratt's little brother, Carmen doesn't make fun of Pratt's little brother, or (*b*), although Whitney makes fun of Whitney's little brother, Carmen doesn't make fun of Carmen's little brother. In other words, each additional anaphoric clause has the understood pronominal references coreferential with its own subject or coreferential with the initial antecedent clause. Thus, for example, the final clause of (30) cannot have the interpretation that Carmen doesn't make fun of Whitney's little brother.

This state of affairs is predicted on our hypothesis since anaphoric clauses are assigned the presuppositions of antecedent clauses. That is, the antecedent clause of (30) has associated with it both of the presuppositions listed in (29), as before. We assign to all following anaphoric clauses either (29a) or (29b), and thus the focus items of all the anaphoric clauses will specify either the variables of (29a) or the variables of (29b). The final clause of (30) cannot have the interpretation that Carmen doesn't make fun of Whitney's little brother, since no presupposition such as (31) will be assigned to that clause:

(31) [x makes fun of Whitney's little brother]

The crucial point, then, is that all anaphoric clauses are assigned only those presuppositions which can be formed from the antecedent clause and no others.

A theory utilizing the notion of sloppy identity, on the other hand, generates sentences with impossible interpretations. For example, consider the representations in (32):[13]

(32) (a) CLAUSE 1: [Pratt$_i$ [makes fun of his$_i$ little brother]]
    (b) CLAUSE 2: [Whitney$_j$ [makes fun of his$_j$ little brother]]
    (c) CLAUSE 3: [Carmen$_k$ [doesn't make fun of his$_j$ little brother]]

S-deletion can occur in Clause 2 to produce *Whitney does it* since the relevant portion of the clause, *makes fun of his$_j$ little brother*, can be considered identical to the analogous portion of Clause 1, given a notion of sloppy identity. Further, deletion can occur in Clause 3 to produce *Carmen doesn't do it* since the relevant portion of that clause is identical with the analogous portion of Clause 2, and is identical (on sloppy identity) with the analogous portion of Clause 1 as well. Hence, it is possible to produce (30) with an interpretation paraphraseable as "Pratt makes fun of Pratt's little brother, and although Whitney makes fun of Whitney's little brother, Carmen doesn't make fun of Whitney's little brother."

Thus, a theory incorporating a notion of sloppy identity, as Ross states it, is insufficiently constrained, and a wider range of interpretations can be derived than is actually possible. On the hypothesis outlined here, we seek to constrain the possible interpretations of anaphoric expressions by requiring that anaphoric clauses be assigned presuppositions of the antecedent clause and no others.

6. The hypothesis sketched in this paper represents an initial step toward a theory of interpretation of anaphoric expressions such as *it*, and there is no doubt that

---

[12] I am indebted to Morris Halle for bringing such sentences to my attention.

[13] The bracketed expressions are intended to represent syntactic phrase markers of the clauses of (30) in the manner illustrated in (23). We give only enough detail to make the point at hand.

the principles discussed here need to be expanded and elaborated. For example, consider a sentence such as (33):[14]

(33) Prátt is afraid to call up girls, but yóu would never be such a fool

The speaker who utters (33) implies that to be afraid to call up girls is to be a fool. Note that *such* in the second clause of (33) is an anaphoric expression which modifies, in some sense, the NP *a fool*. We might, then, associate in some manner the presupposition of the antecedent clause with the anaphoric clause (34):

(34) . . . but you would never be *such* a fool
$\updownarrow$
[*x* is afraid to call up girls]

Hence, the presupposition of the antecedent clause would provide a specification of the anaphoric phrase *such a fool.*

We have restricted ourselves here, however, to a narrow range of sentences, and it remains to be seen whether our hypothesis can be generalized in a natural fashion to cover a wider range of data.

REFERENCES

Akmajian, A. (1968), "An interpretive principle for certain anaphoric expressions," unpublished paper, M.I.T.

Akmajian, A. (1970), *Aspects of the Grammar of Focus in English*, unpublished Ph.D. dissertation, M.I.T.

Anderson, S. R. (1970), "How to get *even*," in *Language Research Reports*, 2, Cambridge, Mass.: Language Research Foundation; also in *Language* (1972), *48*, 893–906.

Chomsky, N. (1971), "Deep Structure, Surface Structure, and Semantic Interpretation," in Jakobovits and Steinberg.

Jackendoff, R. S. (1969), *Some Rules of Semantic Interpretation for English*, unpublished Ph.D. dissertation, M.I.T.

Jackendoff, R. S. (1972), *Semantic Interpretation in Generative Grammar*, Cambridge, Mass.: M.I.T. Press.

Jakobovits, L. A., and P. D. Steinberg, eds. (1971), *Semantics: An Interdisciplinary Reader in Philosophy, Psychology, Linguistics and Anthropology*, Cambridge: Cambridge University Press.

Lakoff, G. (1971), "On Generative Semantics," in Jakobovits and Steinberg.

Ross, J. R. (1967), *Constraints on Variables in Syntax*, unpublished Ph.D. dissertation, M.I.T.

Ross, J. R. (1969), "Guess who?" in *Papers from the Fifth Regional Meeting of the Chicago Linguistics Society*, University of Chicago Linguistics Department.

[14] I am indebted to David Vetter for pointing out such cases to me.

conjoined questions and conjoined relative clauses in serbo-croatian[1]

Wayles Browne

Massachusetts Institute of Technology
and
Institut za lingvistiku, Filozofski fakultet, Zagreb

1.1. A direct *yes-no* question in English, as is well-known, has inversion of subject and first auxiliary, as illustrated in (1):

(1) Do you study by yourself?

In Serbo-Croatian, *yes-no* questions normally contain the question marker *li*, as in (2a), or *da li*, as in (2b):

(2) (a) *Učite   li sami?*
        you study   self
        'Do you study by yourself?'
    (b) *Da li učite sami?*

Li requires the finite verb (*učite* here) to be put first in the clause, and *li*, being an enclitic, immediately follows this first element. *Da li* comes at the beginning of the clause and does not require any word-order changes, except that any enclitics present must follow it directly since it counts as the first element of the clause.

1.2. We will say that a clause is FORMULATED AS A (direct, *yes-no*) QUESTION if it follows the surface structure patterns set forth in 1.1.

1.3. In Serbo-Croatian, when clauses are linked by the disjunctive coordinating

[1] My thanks to A. Nakić and D. Vićan for generous help with examples. See Browne (1971) for a practically-oriented discussion of the differences between Serbo-Croatian and English, with further examples.

conjunction *ili* 'or', only the first one can be formulated as a question. The examples in (3) are, then, ungrammatical:

(3) (a) **Učite li sami ili idete   li u   školu?*
                          you go   to school
      (b) **Da li učite sami ili da li idete u školu?*

Rather, conjuncts subsequent to the first are formulated as statements, as can be seen by comparing (4) and (5):

(4) *Učite li sami ili idete u školu?*
(5) *Idete u školu*
      'You go to school'

The absence of (3) from the language and the existence of (4) both appear to be most curious facts, especially when compared with the situation in English and other languages in which *yes-no* questions conjoin with one another and not with non-questions, and one suspects that the two facts are connected. Suspicions deepen when we consider the semantics of (4): it is translated by two conjoined clauses which are both formulated as questions—'Do you study by yourself or do you go to school?' —and it asks for an answer to the second member just as much as to the first.

There is further evidence that the conjuncts other than the first are indeed questions on some nonsurface level. For this we turn to the behavior of certain indefinites. The relative interrogatives (*k*-words—cf. English *wh*-words) can be used as indefinites in questions and conditionals but not in affirmative declaratives. Thus, with *(t)ko* 'who; anyone, someone', (6a) is possible but (6b) is not:[2]

(6) (a) *Da li vas (t)ko podučava?*
                  you   teaches
          'Does anyone teach you?'
      (b) **(T)ko vas podučava*
          'Anyone teaches you'

This indefinite can occur in the declarative-looking second conjunct when the first conjunct is a question (or conditional) but not otherwise:

(7) (a) *Učite li sami ili vas (t)ko podučava?*
          'Do you study by yourself or does someone teach you?'
      (b) **Učite sami ili vas (t)ko podučava*
          'You study by yourself or someone teaches you'

1.4. The only genuine examples of conjoined questions seem to be those conjoined with *ili*. *Ali* 'but', *a* 'but, and' appear not to be used between questions. *I* 'and' can join sentences having no direct relation to one another; that is, it is a much looser tie. When it joins questions, all the conjuncts are formulated as questions, as in (8):

(8) *Da li učite sami, i da li dobro napredujete?*
                          well   you progress
      'Do you study by yourself, and are you progressing well?'

2.1. A Serbo-Croatian clause is FORMULATED AS A RELATIVE CLAUSE if it begins with a relative word or a phrase containing one. There are relative words that play the role of noun phrases (*koji* 'which, who') and of various other types of constituents.

---

[2] Here *vas* is enclitic and comes after the first element, whatever that may be.

Certain details differ from English and other languages: for example, there is no extraposition, and relative words cannot be extracted from prepositional or noun phrases to be moved to the front by themselves, as shown in (9):

(9) (a) *zemlja   o   kojoj znamo   vrlo malo*
       a country about which we know very little
    (b) **zemlja kojoj znamo vrlo malo o*

Relative clauses on the same item can be joined by various coordinating conjunctions such as *a, ali, ili, i*.

Consider the examples in (10):

(10) (a) *zemlja o kojoj znamo vrlo malo   a   koju smatramo   važnom*
                                      and, but which we consider important
     (b) *zemlja o kojoj znamo vrlo malo a smatramo je važnom*
                                                          it

As shown by the alternants (10a) and (10b), the second (third, etc.) of a conjoined series can but need not be formulated as a relative clause. If it is not, then a personal pronoun (*je* here), whose antecedent is the same as that of the corresponding relative clause, appears in the normal place in the clause.[3] Again, compare the corresponding English examples in (11), in which each conjunct must be formulated as a relative clause:

(11) (a) a country about which we know very little but which we consider important
     (b) *a country about which we know very little but we consider it important
     (c) a country which we know very little about but (which) we consider important

Example (11c) shows conjunction reduction of two similar object pronouns and is not parallel to the Serbo-Croatian situation.

2.1.1. The fact that personal pronouns appear in conjoined relative clauses might be exploited in order to argue that the personal pronouns represent a stage on the way toward the relative pronouns, that is, that the derivation runs as in (12):[4]

(12) *zemlja* (Rel *znamo . . . o zemlji a smatramo zemlju važnom*)
     → Pronominalization →
     zemlja (Rel *znamo . . . o njoj a smatramo je važnom*)
     → Relative formation →
     zemlja (*o kojoj znamo . . . a smatramo je važnom*)

According to (12), first a rule would form personal pronouns, and then the relativization rule, where applicable, would incorporate them into relative pronouns.

The argument in favor of pronominalization preceding relative formation is strengthened by another fact. Relative clauses also exist which begin with *što* 'what, that' and which contain a personal pronoun referring back to the antecedent, as in (13):

(13) *prednosti   što   ih   autor   opisuje*
     advantages that them the author describes

Što would then be the spelling of a "Rel" into which no personal pronoun had been incorporated.[5]

---

[3] This personal pronoun is deleted in subject position, just like any other unstressed personal pronoun.

[4] Here "Rel" indicates a marker of relativehood. *Njoj* is the case form of 'it' used after *o*.

[5] These clauses are possible only when certain conditions, so far unclarified, are fulfilled, depending in part on the antecedent's characteristics and its position in its own clause.

2.1.2. Unfortunately, however, it is not clear how to rule out the other possibility, namely, that pronominalization follows relative formation and affects those constituents which relative formation has left untouched.

3.1. We have seen that obligatorily in conjoined *yes-no* questions and optionally in conjoined relatives the conjuncts after the first one lack the distinguishing surface structure patterns of questions (relatives). This, we suggest, results from a process of conjunction reduction of grammatical elements like that observed by Kiparsky (1968) for Indo-European tense, mood, and case. At some stage of the derivation of a question, there is a marker (say, "Q") present in the clause, and relative clauses contain a marker "Rel." These markers can be spelled out in various ways, and they trigger such rules as verb-fronting in *li*-questions and *wh*-fronting in relatives. But before certain of these rules operate, conjunction reduction can remove some of the "Rel" or "Q" markers, leaving behind a clause with no outward, visible sign of its relative or interrogative nature.

3.1.1. We can propose an explanation for the obligatoriness of conjunction reduction in questions. Both question markers, *li* and *da li*, require that something be put first in the clause. However, first position is already occupied by the conjunction *ili*, and a clash would result if the question marker were to remain.

3.1.2. Such an explanation is per se not conclusive. Relatives and subordinating conjunctions must come first in a clause, as shown with *da* in (14a), and yet the question marker can be put before a subordinator, as in (14b), as can coordinating conjunctions.

(14) (a)   *Da   predjemo ulicu*
            that we cross street
            'Let's cross the street'
      (b)   *Da li da predjemo ulicu?*
            'Shall we cross the street?'

But it still may be that there is some constraint that rules out the possibility of an *ili* and a *da li* or an *ili* and a verb + *li* in first place. We may think of an order chart: *da li* (and V + *li*) can be followed by a relative or subordinator but cannot be preceded by anything except such an insubstantial conjunction as *i*.[6]

3.2. In the case of questions, some recent work in grammar (Sadock (1969), for example) attributes their properties solely to their being embedded in abstract higher sentences such as "I ask you . . ." and structures to that effect. It might also be held that the configuration in which a clause is located is sufficient to define it as relative. The facts of Serbo-Croatian by no means argue against such hypotheses of configuration-determinedness. They do, however, suggest that the various rules of syntax which give clauses their shape are not sensitive merely to the larger configuration in which a clause finds itself: the clause itself must get some feature or marker assigned to it, which can then take part in syntactic operations. The reason is that our nonfirst conjuncts have the same upper context as first conjuncts; that is, they are embedded in their higher sentences in just the same way. And if we suppose that the rules are merely string-sensitive, that is, look merely for a left-hand context containing a verb of asking or an antecedent, then the problem arises of why nonfirst conjuncts have any interrogative or relative properties at all (see (7a) and (10a)).

---

[6] We know that *i* never counts as the "first element" for the purposes of placing enclitics, unlike *ili, ali,* and some other conjunctions, which do count as such optionally.

REfERENCES

Browne, W. (1971), "On Conjoined Questions and Conjoined Relative Clauses in English and Serbo-Croatian," in R. Filipović, ed., *Studies 3*, Yugoslav Serbo-Croatian–English Contrastive Grammar Project, Zagreb.

Kiparsky, P. (1968), "Tense and mood in Indo-European syntax," *Foundations of Language*, *4*, 30–57.

Sadock, J. M. (1969), "Hypersentences," *Papers in Linguistics*, *1*, 283–370.

conoitions
on transformations[1]

Noam Chomsky

Massachusetts Institute of Technology

1. From the point of view that I adopt here, the fundamental empirical problem of linguistics is to explain how a person can acquire knowledge of language. For our purposes, we can think of a language as a set of structural descriptions of sentences, where a full structural description determines (in particular) the sound and meaning of a linguistic expression. Knowledge of a language can be expressed in the form of a system of rules (a grammar) that generates the language. To approach the fundamental empirical problem, we attempt to restrict the class of potential human languages by setting various conditions on the form and function of grammars; the term "universal grammar" has commonly been used to refer to the system of general constraints of this sort. With a narrow and restrictive formulation of the principles of universal grammar, it may become possible to account for the remarkable human ability, on the basis of limited and degenerate evidence, to select a particular grammar that expresses one's knowledge of language and makes possible the use of this knowledge.

For heuristic purposes we may distinguish two aspects of universal grammar: (*a*) conditions on form, and (*b*) conditions on function—that is, (*a*) conditions on the systems that qualify as grammars, and (*b*) conditions on the way the rules of a grammar apply to generate structural descriptions. In the terminology of Chomsky (1965, Chapter 1) and earlier work, these are, respectively, conditions on the class $G_1, G_2, \ldots$ of admissible grammars and on the function f that assigns the structural description $SD_{f(i,j)}$ to the sentence S_i generated by the grammar G_j. The distinction is one of convenience, not principle, in the sense that we might choose to deal with particular phenomena under one or the other category of conditions. The distinction might be carried over to particular grammars as well. That is, while it has generally

[1] For very helpful comments on an earlier draft of this paper, I am indebted to Ray Dougherty, Morris Halle, Richard Kayne, and Howard Lasnik, among others. I am indebted to the Guggenheim Foundation for a fellowship grant that enabled me to complete the work presented here.

been assumed that particular grammars contain specific rules whereas conditions on the functioning of rules are assigned to universal grammar, there is no logical necessity to make this assumption. It is possible that particular grammars differ in conditions of application, just as it is possible that some specific rules actually belong to universal grammar.[2]

To illustrate, we can consider the enumeration of distinctive features or the specification of the form of phonological rules to be conditions of the first sort, that is, conditions on the form of grammars. Or consider the definition of a grammatical transformation as a structure-dependent mapping of phrase markers into phrase markers that is independent of the grammatical relations or meanings expressed in these grammatical relations. This definition makes certain operations available as potential transformations, excluding others. Thus an operation converting an arbitrary string of symbols into its mirror image is not a grammatical transformation, and transformations generally apply to phrase markers that meet some condition on analyzability with no regard to other associated properties.

To take a standard example, the Passive transformation (reducing it to essentials) applies to any phrase marker that can be "factored" into five successive substrings in such a way that the second and fourth are noun phrases, the third a verb of a particular category (perhaps determined by some semantic property), and the first and fifth anything at all (including nothing). Thus the structural condition defining the transformation can be given in the form (Z, NP, V_x, NP, Y). The transformation rearranges the noun phrases in a fixed way. It will, therefore, apply to the phrase markers underlying the sentences of (1), converting them to the corresponding passive forms:

(1) (a) Perhaps–John–read–the book–intelligently
    (b) John–received–the book
    (c) John–regards–Bill–as a friend
    (d) John–painted–the wall–gray
    (e) John–expects–the food–to be good to eat

Evidently, the semantic and grammatical relation of the main verb to the following noun phrase varies in these examples (there is no relation at all in (e)), but these relations are of no concern to the transformation, which applies blindly in all cases, producing *Perhaps the book was read intelligently by John, The book was received by John, Bill is regarded as a friend by John, The wall was painted gray by John, The food is expected to be good to eat by John.* By requiring that all transformations be structure-dependent in this specific sense, we limit the class of possible grammars, excluding many imaginable systems.

I will presuppose here, without further discussion, a set of additional conditions on the form of grammar constituting what I have called the "extended standard theory" (see Chomsky (1970b; 1972a)). Other conditions on the choice of possible transformations that also seem to me plausible and suggestive, if controversial, are outlined in Emonds (1970).[3]

The conditions on the form of grammar mentioned so far are quite abstract and still permit much too wide a range of potential grammars. One might therefore

---

[2] For discussion of limited generality of conditions, see Ross (1967), Chomsky (1968), and Postal (1971).

[3] As already noted, the distinction between conditions on form and conditions on function is, in part, one of convenience. Thus Emonds' constraints could be formulated as conditions on the applicability of arbitrarily chosen transformations.

look for much more specific restrictions. An example, to which I return, is the "Complementizer Substitution Universal" in (2):[4]

(2) Only languages with clause-initial COMP permit a COMP-substitution transformation

This principle presupposes that COMP is a universal element that may appear in various sentence positions and asserts that an item can be moved into COMP position only when COMP is initial. In particular, "*wh*-words"—the relativized constituents in relative clauses or questioned constituents in interrogatives—can be moved only to the left, such movement being permitted only when there is an initial COMP in the phrase to which the transformation is being applied.

It would be quite natural to explore further along these lines. Thus one might try to enumerate "major transformations" such as Question Formation, Imperative, and so on from which languages may draw, with some permitted variation and minor "housekeeping rules" (Bach (1965; 1971)). It may well be that transformations fall into various categories meeting quite different conditions. By constructing a more intricate, more highly articulated theory of grammar in such ways as these, we can perhaps move toward a solution of the fundamental empirical problem.

A second approach attempts to constrain the functioning of grammatical rules and thereby to limit the generative power of grammars of a given form. The earliest suggestions appear in Chomsky (1964)[5] (namely, the condition of "Recoverability of Deletion,"[6] the "*A*-over-*A* Condition," and so on). Another example, to which I will return, is the Insertion Prohibition suggested in Chomsky (1965), which prevents transformations from inserting morphological material into sentences that have already been passed in the cycle. Many examples are discussed in a very important study by Ross (1967), where a number of specific conditions are proposed. These conditions are formulated in such a way as to restrict severely the operation of the rules of grammars while not affecting their form. Thus such conditions contribute toward a solution of the fundamental empirical problem.[7]

In this paper I want to consider conditions on the functioning of grammars once again, specifically, conditions on how transformations apply. As noted, I assume here the general framework of the extended standard theory and, in particular, the lexicalist theory of base structures and nominals discussed in Chomsky (1970a). The work leading to the extended standard theory suggested constraints on base structures and on the relations between derivations and semantic representations but said little about transformations. Here, I will explore some conditions on the application of transformations within the framework of the extended standard theory.

---

[4] J. Bresnan's reformulation (1970) of L. Baker's "Q-Universal" (Baker (1970)).

[5] This work appears in three versions, which differ in their treatment of these problems. The first is in H. G. Lunt, ed. (1964), *Proceedings of the Ninth International Congress of Linguists, 1962*, The Hague: Mouton; the second is in J. A. Fodor and J. J. Katz, eds. (1964), *Structure of Language*, Englewood Cliffs, N.J.: Prentice-Hall; the third is listed in the bibliography. A further revision, in lectures given at Berkeley in January 1967, appears in Chomsky (1968).

[6] On the difficulty of defining this properly and the importance of the issue, see Peters and Ritchie (1973).

[7] Another approach toward solving this problem would be to refine the evaluation measure for grammars. As explained in Chomsky (1965), it seems to me that only limited progress is likely along these lines. It has been suggested in recent work that no evaluation measures are necessary, and this is surely a logical possibility (see Chomsky (1965, pp. 36–37)). Those who offer this suggestion, however, typically propose theories of grammar that make infinitely many grammars available compatible with any imaginable data, so that an evaluation measure is necessary in these cases. The point is, I suspect, that "natural" evaluation measures are generally presupposed, without analysis.

As an example of a possible condition on transformations, consider the "*A*-over-*A*" principle, stated in (3):[8]

(3) If a transformation applies to a structure of the form

$$[_\alpha \ldots [_A \ldots] \ldots]$$

where α is a cyclic node, then it must be so interpreted as to apply to the maximal phrase of the type *A*

Consider again the Passive transformation with a structural condition imposing a factorization into (*X*, NP, V, NP, *Y*). So formulated, the rule would apply to the examples in (4), with the factorization indicated by –, giving the impossible forms in (5):

(4) (a) John and–Bill–saw–Mary
  (b) The man who saw–Mary–bought–the book
  (c) John's winning–the race–surprised–me
(5) (a) *John and Mary was seen by Bill
  (b) *The man who saw the book was bought by Mary
  (c) *John's winning I was surprised by the race

But the misapplication of the rule in these cases is blocked by the *A*-over-*A* Condition (3). This principle requires that *John and Bill*, *the man who saw Mary*, and *John's winning the race* are the factors selected by the first NP in the structural condition of the Passive in the case of (a), (b), and (c), respectively.

Notice that the condition (3) does not establish an absolute prohibition against transformations that extract a phrase of type *A* from a more inclusive phrase of type *A*. Rather, it states that if a transformational rule is nonspecific with respect to the configuration defined, it will be interpreted in such a way as to satisfy the condition. Thus it would be possible to formulate a (more complex) rule with a structural condition imposing the factorization indicated by – in (4); such a rule might extract *Bill*, *Mary*, and *the race*, respectively. Alternatively, one might interpret the *A*-over-*A* constraint as legislating against any rule that extracts a phrase of type *A* from a more inclusive phrase *A*. The former interpretation, which in effect takes the *A*-over-*A* Condition to be an integral part of an evaluation measure, is perhaps more natural, and I will adopt it tentatively here, for this and other conditions to be discussed. Thus the *A*-over-*A* Condition as interpreted here does not prevent the application of *wh*-Movement to form (6) from (7), or the application of Pseudo-Cleft Formation to form (8) from (9), or the application of Conjunct Movement to form (10) from (11):[9]

(6) Who would you approve of my seeing
(7) You would approve of [my seeing who][10]
(8) The only person John admires is himself

---

[8] This is the formulation in Chomsky (1968), where a number of examples and problems are discussed. We may assume here that the cyclic nodes are S and NP.

[9] In principle. On the dubious status of this rule, see Dougherty (1970). We will return briefly to such examples as (6) and (8).

[10] The impossibility of *Whose would you approve of seeing John* from *You would approve of whose seeing John* can perhaps be attributed to a principle that requires that if the specifier of a noun phrase or adjective phrase (in the sense of Chomsky (1970a)) is extracted, then the whole phrase must be extracted: thus the same principle would prevent the formation of *Which did you see books* from *You saw which books*, or *How is John tall* from *John is how tall*. See Ross (1967) for relevant discussion.

(9)   [The only person [John admires himself]] is Predicate
(10) John met Bill
(11) [John and Bill] met

In contrast, we interpret the Complementizer Substitution Universal (2) as imposing an absolute restriction against rules that move an item to the right to a COMP position. But the *A*-over-*A* principle, rather than legislating against the existence of certain rules, permits an ambiguous and unspecific formulation of such rules as Passive, constraining their application in a specific way. The logic of this approach is essentially that of the theory of markedness.

Suppose that we were to formulate the Passive with the structural condition (12):

(12) (X, NP, VY, NP, Z)

Then the rule will apply to either of the italicized noun phrases in (13) to give (14a) or (14b):

(13) PRO took *advantage* of *Bill*
(14) (a) Advantage was taken of Bill
      (b) Bill was taken advantage of

The *A*-over-*A* Condition does not prevent the desired ambiguous application in this case. The same formulation of Passive[11] permits "pseudo-passives" such as *The plan was argued about all day* and *The brat insists on being given in to*. For this formulation of the rule to apply correctly, it is necessary to add the condition that the third term in the factorization (12) be a semantic unit. For example, the sentence *England was lived in by many people* is more natural than *England was died in by many people*, but only when *live in* is interpreted as "reside" and not as in "we really lived in England" in the sense of "in England, we really lived."[12]

Quite generally, the terms of the structural condition of a transformation are either variables or single nonterminals, the case in question being one of the rare exceptions. A single nonterminal is a semantic unit—it has a "reading," in the sense of Katz and others. Thus we might consider the general condition (15):

(15) Each factor imposed by a transformation either is a morphological or semantic unit or corresponds to a variable in the structural condition of the transformation

This condition, along with the *A*-over-*A* Condition (3), permits Passive to be formulated with the structural condition (12), constraining the application of the rule properly in quite a range of cases.

2. To pursue the matter further, let us assume (following, in essentials, Bresnan (1970)) that there is a universal element COMP and that the base system of English includes the rules in (16):[13]

---

[11] Again, oversimplified, overlooking auxiliaries, the agent phrase, and the composite nature of the rule discussed in Chomsky (1970a). Using the terminology suggested there, the structural condition should contain a term after the first NP which can be an arbitrary sequence of specifiers.

[12] See Chomsky (1965, pp. 104, 218). Recall that although transformations are independent of grammatical or semantic relations, they do, of course, reflect properties of lexical items and lexical categories.

[13] More precisely, these "rules" may be factored into several rules that provide intermediate structures that need not concern us here. Much of what we shall suggest will hold under certain other assumptions about English grammar as well; I give these, without further justification, for concreteness. In (16), P stands for "Preposition," T for "Tense," M for "Modal"; and *to* and *ing* are the items that appear (excluding tense and modal), respectively, in *for him to remain is a nuisance, his remaining is a nuisance* (where *for* and possessive, respectively, are assigned to the accompanying noun phrases, the presence of *for* depending on the main verb). We may assume that one realization of M is the element *subjunctive* discussed in Culicover (1971) in his analysis of imperatives and related structures (and thus subjunctives are assumed here to be tensed). We return to some more specific rules later.

(16)

$$\text{(a) } S \rightarrow COMP\ NP \begin{Bmatrix} T(M) \\ (for)\text{-}to \\ \text{'}s\text{-}ing \end{Bmatrix} VP$$

(b) COMP $\rightarrow$ P NP $\pm$ WH

We assume that the NP or P NP of COMP can be replaced by the *wh*-phrase of questions and relatives (Emonds' structure-preserving hypothesis determines which of these positions is filled). Following Baker (1970), I assume that $+$WH (essentially, his "Q") underlies direct and indirect questions, while $-$WH underlies relatives.[14] We impose the condition that no lexical item can be inserted into COMP by base rules; that is, we require that the terminal string dominated by COMP in the base is null. If a $-$WH COMP is not filled by a *wh*-phrase, it will optionally be realized as *that* (otherwise null) if the auxiliary contains Tense. We may assume that *whether* derives from *wh*-Placement on *either* and *wh*-Movement (see Katz and Postal (1964)) and that free relatives such as *I read what he gave me* derive from full relatives with unspecified heads (*I read* [$_{NP}$PRO[$_S$*he gave me it*]]—see Bresnan (1972) for a detailed analysis). Further details and appropriate rules will be given as we proceed.

Let us return to the Passive transformation which, reduced to essentials, applies to a phrase marker of the form NP–V–NP–X, rearranging the NPs. Consider the sentence (17):

(17) I believe the dog is hungry

This can be analyzed into the successive substrings *I, believe, the dog, is hungry*, which are NP, V, NP, X, respectively, so that the transformation should yield **The dog is believed is hungry (by me)*. In exactly the same way, the sentence *The dog is believed to be hungry (by me)* derives from (18), with the analysis indicated:

(18) [$_S$[$_{NP}$I][$_{VP}$[$_V$believe][$_S$[$_{NP}$the dog][$_{VP}$to be hungry]]]]

Notice that there is no problem in explaining why the Passive transformation, with its domain defined in terms of a structural condition on phrase markers in the conventional way, applies to (18); the problem, rather, is to explain why it does not apply to (17).[15]

The most obvious distinction between (17) and (18) is that the embedded sentence in (17) is tensed (finite) while the corresponding sentence of (18) is nontensed. Suppose, then, that we propose the tentative principle in (19):

(19) Items cannot be extracted from tensed sentences

[14] Presumably, either may underlie nominal complements, as in *the idea that S, the question whether S*. Conditions for *wh*-Movement vary slightly, particularly in appositive clauses. See Postal (1971, pp. 71–72) for some discussion.

[15] Under any formulation of the theory of transformations so far proposed, it would require an extra condition on the transformation to exclude (18) from the domain of the Passive with the structural condition (X, NP, V, NP, Y). One might imagine a different theory in which the domain of a transformation is defined not by a structural condition of the familiar sort but rather by a condition on grammatical relations: thus "Passive" in this theory might be defined not in terms of the structural condition (X, NP, V, NP, Y), but in terms of the total configuration which expresses subject and object as relational terms. Under this revised theory, Passive would not apply to (18) unless the configuration were modified by a transformation raising the subject of the embedded sentence to the object position in the matrix sentence. There is, however, no empirical motivation for such a revision of the theory of transformations. It would, furthermore, be ill-advised in the case of Passive because of pseudo-passives (see the discussion following (14)), double passives such as (14), indirect object constructions, and so on.

Note that COMP will not block factorization of (18) in accordance with the structural condition of the Passive transformation if the terminal string dominated by COMP is null, as we have assumed.

The principle of Insertion Prohibition mentioned earlier states that morphological material cannot be inserted into sentences that have been passed in the cycle. If, in fact, Insertion Prohibition is restricted to tensed sentences, we can generalize (19) to incorporate this principle.

Let us restrict our attention initially to rules of extraction that move an item to the left (as in the case of Passive) and to rules of insertion that move an item from the left into an embedded phrase. With this restrictive assumption, we can generalize (19) to (20), incorporating the Insertion Prohibition; we henceforth refer to (20) as the "Tensed-S Condition":[16]

(20) No rule can involve X, Y in the structure

$$\ldots X \ldots [_\alpha \ldots Y \ldots] \ldots$$

where α is a tensed sentence

To understand the application of the Insertion Prohibition as a special case of this principle, consider the sentences in (21):

(21) (a) The candidates each hated the other(s)
      (b) The candidates each expected the other(s) to win
      (c) The candidates each expected that the other(s) would win

Dougherty (1970) has argued that such a sentence as *The men hated each other* derives from *The men each hated the other(s)* (ultimately, from *Each of the men hated the other one(s)*) by a rule that moves *each* into the determiner position in *the other(s)*.[17] Assuming this, note that the sentences of (21) should be transformed into those of (22):

(22) (a) The candidates hated each other
      (b) The candidates expected each other to win
      (c) *The candidates expected that each other would win

Only the first two cases are permitted; (22c) is blocked, as required, by the Tensed-S Condition.

Before turning to other examples, let us consider some facts that lead us to a supplementary principle. Suppose that (23b) derives from the underlying form (23a):

(23) (a) John expected [$_S$PRO to win]
      (b) John expected to win

Now notice that from (24a) we can derive (24b), whereas from (25a) we cannot derive (25b):

(24) (a) The candidates each expected [$_S$PRO to defeat the other]
      (b) The candidates expected to defeat each other
(25) (a) The men each expected [$_S$the soldier to shoot the other]
      (b) *The men expected the soldier to shoot each other

---

[16] A weaker assumption would be that α is a language-specific parameter in the condition. In this exploratory study I will do no more than suggest a number of possibilities and investigate their consequences in English.

Notice that one rule that obviously does not satisfy the condition is Coreference Assignment (however it is formulated). Thus the pronoun can be anaphoric in *John said that he would leave*, for example. The same rule also applies within coordinate structures (for example, *John said that he and Bill would leave*) and others that block various other types of rules.

[17] I presuppose Dougherty's work (1970) here with no further specific reference. Notice that if one were to accept the alternative analysis of Jackendoff (1969), principle (20) would again apply— in this case, not to a movement rule but to a rule of interpretation.

To account for this difference, let us postulate a second principle, the "Specified Subject Condition" (26), where by "specified subject" we mean a subject NP that contains either lexical items or a pronoun that is not anaphoric:

(26) No rule can involve X, Y in the structure

$$\ldots X \ldots [_\alpha \ldots Z \ldots -WYV \ldots] \ldots$$

where Z is the specified subject of WYV in α

We shall return to this principle later to give a more careful formulation. As set forth here, it suffices to distinguish (25), with the specified subject $Z = $ *the soldier* in the embedded sentence α, from (23) and (24), which have no specified subject in that position.[18]

Within the extended standard theory, as developed in the references cited earlier, both NP and S are nodes to which cyclic operations apply, and the notion "subject of" is defined not only in S but also in such NPs as (27), where *John*, in all cases, is the "subject," in an extended sense of this term:

(27) (a) John's refusal to leave
(b) John's picture of Bill
(c) John's strategy for victory

Correspondingly, in (26) α can be either NP or S. Examples (24) and (25) illustrate the application of (26) where $\alpha = $ S. The examples in (28)–(31) illustrate the application of this condition where $\alpha = $ NP:

(28) (a) The men each saw [$_{NP}$pictures of the other]
(b) The men saw pictures of each other
(29) (a) The men each saw [$_{NP}$John's pictures of the other]
(b) *The men saw John's pictures of each other
(30) (a) COMP you saw [$_{NP}$pictures of who]
(b) Who did you see pictures of
(31) (a) COMP you saw [$_{NP}$John's pictures of who]
(b) *Who did you see John's pictures of

The rule of *each*-Insertion applies to (28a) but is blocked by the Specified Subject Condition in (29). The rule of *wh*-Movement applies to (30a) but is blocked by the same condition in the case of (31).[19]

Let us next turn to the rule of *it*-Replacement that produces such sentences as *John is easy to please*. Consider the examples in (32) and (33):

(32) (a) It is pleasant for the rich for poor immigrants to do the hard work
(b) It is a waste of time for us for them to teach us Latin

[18] Helke (1971) observes that *each*-Movement is not permitted in such cases as *The candidates each expected the others to clash* (**The candidates expected each other to clash*), *The candidates each expected the others to work together* (**The candidates expected each other to work together*). However, it seems that this results from the operation of independent rules that also exclude **The men walked between each other* from *The men each walked between the others*. What seems to be involved is a restriction on *each*-Movement in the case when the NP *the other* has the features [+ totality, − individual] in the system of Dougherty (1970), where some relevant examples are discussed.

[19] Some speakers (myself included) find a three-way gradation of acceptability, with (30b) better than *Who did you see the pictures of*, which is in turn preferable to (31b). A refinement of condition (26) incorporating the feature [definite] as well as the property of lexical specification might be proposed to accommodate these judgments. Specified subjects in NPs are [+ definite]. If (26) is revised to include [+ definite] as well as specified subjects, then (31b) will involve a double violation and *Who did you see the pictures of* only a single violation. This might account for the gradation of acceptability.

(33) (a) It is pleasant for the rich to do the hard work
    (b) It is a waste of time for us to learn Latin
    (c) It is easy for us to learn Latin

The rule of *it*-Replacement applies to the examples of (33) to give the corresponding forms in (34), but it does not apply to (32) to give (35):

(34) (a)   The hard work is pleasant for the rich to do
    (b)   Latin is a waste of time for us to learn
    (c)   Latin is easy for us to learn
(35) (a)   *The hard work is pleasant for the rich for poor immigrants to do
    (b)   *Latin is a waste of time for us for them to teach us

These data follow from our previous assumptions if we suppose that the phrases *for the rich* and *for us* in (32) and (33) form part of the predicate of the matrix sentence, with the subject PRO of the embedded sentence deleted in (33), exactly as in the case of (23). (The lexical item *easy* differs from *pleasant* and *waste of time* in that the rule of deletion is obligatory in the case of *easy* in this context.) Thus we take the structures underlying (33) to be of the form (36), as is clearly true (under our general assumptions) in the case of (32):

(36) It–is Predicate for NP–[$_s$NP–VP]

This assumption is not unnatural on other grounds as well. Thus the leftmost *for*-phrase in all the cited examples is more readily detachable than the *for*-phrase in (37), for example:

(37) It is intolerable for John to have to study Latin

Compare the variants (38) with (39):

(38) (a) For the rich, it is pleasant for poor immigrants to do the hard work
    (b) For us, it is a waste of time to learn Latin
    (c) Latin is a waste of time to learn, for us
    (d) Latin is easier to learn for us than for John
    (e) It is easier to learn Latin for us than for John
(39) (a) For John, it is intolerable to have to study Latin
    (b) It is intolerable to have to study Latin, for John
    (c) It is more intolerable to have to study Latin for us than for John

The examples in (39), if acceptable at all, are interpreted somewhat differently from (37): in (39), it must be understood that John finds it intolerable to have to study Latin, but this is not the case in (37). On the other hand, such examples as (38) seem true stylistic variants of the corresponding forms of (32)–(34). We might capture this fact by limiting stylistic inversion to a *for*-phrase of the predicate of the matrix sentence.

There are, moreover, selectional relations between a predicate that appears in the matrix form (36) and the subject of the embedded S, a property that further differentiates these structures from (37). Compare (40) and (41):

(40) (a)   It is intolerable for there to be snow in June
    (b)   It is intolerable for the car to be so poorly constructed
(41) (a)   *It is easy for there to be snow in June
    (b)   *It is easy for the car to be so poorly constructed

These facts, too, might be expressed by assigning the *for*-phrase to the matrix sentence in the examples (33), with deletion of the subject PRO of the embedded S after it is assigned coreference with the NP of the matrix *for*-phrase. (In such cases as *It is easy to learn Latin*, we might assume that the matrix predicate contains a nonspecified phrase *for-Δ* which is deleted, as is the nonspecified agent in agentless passives). We can then restrict the selectional features to the predicate phrase of the matrix sentence.

We return to these structures later.

Consider next the "Unlike Person Constraint" discussed by Postal (1966; 1969). We might formulate this as a rule that assigns the feature * (deviant) to a sentence S dominating $PRO_i - V - PRO_j - X$, where PRO_i and PRO_j are both first person or both second person. Thus we cannot have such sentences as (42):

(42) (a) *I saw me
    (b) *I watched us leaving (in the mirror)
    (c) *We watched me leaving
    (d) *You (all) noticed you standing there (by yourself)

The point is clearly more general (see Postal (1969)). Thus in (43) we interpret the two pronouns as different in reference, and in (44) we interpret the NPs as non-intersecting in reference; that is, we assume that the officers are not included among the soldiers doing the shooting (we do not interpret this sentence as referring to a situation in which some of the officers shot others):

(43) He saw him
(44) The soldiers shot the officers (among them)

The point seems to be that a rule of interpretation RI applying to the structure NP–V–NP (among others) seeks to interpret the two NPs as nonintersecting in reference,[20] and where this is impossible (as in the case of first and second person pronouns—see (42)), it assigns "strangeness," marking the sentence with *. But consider the sentences in (45):

(45) (a)   *We* expect them to visit *me*; *I* expect them to visit *us* (*me*)
    (b) **We* expect *me* to visit them; *I* expect *us* (*me*) to visit them
    (c) **We* expect *me* to be visited by them; *I* expect *us* (*me*) to be visited by them
    (d)   *We* believe *I* may still win; *I* believe *we* (*I*) may still win

In (45a) and (45d), the rule RI is blocked (by the Specified Subject Condition and the Tensed-S Condition, respectively). Therefore in these sentences the pair of italicized NPs may intersect in reference; the sentences are not marked with * by RI. But the rule RI applies to (45b) and (45c), assigning *, just as it applies to the examples of (42). Although the matter is more complex, this appears to be a plausible first approximation to a correct analysis. Notice that it is difficult to see how RI can be construed naturally as anything other than a rule of semantic interpretation, operating at a fairly "superficial" level (at or close to surface structure), at least if we wish to incorporate (44) and (45) under the generalization. Exactly the same considerations apply if we restrict our attention to the Unlike Person Constraint.

Observe that we have now applied the principles to two kinds of rules, namely, syntactic operations moving constituents and rules of semantic interpretation. Some

[20] This particular formulation presupposes the analysis of reflexives in Helke (1971). His approach to reflexives and inherent anaphora (*John lost his mind, John craned his neck*, and so on) fits very well into the present framework.

further possibilities are suggested by observations of Lasnik (1971). He points out that the sentences (46a,b) are ambiguous in a way in which (47) is not:

(46) (a) I didn't see many of the pictures
     (b) I didn't see pictures of many of the children
(47) I didn't see John's pictures of many of the children

The first (more normal and less sophisticated, I believe) interpretation of (46a) in colloquial English associates *not* and *many*; under this interpretation, the sentence means "I saw few of the pictures," "Not many of the pictures are such that I saw them." Thus the sentence would be false, under this interpretation, if I had seen 50 of the 100 pictures (assuming 50 pictures to be "many" under the contextual conditions of the utterance), while it would be true if I had seen only 3 of the 100 pictures. Some speakers also accept a second interpretation of (46a), with the meaning "Many of the pictures are such that I didn't see them." Under this interpretation, which associates *not* with *see*, the sentence would be true if I had seen exactly 50 of the 100 pictures, since there would be 50 that I hadn't seen.

The same ambiguity arises in the case of (46b). Under the interpretation which associates *not* with *many*, the sentence means "I saw pictures of few of the children," "Not many of the children are such that I saw pictures of them." It would be false if I had seen pictures of 50 of the 100 children, true if I had seen pictures of 3 of the 100 children. Under the second interpretation, the sentence means "Pictures of many of the children are such that I didn't see them," which is true if I had seen pictures of 50 of the 100 children. For speakers who do not accept the second interpretation of (46a) and (46b), it seems that (47) is unacceptable. For speakers who assign both interpretations to the sentences of (46), (47) is acceptable with the unique interpretation that associates *not* with *see*; thus it means "John's pictures of many of the children are such that I didn't see them." The sentence (47), then, has no interpretation under which it is false, given that I had seen John's pictures of exactly 50 of the 100 children.

The observations are moderately subtle, but I believe that Lasnik's judgments are correct. Notice that the facts, as stated, follow from the Specified Subject Condition, which does not permit association of *not* with *many* in (47). If (following Lasnik) we regard the assignment of scope of negation as a matter of semantic interpretation, the Specified Subject Condition again blocks a semantic rule. If, on the other hand, it is claimed that a rule of *not*-Movement extracts *not* from the NP object to give the first (normal) interpretation of the sentences of (46), this syntactic rule is blocked in (47) by the same condition.

Lasnik suggests also the following, slightly different example. Consider the sentences in (48):

(48) (a) You didn't understand the proofs of enough of the theorems (for me to be
         justified in giving you an A)
     (b) You didn't understand Euclid's proofs of enough of the theorems (for me
         to be justified in giving you an A)

The word *enough* differs from *many* in that *not* must be associated with it (rather than with *understand*) in (48a). That is, only what I have called the "normal" interpretation is possible in the case of (48a), which must mean something like "You understood proofs of some (but not enough) of the theorems. . ." It follows, then, that (48b) receives no direct interpretation at all (though an interpretation can be forced, as it can also be, say, in (31b)), just as (47) receives no interpretation for speakers who accept only the "normal" interpretation of (46). This appears correct and is a further example of the application of the Specified Subject Condition.

3. Consider next the sentence (49) which, we assume, derives from (50) by *wh*-Placement (on *something*), *wh*-Movement, and Auxiliary Inversion:

(49) What did you tell me that Bill saw
(50) COMP you told me [$_S$COMP Bill saw something]

The rule of *wh*-Movement in this case appears to violate both the Tensed-S Condition and the Specified Subject Condition.

Before turning to the problem posed by *wh*-Movement, let us consider the notion "transformational cycle" somewhat more carefully. The Insertion Prohibition, now sharpened as a special case of the Tensed-S and Specified Subject Conditions, is a step toward a stricter interpretation of the cycle: it asserts that once a stage of the cycle has been passed, we cannot introduce material into it from the outside under the stated conditions. To further sharpen the notion "transformational cycle," suppose that we impose the general condition (51):[21]

(51) No rule can apply to a domain dominated by a cyclic node A in such a way as to affect solely a proper subdomain of A dominated by a node B which is also a cyclic node

In other words, rules cannot in effect return to earlier stages of the cycle after the derivation has moved to larger, more inclusive domains. We will refer to (51) as the "Strict Cycle Condition."

From this condition it follows that *wh*-Movement must be a cyclic rule, since it applies in indirect questions and relatives.[22] The condition (51) seems fairly natural, and we will proceed to investigate its consequences.

Returning now to (50), we first assign *wh* and apply *wh*-Movement on the innermost cycle, which gives (52):

(52) COMP you told me [$_S$[$_{COMP}$what]Bill saw]

On the next cycle, we want to move *what* to the COMP position of the matrix sentence, to give (49).[23] The Specified Subject Condition is no longer a barrier, but we are left with a violation of the Tensed-S Condition. An investigation of the conditions of the violation indicates that they are quite narrow: an item can "escape" from a tensed sentence if it has been moved into the COMP position on an earlier cycle and is moving into the COMP position on the present cycle. Furthermore, in no case does an item in COMP position move to anything other than the COMP position.[24] These specific properties of COMP may be considered alongside the property formulated as the Complementizer Substitution Universal. With the appropriate

---

[21] The condition should perhaps be restricted to major transformations in the sense of Bach (1965; 1971), excluding his "housekeeping rules." A slightly different formulation of (51) would make it impossible for a rule applying to the domain dominated by A to affect solely items that were originally dominated by B. These alternatives lead to slightly different empirical consequences in areas that do not concern us here.

[22] It has been argued repeatedly that *wh*-Movement cannot be a cyclic rule, but I am aware of no conclusive arguments. To my knowledge, none of the arguments that appear in the literature apply to the formulations given here. However, at a later point I will deal with some considerations that might suggest that *wh*-Movement is post-cyclic.

[23] We shall return to the rule for inserting *that* in (49).

[24] In fact, this must be stipulated, quite apart from the Tensed-S Condition, to prevent improper passivization of, for example, *John asked what to read* to **What was asked to read by John*. On the other hand, *What did John ask to read* is permitted by the conditions.

reformulation of our conditions (which we give as (55)), *wh*-Movement can apply to (52), giving (53), which becomes (49) by Auxiliary Inversion and *that*-Insertion:

(53) What you told me [$_s$COMP Bill saw]

Suppose now that we replace some of the base rules in (16) to obtain the more detailed analysis (54) (following Bresnan (1970)):

(54) S → COMP S′
    S′ → NP Aux VP
    $\vdots$

Suppose further that we continue to take S (but not S′) to be the domain of cyclic rules. Under this assumption we can reformulate the Tensed-S and Specified Subject Conditions, together with the narrow restrictions on COMP, as in (55):

(55) No rule can involve X, Y in the structure

$$\ldots X \ldots [_\alpha \ldots Z \ldots -WYV \ldots] \ldots$$

    where (a) Z is the specified subject of WYV
        or (b) Y is in COMP and X is not in COMP
        or (c) Y is not in COMP and α is a tensed S

This modification of the conditions in effect asserts that an item can be extracted from a tensed sentence or across a specified subject only if there is a rule that moves it into the COMP position. Thus a *wh*-word can be extracted, as in (49)-(50), but the subject of the embedded sentence cannot be passivized in *I believe the dog is hungry*. Notice, however, that *wh*-Movement will not be permitted across a specified subject in (31a), which we restate here as (56), to give the ungrammatical **Who did you see John's pictures of*:

(56) COMP you saw [$_{NP}$John's pictures of who]

The relevant difference between (56) and (50) is that (56) has no COMP node in an NP. Therefore the *wh*-word in (56) cannot escape from the NP.

It is observed in Chomsky (1964) that *wh*-Movement can be applied only once to a constituent of the form S. We cannot, for example, question (or relativize) an item that is within an indirect question to derive (57) from (58):[25]

(57) *What did he wonder where John put
(58)   COMP he wondered [$_s$COMP John put what where]

To derive (57) from (58), we must first place *where* in the COMP position of the embedded sentence. But in that case, *what* cannot enter the COMP position, which is filled by *where*, and thus cannot be extracted on the next cycle. The principles of the cycle presupposed so far in this discussion permit no other ordering of rule applications to give (57).

4. As the rules and conditions now stand, we can derive (59) from (60) because the embedded S is not tensed:

(59) What crimes does the FBI know how to solve
(60) COMP the FBI knows [$_s$COMP PRO to solve what crimes how]

---

[25] Some speakers seem to accept such forms as *What did he wonder whether John saw, What crimes did he wonder how they solved*. For me, these are unacceptable. It would be possible to add special rules to allow for these examples by a complication of the particular grammar, given the suggested interpretation of the conditions.

The item *how* is moved into COMP position in the internal cycle, but *what crimes* can be extracted on the next cycle. This is a dubious result, however. Though judgments vary, there seem to me to be severe restrictions on cases such as (59). Thus, (61) seems to me unacceptable, surely much less acceptable than (59); and from (62) the predicted derived sentences (63) and (64) both seem unacceptable, though the immediately underlying forms (65) and (66) are all right:

(61) *What crimes does the FBI know whether to solve
(62) COMP John knows [$_s$COMP PRO to give what books to whom]
(63) *What books does John know to whom to give
(64) *To whom does John know what books to give
(65) John knows what books to give to whom
(66) John knows to whom to give what books

Notice also that (67) does not derive as predicted from (60), but rather only from (68), analogous to (69a) from (69b):

(67) How does the FBI know what crimes to solve
(68) COMP the FBI knows [$_s$COMP PRO to solve what crimes] how
(69) (a) How does the FBI know the code
     (b) The FBI knows the code how

It may be, then, that the *know how to* examples such as (59) are unique in permitting further *wh*-Movement from the embedded sentence and that the general case is that the conditions on transformations prevent movement of a *wh*-phrase over a *wh*-COMP.

In fact, the elaboration of the Specified Subject Condition that we will develop later on will suffice to prevent *wh*-Movement in the cases considered here.[26] However, it may be that there is an independent condition that suffices to prevent *wh*-Movement in these cases. Support for this conjecture is provided by the fact that example (70) must be ruled out as ungrammatical:

(70) *John knows what who saw

The source, *John knows who saw what*, is grammatical, but (70) and other examples like it indicate that *wh*-Movement cannot move a *wh*-phrase across a *wh*-subject (just as it cannot move a *wh*-phrase across a *wh*-COMP). Notice, however, that *wh*-Movement over a *wh*-phrase P is permissible if P is contained in the predicate phrase, that is, to the right of the verb in the clause in question, as we can see from such examples as (71) and (72):

(71) John remembers where Bill bought which book
(72) John remembers to whom Bill gave which book

[26] Thus one could, under this modification, permit the unique case (59) by stipulating that (60) is unique in not containing PRO (or the element Δ, as in agentless passives, which also blocks *wh*-Movement by the Specified Subject Condition). One would thus be arguing that this is a special property of the locution *know how*, perhaps related to the fact that *know-how* can be a nominal compound (*He showed a remarkable degree of know-how*) but not *know-what*, *know-why*, *wonder-why*, and so on. A further modification that we shall discuss will not permit this explanation, given that the subject of the embedded sentence is PRO, and will require something like condition (73). Observe that even with (73), we still need to invoke the strict cyclic interpretation of *wh*-Movement to block such cases as (57). Thus (73) alone would not suffice to prevent movement of *what* in (57) to the COMP position of the matrix sentence followed by movement of *where* to the COMP position of the embedded sentence.

These examples, to which we shall return, are of a type discussed in Baker (1970). Though judgments vary slightly, such forms are surely more satisfactory than (70). (See also (65), (66).) Thus (71) would have the interpretation (roughly) "John remembers that Bill bought the *i*th book in the *i*th place," and similarly for (72).

Speculating, we might propose a further condition on transformations to accommodate these judgments. The obvious suggestion is based on the observation that the subject NP is "superior" to any phrase in the predicate in the sense that it is closer to the root of the tree structure. More precisely, we say that the category A is "superior" to the category B in the phrase marker if every major category dominating A dominates B as well but not conversely.[27] Suppose that we then add the stipulation (73) to the set of general conditions that we are considering:

(73) No rule can involve X, Y in the structure

$$\ldots X \ldots [_\alpha \ldots Z \ldots -WYZ \ldots] \ldots$$

where the rule applies ambiguously to Z and Y and Z is superior to Y

The condition requires that a rule must select the superior term where that rule is ambiguous in application, that is, where the structure given in (73) will satisfy the structural condition defining the rule in question with either Z or Y selected as the factor satisfying a given term of this condition. Like the *A*-over-*A* Condition, (73) restricts the ambiguity of rule application. Like (51), it provides a stricter interpretation of the notion of the cycle. It should be noted that in all of the cases of the general form given in (73) that we are considering, the category X is superior to Y in the sense just defined; and where Z is the specified subject, it is superior to Y.

The condition (73) blocks (70) while permitting (71) and (72). Furthermore, the condition (73) suffices to block the examples (61)–(64), independently of other constraints. Thus consider (62), which we restate here as (74):

(74) COMP John knows [$_S$COMP PRO to give what books to whom]

On the first cycle, *wh*-Movement gives either (75) (= (65)) or (76) (= (66)):

(75) John knows what books to give to whom
(76) John knows to whom to give what books

But on the next cycle condition (73) prevents movement of the embedded phrase *to whom* in (75), just as it prohibits movement of the embedded phrase *what books* in (76). The reason, in both cases, is that the *wh*-phrase in COMP of the embedded cycle is superior to these categories, not being dominated by the major category S'. If *wh*-Movement moves the superior *wh*-phrase *what books* of (75) or *to whom* of (76) to initial position in the sentence, then the sentence will be marked ungrammatical by virtue of the unfilled COMP of the embedded clause and related considerations that we will examine later. This COMP position cannot be filled by subsequent application

[27] We use the term "major category" in the sense of Chomsky (1965, p. 74), that is, N, V, A and the categories that dominate them. See Chomsky (1970a) for a further elaboration of this notion.

To simplify subsequent exposition, we will want to say that in the sentence [*the men each*] *saw the other* and others like it, the word *each* is superior to *the* of *the other*. Let us therefore extend slightly the notion "superior" so that A is "superior" to B if every major category dominating $MMC(A)$ dominates $MMC(B)$ as well but not conversely, where $MMC(X)$ is the minimal major category dominating X (X itself, if X is a major category). We assume now that the NP *the men each* is the minimal major category dominating *each* in the sentence cited. Thus *each* in this sentence is superior to *the*, as intended. Other elaborations are possible, but this will suffice for expository purposes below.

of *wh*-Movement by virtue of the general condition (51) that provides the strict interpretation of the cycle. Thus all possibilities are excluded except (75), (76).

To further explore structures of the general form given in (73), let us say that if X is superior to Y in a phrase marker P, then Y is "subjacent" to X if there is at most one cyclic category $C \neq Y$ such that C contains Y and C does not contain X. Thus, if Y is subjacent to X, either X and Y are contained in all the same cyclic categories (and are thus considered at the same level of the transformational cycle) or they are in adjacent cycles. In the sentences of (77), *who* is subjacent to both nodes COMP, but in (78) and (79) it is subjacent only to the node COMP of the embedded sentence:

(77) (a) COMP he believes [$_S$COMP John saw who]
   (b) COMP he wonders [$_S$COMP John saw who]
(78) (a) COMP he believes [$_{NP}$the claim [$_S$COMP John saw who]]
   (b) COMP he considered [$_{NP}$the question [$_S$COMP John saw who]]
(79) (a) COMP he believes [$_S$COMP John saw [$_{NP}$a picture of who]]
   (b) COMP he wonders [$_S$COMP John saw [$_{NP}$a picture of who]]

From (77a) we can derive *Who does he believe that John saw* by iteration of *wh*-Movement. From (77b) we can derive *He wonders who John saw*. From (79a) we can derive *Who does he believe that John saw a picture of*, again by iteration of *wh*-Movement; from (79b) we derive *He wonders who John saw a picture of*. In the case of (77) and (79), *who* can move to any of the COMP positions; *who* moves ultimately to the external COMP position in (77a) and (79a) and to the internal COMP position in (77b) and (79b). The other four possibilities are excluded, namely, **He believes who John saw*, **Who does he wonder that John saw*, **He believes who John saw a picture of*, and **Who does he wonder that John saw a picture of*. We return to this matter when we consider contextual features of lexical items.

Turning now to (78), we observe that only the embedded COMP position can be occupied by *who*. Thus we can derive from (78b) the sentence *He considered the question who John saw*. No such operation is possible in the case of (78a) because of contextual features of the lexical item *claim*, as we shall discuss at a later point.

Given appropriate contextual features for nouns and verbs, we might account for all of these facts by adding the condition (80), which would restrict rules to adjacent cycles or the same cycle:

(80) No rule can involve X, Y, X superior to Y, if Y is not subjacent to X

Certain examples that we will consider suggest that (80) does not apply to *each*-Movement. The examples, however, are somewhat marginal, and it may furthermore be possible to account for them, under the assumption (80), by a sharpening of the notion "cyclic category." Let us tentatively stipulate, however, that condition (80) applies only to extraction rules, that is, to rules that move some item from the position Y to the superior position X.

5. We can combine conditions (51) and (80) as (81) (slightly reformulating (80)):

(81) Consider the structure α, where α is a cyclic node:

$$[_\alpha \ldots X \ldots]$$

Suppose that the structural description Σ of a transformation T applies to α, where X is the maximally superior category that satisfies some term of Σ. Then T applies to α only if α is the only cyclic category containing X (condition (51)). If, furthermore, T is an extraction rule moving some category in . . . to the position X, then some constant term of Σ must hold of a category subjacent to X in α for T to apply to α (modification of condition (80))

We will tentatively suppose that condition (81) is a general property defining cyclic application of transformations.

The examples of (77) and (79) are not affected by the condition (80) incorporated in (81), and we can thus apply iterated *wh*-Movement as desired. But in (78), though *wh*-Movement can apply on the innermost cycle, it cannot apply on the next cycle since NP does not have a COMP. Furthermore, *wh*-Movement cannot apply on the outermost cycle because of the condition (80) incorporated in (81).[28] In this way, we can explain many of the examples that fall under the Complex Noun Phrase Constraint (Ross (1967)); many others fall under the *A*-over-*A* principle.

Notice that this argument is similar to the one that explains the distinction between (50) and (56). For clarity, we repeat the essential point. The sentences (82) and (83) derive from (84) and (85), respectively:

(82)   Who did he expect Bill to see
(83)   *Who did he find Bill's picture of
(84)   COMP he expected [$_S$COMP Bill to see who]
(85)   COMP he found [$_{NP}$Bill's picture of who]

Apart from the element COMP, (84) and (85) are alike, phrase by phrase, from the point of view of rule applicability: *Bill* is the "subject" of *see who* in (84) and of *picture of who* in (85), in our extended sense of the term "subject," and *who* is the "object" in both cases. But (82) is derivable from (84) by iteration of *wh*-Movement, whereas *wh*-Movement cannot apply in (85), on the first cycle because there is no COMP in NP and on the second cycle by virtue of the Specified Subject Condition (55a).

If we are correct in assuming the condition (81), which restricts extraction to adjacent cycles, it follows that although *wh*-phrases can be extracted from such structures as *a picture of___, stories about___, requests for___*, as in (86), it will not be possible to extract a *wh*-phrase when one of these structures is embedded in another, as in (87), because of the absence of a COMP node in noun phrases. On the other hand, on the same assumptions the forms in (88) are permitted since no extraction rule is involved:

(86)   (a)   Who did you see a picture of___
         (b)   Who did you hear stories about___
         (c)   What do you write articles about___
         (d)   What do you generally receive requests for___
(87)   (a)   *Who did you hear stories about a picture of___
         (b)   *What do you receive requests for articles about___
(88)   (a)   We heard stories about pictures of each other
         (b)   We received requests for articles about each other

Judgments are insecure, but the conclusion seems to me plausible. On the other hand, Ross (1967) cites such examples as (89) as grammatical:

(89)   What books does the government prescribe the height of the lettering on___

---

[28] If we accept the analysis of factives suggested in Kiparsky and Kiparsky (1970), then, as shown there, the fact that there is no *wh*-Movement from factives will follow from the special case of the Complex Noun Phrase Constraint that follows from (80), (81).

Examples (87) and (89) appear to be parallel from the point of view of rule applicability. I see no obvious explanation for an apparent difference in degree of acceptability.

From the same assumptions it follows that such sentences as (90) involve repeated cyclic application of *wh*-Movement:

(90) What did John believe that Bill asked Mary to give her sister to read

It also follows that the surface structure position of the *wh*-phrase will be significant for interpretation and for determination of acceptability, as we might expect under the general assumptions of the extended standard theory.

In Chomsky (1968, Chapter 2, note 23) it is suggested that the *A*-over-*A* principle might be extended to the effect that a transformation must select the minimal phrase of the type S as well as the maximal phrase of the type *A* contained in S. This would account, for example, for the fact that from *John was convinced that Bill would leave before dark* we can derive *John was convinced that before dark Bill would leave* but not *Before dark John was convinced that Bill would leave*. Notice that the Subjacency Condition (81) on extraction rules in effect achieves the same results as the proposed extension of the *A*-over-*A* Condition.

6. The conditions that we have been examining can be extended to accommodate other examples. Notice that in none of the cases considered so far is the rightmost term *Y* involved in a rule properly contained in the subject of a phrase.[29] But there are additional constraints on items in subject position, as has been noted repeatedly (see Chomsky (1964), Ross (1967)). Thus, consider the sentences (91)–(98), where in each case the (a) structure underlies the corresponding (b) forms:

(91) (a)   COMP John heard [$_{NP}$stories about who]
    (b)   Who did John hear stories about
(92) (a)   COMP [$_{NP}$stories about who] terrified John
    (b)   *Who did stories about terrify John
(93) (a)   COMP you expect [$_S$COMP PRO to hear [$_{NP}$stories about who]]
    (b)   Who do you expect to hear stories about
(94) (a)   COMP you expect [$_S$COMP[$_{NP}$stories about who] to terrify John]
    (b)   *Who do you expect stories about to terrify John
(95) (a)   COMP it surprised John [$_S$COMP Mary saw what]
    (b)   What did it surprise John that Mary saw
(96) (a)   COMP [$_{NP}$[$_S$COMP John saw what]] surprised Mary
    (b)   *What did that John saw surprise Mary
(97) (a)   COMP it surprised John [$_S$COMP PRO to see [$_{NP}$pictures of who]]
    (b)   Who did it surprise John to see pictures of
(98) (a)   COMP [$_{NP}$[$_S$COMP PRO to see [$_{NP}$pictures of who]]] surprised John
    (b)   *Who did to see pictures of surprise John

We might account for these discrepancies between subject and predicate position by the condition that in structures of the general form (73) α may not be a subject phrase properly containing *Y*. The stipulation that only *proper* inclusion blocks the rule is, of course, necessary to permit a full subject to be extracted, as in *Who did you*

---

[29] To be more precise, if we take *Y* = *the* as the rightmost term involved in the *each*-Movement rule, then what should be said is that in each case so far considered, where *C* is the minimal major category containing the rightmost term *Y* involved in a rule, then *C* is not properly contained in the subject of a phrase.

expect to be here, Who did you suppose would be here.[30] With this condition, *who* will not be extractable from the subject phrase *stories about who* in (92), (94).[31] The same condition will prevent extraction of the *wh*-phrase to form (96b), (98b). More exactly, in the case of (96a) and (98a), the *wh*-phrase can be moved to the position of the internal COMP but then cannot be extracted further since it is properly contained in a subject phrase. (The ungrammatical status of the intermediate forms so produced is determined by considerations to which we will turn when we consider rules of interpretation.) In the case of (94), the condition just proposed prevents movement of *who* to COMP on the internal cycle (exactly as in the case of (92)), and the Subjacency Condition (81) prevents *who* from being moved to the external COMP on the next cycle. There is a redundancy in this case since the Subject Condition also prohibits the movement of *who* to the external COMP; a similar redundancy applies in the case of (96), (98).

We can eliminate the redundancy by restricting the condition on subjects to the case where Y is subjacent to X. This will not affect any examples involving *wh*-Movement, since in any case where Y is not subjacent to X the extraction rule is blocked. We will also assume, as noted, that the relevant conditions apply to the minimal major category containing $Y (= MMC(Y))$, not Y itself, an assumption that in this discussion has empirical effects only in the case of *each*-Movement. To simplify exposition, we will therefore modify the definition of "subjacency" exactly as we modified the definition of "superior" in note 27, saying that where X is superior to Y, Y is "subjacent" to X if there is at most one cyclic category $C \neq MMC(Y)$ such that C contains $MMC(Y)$ and C does not contain X (and therefore does not contain $MMC(X)$). With these modifications, the Subject Condition reads as in (99):

(99) No rule can involve X, Y in the structure

$$\ldots X \ldots [_\alpha \ldots Y \ldots] \ldots$$

where (a) α is a subject phrase properly containing $MMC(Y)$
and (b) Y is subjacent to X

Condition (b) of (99), rather than being merely a device to avoid redundancy, is in fact necessary, as we can see from the examples in (100) (which were pointed out to me by R. Kayne):

(100) (a) We expect [$_S$[$_{NP}$pictures of each other] to be on sale]
      (b) We expect [$_S$[$_{NP}$each others' arguments] to be valid]

In such cases the rule of *each*-Movement can apply since the subjacency requirement (99b) prevents the rule from being blocked by the Subject Condition (99a). That is, the position Y to which *each* moves is not subjacent to the position X filled by *each* in the matrix sentence of the structure underlying the examples of (100). Rather,

---

[30] To incorporate such phrases as *what books, whose books*, we might again use the notion "minimal major category," or we might rely on the considerations of note 9. Again, we must stipulate that proper inclusion of the minimal major category containing Y blocks the application of the rule, for the reasons just noted.

[31] This analysis of course assumes, as throughout, that there is no raising rule assigning the subject *stories about who* of the embedded sentence of (94) to the object position of the matrix sentence. If there were such a rule, *wh*-Movement should apply, giving (94b), analogous to *Who did you see pictures of last night, Who did you tell stories about at the campfire.* These forms, though hardly elegant, seem to me much more acceptable than (94b), as we would expect on the assumption that there is no rule of subject raising to object position.

there are two cyclic categories (namely, NP and S) containing MMC(Y) ($=$ *the other*(*s*)) and not containing X ($=$ *each*) in the underlying structure. But the definition of "subjacency" implies that in the cases excluded by (99), the subject phrase α is the only cyclic category containing (and by (99a), properly containing) MMC(Y) and not containing X.

Comparing (94) and (100), we observe that *wh*-Movement does not apply under conditions in which *each*-Movement does apply in these cases. We have already noticed this in the case of (87) and (88). The reason, again, is the Subjacency Condition (81) on extraction rules.

The rule RI (see the discussion accompanying (43)–(45)) and the copying rule that forms reflexives (see note 20) should apply under the same conditions as *each*-Movement. Therefore the sentences (101) should be marked "strange" by RI and the sentence (102) should be grammatical:

(101) (a) We (I) expected pictures of me to be on sale
     (b) We (I) expected my arguments to be valid
(102) I expected pictures of myself to be on sale

To my ear, (101b) is perfectly acceptable, and (101a) and (102) seem acceptable as well. Assuming these judgments, it follows that RI has not applied in (101), although the structures are exactly analogous to (100), in which *each*-Movement has applied. Perhaps the difference might be traced to the *A*-over-*A* Condition, if RI is formulated so that both *pictures of me* and *me* in (101a) and both *my arguments* and *my* in (101b) are subject to inspection for possible overlap of reference by RI; if so, then the *A*-over-*A* Condition will block inspection of *my*, *me*, and RI will not assign strangeness. If this assumption is correct, we should also expect both cases of (103) to be acceptable:

(103) (a) I saw a picture of me hanging on the wall
     (b) I saw a picture of myself hanging on the wall

My judgments are uncertain in these cases.

Consider next the sentences in (104):

(104) (a) They each expect [$_S$[$_{NP}$the others] to win]
     (b) They each were quite happy [$_S$[$_\alpha$for the others] to win]
     (c) They each were quite happy [$_S$[$_\alpha$for pictures of the others] to be on sale]

The rule of *each*-Movement applies to (104a), giving *They expect each other to win*. The Subject Condition (99) is inapplicable because the subject of the embedded sentence of (104a) does not properly contain the phrase *the others* ($=$ MMC(Y)). The rule of *each*-Movement also applies to (104c), which is like (100a) in all relevant respects, to give *They were quite happy for pictures of each other to be on sale*.

Consider now the structure (104b). If *each*-Movement were to apply, it would give *They were quite happy for each other to win*. This seems to me ungrammatical. Assuming this judgment, it must be that the Subject Condition (99) prevents the application of *each*-Movement to (104b). This will be the case here only if α is a subject phrase properly containing MMC(Y) and furthermore Y ($=$ *the*) is subjacent to X ($=$ *each*). Assuming that MMC(Y) $=$ *the others*, the first of these conditions holds. As distinct from (104a), the subject of the embedded sentence of (104b) does properly contain MMC(Y) ($=$ *the others*). But it also must be the case that, as distinct from (104c), Y ($=$ *the*) is subjacent to X ($=$ *each*) in (104b). That is, whereas in (104c) there are two cyclic categories properly containing MMC(Y) and excluding X (namely, α and S), in (104b) there is only one cyclic category properly containing

MMC(Y) and excluding X (namely, S). Thus the rule of *for*-Placement must be formulated so that it does not produce (105), with α = NP and *the others* an NP, but rather produces (106), with α = PP:

(105) $[_{NP}$for $[_{NP}$the others$]]$
(106) $[_{PP}$for $[_{NP}$the others$]]$

Notice that if we were to assume that *the others* is not a category within α, then the Subject Condition would no longer apply since under this assumption α = MMC(*the*). But assuming the analysis (106), the examples of (104) and others like them will be properly handled by the Subject Condition (99).

Consider next the sentences in (107):

(107) (a) We like $[_S[_{NP}$pictures of each other] to be on sale]
 (b) We hate it $[_S[_\alpha$for pictures of each other] to be on sale]
 (c) We hate it $[_S[_\alpha$for each other] to win]

Sentence (107a), which is analogous to (100a), is grammatical because of the Subjacency Condition (b) of (99), which prevents *each*-Movement from being blocked in this case. Sentence (107b) is also unaffected by the Subject Condition (99) and for the same reason.

Now we turn to case (107c). If *it*–S is analyzed as an NP in case (c), then the sentence should be grammatical since *the* is no longer subjacent to *each* in the underlying form *We each hate it for the other(s) to win*. If *it*–S is not analyzed as an NP in these structures, then (107c) will be ruled ungrammatical on the same grounds as (104b). To exclude (107c) on the assumption that *it*–S is an NP here, we might modify the definition of "subjacency" to (108):

(108) (a) Category A "L-contains" category B if and only if A properly contains B and for all $C \neq A$, if A contains C and C contains B, then $A = \ldots C \ldots$, where $\ldots$ contains a lexical item
 (b) B is "subjacent" to A if and only if A is superior to B and there is at most one cyclic category C such that C L-contains MMC(B) and C does not contain A

This is a fairly natural extension of the former definition of "subjacency," making use of the notion "L-contains" in place of "contains."

Returning to (107c), suppose now that the *it*–S structure is an NP. Then the structure underlying (107c) is (109):

(109) We each hate $[_{NP}$it $[_S[_\alpha$for the others] to win$]]$

The only cyclic category that L-contains *the others* and excludes *each* is S; therefore, *the* is subjacent to *each*. Furthermore, α properly contains MMC(*the*) (= *the others*); therefore, *each*-Movement is blocked by the Subject Condition (99). Notice that this conclusion does not depend on the assumption that α is analyzed as in (106) rather than (105), but only on the assumption that *the others* is an NP in α and *for* is not a lexical item. Similarly, under the new definition of "subjacency" in terms of "L-contains" (108b), it is no longer necessary to select (106) over (105) in order to prevent *each*-Movement in (104b).

Structures of the form NP *hates it for* ... seem awkward to me, but many speakers find them quite acceptable and examples are not uncommon in the literature. This discussion suggests that such forms seem to provide no difficulty for the theory so far developed. Since the examples seem to me somewhat questionable, however,

I will not try to fix specific suggestions at this point. It would be interesting to find clearer examples on the basis of which to decide among the slightly different alternative analyses and formulations of the conditions that have been examined in this connection.

7. To review this discussion so far, we assume the A-over-A Condition and the related condition (73), and we assume that cyclic application of rules is governed by the general convention (81). In addition, we revise (55) to (110), incorporating the Subject Condition (99):

(110) No rule can involve X, Y (X superior to Y) in the structure

$$\ldots X \ldots [_{\alpha} \ldots Z \ldots -WYV \ldots] \ldots$$

where (a) Z is the specified subject of WYV

or (b) α is a subject phrase properly containing $\text{MMC}(Y)$ and Y is subjacent to X

or (c) Y is in COMP and X is not in COMP

or (d) Y is not in COMP and α is a tensed S

With this revision, (110) incorporates Ross's Sentential Subject Constraint, insofar as the latter does not already fall under the A-over-A Condition. Other examples might be accounted for by specific properties of certain constructions. In coordination, for example, it is generally the case that operations must apply uniformly through the coordinated terms; for instance, verbal affixes must be assigned uniformly, so that we have *John has flown planes and driven cars* but not **John has flown planes and drive cars*. Correspondingly, in a structure such as (110) where Y is a term of a conjunct, no rule, syntactic or semantic, can involve X and Y (but see note 16). For example, there is an echo question *John saw Bill and who*, but *wh*-Movement cannot apply to give **Who did John see Bill and* or *The man who John saw Bill and*.

Though there remain many recalcitrant cases and large areas where even the gross phenomena are unexplained, it seems that the approach just outlined offers considerable promise for a unified and systematic treatment of conditions on transformations, if the specific hypotheses that have been proposed in the course of this discussion can be sustained.[32]

---

[32] In some cases it is not at all clear that conditions of the sort we are discussing are the appropriate device for explaining certain distinctions. Consider Ross's (1967) example—*handsome though I believe that Tom is* versus **handsome though I believe the claim that Tom is*. The distinction can be explained by the case of Ross's Complex Noun Phrase Constraint that falls under the condition of subjacency on extraction (81). However, other examples that seem to me about as bad are *handsome though they told me that Tom is, handsome though my friends suggested that Mary thinks that Tom is,* and so on. If this is so, it is not clear what considerations apply. Perhaps *I believe*, like *I guess* and a few other items, can be analyzed as pre-sentence qualifiers rather than as matrix phrases. The relative order of pre-sentence elements and COMP raises certain problems: *I wonder whether at sunset they'll still be out sailing, *I wonder at sunset whether they'll still be out sailing, At sunset who'll still be out sailing, *Who at sunset will still be out sailing; I wonder why, having offered his support, John then backed down, *I wonder, having offered his support, why John then backed down, Having offered his support, why did John then back down, Why, having offered his support, did John then back down.* Note also that the preposing rule in such cases seems to share some but not all the properties of root transformations, in the sense of Emonds (1970).

Observe that to accommodate comparative deletion (which, as D. Vetter noted, obeys the Complex NP Constraint), one might assume that it involves a movement rule with deletion in the position of the COMP *than.* Thus *John is taller than Mary claims that he is* (cf. **John is taller than Mary believes the claim that he is*) would derive, by successive movement of *tall* through the indexed COMPs, from *John is taller than₂ Mary claims that₁ he is tall*, with [*than, tall*] becoming *than.* That

As already noted, under the analysis proposed here there is no necessity for a rule raising the subject of an embedded sentence to the object position of the matrix sentence (and, furthermore, it is questionable whether such a rule could even be added). One might then raise the question whether cyclic transformations should not be constrained so as to forbid operations that never change the terminal string of a phrase marker but only its structure, as in the original formulations of subject raising to object position (see, for example, Kiparsky and Kiparsky (1970)).[33] Perhaps all such operations can be restricted to the readjustment rule component of the grammar, which relates syntax and phonology (see Chomsky and Halle (1968)). There is no reason to suppose that such rules of regrouping will receive a natural formulation within the theory of grammatical transformations. One might expect such regrouping to apply most regularly to form words from syntactically separate items, and it may be that some languages (Japanese is a case that comes to mind) make much greater use of regrouping rules than of transformations in a stricter sense.

8. Putting aside these speculations and returning to the main topic, consider again the Specified Subject Condition, case (a) of (110), which we restate as (111):

(111) No rule can involve X, Y (X superior to Y) in the structure

$$\ldots X \ldots [\ldots Z \ldots -WYV \ldots] \ldots$$

where Z is the specified subject of WYV

---

than is a COMP follows from the parallelism between adjectival and nominal phrases discussed (within the framework of the lexicalist hypothesis) in Bowers (1969) and Selkirk (1970).

Langendoen (1971) suggests that relative pronouns not moved to initial position yield more acceptable sentences in tenseless than in tensed clauses: thus he proposes that *Many people do things to teach children to do which* (namely, those things) *constitutes a crime in California* is preferable to *The vase that John broke which* (namely, the vase) *annoyed Harry had only sentimental value.* This, if correct, might be explained in terms of the proposed conditions, where the rule associating antecedent and *wh*-word is blocked where the relative clause is a finite (tensed) clause with a specified subject. Langendoen also mentions a number of other examples which, it seems, might be covered by an appropriate formulation of the *A*-over-*A* Condition, though it remains for this to be demonstrated. See Ross (1967) and Postal (1971) for relevant and illuminating discussion.

[33] It is pointed out by McCawley (1970) that if English is a VSO language, then raising to subject and to object positions can be formulated as a single rule. There is, however, no persuasive independent evidence for the assumption, so far as I can see. If there is no rule of raising to object position, then there remains no substantial argument for the VSO analysis.

As already noted, it is difficult to incorporate a rule of raising of the familiar sort within the present framework (see (94), (104b), note 31). There are other examples too which indicate that the allegedly raised subject continues to behave as the subject of the embedded sentence rather than the object of the matrix sentence. Thus, consider *The men each were told to expect John to kill the other(s).* If *John* is raised on an internal cycle, it will no longer be a subject when the matrix cycle is reached so that *each*-movement should apply to give **The men were told to expect John to kill each other.* Similarly, we have *We were told to expect John to kill me* but not **We were told to expect to kill me,* the former inconsistent with subject raising unless we assume that when the subject is raised a "trace" is left behind, perhaps in the form of a PRO controlled by the raised subject and ultimately deleted. While this is not impossible (in fact, we will suggest it as a possibility for certain cases), such a device would not account for (94) or (104b). Furthermore, it seems pointless in the case of a rule which in any event does not modify the form of the terminal string. Another problem is suggested by some observations of John Kimball, who points out that from *It was easy for Jones to force Smith to recover* we can derive *Smith was easy for Jones to force to recover,* but from *It was easy for Jones to expect Smith to recover,* we cannot form **Smith was easy for Jones to expect to recover.* Assuming subject raising, the two sentences are identical at the point where *it*-Replacement takes place. If there is no subject raising, the rule of *it*-Replacement can make the required distinction by permitting the NP moved to be followed by S (as in *Bill is easy to persuade that the moon is made of green cheese*).

In the cases so far considered, the notion "specified subject" could be taken as "subject specified with lexical entries," where nonanaphoric pronouns are taken as lexical (see, for example, (45a)). Thus the distinction was between (a) lexically specified subjects such as *Bill*, *the man*, and fully specified referring pronouns, on the one hand, and (b) the deleted and controlled subject PRO, on the other. But consideration of a wider range of examples shows that the notion "specified subject" must be further refined.

W. Leben points out that the example (112), derived from (113), is unexplained if "specified subject" in (111) means "lexically specified subject":

(112) *We persuaded Bill to kill each other
(113) We *each* persuaded Bill [COMP PRO to kill *the* other(s)]

In (113) the italicized terms are X, Y of (111) and PRO is Z. But the rule of *each*-Movement involving X, Y is blocked, even though Z is not lexically specified.

It might be supposed that the intervening lexically specified object *Bill* blocks *each*-Movement here. However, this is evidently not so, as we can see from (114), which derives from (115):

(114) We promised Bill to kill each other
(115) We *each* promised Bill [COMP PRO to kill *the* other(s)]

We might try to explain such cases by imposing on *each*-Movement the condition that it be strictly within a single clause, thus assuming that (114) derives from (116):

(116) We promised Bill [COMP PRO each to kill the other(s)]

This would require that, say, (117) derives from (118), conflicting with the fact that (119) must be blocked:

(117) We wanted to kill each other
(118) We wanted [COMP PRO each to kill the other(s)]
(119) (a) *We each wanted to kill each other
       (b) *We would have both wanted to kill each other

Apart from the difficulty of excluding (119), examples like (104) and (107) indicate that *each*-Movement cannot be restricted to a single clause. (Notice that we would not want to assume that *each other* is generated by the base in the embedded subject position in the latter cases since we want to exclude this possibility in general so as to avoid *each other saw Bill* and the like.) Furthermore, it would be highly undesirable to extend the general theory of transformations so as to permit transformations to be restricted to a single clause, and so far as I can see, there are no strong empirical reasons motivating such an elaboration of the theory, given the general framework that we are exploring here.[34]

---

[34] In the absence of other considerations, the general point that the theory of transformations should not be extended to permit this option is compelling, if not decisive. Specific arguments are somewhat inconclusive because there are some unresolved questions about the interpretation of *each other* and of quantifiers in general. Thus I think it is clear that there are general grounds for supposing that quantifiers are interpreted at least in part in terms of surface structure position (see Chomsky (1972a) for some review of this question). Specifically, in the case of *each other* there is independent evidence for this assumption. Thus Dougherty (1970) points out that *each other* does not imply a pairwise relation, as does its presumed source: for example, *The kids met each other at the beach every day last summer* does not strictly imply a pairwise meeting, as does *The kids each met the others at the beach every day last summer* (example from M. Helke). Similarly, consider such examples as *We each saw a picture of the other(s)*, *We each saw pictures of the other(s)*, *We saw a*

The rule RI imposes disjoint reference patterns in exactly the same way as *each-*Movement, as we can see from (120), where (a) is parallel to (112) and (b) to (114):

(120) (a)   *I (we)* persuaded Bill to kill *us*
        (b) **I (we)* promised Bill to kill *us*

Evidently, the crucial factor in these examples is the question of control of the embedded subject PRO (to use terminology suggested by Postal). In (112) PRO is controlled by the object of the matrix sentence, a term unrelated to the italicized pair *X, Y* involved in the rule. In (114) PRO is controlled by the subject of the matrix sentence, which incorporates the term *X* of the pair *X, Y*.[35] When PRO is not controlled by the minimal major category containing *X*, then the rule involving *X* and *Y* is blocked. The same assumption accounts for (120), with grammaticalness reversed, as usual.

On the same assumptions, we would expect that grammaticalness would be reversed in the case of *each-*Movement from the direct objects of *persuade* and *promise*. That this is indeed the case is shown by the examples in (121) and (122), suggested in a different context by Fauconnier (1971) (his examples are the French analogs, but the properties are the same):

(121)   I ordered the boys to have each finished the work by noon
(122) *I promised the boys to have each finished the work by noon

In (121), PRO in the embedded sentence is controlled by the object phrase *each of the boys* of the matrix sentence, so that *each-*Movement is permitted. (Compare (112), where PRO of the embedded sentence is controlled by the object phrase *Bill* of the matrix sentence and *each-*Movement from the subject is not permitted.) In (122), PRO of the embedded sentence is controlled by the subject phrase *I* of the matrix sentence so that *each-*Movement from the object *each of the boys* is not permitted. (Compare (114), where PRO of the embedded sentence is controlled by the subject phrase *we each* of the matrix sentence and *each-*Movement from the subject is permitted.)

Notice that when the embedded subject is not PRO but is lexically specified, then it is of course not controlled by the category containing *X*. Hence all cases considered here will be accommodated by the principle (111), if we take "specified subject" in (111) to mean "subject not controlled by the category containing *X*."[36]

---

picture of each other, We saw pictures of each other. See also note 40. There has been, to my knowledge, no analysis of quantifiers adequate to account for cases of this sort in a principled way.

If we assume that PRO does not take quantifiers in the base where it is subject to control, it follows that such sentences as **I argued with Bill about shaving each other*, **I had an understanding with John to kill each other*, **I received a letter from John about killing each other* are excluded (along with (119)), although the same sentences with *ourselves* replacing *each other* are grammatical (see Helke (1971)). The conclusion seems plausible to me in this case. However, such sentences as *We worked together to kill each other*, if grammatical, would indicate that PRO in the embedded sentence can take inherent *each*, even when subject to deletion under control. One would suspect that the solution lies in a theory of interpretation of quantifiers in terms of their surface structure positions.

[35] For a very suggestive discussion of how control is determined in such cases, see Jackendoff (1969; 1972). The subject of the matrix sentence is MMC(*X*) in this case.

[36] Bresnan (1971) points out the contrast **Such things are not good* [*for there to be children involved in*] versus the grammatical *Such things are not good for children* [*to be involved in*], where the brackets bound the embedded phrases. Note that this distinction follows from the Specified Subject Condition as here formulated since the transformationally introduced element *there*, though not a lexical item, is not controlled by any outside category and therefore blocks *it-*Replacement. The distinction will also follow, on other grounds, if one adopts the rule of PRO-Replacement to be taken up later (see the discussion accompanying (170)–(179)).

Making this revision explicit, we restate (110) as (123):

(123) No rule can involve X, Y (X superior to Y) in the structure

$$\ldots X \ldots [_\alpha \ldots Z \ldots -WYV \ldots] \ldots$$

where (a) Z is the subject of WYV and is not controlled by a category containing X

or (b) α is a subject phrase properly containing $MMC(Y)$ and Y is subjacent to X

or (c) Y is in COMP and X is not in COMP

or (d) Y is not in COMP and α is a tensed S

In earlier examples, we took Z to be lexically specified. An NP is lexically specified (in the sense of our earlier discussion) if and only if it is not controlled. Thus in earlier discussion we could just as well have referred to Z as the subject of WYV which is not controlled. The modification incorporated into (123a), then, broadens the scope of the condition to include all cases in which Z is not controlled by a category containing X, including, as a special case, a subject Z which is not controlled at all, that is, is lexically specified in the earlier sense.

9. Examples of the sort that we have been considering have been used to motivate various pruning conventions in earlier work. Thus, in the sentences of (124), the rule of *each*-Movement does not apply; and in (125), the rule RI of semantic interpretation does not apply (so that the sentences are grammatical):

(124) (a) The men *each* expected him to want to kill *the* others
      (b) The men *each* expected to want him to kill *the* others
      (c) The men *each* wanted to hear his stories about killing *the* others
(125) (a) *I* (*we*) expected him to want to kill *us*
      (b) *I* (*we*) expected to want him to kill *us*
      (c) *I* (*we*) wanted to hear his stories about killing *us*

But if *him*, *his* do not appear, *each*-Movement can apply in (124) and RI will apply in (125) (assigning *).

We have explained these facts by means of the Specified Subject Condition (123a). Alternatively, one might suggest that *each*-Movement and RI apply only in a single clause,[37] adding the convention that when the subject *him*, *his* does not appear, the S node is pruned so that only a single clause remains and the rules apply. However, examples such as (112), (114), (120), as well as (124c) and (125c), indicate that it is control of the subject by the term X of the matrix phrase, rather than a pruning convention of the kind discussed in the literature, that is the determining factor. Indeed, it may be that pruning can be dispensed with. If so, it may be that the only deletion of S nodes is by late rules that delete repeated phrases (for example, Ross's "sluicing," or VP deletion, that is, optional deletion of an intonationally marked VP), rules that are

---

[37] Assuming that the difficulties noted earlier (see discussion following (119)) have been overcome. Note that the Specified Subject Condition accounts for the facts just noted in a uniform manner. In contrast, a pruning convention could at best account for cases (a) and (b) of (124)–(125). Clearly, the NP node cannot be pruned if *his* is deleted in *his story about killing the others*, *his story about killing us* since these phrases continue to function as NPs with respect to further operations. Notice that application of *each*-Movement to (124c) with *his* deleted is much more natural if *hear* is replaced by *tell*, so that the subject of *kill* is understood to be *the men*, and there is a relation similar to semantic agency between *the men* and *stories*. The Specified Subject Condition as stated does not suffice to account for the full range of such facts. We shall return briefly to the matter of agency.

possibly the final ones of the grammar. I will not pursue the matter here, but it may well be that the results on cycling functions in Peters and Ritchie (1972) can be applied, under these assumptions, to demonstrate that transformational grammars are quite limited in weak generative capacity. At the very least, this might be true of the interesting sublanguages generated prior to optional final ellipsis.

Notice that the modification (123a) does not affect the cases of *wh*-Movement so far discussed, apart from examples such as (62)–(64). Due to the fact that *wh*-Movement, being cyclic, moves the *wh*-phrase to the COMP position of the clause in which the *wh*-phrase appears, the specification of the subject Z in (123) has no bearing on *wh*-Movement in these cases. Thus both cases of (126) are grammatical, as distinct from the pairs (112), (114) and (120a,b):

(126) (a) Who did they persuade Bill to kill
        (b) Who did they promise Bill to kill

Thus we have the pattern in (127):

(127) (a) *We expect John to see each other   (*each*-Movement does not apply)
        (b)   We expect John to see us   (RI does not apply)
        (c)   Who do we expect John to see   (*wh*-Movement applies twice)
        (d) *We heard John's stories about each other   (*each*-Movement does not apply)
        (e)   We heard John's stories about us   (RI does not apply)
        (f) *Who did we hear John's stories about   (*wh*-Movement does not apply)

In all cases of (127), if *John* (the specified subject Z of (123a)) is dropped, then the rules apply, reversing the asterisk except in case (127c).

The modification (123a) has some implications for examples of a different sort. Consider the sentences (128) and (129):

(128) We heard about plans to kill Bill
(129) We received instructions to kill Bill

Sentence (128) means that we heard about plans for some indeterminate person(s) to kill Bill. Sentence (129), in its more natural interpretation, means that we received instructions that we should kill Bill, though perhaps it also has an interpretation analogous to (128), namely, that instructions for someone to kill Bill arrived in our possession. Clearly, (128) cannot have the interpretation analogous to the more natural interpretation of (129), namely, that we heard about the plans that we should kill Bill (it is not, of course, excluded that the indeterminate killer(s) in (128) should be among those designated by *we*). We can express these facts by postulating the underlying forms (130)–(132) and excluding (133). The element Δ in (130) and (132) is an indeterminate subject which deletes; PRO is controlled by the subject *we* and deletes by Equi-NP Deletion.

(130) We heard about [plans [Δ to kill Bill]]
(131) We received [instructions [PRO to kill Bill]]
(132) We received [instructions [Δ to kill Bill]]   (?)
(133) We heard about [plans [PRO to kill Bill]]   (*)

Consider then the sentences (134) and (135):

(134) (a) We heard about plans to kill each other   (*)
        (b) We received instructions to kill each other

(135) (a) We heard about plans to kill me
      (b) We received instructions to kill me

If the underlying source for (134a) is analogous to (130) (with *we each* replacing *we* and *the other* replacing *Bill*), then (134a) should be blocked by (123a) since Δ is not controlled by the NP *we each* containing *each*.[38] And (135a) should be grammatical since RI is blocked for the same reason. Sentence (134b) should be grammatical with the interpretation expressed by (136) (analogous to (131)) but not with that expressed by (137) (analogous to (132)); and (135b) should be grammatical with the interpretation expressed by (138) (analogous to (132)) but not with that expressed by (139) (analogous to (131)). These conclusions seem to me correct.

(136) We each received [instructions [PRO to kill the other]]
(137) We each received [instructions [Δ to kill the other]]
(138) We received [instructions [Δ to kill me]]
(139) We received [instructions [PRO to kill me]]

Consider next (140):

(140) (a)   We received plans to kill Bill
      (b) *We received plans to kill each other
      (c)   We received plans to kill me

Sentence (140a) is unlike (129) in that it cannot have the interpretation "We are to kill Bill"; thus it cannot have the source analogous to (131) (with *plans* replacing *instructions*). Accordingly, (140b) is ungrammatical and (140c) is interpretable, in contrast to (134b) which is grammatical under the interpretation (136) and (135b) which is uninterpretable with the underlying source (139). Judgments are somewhat uncertain, but it seems to me that these conclusions are correct. If so, these cases, too, indicate that it is the Specified Subject Condition (123a) rather than a standard pruning convention that is operative here.

The conditions we have suggested have certain other consequences. Consider the sentences in (141)–(143) (compare (86)–(88)):

(141) (a) We heard a story about some pictures of me   (?)
      (b) Who did you hear a story about some pictures of   (*)
      (c) The men heard a story about some pictures of each other   [G]

---

[38] This assumes that deletion of the indeterminate subject follows *each*-Movement. Similarly, as the examples in (135) show, deletion of the indeterminate subject follows RI. If this line of reasoning is correct, then "deletion of Δ" should be construed as a principle of interpretation. That is, we can think of Δ in these examples as being a null element; there is no rule of deletion. The rules of interpretation will assign a null element dominated by an NP subject the interpretation of an indeterminate subject.

If (129) cannot be interpreted as meaning "Instructions for someone's killing Bill arrived in our possession," then the rules of interpretation (or of selection) will have to be formulated to block (132). Notice that if the judgments given in this discussion are correct, then selection of PRO or Δ in the embedded sentence will involve both the head noun to which it is complement and the verb of which the phrase N-complement is the object, as is indicated by (134), (135), and (140).

It might be asked why *plans* and *instructions* in these examples are not preceded by the indeterminate subject Δ, as determiner, blocking *each*-Movement and RI in all cases. The reason is that NPs, as distinct from sentences, do not have obligatory subjects. This fact is noted by Wasow and Roeper (1972), who use it to give an explanation of some properties of action nominals (*the singing of songs*) as distinct from gerundive nominals (*singing songs*), in an interesting corroboration of the lexicalist hypothesis concerning the structure of complex noun phrases.

(142) (a) We heard interesting claims about pictures of me   (?)
      (b) Who did we hear interesting claims about pictures of   (*)
      (c) The men heard interesting claims about pictures of each other   (G)
(143) (a) We heard interesting claims about me   (?)
      (b) Who did we hear interesting claims about   (G)
      (c) The men heard interesting claims about each other   (G)

The conditions suggested so far imply the judgments given in brackets
(* = ungrammatical, G = grammatical). In the case of the examples (a), the judgment should be G if RI is formulated so as to be subject to the *A*-over-*A* principle,
* otherwise (see discussion of (101)). In the case of the examples (b), the Subjacency
Condition (81) blocks *wh*-Movement in the case of (141b) and (142b), but not (143b).
In the case of the examples (c), the rule of *each*-Movement is permitted in each case.
While judgments are not entirely trustworthy, the conclusions seem to me plausible.

R. Dougherty notes a variety of other examples that can be explained along
similar lines in terms of the Specified Subject Condition. Consider the underlying
structures (144) and (145):

(144) They will obey [any request [COMP PRO to kill X]]
(145) They will okay [any request [COMP PRO to kill X]]

From (144) we derive *They will obey any request to kill* X; from (145) we derive
They will okay any request to kill X. In the former case, under its most natural interpretation, they are to kill X; but in the latter, someone indeterminate is to do so. That
is, in (144), but not (145), the matrix subject *they* controls PRO. Correspondingly, we
have the examples in (146) and (147):

(146) (a) *Who will they obey any request to kill
      (b) *Who will they okay any request to kill
      (c) They will obey any request to kill each other
      (d) *They will okay any request to kill each other
(147) (a) *We will obey any request to kill us
      (b) We will okay any request to kill us

Examples (146a,b) are excluded by virtue of the Subjacency Condition on extraction and the lack of COMP in the NP *any request to kill* X. Example (146c), however,
is not blocked by these circumstances since it is not formed by an extraction rule.
But (146d) is again excluded, in this case by the Specified Subject Condition since
the matrix subject *they* does not control the subject of the most deeply embedded S.
For the same reason, the rule RI is blocked in the case of (147b) and the sentence is
grammatical, but RI is applicable in the case of (147a) and the sentence is marked
"strange."

Similarly, consider the underlying forms (148) and (149):

(148) It appeared to John [COMP they to like X]
(149) They appealed to John [COMP PRO to like X]

By *it*-Replacement, (148) yields (150), while (149) is transformed finally into (151):

(150) They appeared to John to like X
(151) They appealed to John to like X

In (149) the embedded subject PRO is controlled by *John*. In (150), on the other
hand, *John* does not control the subject of the embedded sentence. (Rather, either

there is no subject after *it*-Replacement or there is a "trace" controlled by the matrix subject *they*, under an analysis that we will consider later.) Correspondingly, we have the distribution of data in (152) and (153):

(152) (a) Who did they appear to John to like
      (b) Who did they appeal to John to like
      (c) They appeared to John to like each other
      (d) *They appealed to John to like each other
(153) (a) *We appeared to John to like us
      (b) We appealed to John to like us

Iterated *wh*-Movement gives (152a) and (152b). The rule of *each*-Movement from the matrix subject *they each* is permitted in (152c); but it is blocked in (152d) by the Specified Subject Condition since *John*, rather than *they each*, controls the subject of the embedded sentence. Similarly, the rule RI is blocked in the case of (153b) by the Specified Subject Condition but is applicable in (153a) where it assigns *.

Dougherty (1970) also notes that the *respectively* Interpretation Rule appears to obey the same constraints. Thus consider the examples in (154):

(154) (a) We will obey any request to kiss our respective wives
      (b) *We will okay any request to kiss our respective wives
      (c) We appeared to John to like our respective wives
      (d) *We appealed to John to like our respective wives

Association of *respective* with the matrix subject *we* is permitted in cases (a) and (c) but blocked in cases (b) and (d) by the Specified Subject Condition since the subject of *kiss*, *like* is not controlled by the matrix subject *we*.

In all of these cases, it is control of the embedded item PRO that determines applicability or nonapplicability of rules. In particular, it seems quite impossible, in these cases too, to rely on any familiar notion of pruning to make the appropriate distinctions.

Before leaving this topic, I will merely mention examples which indicate a possible further refinement of the notion "specified subject," without pursuing the matter. Y. Bordelois notes the following examples (with (155) from Kayne (1969)):

(155) Why are John and Mary letting the honey drip on each other's feet
(156) *Why are John and Mary letting Bill drip honey on each other's feet
(157) Why are they letting the baby fall on each other's laps
(158) *Why are they letting Bill drop the baby on each other's laps

The rule of *each*-Movement is blocked in examples (156) and (158) by the Specified Subject Condition. However, (155) and (157) seem considerably more acceptable, even though they too contain a specified subject that should block *each*-Movement. The examples suggest that a notion of "agency" is involved and that perhaps the notion "specified agent" is the critical one rather than formal subject. Notice, incidentally, that this conclusion, if correct, would not affect the hypothesis that transformations do not refer to semantic relations but only to bracketing of phrase markers (see the opening discussion) even if the semantic notion "agency" plays a role in determining applicability of transformations. Similarly, reference in (123) to the semantic notion of "control" does not affect this conclusion.

10. The Specified Subject Condition, as we have now formulated it in (123a), asserts that in a structure of the form (159), no rule can involve X and Y if Z is the subject of the phrase WYV and Z is not controlled by the category containing X:

(159) $\ldots X \ldots [\ldots Z \ldots -WYV \ldots] \ldots$

The condition on Z has the two subcases (a) and (b) of (160):

(160) (a) Z is not controlled at all[39]
      (b) Z is controlled by a category not containing X

Notice that if X (or the minimal major category containing it) is not a possible controller, then case (160b) will always hold in examples of the sort we are discussing, given that Z is the anaphoric item PRO. We might therefore consider adding to (160b) the provision (161):

(161) where the minimal major category containing X (i.e., MMC(X)) is a possible controller

A possible argument against this modification is provided by such sentences as (162):

(162) (a) John made a fortune by cheating *his friends*
      (b) John made a fortune while living *in England*

A *wh*-phrase in the italicized position of (162) is not subject to *wh*-Movement, although *each*-Movement into this position is permissible. Thus we have the examples in (163):

(163) (a) *Who did John make a fortune by cheating
      (b) *Where did John make a fortune while living
      (c)   They get their kicks by cheating each other
      (d)   They were apprehended while shooting at each other[40]

These judgments regarding grammaticalness follow from the Specified Subject Condition (159), (160). In all four cases of (163), the subject PRO of the embedded phrases *by . . .* and *while . . .* is controlled by the matrix subject. In cases (c) and (d), the matrix subject fills the position X of (159) (more precisely, the position MMC(X)), so that case (160b) is inapplicable and the rule of *each*-Movement applies. In cases (a) and (b) of (163), however, X of (159) is COMP, not the subject *John* which controls Z (= PRO). Therefore (160b) applies and the rule of *wh*-Movement is blocked, as indicated in (163a,b). But if we add the provision (161) to (160b), then the Specified Subject Condition no longer applies since COMP is not a possible controller. We are thus left without an explanation for the ungrammaticalness of (163a,b). Condition (161) is, then, unacceptable unless there is an alternative explanation for (163a,b).

Let us assume that there is an alternative explanation in this case and consider the provision (161). We have discussed two cases in which X is not a possible controller and in which (161) will therefore be relevant, namely, the rule of *it*-Replacement, where $X = it$, and the rule of *wh*-Movement, where $X =$ COMP. Let us examine each of these, under the tentative assumption that (160b) is qualified by (161).

---

[39] Specifically, Z is a lexical item, an item (such as *there*) introduced by a transformation and not subject to control, a nonanaphoric pronoun, or the indeterminate element Δ. See note 38.
[40] Not synonymous with "Each was apprehended while shooting at the other," since for (d) to be true they must have been apprehended simultaneously. See note 34.

In discussing *it*-Replacement previously (see (32)–(41)), we argued that (164b) derives from (164a), whereas the corresponding form (165b) cannot be derived from (165a) because of the Specified Subject Condition (160a):

(164) (a)   It is pleasant for the rich [_SCOMP PRO to do the hard work]
      (b)   The hard work is pleasant for the rich to do
(165) (a)   It is pleasant for the rich [_SCOMP poor immigrants to do the hard work]
      (b)   *The hard work is pleasant for the rich for poor immigrants to do

This earlier discussion preceded our extension of the Specified Subject Condition to include (160b) alongside of (160a). But notice that (160b) prevents *it*-Replacement in (164) as well since PRO of the embedded sentence is controlled by the phrase *the rich* rather than by $X = it$.[41] The problem would be resolved by the modification of the Specified Subject Condition just proposed, namely, the provision (161) added to case (160b).

Notice, incidentally, that we cannot assign the provision (161) to both cases of the Specified Subject Condition for if (160a) is qualified in this way then (165b) will no longer be blocked.

The same point is illustrated by the examples (167), deriving from (166) (from Postal (1971)):

(166) (a)   It is tough for me [COMP PRO to stop [COMP Bill's looking at Harriet]]
      (b)   It is tough for me [COMP PRO to stop [COMP PRO looking at Harriet]]
(167) (a)   *Harriet is tough for me to stop Bill's looking at
      (b)   Harriet is tough for me to stop looking at

If the provision (161) qualifies (160b) but not (160a), then (167b) can be derived from (166b) but (167a) cannot be derived from (166a), explaining the distinction.[42]

Notice that (168) does yield (169) under *it*-Replacement:

(168) It is tough for me [COMP PRO to stop Bill from [COMP PRO looking at Harriet]]
(169) Harriet is tough for me to stop Bill from looking at

[41] I am indebted to R. Kayne for bringing this fact to my attention.
If we were to accept the analysis of such phrases proposed by Bresnan (1971), this problem would not arise since the embedded structure is analyzed as VP rather than as S in the underlying structure. This approach necessitates a richer system of interpretive rules to determine the subject of the embedded structure and corresponding modifications of most of the material presented here. I have not investigated the consequences of such modifications.

[42] It might be argued that the most deeply embedded cyclic category in (166) is an NP (see the discussion of (202)). In that case, the *A*-over-*A* Condition should prevent extraction of *Harriet* in (166), although *it*-Replacement would produce *Bill's looking at Harriet is tough for me to stop* from (166a) and *Looking at Harriet is tough for me to stop* from (166b). (Notice that the alternative form *To stop (Bill's) looking at Harriet is tough for me* is irrelevant to this discussion.) However, the issue is complicated by the fact that extraction of NPs from such nominal structures seems marginally possible (see the discussion of (6) and (186b)).
The *A*-over-*A* Condition should prevent the derivation of **John is fun to see pictures of* from *It is fun* [COMP PRO *to see* [*pictures of John*]] (permitting only *Pictures of John are fun to see*), despite the fact that there is no specified subject in the underlying NP *pictures of John*. Similarly, consider the sentence *It is fun to take pictures of John*. This is ambiguous: it can be interpreted with the NP *pictures of John* as object of the verb *take* (meaning "remove" or "steal") or with the NP *John* as object of the verbal expression *take pictures* (meaning "photograph"). Under the former interpretation we can derive *Pictures of John are fun to take* but not **John is fun to take pictures of*. The latter is derivable only when *take pictures* is analyzed as the verbal expression so that the *A*-over-*A* Condition does not block extraction of *John*, there being no NP *pictures of John*.

The distinction between (169) and (167a) (which would be a near paraphrase of (169) were it grammatical) is that in (168), but not (166a), the most deeply embedded subject is PRO; thus, the provision (161) applies, rendering the Specified Subject Condition inapplicable and permitting *wh*-Movement.

This analysis is weakened, however, by the fact that extraction of *Harriet* in (166b) and (168) violates the Subjacency Condition (81) on extraction rules. To preserve this general convention, we must suppose that *Harriet* is moved to the position of *it* in (166b) and (168) by two cyclic rules, one applying in the cycle containing the main verb *stop* and the second applying in the matrix cycle.

In fact, there is another approach to the analysis of these structures that preserves the general convention (81) and at the same time dispenses with the provision (161), thus further weakening the hypothesis that the latter is required. Recall that the acceptable sentence (164b) is prohibited by the extension (160b) of the Specified Subject Condition unless the provision (161) is added. Now note that (164b) would be permitted if the NP *the hard work* were moved into a position not preceded by PRO on the internal cycle. Then, exactly as in the case of *wh*-Movement, the NP *the hard work* could be extracted on the next cycle, irrespective of the control of PRO, since the structure would not in any event be of the form (159) to which the Specified Subject Condition applies. It cannot be that the NP *the hard work* moves to the position of the embedded COMP in (164a) (as a *wh*-phrase would) or (165b) would not be blocked; furthermore, (123c) would prevent *it*-Replacement by *the hard work* on the next cycle under this assumption. The only remaining possibility, then, is that the NP *the hard work* replaces PRO itself by a new rule of PRO-Replacement, analogous to the rule of *it*-Replacement itself, giving the intermediate form (170):

(170) It is pleasant for the rich [$_S$COMP the hard work to do]

The assumption that there is such a rule of PRO-Replacement is not unreasonable. Notice that we already require a rule that will move the NP *the hard work* from (170) to the subject position of the matrix sentence to replace *it*, namely, the rule that gives (172) from the corresponding cases of (171):

(171) (a) It is likely [$_S$COMP John to leave]
       (b) It seems [$_S$COMP John to be a nice fellow]
(172) (a) John is likely to leave
       (b) John seems to be a nice fellow

Adding the new rule of PRO-Replacement permits, at very little cost, generalization of the obligatory rule that gives (172). It must be stipulated that if PRO-Replacement has applied, say, in the most deeply embedded structure of (166b), then further application is obligatory (as it is with the rule of *it*-Replacement with which PRO-Replacement can probably be merged). We must then make this combined rule obligatory when the NP that is to replace *it* is in subject position in the embedded sentence.[43]

[43] If the subject position of the embedded sentence is filled by a lexical item, then the general condition of Recoverability of Deletion will block the rule of PRO-Replacement. This will, then, suffice to prevent illegitimate *it*-Replacement to give (165b) from (165a). Notice that the rule of *it*-Replacement must be formulated so that while obligatory in (171) and (170), it is inapplicable to (165a), which cannot yield **Poor immigrants are pleasant for the rich to do the hard work*. Thus we must assume that (170) is structurally distinguishable from (165a). The simplest proposal is that the rule of PRO-Replacement, which yields (170), does not replace PRO with *the hard work* but rather combines the two, assigning the feature PRO to the NP *the hard work* which moves into the position of PRO. Then the rule of *it*-Replacement will be obligatory with matrix predicates of the sort that

It is possible that some of the limitations on *it*-Replacement may be explicable in these terms. For example, J. Kimball has noted that there are very few examples of sentences of the form (164b) derived from passives in the embedded sentence. (One of the few examples, noted in Chomsky (1964), is *Such flattery is easy to be fooled by*; there are others with closely related verbs.) For example, we cannot form such sentences as **The poor are pleasant for the rich to be served by* from *It is pleasant for the rich [to be served by the poor]*. To express this fact, it would be sufficient to have PRO-Replacement precede Passive, or, more exactly, precede the subrule of Passive that preposes NP, the latter being actually a special case of PRO-Replacement, in effect.

An additional argument in support of PRO-Replacement is that it accounts for some observations of Bresnan (1971) regarding stress contours. Bresnan points out that if the rules of stress assignment are part of the transformational cycle (as she convincingly argues), then it would be necessary to exclude from the cycle the categories marked with brackets in such cases as (164a), (166b), and (168); otherwise, the Nuclear Stress Rule will incorrectly assign primary stress to the term that replaces *it*. Her proposal is to take the bracketed expressions as VPs, an approach which, as noted earlier, has far-reaching effects on the formulation of many rules. Within the present framework, we can achieve the same result by continuing to take the bracketed categories in these examples to be S and postulating the cyclic rule of PRO-Replacement.

There are, however, certain problems that arise if we assume the rule of PRO-Replacement. Consider the sentences in (173), which derive ultimately from the corresponding cases of (174):[44]

(173) (a) *The men are easy for each other to please
      (b) *John seems to the men to like each other
      (c) Toys are fun for the kids to give each other (?)
(174) (a) It is easy for the others [COMP PRO to please each of the men]
      (b) It seems to each of the men [COMP John to like the others]
      (c) It is fun for each of the kids [COMP PRO to give toys to the others]

Of the sentences in (173), (b) is the worst and (c) seems to me better than (a). Assuming tentatively the classification given in (173), consider the implications. In the case of (174a), the phrase *each of the men* replaces *it* on the external cycle. The rule of *each*-Movement then gives (173a). One way to block the latter would be to order

---

appear in (171) and with all matrix predicates when the subject of the embedded S, which replaces *it*, contains the feature PRO. Under all other circumstances, the rule of *it*-Replacement is inapplicable. This complication is the cost of the rule of PRO-Replacement. We will see in a moment that, under the analysis we are now considering, the assumption that the NP *the hard work* retains the feature PRO in (170) might serve an additional function as well.

Notice that the Tensed-S Condition will in any event block *Books are difficult to believe that Tom reads*, although *This is the book that it is difficult to believe that Tom read* is derivable, by iteration of *wh*-Movement.

I will not explore the many further problems in characterizing the domain of applicability of *it*-Replacement.

[44] Compare (173a) with **The men are happy for each other to leave*, blocked for reasons discussed earlier (see (104b)). Notice that in the latter case, the *for*-phrase is presumably part of the embedded sentence, whereas in the case of (173a), it is part of the predicate of the matrix sentence. Thus we cannot form **The men were happy to leave, for Bill* as a variant of *The men were happy for Bill to leave* although *The men were easy to kill, for Bill* is a possible variant of *The men were easy for Bill to kill*. (See the discussion of (32)–(41).) Similarly, the other properties of *easy*-constructions discussed earlier distinguish these from *The men were happy to leave*, and so on.

the rule of *each*-Movement before the rule of *it*-Replacement.[45] Let us assume this ordering of rules, tentatively.

Turning then to (174b), we see that the phrase *John* replaces *it*, after which *each*-Movement would give (173b). But (173b) is blocked, as required, if *each*-Movement precedes *it*-Replacement, as we are tentatively assuming.[46]

Consider then (174c). On the inner cycle, Indirect Object Movement gives (175):

(175) It is fun for each of the kids [COMP PRO to give the others toys]

If there is no rule of PRO-Replacement, then we turn to the external cycle. The rule of *each*-Movement applies, followed by *it*-Replacement, giving (173c). Application of *each*-Movement is permitted by the condition on control since *each of the kids* controls PRO. The qualification (161) on case (160b) of the Specified Subject Condition makes this condition inoperative, thus permitting *it*-Replacement, giving (173c).

Suppose, however, that we rely on the rule of PRO-Replacement instead of the qualification (161). Then PRO-Replacement, applying on the inner cycle, gives (176), which is then subject to obligatory *it*-Replacement on the next cycle:

(176) It is fun for each of the kids [COMP toys to give the others]

Assuming the analysis of note 43, the item *toys* is actually a complex structure containing the feature PRO. Assuming still that *each*-Movement precedes *it*-Replacement, then *each*-Movement must apply to (176) at this point if we are to derive (173c). However, *each*-Movement will apply only if the position of PRO in (175), now occupied by the complex structure [toys, PRO] (= *toys*) in (176), is still controlled by the phrase *each of the kids* of the matrix sentence of (176); otherwise, *each*-Movement will be blocked by the Specified Subject Condition, which is no longer rendered inoperative by (161). In effect this means that we regard control as an enduring property of the paired positions in such cases (relying, presumably, on the continued presence of PRO in the complex structure [toys, PRO]). Furthermore, we must reformulate the Specified Subject Condition slightly so that a position is not considered to be lexically specified, thus falling under the condition, if it is controlled. These consequences, while not intolerable, nevertheless do not seem to me particularly desirable.

Suppose then that we were to drop the assumption that *each*-Movement precedes *it*-Replacement. Now there is no problem with (174c), assuming the rule of PRO-Replacement or not. We might account for (173b) by assuming that when the NP *John* replaces *it* in (174b), it leaves behind a "trace" which it controls. The trace might be PRO, or it might be the null element if we think of the transformation as moving only the terminal symbol *John* to the NP subject position of the matrix sentence, leaving unaltered the nodes that originally dominated it (see note 38). If the trace is PRO, it will be deleted by a final rule that deletes controlled PRO in such sentences as

---

[45] Other avenues might be explored in attempting to account for the questionable or ungrammatical status of (173a). Thus a relation analogous to that of antecedent-anaphoric pronoun holds between the phrases *each of the men* and *the others* in the underlying structure (174a), and there might be conditions preventing an antecedent from being subjacent to and to the right of a term associated with it by such a relation. Also, one might explore a variant of some Crossover Principle of the type discussed by Postal (1971). These approaches seem to me dubious, however, if not completely impossible, because of such examples as (178) and (179), which require *it*-Replacement from (174a).

[46] Notice that in the case of (174b), we do not have the alternative possibilities for explanation noted in the preceding footnote for the case of (174a).

We expected to leave. The controlled trace blocks *each*-Movement, so that (173b) is ungrammatical.

This approach will not work in the case of (173a), however. Applying PRO-Replacement on the inner cycle in (174a) and then *it*-Replacement on the outer cycle, we derive (177):

(177) Each of the men is easy for the others [COMP PRO to please]

There is, however, no reason why *each*-Movement should not apply to this to give the unwanted (173a). If *each*-Movement does not apply in (177), we derive (178), which seems acceptable:

(178) Each of the men is easy for the others to please

Thus, if we assume (173a) to be ungrammatical and (173c) to be grammatical, it would appear that PRO-Replacement entails that *each*-Movement precedes *it*-Replacement and that it is necessary to carry out the modifications suggested after (176). This conclusion might be regarded as an argument against PRO-Replacement, hence an argument in support of the provision (161) on (160b), which seems necessary if there is no rule of PRO-Replacement. (Indirectly, it is also an argument against the Subjacency Condition (81) on extraction rules, which appears to be violated if we do not presuppose PRO-Replacement.) The argument is no stronger than the assumptions regarding the status of (173a) and (173c) and also depends on the assumption that there is no other way to prevent *each*-Movement to the *for*-phrase in (177). The latter assumption might in fact be challenged. Consider (179):

(179) The men are each easy for the others to please

It seems to me that (179) is as acceptable as (178), and better than (173a). But if our general assumptions about *each*-Movement are correct, then (179) derives from (178) by one of the cases of *each*-Movement (see (121), (122)). If so, then *each*-Movement must be able to apply after *it*-Replacement. Then we can account for (173b) and (173c) as already explained, and we are left with the unexplained distinction between (179) and (173a). We must, in short, suppose that some other consideration makes the *for*-phrase in (174a), (173a) immune to insertion of *each*. If this is correct, then these considerations provide no argument against PRO-Replacement and in support of (161).

I have explored the interconnections among various assumptions, reaching no firm conclusion. It seems reasonable to make the tentative assumption that PRO-Replacement operates and that *it*-Replacement in (174b) leaves a "trace," and, finally, that we can dispense with the qualification (161) and preserve the principle (81) of Subjacency. On this assumption, we leave unexplained the ungrammaticalness of (173a) (as compared with (179)), but all of the other cases examined fall into place.

Let us turn now to the second general case to which the provision (161) applies, namely, the case of *X* in COMP, where *X* again is not a possible controller.

Consider the sentences (180)–(182):

(180) COMP they expected [COMP Bill to kill who]
(181) COMP they expected [COMP PRO to kill who]
(182) COMP they each expected [COMP who to kill the others]

In the case of (180), cyclic iteration of *wh*-Movement gives *Who did they expect Bill to kill.* The cyclic property of *wh*-Movement prevents violation of the Specified Subject Condition, case (160a). In the case of (181), the same process gives *Who did they expect to kill.* However, with the subcondition (160b) of the Specified Subject Condition qualified by provision (161), we no longer need to appeal to the cyclic property of *wh*-Movement to explain why application of *wh*-Movement to (181), placing *who* in the external COMP, is not a violation of the Specified Subject Condition.

Recall that we cannot extend provision (161) to case (160a) of the Specified Subject Condition, that is, to the case of a lexically specified subject. We have already noted this with regard to *easy-to*-VP constructions (see (165)–(167)). Depending on the status of such examples as (6), we may be able to illustrate the same point directly in the case of *wh*-Movement itself. Consider the structures (183)–(186):

(183) (a) +WH you counted on [COMP PRO going to college]
      (b) +WH you counted on [COMP your son's going to college]
(184) (a) +WH you counted on [COMP PRO doing what]
      (b) +WH you counted on [COMP your son's doing what]
(185) (a) Did you count on going to college
      (b) Did you count on your son's going to college
(186) (a) What did you count on doing
      (b) What did you count on your son's doing   (?)

Overlooking details that are irrelevant here, the structures (183) yield the corresponding cases of (185), as expected. The rule of *wh*-Movement applied to (184a) gives (186a). Sentence (186b) is analogous to (6). As noted earlier, it constitutes a violation of an "absolute" interpretation of the *A-over-A* Condition, though not of the interpretation we have tentatively adopted. If, in fact, COMP is empty in such structures as (183), (184), as we will suggest directly, then (186b) is also a violation of the Specified Subject Condition since *wh*-Movement will then not apply on the internal cycle. Such examples as (6), (186b), and others (for instance, *What did you talk about Bill's doing*, *What did you insist on Bill's doing*, *What did you stop Bill's reading*) seem marginal, for the most part. If they are ungrammatical (perhaps with a few idiomatic exceptions, as permitted by the interpretation of the conditions suggested with regard to (6)–(14), then the array of data (183)–(186) again illustrates the impossibility of adding provision (161) to subcondition (160a) of the Specified Subject Condition since this would now permit all such cases as (186b).

Let us return now to (182). Iteration of *wh*-Movement gives (187):

(187) Who they each expected to kill the others

But then *each*-Movement should be applicable, giving (188) ultimately (this example from R. Kayne):

(188) *Who did they expect to kill each other

But (188) does not have the interpretation of (187). Rather, it can derive, if at all, only from *They expected* [*each of who to kill the other*], by *each*-Movement on the internal cycle (analogous to the questionable *Who did Bill expect to kill each other*). The example is analogous to the case of (173a,b), where we considered (but ultimately rejected) the assumption that *each*-Movement precedes *it*-Replacement as an explanation for the ungrammaticalness of the forms. The analogous assumption that *each*-Movement precedes *wh*-Movement would suffice to account for (188), but the assumption does not suffice in general, as we can see from the derivation (189):

(189) (a) COMP Bill wanted [COMP they each to expect [COMP who to kill the others]]
      (b) COMP Bill wanted [COMP they each to expect [who to kill the others]]
      (c) COMP Bill wanted [COMP they to expect who to kill each other]

(d)   COMP Bill wanted [who they to expect to kill each other]
(e)   *Who did Bill want them to expect to kill each other

On the innermost cycle, *wh*-Movement applies to (a) of (189), giving (b). On the second cycle, assuming *each*-Movement precedes *wh*-Movement, we derive first (c) by *each*-Movement and then (d) by *wh*-Movement. Finally, on the last cycle we derive (e) by *wh*-Movement and the obligatory rules of Auxiliary Inversion and Case Assignment.[47] Therefore the assumption that *each*-Movement precedes *wh*-Movement does not suffice to exclude the unwanted derivations in such cases.

In investigating *it*-Replacement, we noted that to exclude (173b) we might assume either that *each*-Movement precedes *it*-Replacement or that when an NP replaces *it* by *it*-Replacement it leaves behind a trace which is controlled by the moved NP; we finally opted tentatively for the latter conclusion. Although the device of rule ordering does not suffice in the analogous cases just discussed, the device of leaving a trace does. Suppose, then, that we assume that the rule of *wh*-Movement leaves a controlled PRO (or a null symbol dominated by its former categories—see the discussion that precedes (177)) in the position from which it moves. Then *each*-Movement cannot apply to give (189c) from (189b) because of the Specified Subject Condition, subcase (160b). Similarly, (188) cannot be derived from (187).[48] As we shall see, this assumption permits a fairly simple rule of interpretation for *wh*-Questions and might be supported on other grounds as well.[49]

[47] We have not explicitly formulated the latter. The simplest assumption would appear to be that pronouns are always in the objective case, except in the subject position of a tensed sentence where a special rule marks them with the appropriate "nominative" inflection.

[48] The final rule of PRO-Deletion must now delete PRO in *They expected* PRO *to leave, Who did they expect* PRO *to leave,* and *Who did they expect* PRO *would leave* (assuming that PRO rather than null is the "trace"), but not in *John expected that* [PRO, singular, masculine] *would win the prize,* where the set of bracketed features is read *he*. The latter may or may not be controlled by *John*. The technical problem of making the appropriate distinction can be handled in a number of fairly obvious ways, and I will not explore the matter here.

[49] For example, assuming that *wh*-Movement leaves a trace PRO, we might then stipulate that every rule that moves an item from an obligatory category (in the sense of Emonds (1970)) leaves a trace. If the trace is not specified as PRO in the movement rule itself, then the trace is *, in which case the sentence would be blocked as ungrammatical unless the position with * is filled by some subsequent rule. It is easy to show that on this assumption Emonds' observations on the obligatory character of NP-preposing in Passive in sentences and its optional character in noun phrases follow directly on the basis of the assumption that in simple N-V-N sentences the subject position is filled by a full NP in the underlying structure. In Emonds' analysis, the subject position is empty in the base and is filled by a rule that moves NP from the agent position. (This rule then replaces the rule of Subject Postposing, one component of Passive). He then stipulates that an obligatory category, such as "subject," must be filled somewhere in a derivation, thus explaining the difference between Passive in NP and S. But the assumption that the obligatory category "subject" is obligatorily null in the base seems curious. And there are further difficulties. As R. Kayne points out, this assumption requires us to relate adverbials to an item in agent position, as in *The offer was sent by John with great glee*. But in general, adverbials relate only to items in subject position: compare *John received the offer with great glee, John was sent the offer with great glee,* where the latter, if interpretable at all, does not associate the adverbial with *John*.

A further step would be to distinguish, in some principled way, between the rules that leave PRO and * as a trace. I will not pursue here the various possibilities that suggest themselves.

To relate this discussion to other currently debated issues, note that the device of leaving a trace which functions in subsequent rules amounts to admitting a certain "derivational constraint" into the grammar. As the notion "derivational constraint" has been used in recent work, there would appear to be no condition on derivations, hence no grammatical rule operating within a derivation, that is not a derivational constraint. The only interesting problem, clearly, is to discover what specific kinds of rules (that is, derivational constraints) are empirically motivated. For my views on this matter, see Chomsky (1972a).

There is one other alternative that immediately comes to mind in the case of (188) and (189e), namely, that the rule of *wh*-Movement be extracted entirely from the cycle of transformational rules and applied only after all of the cyclic rules have applied. Under this assumption, it will follow at once that (188) cannot be derived from (187) or (189e) from (189a) by virtue of the Specified Subject Condition, case (160a), which will block *each*-Movement. Thus the assumption would be that there are two independent and ordered cycles, the first containing all cyclic rules apart from *wh*-Movement and the second containing *wh*-Movement.[50] We must still suppose *wh*-Movement to be cyclic, in particular because of such examples as (180), which will otherwise violate the Specified Subject Condition, case (160a).

Although the possibility just suggested is attractive in some respects, I will not pursue it further here and will assume in the following discussion that the rule of *wh*-Movement leaves behind a trace in the sense discussed.

11. The Specified Subject Condition has a certain naturalness. Note that in several (though not all) of the cases in which it applies to a structure of the form (190), the rule involving (X, Y) might also have involved (Z, Y), were Z appropriately selected:

(190) $\ldots X \ldots [\ldots Z \ldots - WYV \ldots] \ldots$

Thus (191) derives from (192):

(191) The men expected [the police to arrest each other]
(192) The men expected [the police each to arrest the other(s)]

The Specified Subject Condition imples that (191) must have the interpretation indicated by (192), not that given by the underlying representation (193), which cannot be transformed into (191) because of the Specified Subject Condition:

(193) The men each expected [the police to arrest the other(s)]

Thus the Specified Subject Condition, in some cases, has the effect of reducing ambiguity, or, to put it differently, of increasing the reliability of a reasonable perceptual strategy that seeks the nearest NP to a verb (or the head noun of a nominal phrase) as its subject. Similar observations apply in the case of the *A*-over-*A* condition (3). (See also the discussion of (203).) The foregoing of course assumes that the deep structure position of *each* plays some role in interpretation. See, however, notes 17, 34. If deep structure position plays no role, then the considerations just mentioned in effect guarantee a correspondence between deep structure position and scope as determined by surface structure interpretation rules, a rather natural consequence.

12. The rules we have discussed so far involve an item Y in an embedded phrase and an item X superior to it and to its left, as in the structure (190). We have noted various conditions under which X and Y may or may not be involved in a rule in this case. Suppose that we generalize these conditions, eliminating the left-right asymmetry.

---

[50] The latter cycle might also contain the root transformation of Topicalization and perhaps various rules of preposing of adverbials and other structures. See note 32.

Bresnan (1971) suggests that the rules of stress assignment (hence, presumably, all the rules of the phonological component) belong to the transformational cycle, and she discusses the implications of this view with respect to the ordering of *wh*-Movement. The question also bears on the description of Pronominalization, as has been frequently pointed out. (See particularly Postal (1971).) To my knowledge, the considerations just discussed provide the only reason for supposing that *wh*-Movement may not be part of the regular cycle of transformational rules, assuming that the general framework discussed here can be sustained.

Thus we simply drop from (123) the requirement that X be to the left of the embedded phrase $[_\alpha$ and leave all conditions otherwise unchanged. I do not know of many convincing examples that bear on the correctness of this generalization. For example, one consequence will be that the Specified Subject Condition will block (194) but not (195):

(194) *John's pictures of each other intrigued the children
(195) Pictures of each other intrigue the children

Although (194) surely is much worse than (195), leftward movement of *each* still seems at best clumsy, so that the example is perhaps not too illuminating. However, there are more interesting cases when we consider the Subjacency Condition (81). This condition implies (196):

(196) No rule can move an item from position Y to position X in the structure

$$\ldots[_\beta \ldots [_\alpha \ldots Y \ldots] \ldots] \ldots X \ldots$$

where $Y \neq \alpha$ and α, β are cyclic categories, unless some constant term of the structural description of the rule holds of a phrase in β that is subjacent to X

In particular, we cannot derive sentences such as those in (197):

(197) (a) John believes $[_\beta$that $[_\alpha$a man ____] was here . . .] despite the evidence to the contrary *who comes from Philadelphia*
      (b) $[_\beta[_\alpha$one ____] of the men . . .] will meet you at the station *who is a friend of mine*
      (c) the girl $[_\beta$to whom $[_\alpha$it ____] was obvious . . .] slapped the dean *that he was after her* [51]

In (197), ____ indicates the position from which the italicized item is extracted by various types of extraposition, and . . . indicates the position to which the italicized item can properly be moved. These examples are of the form (196), where the italicized phrase is in the position X, having been moved illegitimately from the position Y marked by ____.

On the other hand, consider such sentences as (198):

(198) (a) $[[_\beta$the only people $[_\alpha$they really like ____]] are Bill and Mary
      (b) $[[_\beta$the only people $[_\alpha$they really like ____]] are each other

On the assumption (proposed in Chomsky (1970a) and developed in detail in Akmajian (1970)) that (a) and (b) of (198) derive from a source with a subject containing *They really like Bill and Mary*, *They really like each other*, respectively, by substitution of the object of α into the predicate position of the matrix sentence, the derivation is permissible, under (196), if the structural description of the rule that forms (198) makes explicit reference to the position occupied by *the only people* in (198).

If the analysis given so far is correct, then, there appears to be no left-right asymmetry for extraction rules. Though relevant examples are few, to my knowledge, it seems plausible to offer the general working hypothesis that there is no left-right asymmetry at all with respect to the conditions that have been discussed here.

Left-right asymmetry of rules is not unknown, of course, anaphora being the most obvious example, and the Complementizer Substitution Universal (2) being

---

[51] Example from Bach (1971). If, as Emonds (1970) proposes, there is no rule of extraposition of the assumed form, then the issue does not arise in the case of (197c).

another one. Ross (1967) has suggested that leftward movement rules and rightward movement rules differ in that the former can move an item arbitrarily far to the left, crossing arbitrarily many clause boundaries, whereas the latter cannot extract an item from a clause. Notice that this asymmetry of boundedness follows from the asymmetry of the Complementizer Substitution Universal. That is, we have proposed that leftward and rightward extraction rules are bounded by the Subjacency Condition, but items that move to COMP position will escape this limitation, for reasons that we have discussed. Assuming that complementizer substitution is only leftward (that is, the Baker-Bresnan Complementizer Substitution Universal (2)) and that an item in the COMP position can move upward to (and only to) another COMP position, unhindered by the Specified Subject and Tensed-S Conditions, it follows that there can be, in effect, unbounded movement to the left by iteration of Complementizer Substitution. Thus the two cases of asymmetry are not independent. Rather, the asymmetry of boundedness follows from the asymmetry of the Complementizer Substitution Universal, in the special case of rules that substitute an item in the COMP position. The available data would appear to bear out this limitation.

13. Let us now turn to the transformational rules. We have so far assumed the cyclic rules that I restate as (199) and the root transformations (200):

(199) (a) *wh*-Placement on NP, PP, AP, or *either*

     (b) *wh*-Movement: in the structure

$$[_S[_{COMP} X_1, X_2, X_3, \pm WH], X_5, wh, X_7]$$

     the sixth term fills the position of X_2 and is replaced by PRO

     (c) [*wh*, NP] becomes null in the context

$$[_{NP} NP\underline{\quad}\ldots]\ (\text{i.e., in relatives})^{52}$$

     (d) −WH becomes *that* in the context

$$\begin{cases}[_\alpha X[_S\underline{\quad} YT\ldots]\ldots] & (i)^{53}\\ [_\alpha Z[_N N\underline{\quad} S']]\ (\text{obligatory}) & (ii)\end{cases}$$

     where X or $Y = $ NP and α is the adjacent cyclic node

     (e) NP becomes NP*'s* in the context $\underline{\quad}ing$ VP and becomes *for* NP in the context $\underline{\quad}to$ VP (obligatory)

     (f) *for* becomes null after *expect*, . . . (obligatory)

     (g) Passive, etc.

(200) (a) Auxiliary Inversion

     (b) *whether* becomes null[54]

---

[52] I assume here that a relative structure, at this stage of derivation, has the form NP S. This is not obviously correct, and if the structure is in fact different, the condition for (c) will have to be correspondingly reformulated.

[53] Notice that this rule and the preceding one, as formulated, exploit the interpretation of conditions discussed earlier (see discussion of (6)–(14)). That is, the change effected by the rules is internal to a cycle already passed. It is, in any event, unclear whether the relevant conditions apply to "housekeeping rules" such as (c) and (d).

[54] Both cases of (200) are obligatory and restricted to the matrix sentence. Note that there is no way to generate *that* as the COMP of a matrix sentence. Thus we cannot have either *that* S' or *whether* S' as full sentences. I will assume here that *yes-no* questions derive by (199a,b) from something of the form +WH *either* . . ., along the lines of Katz and Postal (1964). The assumption is in no way crucial.

I assume that *wh* is a feature that can be placed on a node (and, by convention, on all nodes it dominates—see Dougherty (1970) on the matter of "feature percolation"). By (199a) we can assign *wh* either to *someone* or to *to someone* in the sentence *I gave the book to someone.* The rule of *wh*-Movement (199b), which we may take to be optional, will form either *Whom did I give the book to* or *To whom did I give the book*, depending on whether *wh* is applied to the PP or the NP.[55] The structure-preserving condition will insure that P and NP move into the proper position in COMP.

Rule (199c), which is optional, permits the *wh* noun phrase introducing a relative to be deleted (*the man whom I met, the man I met*). Some conditions on the application of this rule follow from the operation of a surface filter to which we return.

Case (i) of (199d), which is also optional, permits *that* as a realization of COMP when the auxiliary contains tense. The requirement that *X* or *Y* must be NP permits *The book that fell on the floor, What did you tell me that Bill read* while excluding **What did you tell me that fell on the floor.* It is ad hoc and presumably indicates some error in the analysis since one would expect this distinction to be predictable on other grounds. After certain verbs, $-$WH in the circumstances of case (i) must be *that.* Compare *John said (that) he had to do his homework this evening, John complained that he had to do his homework this evening, *John complained he had to do his homework this evening.* As noted by Dean (1967), such verbs as *complain, quip*, which require a following *that* as COMP, also block *wh*-Movement; that is, we do not have **What did John complain that he had to do this evening, *What did John quip that Mary wore.* There are a number of ways that come to mind for expressing this generalization, but I see no interesting explanation. Again, this lack may indicate a defect of the analysis.

Case (ii) of (199d) excludes such forms as **the claim John is here* (while permitting *We claim John is here*—N̄ is to be understood in the sense of Chomsky (1970a)). This is one of a set of such conditions (for example, *I am glad John is here, I am sure John is here, *I am delighted John is here, *It surprises me John is here, *I am aware John is here*—again, there is undoubtedly more to this, perhaps an entirely different analysis).

Rules (199e), (199f) must also be given in a more general form (incorporating as well *John's refusal, John's book*, and so on). They provide, for example, for such

---

[55] Here and in what follows, I omit discussion of echo questions. Note that rule (199a) is hardly more than a notational device. We might eliminate it, assuming rather that *wh* is assigned by base rules or dispensing with the element *wh* entirely and reformulating (199b) so that the contexts of *wh*-placement appear in place of *wh* in the structural description. This approach would involve slight modifications of later rules.

The fact that *wh*-Movement, though optional, must apply in indirect questions and relatives follows from considerations to which we turn in a moment. Notice that if *wh*-Placement is applied to the PP *to someone* in the sentence *You expected to give the book to someone*, then after the internal cycle we have COMP *you expected [[wh, to whom] PRO to give the book]*, where *[wh, to whom]* is the structure *to whom* dominated by the feature complex *[wh, PP].* The *A*-over-*A* principle prevents extraction of *whom* on the next cycle, blocking **Whom did you expect to to give the book*, with the "dangling preposition" *to.* This observation is redundant, however, since the rules of interpretation to be given will in any event block interpretation of sentences with dangling prepositions in COMP. The same will be true if we eliminate the notational device of *wh*-Placement entirely.

Notice that in the formulation of rules given here, there may be nodes P and NP in COMP that dominate no terminal string and therefore play no role in interpretation or in factoring terminal strings for transformation. There are other conventions and correspondingly different formulations of the rules that might be adopted in these cases. Note that *wh*-Movement of "intransitive" prepositions also gives structures that are uninterpretable by the rules to be given. We overlook here the interesting and important question of the full set of rules of rewriting of COMP, sufficient to account for all cases of *wh*-Movement.

distinctions as *I expected John to leave, What I expected was for John to leave* and *What we hoped for was for John to win, We hoped for John to win* (with PP simplification —there is much variation in judgment in such cases).[56]

We assume further the base rules (54) (a refinement of (16)). Following essentially Emonds (1970), we assume that of the COMP-Aux pairs, only a null COMP with the auxiliary *-ing* appears as an NP. Thus we assume, at the deep structure level, the following analyses:

(201) (a) I–expect–[COMP John will leave] (NP–V–S)
          (I expect (that) John will leave)
      (b) I–expect–[COMP John to leave] (NP–V–S)
          (I expect John to leave)
      (c) we–argued–about–[COMP John ing leave so early] (NP–V–P–NP)
          (We argued about John's leaving so early)

In fact, *-ing* nominals can appear quite freely as noun phrases, though *that*-S and *for*-NP-*to*-VP cannot (for example, alongside of (201c), **We argued about that John left so early*, **We argued about for John to leave so early*). Noting this, let us add the base condition (202):

(202) In the structure [$_{NP}$[$_S$COMP NP Aux VP]], Aux = *ing* and (16b) does not apply. In effect, then, S = S' when S is immediately dominated by NP.

There will be a number of other conditions of this sort.[57]

14. We have so far listed the relevant conditions, base rules, and transformations. To insure that only the right forms are generated, we add the Surface Exclusion Filter (203):[58]

[56] Alternatively, we might drop (f) and reformulate (e) so that insertion of *for* depends on the governing lexical item. Another possibility would be to distinguish two cases of *to*, determined by selectional rules relating to the governing lexical item, one of which requires *for*, the other of which excludes *for*. I will not pursue these questions here.
Derived nominals with complements of the form (*for* NP) *to* VP do not correlate entirely with such complements in the corresponding sentence (*We believe John to be a nice fellow*, **Our belief (for) John to be a nice fellow*; **We desire (for) John to win, Our desire for John to win*). It seems that derived nominals take *for* only when they also take prepositional phrases with *for* (*our desire for victory (for John to win), (to win)*—similarly, *wish, hopes, plans*, and so on). In Chomsky (1972a) I suggested that the impossibility of **John's belief of Bill to win* was a consequence of the lexicalist hypothesis regarding derived nominals. The considerations just mentioned, however, indicate that the example was irrelevant to that issue since **John's belief for Bill to win* is also impossible.
[57] We might go on, following Emonds (1970), to hold that instead of extraposition there is a rule of *it*-Replacement that gives *For John to leave would surprise me, That John left surprised me*, and so on; we might also hold that the Passive transformation does not apply to such forms as (201a,b) to prepose the embedded S. Forms such as *That John left is (widely) believed* then derive the *it*-Replacement from *It is (widely) believed that John left* (which we shall refer to as "sentence (a)") under these assumptions. If this is a root transformation, in Emonds' sense, it follows that we cannot have *I wonder whether that S' is widely believed*, though *I wonder whether the fact that S' is widely believed* is all right. Speculating as to the sentence (a), we might take it to be in effect a base form, if VP → Aspect $\overline{V}$, where Aspect → (Perfect)(Progressive)(Passive). This analysis would require that both components of Passive are obligatory if Aspect contains Passive (and, of course, NP-Preposing is inapplicable if there is no NP following the verb, as in (a)); that a rule of interpretation relates *it* and sentential complements (thus there is no interpretation for **It is died by John*, but there is for (a)); that *believe* and so on must have a subject at the deep structure level, either a lexical subject or Δ, which will delete (by the rule of Agent Deletion) if it moves to the agent position (excluding *It believes that S); that *it* appears in the position of an otherwise unfilled subject.
[58] In the terminology of Chomsky (1972a), V_T contains the features [+ verb] and also [+ tense], that is, it is a tensed verb or auxiliary. The proposal here is similar to but not quite identical with that of Perlmutter (1971).

(203) The structure $[_{NP}NP\ V_T\dots]$ is excluded, where V_T is an element containing tense (T)

Before illustrating the rules, let us consider the status of the filter (203). Bever (1970) has made the interesting suggestion that certain formal properties of grammar might be functionally motivated, in the sense that their effect on strings is to facilitate perceptual strategies. (As we have already observed, the Specified Subject Condition (123a) might be regarded in this way.) As one example, Bever discusses some of the rules that determine the presence or absence of *that* as a complementizer. The filter (203) accommodates several cases of this sort. By virtue of (203), a left-right analytic routine can operate reliably on the assumption that a noun phrase–verb phrase structure, unless it is preceded by *that* or morphologically marked, is always a full sentence, not a noun phrase. This is a natural candidate for a performance strategy. It would also be rather natural for performance strategies to affect grammars at the level of surface structure filters. So few persuasive examples exist that no firm conclusions can be drawn, but the question that Bever raises is an intriguing one, and (203) is a suggestive example.[59]

[59] Bever's other examples do not involve conditions on the form of grammars. Thus he observes that acceptable adjective order (which is inexpressible in any natural way in a transformational grammar) can be determined in accord with a natural perceptual strategy, and he suggests an alternative to a proposal of Miller and Chomsky (1963) concerning embedded sentences. (The question is irrelevant here, but his alternative seems to me considerably more ad hoc than the proposal he rejects. He states that the latter does not explain the distinction between single and multiple self-embedding, but in fact it does when supplemented by the very natural proposal that there are perceptual stategies for the analysis of such structures as relative clause and that in the case of any analytic procedure it is difficult to call upon this procedure in the course of executing it. See Chomsky, (1965, p. 14).)

Bever's paper has been widely interpreted as questioning the distinction between competence and performance and as denying that grammatical rules relating deep and surface structure are involved in language use. In fact, he presupposes a relation between "internal structure" and "external structure" in language use, and if in fact knowledge of language includes a specification of a pairing between deep (internal) and surface (external) structures determined by transformational rules, it would be surprising to discover that this is not the pairing involved in language use. In any event, Bever's discussion provides no reason for doubting this identity. As to the competence-performance distinction, Bever presupposes it throughout, with his reference to "epistemological systems" (in particular, grammars that describe competence). In fact, his discussion provides independent support for the appropriateness of the competence-performance framework, as conventionally formulated, precisely because the properties of acceptable sentences that he accounts for in terms of performance strategies are grammatically inexpressible (in any natural way). For discussion, see Chomsky (1965; 1971). Bever's comments on the nature of the evidence for transformational grammars seem to me misleading, and in part incorrect, for reasons elaborated in Chomsky (1965).

It is difficult to imagine a coherent alternative to the conventional competence-performance distinction. However, it is possible that grammatical transformations are not the appropriate device for expressing the relationship between "external structures" and "internal structures." Thus one might imagine that this relationship is captured by some set of "perceptual strategies," now unknown. Were knowledge of language to be more adequately expressed in such a system, we could dispense with the theory of transformational grammar. This possibility seems to me quite remote, given present knowledge or conjectures, but it is conceivable. It has been occasionally suggested that transformational grammar is a system of "strategies of prediction" used in determining grammaticalness but not otherwise involved in language use (see Langendoen (1970)). Though possible in principle, this is a most implausible hypothesis. It amounts to the belief that there are separate systems for expressing, on the one hand, strategies of perception and production and, on the other, strategies of prediction; only the former are used in the normal experience of a speaker-hearer, but the latter come into operation when an informant is asked to perform such tasks as judging the acceptability of sentences. The obvious question is why the second system should exist at all since it is rarely if ever used by nonlinguists. Surely the more natural assumption is that there is a mentally represented grammar expressing knowledge of language and used in production, perception, and prediction. One would surely want strong evidence before abandoning this very conservative hypothesis.

15. We illustrate the rules (199)–(200) by a few sample derivations (in which irrelevant details are omitted).

Consider the base structure (204):

(204) [$_{NP}$the person [$_S$[$_{COMP}$P NP $-$WH][$_{S'}$Bill saw the person]]]

On the innermost cycle, *wh*-Placement (199a) applies to the NP *the person*, which replaces the NP of the COMP by *wh*-Movement (199b). Turning to the next cycle, namely, the cycle of the whole NP structure (204), we first replace the *wh*-phrase *the person* by *who* and then turn to (199c), the first applicable rule of those in (199).[60] If this optional rule does not apply, then (199d) is inapplicable and we derive *the person who Bill saw*. If (199c) deletes *who*, then (199di) is applicable. If it applies, we derive *the person that Bill saw*; if not, *the person Bill saw*.

Consider next the base structure (205):

(205) [$_{NP}$the person[$_S$[$_{COMP}$P NP $-$WH][$_{S'}$the person saw Bill]]]

Again, on the innermost cycle *wh*-Placement and *wh*-Movement apply, giving (206):

(206) [$_{NP}$the person[$_S$[$_{COMP}$P[*wh*, the person]$-$WH][$_{S'}$saw Bill]]]

On the next cycle, if (199c) is not applied, we derive *the person who saw Bill*. If (199c) does apply, then (199d) is applicable. If (199d) applies, we derive *the person that saw Bill*; if not, we derive **the person saw Bill*, which is excluded by the Surface Exclusion Filter (203). Hence there are only two possible surface forms corresponding to (205), as compared to three in the case of (204).

Now consider the underlying structure (207):

(207) [$_{NP}$[$-$WH Bill is here]]is surprising

On the innermost cycle no rule applies to (207). On the NP cycle, rule (199di) can apply, giving *that Bill is here is surprising*. If this optional rule does not apply, the resulting form, **Bill is here is surprising*, is excluded by the Surface Filter (203). This is a case of (203) that is different from the one in the derivation initiated by (205). The example here, of course, is beside the point if, as suggested earlier, the sentence in question is derived by *it*-Replacement.

Consider next the base form which, after *wh*-Placement, becomes (208):

(208) [$_{COMP}$NP $+$WH][you will tell me[$_\alpha$[$_{COMP}$NP $-$WH][Bill saw who]]]

On the innermost cycle α, *who* moves to the NP position in the COMP, before $-$WH. This gives (209):

(209) [$_{COMP}$NP $+$WH][you will tell me[$_\alpha$[$_{COMP}$who $-$WH][Bill saw]]]

Unless there is further *wh*-Movement on the next cycle, this structure will be excluded by the rule of interpretation (to be given later) that obligatorily interprets a *wh*-phrase in a $-$WH COMP as a relative; this is impossible here since $\alpha \neq$ NP and there is no antecedent. Suppose, however, that *who* is moved on the next cycle, giving (210):

(210) [who $+$WH][you will tell me[$-$WH[Bill saw]]]

---

[60] On notations for expressing the obligatory character of Relativization, see Chomsky (1965).

The first applicable rule is (199d). (Note that Y = NP). If it applies, we derive (with Auxiliary Inversion) *Who will you tell me that Bill saw*; if it does not apply, *Who will you tell me Bill saw.*[61]

Suppose that we had $-$WH as the initial COMP instead of $+$WH in (209). Then the result corresponding to (210) will also be uninterpretable since the obligatory relative interpretation of a *wh*-phrase in a $-$WH COMP is inapplicable.

Suppose that we have *Who saw Bill* instead of *Bill saw who* in (208). Then the only possible outcome is *Who will you tell me saw Bill*. Rule (199di) is inapplicable in this case since $Y \neq$ NP.

The base structure (211) will yield *I believe (that) John saw Bill*, with the presence of *that* depending on whether or not (199di) applies:

(211) I believe [$-$WH John saw Bill]·

In contrast, consider (212):

(212) I wonder [$+$WH Bill saw who]

Applying *wh*-Movement on the innermost cycle, we derive *I wonder [who Bill saw]*. If the initial COMP of the matrix sentence is $-$WH, this stands as a grammatical sentence. But if the initial COMP is $+$WH, then no interpretable sentence is generated. (Recall that on our present assumptions, *Do I wonder who Bill saw* comes from a different source, with *either* in the matrix sentence; see note 54). The rules of interpretation that we shall discuss provide that a $+$WH COMP is interpretable (namely, as a question) just in case the COMP is filled with a *wh*-phrase. If *wh*-Movement does not apply on the outermost cycle in (212), then the initial $+$WH COMP is not filled by a *wh*-phrase and the sentence is uninterpretable. If *wh*-Movement does apply, giving, with Auxiliary Inversion, *Who do I wonder $+$WH Bill saw*, then the embedded $+$WH COMP contains no *wh*-phrase and the sentence is again uninterpretable.

Compare (211), (212) with (213), (214):

(213) I believe [$-$WH John saw who]
(214) I wonder [$+$WH John saw Bill]

In the case of (213), *wh*-Movement on the innermost cycle gives *I believe [who $-$WH John saw]*. This cannot stand as is because, as already noted, a *wh*-phrase in a $-$WH COMP must be interpreted as a relative, which is impossible in this case. But if the initial COMP of the matrix sentence contains $+$WH, we can derive *Who do I believe (that) John saw* by *wh*-Movement on the external cycle. In the case of (214), no grammatical sentence is generated since we have a $+$WH COMP not containing a *wh*-phrase. The words *believe* and *wonder* differ lexically in that, as the sense indicates, the former requires $-$WH COMP and the latter requires $+$WH COMP, leading to the grammatical consequences just noted.

Consider finally the verb *ask*, which appears in a variety of structures. In the first place, like *wonder*, it appears in (215), analogous to (212):

(215) John asked [$+$WH Bill saw who]

As in the case of *wonder*, we can derive *John asked who Bill saw* from (215) if the initial COMP is $-$WH, but no grammatical sentence results if the initial COMP is $+$WH (in particular, not **Who did John ask (that) Bill saw*).

---

[61] There are further considerations determining the applicability of (199di). Thus, it seems to me that omission of *that* is unacceptable in *What did you persuade Bill___John should see* or *What did you urge___I see*, for example.

The verb *ask*, however, can take − WH COMP in the embedded sentence if the latter is subjunctive, as in *John asked that Bill leave early*. Consider, then, (216):

(216) John asked [− WH Bill see who]

This case is analogous to (213) rather than (212). Thus we can derive *Who did John ask that Bill see* but not **John asked who Bill see*.

The verb *ask*, as distinct from *believe* and *wonder*, can take controlled PRO in the embedded sentence, as in *John asked to see Mary* from (217):

(217) John asked [− WH PRO to see Mary]

Suppose, however, that we have + WH rather than − WH in (217). Then, exactly as in the case of (214), no grammatical sentence can be derived. But suppose that we have + WH in place of − WH and *who* instead of *Mary*, that is, (218):

(218) John asked [+ WH PRO to see who]

This is now analogous to (212) and (215). For the reasons already noted, from (218) we can derive (219) but not (220):

(219) John asked who to see
(220) Who did John ask to see

Of course, *ask* can also take − WH COMP, as in (216), (217). Thus we have the underlying form (221):

(221) John asked [− WH PRO to see who]

From (221) we can derive (220) but not (219). Thus (219) and (220), though both grammatical, derive from different sources: (219) derives from (218), and (220) derives from (221), with matrix-initial + WH. The answer to (220) might be *John asked to see Mary*, which derives from (217). As is generally the case with answer-question pairs of the simplest sort, (217) is identical to (221) except that it contains *Mary* instead of *who*.

The preceding examples illustrate uses of *ask* with only S as complement, but *ask* can also take NP S as complement: *John asked me why Bill left*. Consider, then, the underlying forms in (222)–(226), analogous to (215), (216), (217), (218), (221), respectively:

(222) John asked me [+ WH Bill saw who]
(223) John asked me [− WH Bill see who]
(224) John asked me [− WH PRO to see Mary]
(225) John asked me [+ WH PRO to see who]
(226) John asked me [− WH PRO to see who]

In the case of (222), we derive *John asked me who Bill saw* but not *Who did John ask me (that) Bill saw*. (In fact, as in the case of (215), there is no grammatical sentence derivable if the initial COMP of the matrix sentence in (222) contains + WH.)

Consider next (223). As in the case of (216), we should be able to derive *Who did John ask me that Bill see*, but not **John asked me who Bill see*. For me, the first is also excluded, but in this case because the verb *ask* with NP S complement does not take subjunctive in the embedded sentence, as we can see from the ungrammaticality of **John asked me that Bill leave early* (compare *John asked that Bill leave early*).

The next example, (224), is analogous to (217). Thus we can derive *John asked me to see Mary* (*see* in the rough sense of "visit," as in *John asked me to see the head nurse when I arrive*). Notice that in this case PRO is controlled not by the subject of the matrix sentence but by the NP following the verb *ask*, as in *John asked me to throw the ball* and so on.

Consider next the example (225), analogous to (218). From (225) we can derive (227) but not (228):

(227) John asked me who to see (visit)
(228) Who did John ask me to see (visit)

As in the analogous case of (221), from (226) we can derive (228) but not (227).

As before, these conclusions are semantically correct. We can see this particularly clearly in the present case by considering the matter of control of PRO. As already noted, in the case of (224) PRO is controlled by *me*: I am to see (or visit) Mary. This is in general the case when *ask* takes NP S complement where the COMP of S is − WH. But where the COMP of S is + WH, the subject of *ask*, rather than the NP following it, controls PRO. We can see this in the case of (229), as contrasted with (230) in which the embedded COMP is − WH:

(229) John asked me whether to visit Mary
(230) John asked me to visit Mary

In the case of (229), John is to visit Mary; in the case of (230), I am to visit Mary. Similarly, in the case of (227) John is to see (visit) someone, whereas in the case of (228) I am to do so. This result is as predicted, given that (227), like (229), derives from an underlying structure with + WH in the embedded COMP, whereas (228), like (230), derives from an underlying structure with − WH in the embedded COMP.

Summarizing, *ask* takes an S complement or an NP S complement. In the latter case, a lexical property indicates that the embedded COMP can be − WH only if the subject of the embedded sentence is PRO. Where the subject of the embedded S is PRO, PRO is controlled necessarily by the subject of *ask* if the complement is merely S; PRO is controlled by the subject of *ask* if the complement is NP S and the COMP of the embedded S is + WH; PRO is controlled by the NP following *ask* if the COMP of the embedded S is − WH. (We might seek a further explanation of these facts, but that is another matter). Given the idiosyncracies noted, the distribution of grammatical and ungrammatical sentences and their interpretations follows from the rules already given.

In (199) we assumed, without argument, that Passive follows *wh*-Movement. Supposing this to be true, consider the sentence (231):

(231) Who is John believed to like

The underlying source, after *wh*-Placement, is (232a), and the rule of *wh*-Movement on the first cycle gives (232b):

(232) (a) COMP Δ believe [COMP John to like who]
     (b) COMP Δ believe [who John to like]

The rule forming passives will not apply to (232b). But if *wh*-Movement precedes Passive, placing *who* in the initial COMP, then Passive will apply, forming (231) ultimately.

However, this argument for ordering *wh*-Movement before Passive fails because there is another possible derivation of (231). Since *wh*-Movement is optional, we may assume that it does not apply on the internal cycle. Turning to the outer cycle, we might form (231) by Passive followed by *wh*-Movement, if *wh*-Movement is not blocked under these circumstances by some version of the Specified Subject Condition, as discussed earlier.

The issue is clarified if there is an extra cycle. Thus consider the underlying structure (233):

(233) COMP Δ expected [COMP John to try [COMP PRO to win the race]]

Passive can apply to (233) on the external cycle to give (234):

(234) John was expected to try to win the race

Suppose that in (233) we have *which race* in place of *the race*. Then *wh*-Movement on the internal cycles will given (235):

(235) COMP Δ expected [which race John to try [COMP PRO to win]]

Turning to the outermost cycle, if *wh*-Movement precedes Passive, we derive (236) by applying both rules (followed by Agent Deletion and Auxiliary Inversion):

(236) Which race was John expected to try to win

If Passive precedes *wh*-Movement, however, we cannot derive (236), which is grammatical. Notice that in this case the alternative analysis suggested in the case of (231) is excluded. If *wh*-Movement has not already produced (235) by the time we reach the external cycle, then it will not be applicable at all, by the Subjacency Condition (81) on extraction. Therefore the ordering of (199) is correct, on the assumption that the hypotheses proposed so far (some rather tentatively) are correct. Notice that the same example indicates that the "trace" left by *wh*-Movement must not be a non-null terminal symbol. Therefore, it must either be null (see the discussion that precedes (177)) or, if PRO, a feature of a complex nonterminal symbol.

Notice that Passive must also apparently be permitted to precede *wh*-Movement if such sentences as *Who was John killed by* are to be derived in the most natural way. It may be, then, that the two rules are unordered relative to one another, that is, that they may apply in either order.

16. It remains to discuss lexical subcategorization and rules of interpretation. We suppose (again following Bresnan (1970)) that lexical items are subcategorized with respect to the choice of COMP and Aux in embedded complement sentences. For example, the item *ask* in the sense of "ask a question," as in *You asked me who John saw*, must take a +WH COMP in the embedded sentence; but in the sense of "request" it will take a −WH COMP with subjunctive, as in *I ask that you leave at once*. (See examples (215)–(221)). On the other hand, the verb *tell* can freely take ±WH as COMP in the embedded sentence.[62] Thus we have the indirect question (237), the free relative (238a), and the sentential complement (238b):

(237) I told him who would leave
           (I told him [+WH someone would leave])
(238) (a) I told him what Bill asked me to tell him
              (I told him [PRO [−WH Bill asked me to tell him something]])
          (b) I told him that it is raining
              (I told him [−WH it is raining])

---

[62] When it has an indirect object, as in (237), (238). Otherwise, as Bresnan notes, it can take only +WH (*Susie didn't tell whether they had eaten*, **Susie didn't tell that they had eaten*, *Susie didn't tell us that (whether) they had eaten*).

To be more precise, only cases (237) and (238b) are determined directly by the lexical subcategorization of *tell*. Case (238a) is a special case of the base structure NP–*tell*–NP′–indirect object, where NP′ happens to be a relative with an unspecified antecedent, analogous to *I told him the story he likes, I told him something.* (In these cases, as in (238a), Indirect Object Movement has applied.)

Notice that further specifications are necessary to determine under what conditions indirect questions are appropriate. For example, the examples in (239) seem preferable to those in (240):

(239) (a) I will know whether I pass as soon as he walks in
     (b) I will tell him whether you'll apply
     (c) I didn't tell him whether it would rain
(240) (a) I knew whether I would pass
     (b) I told him whether you will (would) apply
     (c) I told him whether it would rain

Lexical specifications account for such facts as the following. Although (241a) cannot be derived from (241b), as we have seen earlier, (242a) can be derived from (242b), though not from (242c); and (243)a derives properly from (243b), though not from (243c):

(241) (a) *What did you tell him who saw
     (b) +WH you told him [+WH someone saw something]
(242) (a) What did you tell him (that) Bill saw
     (b) +WH you told him [−WH Bill saw something]
     (c) +WH you told him [+WH Bill saw something]
(243) (a) You told him what Bill saw
     (b) −WH you told him [+WH Bill saw something]
     (c) −WH you told him [−WH Bill saw]

Sources (242c) and (243c) are ruled out for (242a) and (243a), respectively, by the principles of interpretation to which we now turn.[63]

In all cases other than those enumerated, the sentence receives no interpretation.

A +WH COMP is interpreted only when it contains a *wh*-phrase. A −WH COMP containing no terminal string is interpreted as a clause introducer; if it introduces a relative clause (that is, after application of (199c)), the interpretation is that of relatives. A −WH COMP with a terminal string other than a *wh*-phrase might be interpreted as topicalization; we have not dealt with this process here, but it appears to be similar to *wh*-Movement except for the condition that there is an interpretation only in a root sentence in the sense of Emonds (1970).

Consider next the rules of interpretation for *wh*-phrases. First, in a −WH COMP, the interpretation is always as a relative clause,[64] with the antecedent appropriately associated with the position marked by the trace left by *wh*-Movement. (Details of relative clause interpretation need not concern us here; it is sufficient to

---

[63] Compare (238a) with (243) from *You told him* [PRO[−WH *Bill saw something*]]. The latter is excluded on the same grounds that exclude *I told him the picture of Mary*, and so on.

[64] We assume that noun phrases with relative clauses have a different structure than those with sentential complements to nouns. Thus we have been assuming such structures as the following, at the surface level: [NP[NP*the man*][S*that I saw*]], [NP*the*[N̄*claim*[S*that John saw Bill*]]], [S*we*[VP[V̄*claim*[S*that John saw Bill*]]]], where N̄ and V̄ are as in Chomsky (1970a) (and NP = N̄, VP = V̄).

Since [NP NP[*wh* +WH] . . .] cannot be interpreted as a question, only −WH can introduce a relative.

note that the formal structures that provide a full interpretation are appropriately determined.) A free relative (for example, *I read what you gave me*) is derived when the antecedent is the indeterminate element, which deletes.

Let us look at the item *urge*, which takes a −WH COMP and subjunctive in Aux, as in (244):

(244) I urge that Bill visit the museum

Consider now the underlying structure (245) (where *wh*-Placement has applied on the internal cycle):

(245) COMP I urge [[NP −WH][Bill visit *what*]]

On the first cycle, *wh*-Movement will apply, giving (246):

(246) COMP I urge [[what −WH][Bill visit]]]

Turning to the external cycle, if the initial COMP is +WH, *wh*-Movement must apply (or we will have an unfilled +WH COMP). This yields, ultimately, (247):

(247) What did I urge that Bill visit

If the initial COMP is −WH in (245), *wh*-Movement will be impossible on the external cycle because the initial −WH COMP is uninterpretable as a relative. If no *wh*-Movement takes place, the resulting form is (246), and there is again no interpretation since here too there is a −WH COMP containing a *wh*-phrase but not interpretable as a relative. Therefore a grammatical sentence (one which is generated by the rules, is not assigned * in the course of the derivation, and receives an interpretation) is generated from (245) only if the initial COMP is +WH and *wh*-Movement takes place on both cycles.

Consider next the rules for interpreting a *wh*-phrase in a +WH COMP. There are several cases, depending on the choice of *wh*-phrase. (Perhaps the cases can be combined, but this will not concern us here.) Thus [*whether* +WH] will be interpreted as "is it the case that" (as in NP *wondered whether it would rain*). The NPs *who* and *what* are interpreted in accordance with (248):

(248) The phrase [$_\alpha$[*wh*, NP] +WH] ... PRO ...] is interpreted with PRO a variable bound by the node [*wh*, NP] and ... the semantic interpretation determined by the derivation of α[65]

Thus, for example, *I wonder who John saw* would mean "I wonder for which *x*, John saw someone *x*." The principle can be extended to other *wh*-phrases, such as *how, when, which, what* (as in *which (what) books*), and can be formalized, but we will carry the matter no further here.

The only remaining case is that of a *wh*-phrase that is not in a COMP. Again overlooking here the matter of echo questions, we can interpret such phrases with the principle (249):

(249) Assign a *wh*-phrase not in COMP to some higher structure [$_{COMP}$ ... +WH] and interpret as in (248) where the interpretation is uniform in this COMP node

---

[65] We leave open, as irrelevant here, the question of which aspects of the derivation (deep structure, surface structure, both, and so on) determine the semantic interpretation. In the case in question, PRO is controlled by the complex symbol [*wh*, NP] which has moved from the position occupied by PRO by *wh*-Movement; that is, PRO is the "trace" remaining from *wh*-Movement, in the terminology used earlier. The principle (248) can be generalized to other cases where a controlled PRO functions as a variable.

Thus the sentence (250) will have the interpretation (251), and (252) will have the interpretation (253):

(250) I wonder who saw what
(251) I wonder for which x, for which y, someone x saw something y
(252) I remembered what John had given to whom; I remembered to whom John had given what
(253) I remembered for which x, for which y, John had given something x to someone y

But sentence (254) will receive no interpretation at all since (248) cannot apply uniformly in the node containing *whether* (since it does not apply to *whether*):

(254) I wonder whether Bill saw what

In fact, (254) is interpretable only as an echo question.

Notice that principle (249) in effect overcomes the formal restriction against moving two *wh*-phrases into the same COMP position. That is, it permits interpretations that proceed as if this double movement had taken place.

In the examples just cited, the *wh*-phrase not in COMP position was assigned, for interpretation, to the immediately dominating COMP. However, principle (249) is not restricted to this case.[66] An example discussed by Baker (1970) illustrates additional possibilities. Consider the sentence (255):

(255) Who remembers where we bought which book

Principle (249) (appropriately extended to *which book, which place* = *where*) permits either of the interpretations in (256) and only these:

(256) (a) For which x, x remembers for which z, for which y, we bought y at z
    (b) For which x, for which y, x remembers for which z we bought y at z

A possible answer, under the interpretation (a), would be *John remembers where we bought which book*. A possible answer under the interpretation (b) would be *John remembers where we bought the physics book and Bill remembers where we bought the novel.*[67]

Notice that in the case of (256b), principle (249) in effect overcomes the restriction against moving a *wh*-phrase from a phrase to which *wh*-Movement has already applied into a higher phrase of the phrase marker, just as in the case of (250)–(253) (and, in fact, both cases of (256) as well) principle (249) overcomes the formal restriction against moving two *wh*-phrases into the same COMP position.

Observe also that with no artificial notational devices, we can interpret sentences directly in terms of the surface structure position of the *wh*-phrase and the nature of

---

[66] Notice that (249), as formulated, explicitly violates (123), just as the rule of Coreference Assignment does (see note 16). Recall again that under the proposed interpretation of universal conditions (see discussion of (6)–(14)), it is possible to formulate particular rules to which they do not apply. If this formulation of (249) is correct, then there should be an interpretation, analogous to (250), for such sentences as *I wonder who heard John's stories about what, I wonder who wrote which textbook and which novel.*

[67] Such examples as (255) appear, with the same ambiguity, in indirect questions, whether or not they are dominated by a "question word": *I wonder who remembers where we bought which book, It is uncertain who remembers where we bought which book.* Notice, therefore, that there is no generalization to be gained by supposing that an obligatorily deleted "performative" question verb appears in the structure underlying (255) as the matrix verb, as has occasionally been suggested.

the COMP in which it appears.[68] This would seem to be the simplest possible situation. It is also what one would expect, given the framework of the extended standard theory.

There are further complexities when we consider a richer array of cases similar to (255). Moreover, there are other cases that we have still not dealt with. To mention one, consider the fact (noted by Bresnan (1970)) that we cannot have such forms as *I don't know who Bill to ask____* or *It is not known who to see ____*, although *I don't know who to ask ____* is acceptable (where ____ indicates the position from which *who* was moved). These are indirect questions with a +WH COMP. It appears that when a +WH COMP takes an S′ with the auxiliary *to*, deletion of the subject of the S′ by Equi-NP Deletion is obligatory (and there is an interpretation roughly as "should" —for example, *I wondered whether to leave* (*how to answer*)). We might express this by adding a Surface Exclusion Filter barring +WH NP *to*. Notice that we might also express the obligatory character of the interpretation rules by surface filters, in various ways which I will not elaborate.

17. Though many questions have been left open and, obviously, many problems remain, nevertheless it seems to me that the approach explored here is quite plausible. Given the extended standard theory, with its restrictions on the possibilities for base structures, on the ordering of lexical and nonlexical transformations, and on the relations between semantic interpretations and derivations, we have been able to sharpen some earlier proposals and to accommodate a number of particular suggestions concerning universals, as well as a fairly wide range of data, under some fairly natural and simple assumptions. The illustrative examples exploit all of the devices available in this theory to determine grammaticalness, namely, rules of the categorial component of the base, lexical insertion transformations involving contextual features, nonlexical transformations of various sorts, surface filters, and rules of interpretation involving deep and surface structures.[69] Only if a derivation satisfies all of these conditions does its final terminal string qualify as a grammatical sentence. We have considered the possibility that surface filters might be regarded as a point of contact between a performance theory and a competence theory, as might some of the conditions on transformations. One might look into the effects of enriching one or another component of the theory. (For example, would more extensive reliance on rules of interpretation suffice to characterize the grammatical sentences without the distinction between +WH and −WH or, say, permit us to eliminate *wh*-Movement in favor of an expansion of COMP in the base?)[70] There is, furthermore, little doubt that additional restrictions and conditions must be discovered if the fundamental empirical problem mentioned at the outset is to become a realistic topic of inquiry.

[68] Notice, in particular, that there is no necessity for any additional devices to exclude other possible interpretations (for example, "For which x, for which z, x remembers for which y, we bought y at z" in the case of (255).

[69] It remains an open question whether rules of interpretation and filters must also apply to what have been called "shallow structures."

[70] The latter suggestion, though attractive in some respects, faces difficulties in the case of such examples as *Which pictures of each other were the men looking at, The pictures of each other that the men were looking at*. The latter might be used to support the view that the antecedent of a relative is actually raised from the relative by a movement rule, with an appropriate *wh*-phrase left behind. I believe that this possibility was first suggested by M. Brame, to explain why it is possible to have such noun phrases as *the headway that he made* though *headway* is otherwise impossible as a noun phrase, and similarly in the case of many other idioms.

REFERENCES

Akmajian, A. (1970), *Aspects of the Grammar of Focus in English*, unpublished Ph.D. dissertation, M.I.T.

Bach, E. (1965), "On Some Recurrent Types of Transformations," in C. W. Kreidler, ed., *Sixteenth Annual Round Table Meeting on Linguistics and Language Studies*, Georgetown University Monograph Series on Languages and Linguistics 18.

Bach, E. (1971), "Questions," *Linguistic Inquiry*, 2, 153–166.

Baker, C. L. (1970), "Notes on the description of English questions: the role of an abstract question morpheme," *Foundations of Language*, 6, 197–219.

Bever, T. G. (1970), "The Cognitive Basis for Linguistic Structure," in J. R. Hayes, ed., *Cognition and Language Learning*, New York: Wiley.

Bowers, J. (1969), "Some Adjectival Nominalizations in English," unpublished paper, M.I.T.

Bresnan, J. (1970), "On complementizers: towards a syntactic theory of complement types," *Foundations of Language*, 6, 297–321.

Bresnan, J. (1971), "Sentence stress and syntactic transformations," *Language*, 47, 257–281.

Bresnan, J. (1972), *The Theory of Complementation in English Syntax*, Ph.D. dissertation, M.I.T.

Chomsky, N. (1964), *Current Issues in Linguistic Theory*, The Hague: Mouton.

Chomsky, N. (1965), *Aspects of the Theory of Syntax*, Cambridge, Mass.: M.I.T. Press.

Chomsky, N. (1968), *Language and Mind*, New York: Harcourt Brace Jovanovich.

Chomsky, N. (1970a), "Deep Structure, Surface Structure, and Semantic Interpretation," in R. Jakobson and S. Kawamoto, eds., *Studies in General and Oriental Linguistics* (Commemorative Volume for Dr. Shiro Hattori), Tokyo: TEC Corporation for Language Research.

Chomsky, N. (1970b), "Remarks on Nominalization," in R. Jacobs and P. Rosenbaum, eds., *Readings in English Transformational Grammar*, Waltham, Mass.: Ginn.

Chomsky, N. (1971), *Problems of Knowledge and Freedom*, New York: Pantheon.

Chomsky, N. (1972a), "Empirical Issues in the Theory of Transformational Grammar," in S. Peters, ed., *Goals of Linguistic Theory* (Proceedings of the Linguistics Conference at the University of Texas, Oct. 1969), Englewood Cliffs, N.J.: Prentice-Hall.

Chomsky, N. (1972b), *Studies on Semantics in Generative Grammar*, The Hague: Mouton. (This contains Chomsky (1970a; 1970b; 1972a).)

Chomsky, N., and M. Halle (1968), *Sound Pattern of English*, New York: Harper & Row.

Culicover, P., (1971), *Syntactic and Semantic Investigations*, unpublished Ph.D. dissertation, M.I.T.

Dean Fodor, J. (1967), "Noun Phrase Complementation in English and German," unpublished paper, M.I.T.

Dougherty, R. (1970), "A grammar of coordinate conjoined structures: I," *Language*, 46, 850–898.

Emonds, J. (1970), *Root and Structure-Preserving Transformations*, unpublished Ph.D. dissertation, M.I.T.

Fauconnier, G. R. (1971), *Theoretical Implications of some Global Phenomena in Syntax*, unpublished Ph.D. dissertation, University of California, San Diego.

Helke, M. (1971), *The Grammar of English Reflexives*, unpublished Ph.D. dissertation, M.I.T.

Jackendoff, R. S. (1969), *Some Rules of Semantic Interpretation for English*, unpublished Ph.D. dissertation, M.I.T.

Jackendoff, R. S. (1972), *Semantic Interpretation in Generative Grammar*, Cambridge, Mass.: M.I.T. Press.

Katz, J., and P. Postal (1964), *An Integrated Theory of Linguistic Descriptions*, Cambridge, Mass.: M.I.T. Press.

Kayne, R. (1969), *The Transformational Cycle in French Syntax*, unpublished Ph.D. dissertation, M.I.T.

Kiparsky, P., and Kiparsky, C. (1970), "Fact," in M. Bierwisch and K. E. Heidolph, eds., *Progress in Linguistics*, The Hague: Mouton.

Langendoen, D. T. (1970), "Generative Grammar from a Functional Perspective," unpublished paper, C.C.N.Y.

Lasnik, H. (1971), "A general constraint: some evidence from negation," *Quarterly Progress Report of the Research Laboratory of Electronics, 101*, M.I.T., 215–217.

McCawley, J. D. (1970), "English as a VSO language," *Language, 46*, 286–299.

Miller, G. A., and N. Chomsky (1963), "Finitary Models of Language Users," in R. Luce, R. Bush, and E. Galanter, eds., *Handbook of Mathematical Psychology*, Vol. II, New York: Wiley.

Perlmutter, D. (1971), *Deep and Surface Structure Constraints in Syntax*, New York: Holt, Rinehart and Winston.

Peters, S., and R. W. Ritchie (1973), "On the generative power of transformational grammars," *Information Sciences, 6*, 49–83.

Postal, P. (1966), "A note on 'understood transitively'," IJAL, *32*, 90–93.

Postal, P. (1969), Review of A. McIntosh and M. A. K. Halliday, *Papers in General, Descriptive and Applied Linguistics*, in *Foundations of Language, 5*, 409–439.

Postal, P. (1971), *Cross-Over Phenomena*, New York: Holt, Rinehart and Winston.

Ross, J. R. (1967), *Constraints on Variables in Syntax*, unpublished Ph.D. dissertation, M.I.T.

Selkirk, L. (1970), "On the Determiner Systems of Noun Phrase and Adjective Phrase," unpublished paper, M.I.T.

Wasow, T., and T. Roeper (1972), "On the Subject of Gerunds," *Foundations of Language, 8*, 44–61.

on accounting
for illocutionary forces[1]

Bruce Fraser

Boston University

1. INTRODUCTION

Native speakers of English know that the utterance of the sentence *John may leave now* normally counts as a simple prediction of the future, a report of John's freedom of movement, or the giving of permission, to name three of the most likely ways in which the sentence may be used. In the terminology of Austin (1962), the utterance (in the appropriate circumstances) can have the illocutionary force of a prediction, a report, and the giving of permission; therefore, the speaker can perform the illocutionary acts of predicting, reporting, and permitting. Native speakers also know that the utterance of this sentence does not normally count as a plea, a request for information, or an oath, although certain circumstances of utterance might permit such uses. In this paper we will be concerned with sketching a framework to account for the ability of native speakers to associate the possible standard uses of a sentence (its illocutionary forces) with the sentence itself.

We will be talking here about "sentences" and "utterances." We will refer to the "forces of a sentence" and mean by this the different illocutionary acts which the sentence is normally used to perform.[2] Some of these forces follow from the nature of the sentence alone, others from the sentence together with a knowledge of the rules of conversation. We will also refer to the "forces of an utterance" and mean by this

[1] The work reported here was supported in part by NASA Contract NAS 9-11157 and Ford Foundation Grant Number 700-0656 to the Language Research Foundation. I am indebted to J. J. Katz, R. M. Harnish, and J. Searle for considerable fruitful discussion of the ideas presented in this paper.
    [2] I will employ various terminological simplifications; for example, I will often refer to illocutionary forces simply as forces and to illocutionary acts simply as acts. I will assume that all sentences have more than one force and will usually use the plural term. In addition, though utterances can have forces, sentences can have only potential forces. I will often omit the word "potential."

the acts the speaker actually performs by uttering the sentence on a particular occasion. While our immediate interest is in characterizing the ability of a speaker to determine the illocutionary forces of an arbitrary English sentence, and only English examples will be used, any theory which emerges should be general enough to deal with not only English but the range of human languages.

Throughout the discussion the notion of "standard" or "normal use" is appealed to, but no definition or even heuristic is provided to characterize it. To pick an extreme case, the sentence *Harry is ill* is normally used to perform the illocutionary acts of stating, reporting, and warning but is certainly not normally used as an example of a three-word sentence. The sentence *I promise I'll find you* has the superficial appearance of a promise but we might want to argue that in standard use it counts as a threat as well; if so, our theory will have to account for such extensions of use.

The overall framework to be developed here is relatively simple and straight-forward in outline. First, following Searle (1969), it will be assumed that every illocutionary act can be analyzed into a set of necessary and sufficient conditions such that, when the utterance of some sentence meets these conditions, we will agree that this particular illocutionary act has been successfully performed. The conditions on illocutionary acts are both linguistic and contextual.

Second, it is assumed that it is the meaning of a sentence rather than its syntactic form or phonological shape that contributes to the determination of the illocutionary force of a sentence. In particular, it is assumed that the semantic representation of the sentence contains an illocutionary force indicator, "F," which specifies the extent to which the sentence contributes to the illocutionary force.

Third, it is assumed that, in general, sentence meaning underdetermines sentence force. For example, the sentence *Should you take that cookie* has the illocutionary force of a request for information by virtue of its meaning. It also has the illocutionary force of a suggestion,[3] namely, a suggestion not to take that cookie, but not only because of its meaning. (We will discuss such cases in Section 5.) Following Grice (1967), it is assumed that that part of the illocutionary force of a sentence not accounted for by sentence meaning must be handled by some theory of conversation.

We can view the process of pairing a sentence and its forces as the following series of steps:

(*a*) Determine the semantic reading (the meaning) of the sentence
(*b*) Determine those illocutionary acts whose linguistic conditions are satisfied by virtue of the sentence meaning
(*c*) Represent the names of these acts as the set F_m
(*d*) Determine those illocutionary acts whose conditions are satisfied by virtue of the sentence meaning and general principles of conversation
(*e*) Represent the names of these acts as the set F_p
(*f*) Combine F_m and F_p as the set F which represents the total forces of the sentence because of what it means and the normal rules of conversation

In the discussion to follow, we will attempt to clarify some of the details of this pairing process.

In Section 2 we deal with the structure of illocutionary acts, first as seen by Austin and then by Searle, and then we look at another, revised version. Section 3

---

[3] "Suggestion" is used here to refer to the class of acts which includes suggesting, recommending, advising, opining (if one actually does this), inviting, and so on. "Request" will be used to refer to the class of acts which includes requesting, ordering, commanding, pleading, demanding, asking, and so on. (See Fraser (1973).)

contains a discussion of the ways in which the sentence meaning contributes to sentence force. Section 4 is a discussion of Grice's schema for a theory of conversation. In Section 5 several specific examples are discussed in the light of the preceding discussion. Section 6 is the conclusion.

2. STRUCTURE OF ILLOCUTIONARY ACTS

Illocutionary acts are only one of a number of speech acts that may be performed in the utterance of a sentence. In the typical speech situation, the speaker will be performing at least the following: (*a*) a phonetic act (the uttering of certain sounds belonging to the phonological system of the language being used); (*b*) a phatic act (the uttering of a well-formed sentence of the language); (*c*) a propositional act (the expression of a proposition), which involves a reference act (reference to some object(s) in the real world) and a predication act (the ascribing of some property, state, or action to the referents); (*d*) an illocutionary act (the use of an utterance in a certain way, for example to promise, threaten, plea, or invoke); and (*e*) a perlocutionary act (the production of certain post-utterance effects upon the feelings, thoughts, or actions of the hearer or speaker). The major divisions are the propositional act (the act of saying something), the illocutionary act (the act of doing something with the utterance), and the perlocutionary act (the act of causing some effect by virtue of the utterance having been uttered). The lines distinguishing these three types are not nearly so clear as has been suggested in the literature,[4] but we will not probe the issue here.

2.1. Austin, who coined the term "illocutionary act," unfortunately never provided a clear analysis of the concept. He writes (1962):

> To determine what illocutionary act is so performed we must determine in what way we are using the locution: asking or answering a question . . . pronouncing a sentence . . . and the numerous like. (I am not suggesting that this is a clearly defined class by any means.) . . . When we perform a locutionary act we use speech; but in what way precisely are we using it on this occasion? For there are very numerous functions of or ways in which we use speech . . . it makes a great difference whether we were advising or merely suggesting, or actually ordering, whether we were strictly promising or only announcing a vague intention, and so forth. These issues penetrate a little but not without confusion into grammar, but we constantly do debate them, in such terms as whether certain words (a certain locution) 'had the force of' a question, or ought to have been taken as an estimate, and so on (pp. 98–99).

For Austin, some illocutionary acts (such as warning someone) might be performed by nonverbal means (such as waving a stick), but he emphasizes that such acts are acts performed *in* doing something, as opposed to acts *of* doing something. It is not always the case that every act one might perform *in* saying something is necessarily the performance of an illocutionary act, as, for example, joking, insinuating, bragging. Illocutionary acts reflect an *intent* on the part of the speaker to cause a certain effect.

Austin points out that the illocutionary act as distinct from the perlocutionary act is connected with the

[4] Austin (1962), Searle (1969), and Fraser (1972).

production of effect in a certain sense. I cannot be said to have warned an audience unless it hears what I say and takes what I say in a certain sense. . . . Generally the effect amounts to bringing about the understanding of the meaning and of the force of the locution. So the performance of an illocutionary act involves the securing of 'uptake' (p. 116).

The degree of uptake required will vary from act to act. It ranges from an actual hearer response in the case of making a bet (for example, *I bet you $5 that Santa Claus is a Republican* does not count as the act of betting until the hearer signals his agreement to the offer of a bet) to the hearer's understanding of the intent (for example, *Shouldn't you be going home now* may be intended as a request for the hearer to leave rather than a question about his obligations) to no requirement for a hearer at all (for example, in the case of the christening of a child).

Austin has also suggested the following:

The verbs we have classified . . . as names of illocutionary acts seem to be pretty close to 'explicit performative' verbs, for we can say 'I warn you that' and 'I order you to' as explicit performatives; but warning and ordering are illocutionary acts. . . . But what is the relation between performatives and these illocutionary acts? It seems as though when we have an explicit performative we also have an illocutionary act . . . (pp. 130–131).

As we shall discuss, there does appear to be this close relationship; in fact, we will argue that the meaning of a performative verb plays a major role in the analysis of the associated illocutionary act.

Austin sees an illocutionary act as a conventional act. For example:

There must exist an accepted conventional procedure having a certain conventional effect, that procedure to include the uttering of certain words by certain persons in certain circumstances . . . (p. 14).

Speaking of the 'use of "language" for arguing or warning' looks just like speaking of 'the use of "language" for persuading, rousing, alarming'; yet the former may, for rough contrast, be said to be *conventional*, in the sense that at least it could be made explicit by the performative formula; but the latter could not (p. 103).

We must notice that the illocutionary act is a conventional act: an act done as conforming to a convention (p. 105).

. . . we also perform *illocutionary acts* such as informing, ordering, warning, undertaking, etc. i.e., utterances which have a certain (conventional) force (p. 108).

Strictly speaking, there cannot be an illocutionary act unless the means employed are conventional, and so the means for achieving its ends non-verbally must be conventional (p. 118).

Illocutionary acts are conventional acts: perlocutionary acts are *not* conventional; acts of *both* kinds can be performed—or, more accurately, acts called by the same name (for example, acts equivalent to the illocutionary acts of warning or the perlocutionary acts of convincing)—can be brought off non-verbally; but even then to deserve the name of an illocutionary act, for example a warning, it must be a conventional non-verbal act: but perlocutionary acts are not conventional, though conventional acts may be made use of in order to bring off the perlocutionary act. A judge should be able to decide, by hearing what was said, what locutionary and illocutionary acts were performed, but not what perlocutionary acts were achieved (p. 115).

There are more instances in which Austin refers to illocutionary acts as conventional acts, but the sampling just given seems to indicate that he is using the notion of convention to refer to (*a*) those types of illocutionary acts, for example, bidding in bridge, christening, declaring a runner out in baseball, which are clearly conventional; (*b*) all illocutionary acts, including those such as warning and promising, which do not appear to be conventional in the formal sense of the term (see, for example, Lewis (1969)); (*c*) the linguistic means by which one performs the illocutionary act.

Strawson (1964) writes with regard to the class of acts in (*b*) that they are

> not essentially a conventional act, an act done as conforming to a convention; it may be that the act is conventional, done as conforming to a convention, only insofar as 'the means used to perform it' are conventional. To speak only of those conventional means which are also *linguistic* means, the extent to which the act is one done as conforming to conventions may depend solely on the extent to which conventional linguistic meaning exhausts illocutionary force (pp. 456–457).

While a discussion of the conventional nature of illocutionary acts is well beyond the scope of this paper, it seems clear that run-of-the-mill illocutionary acts (promising, warning, admitting, offering, asking, commanding, begging, and so on) are not conventional in the same sense as special cases like marrying, christening, sentencing, and redoubling. The reader is referred to Strawson (1964) for an excellent discussion of these points.

Although the notion "illocutionary act" is intuitively clear from Austin's writing, his statements, with the exception of the comments about the conventional nature of illocutionary acts, assist one in determining whether or not a particular utterance (e.g., *I will be home at 5*) counts as the performance of a particular illocutionary act (promising), but they would not be included in any analytical account of illocutionary acts.

2.2. Searle (1969), in developing his theory of speech acts, views the ability to use language as rule-governed behavior. His book is an attempt

> to explore, to spell out some of the implications of, and so to test that hypothesis (p. 16).

The form that this hypothesis will take is that

> speaking a language is performing speech acts, acts such as making statements, giving commands, asking questions, making promises and so on; and more abstractly, acts such as referring and predicting; and, secondly, that these acts are in general made possible by and are performed in accordance with certain rules for the use of linguistic elements (p. 16).

The plan of Searle's approach is clearly stated:

> The procedure which I shall follow is to state a set of necessary and sufficient conditions for the performance of particular kinds of speech acts and then extract from those conditions sets of semantic rules for the use of the linguistic devices which mark the utterances as speech acts of those kinds (p. 22).

Three points are important here, namely, that illocutionary acts can be analyzed into a set of necessary and sufficient conditions for their successful performance, that there are semantic rules derived from these conditions which are part of the speaker's language ability, and that sentences have linguistic features which mark them as having one illocutionary force as opposed to some others. We will examine Searle's conditions now and will turn to the linguistic marking in the next section; we will not deal with his notion of semantic rules in this paper.

Searle attempts to characterize the necessary and sufficient conditions on illocutionary acts by stating these conditions as a set of propositions such that the conjunction of the members of the set entails the proposition that a speaker made a successful and nondefective performance of that act, and the proposition that the speaker performed such an act entails this conjunction. In his analysis there are basically four conditions:[5] (*a*) the propositional content condition, (*b*) the preparatory conditions, (*c*) the sincerity conditions, and (*d*) the essential condition.

The propositional content condition specifies the nature of the proposition expressed in an utterance that is to count as the performance of a particular illocutionary act. For example, the propositional content of a promise must predicate some future act, not necessarily but usually to be carried out by the speaker; for a request, some future act of the hearer; for an assertion, some proposition; and for an admission, some past act of the speaker. We will see in Section 4 that the propositional content condition of an illocutionary act may be satisfied in a number of ways. In particular, the required propositional content need not be explicitly expressed in the utterance.

The preparatory conditions specify the pre-utterance requirements on the speaker and hearer which are necessary for the successful and nondefective performance of the act. For a promise, for example, these conditions include the favorable disposition of the hearer toward the act and the awareness on the part of both the speaker and the hearer that the speaker will probably not perform the act in the normal course of events; for a request the preparatory conditions include the ability of the hearer to perform the act requested, the belief of the speaker in the hearer's ability, and the awareness condition of promising already mentioned; for an assertion the speaker should have reasons for believing in the truth of what he asserts and it should not be obvious that the hearer already knows (needs to be reminded of, etc.) what is asserted.

The sincerity conditions, analogous to Austin's Γ Conditions on Infelicity, specify nonlinguistic conditions which are necessary in order for the act to be "happily" performed. Sincerity conditions can be violated without voiding the act; such violation does, however, cause the act to become defective (as, for example, an insincere promise, an empty threat, deceptive advice, hollow praise). For a promise, these conditions include that the speaker intend to perform the act; for a request, the speaker must believe that the hearer can perform the act; for an assertion, the speaker must believe what he says.

Finally, the essential condition specifies what the speaker intends as the point of the utterance. This condition is the *sine qua non* of the illocutionary act. For a promise, the essential condition is that the speaker intends the utterance to count as placing him under the obligation to bring about the specified act; for a request, the utterance must count as an attempt to get the hearer to carry out the specified act; for an assertion, the utterance must count as an attempt to get the hearer to believe that the speaker has accurately represented the state of affairs; and for a question, it must count as an attempt to elicit certain information from the hearer.

In his attempt to establish a set of necessary and sufficient conditions for the successful and nondefective performance of an illocutionary act, Searle is lumping together both the essense of each illocutionary act and a set of conditions which would follow from this act and many other illocutionary acts but are not, as such, part of this particular act. It is clear that Searle views a "successful" act and a "nondefective" act as separable:

----

[5] There are several others involving input/output conditions and shared language, but these are not relevant to our discussion.

There are various kinds of possible defects of illocutionary acts but not all of these defects are sufficient to vitiate the act in its entirety. In some cases, a condition may indeed be intrinsic to the notion of the act in question and not satisfied in a given case, and yet the act will have been performed nonetheless. In such cases I say the act was 'defective' (p. 54).

Unfortunately, there are no guidelines given as to how to distinguish between a successful-defective act and a successful-nondefective act. All we are told is that the conditions presented, when taken together, are necessary and sufficient as both a successful *and* nondefective illocutionary act.

This merging of conditions seems to me to be a mistake. In my view, any adequate analysis of illocutionary acts must deal only with conditions for the successful performance of the act in question, and the notion of a defect should be accounted for within some larger theory of conversation. I speculate that Searle lumped these two types of conditions together because he was dealing with examples containing an explicit performative verb denoting the intended act (for example, *I promise that* p; *I request that* q). He was concerned with an analysis

directed at the center of the concept of promising . . . ignoring marginal, fringe, and partially defective promises . . . in the analysis I confine my discussion to full blown explicit promises and ignore promises made by elliptical turns of phrases, hints, metaphors, etc. . . . I am also dealing only with categorical promises and ignoring hypothetical promises, for if we get an account of categorical promises it can easily be extended to deal with hypothetical ones. In short, I am going to deal only with a simple and idealized case . . . This method, one of the constructing of idealized models, is analogous to the sort of theory construction that goes on in most sciences, e.g., the construction of economic models, or accounts of the solar system which treat planets as points. Without abstraction and idealization there is no systematization (p. 56).

I do not take issue with his program to consider the simple idealized case and abstract away. However, as frequently occurs, the idealization and abstraction fail to recognize many cases which do not fit nicely into the emerging theory and which, upon further examination, demand a change.

In terms of the four conditions presented by Searle, I would argue that the sincerity conditions, always, and the preparatory conditions, often, do not constitute part of the necessary or sufficient conditions for the *successful* performance of a particular illocutionary act. As an example, let us consider Searle's analysis of requesting, which I summarize here from his page 66:

CONDITIONS ON REQUESTING

Propositional Content:	Speaker expresses a proposition predicating some future act of the hearer.
Preparatory:	(i) The hearer is able to do the act. The speaker believes that the hearer is able to do the act.
	(ii) It is not obvious to both the speaker and the hearer that the hearer will not do the act in the normal course of events of his own accord.
Sincerity:	The speaker wants the hearer to do the act.
Essential:	The speaker intends the utterance to count as an attempt to get the hearer to do the act.

The sincerity condition is surely not necessary to the successful performance of the act of requesting. I can utter *Please get me that pad of paper* as a bona fide request without wanting you to get me the paper—perhaps I want you to move out of my line of vision but am embarrassed to say so; perhaps I am making the request because I was asked to by someone else but do not tell you this; perhaps I think the request is in your best interests although I really don't care one way or the other whether you get the pad. That one normally associates a desire on the part of the speaker to be a part of the notion of requesting follows, I suspect, from a very general principle of human interaction: one normally performs cognitive actions with intention; if the intention is, as in the case of requesting, to attempt to get someone to do something, then a reasonable inference, perhaps the most reasonable, is that the speaker wants the action to be carried out.

The preparatory conditions of requesting again do not seem necessary to the performance of such an act. I can successfully request you to pick up a particular piece of machinery even though you are not able to and I know this in advance— perhaps you intend to take this instrument with you on the night plane to California and I want to convince you that it would be a mistake. Similar examples can be developed for the condition of nonobviousness. Here again I think the preparatory conditions reflect what the ordinary speaker of English expects to be the case if a request is made to perform some act, but these conditions do not seem to be part of the essence of requesting.

On the other hand, the propositional content and essential conditions are exactly what is involved in requesting and, as such, are part of the analysis of this illocutionary act.

2.3. One must, of course, justify the set of conditions chosen in the analysis of each illocutionary act. There is, I think, a straightforward way of establishing these conditions, which rests on the assumption that each performative verb (*promise, admit, request,* and so on) specifies exactly these conditions in its syntactic and semantic analysis. In general, the syntactic conditions for well-formedness on the embedded complement of a performative verb determine the propositional content conditions on the corresponding illocutionary act: the properties of the embedded proposition (for example, *I will be on time* in the sentence *I promise that I will be on time*) are the propositional content conditions on the act. The performative verb itself determines any other conditions on the act, in particular the specification of the intent of the act (for a promise, for example, the speaker must intend to place himself under an obligation to see that the action specified in the proposition is carried out), as well as any features of the act which involve the attitudes and roles of the speaker and hearer (for a promise, for example, the action should be in the best interest of the hearer, as opposed to a threat).

There are problems with this simplified program for determining the conditions on illocutionary acts, not the least of which is the difficulty of ascertaining just what is "meant" by a particular performative verb, as well as the fact that certain performative verbs (for instance, *veto, reject, pronounce*) do not permit embedded complements.[6] At this point, however, let us push the issue of the conditions on illocutionary acts to the issue of determining the semantic analysis of the corresponding performative verb.

In summary, we began this section by indicating certain features of illocutionary acts as Austin viewed them initially, but with the understanding that he failed to provide any structure for the concept. We then examined the view taken by Searle

---

[6] Curiously, nearly all of the performative verbs which do not take embedded sentential complements denote conventional illocutionary acts such as marrying, vetoing, christening, and rendering an umpire's decision.

(1969), who posits four types of conditions on the successful and nondefective performance of a given illocutionary act. We suggested that the analysis of an illocutionary act involved only those conditions necessary and sufficient for the successful performance of the act and that the putative defects belonged in a more general theory about human interaction, in particular a theory of conversation. The result was to remove the sincerity condition and in some cases part or all of the preparatory conditions, leaving his propositional and essential conditions intact. Finally, we suggested that the determination of the conditions on illocutionary acts will be a function of the semantic analysis of the corresponding performative verb.

3. THE ROLE OF SENTENCE MEANING IN DETERMINING FORCE

In the preceding section we were concerned with the overall structure of illocutionary acts, in particular the sort of conditions that are necessary for the successful performance of a given act. In this section we turn to the question of how the linguistic knowledge of the native speaker determines that a sentence such as *Can you pass the salt?* normally has the force of a question and a request but not of a plea or of a raising in bridge.

We will represent the sentence forces arising from linguistic considerations by F_m, a set which specifies as narrowly as possible the ways in which the sentence is normally taken on the basis of its linguistic features only. The members of the set F_m are the names of the illocutionary acts (christening, admitting, promising, asserting, and so on), some of which are hierarchically related (for example, to admit is necessarily to assert but not conversely). F_m may contain one member (for example, F_m (*I pronounce you man and wife*) = marrying) or several members (for example, F_m (*Can you pass the salt*) = question; request). I take F_m to be part of the semantic representation of a sentence: part of what it is to understand a sentence is to know the ways in which it may normally be used. The matter of exactly how this term fits into the semantic representation I leave open (but see Katz (1972)). The issue at hand is how to determine the analysis of F_m for a given sentence.

The first step in this analysis is to reduce the task of finding F_m for a given sentence to that of finding F_m for each semantic interpretation of a given sentence. For example, to find F_m for *John can go*, we have to determine F_m for the reading *John has the ability to go* (F_m = assertion) and for the reading *John has my permission to go* (F_m = giving permission). For this sentence F_m is therefore (assertion; giving permission).

Semantic ambiguity is not the only reason that F_m may contain more than one member. A sentence such as *I will be there on time*, while presumably unambiguous (at least we will consider it so), counts as a promise, threat, warning, and so on. F_m for a particular sentence will reflect *all* semantic interpretations of that sentence. This is quite in line with the fact that speakers can predict the use of a sentence without knowing which of the possible sentence meanings will be intended by the speaker on a particular occasion of utterance.

I am in agreement with Searle when he writes:

> The speech act or acts performed in the utterance of a sentence are in general a function of the meaning of the sentence. The meaning of a sentence does not in all cases uniquely

determine what speech act [illocutionary act] is performed in a given utterance of that sentence, for a speaker may mean more than what he actually says (p. 18).

What this claim entails is that syntactic variations such as those in (1) will not cause variations in sentence force:

(1) (a) John saw Mary / Mary was seen by John
    (b) He called up his friend / He called his friend up
    (c) I gave a book to Harvey / I gave Harvey a book
    (d) We talked to Mary in the park / In the park we talked to Mary

This claim does *not* mean that differences in syntactic form which entail differences in sentence meaning will not vary sentence force. The pairs in (a) and (b) of (2) clearly have different F_ms while the pair in (c) may or may not:

(2) (a) John can see the dog / Can John see the dog?
    (b) You will take the A train / Take the A train, will you?
    (c) I saw Ned / It was Ned that I saw

Analogously, variations in the phonological shape of a sentence which do not alter meaning do not contribute to the determination of the sentence force. Whether *ballet* is pronounced with initial or final stress, for example, will not alter the sentence force, nor will noncontrastive levels of pitch. However, certain phonological phenomena which do contribute to sentence meaning, for example emphatic stress or rising sentence-final intonation, do play a role in the determination of sentence force. We will not consider phonological material in the subsequent discussion.

The determination of F_m for a given sentence may be said to occur in the following way. On the one hand we have an analysis of illocutionary acts—for each act a set of necessary and sufficient conditions for its successful performance. On the other hand we have the semantic reading(s) of the sentence. To determine if a given sentence has a particular force, the semantic reading is examined for the presence or absence of the conditions on each act. We will stipulate that a sentence has force F_i associated with the illocutionary act A_i if it at least satisfies the propositional content conditions of A_i. Of course, if, as we have suggested, illocutionary acts are not independent notions but are instead heavily interrelated and hierarchically arranged, there will emerge a strategy for comparing the sentence reading with the analysis of illocutionary acts. For example, since to confess that *p* entails having asserted that *p*, any semantic reading which denies the force of assertion to the sentence *ipso facto* denies the force of confession. Analogously, because the tense of a prediction must be future while that of an admission must be past, the semantic reading which permits the prediction force immediately precludes the other.

It should be obvious that our stipulation of a sufficient condition for a sentence to have some force F_i is a minimum condition and that a sentence may more or less precisely specify its range of forces. At one end of the spectrum we have the so-called performative sentences, such as *I promise to leave on time*, *I confess that I did it*, *I sentence you to listen to Nixon's speeches*, in which the main verb of the sentence is a performative verb. Such sentences clearly have a reading in which the conditions of the respective acts of promising, confessing, and sentencing are necessarily met: we defined the conditions of the acts as just those conditions on the embedded sentence of these verbs when used performatively and the other conditions as those semantically entailed by the performative verb. We find in addition that most performative verbs can be used in the habitual sense. *I promise to be home on time* can be both a promise and a report about the speaker's habitual actions; for example, it can be a child's answer to the question *How come you are allowed to leave just before dinner to go out and play?* Thus, the F_m of this sentence is (promise; report).[7]

At the other end of the spectrum are cases in which sentence meaning under-determines sentence force: only the propositional content conditions are met, and those other conditions on illocutionary acts which serve to give them a more precise character are missing. A sentence like *I will try* has the force of promising, threatening, and predicting: these acts all have the propositional content condition that the speaker predicate some future act. But further specification is lacking, for example, that for a promise the act must be volitional, the speaker must be undertaking an obligation to carry out the act, and the act must in some sense be beneficial to the hearer.

A third type of example involves sentences like *I undertake the obligation to go*, which contains the performative verb *undertake the obligation* and has the corresponding force. This sentence also meets the propositional content conditions of a promise as well as the condition that the speaker undertakes the obligation to see that the act is carried out; it lacks only the condition of hearer benefit. Promising and undertaking an obligation differ in that the former but not the latter requires the favorable disposition of the hearer toward the action predicated in the utterance. The example sentence explicitly has the force of undertaking an obligation and less explicitly the force of promising.

Up to this point we have referred to the semantic reading of a sentence in general terms. We will now distinguish between the propositional content of a sentence and those syntactic aspects of a sentence which contribute to sentence meaning and thus sentence force. The distinction can be illustrated by considering examples such as those in (3):

(3) (a) You will march to the Commons (declarative syntactic form)
    (b) Will you march to the Commons (interrogative syntactic form)
    (c) You, march to the Commons (imperative syntactic form)

These may be considered to have the same underlying propositional content, approximately stated as *You will march to the Commons*, while the syntactic form of each determines in part how the proposition is to be taken.

While the syntactic type of a sentence does not necessarily require that the sentence qualify for one group of illocutionary acts rather than another, there is a fairly close partitioning of illocutionary acts into three classes. In general, a declarative sentence entails that the speaker intends the utterance of that sentence to count as an attempt to convey to the hearer that the underlying proposition accurately represents the actual state of affairs or did so represent it or will at the future time specified represent it. An interrogative sentence entails that the speaker intends the utterance of the sentence to count as an attempt to elicit from the hearer the information missing in the under-lying proposition. An imperative sentence entails that the speaker intends the utterance of the sentence to count as an attempt to get the hearer to act in accordance with the state of affairs specified in the underlying proposition. We can view the sentence type as indicating what the utterance of the sentence is intended to count as at the highest level of specification (Searle's essential condition). It is important to recognize,

---

[7] *Promise* can also have the force of "assure," as in *I promise that I saw him there*, and the force of "threaten," as in *I promise you that you will never get out of here alive*. These extended uses of *promise* are not treated here.

however, that sentence type crossclassifies with propositional content: with a few notable exceptions (for example, imperative types do not permit past tense propositions) an arbitrary proposition can occur in any of the syntactic types. In addition, sentences with performative verbs are of the declarative type but can obviously be used to perform any type of illocutionary act.

Once the syntactic type of the sentence determines the first order approximation of the range of illocutionary forces for a sentence, the propositional content will, in general, serve to narrow down the possibilities. For example, a sentence of the declarative type which does not contain a performative verb predicts that the sentence has the force of asserting but leaves open which of the more specifically defined forces it might fall into (for example, reporting, stating, claiming). However, examination of the conditions on various kinds of assertions shows restrictions such as the fact that a confession requires that the speaker predicate some previous voluntary act of himself: *I will be there on time, He did it, I could have done it* do not normally count as confessions. (That the act must be of a reprehensible nature is not involved in the specification of the propositional content conditions on the act of confessing although it is certainly part of the analysis.) An admission requires only that the act be a prior one: *John will be there* does not normally count as an admission. A prediction leaves open all but the condition that the act be in the future. Certain adverbials and other phrases also serve this role. For example, while *I will be there* counts as a promise and a prediction, *Possibly I will be there* lacks the force of a promise: *possibly* prevents the assumption that the speaker, in uttering the sentence, is undertaking the obligation to be there. *Can you pass the salt* has the force of a question and a request; *Can you pass the salt to me* still has both but the request force is much the preferred interpretation. And *or else* after *Come here* renders the suggestion force impossible.

What I am proposing is a procedure to determine the forces of a sentence from information about its syntactic type and its propositional content. The information about syntactic type determines a class of illocutionary acts because of what it entails about what the speaker intends the utterance to count as (for example, an attempt to reflect the state of the world, to determine something about the state of the world, or to bring about a change in the state of the world). The information about propositional content determines further which of the more specifically defined acts the sentence may count as *by virtue of its meaning*. This last qualification is extremely important because of the pragmatic considerations discussed in the sections to come. The F_m associated with each sentence is intended to specify the forces of the sentence because of what the sentence means.

4. THE ROLE OF CONTEXT IN DETERMINING FORCE

All sentences can be said to have some particular force(s) solely because of what they mean: sentences with performative verbs are the paradigm examples, but most of the examples already discussed will fall under this claim with little difficulty. However, sentences may have a particular force both because of what they mean *and* certain general principles of conversation. A good example is found in the so-called rhetorical questions so frequently used in political speeches. For the utterance *Should we let Richard Nixon serve another four years in the White House?* the apparent force is that of a question, analogous to *Should we paint the house green or white?* However, if both the speaker and the hearer know that the speaker believes the answer to the literal question to be no, the force of this utterance is not that of a question but rather of an expression of opinion, equivalent to the force of *We should not permit*

Richard Nixon to serve . . . . The fact that such *should* questions can count in standard usage as expressions of opinion I take to be part of linguistic competence, therefore falling within the scope of our inquiry. Any adequate theory pairing sentences with their forces must reflect this fact about *should* questions.

In order to see the nature of the conversational principles that may play a role in determining sentence force, we turn to the theory of conversation presented by Grice (1967). Grice distinguishes between what is *said* in the uttering of a sentence and what is implicated. If, for example, I utter the sentence *It is getting late*, I have "said" merely that it was late. What I have suggested, implied, meant, and so on—hence the cover term "implicate"—may have been equivalent to the uttering of *I am tired, Let's go now*, or *I hope we begin soon*, for example. But whatever it is that I "implicated" by this utterance, I did not "say" it. It is Grice's hypothesis that such implication is not arbitrary but derives from a knowledge of what was said and certain principles of conversation. I shall outline his theory here only in sufficient detail to permit discussion of the examples in the next section. What we shall want to conclude is that the force of a sentence is often not simply a function of what the sentence means, but a function of what it may implicate and the force of the implicated sentence. Such forces, associated with a sentence because of pragmatic considerations, we shall refer to as F_p.

In Grice's theory, what is implicated in the utterance of a sentence is divided into (*a*) what is conventionally implicated, and (*b*) what is nonconventionally implicated. Conventional implication occurs because in some cases the conventional meaning of the words used will determine what is implicated, besides helping to determine what is said. We will not concern ourselves with this type of implication here. Nonconventional implication has several subclasses, according to Grice, although only one is mentioned and discussed, that is, conversational implication.[8]

In an attempt to establish the rules binding the participants in normal conversation, Grice establishes one super-principle, the Cooperation Principle, and four subordinate maxims, namely, Quantity, Quality, Relation, and Manner. In abbreviated form, these can be stated as follows:

COOPERATION PRINCIPLE: Make your conversational contribution such as is required, at the stage at which it occurs, by the accepted purpose or direction of the talk-exchange in which you are engaged.

Relating to what *is said*
QUANTITY:
    (*a*) Make your contribution as informative as necessary
    (*b*) Do not contribute more than necessary
QUALITY: Try to make your contribution one that is true
    (*a*) Do not say what you believe to be false
    (*b*) Do not say that for which you lack adequate evidence
RELATION: Be relevant

Relating to how *it is said*
MANNER: Be perspicuous
    (*a*) Be clear
    (*b*) Be unambiguous
    (*c*) Be as brief as possible
    (*d*) Be orderly

[8] Grice has both particularized and generalized conversational implications, but we will ignore these distinctions, if in fact they exist.

The maxim of Quality is held to be somewhat more important and the maxim of Manner somewhat less important than the others.

It is Grice's position that not only are these principles followed, but that it is reasonable that we should follow them in the interests of efficient conversational intercourse:

> That anyone who cares about the goals which are central to the conversation/communication (e.g., giving and receiving information, influencing and being influenced by others) must be expected to have an interest, given suitable circumstances, in participation in talk-exchanges which will be profitable only on the assumption that they are conducted in general accordance with the Cooperation Principle and the maxims (ch. 2, pp. 11–12).

A conversational implication is characterized as follows. In uttering that p, the speaker conversationally implicates that q if:

(a) the speaker is presumed to be observing the maxims, or at least the Cooperative Principle

(b) the assumption that the speaker thinks that q is required to make the saying of that p consistent with (a)

(c) the speaker and hearer recognize that the hearer can work out that the assumption in (b) is required

A conversational implication is not part of the meaning of a sentence but must be worked out from the meaning and a general program such as that just sketched. There must be some clear line of reasoning, which might run as follows:

> He [the speaker] has said that p
> There is no reason to suppose that he is not observing the maxims or at least the CP
> He could not be doing this unless he thought that q
> He knows (and knows that I know that he knows) that I can see that the supposition that he thinks that q is required
> He has done nothing to stop me (from) thinking that q
> Therefore he intends me to think, or is at least willing to allow me to think, that q
> So he has implicated that q (ch. 2, p. 14)

This sketch of Grice's approach, though hardly doing justice to his numerous examples and detailed discussion, should suffice as an indication of the sort of pragmatic theory which might be developed to predict what we consistently observe to be the case, namely, that what is said and what is implicated are often very different things.

That such a theory is relevant to the determining of utterance force is clear when one considers examples such as the following (from Grice, ch. 2, p. 16). Suppose I ask you for your opinion of Mr. Jones, your student, who is an applicant for a linguistic teaching position, and you reply, "Mr. Jones dresses very carefully when he teaches." Now, if I assume you are still functioning as a participant in the conversation, thus abiding by the Cooperation Principle, I must assume you are violating one of the maxims. It cannot be the maxim of Relation since your reply was relevant; the reply was presumably also truthful (Quality), and I can find no fault in the way (Manner) you answered me. I may conclude, however, that since you know the student well and are capable of providing more information, there is a reason for your violation of the maxim of Quantity. Your failure to impart further details, when presumably you recognize that more information would be appropriate, is understandable if you think that Jones is not suitable for the job. Thus, I conclude you are implicating that Jones does not have your recommendation. Why you might choose this way of telling me is yet another issue, which we leave unexplored here. The original sentence, *Mr. Jones dresses very carefully when he teaches*, has the force of an assertion. The force of the implicated sentence, *Jones isn't the right person*, is that of a negative recommendation—a very different sort of force.

I do not want to argue that this implicated sentence and thus its associated force are actually part of the illocutionary force of the original sentence. On the contrary, this force of negative recommendation appears to be clearly a function of the utterance (or writing) of the sentence in a particular context. There are, however, certain forces which, in my view, should be associated with a sentence, as members of F_p. Such forces follow from general principles of conversation, the character of illocutionary acts, and general properties of the sentence; in particular, they do not depend on the details of the context. We will consider several of these cases in the next section but will not attempt to draw a line between where F_p ends and the force of the utterance of the sentence begins.

5. SOME EXAMPLES

In light of the notion of illocutionary force as amended in Section 2, the contribution to sentence force discussed in Section 3, and the availability of some theory of conversation along the lines outlined in Section 4, we now turn to three examples. These cases do not exhaust the range of possibilities but will serve to provide some idea of the type of variation encountered.

5.1. "Can You Pass the Salt?"

Sentences such as *Can you pass the salt? Would you give me the book?* and *Won't you help me?* are well recognized to have at least two forces—that of a request for information (henceforth, a question), and that of a request for action (henceforth, a request). There are two possibilities: either such sentences have two deep structures, one paired with each force, or they have one deep structure and one of the forces derives from the other. I will explore the former alternative here, although I have serious reservations about its correctness. (See Katz (1972) for discussion of the latter alternative.) On the approach we are now examining, the question force is associated with a deep structure of an interrogative sentence; the request force is associated with a deep structure of an imperative sentence. Leaving aside the question of whether or not there is an imperative marker, I suggest that imperative sentences have the general form

MITG MKR—*you*—VP

where the MITG MKR is a marker of mitigation and stands for a class of morphemes which indicate the politeness level of the sentence. The class includes *can, could, will, would, couldn't, can't, won't*, and ϕ, but not *wouldn't, must, shall, have*, and so on. The case of the ϕ mitigation marker is that of the simple imperative (as in, for example, *You—go home*). This is the only case where the *you* can be deleted (*go home* but not **can go home*). Two points should be made here. First, I am claiming that there is no *will* or future Aux in the deep structure of imperative sentences. (Keep in mind that "imperative" refers to a sentence syntactic type, not to its possible use.) Second, the *n't* of *can't, won't*, and *couldn't* are not separable from the unnegated modal and do not arise as the result of a contraction process.

To support the analysis that includes two deep structures and the analysis of the imperative sentence, I present points (*a*)–(*k*). I believe that (*a*) and (*b*) clearly argue that there must be two deep structures, unless the force of the sentence is included as part of the deep structure.[9] The remaining points, while not conclusive, do offer support in favor of the analysis proposed here.

(*a*) The morpheme *please* can precede the VP of a request but not a question, as shown in (4):

(4) (a)   Can you please pass the salt
    (b)   *Can you please metabolize your blood sugar faster

(*b*) *Can* (*will*, etc.) *you* can be postposed to sentence-final position in requests but not questions, as shown in (5):

(5) (a)   Give me some milk, could you
    (b)   *Resemble your uncle, could you

These sentence-final "tags" do not, in this analysis, derive from some underlying declarative sentence, as, for example, *You could give me some milk* underlying *Give me some milk, could you*. Not only are the meanings of these two sentences different, but such a derivation fails to correspond with the ordinary Tag Question Transformation which effects a polarity change (for example, *You have the cash, don't you?*). The case where the mitigation marker is ɸ results in a postposed sentence of the form VP *you* (*Give me some milk, you*). That these examples may have differing intonation patterns is of no concern: the *can you* VP cases clearly have the surface structure of an interrogative sentence and, accordingly, receive the appropriate intonation contour.

(*c*) The posited analysis whereby the *can you* request cases are derived from an imperative sentence type automatically accounts for the fact that the main verb of the sentence must denote a voluntary action on the part of the subject, thus excluding verbs such as *resemble, want, metabolize,* and *hear*. Questions have no such restriction.

(*d*) The subject NP in requests such as those we are discussing can be only *you* or the indefinite *somebody/someone*. Questions have no restriction on the subject.

(*e*) Adverbs such as *willingly, easily,* and *voluntarily* cannot occur in the requests but can in the questions.

(*f*) The *can* (*will*) of the request cannot be paraphrased by its synonymous form *be able* (*intend to*). For example, the sentences in (6) do not normally have the force of a request:

(6) (a) Are you able to give me the wrench
    (b) Do you intend to leave that for me

(*g*) *Can* (*will*, etc.) cannot be emphatically stressed in requests. For example, the sentences in (7) do not normally have the force of a request:

(7) (a) CAN you help me
    (b) WOULD you hand me the bean bag

(*h*) *Can't* and *won't* and *couldn't* in request cases are not synonymous with their uncontracted forms *cannot, will not,* and *could not*. For example, the pairs in (8) and (9) are not synonymous (although it is not clear to me whether the second member of each pair is normally taken as a request):

---

[9] Arguments against any such analysis, in particular the performative analysis, are presented in Fraser (1971; 1972).

(8) (a) Can't you give me something to ease the pain
　　(b) Can you not give me something to ease the pain
(9) (a) Won't you take this away from me
　　(b) Will you not take this away from me

(*i*) The distribution of *some* and *any* is different in requests and questions. In general, both forms can occur in questions, but, as shown in (10), only *some* can occur in requests:

(10) (a) Would you please send me something (*anything) to ease the pain
　　(b) Could you eat some (*any) of your dinner now

(*j*) A request is not well formed unless an indefinite object actually exists; a question does not require this. For example, (11) clearly has the force of a question, but it has the force of a request only if unicorns are assumed to be available:

(11) Will you send me a unicorn in the morning mail

(*k*) The various modals, including φ, appear to fall into an order of decreasing politeness as follows: *could, would, can, will, won't, can't,* φ. If this or some other relative ordering holds for native English speakers, it must be accounted for somewhere in the grammar. By treating the *can, will,* and so on of the request cases not as modals but merely as markers of degree of mitigation (politeness), this fact can be associated directly with the analysis of imperatives.

These observations, I believe, argue strongly that the request and question forces of the *can you* sentences derive from different deep structures—the question case from an interrogative sentence type, the request case from an elaborated analysis of the imperative syntactic type. If this analysis is accepted, then an accounting of the two forces is obvious: each is determined by the sentence type. Of course, all the grammar can say about a sentence such as *Will you please bring the paper in here* is that it has the force of a request. The determination of whether its actual use counts as a command, request, order, or plea lies with the context of the utterance.

5.2. "May I Have the Salt?"

Sentences of this type enjoy a force ambiguity similar to that just discussed. *May I have the salt?* may count as a request for information about my freedom to have the salt, as a request for permission to have the salt, and as a request to be given the salt.

I take the modal *may* to have at least two semantic interpretations. One is found in sentences like *John may or may not arrive on time,* which comments on the possibility of the denoted action. The first force of a request for information arises when this meaning of the modal is present. The other interpretation is that of "permission." However, I cannot find syntactic evidence to argue in support of two deep structures to account for the permission and request forces of these sentences. *Please* occurs before the verb phrase in both cases, as in (12):

(12) (a) May I please leave to go to the john (permission only)
　　(b) May I please hold the baby for a minute (both forces)

And the *may I* postposes in neither case. In fact, none of the arguments of the previous section serve to distinguish the two cases. There seems to be good reason, actually, to argue that these two forces arise from only one deep structure, with the permission force, the primary interpretation, arising from the meaning of *may* and the sentence type, and the request force being derived.

To see how this might work, we must first recognize that not all *may I* sentences have the force of requests. In particular, this force is possible only in those cases where the verb denotes a state which can arise without the speaker necessarily performing any action (for example, verbs like *have*, *get*, *hold*, *hear*, *see*, and *feel*, as well as passive verb phrases such as *May I now be escorted to my seat*). *May I* sentences with these verbs all have the permission force; it is just that they can also have the request force.

We can provide an alternative explanation for the request interpretation of a sentence such as *May I have the salt* along the following Gricean lines. Assuming this sentence is uttered at the dinner table among friends, the hearer (we could have chosen the speaker as well) might reason as follows:

The speaker has requested permission for the salt
I infer that the speaker wants the salt[10]
In the present context, I can bring it about that the speaker gets the salt and therefore fulfill his (inferred) desire
The speaker and I both recognize my capability to do this and such cooperation is expected among friends
I infer that the speaker has implicated the request *Please pass me the salt*

It appears that an integral part of the working-out schema for such sentences involves both the relative roles of the speaker and hearer and the relative ease with which the hearer can bring about the state requested. As a general rule, we can stipulate that these two aspects bear an inverse relationship: as the role of the speaker moves from one of authority to one of a petitioner, the act must become correspondingly easier for the hearer. In addition, the necessity for the hearer to feel "cooperative" appears to subside as the authority of the speaker increases. For the president of a large company, for example, the utterance of *May I see those packing slips that are down three flights behind fourteen crates and under a pile of books* counts as a request (he is implicating the request *Please bring me those slips . . .*), while the same utterance by one packing clerk to another would probably not count as a request, or at least would not be accepted as a request, and might elicit an answer like "Sure, you know where they are . . . and would you bring me back a cup of coffee, regular." Conversely, the lowest petitioner can have a *may I* sentence count as a request to the highest authority, providing the task is easy enough, as, for example, *May I have the time*.

The working out of the hearer reasoning here does not seem adequate. In particular, because we have no principles to determine the direction of such reasoning, it suffers from the same sorts of criticism as the examples in Grice. However, it would appear that some explanation along these lines will ultimately account for this type of example, and the account here is offered as a first attempt.

To summarize, the force of requesting permission is directly a function of the meaning of the sentence with the "permission" modal. The force of requesting hearer action follows from the permission force and some rules of conversation, in particular that people generally want what they ask for and that expressions of desire can count

---

[10] Desire for x is not a necessary condition for the successful request for permission for x. I may, for example, ask your permission to hold the box, not because I want to hold it but because I am afraid that you might drop it. This is to suggest that it is the hearer who infers that the speaker wants what he requests, since this does seem a reasonable inference.

as requests under the right circumstances. The fact that *may I* sentences normally count as requests because of their meaning and rules of conversation appears to be part of what the native speaker knows about these sentences. This fact belongs in the grammar, as a part of the semantic representation F_p.

5.3. "Why Are We Stopping Here?"

The third and final example involves sentences such as *Why are we stopping here?* and *Why aren't we taking the left fork here?* which have the force of both a question and a suggestion. The latter sentence, for example, can count as a question about the reasons dictating the taking of some road other than the left fork or as a suggestion that we should take the left fork. Again, the issue is how to account for the non-question force. I can find no compelling evidence to suggest that there are two deep structures, one for each force. On the other hand, these *why* cases are unlike the *may I* questions in that the suggestion force seems to arise only if the question force is denied.

To see this, let us consider *should* questions which also have the force of both a question and a suggestion. Suppose, for example, that an older businessman utters *Should you be doing that?* to a teenager using a can of spray paint to decorate a car during an anti-war demonstration. The primary interpretation of the utterance is that the speaker is inquiring about the appropriateness of the paint job. In this context, particularly because of the roles of the people involved, the speaker cannot be seriously asking the question: the context denies the literal interpretation of the utterance because both speaker and hearer know that the painting is inappropriate. The hearer might reason in the following way:

The speaker has inquired if it is appropriate for me to be painting this car
We both recognize that it is not appropriate and we both recognize that the other is aware of this
Thus, the speaker cannot be seriously asking me the apparent question and the question is only rhetorical
Rhetorical questions should be reinterpreted as the statement of the same proposition but with a polarity change (positive questions become negative statements and negative questions become positive statements)
Thus, the speaker is really "saying" *You shouldn't be painting that car*
The sentence *You shouldn't be painting that car* has the force of a suggestion to cease the painting
Thus, I infer that the speaker is suggesting that I stop my painting

There is clearly one large jump in the reasoning, namely, that because the question interpretation is denied this sentence is interpreted as a rhetorical question. That this is the case seems true; why this should be so, which questions permit this interpretation and which don't, and the role of intonation in such examples, I leave as uncharted areas.

To return now to the *why* questions, suppose the same businessman asked *Why are you painting that car?* The hearer might reason in the following way:

The speaker has asked me for a reason for my painting this car
Both he and I recognize that there is no reason which will satisfy the speaker (there may be one satisfactory to the painter)
Thus, the speaker cannot be seriously asking me the apparent question and the question is rhetorical

The rhetorical interpretation of this question is *You are painting that car for no satisfactory reason = You are not painting that car for any satisfactory reason*
The utterance of *You're not painting that car for any reason* appears to violate the maxim of relevance; nothing in the prior discourse raised the subject of the car painting nor is this normally a conversation-initial utterance
Thus, the speaker must be implicating something
The speaker would not be commenting on the reasonableness of the act unless he thought "If an act does not have a satisfactory reason, then it should not be done"
Thus, the speaker is implicating "You should not paint the car"

Note that for the *why* questions, the path for accounting for the suggestion force is not direct: after determining that the question is rhetorical, we reduce the issue to that of a *should* statement by the speaker; we then must determine how such a statement should be interpreted. The specific way in which the utterance of a *why* question is used on a particular occasion is surely not part of the force of the sentence and not part of the grammar. That such sentences can be used rhetorically and that their interpretation involves the notion of appropriateness is part of what it is to understand a *why* sentence and should be viewed as part of linguistic competence. It is thus a part of the semantic representation of the sentence, that is, what we have designated as F_p.

6. CONCLUSION

The main thrust of this paper has been to focus on the problems involved in associating the illocutionary forces of a sentence with the sentence itself. I have sketched out some of the issues involved in analyzing illocutionary acts, in determining the extent to which the sentence meaning contributes to sentence force, and some of the pragmatic machinery that may be necessary in determining the standard uses of a sentence, an ability I take to be part of the native speaker's linguistic competence. The degree to which we lack knowledge in this area is truly staggering. We have barely begun to understand the correspondence between sentences and their forces; we do not know what aspects of sentence meaning are most relevant, the degree of generality of pairing sentences with their forces, how we should best analyze illocutionary acts, the extent to which they can be said to be related, or the extent to which a theory of conversation interacts with linguistic theory or to what extent some aspects of conversation are, in fact, part of linguistics as well. These, and numerous other questions, await investigation.

REFERENCES

Austin, J. (1962), *How to Do Things with Words*, Cambridge, Mass.: Harvard University Press.
Fraser, B. (1971), "An Examination of the Performative Analysis," Indiana University Linguistics Club, Bloomington, Ind.
Fraser, B. (1972), "Sentences and Illocutionary Forces," unpublished paper.

Fraser, B. (1973), "A Partial Analysis of Vernacular Performative Verbs," in R. Shuy and C.-J. Bailey, eds., *Towards Tomorrow's Linguistics*, Washington, D.C.: Georgetown University Press.

Grice, P. (1967), *Logic and Conversation*, unpublished William James Lectures, Harvard University.

Katz, J. (1972), *Semantic Theory*, New York: Harper & Row.

Lewis, D. (1969), *Convention*, Cambridge, Mass.: Harvard University Press.

Searle, J. (1968), "Austin on Locutionary and Illocutionary Acts," *The Philosophical Review*, 77, 405–424.

Searle, J. (1969), *Speech Acts*, Cambridge: Cambridge University Press.

Strawson, P. F. (1964), "Intention and Convention in Speech Acts," *The Philosophical Review*, 73, 339–360.

person marking
in walbiri[1]

Kenneth Hale

Massachusetts Institute of Technology

1. INTRODUCTORY OBSERVATIONS

Walbiri distinguishes finite and infinitive verb forms. Infinitive forms appear in subordinate clauses, while finite verb forms appear both in main clauses and in subordinate clauses. The subordinate (or second) clause in (1) has an infinitive verb form, while the subordinate clause in (2) has a finite verb:[2]

[1] This work was supported in part by the National Science Foundation (Fellowship No. 48058; Grant No. GS-1127) and in part by the National Institutes of Health (Grant No. MH-13390-04).

I am honored to be able to dedicate this work to Morris Halle, who has been of tremendous help to me in my attempts to learn about the nature of linguistic inquiry. I only wish the present work were less unfinished, less tentative, and therefore more worthy of him. However, I think it is in the nature of work on languages radically different from one's own that almost inevitably such studies are primarily suggestive (rather than conclusive) and somewhat elementary in scope. I hope this paper will serve as a basis for further research.

[2] Most of my Walbiri data come from Yuendumu, N.T., Australia. I am especially indebted to Sam Tjapangaḍi Johnson, Mick Tjupurula Connell, and Dinny Tjapaltjari Anderson for their efforts to teach me their language.

The consonants of Walbiri can be tabulated as follows:

	BILABIAL	APICO-ALVEOLAR	LAMINO-ALVEOPALATAL	APICO-DOMAL	DORSO-VELAR
stops	*p*	*t*	*tj*	*ṭ*	*k*
nasals	*m*	*n*	*nj*	*ṇ*	*ŋ*
laterals		*l*	*lj*	*ḷ*	
flaps		*r*		*ḍ*	
glides	*w*		*y*	*r*	

The vowels are: relatively high front (unrounded) /i/, relatively high back (rounded) /u/, low (unrounded—ranging from front to back, but typically rather central) /a/. Vowel length is distinctive (for example, /ŋurpa/ 'unknowing', /ŋu:rpa/ 'throat, larynx'). Stress is on the first vowel of the word. The orthography I have used here, in the main, conforms with practical orthographies used widely in Central Australia.

Published works on Walbiri include Capell's sketch (1962) and Reece's grammar (1970).

(1) *wawiri-tjara ka-ṇa-palaŋu nja-nji, maṇa ŋa-ṇinjtja-kura*
    kangaroo-dual present-I-them see-nonpast, grass eat-infinitive-complementizer
    'I see two kangaroos eating grass'
(2) *wawiri-tjara ka-ṇa-palaŋu nja-nji, kutja-ka-pala maṇa ŋa-ṇi*
    kangaroo-dual present-I-them see-nonpast, relative-present-dual grass eat-nonpast
    'I see two kangaroos eating grass'

In both (1) and (2), the verb of the main (or first) clause is finite. In the subordinate clause of (1), the verb form consists of a stem /ŋa-/ 'eat' followed by the infinitive ending /-ṇinjtja-/, and the combination is followed by the complementizer /-kura/ 'object relative'. In the main clauses of (1) and (2), and in the subordinate clause of (2), the verb form consists of a stem (/nja-/ 'see', /ŋa-/ 'eat') followed by an inflectional suffix /-nji ~ -ṇi ~ .../ 'nonpast tense'.[3] In the finite clauses, moreover, there is an auxiliary element /ka-/ 'present' which, in conjunction with the verbal inflection, marks a general (as opposed to specifically "immediate") present tense. The subordinate finite clause has, in addition, the complementizer /kutja-/ 'relative' prefixed to the auxiliary base.

In the discussion to follow, I will be concerned exclusively with finite clauses, and when I speak of sentences, unless I indicate otherwise, I will mean clauses which contain auxiliaries and finite verbs. For the most part, I will restrict my discussion to simple sentences, or at least to sentences whose surface structures are simple in the sense that they do not contain embeddings.

As is evident from the examples already given, the modal categories of tense, mood, and aspect are represented discontinuously in the surface structures of Walbiri sentences by elements appearing in a constituent which I have referred to as the "auxiliary" and by suffixes in the verb word. As further illustration, consider the sentences (3a–c):

(3) (a) *ŋatju ka-ṇa puḷa-mi*
        I present-I shout-nonpast
        'I am shouting; I shout'   (Continued)

---

[3] Speaking in extremely superficial terms, it is possible to recognize five verbal conjugations in Walbiri according to the alternants which various grammatical endings exhibit in combination with them. In the following table, each of the five conjugations is represented by a model verb under which the appropriate endings are placed in columns:

/waŋka-/ 'to speak'	/paka-/ 'to strike'	/nja-/ 'to see'	/ŋa-/ 'to eat'	/ma-/ 'to take'	
-mi	-ṇi	-nji	-ṇi	-ni	NONPAST
-tja	-ṇu	-ŋu	-ṇu	-nu	PAST
-nja	-ṇinja	-ŋanja	-ṇinja	-nanja	PRESENT
-tju	-ku	-ŋku	-lku	-nku	FUTURE
-ya	-ka	-ŋka	-njtja	-nta	IMPERATIVE
-njtja	-ṇinjtja	-njtja	-ṇinjtja	-ninjtja	INFINITIVE
IMPERATIVE + -ḷa					IRREALIS

The suffixes glossed 'present' and 'future' are of rather limited use in the major Walbiri communities, although they are recognized by most speakers. (The present is found in songs over the entire area.) In modern spoken Walbiri, the nonpast is used, in conjunction with auxiliaries, to indicate present and future tense in the majority of syntactic circumstances.

The nonpast ending in the conjugation represented by /waŋka-/ 'to speak' is /-mi/ or zero; I use /-mi/ consistently in the text of this paper. Also, the nonpast in the /paka-/ and /ŋa-/ conjugations is either /-ṇi/ or /-ni/; I use the former.

It is possible to reduce the number of conjugations to three by combining two of the monosyllabic conjugations with the two polysyllabic ones (see Hale (1969b)). Furthermore, it is possible to relate conjugation membership to transitivity to a degree which is significantly greater than chance. This has some possible significance, if not synchronically, then at least historically (see Hale (1970)).

(b) *ŋatju lpa-ṇa puḷa-tja*
     I past-I shout-past
     'I was shouting; I shouted'
(c) *ŋatju kapi-ṇa puḷa-mi*
     I future-I shout-nonpast
     'I will be shouting; I will shout'

In each of these sentences, the co-occurrence of a particular auxiliary "base" (/ka-/ 'present', /lpa-/ 'past', /kapi-/ 'future') with a particular verbal ending (/-mi/ 'nonpast', /-tja/ 'past') marks a specific modal category. I will not be concerned here with a discussion of Walbiri modal categories, but rather with another aspect of the auxiliary constituent. The auxiliary is also the location of suffixes agreeing in person and number (and case, to some extent) with noun phrases appearing elsewhere in the sentence: in (3a–c), the auxiliary contains the suffix /-ṇa/ '1st person singular (subj)' in agreement with the subject /ŋatju/ 'I'; similarly, the suffix /-palaŋu/ '3rd dual (obj)' appearing in the auxiliaries of the main clauses of sentences (1) and (2) is in agreement with the object /wawiri-tjara/ 'kangaroo-dual'. It is with the person-marking suffixes that the present discussion will be primarily concerned.

The sentences used in illustration so far illustrate the general outlines of the internal structure of the auxiliary constituent. The central ingredient is what I will refer to as the "base" (represented by /ka-/, /lpa-/, /kapi-/ in (3)); person-marking suffixes follow the base, and a complementizer (for example, /kutja-/ in (2)) may precede the base. In order to maintain this internal analysis, it will be necessary to recognize a phonologically null auxiliary base, which I will represent by φ- in examples. Like its phonologically constituted counterparts, the zero base serves as a peg for the attachment of person markers and complementizers.[4]

Compare the aspectually indefinite or nonspecific sentences (3a–c) with the aspectually definite sentences (4a,b):

(4) (a) *ŋatju φ-ṇa puḷa-mi*
         I φ-I shout-nonpast
         'I'll shout; let me shout'
    (b) *ŋatju φ-ṇa puḷa-tja*
         I φ-I shout-past
         'I shouted'

And compare the subordinate clause of (2) with that in (5):

(5) *wawiri-tjara kapi-ṇa-palaŋu pura-mi, kutja-φ-ṇa-palaŋu pantu-ṇu*
     kangaroo-dual future-I-them cook-nonpast, relative-φ-I-them spear-past
     'I'm going to cook the two kangaroos that I (have) speared'

----

[4] I give here a list of auxiliaries together with the verbal endings (by gloss) with which they co-occur. Approximate meanings are given in single quotes: /φ . . . NONPAST/ 'immediate future, optative'; /φ . . . PAST/ 'past definite, preterite'; /φ . . . PRESENT/ 'immediate present, demonstrative aspect'; /φ . . . FUTURE/ 'immediate future, optative'; /φ . . . IMPERATIVE/ 'imperative'; /ka . . . NONPAST/ 'present, progressive, usitative'; /kapi . . . NONPAST/ 'future'; /lpa . . . PAST/ 'indefinite (imperfect) past, narrative past'; /katjika . . . NONPAST/ 'potential, present conditional (apodosis)'; /kalaka . . . NONPAST/ 'admonitive'; /katjilpa . . . IRREALIS/ 'present conditional (protasis)'; /katji- . . . NONPAST/ 'future conditional (protasis)'; /katji . . . IRREALIS/ 'past conditional (protasis)'; /kapi . . . IRREALIS/ 'past conditional (apodosis)'.

The principal complementizers (combinable with the auxiliary bases /φ/, /ka/, or /lpa/) are: /kutja-/ 'relative', /yuŋu- (yiŋa- ~ yi-)/ 'jussive, purposive', and /kula-/ 'negative'. It is probable that /katji-/, listed as an auxiliary base, should also be regarded as a complementizer; however, the relationship among /katji-/, /katjika-/, and /katjilpa-/ is no longer a straightforward one.

From a gross morphological point of view, the zero base is no different in its behavior from the phonologically constituted auxiliary bases and, like the latter, it co-occurs with the verbal endings to render particular modal meanings.

I will assume in what follows that the basic subconstituent in the auxiliary is the base (or possibly a complementizer together with the base) and that the person markers are introduced into the auxiliary transformationally. That is to say, I will assume that there is a point in the derivation of Walbiri finite clauses at which the person-marking suffixes are not present in the auxiliary. The purpose of this paper is to point out a number of facts of Walbiri person-marking which must in one way or another be accommodated in those parts of the grammar which provide for the correct surface form of Walbiri auxiliaries. Before entering into the central topic, however, I would like to digress momentarily in order to discuss the external syntax of the auxiliary with a view to determining its basic position within the sentence. This basic position will presumably be that which the auxiliary occupies at the time the person markers are inserted into it.

2. THE POSITIONING OF THE AUXILIARY

I have implied in the foregoing discussion that the auxiliary is a "constituent" of Walbiri finite clauses. I will make this assumption explicit by proposing that the parts of the auxiliary are exhaustively dominated by a node "Aux" and that the Aux node is in turn immediately dominated by the sentence node "S." My concern here will be with the relative order position of Aux among the other constituents of a sentence.

In the sentences of (3) and (4), the auxiliary follows the subject /ŋatju/ 'I'. However, in the main clauses of (1) and (2), where the first person subject pronoun has been deleted (as is normally the case for nonemphatic pronouns), the auxiliary follows the object /wawiri-tjara/ 'kangaroo-dual'. If the subject pronoun were deleted from, say, (3a), then the auxiliary would follow the verb, as in (6):

(6) *puḷa-mi ka-ṇa*
   shout-nonpast present-I
   'I am shouting; I shout'

And the auxiliary would also follow the verb if the relative order of subject and verb in (3a) were inverted:

(7) *puḷa-mi ka-ṇa ŋatju*

The generalization which can be made, of course, is that in the surface structures exemplified here, the auxiliary is consistently in second position, that is, it follows the first constituent of the sentence. And, in general, while the relative ordering of the major constituents of a sentence is relatively free, the surface position of Aux is relatively fixed. Take, for example, the nonauxiliary constituents of a sentence like (8):

(8) *ŋarka-ŋku ɸ-palaŋu wawiri-tjara kuḷaḍa-ḷu pantu-ṇu*
   man-ergative ɸ-them kangaroo-dual spear-instrumental spear-past
   'The man speared two kangaroos with a spear'

These constituents can permute freely, subject to conditions having more to do, strictly speaking, with considerations of style and the well-formedness of discourses than with the syntax of the sentence. The auxiliary, however, is consistently in second position, as we see in (9):

(9) (a) *wawiri-tjara ɸ-palaŋu kuḷaḍa-ḷu pantu-ṇu ŋarka-ŋku*
    (b) *kuḷaḍa-ḷu ɸ-palaŋu wawiri-tjara pantu-ṇu ŋarka-ŋku*
    (c) *pantu-ṇu ɸ-palaŋu ŋarka-ŋku wawiri-tjara kuḷaḍa-ḷu*
    ⋮

It is evident that the deep structure position of Aux cannot be identified with its surface structure position since second position, in the sense required for the ultimate positioning of Aux, can be defined only rather late in the derivation of a particular sentence, at a point subsequent to the possible application of rules which delete (as in (6)) or permute (as in (9)) other sentence-internal constituents. In fact, if the positioning of Aux is to be regarded as a rule at all, as I will assume, its application must be extremely late in the derivation of a sentence and must even, as I shall show, make reference to phonological information.

I would like to suggest that the auxiliary is basically initial in Walbiri and that it is moved into second position by a rule which I shall call Aux-Insertion. This suggestion is supported to some extent by the observation that, under certain phonologically specifiable circumstances, the auxiliary may actually appear in sentence-initial position (as it does in the subordinate clauses of (2) and of (5), for example). If an auxiliary base, or the combination of complementizer plus base, is disyllabic or longer, then Aux may remain in initial position. Thus, while the auxiliary must appear in second position in the surface structures of (10), because the auxiliary bases are less than disyllabic in length, the auxiliary of (11) may appear either in initial position or in second position since the future base /kapi-/ is disyllabic:

(10) (a) *wawiri ka-ṇa pura-mi*
         kangaroo present-I cook-nonpast
         'I am cooking the kangaroo'
     (b) *wawiri ɸ-ṇa pura-tja*
         kangaroo ɸ-I cook-past
         'I cooked the kangaroo'
(11) (a) *kapi-ṇa wawiri pura-mi*
         future-I kangaroo cook-nonpast
     (b) *wawiri kapi-ṇa pura-mi*
         kangaroo future-I cook-nonpast
         'I will cook the kangaroo'

Similarly, in the negatives corresponding to (10a,b), the auxiliary may remain in initial position since the negative element (which, like a complementizer, is prefixed to the auxiliary base) is disyllabic:

(12) (a) *kula-ka-ṇa wawiri pura-mi*
         negative-present-I kangaroo cook-nonpast
         'I am not cooking the kangaroo'
     (b) *kula-ɸ-ṇa wawiri pura-tja*
         negative-ɸ-I kangaroo cook-past
         'I did not cook the kangaroo'

In fact, there are circumstances in which the negative auxiliary may not be inserted into second position at all, namely, when, as a result of permutation or deletion occurring prior to Aux-Insertion, the verb immediately follows the negative auxiliary. Thus, while (a), (b), and (c) of (13) are possible, (d) and (e) are not:[5]

(13) (a) *ŋatju kula-ka-ṇa puḷa-mi*
     (b) *kula-ka-ṇa puḷa-mi ŋatju*
     (c) *kula-ka-ṇa puḷa-mi*
          'I am not shouting'
     (d) **puḷa-mi kula-ka-ṇa ŋatju*
     (e) **puḷa-mi kula-ka-ṇa*

Aux-Insertion operates in finite clauses, whether they are subordinate or main. In the subordinate clause of sentence (2), the auxiliary may remain initial because of the phonological weight added to the auxiliary base by the prefixed relative complementizer /kutja-/, but it could also be moved, as in the variant (14):

(14) *wawiri-tjara ka-ṇa-palaŋu nja-nji, maṇa kutja-ka-pala ŋa-ṇi*

To account for these various observations, I will assume that the auxiliary is basically initial in Walbiri and that it is moved into second position by the Aux-Insertion Rule. Furthermore, Aux-Insertion is (*a*) obligatory if the portion of the auxiliary preceding the person markers is less than disyllabic (that is, monosyllabic or phonologically null), (*b*) blocked if the auxiliary is the negative and is immediately followed by the verb, and (*c*) optional otherwise. The insertion must be ordered in the grammar to follow all syntactic operations which have an effect on the ordering of nonauxiliary constituents.[6]

It is appropriate to think of Aux-Insertion as having the effect of making the auxiliary enclitic to the first nonauxiliary constituent of the sentence. The auxiliary is unstressed and, particularly where the base is monosyllabic or phonologically empty, it forms a prosodic unit with the preceding word.[7] I have left inexact the

[5] It is conceivable that what is responsible for this is the fact that the verb must be within the "scope" of the negative and, further, that material which is in the scope of the negative must be to its right.

[6] It is also possible in Walbiri to extrapose noun phrases to the left of the main body of the sentence. In such cases it is within the main body of the sentence that Aux-Insertion operates, as in the following:

wawiri njampu, ŋatjulu-ḷu ɸ-ṇa pantu-ṇu
kangaroo this, I-ergative past-I spear-past
'This kangaroo, I speared'

I assume that this operation of left-dislocation precedes Aux-Insertion and that it extraposes the noun phrase to the left of the initial Aux. For the purposes of Aux-Insertion, the extraposed noun phrase is no longer a part of the sentence.

[7] This refers not only to the behavior of Aux and the preceding word with respect to stress and intonation (a word and following enclitic Aux are stressed as if they comprised a single word), but also to the phenomenon of vowel assimilation according to which a suffixal high vowel assimilates to a preceding final high vowel (for example, /kaḷi-ku/ → [kaḷi-ki] 'boomerang-dative'—see Hale (to appear)). Enclitic person markers behave like suffixes in this regard. For example, (a) becomes (b) by vowel assimilation:

(a) *maliki-ḷu ɸ-tju yaḷku-ṇu*
     dog-ergative past-me bite-past
     'The dog bit me'
(b) *maliki-ḷi ɸ-tji yaḷku-ṇu*

And (c) becomes (d):

(c) *kuyu ɸ-ḷipa ŋa-ṇu*
     meat past-we eat-past
     'We ate meat'
(d) *kuyu ɸ-ḷupa ŋa-ṇu*

notion "sentence constituent" in referring to the operation of Aux-Insertion, and the examples I have given so far would lead one to believe that the rule inserts the auxiliary immediately to the right of the first nonauxiliary "word" of a sentence. This is not correct, however, since a noun phrase consisting of more than one word functions as a unit with respect to Aux-Insertion, as can be seen from (15):

(15) (a) *wawiri njampu kapi-ṇa pura-mi*
          kangaroo this future-I cook-nonpast
          'I will cook this kangaroo'
     (b) *tjaṇṭu wiṛi-ŋki φ-tji yaḷku-ṇu*
          dog big-ergative φ-me bite-past
          'The big dog bit me'

I feel, therefore, that the correct formulation of Aux-Insertion will make reference to constituents of sentences rather than to words; that is, the auxiliary is inserted to the right of the immediately following single constituent which is immediately dominated by the sentence node S, regardless of the number of words that single constituent might itself contain. Thus, an auxiliary will be inserted to the right of a noun phrase, regardless of its internal complexity. It is possible, however, to break up a noun phrase so that its erstwhile subconstituents become separate sentence constituents. This is even stylistically preferred. When it happens, the parts of the former noun phrase are free to scramble among the other sentence constituents and, of course, they function as separate constituents with respect to Aux-Insertion, as shown in (16):

(16) (a) *njampu kapi-ṇa pura-mi wawiri*
     (b) *wawiri kapi-ṇa pura-mi njampu*

Where a noun phrase is marked for case, by means of a phonologically con-stituted case ending, typically the inflection is attached to the noun phrase as a whole if the latter is still intact, as in (15b). But if a noun phrase is broken up, the case ending appears on each of its subparts, as in (17):

(17) (a) *tjaṇṭu-ŋku φ-tju yaḷku-ṇu wiṛi-ŋki*
          dog-ergative φ-me bite-past big-ergative
     (b) *wiṛi-ŋki φ-tji yaḷku-ṇu tjaṇṭu-ŋku*
          big-ergative φ-me bite-past dog-ergative

While an auxiliary is inserted to the right of a noun phrase, it is not inserted to the right of a sequence consisting of both a noun phrase (an object, say) and a verb. I take this to mean either that there is no verb phrase constituent in Walbiri or that, at the time Aux-Insertion applies, there is no such constituent. A verb and its nominal complement(s) do not form a constituent with respect to Aux-Insertion, nor can it be argued that they form a constituent for the purposes of the earlier operation of permutation. I will assume, therefore, that the verb and the complement are each dominated immediately by the S node, at least at this point in the derivation of sentences.

To summarize, the auxiliary is basically initial in Walbiri finite clauses. Since the most reasonable assumption about the insertion of person markers into the auxiliary is that it takes place prior to deletion or permutation of the noun phrases with which the auxiliary ultimately agrees, it follows that the auxiliary is in its original initial position at the time person marking is effected, for Aux-Insertion follows deletion and permutation.

3. SUBJECT PERSON MARKERS

I will begin the discussion of person marking proper with the simplest possible case, namely, simple intransitive sentences of the type represented by (3), in which the sole noun phrase constituent is the subject. The sentences of (3) are all instances of the first person singular, and the person marker /-na/ appearing in the auxiliary can be said to agree with the subject pronoun /ŋatju/. Similarly, the person marker /-npa/ in the auxiliary of (18) can be said to agree with the second person singular pronoun /njuntu/:

(18) *njuntu ka-npa puḷa-mi*
       you present-you shout-nonpast
       'You are shouting; you shout'

The entire list of non-third person pronouns is given in (19), together with the corresponding suffixes for subject person agreement. I will henceforth refer to the person-marking suffixes as (pronominal) clitics. The numbers appearing to the left of the pronouns in (19) are glosses used for the sake of brevity. They are to be interpreted as follows: 1 'first singular', 2 'second singular', 11 'first dual exclusive', 12 'first dual inclusive', 22 'second dual', 111 'first plural exclusive', 122 'first plural inclusive', 222 'second plural'.[8] (The hyphenation appearing within the 22, 111, and 222 clitics will be explained later, as will the parenthesized element in the 22 clitic.)

(19)

	PRONOUN	SUBJECT CLITIC
1	*ŋatju(lu)*	*-ṇa*
2	*njuntu(lu)*	*-n(pa)*
11	*ŋatjara*	*-ḷitjara*
12	*ŋali(-tjara)*	*-ḷi*
22	*njumpala*	*-n(pa)-pala*
111	*ŋanimpa*	*-ṇa-lu*
122	*ŋalipa*	*-ḷipa*
222	*njurula*	*-nku-lu*

Third person subject agreement is exemplified in the sentences in (20):

(20) (a) *ŋarka ka puḷa-mi*
            'The/a man is shouting'
      (b) *ŋarka-tjara ka-pala puḷa-mi*
            '(The) two men are shouting'
      (c) *ŋarka-patu ka-lu puḷa-mi*
            '(The) several men are shouting'
      (d) *ŋarka ka-lu puḷa-mi*
            '(The) men are shouting'

Third person singular agreement is represented by a zero in the auxiliary, third dual agreement by the clitic /-pala/, and third plural by /-lu/. Thus we have the clitics in (21):

---

[8] The alternations /ŋatju ∼ ŋatjulu/ in the 1 pronoun and /njuntu ∼ njuntulu/ in the 2 pronoun are free in uninflected forms. The shorter alternant appears with the possessive suffix /-njaŋu/; the dative /-ku/ combines with either alternant, while the ergative /-ḷu/ regularly combines with the longer form, as do the locative /-ḷa/ and comitative /-ḷatjinta/. The alternation /ŋali ∼ ŋalitjara/ in the 12 pronoun is free in all environments.

(21)   3   zero
       33   -*pala*
      333   -*lu*

Four numbers are recognized for count nouns of the type represented by the subjects of (20a–d), namely, singular, dual, paucal, and plural.[9] Paucal number (represented by the suffix /-patu/) is also possible for the non-third person pronouns (/ŋanimpa-patu/, /ŋalipa-patu/, and so on). However, the two plurals are not represented by distinct clitics in the auxiliary. In speaking of agreement, then, I will use the term "plural" to refer generally to both plural categories.[10]

The noun phrases in the sentences of (20) consist of nouns alone. The same facts of third person subject agreement could have been illustrated by means of subject noun phrases consisting of nouns together with determiners, as in (22), or of determiners alone, as in (23):

(22) (a) *ŋarka njanuŋu ka puḷa-mi*
           'The aforementioned man is shouting'
      (b) *ŋarka njanuŋu-tjara ka-pala puḷa-mi*
           'The two aforementioned men are shouting'
(23) (a) *njanuŋu ka puḷa-mi*
           'The aforementioned one is shouting; he/she is shouting'
      (b) *njanuŋu-tjara ka-pala puḷa-mi*
           'The aforementioned two are shouting; they (dual) are shouting'

Walbiri has a semantically rich system of determiners, but the categories which are relevant to third person subject agreement are limited to person and number as summarized in (21).[11]

It would be a mistake to imply that a noun phrase with a nominal head always requires third person agreement. The noun phrases of (22) do in fact require such agreement but this is because the determiner /njanuŋu/ 'the, the aforementioned' is strictly third person. Sentences like those in (24) are not only allowed, but fairly common:

---

[9] For the most part, plural number is unmarked in nouns (that is, the singular and plural are identical), although a few nouns can reduplicate to mark the plural: *kuḍu* 'child', *kuḍukuḍu* 'children'; *kanta* 'woman', *kantakanta* 'women'.

[10] Noncount nouns, expectably, behave as singulars with respect to agreement:

payi ka paŋka-mi
wind present run-nonpast
'The wind is blowing'

[11] Walbiri indefinite determiners are /tjinta/ 'singular, one', /tjirama ~ tjirima/ 'dual, two', /wirkaḍu, maŋkurpa/ 'paucal, few, several', /panu/ 'plural, many'. Demonstratives (combinable with the suffixes /-tjara/ 'dual', /-patu/ 'paucal', and less frequently /-ra/ "plural") are /njampu/ 'this', /yalumpu/ 'that mid-distal, that near addressee', /yali/ 'that distal, removed from speaker and addressee', /yinja/ 'that ultra-distal'. Nondemonstrative definite determiners (also combinable with dual and paucal suffixes) are /njanuŋu/ 'the, he/she/it, previously mentioned in discourse', /yaŋka/ 'the, he/she/it, evocative, the same', and /ŋula/ 'that, mentioned in prior clause or closely preceding sentence'. Interrogative determiners are definite /njarpaṟa/ 'which' and indefinite /ŋana/ 'who', /njiya/ 'what', /njatjaŋu/ 'who/what nonsingular, how many'. This is not a complete inventory of Walbiri determiners. The glosses given here are to be regarded as approximate only.

(24) (a) *ŋarka ka-ṇa puḷa-mi*
　　　　man present-I shout-nonpast
　　　　'I man am shouting'
　　(b) *ŋarka ka-npa puḷa-mi*
　　　　man present-2 shout-nonpast
　　　　'You man are shouting'
　　(c) *ŋarka-tjara ka-ḷitjara puḷa-mi*
　　　　man-dual present-11 shout-nonpast
　　　　'We men (dual exclusive) are shouting'

I propose that it is the determiner, rather than the nominal, which determines the person of a given noun phrase and, further, that noun phrases consisting only of nouns are derived by deletion of a determiner (probably under conditions similar to those which allow for the deletion of pronouns in sentences of the type represented by (16)). According to this proposal, the subjects of (a), (b), and (c) of (24) are, abstractly, /ŋarka ŋatju/, /ŋarka njuntu/, and /ŋarka ŋatjara/, respectively; and the pronouns /ŋatju/, /njuntu/, /ŋatjara/ are determiners, strictly speaking. In fact, noun phrases of the form /ŋarka ŋatju/ 'I man', /yapa ŋatju/ 'I person', with retention rather than deletion of the determiner, are possible, albeit rare, in actual usage.[12]

This proposal extends, of course, to noun phrases of the type represented by the subjects of (20a–d): they are assumed to be derived by deletion of a third person determiner. It is arguable that some noun phrases consisting of a determiner alone are derived by deletion of the noun under identity with a noun in a prior clause. However, where no such source can be suggested, as is typically but not exclusively the case in non-third person noun phrases consisting solely of the pronoun (= determiner), some other provision must be made. At least two proposals come to mind. First, one might assume that the rules of the base allow a noun to be chosen optionally in the expansion of NP (that is, the rule expanding NP is roughly of the form NP → (N) Det, where "Det" is the node dominating determiners, including what are commonly referred to as pronouns). Alternatively, one might assume that both the noun and the determiner are obligatory but that some nouns are fully abstract (that is, phonologically vacuous) and therefore deleted in surface structures universally. I will not commit myself on either of these two proposals since I know of no clear evidence which bears on the issue. In any event, nothing would be lost in a discussion of Walbiri person marking by pretending that noun phrases consisted always and only of determiners if, as I have asserted, it is true that the categories which are expressed in pronominal clitics are also distinguished in determiners.[13]

---

[12] The demonstrative determiners /njampu/ and /yalumpu/ can also be used as first and second person determiners, respectively.

[13] Proper nouns and indefinite noun phrases typically appear without overt determiners in Walbiri. However, the definite /njanuṇu/ 'the' can appear with proper nouns, and there is a set of indefinite determiners (see note 11) which might underlie indefinite noun phrases which appear in surface structures without overt determiners. In actual fact, a sentence like the following is ambiguously either definite or indefinite in isolation:

ŋarka ka puḷa-mi
man present shout-nonpast

It is probably correct to view such sentences as resulting from the deletion of either a definite or indefinite determiner. The latter, like the so-called independent pronouns, appear overtly only under conditions of emphasis or the like.

4. A PROVISIONAL THEORY OF WALBIRI PERSON MARKING

With this introduction it becomes possible to characterize, in rough outline, the form which simple intransitive sentences exhibit prior to the application of the agreement rules. The essential proposals are that the auxiliary, into which pronominal clitics are inserted, is initial, and that the subject noun phrase consists of at least a determiner.

The structure of sentence (3a) prior to agreement might be represented roughly as in (25):[14]

(25)

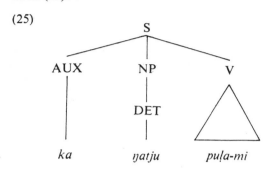

Similarly, the pre-agreement structure of (22a) (and of (20a), as well, on one of its readings) might be represented as in (26):

(26)

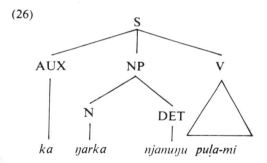

I will assume momentarily that these structures, and the general class which they represent, can reasonably be regarded as the objects over which agreement is defined, and I will turn now to the question of how agreement is to be stated in a formal grammar of Walbiri. I will not be able to comment in any substantive way on certain of the issues involved, but I will nonetheless be able to make a number of observations which help to select among theoretically possible competing alternatives.

An initially suggestive conception of agreement, which I will refer to as the "constituent-copying" alternative, holds that the pronominal clitics are direct duplicates of the determiners that appear in the noun phrases with which they are construed, differing only in their phonological realization (or "spelling"). Agreement is then accomplished by means of rules inserting determiner copies from the appropriate

---

[14] I will continue to assume that there is no VP node or at least that it is irrelevant to the concerns of this paper. I will also not address myself to the question of the source of tense inflections on the verb.

noun phrases into the auxiliary and adjusting their phonological constituency in required ways.

In order to place into clear perspective certain important aspects of Walbiri person marking, I will consider this alternative in a strictly literal manner. Thus, for example, I will assume that a determiner copy which is inserted into the auxiliary (and, presumably, sister-adjoined to the auxiliary base) is an *exact* duplicate of the determiner in the noun phrase with which it is construed, including its phonological representation. Furthermore, I will assume that the phonological rules which readjust the spelling of Aux-dominated determiners are defined solely in terms of phonological matrices and their domination by categorical nodes (Det, Aux) and perhaps also in terms of their relative order positions within Aux. According to this literal interpretation, the effect of the copy rule on (25), for example, would be the derived structure (27):

(27)

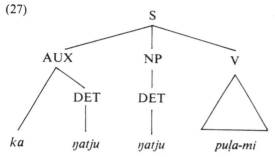

Subsequently, a phonological readjustment rule would "respell" the Aux-dominated occurrence of /ŋatju/ as the clitic /-ŋa/.

Under the constituent-copying alternative as I have outlined it here, all person agreement is effected in this manner and all pronominal clitics are derived by respelling Aux-dominated determiner copies: /ŋatju/ → /-ŋa/, /njuntu/ → /-npa/, /ŋatjara/ → /-litjara/, /njanuŋu/ → φ, /njanuŋu-tjara/ → /-pala/, and so on. The initial appeal of this analysis is that it incorporates, in a very concrete way, the basically correct observation that the determiner is the primary locus of the category of person. It accomplishes this by relating pronominal clitics *directly* to specific determiners, by identifying the former as phonological respellings of the latter. I will now attempt to show, however, that this direct identification of clitics with determiners is mistaken and that an adequate account of Walbiri person marking must be somewhat more abstract than the constituent-copying alternative under the strictly literal interpretation.[15]

That the relationship between pronominal clitics and determiners cannot be so simple and direct is shown, for example, by the behavior of conjoined noun phrases in agreement. Consider the forms in (28):

(28) (a) *njuntu manu ŋatju ka-li puḷa-mi*
          you and I present-12 shout-nonpast
          'You and I are shouting'   (*Continued*)

[15] It is, nevertheless, almost certain that there is historical reality in a concrete morphic identification between certain clitics and determiners. For example, the similarity between /ŋalipa/ '122' and the object clitic /-ŋalpa/ '122', or between /ŋanimpa/ '111' and /-ŋanpa/ '111' (which we mention later), is certainly not entirely accidental. A hypothetical account of the evolution of the Walbiri system of person marking, consistent with the existence of such similarities, will be suggested later.

(b) *njuntu manu yali ka-n-pala puḷa-mi*
    you and that present-22 shout-nonpast
    'You and that one (removed) are shouting'
(c) *ŋatju manu yali ka-ḷitjara puḷa-mi*
    I and that present-11 shout-nonpast
    'That one and I are shouting'
(d) *njampu manu yali ka-pala puḷa-mi*
    this and that present-33 shout-nonpast
    'This one and that one are shouting'

In none of the sentences of (28) can it be said that the pronominal clitic corresponds directly to a determiner present in the subject noun phrase. But in each sentence, in an intuitively clear sense, the clitic agrees in person and number with the subject noun phrase as a whole. The combination of /njuntu/ '2' and /ŋatju/ '1' in (28a) amounts to dual number and simultaneous first and second person (that is, "inclusive person," in the established terminology), and this is precisely the combination of categories expressed by the clitic /-ḷi/ '12'. Exactly the same kind of analysis applies to the other data of (28) and to their logical extensions. While these data are consistent with the claim that determiners play the central role in determining the person of noun phrases in which they appear, they suggest that agreement in Aux is not with the person and number of individual determiners but rather with the person and number of whole noun phrases.[16]

The constituent-copying alternative would be a serious proposal for Walbiri agreement if it could be shown that the entire battery of operations involved in effecting agreement could, without loss of significant generalizations, be formulated in such a way as to avoid entirely any reference to the categories of person and number as abstract features of noun phrases and independent of their morphic realization. I see no obvious way in which the behavior of conjoined noun phrases can be accommodated in the constituent-copying alternative. But even assuming that conjoined noun phrases could be handled, the direct identification of clitics with determiners seems particularly misguided when one considers the total range of possible third person noun phrases. A rich variety of categories expressed in third person determiners are simply not reflected in the clitics of agreement. And in general, only the categories of person and number (and case) are directly relevant to agreement, regardless of any additional categories which might be expressed in the determiners of noun phrases with which the pronominal clitics are construed. This prevailing fact of Walbiri agreement constantly makes itself felt in any serious attempt to formulate a

---

[16] There is some evidence which suggests that certain determiners, or independent pronouns, are provided by transformational rule subsequent to the insertion of lexical items into preterminal strings. For some if not all speakers of Walbiri, conjoined noun phrases, consisting of both nominal and pronominal conjuncts, may undergo a process which might be termed "conjunct absorption." In a conjoined expression of the type represented by /tjapaŋaḍi manu ŋatju/ 'Tjapangardi and I', the pronominal conjunct, together with the conjunction /manu/, may be replaced by a pronoun which embodies the person and number of the noun phrase as a whole: in this example the noun phrase as a whole is dual in number and first inclusive in person; hence, the subsequence /manu ŋatju/ 'and I' may be replaced by /ŋatjara/ '11'. This fact could be taken as establishing the existence of a rule which actually creates a pronoun and could conceivably be of significance in determining the proper analysis of Walbiri agreement in relation to conjoined expressions. One might, for example, propose that conjunction absorption is a necessary prior step in effecting agreement. Since the pronoun which is created by absorption embodies the correct person and number, one could argue that it is a copy of this composite pronoun which is inserted into the auxiliary. This proposal is somewhat weakened by the fact that both absorbed and unabsorbed pronominal conjuncts are allowed in Walbiri sentences, that is, absorption is optional. Nevertheless, the proposal will be briefly reconsidered later in the context of a comparison of the Walbiri system of person marking with that of Warramunga.

determiner-copying transformation and a set of respelling rules for converting determiners into their ultimate clitic forms.

In short, the failure of the constituent-copying alternative, under the strictly literal interpretation, is in its inability to refer directly to the relevant grammatical categories of person and number. Because it allows reference only to constituents and their phonological constituency, it cannot account in any simple and direct fashion for the fact that morphologically and syntactically distinct noun phrases can behave identically with respect to agreement—for example, each of the following noun phrases is 'first person plural inclusive' and, accordingly, requires /-lipa/ '122' in subject agreement: /ŋalipa/ '122', /ŋatjara manu njuntu/ '11 and 2', /ŋatju manu njumpala/ '1 and 22', /ŋatjara manu njumpala/ '11 and 22', /ŋatju manu njurula/ '1 and 222', /ŋali manu yalumpu-tjara/ '12 and those two near', and so on.

The plausibility of the determiner-copying conception of Walbiri agreement would be further diminished if it could be shown that phonologically identical determiners allowed distinct forms of agreement, corresponding to differences in person or number not overtly expressed in the determiners themselves. This is apparently the case for some Walbiri determiners, although the relevant data are amenable to alternative analyses.[17]

Consider, for example, the case of number in third person determiners. Typically, the singular and plural numbers are unmarked, while dual and paucal numbers are marked, for example, /njampu/ 'this singular', /njampu-tjara/ 'these dual', /njampu-patu/ 'these paucal', /njampu/ 'these plural'. The singular and plural are identical, /njampu/, but the former requires singular agreement and the latter requires plural agreement. This state of affairs holds generally for the definite third person determiners. One could, of course, allow the respelling of Aux-dominated /njampu/ and all other unmarked definite third person determiners to be freely either zero or /-lu/, to be interpreted later as singular and plural, respectively. But, quite apart from the implied claim that the semantic interpretation of number follows the phonological respelling of certain formatives, this would yield strictly ungrammatical results in certain cases, as, for example, with a zero subject clitic in the auxiliary of a sentence whose verb requires a plural subject (/mati-/ 'to go in procession', for instance) or a zero subject clitic in agreement with a noun phrase whose head noun is specifically plural in form (as is possible for a few nouns, such as /kudu/ 'child', /kudukudu/ 'children'; /pulka/ 'old man', /pulkapulka/ 'old men'). While the category of number may not be overtly distinguished in determiners, it is consistently distinguished in subject agreement. A similar situation exists in the case of person. Thus, the determiners /njampu/ 'this' and /yalumpu/ 'that near' are used not only as third person demonstratives but as, respectively, first and second person demonstratives as well. In the latter case, they

[17] In the case of identity between singular and plural determiners in Walbiri, one could, for example, argue that plural determiners are in fact overtly marked (and therefore distinct from singulars) by the suffix /-ra/ (see note 11) but that this suffix is optionally (and preferably) deleted, resulting in superficial morphological identity between singular and plural. I doubt whether this remedy will work in general, however. In Walmanpa, one of Walbiri's neighbors to the east, the category of number is normally totally unmarked in independent pronouns. While dual number can be marked by the suffix /-tjara/, optionally, I know of no overt marker for plural number in independent pronouns. In general, in Walmanpa sentences, the independent pronoun is noncommittal with respect to number, while the corresponding pronominal clitics mark the same categories of number as do their Walbiri cognates. Thus, /ŋayu/, the first person pronoun, can be said properly to "agree" with any of the subject pronominal clitics /-na/ '1', /-tja/ '11', /-li/ '12', /-na-lu/ '111', and /-lpa-lu/ '122'. And similarly, /njuntu/, the general second person pronoun, can be said to agree with the clitics /-n/ '2', /-npala/ '22', and /-nkulu/ '222'. I have heard at least one Walmanpa speaker carry this practice over into her Walbiri speech, allowing /ŋatju/ to agree with /-na-lu/, for example.

I am grateful to the late Jack Walker (of Warrabri, N.T.) and to Donald Spencer (of Tennants Creek, N.T.) for information on Walmanpa.

require the correspondingly appropriate agreement. I illustrate with the sentences in (29):

(29) (a) *njampu ka-ṇa puḷa-mi*
            this present-1 shout-nonpast
            'I here am shouting'
     (b) *njampu-tjara ka-ḷitjara puḷa-mi*
            this-dual present-11 shout-nonpast
            'We two here (exclusive) are shouting'
     (c) *yalumpu ka-npa puḷa-mi*
            the present-2 shout-nonpast
            'You there are shouting'
     (d) *yalumpu-tjara ka-n-pala puḷa-mi*
            that-dual present-22 shout-nonpast
            'You two there are shouting'

5. A REVISED CONCEPTION OF WALBIRI PERSON MARKING

The observations made up to this point indicate rather clearly that the mechanisms which effect agreement in Walbiri must be permitted to make direct reference to the categories of person and number and, further, that these categories are abstract in the sense that they are not always overtly expressed in noun phrases. I suggest, therefore, that the rules of agreement should be defined, in part, over abstract features of person and number. I am not committed to any particular feature representation of these categories since my interest here is only in arguing that a feature representation is necessary in an adequate account of Walbiri agreement.

For the sake of the present discussion, I will assume that there are at least two person features, [I] 'first' and [II] 'second' and that the Walbiri system of persons can be represented as in (30) in the feature notation:

(30) $\begin{bmatrix} +\text{I} \\ -\text{II} \end{bmatrix}$ first person

$\begin{bmatrix} +\text{I} \\ +\text{II} \end{bmatrix}$ first and second person (i.e., first inclusive person)

$\begin{bmatrix} -\text{I} \\ +\text{II} \end{bmatrix}$ second person

$\begin{bmatrix} -\text{I} \\ -\text{II} \end{bmatrix}$ third person

And I will assume, for the purposes of agreement, that there are two features for the category of number, [sg] and [pl], as shown in (31):

(31) $\begin{bmatrix} +\text{sg} \\ -\text{pl} \end{bmatrix}$ singular

$\begin{bmatrix} -\text{sg} \\ -\text{pl} \end{bmatrix}$ dual

$\begin{bmatrix} -\text{sg} \\ +\text{pl} \end{bmatrix}$ plural

The notation [−sg, +pl] and the gloss 'plural' are used here to embrace both the lesser (plaucal) and the greater plurals: these are not distinguished in agreement.

I suggest that these features are inherent to determiners but that they are duplicated in an immediately dominating NP node. Thus, for example, subsequent to this duplication of features, the noun phrase /ŋatju/ '1' will appear approximately as in (32):

(32) NP

$$\begin{bmatrix} +\text{I} \\ -\text{II} \\ +\text{sg} \\ -\text{pl} \end{bmatrix}$$

|

DET

$$\begin{bmatrix} +\text{I} \\ -\text{II} \\ +\text{sg} \\ -\text{pl} \end{bmatrix}$$

|

ŋatju

In the case of conjoined noun phrases, the dominant NP node acquires person and number features from the conjoined NP nodes under it according to principles which might be stated very roughly as in (33) and (34):

(33) PERSON
   (a) If [+I] is present among the conjoined NPs, the dominating NP is [+I]
   (b) If [+II] is present among the conjoined NPs, the dominating NP is [+II]
   (c) If only minus values of person features are present among the conjoined NPs, the dominating NP is [−I, −II]

(34) NUMBER
   (a) If [+pl] is present among the conjoined NPs, the dominating NP is [+pl] (and therefore [−sg], redundantly)
   (b) If [+pl] is not present among the conjoined NPs, then the dominating NP is [−sg, −pl] if the total of minus values for number features among the conjoined NPs is 2; the dominating NP is [−sg, +pl] if the total of minuses exceeds 2 (accordingly, two singulars give a dual; a singular and a dual give a plural)

According to these principles, the conjoined expression /njuntu manu ŋatju/ '2 and 1' has roughly the form in (35), leaving nonessential details aside:

(35)

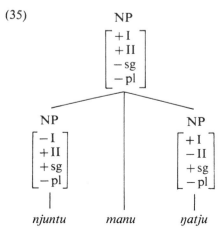

I propose that the agreement rule in Walbiri copies the person and number features into the auxiliary from the NP node which exhaustively dominates the noun phrase with which the auxiliary agrees. The rule does not copy an actual constituent but rather a bundle of features. I will refer to this conception of Walbiri agreement as the "feature-copying" alternative. The remainder of this discussion will be devoted to further exemplification of the fact that Walbiri agreement requires direct reference to the categories of person and number.

While the feature-copying alternative does not involve the duplication of an actual constituent, it must be formulated in such a way as to create a constituent in the auxiliary, for it is a fact that the person markers appear as a sequence of clitics following the auxiliary base, and, as I will show later, some of the clitics are subject to reordering. I am not sure how this fact should be represented formally, but I will assume that the feature-copying operation simply creates a constituent in the appropriate position in the auxiliary and, therefore, that what appears only as an assemblage of features in the noun phrase is an actual constituent in the auxiliary. Under this revised conception of agreement, the pre-agreement structure of sentence (3a) will be represented roughly as in (36):

(36)

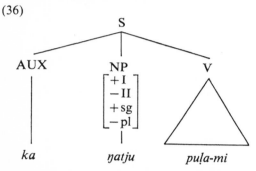

After agreement, it will appear roughly as in (37):

(37)

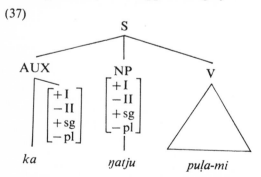

Ultimately, the Aux-dominated abstract constituent $[+I, -II; +sg, -pl]$ will be spelled /-ṇa/. The feature-copying alternative specifically denies that the pronominal clitics are merely alternants of determiners. And, assuming that determiners are entered in the lexicon, the feature-copying alternative asserts that the phonological shapes of pronominal clitics, derived by means of rules which spell abstract constituents, are not related by rule to the phonological shapes of determiners. It is consistent with this alternative that while some morphological identifications can be made between subparts of determiners and subparts of clitics (for example, the sequence /-tjara/ appears in the determiner /ŋatjara/ '11' and the corresponding clitic /-ḷitjara/), by and large such identifications are highly irregular and often extremely tenuous. It is questionable whether they play any role whatsoever in the synchronic grammar of Walbiri. By contrast, there are morphological identifications among the clitics themselves which are synchronically valid. The second and third person subject clitics share morphological material: the category of number is represented identically in the two sets, as we see in (38):

(38) SECOND PERSON   THIRD PERSON
    -n(pa)   zero   singular
    -n(pa)-pala   *-pala*   dual
    -nku-lu   *-lu*   plural

The first person plural exclusive clitic is subject to a similar subanalysis: /-ṇa-lu/. By inspection alone it is reasonable to suggest that /-pala/ and /-lu/ here mark dual and plural number, respectively. But it is possible to show further that the bipartite analysis of these particular clitics is synchronically real and must therefore be provided by the rules which give concrete phonological shape to the pronominal clitics; that is, the rules must provide that each of the nonsingular clitics here consist of a person marker (phonologically null in the case of the third person) followed by a number marker.

It is tempting to suggest that the remaining first person nonsingular clitics, /-ḷitjara/ '11', /-ḷi/ '12', and /-ḷipa/ '122', are amenable to subanalysis as well, since they clearly share the subportion /-ḷi/. This may be etymologically correct, but a bipartite analysis in this case is not synchronically justifiable since the subparts do not function as separate units in connection with any later morphological operation.

That the subanalysis of clitics given in (38) is correct is shown in part by the fact that the subsequence identified with person in the second person forms can be manipulated separately from the subsequence identified with person. Let us assume that the second person subject clitics, prior to their ultimate spelling, have an abstract bipartite structure as in (39):

$$(39) \quad \begin{bmatrix} -\mathrm{I} \\ +\mathrm{II} \end{bmatrix} \begin{bmatrix} +\mathrm{sg} \\ -\mathrm{pl} \end{bmatrix} \quad 2$$

$$\begin{bmatrix} -\mathrm{I} \\ +\mathrm{II} \end{bmatrix} \begin{bmatrix} -\mathrm{sg} \\ -\mathrm{pl} \end{bmatrix} \quad 22$$

$$\begin{bmatrix} -\mathrm{I} \\ +\mathrm{II} \end{bmatrix} \begin{bmatrix} -\mathrm{sg} \\ +\mathrm{pl} \end{bmatrix} \quad 222$$

All three forms in (39) share, abstractly, an identical initial subconstituent marking second person which is later spelled as one or another of the alternants /-n(pa)/, /-nku-/, depending on what follows it. Notice that singular number is also given an abstract feature representation in (39), but it does not receive concrete phonological realization. This entails a rather strong claim, which may be entirely mistaken, namely, that singular number is marked in Walbiri. Since singular number is nowhere overtly marked by separately identifiable morphological material, it may be incorrect to assume that singular forms should be identified as being singular in number. It may be the case, rather, that the observation that singular number is never overtly marked in Walbiri is a true linguistic fact and that singular number is determined for a particular form by the *absence* of either dual or plural number. This is an issue which I simply cannot address meaningfully at this point, and I will assume that some zeros do in fact have underlying feature assemblages. I will therefore consider the analysis in (39) to be correct for Walbiri second person subject clitics at a point in their derivation prior to their ultimate phonological spelling.

It is appropriate to extend this assumption about morphological zeros to the third person subject clitics as well, attributing to them an abstract, prephonological morphology exactly parallel to that of the second person forms, as shown in (40):

$$(40) \quad \begin{bmatrix} -I \\ -II \end{bmatrix} \begin{bmatrix} +sg \\ -pl \end{bmatrix} \quad 3$$

$$\begin{bmatrix} -I \\ -II \end{bmatrix} \begin{bmatrix} -sg \\ -pl \end{bmatrix} \quad 33$$

$$\begin{bmatrix} -I \\ -II \end{bmatrix} \begin{bmatrix} -sg \\ +pl \end{bmatrix} \quad 333$$

In the clitics in (40), of course, both the initial abstract constituent $[-I, -II]$ and the singular number marker $[+sg, -pl]$ are phonologically vacuous. Other conceptions of the third person clitics are possible, to be sure, but nothing is lost by assuming that their structure parallels (39).

Returning to the original theme, it is possible to show that the analysis of second person subject clitics as represented in (39) is synchronically valid by considering, for one thing, their behavior in the imperative:

(41) (a) *puḷa-ya* φ
         shout-imperative imperative
         'Shout! (you sg)'
     (b) *puḷa-ya* φ-*pala*
         shout-imperative imperative-dual
         'Shout! (you dual)'
     (c) *puḷa-ya* φ-*lu*
         shout-imperative imperative-plural
         'Shout! (you pl)'

The imperative auxiliary, like certain other aspectually definite auxiliaries (see the sentences of (4)), has a zero base (φ) to which the personal clitics are attached. Furthermore, like the other auxiliaries, the imperative is subject to the Aux-Insertion Rule. What is of interest in (41), however, is the shape of the personal clitics: they consist of the number markers alone; the initial portion, marking second person, is absent. It appears, therefore, that Walbiri, like so many other languages of the world, has a rule which deletes the second person subject in an imperative. But it is interesting to note that it is only the second person subject *clitic*, not the second person subject *noun phrase* (that is, determiner) which is deleted in forming imperatives. The deletion of the subject noun phrase, if there is a deletion, appears to be governed by considerations of emphasis and the like, just as in the case of the other so-called independent pronouns. That is to say, imperatives in which the second person subject noun phrase is still present are not only well-formed but even frequent. But whether or not the subject noun phrase is itself deleted, the second person subject clitic is obligatorily deleted, as shown in (42):

(42) (a) *njuntu* φ *puḷa-ya*
         you imperative shout-imperative
         'You shout!'
     (b) *njumpala* φ-*pala puḷa-ya*
         you imperative-dual shout-imperative
         'You two shout!'

(c) *njurula* ɸ-*lu puḷa-ya*
    you imperative-plural shout-imperative
    'You plural shout!'

There are several ways in which this could be accommodated in a grammar of Walbiri. I will consider two very briefly. One alternative would be to allow the deletion rule to apply when the clitics are in place and in the abstract form given in (39). The rule would simply delete the initial constituent, that is, the second person marker [−I, +II]. This would give the correct result in all cases. Another alternative would be to switch the feature [+II] to [−II] in the second person determiners prior to agreement, that is, prior to the application of the rule which copies person and number features into the auxiliary. This would leave the determiners unaffected phonologically since presumably their shapes are already specified in the lexicon, but it would cause them to behave like third person forms with respect to agreement: the clitics would be identical in form to third person clitics, which is in fact the case observationally. The second alternative is initially appealing because it accounts for the morphological identity between second person imperative subject clitics and third person subject clitics, but it would be a possible analysis only if, after agreement, the imperative subject clitics consistently behaved like their morphologically identical third person counterparts, that is, if the category of person were totally neutralized between them. There appear to be circumstances in which it is necessary to appeal to the category of second person in the imperative clitics, although the data are not altogether clear (we shall return to this). In any event I will assume that the first alternative, namely, that which assumes deletion of the initial portion of the second person clitic in an imperative auxiliary, is the correct analysis.

Walbiri imperatives show not only that the subanalysis of second person subject clitics is synchronically real but also that the categories of person and number must be referred to in the derivation of pronominal clitics. This is so regardless of which analysis of the imperative is adopted since any version will be required to make direct reference to second person. To this extent, the behavior of imperatives is more consistent with the feature-copying alternative of agreement than with the constituent-copying alternative strictly interpreted.

6. PERSON MARKING IN TRANSITIVE CLAUSES

I would like now to turn to agreement within simple transitive sentences. In such cases the auxiliary contains both subject and object clitics, and their treatment lends further strength to the observation that an adequate account of Walbiri agreement must permit reference to the categories of person and number.

In true transitive sentences in Walbiri, the subject noun phrase, whether it is "pronominal" (that is, a determiner alone) or nominal, is inflected for ergative case, by means of a suffix /-ŋku ~ -ḷu/.[18] However, the subject clitics in transitive sentences

---

[18] The alternant /-ŋku/ combines with disyllabic stems, /-ḷu/ with stems longer than disyllabic: thus, /ŋarka-ŋku/ 'man-ergative' but /ŋanimpa-ḷu/ '111-ergative'. The disyllabic demonstrative determiners are exceptions to this rule, as are the indefinite nonhuman interrogative determiner /njiya/, the manner pro-form /kutja/ 'thus', and the manner interrogative /njarpa/ 'how'. The indefinite interrogative /ŋana/ 'who' is not exceptional in Western Walbiri, but the corresponding /njana/, found in the speech of some Eastern Walbiris, is. These exceptional forms take the alternant /-ḷu/ instead of the expected /-ŋku/.

The term "disyllabic" must be understood as excluding forms in which one of the vowels is long: that is, a long vowel counts as two syllables for the purposes of the distribution of ergative alternants (thus /ŋu:rpa-ḷu/ 'throat-ergative', not */ŋu:rpa-ŋku/).

are the same as those listed in (19) and (21). Object noun phrases in transitive sentences, again whether pronominal or nominal, are unmarked for case (as are the subjects of intransitive sentences), but the corresponding clitics are different in shape from the subject clitics. The complete list of object clitics appears in (43) (where parenthetic alternants for 12 and 222 are idiolectal and dialectal, respectively):

(43)   1   *-tju*
        2   *-ŋku*
        3   zero
     11   *-tjaraŋku*
     12   *-ŋaliŋki* (~ *-ŋali*)
     22   *-ŋku-pala*
     33   *-palaŋu*
   111   *-ŋanpa*
   122   *-ŋalpa*
   222   *-njara* (~ *-njura*)
   333   *-tjana*

Only one of the clitics, namely, /-ŋku-pala/ '22' can be subanalyzed synchronically. That is to say, the hyphenation corresponds to a morphologically justifiable segmentation in this form, while suggestive and perhaps etymologically correct segmentations in certain of the other nonsingular forms cannot be justified on synchronic grounds.

With an exception to be detailed later, the order of clitics is subject-object, as shown in (44):

(44) (a)   *ŋatjulu-ḷu ka-ŋa-ŋku njuntu nja-nji*
         I-ergative present-1-2 you see-nonpast
         'I see you'
    (b)   *njuntulu-ḷu ka-npa-tju ŋatju nja-nji*
         you-ergative present-2-1 me see-nonpast
         'You see me'
    (c)   *ŋalipa-ḷu ka-ḷipa-tjana wawiri-patu nja-nji*
         we-ergative present-122-333 kangaroo-paucal see-nonpast
         'We (plural inclusive) see the several kangaroos'

The exceptions to this linear ordering constitute the principal synchronic justification for the subanalysis of certain of the nonsingular pronominal clitics. Whenever a subject clitic which is analyzable into a person marker followed by one of the number markers /-pala/ 'dual' or /-lu/ 'plural' precedes one of the object clitics /-tju/ '1' or /-ŋku/ '2', the number marker follows rather than precedes the object clitic, as in (45):

(45) (a)   *ŋanimpa-ḷu ka-ŋa-ŋku-lu njuntu nja-nji*
         we-ergative present-1-2-plural you see-nonpast
         'We (plural exclusive) see you singular'
         (*. . . *ka-ŋa-lu-ŋku* . . .)
    (b)   *njumpala-ḷu ka-npa-tju-pala ŋatju nja-nji*
         you-ergative present-2-1-dual me see-nonpast
         'You two see me'
         (*. . . *ka-n-pala-tju* . . .)
    (c)   *ŋarka-tjara-ḷu ka-zero-tju-pala ŋatju nja-nji*
         man-dual-ergative present-3-1-dual me see-nonpast
         'The two men see me'
         (*. . . *ka-zero-pala-tju* . . .)

Notice that this does not happen when the object is represented by a clitic other than /-tju/ or /-ŋku/, as in (46):

(46) *njumpala-ḷu ka-n-pala-tjana wawiri-patu nja-nji*
    you-ergative present-2-dual-333 kangaroo-paucal see-nonpast
    'You two see the several kangaroos'
    (**njumpala-ḷu ka-npa-tjana-pala wawiri-patu nja-nji*)

I will assume that the basic order of clitics is subject-object but that a special metathesis rule applies to shift a number marker /-pala, -lu/ from the subject clitic to the right of an immediately following object clitic /-tju/ or /-ŋku/. The rule applies not only where the object is first or second person singular but also where it is second person plural /-ŋku-pala/. Thus the underlying subject-object sequence */-ṇa-lu-ŋku-pala/ '1-plural-2-dual' (that is, 111 acts on 22) is converted to /-ṇa-ŋku-lu-pala/ '1-2-plural-dual'. This attests to the reality of the subanalysis of the second person dual object clitic.

Given the subject and object clitics as listed and the metathesis rule, there is only one additional strictly morphological detail which must be accommodated to derive correct surface forms for subject-object clitic sequences, namely, the shape of the second person subject marker /-n(pa) ~ -nku-/. This is always /-nku-/ when in combination with the plural marker /-lu/, even when separated therefrom as a result of metathesis. Thus, we have (47):

(47) *njurula-ḷu ka-nku-tju-lu ŋatju nja-nji*
    you-ergative present-2-1-plural me see-nonpast
    'You plural see me'

But in singular and dual forms the second person subject marker is alternately /-n-/ or /-npa/, depending on what follows. In the singular, it is /-npa/, except before the third dual object clitic /-palaŋu/ '33', where it is /-n-/ (thus, /-n-palaŋu/ '2 acts on 33'). In the dual it is /-n-/ except before the clitic /-tju/ inserted by metathesis, where it is /-npa-/ (thus, /-npa-tju-pala/ '2-1-dual' (that is, 22 acts on 1), as in (45b).[19]

While the strictly morphological facts of subject-object clitic sequences are covered by the remarks just made, this by no means covers everything relevant to sequences of subject and object clitics in the auxiliary. It is not the case that clitic sequences correspond exactly to the possible co-occurrences of subject and object noun phrases. Thus, while it is possible of course to have a dual subject and a dual object in a given transitive sentence, it is not possible, in the auxiliary, to have subject and object clitics which are both of dual form (that is, of a form glossed as dual in the listings here).

In general, not all sequences of clitics are possible. Instead, an adjustment is made within the auxiliary to derive the possible sequences, and as a result a given clitic may disagree, with respect to the category of number, with the noun phrase with which it is construed. This makes a direct equivalence between clitics and determiners highly implausible. Moreover, the correct selection of clitics will require direct reference to the categories of person and number.

In discussing clitic sequences, I will make reference to two dialects which I will term, perhaps inexactly, Eastern (represented in my data by speakers from Warrabri,

---

[19] The /-pa/ associated with alternants of the second person clitic is a residue from a once productive phonological rule which augmented word-final consonants. The same augment is now an inseparable part of such lexical items as, among many others, /tjaŋanpa/ 'possum', /tjukurpa/ 'dreamtime', /tjintirtjintirpa/ 'willy-wagtail' (see Hale (to appear)).

N.T.) and Western (represented by speakers from Yuendumu, N.T.). The more complex and possibly historically prior treatment is the Western one. It is convenient, therefore, to begin with the Eastern treatment.

In both dialects, the essential fact is that a clitic of dual form is replaced by a clitic of plural form under certain circumstances. I will use the term "basic form" whenever the form of a clitic agrees with its semantic reading (or, equivalently, when it agrees in number with the noun phrase with which it is construed). Semantically singular and plural clitics are always in their basic forms; only duals undergo replacement. A dual subject clitic is always in its basic form when it is alone in the auxiliary (that is, in a simple intransitive sentence). Furthermore, a dual subject clitic always appears in its basic form if the object is singular, and a dual object clitic always appears in its basic form if the subject is singular. Only in combinations of nonsingular subject and object does a basically dual form undergo replacement.

In Eastern Walbiri, the rule according to which a dual clitic is replaced by a plural clitic is extremely simple and straightforward. If both the subject and object are nonsingular, only plural clitics are allowed. Thus, a dual subject clitic is replaced by the corresponding plural clitic (keeping person constant) if the object is either dual or plural, and a dual object clitic is replaced by the corresponding plural clitic if the subject is either dual or plural. For example, the basic sequence 11-22 (first dual exclusive acts on second dual) is replaced by 111-222, as in (48):

(48) *ŋatjara-ḷu ka-ṇa-lu-njara njumpala nja-nji*
       we-ergative present-111-222 you see-nonpast
       'We two see you two'

While the basic 11 subject clitic is /-ḷitjara/, it is replaced by /-ṇa-lu/ '111' in (48), and while the basic 22 object clitic is /-ŋku-pala/, it is replaced by /-njara/ '222' in (48), despite the fact that the clitics are construed with the dual noun phrases /ŋatjara/ '11' and /njumpala/ '22'.

Similarly, in (49) basic 33-333 (third dual acts on third plural) is replaced by 333-333:

(49) *maliki-tjara-ḷu ka-lu-tjana wawiri-patu nja-nji*
       dog-dual-ergative present-333-333 kangaroo-paucal see-nonpast
       'The two dogs see the several kangaroos'

While the basic 33 subject is /-pala/, it is replaced by /-lu/ '333' in (49), although it is construed with a dual subject noun phrase.

The neutralization of nonsingular subject-object clitic sequences by replacement of all dual clitics with plurals is consistently applied in Eastern Walbiri, so far as I am aware; it is also the rule in the neighboring Waḷmanpa and Warramunga languages, which, like Walbiri, use pronominal clitics.

It is appropriate, I feel, to look upon the Eastern Walbiri treatment of nonsingular clitic sequences as a neutralization in the category of number. Assuming that the correct combinations are derived by means of a rule which actually replaces dual clitics by the corresponding plural clitics under some circumstances, it is clear that the category of number, as such, plays a direct role in the derivations. The category of person is also involved, but only indirectly: the replacements must keep the category of person constant. In Western Walbiri, the category of person plays a more important role. The replacement of dual clitics by plurals is not general in nonsingular subject-object clitic sequences; rather, it is conditioned in part by the persons involved.

The situation in Western Walbiri is somewhat complicated by the fact that the Eastern usage is accepted by most if not all speakers. This makes it difficult to determine the principles which underlie the strictly Western usage in those cases in which it differs from the Eastern. A considerable amount of study of the matter has revealed a pattern, nonetheless. As I understand it, a dual clitic may co-occur with a plural clitic. That is, if the subject is plural, a dual object clitic may appear in its basic dual form; and if the object is plural, a dual subject clitic may appear in its basic dual form. In fact, this is preferable to replacement. Thus, in Western Walbiri the sequence of clitics in (49) could, and preferably would, appear as the basic 33-333, that is, as /-pala-tjana/.

Where replacement becomes obligatory is in an auxiliary in which both the subject and object are dual. But even here it is not the case that both duals are replaced by plurals. Rather, it appears that only one of the duals is replaced by the corresponding plural, and the principle which governs the replacement is based upon a ranking of persons: 1 higher than 2 higher than 3. In a given combination of dual clitics, the higher ranking clitic remains in its basic form while the lower ranking clitic is replaced. For example, if a first person dual subject co-occurs with a second person dual object, only the dual object clitic (/-ŋku-pala/ '22') is replaced by the corresponding plural /-njara/ '222'). Thus, the sequence of clitics in (48) would appear as /-litjara-njara/ in Western Walbiri. And if a second person dual subject occurs with a first person dual object, only the dual subject clitic (/-n(pa)-pala/ '22') is replaced by the corresponding plural clitic (/-nku-lu/ '222'), as in (50):

(50) *njumpala-ḷu ka-nku-lu-tjaraŋku ŋatjara nja-nji*
      you-ergative present-222-11 us see-nonpast
      'You two see us two'

Similarly, basic 11-33 is replaced by 11-333, basic 33-11 is replaced by 333-11, basic 12-33 by 12-333, basic 33-12 by 333-12, basic 22-33 by 22-333, and basic 33-22 by 333-22.[20] If both the subject and object are third person dual, it is, of course, possible to follow the Eastern Walbiri usage and to replace both dual clitics by plurals; however, it is also possible to replace only one of them. It appears, in fact, that a ranking among third persons must also be recognized. To the extent that I have been able to observe it adequately, ranking among third persons depends upon the relative prominence or importance, in a given discourse or narrative, of the characters to whom the clitics refer. A dual clitic referring to a pair of characters who are the primary ones in a given narrative retains its basic form, while a dual clitic referring to secondary characters is replaced.[21] Thus, in an epic about two snake personalities (the primary characters), a pronominal clitic referring to them appears consistently in its basic dual form. When the two snakes are seen by a pair of women gathering mulga seed (secondary characters), the basic dual subject clitic, referring to the women, is replaced by the corresponding plural. Thus, basic 33-33 is replaced by 333-33 (that is, by /-lu-palaŋu/), as in (51):

[20] In my field notes I have recorded a sequence /-pala-njara/ '33-222' for basic 33-22. This violates the ranking principle. If it is not a mistake in my recording, then I have no explanation for it.
[21] This is not unlike the principle of obviation found in the Algonquian languages of North America. However, the Walbiri data are by no means as clear as the Algonquian case. It could well be that my understanding of the Walbiri facts is entirely mistaken, particularly in view of the fact that I did not devote a great deal of time to studying actual usage with regard to this particular aspect of Walbiri grammar.

(51) *kaṇṭa-tjara-ḷu lpa-lu-palaŋu nja-ŋu waṇa-tjara*
     (woman-dual-ergative past-333-33 see-past snake-dual)
     'The two women saw the two snakes'

But when the snakes attack and eat the women, the subject clitic, referring to the snakes, retains its basic form, while the object clitic, referring to the women, is replaced. Thus, basic 33-33 is replaced by 33-333 (that is, by /-pala-tjana/), as in (52):

(52) *waṇa-tjara-ḷu lpa-pala-tjana ŋa-ṇu kaṇṭa-tjara*
     snake-dual-ergative past-33-333 eat-past woman-dual
     'The two snakes ate the two women'

This concludes the discussion of (nonreflexive) subject-object clitic sequences. It seems abundantly clear that their correct derivation requires reference to the categories of person and number and, further, that virtually nothing is to be gained by regarding pronominal clitics as alternants of determiners.

I would like now to return briefly to the behavior of second person clitics in the imperative. Recall that the second person subject clitics in imperatives are identical in form to the third person subject clitics, which are listed in (53):

(53) zero   singular
     -pala dual
     -lu   plural

As suggested earlier, one conceivable way of accommodating this fact is to permit the clitics to be marked as third person, that is, as $[-I, -II]$. This would be possible if they behaved like true third person forms throughout their Aux-internal derivations. There is some evidence, however, suggesting that they do not. So far as I can tell, they behave like second person forms with respect to the ranking detailed earlier for Western Walbiri; that is to say, they consistently rank higher than third person. If this is true, a natural way to handle the imperative clitics would be to adopt the analysis according to which they have the underlying abstract structure given in (39), like any other second person subject clitic, and to allow the initial subconstituent, that is, the second person marker $[-I, +II]$, to be deleted subsequent to the readjustment of dual number which must make reference to the category of person. This weakly supports the deletion hypothesis for imperatives, as opposed to the feature-changing hypothesis.

7. OTHER CLITIC SEQUENCES

Simple intransitive and transitive sentences provide sufficient material to illustrate the essential facts of Walbiri agreement. It seems appropriate, however, to include other sentence types in this discussion.

There is a class of verbs whose members are basically intransitive, in the sense that their subjects are in the unmarked or absolutive (as opposed to the ergative) case, but which can take dative complements. A noun phrase functioning as the complement of such a verb is especially marked for dative case by means of the suffix /-ku/, as in the sentence in (54):

(54) *ŋatju ka-ṇa-ŋku njuntu-ku waŋka-mi*
     I present-1-2 you-dative speak-nonpast
     'I am speaking to you'

Agreement in such sentences is exactly as in true transitive sentences of the type discussed earlier, with the exception that there is a special clitic for third person singular dative complements, namely, /-ḷa/, as in (55):

(55) ŋatju ka-ṇa-ḷa ŋarka-ku waŋka-mi
     I present-1-3 man-dative speak-nonpast
     'I am speaking to the man'

Except for the third person singular, the dative object clitics are identical to the object clitics listed in (43).

The class of predicators which accept dative complements includes not only intransitive verbs but nonverbal predicators as well, as illustrated in (56):

(56) (a) ŋatju ɸ-ṇa-ḷa njampu-ku wiṛi
          I stative-1-3 this-dative big
          'I am big to (i.e., by comparison with) this one'
     (b) ŋatju ɸ-ṇa-ḷa njampu-ku kiḍanjanu
          I stative-1-3 this-dative father
          'I am father to this one'

Nonverbal predicates require what I will refer to as the "stative" auxiliary, whose base is phonologically null. The stative auxiliary differs from others only in that it may be deleted from main clauses. Thus, the sentences of (56) can also appear as in (57):

(57) (a) ŋatju njampu-ku wiṛi
     (b) ŋatju njampu-ku kiḍanjanu

But when the stative auxiliary is present, it takes pronominal clitics in the same way as does the auxiliary in a finite clause.

There is a small class of transitive verbs (that is, verbs whose subjects are ergative) which require both a direct object and an indirect object. A noun phrase functioning as the direct object of such a verb is in the absolutive case, while a noun phrase functioning as the indirect object appears in the dative. Only the subject and indirect object are represented by clitics in the auxiliary. I illustrate in (58):

(58) (a) ŋatjulu-ḷu ka-ṇa-ŋku kaḷi yi-nji njuntu-ku
          I-ergative present-1-2 boomerang give-nonpast you-dative
          'I am giving you a boomerang'
     (b) ŋatjulu-ḷu kapi-ṇa-ḷa kaḷi punta-ṇi kuḍu-ku
          I-ergative future-1-3 boomerang take-nonpast child-dative
          'I will take the boomerang away from the child'

In (a) and (b) of (58), the direct objects are third person singular; the corresponding clitics would be phonologically null here in any event. But even if the direct object were, say, third person dual (whose clitic is normally /-palaŋu/), it would still not be represented by a pronominal clitic in a "double transitive" sentence of the type represented in (58). Compare, for example, (59):

(59) ŋatjulu-ḷu kapi-ṇa-ŋku kaḷi-tjara punta-ṇi njuntu-ku
     I-ergative future-1-2 boomerang-dual take-nonpast you-dative
     'I will take the two boomerangs away from you'

The fact is, apparently, that there is a constraint upon clitic sequences to the effect that a phonologically constituted direct object clitic cannot co-occur with a dative clitic. The third dual object clitic /-palaŋu/ is suppressed in (59) to conform with this constraint. Normally, if a direct object has a corresponding phonologically constituted pronominal clitic, the latter *must* appear in the auxiliary; but in sentence (59) this requirement is in conflict with the constraint on clitic sequences. Where the direct object is inanimate, apparently, a clitic may be suppressed, as in (59); but where the direct object is animate, a phonologically constituted clitic may not be suppressed. This yields an irresolvable conflict in the case of certain sentences of the type presently under discussion, accounting for the ill-formedness of such strings as those in (60):

(60) (a) *ŋarka-ŋku kapi-zero-*ŋki-tji njuntu punta-ṇi ŋatju-ku*
            man-ergative future-3-2-1 you take-nonpast me-dative
      (b) *ŋarka-ŋku kapi-zero-*tji njuntu punta-ṇi ŋatju-ku*
            man-ergative future-3-1 you take-nonpast me-dative
            'The man will take you from me'

Sentence (60a) is ill-formed because it violates the constraint on clitic sequences within the auxiliary, and sentence (60b) is ill-formed because it violates the requirement that animate objects whose corresponding clitics are phonologically constituted (in this case, /-ŋku/ is the clitic for the object noun phrase /njuntu/ 'you') actually be represented by a clitic in the auxiliary. Notice that the ill-formedness of (60a,b) cannot be handled simply by saying that a verb of the double transitive type cannot take animate direct objects since (61) is perfectly grammatical:

(61) *ŋatjulu-ḷu kapi-ṇa-ŋku kaṇṭa punta-ṇi njuntu-ku*
       I-ergative future-1-2 woman take-nonpast you-dative
       'I will take the woman from you'

The object is animate in (61), but since it is third person singular, its corresponding direct object clitic is phonologically null and, therefore, does not violate the constraint on clitic sequences.[22]

To summarize, there is a constraint which would appear to limit clitic sequences to two members, subject-object. In cases where a sentence contains two object noun phrases (using "object" loosely here to refer both to direct and indirect), only one may be represented in the auxiliary by a phonologically constituted clitic, and this is

---

[22] D. Perlmutter has studied constraints on clitic sequences in Spanish and French (Perlmutter (1971)). He argues that the theory of grammar must allow constraints on surface structure, and he shows that certain limitations on clitic sequences, in Spanish, for example, can be explained only in this way. The Walbiri data, provided they are correct, furnish an additional example in support of Perlmutter's proposal. Certain Walbiri deep structures, which are themselves well-formed, are prevented from receiving surface realization because clitic sequences which they require are, in fact, impossible on the surface.

I feel, however, that it is wise in this connection to appeal to the caution which I mentioned in the first note to this paper. In working on a language radically different from one's own, the possibility of mistakes in primary data is extremely great. In this instance, it could conceivably be the case that the true constraint is a deep structure one which disallows non-third person direct objects in sentences in which a dative also appears. This seems unlikely in view of the fact that datives can arise from a considerable variety of sources, making it extremely difficult, if not impossible, to formulate the constraint. That it is not a deep structure constraint could be proven by showing that non-third person direct objects are permitted to co-occur with datives in infinitive clauses, that is, in clauses which lack auxiliaries and therefore pronominal clitics. My understanding is that such infinitive clauses are grammatical, but I could very easily be mistaken.

In any event, I wish to indicate my indebtedness to D. Perlmutter for several discussions of this material which have helped me to understand its potential significance.

consistently the noun phrase which is in the dative case (that is, the indirect object, in the cases examined here).

This is correct as far as it goes, but it would be incorrect to leave the impression that only two clitics (a subject and an object) may appear in a given auxiliary. In fact, three may appear: a sequence of subject followed by dative object may be further extended by the clitic /-la/. This may arise in one of several ways, two of which I will examine.

There is at least one transitive verb in Walbiri which requires a dative object rather than the usual absolutive object. This is illustrated in (62):

(62) ŋatjulu-lu ka-ŋa-la kali-ki wari-ni
     I-ergative present-1-3 boomerang-dative seek-nonpast
     'I am looking for a boomerang'

It is always possible in transitive sentences to include a benefactive noun phrase as well as the object. This noun phrase appears in the dative case and requires a dative clitic in the auxiliary. Of course, such sentences must conform to the constraint on clitic sequences whereby only the dative noun phrase is represented by a clitic in the auxiliary, as is the case in (63):

(63) ŋatjulu-lu ka-ŋa-ŋku kali paka-ni njuntu-ku
     I-ergative present-1-2 boomerang chop-nonpast you-dative
     'I am cutting a boomerang for you'

Here, only the dative noun phrase /njuntu-ku/ 'for you' is represented by a clitic. However, if a benefactive noun phrase is inserted into (62), there will be two datives in the same sentence. In such cases, both are represented by clitics in the auxiliary, as shown in (64):

(64) ŋatjulu-lu ka-ŋa-ŋku-la kali-ki wari-ni njuntu-ku
     I-ergative present-1-2-3 boomerang-dative seek-nonpast you-dative
     'I am looking for a boomerang for you'

These three-membered clitic sequences are also subject to a constraint: they must be of the form subject-dative-la. Thus, one of the dative noun phrases in such a sentence must be of a form whose corresponding dative clitic is /-la/, that is, it must be third singular. It appears again, however, that an inanimate nonsingular third person can be treated as if it were singular with respect to agreement in such cases. Thus, consider (65):

(65) ŋatjulu-lu ka-ŋa-ŋku-la kali-tjara-ku wari-ni njuntu-ku
     'I am looking for two boomerangs for you'

Here, a third person inanimate dative noun phrase in the dual, /kali-tjara-ku/ 'boomerang-dual-dative', normally requiring the clitic /-palaŋu/, is allowed to take the clitic /-la/ instead. But strings of the form shown in (66) are unacceptable:

(66) (a) *ŋarka-ŋku lpa-zero-tju-ŋku njuntu-ku waru-ŋu ŋatju-ku
        man-ergative past-3-1-2 you-dative seek-past me-dative
        'The man was looking for you for me'
    (b) *ŋarka-ŋku lpa-zero-tju-la njuntu-ku waru-ŋu ŋatju-ku
        man-ergative past-3-1-la you-dative seek-past me-dative

The sentence (66a) is ill-formed because it violates the constraint on clitic sequences (a sequence of two nonsubject clitics is allowed only when the second is

/-ḷa/). Sentence (66b) is ill-formed because the clitic /-ḷa/ cannot be construed with the second person dative noun phrase /njuntu-ku/.

There is a morphological detail concerning clitic sequences of the form subject-dative-*ḷa* which should be mentioned at this point. In sentences of the type represented by (64), if both dative noun phrases are third person singular, both must be represented of course in the auxiliary. However, the sequence /-ḷa-ḷa/ is not permitted. Instead, the second of these dative clitics is replaced by the morph /-tjinta/, as shown in (67):

(67)   *ŋatjulu-ḷu ka-ṇa-ḷa-tjinta kaḷi-ki wari-ṇi ŋarka-ku*
       I-ergative present-1-3-3 boomerang-dative seek-nonpast man-dative
       'I am looking for a boomerang for the man'
       (*. . . *ka-ṇa-ḷa-ḷa . . .*)

Another circumstance in which the clitic sequence subject-dative-*ḷa* arises is the following. An object of a transitive verb is put into the dative to indicate that the action denoted by the verb is not fully carried out, in the sense that it does not have the intended effect on the entity denoted by the object. That is to say, putting the object into the dative cancels the otherwise affective nature of the transitive verb. However, not only does the object go into the dative, but the clitic /-ḷa/ is inserted into the auxiliary as well, in addition to the dative clitic which emanates from the object. This /-ḷa/ does not relate to any noun phrase in the sentence but is merely a part of the morphology associated with the meaning achieved by the change in object case marking.

The sentences in (68) illustrate unaltered (absolutive) and altered (dative) object case markings together with the corresponding difference in meaning:

(68) (a)   *njuntulu-ḷu ɸ-npa-tju pantu-ṇu ŋatju*
            you-ergative ɸ-2-1 spear-past me
            'You speared me'
      (b)   *njuntulu-ḷu ɸ-npa-tju-ḷa pantu-ṇu ŋatju-ku*
            you-ergative ɸ-2-1-*ḷa* spear-past me-dative
            'You speared at me; you tried to spear me'

If the object is third person singular, this operation gives rise to a sequence of the form */-ḷa-ḷa/, which, according to rule (as in the case of (67)), is converted to /-ḷa-tjinta/, as in (69):

(69)   *ŋatjulu-ḷu ɸ-ṇa-ḷa-tjinta wawiri-ki ḷuwa-ṇu*
       I-ergative ɸ-1-3-*tjinta* kangaroo-dative shoot-past
       'I shot at the kangaroo; I tried to shoot the kangaroo'
       (*. . . ɸ-*ṇa-ḷa-ḷa . . .*)

Dative clitics, apart from the third singular, which is special in several respects, are identical in their Aux-internal behavior to the object clitics already discussed. That is, they are subject to the same rules: metathesis (of the number markers /-pala/ and /-lu/) and the systematic replacement of dual clitics by corresponding plurals apply identically in both cases. However, there is one respect in which one class of dative clitics, namely, those associated with benefactives, differs from others. In reality, though, this is a difference in syntax rather than a difference in the behavior of the clitics themselves. First and second person subjects are incompatible with first person inclusive objects (whether absolutive or dative). Hence, the corresponding clitic sequences, /-ṇa-ŋaliŋki/ '1-12', /-npa-ŋalpa/ '2-122', and the like, do not occur. But such sequences of clitics can in fact occur provided the second clitic is a dative emanating from a benefactive. Thus, while one does not normally say the sentences in (70), one can say those in (71):

(70) (a) *ŋatjulu-ḷu ka-ṇa-ŋaliŋki nja-nji ŋali*
     I-ergative present-1-12 see-nonpast us
     'I see us two inclusive'

   (b) *njuntu ka-npa-ŋaliŋki waŋka-mi ŋali-ki*
     you present-1-12 speak-nonpast us-dative
     'You are speaking to us (dual inclusive)'

(71) (a) *ŋatjulu-ḷu kapi-ṇa-ŋaliŋki waḷu ma-ni ŋali-ki*
     I-ergative future-1-12 firewood get-nonpast us-dative
     'I will get us (dual inclusive) some firewood'

   (b) *njuntulu-ḷu ɸ-npa-ŋaliŋki waḷu ma-ni ŋali-ki*
     you-ergative ɸ-2-12 firewood get-nonpast us-dative
     'You should/will get firewood for us (dual inclusive)'

A detailed account of the syntax of Walbiri agreement would go considerably beyond the central purpose of this paper, which is concerned primarily with the question of the relationship between noun phrases and corresponding pronominal clitics. For the present purposes, the essential syntactic facts are given. Clitics appear in the auxiliary in agreement with the subject, with the direct object (provided no dative noun phrase also appears), with dative complements, and with the benefactive (also dative in case). Noun phrases in other functions (such as locative and directional) are not represented by clitics in the auxiliary. In addition, there is a clitic /-ḷa/, identical to the third singular dative, which appears under circumstances not directly related to agreement (as in (68b)). The possible basic clitic sequences are listed in (72):

(72) subject-object
    subject-dative
    subject-dative-*ḷa*

These basic sequences are modified by (*a*) a rule of clitic metathesis which shifts a number marker /-pala/ or /-lu/ to the right of a following /-tju/ or /-ŋku/; (*b*) rules which replace a basically dual clitic by its plural counterpart under certain circumstances; and (*c*) a late morphological rule which replaces a basic sequence */-ḷa-ḷa/ by /-ḷa-tjinta/.

To complete the basic factual account of Walbiri clitic sequences, it is necessary to accommodate the reflexive and the reciprocal. In a reflexive sentence the object is not represented by a noun phrase, but the auxiliary contains a reflexive clitic following the subject clitic, as in (73):

(73) (a) *njuntulu-ḷu ka-npa-njanu mapa-ṇi*
     you-ergative present-2-reflexive rub-nonpast
     'You are rubbing yourself (with red ochre, or the like)'

   (b) *ŋarka-tjara-ḷu ka-pala-njanu patji-ṇi*
     man-dual-ergative present-33-reflexive cut-nonpast
     'The two men are cutting themselves'

With two exceptions, the reflexive clitic is universally /-njanu/. The first of these exceptions is the first person singular, where the reflexive clitic is identical to the nonreflexive object clitic, as in (74):

(74) *ŋatjulu-ḷu ɸ-ṇa-tju patju-ṇu*
    I-ergative ɸ-1-1 cut-past
    'I cut myself'

The second of the two exceptions is the second person singular in the imperative, where the reflexive clitic is likewise identical to the nonreflexive. In (73a) the second person singular reflexive is /-njanu/, but in the corresponding imperative it is /-ŋku/, that is, it is identical to the ordinary second singular object clitic. I illustrate in (75):

(75) *mapa-ka φ-ŋku*
      rub-imperative imperative-2
      'Rub yourself (with ochre, or the like)!'

Dative and benefactive reflexives are identical in form to the objective ones just illustrated. In all cases the reflexive clitic immediately follows the subject. As in the case of nonreflexive dative clitics, dative reflexives may be followed by /-la/ under the appropriate circumstances, as in (76):

(76) (a) *ŋatjulu-lu ka- na-tju-la kali-ki wari-ni*
           I-ergative present-1-1-3 boomerang-dative seek-nonpast
           'I am looking for a boomerang for myself'
      (b) *ŋarka-tjara-lu ka-pala-njanu-la kulada-ku wari-ni*
           man-dual-ergative present-33-reflexive-3 spear-dative seek-nonpast
           'The two men are looking for a spear for themselves'

But dative reflexives may not be followed by other dative or objective clitics. Thus they conform in their occurrence to the sequences tabulated in (72).

The interpretation of a sentence like (73a) or (74) is that the subject and the object are coreferential; similarly, the interpretation of (76a) is that the subject and the beneficiary are coreferential. These interpretations are, of course, consistent with a theory which holds that the deep structures of such sentences contain actual object or benefactive noun phrases which are identical to and coreferential with the subject and which, although ultimately deleted from the surface structure, are responsible for the reflexive agreement. The derivation from such a deep structure might involve marking the coreferential object or benefactive noun phrase as reflexive and allowing the reflexive feature to be copied, along with features of person, number, and case, into the auxiliary by the agreement rule. Subsequently, in such a theory, the reflexive noun phrase itself would be deleted.

This seems, in fact, to be a reasonable account of Walbiri reflexives. However, I am hesitant to commit myself to any analysis of the reflexive until a reasonable account of the reciprocal is established. The fact is, the reflexive and reciprocal are identical in Walbiri save for the fact that the reciprocal interpretation is possible only where the subject is nonsingular. Thus, while only the reflexive interpretation is possible for (73a), both reflexive and reciprocal interpretations are possible for (73b). I see no way at the moment to develop a unified syntactic treatment of the reflexive and the reciprocal; thus, I will limit my remarks to the foregoing description of their gross morphological behavior.

Whatever the correct syntactic analysis of the reflexive ultimately turns out to be, it is clear that it will be necessary to refer to the categories of person and number in order to accommodate the exceptions to the otherwise general rule that the reflexive is represented by /-njanu/ within the auxiliary, that is, in order to account for the fact that the reflexive is represented by the ordinary object (or dative) clitics in the first person singular and in the second singular imperative.

8. SOME CONCLUDING OBSERVATIONS

The two alternatives which we have been considering as possible mechanisms for effecting person agreement in Walbiri are, in a sense, extremes. The constituent-copying conception of agreement holds that pronominal clitics and determiners are merely alternants of one another. The feature-copying conception, on the other hand, holds that there is no direct morphological identification to be made between pronominal clitics and determiners (or pronouns); instead, the latter determine the person and number of noun phrases, and it is the abstract features identified with these categories which are transferred from the appropriate noun phrases into the auxiliary, to be spelled out later as sequences of morphemes. Any morphological similarity between determiners and pronominal clitics is purely accidental under the feature-copying alternative.

I think there can be little doubt but that the constituent-copying alternative, in the literal sense, is impossible for Walbiri. It seems totally clear that the abstract features of person and number must be invoked in an adequate account of Walbiri agreement; furthermore, morphophonological similarities between clitics and determiners appear, as a matter of fact, to be highly unsystematic and of little if any synchronic significance, whatever their historical validity might be.

It is reasonable to question, however, whether the extreme represented by the feature-copying alternative is, in general, the only viable conception of person agreement. Suppose, for example, that pronominal clitics were identical in phonological shape to the independent pronouns (that is, determiners) of corresponding feature composition. That is to say, suppose that the auxiliary in such hypothetical structures as (27) were in fact the ultimate surface form. And suppose further that the other facts of Walbiri were as they actually are: the clitic construed with a conjoined noun phrase is the pronoun which embodies the categories of person and number of the noun phrase as a whole (for example, clitic /-ŋali/, phonologically identical to the independent pronoun /ŋali/ '12', construed with the conjoined expression /njuntu manu ŋatju/ '2 and 1', and similarly for other cases); dual clitics are replaced by plurals under certain circumstances. In short, suppose that, as is actually the case in Walbiri, the abstract features of person and number play a role in determining the correct surface clitic sequences. Given these suppositions, then clearly it would be a mistake to choose a treatment of agreement which failed to reflect the morphophonological identification of clitics with independent pronouns. While it would still be necessary to allow reference to the features of person and number, failure to express the identity of phonological actualization between clitic and independent pronominal feature complexes would amount to a failure to express a linguistic fact of the most obvious kind, that is, a fact of observation at the surface representation of linguistic forms.

To be sure, Walbiri does not conform to the hypothetical picture just drawn. Nonetheless, one could conceive of a version of Walbiri agreement which did in fact have, as an intermediate stage, the hypothetical case. The difference between Walbiri and the latter would then lie precisely in the difference of surface phonological representation between clitic and noun phrase occurrences of the relevant feature assemblages. Along these lines, one could construct a theory of Walbiri agreement which was, in effect, a compromise between the extremes explored in the body of the preceding discussion. The compromise would be a constituent-copying alternative which allowed reference to abstract features at all of the critical points in the derivation of correct clitic sequences.

In thinking about this question, it is instructive to imagine what the historical antecedent of Walbiri agreement might have been like and, if possible, to examine a language which represents synchronically some antecedent stage in the imagined evolution. I think it is reasonable to propose that the source of pronominal clitics in Walbiri is in fact independent pronouns which, at some stage in the prehistory of the language, became unstressed and were attracted into clitic position (that is, second position) in accordance with a principle of clitic placement which is extremely widespread among languages of the world.[23] The process of destressing and cliticizing pronouns eventually became an obligatory rule and, subsequently, independent pronouns were re-created from other sources available to the language, such as oblique forms of pronouns like those found in possessives or in other functions not normally subject to cliticization.[24] Such a sequence of events seems quite suggestive and is, moreover, entirely compatible with the synchronic state of affairs in which pronominal clitics no longer necessarily resemble, in phonological constituency, the determiners which they most closely approximate in grammatical feature composition.

Whether or not such an imagined historical development represents the actual evolution in the Walbiri case, it is a fact that there exists at least one language in Australia—Warramunga, a neighbor of Walbiri to the east—which represents synchronically the initial phase.[25] In Warramunga, the independent pronouns become unstressed and cliticize, that is, become enclitic to the first nonpronominal constituent of the sentence. Warramunga, like Walbiri, allows permutation of the constituents of a sentence: whatever the resulting surface order of nonpronominal constituents, the pronouns appear in second position. Consider, for example, the variants in (77), in which the subject pronoun /aṇi/ 'I' appears:

(77) (a) *kunapa-aṇi waŋari-tji wuṛu-nju*
           dog-I stone-instrumental hit (with missile)-past
      (b) *waŋari-tji-aṇi kunapa wuṛu-nju*
           stone-instrumental-I dog hit-past
      (c) *wuṛu-nju-aṇi kunapa waŋari-tji*
           hit-past-I dog stone-instrumental
           :
           'I hit the dog with a stone'

[23] This principle is operative in a large number of Australian languages, but it is also widespread elsewhere. For example, it is operative in many of the Uto-Aztecan languages of North America, in at least one of the Algonquian languages (namely, Abnaki—see Laurent (1884, p. 119)), and to a limited extent in the Athabaskan language Navajo; its operation in Serbo-Croatian is described in Browne (1966). In Papago, a Uto-Aztecan language of the American Southwest, the surface positioning of the auxiliary appears to be identical to that of Walbiri (see Hale (1969a, note 3)). The principle is, in fact, known as Wackernagel's law and its operation in Indo-European is the subject of a long paper by Wackernagel (1892).

[24] In Waṇman, of Western Australia, the creation of new independent pronouns has been especially interesting. All are based upon the stem /para/, of unknown etymology but certainly not a pronoun historically (O'Grady, Voegelin, and Voegelin (1966, p. 136)). Waṇman is very closely related to languages whose modern independent pronouns are built upon forms which were pronominal historically. It is, in fact, reasonably closely related to Walbiri.

[25] I am indebted to Sandy Nandy and to George Bruce for their help in my brief study of Warramunga. I have also benefited from Capell's sketch (1953). I use here a common spelling of the tribal name—Warramunga—but the speakers whom I consulted pronounced it [waṛumuṇu]. The inventory of consonants and vowels for Warramunga is the same as that for Walbiri, except that (*a*) it lacks the retroflexed flap /ḍ/, and (*b*) it has an opposition between tense and lax stops which, although little understood, clearly plays a role in the phonology: superficially, at least, there are minimal pairs for tensity, such as /paṭa/ 'leave, imperative', /paṭ:a/ 'heel'. Furthermore, so far as I know, Warramunga lacks the length distinction in vowels which is found marginally in Walbiri (a recent development there—see Hale (to appear, note 54 and related text)).

If both the subject and the object are represented by pronouns, both cliticize, and, as in the case of Walbiri pronominal clitics, they appear in the order subject-object. In (78), the pronouns are subject /aṇi/ 'I' and object /aŋku/ 'you (sg)':

(78) (a) *waŋari-tji-aṇi-aŋku wuṛu-nju*
        stone-instrumental-I-you hit-past
     (b) *wuṛu-nju-aṇi-aŋku waŋari-tji*
        hit-past-I-you stone-instrumental
        'I hit you with a stone'

The pronominals are not the only elements which appear in clitic position. Among other clitics is a marker /a/ which, together with an inflection on the verb, marks future tense. This follows the cliticized pronouns, as illustrated in (79) and (80):[26]

(79) (a) *yuwala-tja-aṇi-aŋku-a paki-l*
        spear-instrumental-I-you-future spear-future
     (b) *paki-l-aṇi-aŋku-a yuwala-tja*
        spear-future-I-you-future spear-instrumental
        'I will spear you with a spear'
(80) (a) *kunapa-aṇi-a waŋari-tji wuṛu-φ*
        dog-I-future stone-instrumental hit-future
     (b) *waŋari-tji-aṇi-a wuṛu-φ kunapa*
        stone-instrumental-I-future hit-future dog
        :
        'I will hit the dog with a stone'

Warramunga pronouns, although they normally appear unstressed and cliticized, are in fact independent pronouns in the sense that they can appear as isolated, fully stressed words—as answers to questions, for instance. They can also appear fully stressed as postposed tags to sentences, in which position they serve to reemphasize or to clarify the identification of, say, the subject which is represented by a cliticized pronoun within the sentence itself. Furthermore, subject pronouns may (under conditions, perhaps of style, which I do not adequately understand) appear fully stressed in sentence-initial position. All of this is totally unlike the behavior of Walbiri pronominal clitics.

It is not the case in Warramunga, as it is in Walbiri, that both clitic and independent varieties of a given pronoun can co-occur within the same sentence, except for the rather marginal case in which a reemphasizing tag pronoun appears (separated, incidentally, from the main body of the sentence by a considerable pause). It would seem, therefore, that Warramunga does not have agreement in the Walbiri sense. Rather, I think the correct way to view the Warramunga case is along the lines already suggested, that is, to assume that pronouns are actually moved, rather than copied, into clitic position.

One might expect that if Warramunga cliticization involves the actual movement of pronouns, it would never be necessary to make reference to the categories of person

---

[26] In Warramunga, morpheme-final vowels are deleted before a following morpheme-initial vowel. This rule is applied without fail at the juncture between a morpheme and following suffix or pronominal clitic, although between words the rule is less strictly observed. Thus, for example, the sentences of (79) are as follows, after vowel deletion:

(a) *yuwalatjaṇaŋka pakil*
(b) *pakilaṇaŋka yuwalatja*

and number in deriving correct clitic sequences. This is not the case, however. Once the pronouns are in clitic position, not only is it necessary to apply a variety of phonological rules to derive the ultimate surface forms (including the completely general deletion of morpheme-final vowels in the environment ____ + V and, in addition, a rather diverse array of highly idiosyncratic morphophonological readjustments), but also, as is the case in Eastern Walbiri, there must be neutralization of the distinction between dual and plural number in clitic sequences of nonsingular subject followed by nonsingular object. To effect this neutralization, clearly, reference must be made to the category of number. In this respect the Warramunga system closely resembles the Walbiri one and affords a suggestive model for a possible historical antecedent to the latter.

The similarity between the two systems is also evident in their treatment of conjoined noun phrases. In Warramunga, as in Walbiri, where the subject or object is a conjoined expression, the corresponding pronominal element appearing in clitic position must embody the features of number and person appropriate to the expression as a whole. Thus, the conjoined expression /aṇi *c* aṇi/ 'you and I' (in which *c* represents an intonational feature characteristic of Warramunga noun phrase conjoining, not otherwise marked morphologically), which can appear as such only as an isolated expression or as a tag, is regularly replaced by the corresponding pronoun /ayil/ '12'. The latter, of course, becomes unstressed and moves to clitic position, as shown in (81):

(81)   *kuyu-ayil walpu-nju, aṇi c aṇi*
        meat-12 kill-past, you and I
        'We killed meat, that is, you and I did'

Where a conjoined expression includes both a pronoun and a noun, only the former is subject to cliticization, and it must cliticize unless the expression is isolated or is a tag. However, it is not the case that the pronoun simply cliticizes out of the conjoined noun phrase; rather, the pronoun is replaced by one which embodies the number of the noun phrase as a whole, and it is this composite pronoun which cliticizes. Thus, in the conjoined expression /kiritji *c* aṇi/ 'the woman and I', which can appear as such in isolation or in a tag, the pronoun /aṇi/ 'I' is replaced by the first person exclusive pronoun /atjil/ '11'. This latter cliticizes, but a vestige of the original duality is left in the noun phrase in the form of the dual suffix /-kutjur/ attached to the noun /kiritji/ 'woman', as in (82):

(82)   *kiritji-kutjur-atjil yiŋal kuṛa-yina*
        woman-dual-11 frightened run-past (narrative)
        'The woman and I ran away in fear'

Where only nouns are present in, say, a conjoined subject noun phrase, a pronoun embodying the number of the whole appears in clitic position. Thus, as in (83), /awul/ '33' appears in association with a noun phrase like /kampatju *c* kaṇanti/ '(my) father and mother':

(83)   *kampatju c kaṇanti-awul apirapa-n*
        father and mother-33 come-present
        '(My) father and mother are coming'

Sentences like (83) raise an interesting question. The subject noun phrase /kampatju *c* kaṇanti/ consists of two singular nouns. Therefore, it cannot be said to have contained the pronoun /awul/ as such in its deep structure representation. But then where does /awul/ in (83) come from if, as seems to be the case, the Warramunga system of person marking involves the actual movement of pronouns into clitic position from positions otherwise occupied by (subject or object) noun phrases? The possibility arises that Warramunga might actually represent a system which to some degree approximates the compromise conception of agreement suggested very briefly for Walbiri earlier. We have reason to suspect, for example, that there must exist in Warramunga a process which creates pronouns on the basis of the person and number feature composition of noun phrases. This is the process which creates the pronoun /atjil/ (or at least the abstract feature assemblage which underlies it) to replace /aṇi/ in conjoined expressions of the type represented by /kiritji c aṇi/ 'the woman and I'. If such a process actually exists for cases like this one, then it does not seem unreasonable to extend its application to noun phrases like (kampatju c kaṇanti/. In general, what one might propose for Warramunga is something like the following: if a subject or object noun phrase is not a pronoun and therefore cannot itself cliticize, then a strictly pronominal copy of it is produced; subsequently, all subject and object pronouns, whether they are copies or originals, undergo the process of cliticization.[27] This seems as reasonable a proposal as any for Warramunga. However, I am not at all sure what kinds of evidence could be brought to bear either to support or to contradict it. Thus, I am reluctant to attempt a formalization of any proposal vaguely suggested here.

Let us assume for the sake of the discussion, however, that the proposal just mentioned is correct for Warramunga. What is central here is the claim that pronouns are actually moved into clitic position. I will refer to Warramunga and other languages like it as "clitic-placement languages," at least insofar as the system of person marking is concerned. The question I would like to address myself to now is whether Walbiri is also a clitic-placement language in this respect. Or, to put the question another way, what is the difference between the Walbiri and Warramunga systems of person marking?

Notice that the proposal suggested as most reasonable for Walbiri is somewhat different from that suggested for Warramunga. For Walbiri, I have proposed what is essentially an agreement rule, that is, a rule which effects an agreement, by feature copying, between (subject and object) noun phrases and the auxiliary. Now it is certainly possible to extend the Warramunga proposal to Walbiri. One might suggest, for example, that in Walbiri there is produced a strictly pronominal copy of each subject and object noun phrase, whether pronominal or nominal; subsequently, the copies (but not pronouns originally in the base structure) undergo the process of cliticization. Under this proposal, Walbiri would differ from Warramunga in the following ways: (a) the process of creating pronominal copies would be extended to all subject and object noun phrases; (b) only the pronominal copies would cliticize; and (c) a special set of rules would be needed to provide the phonological actualization of pronominal clitics since there is no systematic correspondence in phonological shape between clitics and independent pronouns. On the other hand, Warramunga and Walbiri would be in agreement in that the surface positioning of person markers is by a movement rule of clitic placement.

Although I certainly cannot take a strong position in this matter, I feel that it is at least worth considering the possibility that the Walbiri system of person marking is synchronically quite different from that of Warramunga. At some future time, it might be possible to argue more strongly than I am now able to that the correct way to view the Walbiri system is in terms of the feature-copying alternative outlined

---

[27] Some details are glossed over here. Third person singular subjects and direct objects are not represented by clitic pronouns, although third person dative is represented by the clitic /aku/. There is, however, some ability to cliticize evident on the part of the third person definite determiner /ŋala/ 'the, this', appearing as /ala/ in clitic position.

earlier, and, further, that there is a significant typological distinction to be made between clitic-placement systems of person marking, like that of Warramunga, and what we might term "agreement" systems of person marking, represented here by Walbiri. To be sure, one might object to this conception of Walbiri person marking on the grounds that the Walbiri person markers do in fact appear in clitic position in surface structures. But the answer to this is that it is really the auxiliary which appears in clitic position: the person markers themselves are attached to the auxiliary base, as is to be expected if it is actually the case that the Walbiri system is one in which the auxiliary can be said to agree in person and number with subject and object noun phrases. Moreover, it is most reasonable to assume that agreement takes place prior to permutations in word order and, therefore, prior to the point at which the auxiliary is itself inserted into clitic position.

If it is correct that Warramunga and Walbiri are typologically different in this way, then the obvious similarities between the two systems—including similarities of syntactic and morphological detail, as well as similarities due to common retention of morphs (such as Walbiri /-tju/ '1 object', /-ŋku/ '2 object' beside Warramunga /atju/ '1 object', /aŋku/ '2 object')—are to be explained in historical terms. Both languages went through a stage in which cliticization of pronouns was a synchronic process in their grammars. For Warramunga, that happens still to be the case. The development which sharply distinguished Walbiri from Warramunga was the creation of a new set of independent pronouns, giving rise to the current state of affairs in which both independent and clitic pronouns, not necessarily at all alike in phonological shape, are permitted to co-occur in the same sentence, a system in which pronominal clitics appear in *agreement* with independent (albeit optionally deletable) pronouns.

REFERENCES

Browne, W. (1966), "On the problem of enclitic placement in Serbo-Croatian," unpublished paper, M.I.T.

Capell, A. (1953), "Notes on the Warramunga Language, Central Australia," *Oceania*, 23, 296–311.

Capell, A. (1962), *Some Linguistic Types in Australia*, Oceanic Linguistic Monographs, 7, Sydney.

Hale, K. (1969a), "Papago /cɨm/," *IJAL*, 35, 203–212.

Hale, K. (1969b), "Walbiri conjugations," unpublished paper, M.I.T.

Hale, K. (1970), "The Passive and Ergative in Language Change: the Australian Case," *Pacific Linguistic Studies in Honor of Arthur Capell*, Pacific Linguistics, Series C, no. 13.

Hale, K. (to appear), "Deep-Surface Canonical Disparities in Relation to Analysis and Change: an Australian Example," in T. Sebeok, ed., *Current Trends in Linguistics*, vol. 11.

Laurent, J. (1884), *New Familiar Abenakis and English Dialogues*, Quebec.

O'Grady, G., C. F. Voegelin, and F. M. Voegelin (1966), "Languages of the world: Indo-Pacific fascicle six," *Anthropological Linguistics*, 8, 1–197.

Perlmutter, D. (1971), *Deep and Surface Structure Constraints in Syntax*, New York: Holt, Rinehart and Winston.

Reece, L. (1970), *Grammar of the Walbiri Language of Central Australia*, Oceania Linguistic Monographs, 13, Sydney.

Wackernagel, J. (1892), "Über ein Gesetz der indogermanischen Wortstellung," *IF, 1*, 333–436.

the base rules
for prepositional phrases

Ray S. Jackendoff

Brandeis University

People seem never to have taken prepositions seriously. One proposal in print (Fillmore (1968)) treats prepositions as case markers, having equal status with the case inflections of Latin or German. Another proposal (Postal (1971)) treats them as realizations of features on noun phrases. Still another (Becker and Arms (1969)) tries to reduce prepositions to a subclass of the category "verb." What all these proposals have in common is that they deny that the category "preposition" has any real intrinsic syntactic interest other than as an annoying little surface peculiarity of English.

The neglect of prepositions arises from the assumption that prepositional phrases invariably take the form P–NP: if this were the case, prepositions would indeed be dull. However, I will show here that such an analysis is not adequate and that prepositional phrases are by no means as trivial as generally supposed.

1. PP → P

Klima (1965) realized that prepositions are more than markers on NPs. He showed that many "adverbs" such as *home*, *downstairs*, and *afterward* can advantageously be identified as "intransitive prepositions," that is, prepositions that do not take an object. Emonds (1970) argued that the traditional "particles" of verb-particle combinations such as *look up*, *give out*, and *show off* are also best analyzed as "intransitive prepositions."

The arguments for the existence of intransitive prepositions are straightforward. First, we note in (1) the close phonological relation (often identity) obtaining between many ordinary prepositions and the words in question:

(1) (a) Chico ran $\begin{cases} \text{into the opera house} \\ \text{in} \end{cases}$

(Continued)

(b) The elevator operator kicked Groucho $\begin{cases} \text{down the stairs} \\ \text{downstairs} \end{cases}$

(c) He didn't play the harp $\begin{cases} \text{after the first act} \\ \text{afterward} \\ \text{before Zeppo walked in} \\ \text{before} \\ \text{inside the hotel} \\ \text{inside} \end{cases}$

In fact, all the particles in verb-particle constructions (*down, up, in, out, through, over, by,* and so on) are phonologically identical to ordinary prepositions. As Emonds points out, this fact can hardly be accidental; if the grammar treated it as such, there would be no more reason to expect this result than a class of particles made up partly of nouns, partly of verbs, partly of modals, and partly of adjectives. By treating particles as a type of preposition, we can claim that particles are related to the corresponding prepositions in much the same way that intransitive verbs such as *eat, drink,* and *smoke* are related to their transitive counterparts.

A second argument concerns the strict subcategorization of verbs such as *put,* which require after the direct object a normal prepositional phrase, a "directional adverb," or a particle, as illustrated in (2):

(2) (a) *Irving put the books

(b) Irving put the books $\begin{cases} \text{on the shelf} \\ \text{there} \\ \text{away} \end{cases}$

(c) Sheila put the clothes $\begin{cases} \text{in the closet} \\ \text{inside} \\ \text{on} \end{cases}$

The particles are distinguished from other directional phrases only in that they may also occur before the direct object, as shown in (3):

(3)

(a) Irving put $\begin{cases} \text{*on the shelf} \\ \text{*there} \\ \text{away} \end{cases}$ the books

(b) Sheila put $\begin{cases} \text{*in the closet} \\ \text{*inside} \\ \text{on} \end{cases}$ the clothes

The occurrence of just these three kinds of constituents with *put* to the exclusion of all other kinds is easily expressed if all three are analyzed as prepositional phrases, thereby simplifying the strict subcategorization of *put*.

A third argument favoring intransitive prepositions concerns the construction illustrated in (4):

(4) (a) Into the opera house raced Harpo
(b) Up the stairs wafted the fragrant smell of airplane glue
(c) On the corner stood a frightened Venusian cookie monster

In such sentences a preposed locational or directional prepositional phrase causes inversion of an intransitive verb with the subject when there are no auxiliary verbs. The only other constituents which can cause this particular inversion are locational and directional "adverbs," particles, and certain participial constructions containing directionals or locationals, as shown, respectively, in (a), (b), and (c) of (5):

(5) (a) There goes Chico
 Outside stood three cases of Romanian beer
 Downstairs rolled the two screaming dentists
 (b) Off came Harpo's fake beard
 Away flew the remnants of your tattered hat
 On trundled the weary heroes
 (c) Bouncing out of the operating room came the happy patients
 Screaming down the hall ran two celebrated linguists
 Wiping his nose in a corner stood a bedraggled hobbit
 Buried here lies the producer of *A Night at the Opera*

Of course, not all particles take part in this construction, particularly not those that impart an idiomatic meaning to the verb, as in (6):

(6) *Up threw John

But nondirectional "adverbs" and nondirectional prepositional phrases do not take part either, as shown in (7):

(7) (a) *Beforehand left John
 (b) *In the twinkling of an eye collapsed the enchanted fortress

The rule forming this construction will be simplified if it has to refer only to the category "PP" (aside from participials) rather than to three independent categories.

In an especially curious construction in English, sentences are formed from a directional phrase followed by *with* and a definite noun phrase. Directional prepositional phrases, "adverbs," and particles are all possible here, as shown in (8):

(8) (a) Into the dungeon with the traitors!
 Down the well with your money!
 (b) Outdoors with these noisy machines!
 Upstairs with this illegal card game!
 (c) Off with his nose!
 Away with the evidence!

Once again, no matter how this construction is derived, it will be simpler if all three types of phrases are considered PPs.

As illustrated in (9), the modifier *right* occurs only with standard prepositional phrases, the particular class of "adverbs" we have been discussing, and particles (in their post-object position):

(9) (a) Mr. Gottlieb staggered right into Mrs. Claypool's stateroom
 The collapse came right after Ricardo's arrival
 (b) The eager dwarves rushed right inside
 Nobody could figure out what had happened right afterward
 (c) The scenery caved right in under Gummo's weight
 Frodo put the ring right on when he saw Mrs. Claypool coming

Right with this sense does not occur in standard English before any other kind of constituent, including adjectives and true adverbs, as shown in (10):

(10) (a) *The scenery right collapsed under Gummo's weight
     (b) *Fredonia went to war with Rohan right quickly
     (c) *Bilbo had become right fat during his stay

Again, the description of *right* can be simplified if all three types of phrases are described as PPs.

These arguments are given in more detail by Emonds (1970), who goes on to describe the Particle-Movement Rule within this framework. What the arguments imply is that the base rule for PP should be altered by the addition of parentheses, as in (11):

(11) PP → P–(NP)

Prepositions, like verbs, will then contain strict subcategorization features in their lexical entries. For example, *down*, *up*, *before*, *in*, and *out* will have the feature [+___(NP)]; *of*, *for*, and *toward* will have the feature [+___NP]; and *home*, *afterward*, and *beforehand* will have the feature [+___].

2. PP → P–PP

Combinations of two prepositions followed by a noun phrase as in (12) are quite common (though frequently overlooked):

(12) (a) Harpo rode the horse out of the barn
     (b) Sam disappeared down into the darkness
     (c) A great howl of pain emerged from inside the rain barrel

Phrases of this form satisfy the five criteria established in the last section for prepositional phrases: (*a*) they begin with words that are obviously of the category "preposition"; (*b*) they occur in the complements of verbs such as *put*, which strictly subcategorize PPs; (*c*) they condition subject-verb inversion under appropriate circumstances, as shown in (13):

(13) (a) Out of the night appeared the nine black riders
     (b) Up into the clouds shot a riderless broomstick
     (c) Back from his successes in the Faroe Islands comes that star of stage and
         screen, Frodo Marx!

(*d*) they occur in the *with*-construction, as in (14):

(14) (a) Up to your bedroom with you, young man!
     (b) Back in the box with you, Jack!

(*e*) they occur with *right*, as can be seen by adding *right* in the appropriate place in any of the sentences in (12), (13), and (14).

To account for these constructions, we can permit prepositions to strictly subcategorize PPs in their complements. For example, *out*, *in*, *up*, and *down* allow an NP, a PP, or nothing; *from* must have a complement, but this may be either an NP or a PP; *away* and *back* allow either a PP or no complement but cannot be followed by an NP.

Given the existence of intransitive prepositions, a string of the form P–P–NP has, in fact, two possible analyses, as shown in (15):

(15) (a)

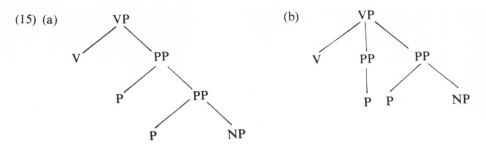

(b)

In (15a) there is a preposition whose complement is a PP; in (15b) there is an intransitive preposition followed by a normal PP. Both of these structures do exist, as illustrated, respectively, in (16a) and (16b):

(16) (a) Chico raced away from Mrs. Claypool
     (b) Otis T. Flywheel raced away in a battered Ford

We observe in (17) and (18) that these sentences give opposite results in terms of acceptability when the PP-Preposing Rule is applied in two conceivable ways:

(17) (a)   Away from Mrs. Claypool raced Chico
     (b)   ?*Away in a battered Ford raced Otis T. Flywheel
(18) (a)   ?*Away raced Chico from Mrs. Claypool
     (b)   Away raced Otis T. Flywheel in a battered Ford

If we make the reasonable assumption that PP-Preposing applies to single complete PPs, the difference between (15a) and (15b) predicts these results: *away from Mrs. Claypool*, being a constituent of the form PP in (15a), preposes as a unit and cannot be separated; *away in a battered Ford*, on the other hand, is analyzed as in (15b), and, since this is not a constituent, only the first PP, *away*, preposes. Furthermore, as shown in (19), only (16b) permits a manner adverb to be interposed comfortably between the prepositions, as might be predicted from the structures (15a,b):

(19) (a)   ?*Chico raced away quickly from Mrs. Claypool
     (b)   Otis T. Flywheel raced away quickly in a battered Ford

Certain combinations of directional prepositions seem to be ambiguous between the constructions (15a) and (15b) since, as illustrated in (20), either of the preposed forms parallel to (17)-(18) is possible:

(20) (a) The kite went up into the clouds
          The bomb plunged down toward the village
     (b) Up into the clouds went the kite
          Down toward the village plunged the bomb
     (c) Up went the kite into the clouds
          Down plunged the bomb toward the village

An adverb may also be interposed with these combinations, as in (21):

(21) (a) The kite went up slowly into the clouds
     (b) The bomb plunged down precipitously toward the village

However, if a locational preposition is substituted for the second directional preposition, only the structure (15a) is possible with the sense intended, as illustrated in (22):[1]

(22) (a)   The kite went up in the clouds
            The bomb plunged down at the village
     (b)   Up in the clouds went the kite
            Down at the village plunged the bomb
     (c) ?*Up went the kite in the clouds
            ?*Down plunged the bomb at the village
     (d)   *The kite went up slowly in the clouds (*in the intended sense*)
            ?*The bomb plunged down precipitously at the ground

These syntactic differences seem sufficient to justify the existence of both structures in (15).

If there are prepositional phrases of the form P–PP, we would expect to find certain structures in addition to (15a). One such is (23), in which the inner PP consists of an intransitive preposition:

(23)

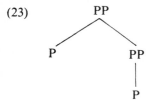

And, in fact, (23) is the appropriate analysis for such phrases as *over here*, *down there*, *back home*, and *from within*.

We might also expect the inner PP itself to expand as P–PP, yielding a string of three prepositions within one constituent. This prediction is borne out by sentences like (24), in which the preposing is a clear indication of constituency:

(24) (a) From out of the darkness hurtled a masked hobbit on a broomstick
     (b) Down from above the altar groaned a mysterious voice

The PPs can iterate further, generating unwieldy but genuine PPs such as (25):

(25) Back out from inside of the hole squirmed Groucho

3. PP → P–NP–PP

We have thus far left open the question of how the phrase structure rule for (15a) generalizes with the phrase structure rule (11). Two possibilities are given in (26):

(26) (a) PP → P–($\begin{Bmatrix} NP \\ PP \end{Bmatrix}$)

     (b) PP → P–(NP)–(PP)

Both (26a) and (26b) are consistent with the investigation up to this point. The second

---

[1] The use of locational prepositions in a directional sense is discussed by Gruber (1965) under the rubric "simplification of secondary expression of goal." Although Gruber reaches somewhat different conclusions, his discussion was instrumental in suggesting to me the analysis presented in this section and the next.

alternative, however, makes an interesting prediction: there should be PPs of the form P–NP–PP. The sentences in (27) do indeed contain phrases which seem likely candidates for such a structure:

(27) (a) A Martian grzch lumbered down the street toward the frightened garbage collector
     (b) A drunken bassoonist staggered into the smoky room from out of the cold
     (c) The mice raced from one end of the park to the other
     (d) Max sent the trilogy to Bill in New York

To justify the existence of this structure, shown in (28a), it is important to distinguish its properties from those of two other structures producing the same string, shown in (28b) and (28c):

(28)

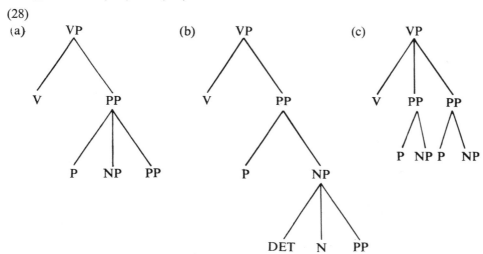

The structure (28b) occurs in such sentences as *they went to the house in the woods*, where *the house in the woods* forms a constituent that can be used independently, for instance as the subject of a sentence. This is clearly impossible, on the other hand, for the phrases in (27), as shown in (29):

(29) (a) *The street toward the frightened garbage collector was littered with broken bassoon reeds
     (b) *The smoky room from out of the cold had too many movie stars and hobbits in it
     (c) *One end of the park to the other was a mess
     (d) *Bill in New York liked reading the trilogy[2]

To show that the relevant phrases in (27) have the structure (28a) rather than (28c), we must show that they can behave as single constituents. The first piece of evidence, presented in (30), comes from the Preposing Rule:

(30) (a) Down the street toward the frightened garbage collector lumbered a Martian grzch
     (b) Into the smoky room from out of the cold staggered a drunken bassoonist

(Continued)

---

[2] This sentence is not to be read with commas around *in New York*.

(c) From one end of the park to the other raced the mice
(d) To Bill in New York, Max sent the trilogy[3]

A sentence that definitely contains the structure (28c) is (31a), which has only the preposed variant (31b) and not (31c); since the two PPs do not form a constituent, only the first can prepose:

(31) (a)   Harpo paraded down the aisle with Margaret Dumont
     (b)   Down the aisle paraded Harpo with Margaret Dumont
     (c)   ?*Down the aisle with Margaret Dumont paraded Harpo

Sentences (27a) and, perhaps, (27b) are ambiguous between structures (28a) and (28c), since, as shown in (a) and (b) of (32), these sentences have forms parallel to (31b). But, as shown in (c) and (d) of (32), the sentences (27c,d) do not have this preposed form and thus can have only the structure (28a):

(32) (a)   Down the street lumbered a Martian grzch toward the frightened garbage
            collector
     (b)   ?Into the smoky room staggered a drunken bassoonist from out of the cold
     (c)   *From one end of the park raced the mice to the other
     (d)   *To Bill, Max sent the trilogy in New York

As in the previous section, we find it possible to interpose a manner adverb between the two PPs just in case they can be split by the Preposing Rule. We illustrate in (33):

(33) (a)   A fearsome grzch lumbered down the street noisily(,) toward the frightened
            garbage collector
     (b)   ?A bassoonist staggered into the smoky room drunkenly(,) from out of the
            cold
     (c)   *The mice raced from one end of the park rapidly(,) to the other
     (d)   *Max sent the trilogy to Bill quickly(,) in New York
     (e)   Harpo paraded down the aisle grandly with Margaret Dumont

Cleft sentences provide further evidence that the relevant phrases in (27) constitute a constituent. Prepositional phrases (except, for some unexplained reason, those consisting of a single intransitive preposition) can appear in the focus position of cleft sentences, as in (34):

(34) (a) It wasn't in Australia that Boromir encountered Chico
     (b) It was around six o'clock that the bassoon turned into a toad
     (c) It was down in the grease pit that Chico found his piano

Strings of the form P–NP–PP can occur in this position as well, given appropriate opportunities for semantic contrast, as in (35):

(35) (a) It wasn't down the street toward Harpo that the garbage collector ran
     (b) It was to Bill in New York that Max sent the trilogy
     (c) It was (only) from Sunday to Thursday that Gandalf's teeth itched

Since, in general, only single constituents can cleft, the sentences in (35) give additional reason to believe in the existence of structures like (28a). Note from (36) that sentence

---

[3] Subject-verb inversion is prevented here by the presence of the direct object.

(31a), which was claimed to have the structure (28c), can cleft one or the other of the PPs but not both at once:

(36) (a)   It was down the aisle that Harpo paraded with Margaret Dumont
      (b)   It was with Margaret Dumont that Harpo paraded down the aisle
      (c)   ?*It was down the aisle with Margaret Dumont that Harpo paraded

Finally, we observe from (37) that strings of the form P–NP–PP can serve as antecedents for appositive relative clauses:

(37) (a) A prepositional phrase can be found across the copula from a measure phrase, which is a significant position
      (b) We progressed from abstract deep structure to generative semantics, which seems like a formidable conceptual distance, in less than two years
      (c) Solving this problem will take from now until doomsday, which is more time than we've got, my dear

Since, presumably, relative clauses have single constituents as their antecedents,[4] (28c) is not a possible structure for the relevant PP strings in (37).[5]

We now have three independent pieces of evidence, from preposing, clefting, and appositive formation, showing that there are single PPs of the form P–NP–PP. Of course, (28a) is not the only possible structure for this form. One could claim, for example, that such strings are analyzed as in (38a) or (38b):

(38)

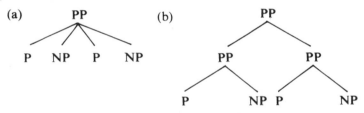

The structure (38a) might be proposed in the belief that *from . . . to* and *across . . . from*, for example, are a sort of discontinuous "compound preposition" which takes two NP or PP arguments. Structure (38b) would be preferred if complex PPs were closely related to conjoined PPs—for instance if *up the hall into the kitchen* were derived from *up the hall and into the kitchen*. However, neither of these structures seems as satisfactory an analysis as (28a). Structure (38a) suffers in that it requires a new base rule and some explanation of why the "compound prepositions" happen all to be formed from the stock of ordinary prepositions. And (38b) suffers in that a conjunction deletion is needed. Furthermore, not all complex PPs can be related to conjoined PPs; for example, none of the PPs in (37) can be replaced by conjunction. On the other hand, when we seek to generalize the already needed base rules PP → P–NP and PP → P–PP, one of the possible ways of combining them predicts

---

[4] The only cases I know where relative clauses have split antecedents are those mentioned by Perlmutter and Ross (1970), in which the two antecedents occupy parallel positions in conjoined clauses. There is no relation between these cases and those given here.

[5] Note that I am arguing only that the PPs form a constituent, not that they form an NP, as is often argued for antecedents of relative clauses. Since so many kinds of constituents (NP, S, AP, AdvP, and now PP) can serve as antecedents for appositives, the latter argument makes the notion NP syntactically rather vacuous.

automatically the existence of forms having the structure (28a). This is therefore the simplest structure we can produce for complex PPs in terms of extra rules needed in the grammar, for it results from an actual simplification of the grammar.

4. THE SPECIFIER

Is it a coincidence that the correct generalization of the base rules for PPs is P–(NP)–(PP) and not P–($\left\{\begin{matrix} NP \\ PP \end{matrix}\right\}$) or P–(PP)–(NP) (which we did not suggest earlier)? There is one other syntactic category which allows NPs rather than just PPs in its complement, namely, the verb. And in verb phrases the NPs in the complement precede the PPs. This suggests that the structure of PPs is in fact not accidental.

The Lexicalist Hypothesis of Chomsky (1970) is an attempt to capture similarities of this sort. The claim is that similarities are to be expected among various constituents and that these similarities are expressed in generalized schemata for the base rules. The first base rule schema can be expressed as (39), where X represents any lexical category and $\overline{X}$ is the node directly dominating it:

(39) $\overline{X} \rightarrow X\text{–Comp}_X$

The realizations of this schema for the various lexical categories are shown in (40):

(40) VP $\rightarrow$ V–(NP)–($\left\{\begin{matrix} NP \\ AP \end{matrix}\right\}$)[6]–(PP)*

$\overline{N} \rightarrow N$ –(PP)*
$\overline{A} \rightarrow A$ –(PP)
$\overline{Adv} \rightarrow Adv$
$\overline{P} \rightarrow P$–(NP)   –(PP)

We see that the complements of N, A, Adv, and P are all subsets of the complement of V. Note that I have not identified $\overline{P}$ with the node PP, for reasons which will appear in a moment.

Chomsky's second base rule schema, (41), claims that for any lexical category X, $\overline{X}$ is preceded by a system of phrases called the "specifier":

(41) $\overline{\overline{X}} \rightarrow \text{Spec}_X$–$\overline{X}$

In the case where X is a verb, $\overline{V}$ is the traditional node VP, $\overline{\overline{V}}$ is the traditional node S, and $\text{Spec}_{\overline{V}}$ includes the subject and Aux nodes, as in (42):[7]

(42) $\overline{\overline{V}} \rightarrow \text{NP–Aux–}\overline{V}$

When X is a noun, $\overline{\overline{N}}$ is the traditional node NP and $\text{Spec}_{\overline{N}}$ includes the traditional determiner system. $\overline{A}$ and $\overline{Adv}$ are the traditional nodes AP and AdvP, and $\text{Spec}_{\overline{A}}$ and $\text{Spec}_{\overline{Adv}}$ both include the system of degree phrases.

Similarly, we should expect a system of phrases to appear within PPs before the preposition, justifying the base rule (43):

[6] This constituent in the expansion of VP is necessary for such VPs as *call Max an idiot* and *cook the meat dry.*
[7] This differs from the analysis in Chomsky (1970). In Jackendoff (1968) I have tried to justify this analysis over Chomsky's.

(43) PP → Spec$_{\overline{\overline{P}}}$–$\overline{\overline{P}}$

And in fact there are such phrases, as illustrated in (44):

(44)

(a) $\left\{\begin{array}{l}\text{Right}\\\text{Far}\\\text{Six miles}\\\text{A long way}\\\text{Halfway}\end{array}\right\}$ down the road Frodo saw an approaching band of grzches

(b) The curious sounds of a harp could be heard $\left\{\begin{array}{l}\text{right}\\\text{far}\\\text{four hours}\\\text{a long time}\end{array}\right\}$ after the landing of the saucer

(c) The class of prepositions is made up $\left\{\begin{array}{l}\text{entirely}\\\text{partly}\end{array}\right\}$ of verbs

PPs take *even*, *only*, *just*, and comparatives, just like all the other phrase nodes (S, NP, AP, AdvP), as shown in (45):

(45) (a) Groucho found swarming hobbits even in the kitchen
  (b) Harpo stopped playing only after a long interval
  (c) Chico got out just before the arrival of the cops
  (d) Zeppo was more out of that movie than (he was) in it

Thus some of the permissible specifier phrases are also specifiers for other constituents, and some (such as *right*) are peculiar to PPs.

This situation is what the Lexicalist Hypothesis leads us to expect: constituents of comparable level (that is, all $\overline{X}$ or all $\overline{\overline{X}}$) should have parallel structure up to a point, but they are likely to differ in some respects. PPs seem like APs in their specifier structure because of the use of measure phrases. In their complement structure they seem like Ss because of the presence of NP. On the other hand, they resemble NPs in that they undergo cleft formation and AdvPs in that they prepose freely. The PP structures we have observed therefore provide a modest confirmation of the Lexicalist Hypothesis.

We have seen that prepositions determine a much larger range of structures than the P–NP construction usually attributed to them. Our rather simple observations make it far more difficult to treat prepositions merely as features on verbs or nouns, phonologically realized through trivial transformations. Prepositions must instead be accorded the right to a small but dignified syntactic category of their own.

REfERENcES

Becker, A. L., and D. G. Arms (1969), "Prepositions as Predicates," in Binnick *et al.*, *Papers from the Fifth Regional Meeting of the Chicago Linguistic Society*, University of Chicago.

Bowers, J. S. (1968), "Adjectives and Adverbs in English," Indiana University Linguistics Club, Bloomington, Ind.

Chomsky, N. (1970), "Remarks on Nominalization," in R. Jacobs and P. Rosenbaum, eds., *Readings in English Transformational Grammar*, Waltham, Mass.: Blaisdell.

Emonds, J. (1970), "Evidence that Dative Movement is a Structure-Preserving Rule," to appear in Ruwet, ed., *Papers from the IRIA Conference*.

Fillmore, C. (1968), "The Case for Case," in E. Bach and R. T. Harms, eds., *Universals in Linguistic Theory*, New York: Holt, Rinehart and Winston.

Gruber, J. (1965), "Studies in Lexical Relations," Indiana University Linguistics Club, Bloomington, Ind.

Jackendoff, R. (1968), "Speculations on Presentences and Determiners," Indiana University Linguistics Club, Bloomington, Ind.

Klima, E. S. (1965), *Studies in Diachronic Syntax*, unpublished Ph.D. dissertation, Harvard University.

Perlmutter, D., and J. R. Ross (1970), "Relative Clauses with Split Antecedents," *Linguistic Inquiry*, *1*, 350.

Postal, P. (1971), *Cross-Over Phenomena*, New York: Holt, Rinehart and Winston.

compositionality, idiomaticity, and lexical substitution[1]

Jerrold J. Katz

Massachusetts Institute of Technology

1. INTRODUCTORY REMARKS

This paper is concerned with two problems involved in compositionality, for which two changes in the present theory of lexical substitution will be proposed as solutions.

One of the main conditions imposed by the theory of grammar on the form of generative grammars requires that the account of the sound-meaning correlations in a language reflect the fact that meanings are related to sound on the basis of the compositional structure of sentences. Thus, in addition to the commonly accepted "completeness condition," which may be stated in the form (1), we have a "compositional condition" on a grammar's explications of sound-meaning correlations which may be stated as (2):

(1) For every sentence S of the language L and every constituent C of S (including S itself), the grammar of L must assign to C a set R_C of semantic representations such that R_C contains a member for each sense of C, and no other semantic representations

(2) For every syntactically complex constituent C of S (including S itself) whose meaning is nonidiomatic, the set of semantic representations R_C assigned to C is a function of the sets of semantic representations assigned to the subconstituents that make up C and their grammatical relations in the sentence S

Condition (2) says that the mapping required by (1) cannot be arbitrary: it must reflect the relations between the syntactic organization of sentences and the conceptual

[1] This work was supported in part by the National Institute of Mental Health, Grant 2 PO1 MH13390-06. I am also indebted to the John Simon Guggenheim Memorial Foundation for aid during the time this article was being written.

organization of their senses. Thus, not just any numerically appropriate assignment of semantic representations to the constituents of a sentence can count as a grammar's explication of a sound-meaning correlation.

More significantly, condition (2) plays an indispensable role in expressing in the theory of grammar the requirement that grammars represent the systematic character of the principles comprising the speaker's competence to produce and understand any novel sentence (within their performance capacities and the limitations of speech situations). Grammars that satisfy (2) will offer some hypothesis about how the sound-meaning correlations in the finite experience of the speaker are extrapolated in the form of principles generating such connections for infinitely many cases.

This systematicity can be illustrated by considering (3) and (4):

(3) Several lazy people ramitized the breeze
(4) Several lazy people enjoyed the breeze

In (3), the meaninglessness of the nonsense verb *ramitize* is passed on to the verb phrase and then to the whole sentence. But a constituent like the subject of (3) is not so affected. Clearly, constituents that do not have a meaningless constituent as one of their subconstituents cannot be directly affected by a meaningless constituent because meaning is determined compositionally. On the other hand, just as the constituents that inherit semantic deviance are those that contain the meaningless construction as one of their subconstituents, so it is these same constituents that would obtain (part of) their meaning from a meaningful word appearing in place of the meaningless one. This is the case in (4). Here the verb phrase and the sentence obtain (part of) their meaning from the meaning of *enjoy*, but the subject does not obtain any component of its meaning from *enjoy* since the verb is not one of its subconstituents. Again, the explanation depends on its being the rule that natural languages correlate sound and meaning compositionally.

Idioms are the "exceptions that prove the rule": they do not get their meaning from the meanings of their syntactic parts. If an idiom is treated as if it were compositional, false predictions are made about its semantic properties and relations. For example, *taxi* and *cab* both have a sense on which they mean "a passenger-carrying automobile that can be hired for transportation"; thus, if the meaning of the syntactically complex *taxicab* were represented as a compositional function of the meanings of its parts, it would be predicted to be semantically redundant on a sense (that is, as having the same semantic property as *naked nude*, for example).

Moreover, the meaninglessness of a part of an idiom does not determine the meaninglessness of constituents containing the idiom (and thus containing the meaningless part of it). Compare a case like (3) with one like (5):

(5) Several lazy people shot the breeze

Although the occurrence of the verb in (5) is meaningless, unlike (3) the meaninglessness is not transmitted to the verb phrase and the sentence. The reason, of course, is that the verb phrase as a whole is the idiom, and therefore it obtains a meaning in the manner of a lexical item rather than as a projection from the meanings of its constituents in the manner of compositional complex constituents.

The pervasiveness of compositional structure in natural languages is thus demonstrated: only by assuming it can idioms as a type of construction be defined, as the contrasting cases, the irregularities at the semantic level.

2. THE PROBLEM OF IDIOMS

The first of the two problems dealing with compositionality which will concern us here arises because idioms are the exceptions to compositionality, and thus any attempt to formulate the compositional condition will require a clause like that included in (2) which says that the meaning of C is nonidiomatic. The use of the term "nonidiomatic" (or "compositional" if the clause is stated positively) prevents the statement of the condition from taking the form of a formal requirement on the structure of generative grammars. Such a statement of the compositional condition is only *partly* a formal requirement: its application depends *in part* on appeals to linguistic intuition to decide whether the meaning of a constituent is nonidiomatic. Without such appeals, the statement as it stands is worse than informal, it is circular.

What we require, then, is some property of all and only idioms that can be stated in terms of the formal structure of grammars. Given such a property, we will no longer have to resort to linguistic intuition in specifying the compositional condition on sound-meaning correlations because the formal property in question can be used to replace informal reference to idiomaticity.

In the discussion in Section 1, such a property was suggested: idioms are the syntactically complex constituents in a language that the semantic component of the grammar treats as lexical items, that is, they are entered in the dictionary as a whole. With one further qualification, we can restate (2). We make a distinction between the lexicon of the syntactic component (in Chomsky's sense) and the dictionary of the semantic component. The latter consists of entries, each of which is a lexicon entry—a pair consisting of a lexical item (suitably represented) and a set of syntactic features—and a set of lexical readings representing the senses of the item in the language. Hence, in speaking of an expression being entered in the dictionary, we can consider it in relation to its senses (or the symbolism that represents them). This is important because some constituents have both an idiomatic and a compositional sense. Consider, for example, (6):

(6) kick the bucket

The expression (6) has an idiomatic sense on which it is synonymous with "die" and a nonidiomatic sense on which it is synonymous with "strike some vessel with the foot." We shall want to refer to cases like (6) as "idiomatic on a sense" rather than as simply "idiomatic."

Now, (2) can be replaced by (7):

(7) For every syntactically complex constituent C of S (including S itself) and any sense of C representable by the reading R, such that there is no entry for C in the dictionary in which R appears as a lexical reading of C, the assignment of R to C is a function of the sets of semantic representations assigned to the subconstituents that make up C and their grammatical relations in S

This, then, leaves us with the problem of how to specify idioms in the lexicon and dictionary. The proposal that will be made in the remainder of this section follows roughly the lines of an earlier proposal set forth in Katz and Postal (1963). We shall seek to bring this previous proposal up to date by allowing for Chomsky's (1965) introduction of syntactic features and local (substitution) transformations to handle lexical insertion. The present proposal will also include other changes that seem desirable in terms of empirical adequacy.

No attempt will be made here to reply to criticisms of the earlier proposal, for two reasons. First, the changes required by the introduction of syntactic features and local transformations for lexical insertion alter general aspects of the framework within which the original questions about idioms were asked and answered, and as a consequence, a number of criticisms become irrelevant with the shift to the new framework. Second, most other criticisms were not really to the point originally, due to one or another misunderstanding of a general nature about the background of the discussion.[2]

We can distinguish two types of idioms: "lexical idioms" belong to the lowest syntactic categories (noun, verb, adjective, and so on) while "nonlexical idioms" belong to higher syntactic categories (phrases, clauses, and sentences). Nouns like *tele+phone* and *photo+graph* are examples of the former type; (6) is an example of the latter.

The treatment of lexical idioms is handled unproblematically on the present conception of the lexicon. These idioms are entered in the lexicon in exactly the same manner as ordinary single morphemes like *run*, *book*, *big*, *and*, and *fast*. Thus, (8) illustrates such an entry:

(8) (*phono+graph* [+N, +Common, ...])

Lexical idioms can be inserted into derivations as a unit by the same lexical substitution rule that permits other lexical items to be plugged into a line of a derivation provided the syntactic features of the item are compatible with those that mark the substitution position. Hence, unlike cases of unidiomatic words like *un+safe*, *re+sell*, and *de+bug*, where the readings are the result of the projection rule operating on the readings of their component morphemes,[3] cases like *tele+phone* are marked as idioms by the fact that the dictionary assigns their readings to whole entries like (8) and these readings are then carried over into phrase markers by operations of lexical insertion.

There is something to be said for handling nonlexical idioms in the same manner, namely, by listing each in the lexicon as a single lexical item associated with a set of lexical readings to represent its senses. On this approach, an expression like (6), on its idiomatic sense, would be regarded as an intransitive verb, to be introduced into derivations by an operation of the lexical insertion rule. Its lexicon entry would then have the form (9):

(9) (*kick+the+bucket* [+V, —____NP, ...])

The advantages of this approach are clear. First, it is simple and natural to have both kinds of idioms handled in the same way. Second, this treatment automatically precludes an item from receiving a compositionally formed reading to represent its

---

[2] For example, Chafe (1968, p. 115) fails to represent correctly the position we took in Katz and Postal (1963) when he claims that we hold that the deep structure of an idiom and its compositional counterpart are identical. Moreover, from our admission of the speculative nature of our suggestion that ill-formed idioms be handled as part of the grammar's account of semi-sentences, Chafe leapt to the conclusion that our theory "does not accommodate idioms whose structure would not be generated . . . by the syntactic component." Finally, he confuses performance and competence when he claims that the inadequacy of our account is shown by the fact (if it is one) that "the interpretation of a particular deep structure as an idiom should happen typically so much more often than the literal interpretation."

[3] See Katz (1972), where the antonymy rules required as the lexicon-dictionary entry for *un-* and *de-* are given (Chapter 4), as well as the lexicon-dictionary entry for *re-* (Chapter 7).

idiomatic sense: (9) accords (6) no internal syntactic structure. Third, this absence of internal syntactic structure correctly predicts that transformations of the kind that apply to the nonidiomatic occurrence of an expression—for example, the passive and relative clause transformations—do not apply to the idiomatic occurrence. Accordingly, we obtain an exceedingly simple explanation of the fact that sentences like (10) and (11) are not ambiguous in the way that a sentence like (12) is:

(10) The bucket was kicked by Ruth
(11) Ruth kicked the leaky old bucket
(12) John kicked the bucket

But this way of handling nonlexical idioms is not adequate. Although for semantic purposes nonlexical idioms should not have an internal phrase structure insofar as this structure does not play a role in the representation of their meaning, there are both phonological and syntactic reasons for such idioms having internal syntactic structure. On the phonological side, the rules that assign a stress pattern to English sentences require information about surface syntactic form in order to assign stress (see Chomsky (1967), for example), and since the stress patterns of idiomatic constituents follow the same regularities as those of nonidiomatic ones, nonlexical idioms must be represented as having the customary constituent structure breakdown in order for them to be assigned their proper phonetic shape. On the syntactic side, consider cases like (13)-(14), (15)-(16), (17)-(18):

(13) Jane laid down the law to Bill
(14) Jane's laying down the law to Bill
(15) The fighter threw in the towel
(16) The fighter threw the towel in
(17) I caught even worse hell from them than you did
(18) I caught hell from them even worse than you did

Such pairs show that some of the syntactic parts of an idiomatic stretch must be separated and labeled with their proper syntactic markers since transformational operations can be performed on them. It is clear that the nominalization transformation treats the verb in (13) and (14) in just the way that it does in ordinary, nonidiomatic constructions. The particle movement transformation in (15) and (16) requires that the particle and the noun phrase be distinguished from the other elements of the idiomatic stretch and be marked as such, again as in nonidiomatic constructions of the same form. Thus, representations such as (9) that analyze an idiom like *kick + the + bucket* as an intransitive verb, with no further syntactic decomposition and classification, cannot be adequate, whatever their prima facie advantages in simplicity and naturalness.

These considerations show that nonlexical idioms cannot receive the same treatment as lexical idioms, that is, they cannot be regarded as members of one or another of the lowest level major categories in syntax with *no* internal syntactic structure. The obvious compromise, then, is to develop a treatment on which these idioms receive as much syntactic structure as is required to permit both the relevant transformational development and the assignment of the proper phonological representation and yet not so much structure that inappropriate transformational development can be defined for them.

Our conception of the knowledge that speakers have of the distribution of idioms is that it is parasitic on knowledge of the behavior of nonidiomatic forms of corresponding syntactic structure. Each idiom thus corresponds structurally to some regular syntactic type in the language, as illustrated in (19):

(19) (a) N–N   paddy wagon, frogman, joy stick, Bronx cheer, good-time Charlie
     (b) A–N   blue movie, red herring
     (c) A–N–N   wild-goose chase
     (d) V–NP   chew the rag, kick the bucket, give a damn
     (e) V–Prt   look up, dump on, clam up
     (f) V–NP–Prep   make light of, give birth to, pay heed to, read the riot act to
     (g) V–Prt–NP   throw in the towel, lay down the law, blow off steam, turn back the clock
     (h) V___NP   rub___the wrong way
     (i) Neg–V___Prep–NP   don't know___from Adam
     (j) S   The fat is in the fire, You can't take it with you, Cat got your tongue?

Speakers determine where an idiom can occur in a sentence by treating the whole stretch as a construction of the same syntactic type as the nonidiomatic expressions to which it corresponds structurally but marking its individual differences specially. The idiomatic forms listed in (19), considered as whole constructions without regard to their internal structure (that is, (a), (b), and (c) considered as nouns, (d) as verb phrases, and so on), typically behave like regular, nonidiomatic constructions of the same syntactic type. For example, the form *blue movie* generally behaves like any noun in that it occurs in frames such as (20) that accept nouns and does not occur in frames such as (21) that do not:[4]

(20) We saw the ____ that titillated you
(21) The child hit and ____ the dog

But, when behavior turns on aspects of their internal structure, nonlexical idioms show their true colors. Often they do not undergo transformational development in cases where a constituent is required to be analyzable into subconstituents in restricted ways. Take, for example, (22):

(22) My neighbor does not like blue French movies

This sentence does not have a sense in which the movies my neighbor does not like are pornographic ones coming from France (or in the French style).

Furthermore, most of the internal structure of a nonlexical idiom is sealed off from the application of transformations. Of course, most idioms undergo some transformations, and some undergo many. But within the structure of a nonlexical idiom, more structure is sealed off than is open to transformational development. Also, idioms of roughly the same surface form can differ in terms of whether the same transformation applies to the same aspect of their common structure.[5] Compare (23) and (24), which are unacceptable, with the perfectly satisfactory (25) and (26):

(23) *Work was knocked off by the laborers
(24) *A storm was danced up by the lady

---

[4] Note also *Jane kicked the bucket on Friday and was buried on Saturday, John saw a purple paddy wagon, Don't clam up when you are asked about it, Who will pay heed to her?* and so on.

[5] I am indebted to B. Fraser for this point and for general discussion of the material in this paper.

(25) The law was laid down by her father and mother
(26) The point was put across by the lawyer

Finally, the behavior of the subconstituents of nonlexical idioms seems not to exhibit any genuine regularity with regard to openness to transformational operations: the transformational future of such subconstituents seems to be determined by some inherent properties rather than by their syntactic relations with other subconstituents.

Given these observations and also the desire to minimize the difference between the treatment of lexical and nonlexical idioms, we require apparatus for generating idiomatic stretches that handles the refractoriness of a subconstituent of a nonlexical idiom to transformational development as an idiosyncratic property of that subconstituent. This requirement indicates that we should treat this case in the same way that we treat other idiosyncratic properties of lexical classification, that is, by introducing a new syntactic feature, namely, [±Idiom].

This addition requires an extension of the present notion of a lexicon entry, although not a very radical one, and also a new clause to the lexical insertion rule. The extension is presented in (27), where X_i, $1 \leq i \leq n$, is the ith morpheme of the phrase idiom and the brackets to the right of X_i contain the feature specification required for the morpheme X_i, including [+Idiom] or [−Idiom], and the more expansive brackets under $X_i[\ ]$, $X_{i+1}[\ ]$, ..., $X_{i+k}[\ ]$, $k \leq n$, contain the feature specification required for the string of morphemes $X_i + X_{i+1} + \ldots + X_{i+k}$:

$$
(27) \quad \begin{pmatrix} X_1[\ ], X_2[\ ], \ldots, X_n[\ ] \\ \vdots \\ [\qquad\quad [\qquad\quad] \\ [\qquad\qquad\qquad] \end{pmatrix}
$$

The number of "levels" in such an entry corresponds roughly to the amount of internal syntactic structure of the nonlexical idiom. Thus, (27) can be regarded as the general form of lexicon entries, with ordinary lexical items and lexical idioms constituting the case where $n = 1$. In cases where $n > 1$, we allow that some X_is (but not all) can be, instead of morphemes, symbols of the nonterminal syntactic vocabulary to which syntactic rules can apply. This will permit us to handle discontinuous nonlexical idioms.

As in the case of lexicon entries of the sort found in Chomsky (1965), the entries for nonlexical idioms are inserted into derivations on the basis of Chomsky's nondistinctness condition.[6] But in the case of lexicon entries having the form of (27), lexical insertion involves successive substitutions of the morphemes $X_1, X_2, \ldots, X_n$ for the sequence of occurrences of Δ under a single node. The syntactic symbols appearing within brackets of one kind or another in a lexicon entry of the form (27) express a condition on some subconfiguration in phrase markers.[7] The symbols inside

---

[6] See Chomsky (1965, section 2.3.2).

[7] I will assume that such syntactic symbols are syntactic features, which means taking the symbols appearing as node labels in phrase markers to be syntactic features. This has already been proposed by Chomsky (1970b, pp. 207–208). Thus, instead of interpreting a substring of the terminal string of an underlying phrase marker that is fully dominated by a node labeled X as belonging to the syntactic class of Xs, it is now interpreted as having the syntactic property specified by the feature [X]. Chomsky points out that this extension of the feature interpretation has the advantage of eliminating the need for ad hoc rules of the form N = [+N], V = [+V] which identify class symbols with the feature symbols corresponding to them. The advantage here is that in this system it is natural to have two or more syntactic symbols appearing as labels of a single nonterminal node in a phrase marker. The need for this will become clear as we proceed.

a pair of brackets to the right of X_i in the first row specify the nondistinctness condition for syntactic features associated with the ith occurrence of Δ in the sequence, and the symbols inside a pair of brackets that properly span $X_{n-r}[\ ],\ldots, X_{n-1}[\ ]$, $X_n[\ ]$ specify the nondistinctness condition for syntactic features associated with the node that fully dominates the subsequence of Δs which the morphemes $X_{n-r},\ldots, X_{n-1}, X_n$ are to replace, respectively.

Let us consider an example. Suppose that (28) is a subconfiguration in an underlying phrase marker:

(28)

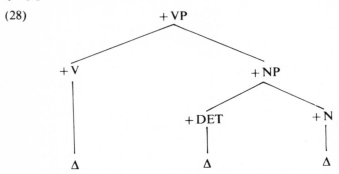

Suppose also that (29) is an entry in the lexicon:

(29) $\begin{pmatrix} kick\ [+\text{V},\ +\text{Idiom}],\ the\ [+\text{Det},\ +\text{Idiom}],\ bucket\ [+\text{N},\ +\text{Idiom}] \\ \qquad\qquad\qquad [+\text{NP},\ +\text{Idiom},\ldots \\ [+\text{VP},\ldots \end{pmatrix}$

We can insert the morphemes *kick*, *the*, and *bucket* sequentially as terminal elements of (28) since the various compatibility conditions in (29) on the nodes in (28) are satisfied.

As mentioned, we also require a new clause for the lexical insertion rule. The function of this clause will be to assign syntactic features, particularly [+Idiom], from some pair of brackets in any lower row of a lexicon entry (of the form (27)) to the node of the phrase marker that fully dominates the sequence of Δs that is determined by the syntactic information in the part of the first row that this pair of brackets spans in the lexicon entry. With the addition of such a clause, the lexical insertion rule will not only replace occurrences of Δ by morphemes but will also assign further syntactic features to the higher nodes of phrase markers.

On the basis of (28), (29), and this new clause, we get (30):

(30)

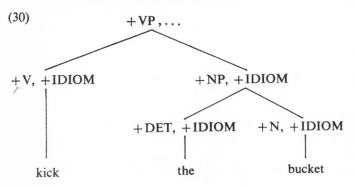

We must now introduce a general convention on transformations. Roughly, this convention says that a transformation does not apply to a phrase marker if the structural change of the transformation specifies a formal operation on a component of the substring that is marked [+Idiom], regardless of the fact that it otherwise satisfies the structural analysis of the transformation. This convention, together with the lexical insertion rule amended by the addition of the new clause for entries of the form (27), provides the simplest compromise between the demand of the phonological component that *all* the internal structure of an idiomatic stretch be represented and the demand of the transformational component that only *some* of the structure be available to transformations. The scheme represents a nonlexical idiom as having all of the structure in the syntactic construction type to which it corresponds (see (19)) by virtue of the fact that nonlexical idioms are inserted into the same configurations of symbols in phrase markers into which any regular expressions of the same type are inserted. On the other hand, the new clause and convention will seal off those aspects of the internal structure of a nonlexical idiom that cannot be open to transformational development by appropriately distributing the occurrences of [+Idiom].

The demands of the semantic component are met by virtue of the fact that lexicon entries are the objects that are associated with sets of lexical readings in the dictionary. Thus a lexicon entry of the form (27) receives a set of lexical readings as a whole. These are then assigned to the node represented by the syntactic symbols in the lowest row when the morphemes are substituted for occurrences of Δ. Accordingly, there are no lexical readings associated with the morphemic components of a nonlexical idiom and thus nothing for the projection rule to combine with to incorrectly obtain a compositional reading of the stretch. But there is a reading for the whole nonlexical idiom and therefore something for the projection rule to use in obtaining derived readings for constituents of the sentence of which the idiom is a part.

Clearly, the scheme works for the cases discussed so far. Neither the passive transformation nor the relative clause transformation will apply to an expression like (6) which is represented as a nonlexical idiom; therefore, such expressions in sentences like (10) and (11) will not bear their idiomatic sense. A sentence like (12), of course, will be ambiguous between the sense that John booted some bucket and the sense that John died because it will have two derivations in the grammar, each determining different semantic interpretations. The proposal is also flexible enough to represent the deep syntactic structure of cases like (13)–(18) in such a way that they can be generated without at the same time allowing sentences like (31):

(31) (a) *It is the law that Jane laid down to Bill
     (b) *In the towel, the fighter threw

Moreover, our scheme can easily represent the deep structures of (32) so that (23) and (24) are ruled out but (25) and (26) are permitted:

(32) (a) They knocked off work
     (b) He danced up a storm
     (c) She laid down the law
     (d) They put the point across

Let us look at the case of (25). Such a sentence can be derived by an application of the passive transformation to an underlying phrase marker in which the NP *the law* in the idiom *lay down the law* is not itself marked [+Idiom]. Thus, we require something like (33) as a lexicon entry for *lay down the law*:

(33)
$$\begin{pmatrix} lay[+V, +\text{Idiom}], down[+\text{Prep}, -\text{Idiom}], & the[+\text{Det}, +\text{Idiom}], law[+N, +\text{Idiom}] \\ & [+\text{NP}, -\text{Idiom}, \ldots &] \\ [+V, +\text{Idiom}, \ldots &] \\ [+\text{VP}, -\text{Idiom}, \ldots &] \end{pmatrix}$$

A type of case we have not yet discussed is one that allows the recursive development of constituents having readings inside a nonlexical idiom, as in (34):

(34)

Bill rubs $\begin{Bmatrix} \text{the unfriendly policeman} \\ \text{Sue and Mary and Tom} \\ \text{everyone whom we like} \\ \text{several of us in the class} \end{Bmatrix}$ the wrong way

Such cases can be accommodated easily in our scheme by lexicon entries such as (35), where the blank in the first row indicates the position in the preterminal string of a phrase marker around which the components *rub* and *the wrong way* of this nonlexical idiom are inserted:[8]

(35) $\begin{pmatrix} rub[+V, +\text{Idiom}], \underline{\quad}[+\text{NP}, -\text{Idiom}], the+wrong+way\,[+\text{Adv}, +\text{Idiom}] \\ [+\text{VP}, -\text{Idiom}, \ldots &] \end{pmatrix}$

On the basis of such a lexicon entry, a sentence like (36) has an underlying phrase marker like (37):

(36) The child rubs the teacher the wrong way

(37)

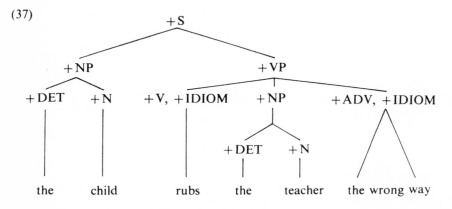

Thus, the lexicon of the syntactic component contains, besides lexicon entries of the familiar type for single morphemes, entries for lexical and nonlexical idioms. Entries for lexical idioms represent the idioms as strings of morphemes with no internal constituent structure, while entries for nonlexical idioms represent them as having

---

[8] We do not require that the constituent occurring between the components of such an idiom itself be either an idiom or a nonidiom since the requirement expressed by [+NP, −Idiom] is met by idiomatic noun phrases like *grease monkeys*. As a whole NP this expression is marked [−Idiom], and thus a sentence like *Our crowd rubs grease monkeys the wrong way* will be generated. Note also that the example in the text is not intended to exclude other requirements on such noun phrases as [+Human].

internal constituent structure. The former type is illustrated by (8) and the latter by (29). In both cases, however, the dictionary entry for the item consists of the lexicon entry together with (that is, associated with) a set of lexical readings representing the senses of the item as a whole. The lexical insertion rule substitutes the whole lexical idiom for a single occurrence of Δ and assigns the set of lexical readings associated with the lexicon entry (in the dictionary) to the occurrence of this lexical idiom as a terminal element of an underlying phrase marker. The rule substitutes the parts of a phrase idiom for different occurrences of Δ and assigns the set of lexical readings associated with the lexicon entry to the node of the phrase marker dominating the entire idiomatic stretch. The projection rule, operating on these lexical readings and the others assigned to the other lexical items, will form and assign derived readings as an account of the compositional structure of the sentence represented by the phrase marker.[9]

This is the account of idioms criticized in Fraser (1970). But Fraser's criticisms do not apply to my theory because he confuses it with Weinreich's. Fraser says that "the sense of the suggestion" in Weinreich (1969) and in Katz (1968)[10] is that idioms be marked to exclude each transformation that does not apply to it (p. 34): ". . . I do not want to suggest that the way we should characterize idioms is to mark each with a set of features designating which operations it will not permit. This is but a terminological hedge from the suggestion of Katz discussed earlier" (p. 39). Thus, on this account of my theory, the idiomatic stretch *blow off steam* would be lexically marked as [− Particle Movement, − Passive, − Action Nominalization] to prevent the generation of strings like (38):

(38) *I blew some steam off the other day

Fraser's account falsely represents my theory, which marks *components* of idiomatic stretches with *a* feature that prevents them from satisfying the structural analysis of a range of transformations, as a theory that marks each *whole* idiomatic stretch with many, perhaps even a huge number of, *different* features. Clearly, the two theories not only offer different solutions to specific problems, but Weinreich's, unlike mine, adds a great number of new symbols to syntactic theory, which constitutes a proliferation intolerable by common standards of simplicity.

Fraser (1970) refers to two "serious objections" against my account of idioms,

---

[9] The projection rule—see Katz (1972, (3.86))—combines the readings of idiomatic and non-idiomatic constituents of sentences in accord with the situation accounted for in (3.86c) case (i) or case (ii). A sentence like (12) illustrates the former situation. Assuming the idiom *kick the bucket* has a lexicon entry something like (29) and this entry is paired with a lexical reading representing the sense of "die" in the dictionary entry for the idiom, the projection rule (3.86) will assign this reading to the VP node of a phrase marker. Now, this assignment and an assignment of a reading(s) to the NP node dominating the subject provide the instances of an R_j assigned to N_j and an R_i assigned to N_i (the S node being the instance of N). A sentence like (36) illustrates the latter situation. A lexical reading representing the sense of "annoys" (from the dictionary entry) will be assigned to the VP node of a phrase marker like (37). This assignment and an assignment of a reading to the NP node dominating the direct object provide instances of an R_i assigned to an N and an R_j assigned to an N_j. In each of these situations, the projection rule will substitute the reading of the NP as the value of the appropriate categorized variable appearing in the reading of the VP if the selection restriction governing the substitution is satisfied.

[10] Here we have a case of a criticism appearing prior to the paper to which it is addressed. The discussion Fraser refers to as "(Katz 1968)" is actually an early version of the present paper, which was not published until now because it was part of a work whose publication was delayed.

but the reader finds only one, which alleges that my account conflicts with the notion of an ungoverned rule. Fraser informs me (personal communication) that somehow the paragraph expressing the second objection was not included in the published article. The missing objection, as it appears in the original manuscript, runs as follows:

> [if we mark] the noun phrase [of *blow off steam*] for the passive transformation, the verb for the action nominalization, what is to be marked with the feature Idiom for the gerundive nominalization? And what if there is a fifth transformation which is applicable? I cannot find one but the point is clear: the use of a single feature may possibly run into difficulty if the number of constituents in an idiom is smaller than the number of transformations which are applicable.

This criticism is mistaken because it assumes that each occurrence of [+Idiom] assigned to a constituent of an idiom marks that idiom for a single transformation. But this is not so. The convention governing the applicability of a transformation to an idiom is that the transformation does not apply if its structural change specifies an operation for a constituent (picked out by the structural index) that has [+Idiom] assigned to it. Thus, the same assignment of [+Idiom] to a constituent of an idiom can preclude the application of many transformations, meaning that the number of constituents in the idiom does not limit the number of transformations that can be prevented from operating on its constituents.

We now turn to Fraser's objection that my account of idioms conflicts with Lakoff's conception of "governed" and "ungoverned" rules. The claim seems to be that a transformation like Particle Movement (39) does not apply to *blow off some steam* but does apply to *make up one's mind* and *lay down the law*, which are identical in syntactic structure:

(39) $X–V–Prt–NP–Y \rightarrow 1\ 3\ 2\ 4$ (optional)
      $\underbrace{1}\quad 2\quad 3\quad 4$

This fact, however, can be turned against Fraser's criticism: it can be used as evidence against his assumption that these cases have the same syntactic structure. We can say that the fact that (38) is ungrammatical but *make one's mind up* and *lay the law down* are not has exactly the same significance as the fact that *To please Jones is eager* is ungrammatical but *To please Jones is easy* is not, namely, that although the cases are very similar at the level of surface structure, their deep syntactic structures are somehow different in a relevant way. Moreover, the account given here can easily handle such a difference. The idiom in (38) would be entered in the lexicon-dictionary with [+Idiom] assigned to the particle *off*, while the particles *up* and *down* in the other cases would be entered without this feature. Given our convention that a transformation cannot apply if the constituent for which its structural change specifies an operation is marked [+Idiom], plus the fact that the structural change in (39) specifies an operation on the particle of an expression, then rule (39) will not apply to *blow off some steam*, whose particle is marked [+Idiom], but will apply to both *make up one's mind* and *lay down the law*.

If this account does indeed work, we will not need systems such as Lakoff's, in which a constituent must be specially marked for the transformations it does not undergo, or systems such as Fraser's, in which a constituent is marked for its position on a frozenness hierarchy whose levels are defined in terms of operations on phrase markers, again, to prevent the application of transformations that otherwise would apply. Such systems, as I have indicated, unnecessarily proliferate symbols by introducing particular features referring to particular transformations or transformational operations. Thus, one advantage of our account is simplicity. Another is that assignment of the feature [+Idiom] says no more than that at certain points departures from regularity occur. It does not say that different regularities have their own special kind of departure, as the other proposals do. The counterpart of our account in other sciences is quite reasonable; it amounts to the case of specifying certain behavior as unlawlike. The counterpart of Lakoff's system is outlandish; it would be a case where we were asked to accept "not behaving in accord with Archimedes' law" as a legitimate hydrodynamical property of substances. Thus, one applauds Fraser's discussion of the cases where Lakoff's distinction is vacuous. It must be counted as one of the virtues of the account given here that it extends Fraser's vacuity criticism to the cases (particle movement, gerundive nominalization, prepositional preposing transformations, and so on) where Fraser himself conjectures that Lakoff's proposal (or something similar) might be necessary.

Even though our account of idioms is far simpler and more natural than Weinreich's, Lakoff's, or Fraser's (Fraser's account will require fewer features than the others but will still need a feature for each rank in the frozenness hierarchy, not to mention an otherwise unmotivated hierarchy of transformational operations), it is empirical and subject to counterexamples. For our account, counterexamples take the form of a pair of transformations T_i and T_j and an idiom I such that T_i has to apply to I by virtue of an operation on one of I's constituents, C, but C has to be marked with the feature [+Idiom] to prevent T_j from applying to I. Although I have looked for such a counterexample and have not found one, this could be due simply to the unclarity of the situation: intuitions in this area are not firm, and there is not enough certainty about the way many transformations are stated.[11]

To conclude this section, I propose in (40) a new definition for the semantic relation "*s* is an idiomatic sense of the constituent C," one based on the account of idioms just presented:

(40) *s* is an idiomatic sense of C in the sentence S (the reading *r* represents an idiomatic sense *s* of C in S) if and only if the semantically interpreted underlying phrase marker of S is such that *r* is assigned to C and C dominates a string of terminal elements representing the constituents $c_1, \ldots, c_n$ and each lacks a reading except for any c_i, $2 \le i \le n-1$, that does not come from the same lexicon entry from which c_1 and c_n come[12]

3. CHOMSKY'S PROBLEM

The second problem relating to compositionality that we want to take up here was suggested by Chomsky.[13] It takes the form of an apparent counterexample to the assumption that any nonidiomatic expression or sentence in a natural language is

[11] Fraser's paper offers some evidence against there being such a counterexample since his fairly systematic survey of the varieties of idioms does not reveal one.

[12] Note that the *except* clause at the end of this definition is included to avoid the obvious difficulties in connection with idiomatic stretches that are discontinuous in the way that *rub the wrong way* is.

[13] Chomsky posed this problem in a lecture and it is now in print in Chomsky (1972, pp. 186–188).

compositional in the sense of principles like (2) and (7). The cases in point are presented in (41) and (42):

(41) John has not been here for a week, but Bill has

(42) John has not been here for a week, but Bill has been here for a week

Chomsky (1972, p. 187) claims that the "natural" way to account for sentences like (41) and (42) is to assume that they are ". . . not formed by deletion operations, and that 'compositional semantics' must be abandoned (or at least restricted), with semantic interpretation in such cases . . . constructed along lines that have been explored by Jackendoff and Akmajian." Chomsky is here claiming both that we must give up syntactic deletion in such cases and that we must adopt Jackendoff and Akmajian's development of his own theory that aspects of semantic interpretation are determined on the basis of information from surface structure.[14] (In the sentence immediately following this quotation Chomsky says "There are other examples that suggest that rather complex aspects of semantic representation must be constructed from surface structure.")

In this section I will argue that Chomsky is mistaken in claiming that the natural solution requires both giving up the use of deletion in connection with these examples *and* adopting the extended standard theory. Either will take care of the problem. In fact, these two moves are rival ways of handling these examples without abandoning compositional semantics. I will argue that the former provides a quite satisfactory solution without lending any support whatever to the extended standard theory.

Both (41) and (42) say the same thing, make the same assertion, about the referent of *John*, namely, that he has been absent from the place in question during the entire week. However, they say *different* things about Bill. Sentence (41) says that Bill was present at the location in question at some time during the week interval, whereas (42) says that he has been present at the location throughout the entire week interval. Accordingly, (41) and (42) differ in meaning. On the basis of principles like (2) and (7), the meaning of any nonidiomatic construction is a function of the meanings of its lexical items and its grammatical relations. From this it follows that constructions having the same lexical items and the same grammatical relations (between the lexical items and the constituents they form) are the same in meaning. Now, neither (41) nor (42) is an idiom, and both have the same lexical items and grammatical relations. Principles like (2) and (7), then, imply that (41) is synonymous with (42). But since we know the two sentences differ in meaning, such principles must be false.

Another form of this argument might be thought to support the claim of Chomsky, Jackendoff, and others that surface structure plays a role in supplying syntactic information required by the semantic component to assign semantic interpretations. On this version of the argument, we are able to preserve the assumption that natural languages are compositional in the sense of (2) and (7) by saying that the underlying phrase markers of a sentence are not the only syntactic objects that supply information

---

[14] See, for example, Chomsky (1970a). In Katz (1972, Chapter 8, Section 3), I offer counterarguments to Chomsky's position in Chomsky (1970a).

required for semantic interpretation.[15] If this is so, the first argument turns out to be unsound because its premise that (41) and (42) have the same lexical items and grammatical relations is false. If surface phrase marker information enters into the range of syntactic information that the semantic component utilizes, then some of the syntactic relations in (41) and (42) are different.

As an account favoring the relevance of surface structure information to semantic interpretation, the argument runs as follows. Since (41) and (42) differ in meaning, we must account for the difference on the basis of their having either different underlying phrase markers or different transformational histories (that is, different surface phrase markers). Insofar as (41) is derived from the same underlying phrase marker as (42), the only difference in their transformational histories being the deletion transformation that produces the ellipsis in (41), we must account for the difference in their senses on the basis of their different transformational histories. Otherwise, we will falsely predict that they are synonymous. Consequently, the assignment of their semantic interpretations makes use of information from their surface phrase markers (or some derived phrase markers), and we cannot restrict semantic interpretation to the underlying phrase markers.

The adequacy of this line of argument as a way out of Chomsky's problem is only as good as the explanation it offers of the difference in meaning between (41) and (42), and actually it explains very little.

The arguments cited by Chomsky in support of his claim about the relevance of surface structure to semantic interpretation indicate how transformations might change syntactic relations in underlying phrase markers, thereby producing different relations in the surface phrase marker mapped onto them. The plausibility of these arguments comes in part from the fact that such surface structure relations seem to satisfy the antecedently specified requirements of the semantic component on underlying phrase markers. But the purported explanation of the difference in meaning between (41) and (42) refers merely to an absence of surface constituents. It remains a mystery as to how this difference in meaning is explained by the fact that the surface structure of one sentence does contain a realization of some of their common underlying constituents while the surface structure of the other does not contain this same realization.

Therefore, let us suggest another way out of Chomsky's problem. We submit that the vulnerable premiss of the argument against compositionality is the assumption that cases of ellipsis like (41) come from transformational operations of deletion on the same phrase marker underlying a sentence like (42). I suggest that what is wrong with this assumption is that it rests on the view that the proper account of such cases is in terms of operations of deletion performed by rules of the transformational component. This view is not indispensable, and, as we shall see, once questioned it turns out to be weak.

The alternative is to allow the lexical substitution rule of the base to have the option of not introducing certain morphemic elements, namely, those that on the received view are transformationally erased if they are identical to another constituent at some fixed position in the terminal string of the same phrase marker. We allow the lexical substitution rule to omit the substitution of certain morphemes under major categories, thereby leaving occurrences of Δ to be carried down from the

---

[15] This challenges the thesis of Katz and Postal (1964) that transformations make no contribution to semantic representation.

preterminal to the terminal string. Underlying phrase markers will thus have some "empty terminal nodes" or "gaps" in their terminal strings.[16] These, however, will exist only in the exact same conditions of constituent identity as those where the erasure transformation applies in the present transformational account of ellipsis.[17]

This alternative requires a simple supplement to the projection rule machinery of semantic theory. We will call this supplement the "interpolation rule" and state it informally as in (43):

(43) Whenever lexical insertion has taken the option of leaving a string of Δs under a node α by virtue of an identity with a configuration under another node β (that is, whenever a "gap" has been left in the terminal string of lexical items so that no lexical readings have been assigned to lexical items in this "unfilled" portion of the string), each derived reading that can be formed from the set of readings assigned to β and the sets of readings assigned to the constituent(s) under the next higher node above α is assigned to this next higher node

On our alternative to the explanation of ellipsis in terms of transformational deletion, a sentence like (44) will have an underlying phrase marker like (45):

(44) Jane is smarter than Ruth

(45)

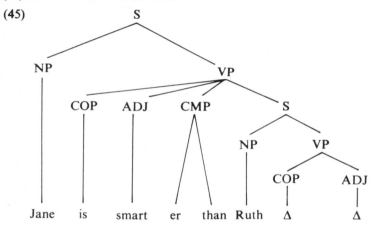

On the basis of the interpolation rule (43), the S node of the embedded sentence structure in (45) will receive a set of derived readings formed from (*a*) the readings assigned to the subject NP *Ruth* and (*b*) those readings that can be formed by the projection rule from the readings assigned to *is* and *smart* from the dictionary. This will explain why (44) means that Jane's intelligence exceeds Ruth's intelligence, rather than, say, her kindness.

We can now explain the semantic difference between (41) and (42) without appealing to surface structure interpretation or giving up compositionality. On our alternative, (41) is *not* derived from the same phrase marker as (42) by an erasure transformation which deletes the verb phrase of the second clause. Rather, (41) and (42) have different underlying phrase markers. The common structure of these phrase markers is shown in (46):

[16] The idea of employing empty terminal nodes seems to have occurred to a number of people at about the same period in the late sixties, who subsequently made different applications of it in their work, in particular, Jackendoff and Akmajian. I wish to thank them both for discussions of this topic.

[17] See Chomsky (1965, Chapter 3).

(46)

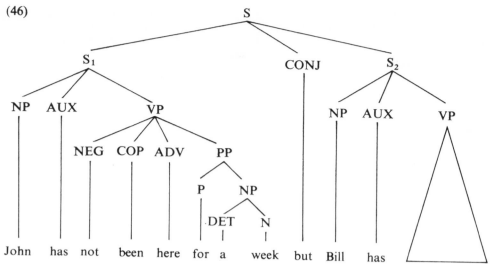

John has not been here for a week but Bill has

In the underlying phrase marker for (42), the verb phrase of the second clause is the same as the verb phrase of the first. But in the underlying phrase marker for (41), the verb phrase of the second clause has the form shown in (47). Note also that, in a full representation, syntactic features would be assigned to each occurrence of Δ in (47) just as they would be in (46) to permit proper lexical insertion. Such bundles of syntactic features determine an "identity" like that of Δ below N in (47), for example, and the noun *week* in (46); this is the basis for the assignment of the lexical reading of *week* to the Δ below N in (47).

(47)

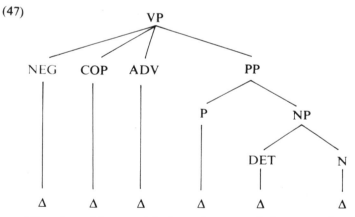

There is nothing special about the semantic interpretation of either clause of (42). Application of the dictionary and projection rule to the underlying phrase marker of (42) will represent the sense of the first clause as, roughly, (48) and the sense of the second clause as, roughly, (49):

(48) $\sim (\exists x)$ (x is a time in the specified week interval & John is at the specified location at x)

(49) (x) (x is a time in the specified week interval & Bill is at the specified location at x)

Similarly, there is nothing out of the ordinary about the semantic interpretation of the first clause of (41). Its sense will also be represented by a reading carrying the information in (48). What needs to be explained is how the second clause of (41) will receive a reading carrying the information in (50):

(50) $(\exists x)$ (x is a time in the specified week interval & Bill is at the specified location at x)

We may assume that the grammatical structure of the verb phrase of the first clause in (41), together with the dictionary and projection rule, determine the assignment of a reading to this verb phrase representing the one-place predicate (51):

(51) $\sim (\exists x)$ (x is a time in the specified week interval & y is at the specified location at x)

Let the reading representing (51) take the form (52), where the antonymy operator A/ expresses the negation, the predicate φ expresses "$(\exists x)$ (x is a time in the specified week interval & ____ is at the specified location at x)," and $X \begin{smallmatrix} [\text{NP, S}] \\ \langle \ \rangle \end{smallmatrix}$ expresses the variable "y":[18]

(52) $A/\left(\begin{smallmatrix} & [\text{NP, S}] \\ \varphi & X \\ & \langle \ \rangle \end{smallmatrix} \right)$

In this notation, the reading representing (48), the reading of the first clause of (41), is (53), where "(John)" expresses the individual constant *John*:

(53) $A/(\varphi(\text{John}))$

We will let the reading of the conjunction in (46) be (54), where "(&)" expresses logical conjunction and the conditions stated within angles under categorized variables express the selection restriction that the senses of the verb phrases conjoined exhibit a negative or antonymic contrast:

(54) $\begin{matrix} [\text{S}_1, \text{S}] \\ X \\ \langle R_{[\text{VP},\text{S}_1, \text{S}]} = \Phi \rangle \end{matrix}$ (&) $\begin{matrix} [\text{S}_2, \text{S}] \\ X \\ \langle R_{[\text{VP}, \text{S}_2, \text{S}]} = A/\Phi \rangle \end{matrix}$

This last aspect is independently motivated insofar as it is needed in order to handle the semantically deviant and the meaningful cases in paradigms like (55), (56), (57), and (58):[19]

(55)
   She is smart but he is $\left\{ \begin{matrix} \text{dumb} \\ \text{unintelligent} \\ \text{not (smart)} \end{matrix} \right\}$

(56) *She is smart but he is $\left\{ \begin{matrix} \text{smart} \\ \text{intelligent} \end{matrix} \right\}$

---

[18] Categorized variables such as the one used to express y first appeared in Katz (1967a) and were first used in this form in Katz (1972). They function as substitution symbols in semantic representation, marking the place at which one reading can be embedded (by the projection rule) within another. The grammatical function over the X determines the constituent whose readings can substitute for the variable if they satisfy the selection restriction which appears within angles under X.

[19] See Katz (1967b, pp. 47–51).

(57) She is not smart but he is (smart)

(58) *She is not smart but he is $\begin{Bmatrix} \text{unintelligent} \\ \text{not (smart)} \end{Bmatrix}$

Now, the reading (59) is assigned to the S node of the second sentence structure in the underlying phrase marker for (41) by the projection rule, in particular, the new clause (43):

(59) A/(φ(Bill))

Since the verb phrase structure of the second sentence structure has the form (47), this constituent has no reading to either satisfy or not satisfy the selection restriction on the second conjunct in (54). In this case the projection rule, by virtue of the clause in the definition of "categorized variable" that replaces the semantic marker "(Selector),"[20] provides the semantic markers that the selection restriction requires as the condition for substitution as the value of the variable. This is to say, the value of the variable is (60), since Φ is (52):

(60)
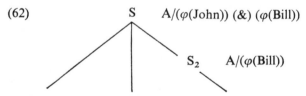
$$\text{A/A/} \begin{pmatrix} [\text{NP, S}] \\ \varphi \quad X \\ \langle \ \rangle \end{pmatrix}$$

The variable in (60) is replaced by the reading of the subject NP *Bill*, and the antonymy rule A/A/$\gamma = \gamma$[21] converts the result into (61):

(61) (φ(Bill))

Therefore we obtain appropriate readings for both of the sentence nodes in question, as shown in (62):

(62)   S   A/(φ(John)) (&) (φ(Bill))

                  S$_2$ A/(φ(Bill))

Given our notational conventions, (61) expresses the sense of (50). Therefore, we obtain readings for the sentences in (41) and (42) that predict exactly the right difference in their meaning, namely, the same sense for their first clauses—that there has been no time during the week interval when John has been here—and different senses for their second clauses—that Bill has been here at some time during the week interval for the second clause of (41) and that Bill has been here for the entire week period for the second clause of (42). Moreover, this alternative neither conflicts with the thesis that the semantic structure of natural languages is compositional nor involves ad hoc appeals to properties of derived phrase markers or of transformational rules of the syntactic component. Finally, this alternative has the further advantage of simplicity: the standard transformational explanation of ellipsis introduces strings of

[20] See Katz and Postal (1964, section 4.2.4), where "(Selector)" is introduced and justified in terms of the conferred sense of pro-forms. That discussion provides some of the independent motivation for this mechanism that is required here. Further such motivation is given in Katz (1972), where "categorized variable" is defined to handle automatically the function for which "(Selector)" was introduced.

[21] See Katz (1966, p. 200).

morphemes as the constituents underlying an ellipsis only to have to erase them later, whereas our explanation does not introduce them at all.[22]

REFERENCES

Chafe, W. L. (1968), "Idiomaticity as an anomaly in the Chomskyan paradigm," *Foundations of Language, 4*, 109–127.
Chomsky, N. (1965), *Aspects of the Theory of Syntax*, Cambridge, Mass.: M.I.T. Press.
Chomsky, N. (1967), "The Formal Structure of Language," in E. H. Lenneberg, *Biological Foundations of Language*, New York: Wiley.
Chomsky, N. (1970a), "Deep Structure, Surface Structure, and Semantic Interpretation," in R. Jakobson and S. Kawamoto, eds., *Studies in General and Oriental Linguistics*, Tokyo: TEC Corporation for Language Research.
Chomsky, N. (1970b), "Remarks on Nominalization," in R. A. Jacobs and P. S. Rosenbaum, eds., *Readings in English Transformational Grammar*, Waltham, Mass.: Ginn.
Chomsky, N. (1972), *Studies on Semantics in Generative Grammar*, The Hague: Mouton.
Fraser, B. (1970), "Idioms within a transformational grammar," *Foundations of Language, 6*, 22–42.
Katz, J. J. (1966), *The Philosophy of Language*, New York: Harper & Row.
Katz, J. J. (1967a), "Recent issues in semantic theory," *Foundations of Language, 3*, 124–194.
Katz, J. J. (1967b), "Some remarks on Quine on analyticity," *The Journal of Philosophy, 64*, 36–52.
Katz, J. J. (1972), *Semantic Theory*, New York: Harper & Row.
Katz, J. J., and P. Postal (1963), "Semantic interpretation of idioms and sentences containing them," *Quarterly Progress Report of the Research Laboratory of Electronics, 70*, M.I.T., 275–282.
Katz, J. J., and P. Postal (1964), *An Integrated Theory of Linguistic Descriptions*, Cambridge, Mass.: M.I.T. Press.
Rosenbaum, P. S. (1967), *The Grammar of English Predicate Complement Constructions*, Cambridge, Mass.: M.I.T. Press.
Weinreich, U. (1969), "Problems in the Analysis of Idioms," in J. Puhvel, ed., *Substance and Structure of Language*, Berkeley: University of California Press.

[22] Note also that if there are transformations that erase constituents in such cases, then there also have to be ordering relations among them and other transformations. (See Rosenbaum (1967, pp. 49–52).) And if these transformations do not appear at all, then these ordering relations also need not appear. There are further advantages to our alternative in connection with pronominalization, but these will have to be left for other investigations.

wHERE EPISTEMOLOGY, STYLE, AND GRAMMAR MEET: A CASE STUDY FROM JAPANESE

S.-Y. Kuroda
University of California at San Diego

1. Bertrand Russell (1940, pp. 195 ff.), discussing language in a philosophical framework, concerns himself with the distinction and relation between two purposes that language serves, namely, (*a*) indicating facts, and (*b*) expressing the state of the speaker.[1] He points out that in some cases the distinction between (*a*) and (*b*) seems to be nonexistent. Thus, when I say "I am hot," "the fact indicated is a state of myself, and the very state that I express . . . " And "where, as in such cases, there is no distinction between [*a*] and [*b*], the problem of truth or falsehood does not arise . . ." Suppose, on the other hand, I say "You are hot" or "John is hot." I am now *expressing* my state and *indicating* yours or John's. Such a statement is "in one sense 'significant' if it can express a state of me; in what is perhaps another sense, it is 'significant' if it is true or false."

We have here one of the basic issues with which epistemology is concerned. From the linguistic point of view, we are not immediately concerned with how the philosopher might develop his theory of knowledge and how the fundamental epistemological issue just noted would be explained in his epistemological system. What draws the linguist's attention is the fact that adjectives like "hot" which express sensations or emotions of the subject are epistemologically quite different from other adjectives, in spite of the fact that they are all alike grammatically.[2] Thus, pairs of

---

[1] Russell also indicates a third purpose, that is, to alter the state of the hearer. This point is not directly related to our concern here.

[2] The adjective *hot*, however, is ambiguous in a certain sense. It may indicate either that the one to whom the subject refers feels hot or that that to which the subject refers has a high temperature that would or could cause someone to feel hot. The two readings are, of course, closely related, and many adjectives of this class are ambiguous in the same way: compare "I am sad," "This picture is sad." However, it is the first type of reading that will be relevant to our discussion.

sentences like "I am tall" and "John is tall" or "I am square" and "John is square" do not reveal the epistemological dichotomy noted in the preceding paragraph.

In Japanese certain words of sensation exist in pairs, one member of a pair being morphologically an adjective and the other a verb, and this morphological distinction corresponds exactly to the epistemological one indicated here. Thus, we have the adjective form *atui* in (1) but the verb form *atugatte* in (2) and (3):

(1)   *Watasi wa atui*
      'I am hot'
(2)   *Anata wa atugatte iru*[3]
      'You are hot'
(3)   *John wa atugatte iru*
      'John was hot'

And one cannot use *atui* with second or third person, as indicated in (4) and (5):[4]

(4)   **Anata wa atui*
(5)   **John wa atui*

On the other hand, the grammatical status of sentence forms such as (6), with a first person subject and the verb form, is somewhat subtle:

(6)   *Watasi wa atugatte iru*

The sentence sounds odd, perhaps because it implies a split ego—one is simultaneously the subject of a sensation and the objective observer of the subject of this sensation. However, the grammatical status of such sentences is not of principal concern in the present paper.

To cite some additional examples, parallel data are obtained with respect to *kanasii/kanasigaru* 'sad', *sabisii/sabisigaru* 'lonely', and also the past forms *atukatta/ atugatta* 'was/were hot'. In these cases too, then, the subjects of the sensation adjectives, as opposed to the corresponding sensation verbs, must be first person.[5]

2. These facts from Japanese are well known and are of considerable epistemological significance. A complete grammatical description of the sensation words, however, is by no means so simple a matter as the preceding sketch might imply. The grammatical features of these words are closely interrelated with other intricate features of the language. In particular, there are two kinds of complications that arise in the description of the sensation words.

In the first place, the restriction observed in the preceding section, namely, that sensation adjectives like *atui* may take only first person subjects, does not necessarily apply if the sentence forms occur, not by themselves as independent sentences, but as segments contained in a larger context. Thus, there are cases in which those sentence

---

[3] The underlying phonological form of the verbalizing suffix added to adjective stems is *gar*. In this example, the verb is accompanied by *iru* and is in the "present progressive" form. The morph *gat* is the result of assimilation to the following "gerund" suffix *te*. Note that this morph is no way related to the infix *kat* that appears in the past forms of adjectives in spite of the phonetic similarity of the past forms of the paired adjectives and verbs: *atukatta:atugatta*. In what follows, I use *sensation adjectives* and *sensation verbs* to refer to those adjectives and verbs that are paired in this way by means of the suffix *gar*.

[4] We are concerned here only with the first kind of reading mentioned in note 2. Sentences (4) and (5) are acceptable under the second kind of reading.

[5] This restriction, however, applies to declarative sentences. In interrogative sentences it is reversed. Thus, while *anata wa atui desu ka* is natural, *watasi wa atui desu ka* is not.

forms are embedded as constituent sentences. For example, with relativization we have both (7) and (8):[6]

(7) *atui hito*
     'hot man'
(8) *atugatte iru hito*
     'hot man'

And with nominalization there is both (9) and (10):

(9) *Mary ga sabisii koto wa dare mo utagawanai*
     'No one doubts that Mary is lonely'
(10) *Mary ga sabisigatte iru koto wa dare mo utagawanai*
     'No one doubts that Mary is lonely'

But there are also cases in which sentence embedding in the customary sense is not involved, at least not in an immediately obvious way. For example, we have both (11) and (12):[7]

(11) *Mary wa sabisii ni tigainai*
     'Mary must be lonely'
(12) *Mary wa sabisigatte iru ni tigainai*
     'Mary must be lonely'

Another example of the same sort involves the expression *no da*, which we now turn to.

3. Syntactically, *no da* is attached to a sentence at the end and forms another one. Semantic description of *no da* is not easy. The closest equivalent in one of the more familiar languages would be *c'est que* in French, though one can still only speculate as to what exactly they have in common.

The *no da* sentence may indicate a reason or cause, as in (13):[8]

---

[6] These two noun phrases do not have the same meaning, however. Example (8) seems to imply that the information one uses to judge that the person in question is hot is available to direct observation by one's senses, while in example (7) one's judgment may perhaps be made on a more indirect basis. However, a complete semantic analysis of these two kinds of noun phrases would inevitably involve some other complex factors as well, and such an analysis is not intended here. Similarly, the pairs of Japanese phrases or sentences that contain a sensation adjective and the corresponding sensation verb in the following discussion are not perfectly synonymous although they are given identical English translations here. However, I shall not necessarily comment on their intricate and varying semantic differences.

[7] A closer approximation to sentence (12) might be 'I assert that necessary information according to which one would judge that Mary is lonely would have to be available to those who could directly observe her at the present moment'. The sentence presupposes that Mary is not observable to the speaker at the moment of speaking. Such a presupposition is absent from (11).

[8] When *no da* clearly indicates a reason or cause, it can be paraphrased by *nazenara . . . kara da*.
Kuno (1970) characterizes *no da* as giving "some explanation for what the speaker has said or done, or the state he is in (p. 14). Kuno goes on to say that such an explanation can but need not be the cause of a stated fact. He cites the interesting pair (a) and (b) to illustrate this point (I have made a stylistic change that is of no concern to us here):

   (a) *Taizyuu ga 10-pondo hetta; byooki na no da*
      'I have lost 10 pounds; I am sick'
   (b) *Byooki da; taizyuu ga 10-pondo hetta no da*
      'I am sick; I have lost 10 pounds'

As Kuno indicates, the *no da* in (a), but not that in (b), may be replaced by *kara da*. In (a) "I am sick"

(13) *Mary wa kanasigatte iru; Fido ga sinda no da*
      'Mary is sad; Fido died'

The second, *no da* sentence explains why Mary is sad and may be translated by means of 'because'. But reason and cause do not explain all uses of *no da*. Some *no da* sentences express effects rather than causes, as in (14):

(14) *Fido ga sinda; sore de Mary wa kanasigatte iru no da*
      'Fido died; so Mary is sad'

Another semantic effect of *no da* may be seen from (15) and (16):

(15) *Mary wa Fido ga sinda no de kanasigatte iru*
      'Mary is sad because Fido died'
(16) *Mary wa Fido ga sinda no de kanasigatte iru no da*
      'Mary is sad because Fido died'

Both sentences are given the same English translation, but (16) and not (15) can be used when the fact that Mary is sad is already known, or, in current terminology, when it is a presupposition, and the speaker is asserting that Fido's death is the cause of this event. Hence (16) (but not (15)) may be translated by (17):[9]

(17) It is because Fido died that Mary is sad

Similarly, compare (18) and (19):

(18) *Bill wa asoko de John ni atta*
      'Bill met John there'
(19) *Bill wa asoko de John ni atta no da*
      'Bill met John there'

That Bill met John can be a presupposition when sentence (19) is used.

Thus, the semantic effects of *no da* are difficult to characterize clearly and completely. The only generalization one can make from the preceding examples is that *no da* somehow serves as a marker to indicate that some "second order" assertion, so to speak, is made with respect to the proposition expressed by the sentence to which *no da* is attached. That is, it serves to indicate that some assertion is made as to how the proposition in question is related to some other proposition or propositions that

---

expresses the cause of the fact that I have lost ten pounds; on the other hand, "I have lost ten pounds" cannot be a cause of the fact that I am sick; in (b) it is, to use Kuno's term, an "explanation" for saying that I am sick.

Besides *kara* there is the word *nazenara* which may also be glossed as 'because'. This word may be added to the second sentence at its head in both (a) and (b). Furthermore, if it is added then *no da* may be replaced by *kara da* in both examples. Thus we have (c) and (d):

    (c) *Taizyuu ga 10-pondo hetta; nazenara byooki da kara da*
    (d) *Byooki da; nazenara taizyuu ga 10-pondo hetta kara da*

In (c) the second sentence gives the reason why the speaker lost ten pounds, while in (d) the second sentence gives the reason why the speaker judges that he is sick.

    [9] But this is not the only possible reading of (16). In my judgment, (16) can be read without taking *Mary is sad* as a presupposition. For example, it can be read so that *Mary is sad* is taken to be an effect of the fact that Fido died. Such a reading is in fact obtained (though not necessarily so) when the *no da* in (16) makes the whole sentence a reason sentence for another that precedes it:

    Mary wa nani mo iwanai; Mary wa Fido ga sinda node, kanasigatte iru no da
    'Mary would not talk; for she is sad, as Fido died'

are stated (or even understood) in a particular discourse context. However, even such a vague characterization may be too narrow.

Whatever the semantic characterization of *no da* may be, of particular interest to us is the fact that inside the *no da* sentence the previously mentioned restriction on the subject of a sensation adjective does not apply. Hence, not only is (20) grammatical, but also (21):

(20) *Mary wa sabisigatte iru no da*
'Mary is lonely'
(21) *Mary wa sabisii no da*
'Mary is lonely'

Sentences like these may be used with the various semantic effects of *no da* sentences we have described. However, sentences like (21), with the sensation adjective, require a further comment. Sentence (21) seems to have these semantic effects: The speaker asserts that he knows that Mary is lonely but his knowledge is not solely or perhaps even not at all based on what he perceives of Mary. The sentence does not tell how he knows what he knows, and it can sound just like an a priori declaration— "Mary must be lonely." He might perhaps be able to judge from past experience that Mary is lonely, using circumstantial evidence of a kind that would not allow a neutral party to draw such a conclusion. Or he might even have been told by Mary that she was lonely.

4. We have observed that the restriction on the subject of a sensation adjective need not be applicable when a sentence form with such an adjective is contained within a larger sentence. Another qualification to be made about the same restriction relates to style. Consider (22) and (23):

(22) *Mary wa sabisii*
'Mary is lonely'
(23) *Mary wa atukatta*
'Mary was hot'

Contrary to what was said earlier, forms like these and like (5) are actually permitted as independent sentences, *provided that* they are used in a particular style, which, for the lack of a better name, I shall call the *nonreportive* style, to contrast with the *reportive* style.

To describe the nonreportive style,[10] it is necessary first to refer to what are generally taken as basic components of linguistic performance. A linguistic act is assumed to take place between a speaker and a hearer: a sentence is uttered by the speaker, who has the intention of being heard by the hearer. There are, however, cases of linguistic performances which do not directly comply with this paradigmatic schema. Monolog is one such unparadigmatic type, and story writing and story telling represent another.

One may try to account for such cases while still holding to the paradigmatic schema. The notions of "speaker," "hearer" can be extended in diverse ways and, if necessary, made somewhat abstract. For example, monolog might be viewed as somewhat displaced linguistic performance in which the hearer is the speaker himself.

Literary works submit to such explanations with varying degrees of plausibility. Consider, to begin with, a story in the first person. In this case "I" appears as the

[10] We shall offer an actual definition in Section 7.

narrator. The "I" need not be the writer of the story, that is, physically the producer of the sentences in this linguistic performance. However one can conceive of a performance in which the writer assumes the role of the speaker "I," and the reader that of the hearer. A first-person story in the strict sense has only one point of view. It is a description of a series of events inside or reflected in one subject of consciousness—real, if autobiographical, or imaginary, otherwise. The reading of a first-person story can be understood as an act relating this real or imaginary subject of consciousness to the reader. In this way first-person stories can be fit into the paradigmatic schema of linguistic performance.

But stories are often not written in the first person, and analysis of their structure as linguistic performance inevitably needs a subtler device. A story may involve more than one point of view. It may shift from one subject of consciousness to another, representing what is inside or reflected in a different consciousness. Sometimes distinct points of view may overlap, or the point of view may even be left indistinct.

5. Consider, for example, the following quote from D. H. Lawrence's *Sons and Lovers*:

> Paul looked into Miriam's eyes. She was pale and expectant with wonder, her lips were parted, and her dark eyes lay open to him. His look seemed to travel down into her. Her soul quivered. It was the communion she wanted. He turned aside, as if pained. He turned to the bush.

Involved here are Paul's and Miriam's consciousness and perhaps also the narrator's point of view. The three points of view are not always clearly separated but rather subtly intermingled. Yet this short passage exhibits a gradual and intricate shifting of the point of view, from Paul's to Miriam's. The starting sentence may be taken as representing the narrator's point of view, but it may also represent Paul's consciousness directed toward Miriam's through his sight. It prepares the reader for the next sentence, which represents Miriam's image as it is reflected in Paul's mind. And then Miriam's eyes in Paul's consciousness and Paul's look in Miriam's are where the two could seem to meet. But the third to fifth sentences represent Miriam's consciousness directed toward herself. In the next to last sentence Miriam's consciousness is returning outward and the narrator's point of view may be coming back. The last sentence can be interpreted as the narrator's indifferent point of view.

6. There seem to be two possible ways to view non-first-person stories: one can assume that they fit the basic paradigm of linguistic performance in terms of speaker and hearer, or one can assume that they do not.

The theory of the omniscient narrator is a familiar solution along the former lines. The omniscient narrator is an imaginary omnipresent subject of consciousness who is assumed to be able to enter each character's mind. The whole story is then assumed to be told by this narrator as a series of events perceived by him. The narrator is the "speaker" with respect to such a non-first-person story, just as "I" is the "speaker" of a first-person story. As a result, non-first-person stories are viewed in the same light as first-person stories.

Along the other line of approach, a story may be assumed to be just a structured collection of information from various subjects of consciousness. One of these can be the narrator, who is not referred to in the story (the omniscient narrator is assumed not to be referred to, either); the others are characters in the story. The role of the writer of a non-first-person story is to assemble (in fact, create) such information and set it in order. This is in no way identifiable with the role of the "speaker" in the paradigm of linguistic performance, as is the "I" in the case of a first-person story or the omni-scient narrator in the case of a non-first-person story. Let us call this latter theory the *multi-consciousness* theory.

I have been contrasting first-person stories and non-first-person stories, but this dichotomy may be somewhat misleading with respect to the essential point to be made here. Some clarification of the term *omniscient* is also in order.

In a first-person story, "I" is, by definition, the narrator; in addition, he may or may not be a character in the story. If he is, he cannot be allowed any superhuman faculty without destroying the naturalness of the story.[11] On the other hand, when "I" does not participate in the story, he can be accorded somewhat more privileged powers while allowing the story to remain natural, but he may not have any non-human kind of perceptual faculty. If this technique is extended to the extreme, we have a non-first-person story with a neutral or effaced narrator. Such a narrator not only does not participate in the story, but also is never referred to. Given his absence from the story, he can be omnipresent. But his faculties are still human: he is not omniscient and cannot enter into characters' minds. The story is told from one point of view, the narrator's. In this sense a non-first-person story with a neutral or effaced narrator can be considered as an extreme form of a first-person story. One could even conceive of an approach that turns such a story into the first-person type by assuming that all sentences of the story are "reports" by an "I" never mentioned in the story.

Let us group together first-person stories and non-first-person stories with a neutral or effaced narrator and call them *reportive*. A story is reportive if it is told by a narrator who may be omnipresent but not omniscient; otherwise, a story is non-reportive. This is the dichotomy that is relevant to us here.

The opposing two theories mentioned previously—the omniscient narrator theory and the multi-consciousness theory—deal with nonreportive stories.[12] Is there any empirical evidence that favors one or the other of these theories? Do they have any different empirically relevant consequences? If not, they are empirically equivalent and provide only two different frameworks of terminology; the choice between the two would be a matter of convenience, not a matter of theoretical adequacy.

Be that as it may, we have two categories of stories, reportive and nonreportive. This categorization, it must be noted, does not refer to the theory of grammar nor to the grammar of a particular language. It presumably belongs to the universal theory of literary art. However, two different grammatical styles exist in Japanese which, it is claimed, parallel this categorization of stories. I shall discuss these in the next section.

7. We are now in a position to return to our discussion of the grammar of Japanese sensation words. As already mentioned, sentence forms like (22) and (23), with a third person subject and a sensation adjective, we originally said to be un-grammatical, but they are in fact permitted in certain non-first-person stories. Such a sentence can be used when the omniscient narrator (if we employ this notion) adopts

---

[11] Fairy tales, fantasy stories, and science fiction are, of course, not pertinent here.

[12] My use of the term *omniscient* may be found to be more restricted than the usual use in literary criticism. It does seem congruent with what N. Friedman (1955) calls Multiple Selective Omniscience (and, as a limiting case, Selective Omniscience); however, what he calls Editorial Omniscience and Neutral Omniscience do not appear to involve essentially my usage of the term. These latter, together with his Dramatic Mode, seem rather to characterize modes of reportive story, in my terms, with a first-person, neutral, or effaced narrator, perhaps omnipresent but not omniscient.

The problem of the narrator and the point of view is a complex one which obviously requires and deserves more extensive treatment. Here, however, I have tried only to give a brief, self-contained sketch of that aspect of the problem which is of immediate concern to us.

the point of view of its third person subject. For example, one might have a line like (24) in a story:

(24)   *Yamadera no kane o kiite, Mary wa kanasikatta*
        'Hearing the bell of the mountain temple, Mary was sad'

On the other hand, if "I" am narrating the story from "my" point of view, then "I" must say (25), using the sensation verb *kanasigaru*, or perhaps (26), using *no da*:

(25)   *Yamadera no kane o kiite, Mary wa kanasigatta*
        'Hearing the bell of the mountain temple, Mary was sad'
(26)   *Yamadera no kane o kiite, Mary wa kanasikatta no da*
        'Hearing the bell of the mountain temple, Mary was sad'

Thus, we must differentiate two grammatical styles in Japanese. The one in which sentences like (22), (23), and (24) are not permitted is employed both in the paradigmatic setting of linguistic performance and in first-person stories where the imaginary "I" narrates. Sentences like (25) and (26) may also be used in a non-first-person story, but then they are understood as a report from a narrator's point of view, a narrator who is not referred to in the story and perhaps omnipresent but not omniscient. Using only sentences like (25) and (26) and avoiding those like (22), (23), and (24), one can write a reportive story without necessarily introducing the first-person narrator "I." The style in which sentences like (22), (23), and (24) are not used will be called *reportive*.

On the other hand, sentences like (22), (23), and (24) may be used only in non-first-person stories. Such sentences, it is claimed, represent the point of view of a character, the referent of the subject of the sentence. In no way can they be interpreted as reports by an "effaced" narrator. One cannot apply a stylistic variation to a story in which such sentences occur to turn it into a first-person story; the story is not reportive. The style which allows sentences like (22), (23), and (24) will be called *nonreportive*.

In brief, the reportive style is the style in which one writes reportive stories and the nonreportive style the one in which one writes nonreportive stories. Note, however, that the reportive and nonreportive styles are here defined as notions belonging to the theory of Japanese grammar, based on grammatical facts in Japanese.

The sentence-final particle *yo* will aid the Japanese speaker to see the difference between these two styles. One function of this particle is to give the connotation "I am telling you." In consequence, sentences with *yo* are inevitably understood to be in the reportive style. A native speaker of Japanese may not be able to respond immediately as to whether forms like (22) and (23) are grammatical and if so in what contexts. But he would be able to judge more readily forms like those in (27)–(30):

(27)   **Mary wa sabisii yo*
(28)   *Mary wa sabisigatte iru yo*
(29)   **Mary wa atukatta yo*
(30)   *Mary wa atugatta yo*

8. The grammatical difference between the reportive and nonreportive styles does not end with the use of the sensation words that we have been discussing. It also manifests itself in the "reflexive" use of the word *zibun*. This word may be compared with the reflexive pronouns in English, as the examples in (31) and (32) suggest:

(31) *John wa kare o hometa*
'John praised him'
(32) *John wa zibun o hometa*
'John praised himself'

It is not a simple matter to formulate an infallible condition as to when *zibun* and other means of anaphora are used. The Klima-Lees rule (Lees and Klima (1963)) gives a good first approximation for English reflexive pronouns: to state the condition informally, a reflexive pronoun is used to express a coreferential relation within a simple sentence while a personal pronoun is used for such a relation across sentence boundaries. However, occurrences of English reflexive pronouns inside complex noun phrases are controlled by rules much harder to discover.[13] The Japanese reflexive *zibun* has wider applicability than the English reflexive pronouns, even if we restrict ourselves to cases in which *zibun* is itself a noun phrase constituent of a sentence, without any intermediary larger noun phrase. In an earlier work (Kuroda (1965)) I gave some conditions for such occurrences of *zibun* (which now no doubt would have to be supplemented and refined). I shall not restate these conditions fully here, for it is not necessary for our present purposes. However, some discussion of this topic is relevant. One condition on *zibun* is that in the object position of a constituent sentence it may be anaphorically coreferential with the matrix subject if the constituent sentence is inside the matrix verb phrase. Thus, *zibun* can be anaphorically coreferential with the matrix subject if it is the object of a verb phrase complement or of a noun phrase complement which is the matrix object. On the other hand, it cannot be so coreferential if it is the object in an adverbial clause. Whether or not it can be coreferential with the matrix subject seems to be dependent on additional syntactic and/or semantic factors in intricate ways which I am not at present in a position to describe. For our present purposes let us simply say that *zibun* contained in a certain class of adverbial clauses as the object cannot be coreferential with the matrix subject. In what follows only this negative condition concerns us. Consider (33):

(33) *John wa Bill ga zibun o hometa toki Mary no soba ni ita*
'John was by Mary when Bill praised himself'

Here *zibun* cannot be coreferential with *John*. Now compare (33) with (34):

(34) *John wa Bill ga zibun o hometa koto o kiite yorokonda*
'John was glad to hear that Bill had praised him/himself'

Here *zibun* is inside the object noun phrase of the verb *kiku* 'hear', and it can be coreferential with the subject of this verb, which in turn is coreferential with *John*, the subject of *yorokonda* 'was glad', and is deleted—hence the ambiguous English translation.

But the condition in question is only applicable in the reportive style. In the nonreportive style the *zibun* in (33) may also be coreferential with *John*, making this sentence ambiguous also. To check this point, the native speaker of Japanese is advised first, without worrying about the stylistic value of the sentence, to confirm that the sentence can be read with *zibun* taken as coreferential with *John*, and then to observe from (35) that the same reading is impossible if *yo* is attached at the end of the sentence:

(35) *John wa Bill ga zibun o hometa toki Mary no soba ni ita yo*
'John was by Mary when Bill praised himself'

---

[13] See Lees and Klima (1963), Warshawsky (1965), Jackendoff (1969).

Sentence (35), used only in the reportive style, has the unique reading indicated by the English translation.

9. To see the subtle stylistic effects which reflexivization may have in Japanese stories, let us consider the following passage:

> *John wa Bill ga zibun o utta toki Mary no soba ni tatte ita. Yuka ni taorete, Mary no hosoi kakato ga me ni ututta. Bill wa subayaku Mary no ude o tukamu to, hikizuru yoo ni site soto e deta. Huyu no yozora wa sumikitte, musuu no hosi ga tumetaku hikatte ita.*

> John was standing by Mary when Bill hit him. Falling to the floor, he saw her slender ankle. Instantly, Bill grabbed her arm and dragged her out. The night sky of winter was clear and innumerable stars were coldly shining.

Reading this story in English, one would conclude that it involves at least two points of view: the second sentence represents John's viewpoint while the last does not. All the sentences except for the second could be interpreted as representing the narrator's point of view. Various other interpretations are also possible, and ambiguities of points of view might even be intended. The last sentence could be interpreted as representing Bill's and/or Mary's point of view, since the stars might have looked cold to one or both of them. But for us the essential difference between the Japanese and the English versions lies in the interpretation of the first sentence. In the English version this sentence may be taken as representing either the narrator's or John's point of view; other interpretations are also possible. Additional information from other parts of the story or from more indirect sources might decide which interpretation is more natural. But the reader of the Japanese version would immediately adopt John's point of view in the first sentence. In particular, he would understand that when John was hit he must have been conscious of the fact—spontaneously if not reflectively—that he was standing by Mary.

Note that the whole story could be written from the narrator's point of view, as a witness to the incident. But then some stylistic change would be necessary. In the English version the minimum change required would be to read the second sentence as: "Falling to the floor, he *must have seen* her slender ankle." In the Japanese version, in addition to a corresponding change in the second sentence, the first sentence would need some stylistic modification. One might delete *zibun* or replace it by *kare* 'he'. But then in this story, retold in the reportive style, we lose the original implication that John was conscious (not necessarily reflectively) of standing by Mary.

10. To repeat, *zibun* as the object of an adverbial clause of a certain kind may refer to the matrix subject in the nonreportive style but not in the reportive style. Actually, the whole story of this constraint is much more complicated and cannot be told fully here, partly because of lack of space but also because the grammatical clarity of the relevant facts deteriorates rapidly with a slight increase in grammatical complexity.

Recall that in the reportive style, sentence forms with a sensation adjective such as (22) and (23) are ungrammatical by themselves but become grammatical if followed by *no da*. Now, if *no da* is added to (33) it seems that *zibun* can refer to *John* even in the reportive style (and even when *yo* is added after *no da*), at least in some contexts.[14]

---

[14] Consider, for example, a discourse context where *John ga Mary no soba ni tatte ita* 'John was standing by Mary' is presupposed. Or, assume that the sentence in question is preceded by *John wa taihen uresi soo datta* 'John was very happy' and gives a reason for John's happiness due to some understood relationship between John and Mary.

Consider also (36) and (37):

(36) *John wa Bill ga zibun o hometa no de okotta*
      'John got angry because Bill praised him/himself'
(37) *John wa Bill ga zibun o hometa no de okotta no da*
      'John got angry because Bill praised him/himself'

This pair parallels the pair (15), (16) and the same remark about the semantic effect of *no da* can be made here. The point that interests us in the present context, however, is that the *zibun* in (37) can be coreferential with *John* in the reportive style, while the potential coreferentiality of *zibun* with *John* in (36) is less clear.[15] This seems to be related to the fact that (38) seems acceptable in the reportive style, although its grammaticality appears to me to be less clear than that of (39):

(38) *Mary wa kanasii no de naita*
      'Mary wept because she was sad'
(39) *Mary wa kanasii no de naita no da*
      'Mary wept because she was sad'

The facts discussed here seem to indicate that there are some relations between the contexts in which a sensation adjective can occur with a third person subject and the contexts in which *zibun* in the object of an adverbial clause can be coreferential with the matrix subject. But to characterize these contexts in the reportive style and to uncover any generalization that holds between them seems to be an intricate matter. One might also hope to arrive at some semantic characterization of the contexts that relates them in some way to the semantic characteristics of nonreportive style.

11. We have seen that the dichotomy between reportive and nonreportive stories is accompanied in Japanese by the distinction between reportive and nonreportive style. The grammars of these two styles differ in their treatment of sensation words, as one would expect from the epistemological characteristics of such words. But the styles differ also in their treatment of the process of reflexivization.

I introduced in Section 6 two opposing theories for nonreportive stories, namely, the omniscient narrator theory and the multi-consciousness theory. Let us consider the possible implications, with respect to these theories, of the fact that nonreportive stories have their own grammar.

Assume a writer writes a first-person story. The narrator "I" of the story must generally be distinguished from the writer. The narrator "I" is an imaginary subject of consciousness. But through the intermediary of this imaginary subject of consciousness, the "speaker-hearer" relationship may be assumed to be established between the writer and the reader. The writer thus "talks" to the reader. Needless to say, we understand terms like "speaker," "hearer," and "talk" in an extended theoretical sense. In particular, the writer may use a style which he could not possibly use in speech. But in this case he might "write" to the reader in the form of a letter or a report. The point is that he can address himself to the reader in a certain form of linguistic performance in the way the narrator expresses himself in a first-person story.

---

[15] If *zibun* in (36) can in fact be coreferential with *John* in the reportive style, then the *node* clauses are to be assumed to be adverbial clauses to which the condition we are concerned with does not apply. The reason for the nonapplication of the condition may have something to do with the fact that *node* may be related syntactically to *no da*.

With a non-first-person story one may also assume that the writer and the reader are related to each other basically in the same way. The writer "talks" to the reader through the intermediary of the narrator, the imaginary subject of consciousness, who is not referred to in the story and who, according to the omniscient narrator theory, may be omniscient. But here the empirical fact intervenes that there exist two distinct styles, reportive and nonreportive. Empirically, there could or could not exist such a distinction of styles. If there were no such distinction, the writer would "talk" to the reader in the same language whether he assumed the role of a natural, an omnipresent, or an omniscient narrator. The differences would lie simply in the writer's assumed personality and faculties, physical and mental, and except for that, the way the writer and the reader are related to each other would remain the same. But the fact is that a different grammar is used for the nonreportive style. This means that if a story is nonreportive, that is, if and only if the narrator is omniscient, the writer will "talk" to the reader in a different language, which can never be used in an actual linguistic performance. This situation makes it impossible for us to establish a uniform relationship, except for the writer's assumed mental and physical faculties, between the writer and the reader of a story through the intermediary of the narrator and, it seems to me, deprives the omniscient narrator of much of his charm. Indeed, the omniscient narrator would serve only as a cover-up for the fact that the writer can, thanks to the existence of a distinct grammar for nonreportive style, communicate with the reader directly and in a way which is essentially different from the paradigmatic linguistic performance. One might say that the secret of the writer's artistic creation lies partially here. The multi-consciousness theory seems to reflect the empirical fact directly.[16]

The spurious status of the omniscient narrator can also be demonstrated by a semantic consideration. Let us compare sentences like (24) with those like (25) and (26). A sentence like (25) or (26) points semantically to the existence of a subject of consciousness whose judgment the sentence is understood to represent. This is a semantic effect of *gatta* and *no da*. Then if the sentence in question is used in the paradigmatic linguistic performance, that subject of consciousness, the one who judges, is of course the speaker. If the sentence appears in a first-person story, the "judger" is "I," the narrator. If some individual, say, John, is explicitly established as a narrator in the story, then the "judger" is John, the narrator. Now, a story in the reportive style could be subtly structured so that no one inside or outside the world the story describes can be definitely identifiable as a narrator. Yet a sentence like (25) or (26), if it appears in a story, has definite referential force directed toward the "judger." Thus, however the narrator might be effaced in a story in the reportive style, a sentence like (25) or (26) points to him. To put it differently, the narrator in the reportive style, however successfully he might otherwise transcend the world the story describes, can be pointed to by a mechanism of reference in grammar which exists independently of any assumption we might make concerning the ontological status of the narrator. In the case of a sentence like (24), on the other hand, which can appear only in the nonreportive style, there is no such referential force directed toward a subject of consciousness whose judgment the sentence is to be taken as representing. One might argue on some nonlinguistic grounds that a sentence like (24), as a sentence (or, perhaps more exactly, as an occurrence of a sentence), must nonetheless represent someone's judgment, and in that sense this type of sentence also

---

[16] The multi-consciousness theory is incompatible with the performative analysis proposed by J. R. Ross (1970), according to which "all types of sentences have exactly one performative as their highest clause in deep structure."

directs us toward this "someone," who might be taken as the "omniscient narrator." But then the referential force thus assumed for a sentence like (24) would only be applicable to the "omniscient narrator," that is, the "omniscient narrator" would be the only one who can be so referred to; conversely, the omniscient narrator could presumably be referred to only in this way. Such an assumed referential device is then totally ad hoc. The omniscient narrator cannot be identified by a linguistic mechanism whose existence we can establish independently of the assumption of his existence in the way the narrator in the reportive style can. The omniscient narrator has no linguistic basis in the way that the narrator in the reportive style does.

12. I started this article with a problem in epistemology and ended with a problem in literary art. Both of those problems have been found to be directly reflected in Japanese grammar. They both represent such fundamental features in the two basic aspects of human mental life relating to language, that is, knowledge and literary art, that one might expect that they cannot fail to imprint their shadow on the grammar of any language. The distinction between the reportive and nonreportive styles might also be found to exist in English grammar, perhaps in a more concealed way. Be that as it may, as language relates to various aspects of our mental life, it reveals its features in different ways to those who study it. These features need not have similar grammatical expressions in all languages. A feature, fundamental from some point of view, may have little overt manifestation in some languages but an obvious representation in others. Conversely, linguistic investigation of a grammatical feature in some language may help the student of another discipline to clarify an aspect of language which is fundamental in that discipline but which has tended to escape him due to his limited knowledge of languages. Language may be approached from many aspects, and different languages look different from different aspects. The present study has reaffirmed that therein lies our fascination with the study of language.

---

addendum

It might be well to add here some remarks on *erlebte Rede* or *style indirect libre*, a notion widely discussed in the European tradition of literary criticism in connection with what I have called the nonreportive style. This notion seems generally taken as one to be compared with direct and indirect discourse and is considered as yet another stylistic technique of "quotation," in an extended sense. To quote Ullmann (1964), for example:

> The essence of free indirect speech [Ullmann's translation of *style indirect libre*] can best be defined in stylistic terms. It is a classical example of the possibility of choice between quasi-synonymous modes of expression. According to traditional grammar, two alternatives are open to the narrator when reporting the speech of other people: direct and indirect style, 'oratio recta' and 'oratio obliqua'. . . . The great change brought about by the advent of free indirect speech is that we can now choose between three,

not two, forms of reporting. The new construction stands half-way between the two orthodox types (p. 95).

The English term "narrated monolog" coined by Cohn for this notion seems to indicate the same approach. In fact, Cohn (1966) states:

> *erlebte Rede* is somewhere between direct and indirect discourse, more oblique than the former, less oblique than the latter. In searching for a better English label, I hesitate between 'narrated consciousness' and 'narrated monolog'; the second term in both these phrases expresses the immediacy of the inner voice we hear, whereas the first term expresses the essential fact that the narrator, not a character in the novel, relays this voice to us . . . (p. 104).[17]

The distinction I intend to make in terms of nonreportive style, however, seems to be of a more general character than that made by *erlebte Rede*. Basically, it is not to be characterized with reference to direct and indirect speech nor in terms of "inner voice." In the example given in Section 9, the first sentence is not necessarily to be understood as rendering John's "inner voice"; it simply presents his *Erlebnis*, and that possibly even spontaneous or unreflected.[18]

Thus, it seems to me that the problem of the nonreportive style should rather be compared with the general problem area raised by the omniscient narrator theory (although I am arguing against it) than the more restricted issue of the different modes of "quotation." In this respect Hamburger's (1968) concern for constructing "die Logik der Dichtung" seems to be more relevant to the intended distinction of the reportive and the nonreportive styles than the notion of *erlebte Rede* itself. She wishes to claim that literary fiction must be characterized as not conforming to the "Aussagesystem der Sprache." She in fact forcefully argues against the omniscient narrator conception when she states:

> Die Rede von der 'Rolle des Erzählers' ist denn auch in der Tat ebensowenig sinnvoll wie es die von der Rolle des Dramatikers oder Malers wäre. . . . K. Friedmann hat gewiss den 'Erzähler' als 'organisch mit der Dichtung selbst verwachsenes Medium' richtig bestimmt. Aber weil sie die funktionale Art dieses Mediums naturgemäss nicht durchschaut hat, ist es nur scheinbar richtig, wenn sie sagt: 'Er ist der Bewertende, der Fühlende, der Schauende. . . . ' Wenn dann dreissig Jahre später J. Petersen diesen Aspekt so ausmalt, dass er den Erzähler mit einem 'Spielleiter' vergleicht, 'der zwischen den Personen auf der Bühne steht und ihnen Stellung, Bewegung und Betonung anweist', ihn aber zugleich 'praktisch in die Rolle des Psychologen versetzt und mit seinen Aufgaben belastet' sein lässt und zwar dadurch dass ihm die Beschreibung und Schilderung seelischer Vorgänge verantwortlich zufällt'—wird es noch deutlicher, dass es sich hier um mehr oder weniger adäquate *metaphorische Scheindeskriptionen* handelt, die sich im literarischen Sprachgebrauch zu gängigen Schlagworten wie 'Autorität' oder 'Allwissenheit des Erzählers' verdichtet und abgenützt haben oder sogar zum Vergleich mit Gottes Allwissenheit mythisiert werden und eben deshalb Kritik hervorgerufen haben. Dieser weitverbreiteten, ja, soweit ich sehe, nahezu alleinherschenden Auffassung liegt die Verkennung des Charakters des fiktionalen Erzählens und seines kategorialen Unterschiedes von der Aussage zugrunde (pp. 116–117).

At present I am not in a position to be able to critically evaluate Hamburger's *Logik der Dichtung* and to see whether the intended distinction between the reportive

---

[17] I am indebted to C. Fillmore for drawing my attention to this article, which is a succinct introduction in English to the notion of *erlebte Rede*.

[18] I use the term "unreflected *Erlebnis*" here in the sense described in Husserl (1950, pp. 104–106, 177–185), for example.

and the nonreportive styles can fit into her conceptual framework. But the direction opened by her phenomenological investigation into the "Logik der Dichtung" seems to me most promising.

REFERENCES

Cohn, D. (1966), "Narrated monologue: a definition of fictional style," *Comparative Literature, 18*, 97–113.

Friedman, N. (1955), "Point of view in fiction," *PMLA, 70*.

Hamburger, K. (1968), *Die Logik der Dichtung*, Stuttgart: Klett.

Husserl, E. (1950), *Ideen zu einer reinen Phänomenologie und phänomenologischen Philosophie*, I, The Hague: Martinus Nijhoff.

Jackendoff, R. S. (1969), *Some Rules of Semantic Interpretation for English*, unpublished Ph.D. dissertation, M.I.T.

Kuno, S. (1970), "Notes on Japanese Grammar," pt. 1, Aiken Computation Laboratory, Harvard University.

Kuroda, S.-Y. (1965), *Generative Grammatical Studies in the Japanese Language*, unpublished Ph.D. dissertation, M.I.T.

Lees, R. B., and E. S. Klima (1963), "Rules for English pronominalization," *Language, 39*, 17–28.

Ross, J. R. (1970), "Declarative Sentences," in R. A. Jacobs and P. S. Rosenbaum, eds., *Readings in English Transformational Grammar*, Waltham, Mass.: Ginn.

Russell, B. (1940), *An Inquiry into Meaning and Truth*, London: G. Allen.

Ullmann, S. (1964), *Style in the French Novel*, New York: Barnes and Noble.

Warshawsky Harris, F. (1965), "Reflexivization I, II," unpublished papers, M.I.T.

can a not unhappy person be called a not sad one?[1]

D. Terence Langendoen

The Graduate Center
and Brooklyn College of
The City University of New York

Thomas G. Bever

Columbia University

... banal statements are given the appearance of profundity by means of the *not un-* formation ... it should also be possible to laugh the *not un-* formation out of existence ... [o]ne can cure oneself of the *not un-* formation by memorizing this sentence: *A not unblack dog was chasing a not unsmall rabbit across a not ungreen field.*

George Orwell

1. ACCEPTABILITY AND GRAMMATICALITY

In this paper we present a current sample of the rationalist-structuralist approach to the study of language.[2] Specific results are discussed that may be of interest to researchers specializing in English syntax. But more important, the present investigation is an example of how to treat linguistic phenomena as the result of interactions among different systems of linguistic knowledge. We argue that certain acceptable sequences are in fact ungrammatical but they are deemed acceptable by virtue of their perceptual comprehensibility. This analysis reduces the generative potential of

---

[1] An earlier version of this paper was read by Langendoen at the 1972 Summer meeting of the Linguistic Society of America under the title "Prenominal Negation in English."

[2] As pioneered by Jakobson and Halle (1956), Halle (1964), and Chomsky and Halle (1968).

universal grammatical formalisms and thus strengthens the claims made about what the child must know to be able to learn language.

The goal of a linguistic grammar is to account directly for the grammatical status and structure of sentences. Many contemporary proposals in linguistics derive critically relevant facts using the assumption that sentence grammaticality is equivalent to string acceptability. Representative samples of acceptability judgments that have been interpreted as grammatical ones are given in (1)–(4):[3]

(1) (a) *A not happy person entered the room
    (b) A not unhappy person entered the room
(2) (a) *Who did you give this book?
    (b) Who did you give this book to?
(3) (a) *Did that the guests slept late inconvenience you?
    (b) Did it inconvenience you that the guests slept late?
(4) (a) *Tomorrow I expected him to be there
    (b) Tomorrow I expect him to be there

But, as Chomsky (1965) has pointed out, sentence acceptability is to be distinguished from grammaticality: acceptability can be characterized *within* grammar "only in terms of some 'global' property that is attributable, not to a particular rule, but rather to the way in which the rules interrelate in a derivation" (p. 12). Accordingly, the decision to interpret differences in acceptability in cases like (1)–(4) as differences in grammaticality has recently led to the development of formalisms that enable one to mark sentences as ungrammatical on the basis of properties of their derivations (derivational constraints) or even on the basis of properties of potential derivations of other sentences (transderivational constraints).[4]

The unnecessary use of such formalisms will lead to a trivialization of linguistic theory: the more descriptive potential a formal device has, the less revealing it is about the specific ability it represents.[5] To accept these powerful formalisms as linguistic universals is to weaken the interest of the specific claims made about language acquisition and the antecedent properties of the child's mind. However, if there is no independently motivated theory of language performance that accounts for differences in acceptability like those in (1)–(4) one must then accept the grammatical formalisms in question.

As a case in point, let us consider sentences which have center-embedding. If sentences such as (5a) were to be classified as ungrammatical and those such as (5b) as grammatical, then the grammar of English would require at least the power of derivational constraints:

(5) (a) *I watched the man the psychiatrist my mother had worked with jump out the window
    (b) I watched the man the psychiatrist had worked with jump out the window

---

[3] Examples (1) are adapted from Klima (1964), examples (2) from Fillmore (1965), examples (3) from Ross (1967), and examples (4) from Postal and Ross (1970).

[4] See, in particular, Lakoff (1969; 1970; 1971).

[5] There has been, so far, no formal proof that derivational and transderivational constraints of the kinds that have been proposed do actually increase the generative capacity of the class of grammars permitted by the theory. In fact, one can imagine derivational constraints which would restrict the generative capacity of linguistic grammars to that of finite-state grammars—for example a constraint that would limit the degree of self-embedding to some fixed finite amount (see the discussion of (5) in the text). However, it is intuitively clear that the ability to make reference at any stage of a derivation to any other stage or to make reference to other possible derivations increases the descriptive power that is available to the grammarian.

Although there is no fully agreed-upon behavioral theory that accounts completely for the difference in acceptability between (5a) and (5b), most researchers have been willing to recognize some behavioral theory[6] as sufficiently plausible so that grammatical mechanisms are not required here.

Similarly, were grammaticality the basis for the differential acceptability of English sentences such as (6) in which Relative Clause Reduction has applied, derivational constraints would be required within a grammar:

(6) (a) *The horse raced into the ring bolted
     (b)   The horse ridden into the ring bolted

However, the behavioral explanation is sufficiently well documented in this case to show that (6a) and (6b) are both fully grammatical.[7] The unacceptability of (6a) is explained by appeal to otherwise motivated perceptual mechanisms.

In each of these cases, the grammar has been relieved of accounting for certain instances of differential acceptability by reference to other systems of linguistic knowledge. A considerable number of systems of language behavior have by now been isolated for study—among them, systems of rhetoric, conversational implicature, speech production, speech perception, and language acquisition. Any or all of these systems may provide a basis for acceptability differences independent of grammar. Paradigm examples have been like the case of center-embedding; that is, the unacceptability of a grammatical sentence, such as (5a), is described in terms of a behavioral process.

In this paper we shall be concerned with the problem posed by the contrast in acceptability between sentence (1a) and sentence (1b). We shall show that both (1a) and (1b) are ungrammatical but (1b) is acceptable and interpretable as a result of independently motivated processes of speech perception and conversational implicature. That is, the case of (1a) versus (1b) is one in which the acceptability of an ungrammatical string is accounted for in terms of its behavioral comprehensibility.

2. GRAMMAR OF NEGATED ATTRIBUTIVE ADJECTIVE PHRASES

Let us first examine the descriptive and theoretical problems that would be entailed by the decision to label (1a) ungrammatical and (1b) grammatical. To begin with, note that the two sentences (7a) and (7b), which correspond directly to structures underlying (1a) and (1b), do not differ in acceptability; both are fully acceptable and presumably also fully grammatical:

(7) (a) A person who was not happy entered the room
     (b) A person who was not unhappy entered the room

Therefore, there must be a restriction on either the Relative Clause Reduction Rule or the Adjective Phrase Preposing Rule to the effect that (1a) cannot be derived from (7a) but that (1b) can be derived from (7b). That the restriction must be on Relative Clause Reduction can be seen from the unacceptability of (8), the analog to (1a) in which the reduced relative clause follows the head of the noun phrase:

(8) *Someone not happy entered the room

---

[6] For example, Miller and Chomsky (1963), Bever (1970).
[7] See Bever (1970), Bever and Langendoen (1972).

As Klima noted, however, Relative Clause Reduction is not restricted if the adjective, besides being preceded by *not*, is also modified either by an intensifier or by a following phrase or clause, as in (9):[8]

(9) (a) A not very happy/unhappy person entered the room
    (b) Someone not very happy/unhappy entered the room
    (c) A person/someone not happy/unhappy about the recent polls entered the room

We therefore may state the restriction on Relative Clause Reduction as follows: a relative clause may not be reduced just in case it ends in the string *not*$\frown$Adjective, unless the adjective is composed of a negative prefix followed by an independently occurring adjective. Formally, Relative Clause Reduction can be stated as in (10):

$$(10) \quad \underbrace{X \;]_s}_{1} \; \underbrace{\begin{bmatrix} \text{Rel} \\ \text{Pro} \end{bmatrix} \text{Tense } be \; Y]_s}_{2} \; \underbrace{Z}_{3} \;\; \Rightarrow$$

$$\qquad\qquad\;\; 1 \qquad\qquad\quad \phi \qquad\qquad 3$$

Condition:[9] Inapplicable if
    (a) $Y = not\frown\text{Adj}_1$, and
    (b) $\text{Adj}_1 \neq [\text{Neg}] + \text{Adj}_2$
Otherwise optional

The requirement that Adjective not be analyzable into $[\text{Neg}] + \text{Adjective}_2$ is necessitated by the fact that sentences like (11) are unacceptable (hence, by hypothesis, ungrammatical):

(11) (a) *Some not insolent students want to see the dean
    (b) *Did he make a not untoward remark about me?
    (c) *His uncle left him a not dismantled clock

The input of (11) to rule (10) satisfies the condition that makes the rule inapplicable: *insolent, untoward, dismantled* are not analyzable into $[\text{Neg}] +$ Adjective since at most *-solent, -toward, -mantled* are categorized as adjective stems.

3. PROBLEMS FOR STANDARD THEORY

Upon closer examination the statement of the rule of Relative Clause Reduction in (10) turns out to be inadequate. First, note that there is an asymmetry in the acceptability judgments having to do with whether the modified element is a noun or an indefinite pronoun. We observed that (8), the analog to (1a) with an indefinite pronoun

[8] Since the intensifier *enough* follows the adjective it modifies, there may be some disagreement as to the acceptability of sentences like (a):

    (a) ?A not large enough box came with the coffeepot

We shall treat such sentences as acceptable. If it should turn out that this is the wrong decision, the rules we propose can be adjusted accordingly.

[9] The subscripts on Adjective are for convenience only, to distinguish the full adjective (e.g., *unhappy*) from the adjective that follows the negative prefix (e.g., *-happy*). The symbol [Neg] should be read "negative prefix."

as head, was, like (1a), unacceptable. However, sentence (12), the analog to (1b), is unacceptable, unlike (1b):

(12) *Someone not unhappy entered the room

Thus the second part of the condition in (10) must be dropped in case the element immediately preceding the relative clause is an indefinite pronoun (*someone, something*).

However generic indefinite pronouns (*anyone, anything*) can be modified by reduced relative clauses of any sort whatever.[10] Consider in this regard the examples in (13), all of which are acceptable:

(13) (a) Anyone not interested may leave
    (b) Anything not easy is worthwhile
    (c) Melvin dislikes anything not fattening

This relaxation of the condition, however, does not extend to generically used nouns, as illustrated in (14):

(14) (a) *Any not interested person may leave
    (b) *Any not easy project is worthwhile
    (c) *Melvin dislikes any not fattening food

Given the facts in (12)–(14), the condition on Relative Clause Reduction must be amended as in (15):

(15) Condition: Inapplicable if
    (a) $X = X' \frown N$ and $Y = not \frown Adj_1$ and $Adj_1 \neq [Neg] + Adj_2$

    (b) $X = X' \frown \begin{bmatrix} \text{Indef} \\ \text{Nongener} \\ \text{Pro} \end{bmatrix}$ and $Y = not \frown Adj_1$

The requirement that Adjective not be analyzable into [Neg] + Adjective$_2$ is not strong enough, however. Consider (16):

(16) *Sheila wants to meet a not unmarried man

Clearly *unmarried* is analyzable into [Neg] + Adjective$_2$, yet (16) is unacceptable. The reason, apparently, is that *married* and *unmarried* denote two mutually exclusive states. It is sufficient for Relative Clause Reduction to be blocked if an explicitly negated negatively prefixed adjective and its unprefixed counterpart do not denote two ends of a continuous scale with respect to the noun being modified.[11] Thus we must alter the condition (15) to read as in (17):

(17) Condition: Inapplicable if
    (a) $X = X' \frown N$ and $Y = not \frown Adj_1$ and
        $\{Adj_1 \neq [Neg] + Adj_2$ or $\{Adj_1$ or $Adj_2 = [Noncontinuous]\}\}$

---

[10] This was pointed out to us by J. R. Ross. See also Ross (1972, pp. 70–71).

[11] Whether an adjective is marked as continuous or noncontinuous is not always clear and perhaps may vary from person to person in some cases. Thus one can imagine a person who categorized people into exactly two classes with respect to holiness—*holy* and *unholy*. Presumably such a person would refuse to accept the phrase *a not unholy man*, whereas another person who considers there to be a holiness continuum would accept it readily.

(b) $X = X^\frown \begin{bmatrix} \text{Indef} \\ \text{Nongener} \\ \text{Pro} \end{bmatrix}$ and $Y = \textit{not}^\frown \text{Adj}_1$

Even with this modification the condition is still too weak. We must also specify that Adjective$_1$ and Adjective$_2$ have exactly the same meaning, save for the contribution of the negative prefix of Adjective$_1$. Examples are legion. Consider (18):[12]

(18) (a) *He emitted a not unearthly scream
  (b) *Sam bought his wife some not unusual clothes

We must therefore build into the restriction on Relative Clause Reduction the additional qualification that the rule is inapplicable if Adjective$_1$ and Adjective$_2$ differ in meaning beyond the difference supplied by [Neg]. Such a qualification, however, is not statable in the theory of Chomsky (1965) (the so-called Standard Theory), assuming that -*earthly* and -*usual* of *unearthly* and *unusual* are categorized as Adjective. To avoid this impasse, we would have to assign to all negatively prefixed adjectives like *unearthly* a special bracketing, analogous to the bracketing of *insolent*, in which -*earthly* is not given the label "Adjective" but rather some special label such as "Adjective-Stem." In this way Standard Theory could account for cases like those in (18).

Such a decision, however, leads to unacceptable consequences for lexical representation and hence cannot be generally applied.[13] Consider, for example, the lexical items *healthy* and *unhealthy*. Both items are polysemous, and in some of their senses, listed in (19), they differ only to the extent supplied by the prefix *un-*:[14]

(19) (a) *healthy* (i)   in a state of good health
          (ii) conducive to good health
          (iii) indicative of good health or of a rational or constructive frame of mind
    (b) *unhealthy* (i)   in a state of ill health
          (ii) conducive to ill health
          (iii) indicative of ill health or of an irrational or destructive frame of mind

Accordingly, phrases of the type *a not unhealthy* N are acceptable when *unhealthy* is used in any of the senses of (19b). But both *healthy* and *unhealthy* also have senses that are unmatched by corresponding senses in the other, as shown in (20):

(20) (a) *healthy*   (iv) sizable
    (b) *unhealthy* (iv) dangerous

---

[12] Our acceptability intuitions about cases like (18) have interesting properties. At first it appears that the sentences are acceptable; then, upon reflection as to their meaning, their unacceptability emerges. Our explanation for this in terms of the general solution proposed in Section 7 is the following: the sentences contain phrases that are superficially analyzable in terms of the perceptual schema (34c), but once they are so analyzed, their interpretation is seen to be anomalous (for example, "He emitted a slightly to moderately earthly scream" for (18a)).

[13] The decision would be right only for those cases in which an adjective stem, by accident, is homophonous with a true adjective with an entirely different meaning. Neither of the cases in (18), however, strikes us as meeting this criterion.

[14] The definitions in (19) and (20) are based on the entries that appear under *healthy* and *unhealthy* in *The American Heritage Dictionary*.

The fact that *healthy* has the additional sense 'sizable' is not problematic.[15] However, the sense 'dangerous' for *unhealthy* does present a problem since phrases of the type *a not unhealthy* N, in which *unhealthy* is used in this sense, are unacceptable, as illustrated in (21):

(21) *Don't take any not unhealthy risks

To adopt the solution that *unhealthy* with the sense 'dangerous' is not analyzable into the negative prefix *un-* and the adjective *healthy* would be incorrect since this sense of *unhealthy* clearly belongs with the others.[16] Therefore Standard Theory has no mechanism to account for the unacceptability of cases like (21).

These cases do not exhaust the list of difficulties for Standard Theory. Consider (22):

(22) (a) *The bishop favored the not impious regent
     (b) *Maude wants to marry a not impotent man

Semantically, the relation of *impious* to *pious* (similarly, *impotent* to *potent*) is that of *unhappy* to *happy*: they mean the same save for the contribution of the negative prefix. But phonologically they differ in the quality of the first vowel. Using Chomsky and Halle's (1968) informal spelling, *pious* is *pIous* and *-pious* is *-pEous*. The *E* of *-pEous* is derived from underlying *-pIous* by a laxing rule (and a subsequent rule which tenses vowels in prevocalic position). The laxing rule applies to a vowel which immediately follows a stressed syllable and which is not the final syllable in the word. Formally, the rule is (23):[17]

(23) $V \rightarrow [-\text{tense}] \ / \ [+\text{stress}]C_0 \underline{\quad} C_0 V$

The effect of rule (23) can also be seen in such examples as *infinite* (from *in+fInIt*—compare *finite*), *barometer* (from *baro+mEter*—compare *meter*), *relative* (from *relAt+ive*—compare *relation*), *bicycle* (from *bI+cIcle*), and *maturation* (from *matUr+ation*—compare *mature*).

Consequently, *pious* and the *-pious* of *impious* do not differ in their systematic phonemic representation: both are represented *pIous*. But if *pious* and *-pious* have the same meaning and are represented alike phonologically, how can Standard Theory account for the unacceptability of (22)? The relevant factor, clearly, is that the two forms differ phonetically as a consequence of the application of the laxing rule in *impious*. However, Standard Theory cannot make reference to that difference in the formulation of a restriction on a syntactic transformation. And even if it could, there would be no way of referring to the pronunciation of the adjective *pious* in a derivation of a sentence that contains only the adjective *impious*. The constraint would have to

---

[15] For some people, however, *not unhealthy* may acceptably be used to mean 'slightly to moderately sizable', as in (a):

(a) The president fled to Venezuela with a not unhealthy share of the profits

The significance of this fact is discussed in note 29.

[16] Roughly, we may say that the sense 'dangerous' for *unhealthy* is derivable from the sense 'conducive to ill health' by generalizing the notion 'ill health' to 'harm'. Such a generalization, however, does not obscure the underlying relation of *unhealthy* to *healthy*.

[17] Rule (23) is obviously related to Chomsky and Halle's rule (118d), the last line of their Auxiliary Reduction Rule I (1968, p. 125), which they develop to handle the reduction of the penult in words like *advisory* (from *advise+Ory*). What our discussion shows is that their rule (118d) has a more extensive application than they supposed.

refer to a quasi-phonetic form that does not appear in the derivation of the sentence in question, a possibility that does not exist within Standard Theory.[18]

One could argue that condition (17) handles most of the cases and that the remaining problems can be listed as idiomatic exceptions to the rule of Relative Clause Reduction. But such a list would provide no explanation of why just these cases are exceptional.

4. A SOLUTION WITHIN GENERATIVE SEMANTICS

Having shown that Standard Theory is incapable of providing a natural account of negated attributive adjective constructions, we will now demonstrate that Generative Semantics is more than adequate to the task. This should not be surprising, given the fact that the theory permits reference to all stages of a derivation at any given stage (derivational constraints) and even to other possible derivations (transderivational constraints).

Recall the problematic cases for Standard Theory, which are illustrated in (18), (21), and (22). In (18) we find examples like *unearthly* and *unusual*, in which the meaning of the full adjective is different from the compositional meaning of the negative prefix and the adjective that follows it (*-earthly* and *-usual*). One possible treatment for such cases within Generative Semantics is to specify a constraint that noun phrases of the type $X \frown not \frown$ Adjective$_1$ Noun, where Adjective$_1$ = [Neg] + Adjective$_2$, are ill-formed just in case the material that corresponds to Adjective$_2$ in a derivation of a noun phrase of the type $X \frown$ Adjective$_2$ Noun is different from the material that corresponds to Adjective$_2$ in the original derivation or in case there is no derivation that leads to a well-formed noun phrase of the latter type.[19] The constraint is both derivational (requiring simultaneous reference to a stage preceding lexical insertion and a stage following relative clause reduction) and transderivational (requiring reference to other derivations or to the nonexistence of other derivations of a certain type).

The case of (21) would receive a similar treatment. Prior to lexical insertion, the material corresponding to *healthy* in the derivation of (21) would be the structure corresponding to the notion 'safe'. This semantic structure is not one of the possible prelexical structures underlying *healthy* in the derivation of the corresponding sentence (24):

(24) *Don't take any healthy risks

Thus (21) is ill-formed.

Finally, consider (22). To account for the unacceptability of this type of sentence, we would simply add to the transderivational part of the constraint that Adjective$_2$ in the phrase $X \frown$ Adjective$_2$ Noun is phonetically the same as Adjective$_2$ in $X \frown not \frown$ [Neg] + Adjective$_2$ Noun after the application of the morphophonemic rules of vowel laxing.

---

[18] See examples (d)–(g) in note 28 for other cases of this sort.

[19] A generative semanticist could argue that his approach to this situation enables one to avoid the ad hoc and arbitrary maneuver of considering *-earthly* and *-usual* to be adjective stems rather than adjectives. For other arguments that claim that Generative Semantics offers an alternative to "arbitrary syntax," see Lakoff (1972) and Postal (1970).

5. A SOLUTION WITHIN EXTENDED STANDARD THEORY

Since the description of the cases under consideration appears to involve the full panoply of power available to Generative Semantics, it is surprising that the Extended Standard Theory (Chomsky (1971)), with one modification, can also account for these cases. It is not usually supposed that the Extended Standard Theory provides as much increased descriptive latitude over the Standard Theory as does Generative Semantics. However, all that must be assumed is that reduced relative clauses receive their semantic interpretation (including semantic amalgamation with the head noun) following the rule of Relative Clause Reduction rather than in deep structure.

This assumption is not unreasonable in view of the possibility that there are real, though subtle, differences in interpretation assigned to the object noun phrases in (25a) and (25b):

(25) (a) I see an elephant that is small
    (b) I see a small elephant

To see these differences, suppose that (25a) and (25b) are the first premises of the two arguments whose second premises are given in (26):

(26) (a) An elephant is an animal
    (b) An elephant is an animal

Substituting *animal* for *elephant* whenever it appears in (25), we obtain (27):

(27) (a) I see an animal that is small
    (b) I see a small animal

For many people, (27a) would be considered a valid inference from (25a) and (26a), but (27b) would be considered an invalid inference from (25b) and (26b). Thus it would appear that (25b), which is derived from the structure that also underlies (25a) by Relative Clause Reduction and Adjective Preposing, differs semantically in an ever-so-slight way from (25a).[20]

Suppose, then, that we accept the view that there is a surface interpretation of

---

[20] We believe, however, that the difference in interpretation between full and reduced relative clauses is rhetorical rather than semantic. That is, both (25a) and (25b) are ambiguous: the substitution of *animal* for *elephant* leads to a valid conclusion in one reading and to an invalid one in the other, and this is true for both examples. The reduced relative clause structure simply highlights the reading in which the substitution leads invalidly to the conclusion. This is so because the surface string Adjective Noun gives perceptual salience to the interpretation in which the adjective is to be judged in relation to the noun rather than in an absolute sense (that is, "small for an elephant"); the surface string in which the adjective is separated from the noun by the relative pronoun and the copula gives salience to the absolute interpretation of the adjective. This case is very much like that of sentences containing two quantifiers for which there is a preferred reading based on which quantifier comes first, as, for example, in *Many arrows hit few targets* and *Few targets were hit by many arrows*. Indeed it may turn out that all of the central cases motivating semantic sensitivity to surface structure can be explained by mechanisms outside the grammar. (See Katz (1972, Chapter 8).)

Adjective-Noun combinations in English, and suppose that we are faced with the question of how to interpret the surface noun phrase configuration (28):

(28)

$$ADJ_1$$

$$X \; not \; [NEG] + ADJ_2 \; N$$

We proceed as follows. First we determine the senses of Adjective$_1$ that are compatible with the noun. We then construct the antonyms of these senses, assign the readings to Adjective$_2$, and declare that the interpretation is that of (29):

(29) X slightly to moderately Adj$_2$ N

The interpretation (29), however, is well-formed (grammatical) only if Adjective$_2$ is lexically represented as having at least one of the senses assigned to it by the interpretive rule. Given the surface noun phrases in (30), this rule would assign the interpretations in (31):

(30) (a) a not unhappy man
     (b) a not unhealthy man
     (c) a not unearthly scream
     (d) a not unhealthy risk
(31) (a) a slightly to moderately happy (in a state of emotional well-being) man
     (b) a slightly to moderately healthy (in a state of good health) man
     (c) a slightly to moderately earthly (not weird, ordinary) scream
     (d) a slightly to moderately healthy (safe) risk

Both (31a) and (31b) are well-formed interpretations since the independent lexical items *happy* and *healthy* within them have the interpretations assigned to them by the interpretive rule. But (31c) and (31d) are not well-formed since *earthly* does not mean 'not weird, ordinary' and *healthy* does not mean 'safe'.

To handle the unacceptability of phrases like *a not impious regent* in (22a), however, the Extended Standard Theory would have to have the power of examining the output of phonological rules such as (23), since the surface structure representations of such phrases would not distinguish them from acceptable phrases like *a not impossible situation*. Rule (23) is either a cyclic rule or a post-cyclic rule since it makes reference to stress placement. In either case the internal labeled bracketing would have been erased, destroying the information necessary for constructing a semantic representation. Therefore the theory would have to be modified further in one of two ways: either it would have to abandon the principle that labeled bracketing is erased after each cycle or it would have to permit the existence of derivational constraints that hold between surface structure and phonetic representation. Either choice would add descriptive power to the theory, thus reducing its explanatory capacity.[21]

---

[21] Presumably, Generative Semantics and Extended Standard Theory would treat cases of phrase-incorporated *not* with predicate adjectives in a similar manner. These cases appear to be governed by the same set of restrictions that applies to the prenominal cases, as exemplified in (a) and (b):

6. A MOVE TO SAVE STANDARD THEORY

To summarize, we have shown that if we are obliged to account within the grammar for the acceptability judgments concerning negated attributive adjective phrases in English, then Standard Theory must be abandoned in favor of either the much more powerful theory of Generative Semantics or a more powerful version of Extended Standard Theory. It is clear that the problem with Standard Theory is the complexity involved in the theoretical extensions needed to make it sensitive to the internal morphology of adjectives with negative prefixes. Suppose we accept this limitation and add to Standard Theory the following universal constraint, which increases the restrictiveness of the theory: *no syntactic transformational rule is permitted to make use of the internal morphological structure of lexical items.*[22] The effect of this restriction on the statement of the rule of Relative Clause Reduction would be the elimination of that part of the condition on inapplicability that refers to the analysis of an adjective into a negative prefix and another adjective. Thus, the rule would now have the form (32):

$$(32) \quad \underbrace{X \ |_{\mathbf{S}}}_{1} \quad \underbrace{\begin{bmatrix} \text{Rel} \\ \text{Pro} \end{bmatrix} \text{Tense } be \ Y \ |_{\mathbf{S}}}_{2} \quad \underbrace{Z}_{3} \quad \Rightarrow$$

$$\quad\quad\quad 1 \quad\quad\quad\quad \phi \quad\quad\quad\quad 3$$

   (a) Harry was often not unfriendly

   (b) *Harry was often not $\begin{Bmatrix} \text{intrepid} \\ \text{impious} \end{Bmatrix}$

Generative Semantics would mark cases like (b) as ungrammatical. Extended Standard Theory would include a generalized form of the interpretive rule (28)–(29) that could apply to predicate adjective structures as well. This, however, has some unfortunate consequences for the treatment of nonechoic, noncontrastive tag question formation, which has usually been taken as a paradigmatic example of a syntactic phenomenon. Consider (c)–(f):

   (c) Harry [was not] unhappy, was he?

   (d) Harry was [not unhappy], wasn't he?

   (e) Harry [was not] happy, was he?

   (f) Harry was [not happy], wasn't he?

Presumably, the surface interpretive rule would allow sentences like (d), (f) to be generated freely with the assumption that *not (un)happy* is a constituent. Sentence (f) would then be marked as semantically anomalous by virtue of the fact that no interpretive rule applies to simple constructions of the type *not* Adjective. That is, (f) would be marked as syntactically well-formed but semantically anomalous. This consequence, of course, is not further proof of the inadequacy of Extended Standard Theory but is certainly at variance with the previously well-motivated assumption that tag formation is a syntactic process.

[22] Note that feature-sensitive transformations such as Subject-Verb Agreement and polarity-adjustment rules (for example, the rule that specifies the conditions under which items like *any*, *ever*, and *at all* occur) are stated in terms of semantico-syntactic features, not word-internal morphemes. Thus the proposed universal restriction would have no adverse effect elsewhere in a Standard Theory account of English syntax. The restriction may have to be slightly modified, however, to allow for such phenomena as separable prefixes, as in German and Dutch.

Condition: Inapplicable if

$$X = X^\frown \left\{ \begin{pmatrix} N \\ \begin{bmatrix} \text{Indef} \\ \text{Nongener} \\ \text{Pro} \end{bmatrix} \end{pmatrix} \right\} \text{ and } Y = not^\frown \text{Adj}$$

Otherwise optional

Rule (32) specifies that (1a) and (1b) are both ungrammatical, despite the acceptability of the latter. This simplifies the grammar but requires an explanation of the acceptability of (1b).

7. A BEHAVIORAL ACCOUNT OF THE MEANING AND ACCEPTABILITY OF A RELATED CONSTRUCTION

In order to understand the basis for the acceptability of (1b), it is necessary to consider the mechanism for the perception of speech. Recent research has isolated various systems of this component. The most pertinent to the present discussion is a set of perceptual strategies, operations which utilize information in surface strings to assign directly their deep structure relations. Recent experimental evidence supports the view that the words in a surface sequence are first assigned their possible lexical classification.[23] Other experimental evidence supports the view that perceptual strategies are schemata which take the lexically labeled strings as input and mark them directly for deep structure relations, without processing intermediate levels of representation.[24] The best-studied example of such a strategy is one which assigns the "actor-action" relation to a clause-initial $NP^\frown V$ string (33):

(33) $NP^\frown V \rightarrow NP_{\text{actor}}{}^\frown V_{\text{action}}$

Of course, strategies such as (33) are not rules which define well-formedness since they allow exceptions. (For example, (33) is inappropriate to passive sentences or to object-first cleft sentences, as is reflected in their relative perceptual complexity.) Rather, such operations appear to be incorporated as an early stage of perceptual processing because of their general validity.

Such strategies also apply to assign relations within phrases. For example, rules like (34) would assign a particular relation correctly in almost every case in English:

(34) (a) $DET^\frown ADJ^\frown N \rightarrow DET^\frown ADJ_{\text{modifier of N}}{}^\frown N$

    (b) $DET^\frown ADV^\frown ADJ^\frown N \rightarrow DET^\frown ADV_{\text{modifier of ADJ}}{}^\frown ADJ_{\text{modifier of N}}{}^\frown N$

    (c) $DET^\frown ADV_1{}^\frown ADV_2{}^\frown ADJ^\frown N \rightarrow$
        $DET^\frown ADV_{\text{modifier of ADV}_2}{}^\frown ADV_{\text{modifier of ADJ}}{}^\frown ADJ_{\text{modifier of N}}{}^\frown N$

The psychological interpretation for such labeled structures is a function of semantic analysis together with the analysis provided by such systems as rhetoric and conversational implicature. Consider, for example, (35):

---

[23] See Garrett (1970) and Conrad (1972).
[24] See Fodor and Garrett (1966), Bever (1970), and Fodor, Bever, and Garrett (in press).

(35) He has a not very expensive apartment

Its literal interpretation is paraphrased in (36); note that *not* simply negates that part of the price dimension denoted by *very expensive*:

(36) He has an apartment which is expensive to a not very extreme degree

However, the interpretation that is often given to sentences like (35) is something like (37):

(37) He has a slightly to moderately inexpensive apartment

Thus the pure semantic interpretation of (35) does not correspond to the interpretation which is more likely to be associated with it. A possible conclusion is that the proposed semantic interpretation is wrong. However, that would incorrectly entail that the pure semantic interpretation of (35) is not a possible interpretation for it.

A more promising line of investigation is provided by Grice's theory of conversational implicatures (Grice (1968)), which assigns interpretation (37) to (35) as a function of the literal interpretation (36) together with inferences based on conversational "maxims." The relevant maxim here would be that of "Quantity": *make your (conversational) contribution as informative as required.*

Suppose (35) is given as an answer to the question (38):

(38) How expensive an apartment does Horace have?

In such a case the literal meaning of (35) is an apparent violation of the maxim of Quantity: it answers a request for positive information about a continuum denoted by the unmarked adjective *expensive* with a denial of only one position on that continuum.[25] This leaves open all the other positions on the "expensive" side of the continuum—"rather expensive," "slightly expensive," and so on. Thus, the questioner is free to assume that the literal interpretation of the answer was not intended because it violates the maxim of Quantity. The task then becomes to determine the intended interpretation. The questioner may reason as follows. If the answerer had intended to communicate any specific degree of expensiveness in conformity with the maxim of quantity, then he or she would have used one of the positive adverbs (e.g., *pretty*, *slightly*) with the adjective in framing the answer. Thus, the questioner can assume that the answerer intended to indicate a range on the "inexpensive" side of the continuum. But that range cannot be the one denoted by *very inexpensive* since what was said was the explicit negation, namely, *not very expensive*. Hence, by exclusion, the questioner is left with the interpretation 'slightly to moderately inexpensive' as the intended meaning.

This line of reasoning and its conclusion are strengthened by an independent rhetorical principle, namely, that one should strive for parallelism: one should not answer a question using *expensive* with a construction using *inexpensive*. Accordingly, (39) as a response to (38) would be heard as slightly abrupt, almost disagreeable:

(39) He has a pretty inexpensive apartment

Thus, if in fact Horace has a pretty (but not very) inexpensive apartment, the respondent to the question (38) has the choice of either the abrupt (39) or the polite but somewhat more prolix (35).

The analysis just given correctly predicts an asymmetry in the natural interpretations of answers to questions framed in terms of marked and unmarked adjectives.

---

[25] It is not necessarily a violation, however, since this may be all the information that is available to the answerer, in which case to say more would be in violation of one of the maxims of Quality.

Consider the question-answer dialog (40)-(41), as compared with the dialog (38)-(35):

(40) How inexpensive an apartment does Horace have?
(41) He has a not very inexpensive apartment

Example (41) does not contain the conversational meaning 'slightly to moderately expensive' but can be taken only literally as containing the meaning 'inexpensive to a not very extreme degree'. This is so because the use of the marked adjective *inexpensive* in the question in (40) conveys the presupposition that Horace's apartment is inexpensive to some degree. The respondent in this case cannot be interpreted as denying this presupposition. Thus the questioner here would conclude that the answer is vague because the answerer could not be more precise (that is, the answerer was actually obeying the maxim of Quality).

In summary, then, we find that phrases of the type Determiner⌢*not* Intensifying-Adverb⌢Unmarked-Adjective⌢Noun have possible nonliteral interpretations which would literally be rendered by Determiner⌢*slightly to moderately*⌢Marked-Adjective⌢Noun. These interpretations are consequences of the application of rules that determine conversational implicatures. Moreover, it appears to be the case that these nonliteral interpretations can be supplied by speakers even in the absence of a conversational setting. To the extent that they can, the rules have become generalized,[26] that is, they are part of a system of surface interpretive rules that are not part of the grammar of English.

8. WHY WE CAN SAY A NOT UNHAPPY PERSON EVEN THOUGH IT IS UNGRAMMATICAL

We can now explain the acceptability of sentences like (1b) in terms of the perceptual mechanisms. Consider the perceptual strategy in (34c). This operates correctly on sequences like (42) to assign the scope of the initial *not* as the following adverb:

(42) the not $\begin{Bmatrix} \text{very} \\ \text{clearly} \end{Bmatrix}$ happy boy

Since such strategies operate on a preliminary lexical-class analysis of the input as it is heard, they sometimes apply behaviorally in instances where their structural index is met only approximately. For example, consider the sentences in (43), each of which contains a negated attributive adjective, while the adjective contains an adverblike prefix.

(43) (a) Harry's not overdeveloped muscles were not up to the task
     (b) We worship a not all-powerful deity
     (c) A not supersaturated solution is what we need
     (d) They are certainly a not underdeveloped tribe

Apparently, the *not* can combine in perception with the prefixes *over-*, *all-*, *super-*, *under-* by the application of (34c), provided that what remains after the prefix has been removed is an adjective that plausibly modifies the noun that follows it. In (43) this proviso is met; in (44) it is not, and the examples are accordingly unacceptable:

(44) (a) *Isidor has a not overweening personality
     (b) *The not overturned decision was the basis for his case

[26] See Grice (1968, pp. 21–23).

The explanation for the acceptability of sentences like (1b) is of exactly the same form. The subject noun phrase is misanalyzed perceptually as in (34c), with *un-* being treated as a negative intensifying adverb that modifies the adjective *happy*.

Immediately most of the problematic acceptability judgments given in Section 3 receive their proper explanation. The most serious problem was that the adjective that remained after separating the negative prefix had to be perspicuous as an independent modifier of the following noun. But phrases containing negated adjectives cannot be misanalyzed in accordance with (34c) unless what follows the negative prefix is perspicuous as an adjective. If the mechanism that assigns lexical-class membership in perception cannot assign adjectival status to the element that immediately follows a negative prefix, then (34c) will not be activated.[27]

Now consider the interpretation that is given to the subject noun phrase of (1b), namely (45):

(45) a slightly to moderately happy person

Given that the negative prefix is classified in perception as an intensifying adverb (in the same class as *very*, but with negative sense), then (45) follows by virtue of the generalized conversational implicatures governing expressions of the type Determiner $\frown$ *not* $\frown$ Intensifying-Adverb $\frown$ Unmarked-Adjective $\frown$ Noun. In fact (1b) does not have a literal interpretation, but of course that is just what we would expect, since on our analysis it is ungrammatical.

9. ACCEPTABILITY AND GRAMMATICALITY—REPRISE

Our analysis of the acceptability of sentences like (1b) represents a departure from the usual assumption that if a sentence is acceptable, it is grammatical.[28] It is commonly accepted that ordinary speech behavior is filled with ungrammatical utterances that are used simply because they are behaviorally simple and comprehensible in specific contexts. On our analysis, (1b) is ungrammatical, but it is acceptable in most contexts due to the applicability of a general perceptual strategy, (34c). The methodological basis for this decision is straightforward. On the one hand, to treat such sentences as grammatical, while treating sentences like (1a) as ungrammatical, places extremely strong formal requirements on grammatical theory—in particular, a transderivational constraint that is sensitive to the output of the phonological component. On the other

---

[27] See note 12 for evidence that in cases like *a not unearthly scream* in (18a) a preliminary lexical-class assignment in conformity with the left-hand side of (34c) may be made, only to be rejected because it cannot be interpreted.

The fact that phrases like *someone not unhappy* in (12) are unacceptable follows from the fact that the schema (34c) operates on pronominal modifiers. The unacceptability of *a not unmarried man* in (16) results from the anomalous character of its interpretation, 'a slightly to moderately married man'. Finally, the unacceptability of *the not impious regent* (22) results from the fact that *-pEous* is not a perspicuous representation of *pIous*.

[28] One precedent for this departure is Chomsky's claim (1970, pp. 193–194) that phrases of the type (a) are ungrammatical but acceptable:

(a) his criticism of the book before he read it

However, Chomsky does not cite any independent evidence from the theory of language use to support his contention; rather, his argument is simply that since his theory (the Lexicalist Hypothesis) predicts that (a) is ungrammatical, it must be so, even if it is acceptable. More recently Otero (1972) has argued that certain Spanish sentences in which the verb agrees in number with the direct object rather than with the subject are acceptable but ungrammatical. He, too, argues that since such

hand, the acceptability of such sentences may be accounted for in terms of an independently motivated perceptual theory. Thus we conclude that both sentences (1a) and (1b) are ungrammatical but that (1b) is acceptable because it is comprehensible.

This methodology is not only straightforward, it also offers a principled basis for the notion of "analogy" within the theory of language behavior. Our claim in Section 8 was that certain adjective prefixes may be misanalyzed perceptually as intensifying adverbs which modify the adjectives to which they are prefixed. The process of perceptual misanalysis would appear to capture what is often meant by "analogy" in linguistic discussions. We now propose that appeal to "analogy" should be restricted to cases in which the analogy is generated within the behavioral systems of language use.[29] This means that analogy may be appealed to only in those cases in which there

---

factors cannot be handled within his grammatical framework, they must *ipso facto* be nongrammatical in nature.

Of course, in the absence of an independently motivated performance theory (or some other theory about a part of linguistic knowledge), the failure of a grammatical device to account for acceptability facts can be taken as evidence that more powerful devices are needed within the grammar. For example, Lakoff and Ross (1972) assume the availability of a grammatical device that is sensitive to the phonological clarity of a morphological relationship. Such a device is needed to account for the relative acceptability of sentences like (b) and (c):

(b) ?Max liquefied the metal faster than Sam could bring it about
(c) *Max killed Boris faster than Sam could have brought it about

Lakoff and Ross argue that (c) is unacceptable by virtue of a *grammatical* process that is sensitive to the clarity of the morphological relation between the causative form of the verb and the corresponding change-of-state form. Thus, *liquefy* in (b) is phonologically close to the corresponding intransitive, *liquefy*, while *kill* in (c) is phonologically distinct from the corresponding intransitive, *die*, thus rendering the sentence unacceptable. Lakoff and Ross simply assume that this unacceptability must be due to ungrammaticality and therefore that the grammar must include a device that can account for it. They use this device to explain the ungrammaticality of (c), in response to Fodor's point (1970) that (c) should be as grammatical as (b) if *kill* is actually derived from *cause to die*.

Independent of the arguments given by Fodor, there is a simpler explanation of the difference in acceptability between (b) and (c) than that offered by Lakoff and Ross. We can assume that both (b) and (c) are ungrammatical but that (b) is partially acceptable by virtue of the relative ease with which the listener can figure out what the *it* in the second clause might refer to. This interpretation would allow other aspects of performance to play a role in the relative acceptability of sequences raised but not explained by Lakoff and Ross. For example, (d) would be predicted as being more acceptable than (e) because of the relative clarity of *flute* in (d):

(d) ?Flutists are strange: it doesn't sound shrill to them
(e) *Flautists are strange: it doesn't sound shrill to them

Similarly, the relative productivity of the form which binds the pronominal referent should also correspond to the relative acceptability of such sentences, which is exactly the phenomenon asserted by Lakoff and Ross. Thus, sentences like (g) are more acceptable than those like (f) because "the productivity of the morphological process . . . also plays a role" (p. 122).

(f) *Iroquoianists are strange: they think it should be a world language
(g) ?Australians are strange: they don't think it's too remote

In sum, if the facts noted by Lakoff and Ross are interpreted as due to behavioral processes, then we can explain the different observations as all due to one fact, namely, *any* property of the morphologically bound form which makes it easier for the listener to isolate it facilitates the interpretation of a later pronoun as referring to it. Thus the interpretation that (b) and (c) are both ungrammatical not only simplifies the grammar, it allows for the direct representation of a significant generalization about linguistic knowledge underlying the distribution of words and morphemes.

[29] Further evidence for the perceptual as opposed to the grammatical character of the analogy we propose is supplied by the observation in note 15. Since the lexical item *unhealthy* cannot mean 'unsizable', there is absolutely no way for a grammar constructed in accordance with Standard Theory to generate sentence (a) of note (15) with the interpretation it has. In perception, however, *healthy*, in the sense 'sizable', is perspicuous in that example.

are independently verifiable mechanisms that could contribute to it, rather than leaving it open as an unconstrained grab bag to be used whenever needed.[30] By restricting analogy in this way, it is at least possible that an explanation for it can be found.

We have shown that if certain strings can be analyzed as ungrammatical but acceptable, the empirical facts about negated attributive adjective phrases can be interpreted in a way that vindicates Standard Theory. This vindication is important primarily because Standard Theory imputes more limited and specific structures to linguistic knowledge. This in turn makes more precise claims about what is in the child's mind that allows the acquisition of language. Of course, it remains to be shown that Standard Theory can be vindicated in all the areas in which it is currently under attack. However, the clarification of the relation between acceptability and grammaticality can provide the basis for a revival of what we consider to be a prematurely rejected theory.[31]

REFERENCES

Bever, T. G. (1970), "The Cognitive Basis for Linguistic Structures," in J. Hayes, ed., *Cognition and the Development of Language*, New York: Wiley.

Bever, T. G., and D. T. Langendoen (1972), "The Interaction of Speech Perception and Grammatical Structure in the Evolution of Language," in R. Stockwell and R. Macaulay, eds., *Linguistic Change and Generative Theory*, Bloomington: Indiana University Press.

Chomsky, N. (1965), *Aspects of the Theory of Syntax*, Cambridge: M.I.T. Press.

Chomsky, N. (1970), "Remarks on Nominalization," in R. A. Jacobs and P. S. Rosenbaum, eds., *Readings in English Transformational Grammar*, Waltham, Mass.: Ginn.

Chomsky, N. (1971), "Deep Structure, Surface Structure, and Semantic Interpretation," in D. Steinberg and L. Jakobovits, eds., *Semantics*, New York: Cambridge University Press.

Chomsky, N., and M. Halle (1968), *The Sound Pattern of English*, New York: Harper & Row.

Conrad, C. (1972), *Studies of the Subjective Lexicon*, unpublished Ph.D. dissertation, University of Oregon.

Fauconnier, G. (1971), *Theoretical Implications of Some Global Phenomena in Syntax*, unpublished Ph.D. dissertation, University of California at San Diego.

Fillmore, C. J. (1965), *Indirect Object Constructions in English and the Ordering of Transformations*, The Hague: Mouton.

[30] As in Chomsky (1970).

[31] For example, the contrast in acceptability between (2a) and (2b) would require a grammatical theory that allows for derivational constraints. But there is good reason to believe that (2a) and (2b) are both grammatical (see Jackendoff and Culicover (1971) and Langendoen, Kalish-Landon, and Dore (1972)). For arguments that (3a) and (3b) are both grammatical, see Grosu (1972). Grosu, in fact, attempts the very ambitious task of showing that all of Ross's constraints are based on perceptual operations. Similarly (4a) and (4b) are interpretable as grammatical, with the unacceptability of (4a) being due to a perceptual operation that attaches an initial adverb to the nearest following verb, leading to an apparent temporal contradiction in the verb phrase (see Katz and Bever (forthcoming)).

Finally, Fauconnier (1971) and Kuno (1972) have argued that the syntactic treatment of pronominalization does not require global constraints of any kind. Thus there are two ways to remove cases that motivate derivational constraints: one can account for the facts by appealing either to an independently motivated performance theory or to independently motivated syntactic devices.

Fodor, J. A. (1970), "Three reasons for not deriving 'kill' from 'cause to die'," *Linguistic Inquiry*, *1*, 429–438.

Fodor, J. A., and M. Garrett (1966), "Some Reflections on Competence and Performance," in J. Lyons and R. Wales, eds., *Psycholinguistics Papers*, Chicago: Aldine Press.

Fodor, J. A., T. G. Bever, and M. Garrett (in press), *The Psychology of Language*, New York: McGraw-Hill.

Garrett, M. (1970), "Does Ambiguity Complicate the Perception of Sentences?" in G. D'Arcais and W. Levelt, eds., *Advances in Psycholinguistics*, Amsterdam: North Holland.

Grice, H. P. (1968), "Logic and Conversation II," unpublished paper.

Grosu, A. (1972), *The Strategic Content of Island Constraints*, unpublished Ph.D. dissertation, Ohio State University.

Halle, M. (1964), "On the Bases of Phonology," in J. A. Fodor and J. J. Katz, eds., *The Structure of Language*, Englewood Cliffs, N.J.: Prentice-Hall.

Jackendoff, R., and P. Culicover (1971), "A reconsideration of dative movements," *Foundations of Language*, *7*, 397–412.

Jakobson, R., and M. Halle (1956), *Fundamentals of Language*, The Hague: Mouton.

Katz, J. J. (1972), *Semantic Theory*, New York: Harper & Row.

Katz, J. J., and T. G. Bever (forthcoming), "The Fall and Rise of Empiricism, or the Truth about Generative Semantics."

Klima, E. S. (1964), "Negation in English," in J. A. Fodor and J. J. Katz, eds., *The Structure of Language*, Englewood Cliffs, N.J.: Prentice-Hall.

Kuno, S. (1972), "Pronominalization, reflexivization, and direct discourse," *Linguistic Inquiry*, *3*, 161–196.

Lakoff, G. (1969), "On Derivational Constraints," in R. I. Binnick, *et al.*, eds., *Papers from the Fifth Regional Meeting of the Chicago Linguistic Society*, Chicago: Department of Linguistics, University of Chicago.

Lakoff, G. (1970), "Thoughts on Transderivational Constraints," unpublished paper.

Lakoff, G. (1971), "On Generative Semantics," in D. Steinberg and L. Jakobovits, eds., *Semantics*, New York: Cambridge University Press.

Lakoff, G. (1972), "The arbitrary basis of transformational grammar," *Language*, *48*, 76–87.

Lakoff, G., and J. R. Ross (1972), "A note on anaphoric islands and causatives," *Linguistic Inquiry*, *3*, 121–125.

Langendoen, D. T., N. Kalish-Landon, and J. Dore (1972), "Dative Questions," unpublished paper.

Miller, G. A., and N. Chomsky (1963), "Finitary Models of Language Users," in R. Luce, R. Bush, and E. Galanter, eds., *Handbook of Mathematical Psychology*, Vol. II, New York: Wiley.

Otero, C. (1972), "Acceptable ungrammatical sentences in Spanish," *Linguistic Inquiry*, *3*, 233–242.

Postal, P. (1972), "A global constraint on pronominalization," *Linguistic Inquiry*, *3*, 35–60.

Postal, P., and J. R. Ross (1970), "A problem of adverb preposing," *Linguistic Inquiry*, *1*, 145–146.

Ross, J. R. (1967), *Constraints on Variables in Syntax*, unpublished Ph.D. dissertation, M.I.T.

Ross, J. R. (1972), "Doubl-ing," *Linguistic Inquiry*, *3*, 61–86.

the syntax
and semantics of quotation[1]

Barbara Hall Partee

University of Massachusetts at Amherst

1. INTRODUCTION

The main concern here will be with sentences in which a verb of saying is in construction with the direct quotation of a whole sentence, as in (1):

(1) The other day Tom said to me, "My grandfather was killed with a knife by a bachelor"

Such constructions are not intuitively very problematical looking. The verb "say" raises none of the semantic puzzles of "know" or "believe," at least not when used with direct quotation; and the syntax of the embedding could hardly be simpler —a quoted sentence has exactly the form it would have as an independent sentence. But since such simplicity is exceptional among embedding constructions, it is perhaps not surprising to discover that it is far from simple to fit these sentences into a generative grammar.

First some delimitation of the data under consideration is in order. I am assuming that quotation is a natural part of natural language, although I am not completely confident of it. Quotation marks are an orthographic device with no exact analog in spoken language. The locution "quote ... unquote" is clearly derivative from the written form and restricted mainly to reading aloud, and the same holds, I think, for "and I quote." The phrase "in so many words" is natural in spoken language but does not indicate strict quotation. For example, sentence (2) could be my report of Bill's utterance of (3):

[1] This is a revision of a paper read at the California May Day Linguistics Conference held at Berkeley in May 1971. I am indebted to Paul Durham, who led me to much of the relevant philosophical literature. Any misuse of it is my own.

(2) Bill said in so many words that I was a fool
(3) Barbara is a fool

Perhaps the nearest thing spoken language has to a natural quotation device is an intonational one, namely, a pause before and after the quoted sentence, plus (imitation of (?)) the intonation the sentence would have in isolation.[2]

Excluded from consideration here are two uses of quotation which, it is postulated, can best be treated separately. The first of these exclusions is word quotation,[3] as in (4) and (5):

(4) Should "pickup" ever be hyphenated?
(5) I used to think that the word "ellipsis" was related to "elide"

The other exclusion is mixed direct and indirect quotation, as in (6):

(6) Captain Davis said that he did not intend to "go soft on those bomb-throwing hippies"

My only justification for this second exclusion (since intractability is not a justification) is the admittedly prejudiced belief that such sentences do not occur in ordinary spoken language.

Having narrowed down the relevant data somewhat, let us look at some of the interesting problems in the linguistic analysis of what remains. Sentence (1) is not synonymous with sentence (7) and certainly not with sentence (8), even if the quoted sentences are taken to be synonymous:

(7) The other day Tom said to me, "A bachelor killed my grandfather with a knife"
(8) The other day Tom said to me, "An unmarried man used a knife to cause the father of one of my parents to die"

The immediate semantic conclusion to be explicated is that it is not the *meaning* of the quoted sentence that is contributing to the meaning of the whole, but rather its surface form. If we want an underlying representation which will set up an appropriate structure for the semantics to apply to, we might then try something like (9); that is, we might include a phonological representation instead of a deep structure or semantic representation so that (1) and (7), and certainly (1) and (8), will be assigned different underlying structures:

[2] One peculiar discrepancy between spoken and written quotation is that spoken quotation most commonly follows the standard word order of (a), while written quotation most commonly follows the inverted word order of (b):

(a) Then John said, "Why don't you mind your own business for a change?"
(b) "I'm sick of arguing," said John

It is commonly claimed that writing is purely derivative from speech, but cases like this, where the most common written form is rarely found in speech, suggest otherwise (at least for cultures with literary traditions).

I believe that a similar discrepancy, unrelated to quotation, exists between speech and writing in the case of pairs like (c) and (d), with the same word order difference:

(c) The butcher rushed in
(d) In rushed the butcher

[3] There are some cases of quoted sentences which should perhaps be subsumed under this exclusion, but I have no sharp distinguishing criteria. I have in mind cases such as in (a) which can be paraphrased with the quotation in apposition to the words "the sentence":

(a) "I am speaking now" is always true when spoken

(9)

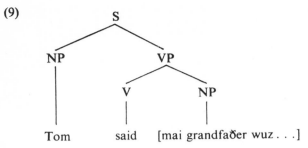

Tom   said   [mai grandfaðer wuz . . .]

This would in fact seem to be a reasonable treatment for a sentence like (10), where the verb is *go* rather than *say*:

(10) Morry aimed the toothbrush at David and went "[æʔæʔæʔæʔ]"

For my dialect,[4] *go* and *say* are distinguished by the complementary restrictions that what follows *say* must be a sentence and what follows *go* must not be.[5] Thus, what follows *go* may indeed be best represented as a string of sounds. But (9) would not account for ordinary quotation because of the evidence presented by sentences like those in (11):

(11) (a) The sign says, "George Washington slept here," but I don't believe he really ever did [*he, did*]
      (b) Whenever Fred sighs "Boy, do I need a drink," he expects you to fix him one [*one*]
      (c) What he actually said was, "It's clear that you've given this problem a great deal of thought, " but he meant quite the opposite [*opposite*]

Representing the quoted sentences as phonological material only would appear to make it impossible to describe the connection between the cited words of the matrix and the relevant parts of the quotation.

2. "THE MEANING OF A SENTENCE IS A FUNCTION OF THE MEANING OF ITS PARTS"

Let us now attempt to relate the data of the preceding section to the general principle enunciated in the title of this section, which will be referred to as the MSFMP principle. At its weakest, this principle is simply the semantic analog of the syntactic

---

[4] What follows is not true of an up-and-coming dialect spoken at least by many college-age Californians in which *go* (usually in the historical present) is the standard verb for reporting speech.

[5] The restriction appears not to be purely syntactic: in my dialect *go* can be used when talking of parrots and tape recorders, even if they happen to produce well-formed sentences, and also to report otherwise normal speech that mimics deviant intonation:

    (a) The parrot went "Polly wants a cracker"
    (b) John went "*How* are *you* to*day*!"

Therefore it is (fortunately) not necessary actually to constrain the grammar so as to prevent the generation of well-formed sentences after *go*. It will be sufficient simply to generate unanalyzed strings of sounds in that position; some strings of sounds will be pronunciations of sentences in English or other languages. This should capture just the right difference between (c) and (d):

    (c) Whoever answered the phone said "¿Quien habla?"
    (d) Whoever answered the phone went "[kyen abla]"

principle that speaker-hearers must have a finite set of rules accounting for an infinite set of possible sentences. That is, we can also *understand* an infinite set of sentences using our finite mental equipment, and that would be impossible if there were not definite principles relating wholes to parts.

But there is a stronger form of the MSFMP principle, one which is by no means such a necessary principle but which is widely accepted as true or at least as the best working hypothesis, namely, what logicians call the principle of a "logically perfect language," relativized to phrase structure grammars:

> *The LPL Principle:* Corresponding to each syntactic rule $A \to BC$ (or equivalently to any deep structure configuration $B \overset{A}{\diagup \diagdown} C$), there must be associated a unique semantic projection rule R which applies to the meanings of B and C as arguments to yield the meaning of A as value.

Starting from syntax, it would seem that the simplest description of a quoted sentence is that it consists of a quotation morpheme plus a sentence, as shown in (12):

(12) NP $\to$ QM + S   (QM = quotation morpheme)

Then the relevant part of the deep structure for (1) would be something like (13):

(13)

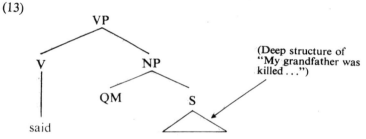

The syntactic function of QM would be twofold: (*a*) to trigger "last-cyclic" transformations, such as interrogative word-order shifting on the cycle of the quoted sentence, and (*b*) to insulate the quoted sentence from further change on subsequent cycles.

But (13) does not supply a sufficient basis for semantic interpretation, since on the standard theory it leads to the prediction that (1) and (7) are synonymous; and a generative semantics version of it could do even worse, predicting (1) and (8) to be synonymous as well.

Therefore the LPL principle is violated by the analysis suggested here. There are various possible next steps. The strategy recommended by Katz and Postal (1964) and followed by most generative semanticists is the following:

> *The "Look Deeper" Principle:* When apparent violations of the LPL principle occur, we have erred in our syntactic analysis of the sentence; that is, we are mistaken about what the parts are or about how they are combined, or both.

Before applying the "Look Deeper" principle to quotation, let us put the matter into perspective by recapitulating the history of the analysis of sentences like (14):

(14) Johnny hasn't yet learned that my brother is my brother

The classical syntactic analysis, (15a), provides an appropriate structure for only one of the two possible semantic interpretations of the sentence, in fact for the less plausible one, namely, that on which Johnny hasn't yet learned a certain tautology. When these examples were noticed by such linguists as Bach and McCawley, the "Look Deeper" principle led to an additional analysis along the lines of (15b), with whatever additional syntax it takes to turn (15b) into (14):

(15)   (a)

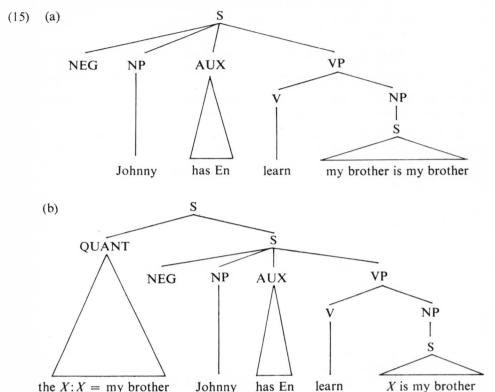

   (b)

The classical analysis, (15a), is appropriate for what Quine (1960) calls the *opaque* construction (with what philosophers refer to as the *de dicto* reading of "my brother"); the generative semanticists have added structures like (15b) to represent the *transparent* construction (with the *de re* reading of "my brother"). What is interesting here is that while the classical analysis has trouble with the *de re* reading of (14), the generative semantics approach, which handles that nicely, will have trouble with the opaque (that is, the normal) interpretation of (16a), on which (16a) and (16b) are not synonymous:

(16) (a) Johnny hasn't learned that bachelors are unmarried men
      (b) Johnny hasn't learned that unmarried men are unmarried men

The problem is that a generative semanticist is committed to deriving "bachelor" and "unmarried man" from the same source if their synonymy is part of the linguistic competence of the speaker of a sentence like (16a) and hence committed to deriving (16a) and (16b) from the same source. But the speaker of (16a) is describing someone who has not attained that particular bit of competence.

Thus, for (16a), the classical approach has an advantage by virtue of its very superficiality, at least on the normal (opaque–*de dicto*) reading. My general thesis is that the classical approach will always have an advantage in *de dicto* cases, where by definition linguistic form as well as (or instead of) content matters. And I see quotation as a paradigm example of a construction which is *always* opaque; the quoted sentence always has a *de dicto* interpretation (if that term can be used for whole sentences; it certainly can be used at least for each NP within a quoted sentence).

Returning now to the "Look Deeper" principle, the only way that comes to mind for applying it to quoted sentences is somehow to add the required surface information to the deepest structure, as, for example, in (17):

(17) (a)   NP → QM S PHON

(b)

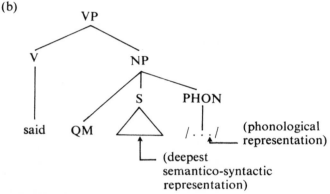

(c) Surface rule:

X ₙₚ [QM S PHON] X
        1   2   3
If 2 = 3, delete 3
If 2 ≠ 3, abort

Since (17) has been set up as a straw man, it is not surprising that it looks ad hoc. I will mention some specific arguments against it in the course of offering some positive suggestions in the next section.

3. LANGUAGE AND METALANGUAGE

Logicians have long observed that one of the advantages of natural languages (which offsets and may even partially explain the rampant ambiguity and vagueness for which natural languages are notorious) is their universality; natural languages provide means for talking about virtually anything, including themselves.[6]

---

[6] Another aspect of the universality principle which might cause trouble for generative semantics is that one can talk about things one knows little or nothing about. Consider the interesting example in (a):

(a) Where is ambergris found?

Such a question can be used equally well by someone who knows what ambergris is but is missing some empirical facts about its occurrence and by someone who is trying to find out what ambergris is. I do not believe that this is an ambiguity, however, and I would consider inappropriate a deep structure which could not accommodate the second use.

The use of English as its own metalanguage is normally illustrated by examples of the sort that have been excluded from this study, that is, examples like (4) and (5). Other typical illustrations are (18) and (19). These are not excluded here by the earlier criteria, but I regard them as noncolloquial and hence slightly nonnatural because they do not involve verbs of saying:

(18) "I am speaking now" is always true when spoken
(19) "John didn't answer three of the questions" is ambiguous in my idiolect

There are, however, other examples which show the language/metalanguage distinction equally well and which do involve the kind of direct quotation viewed here as central—for example, (20) and (21):

(20) "I talk better English than the both of youse!" shouted Charles, thereby convincing me that he didn't
(21) When you said, "You won't be able to answer three of the questions," I guess I took it the wrong way

These sentences show most clearly the conflicting demand that quotation imposes on a theory. On the one hand, the ellipsis of (20) and the semantic content of the main clause of (21) show that the quoted sentence is syntactically and semantically a functional part of the whole sentence. On the other hand, the quoted sentence in (20) may be ungrammatical for the speaker of (20) and hence not generated at all by his "own" grammar; and any *single* semantic interpretation for the quoted sentence in (21) would be inappropriate in the light of the containing sentence. It is these facts that rule out an analysis like (17).

To resolve the apparent conflict, it may be helpful to consider (*a*) certain properties of demonstratives, and (*b*) certain properties of discourse.

Philosophers, especially Donald Davidson and David Kaplan, have made some relevant observations about how demonstratives work in natural language. The idea is that demonstratives (for example, *this, that, here, there, now, I, yay* in "yay big") do not contribute to the meaning of a sentence by virtue of having a meaning or a sense of their own. Rather, for each demonstrative there is some kind of associated algorithm which, given the linguistic context of the demonstrative in the sentence and the linguistic and extralinguistic context in which the sentence occurs, picks out certain objects in or properties of the whole context as referent of the demonstrative. (Demonstratives are always referential.) Consider the examples in (22), in which the utterance of a demonstrative is typically accompanied or followed by a gesture:[7]

(22) (a) A circular staircase looks like this: [gesture]
     (b) He stuck out his tongue and went like this: [gesture]
     (c) A good way to draw a five-pointed star is like this: [gesture]

The gesture is not a part of the sentence, but the demonstrative in the sentence refers to the gesture, not by virtue of a sense, but by way of the convention that the demonstrative always refers to whatever is being demonstrated in the appropriate way.

Sentence (23a) is clearly analogous to the sentences in (22); note especially its similarity to (22b). I would suggest, therefore, that (23b) is really an elliptical form of (23a):

(23) (a) Morry went like this: [vocal noise]
     (b) Morry went: [vocal noise]

_____

[7] I am considering the colon a *sentence-final* punctuation mark.

In such a construction, the vocal noise is not a part of the sentence any more than the gestures of (22).

Syntactically, however, the sentences with *say* are different. Sentence (24) is not well-formed:

(24) *John said like this: "I have a new car"

Say takes direct objects rather than *like* phrases. But the same sort of analysis can still be proposed, and has been by Donald Davidson, who would derive (25b) from something like (25a):

(25) (a) John said this: Alice swooned
(b) John said, "Alice swooned"

But it is clearly not enough to say that the quoted sentence is a separate sentence, with the quotation marks acting as a kind of demonstrative in the outer, or prior, sentence pointing at this separate sentence. We also must account for the syntactic and semantic integration of the quoted sentence into the containing sentence, as illustrated by (11a–c), (20), and (21).

It is at this point that we need to consider discourse: the syntactic and semantic integration just noted consists of three phenomena, all of which can also occur in discourse, even two-person discourse:

(*a*) pronominalization, of NP's, N's, and other constituents
(*b*) ellipsis
(*c*) a phenomenon which, for want of a better name, I will call *semantic anaphora*

Let us repeat earlier examples here and add analogous discourse examples:

(*a*) *pronominalization*

(26) The sign says, "George Washington slept here," but I don't believe *he* really did
(27) Whenever Fred sighs "Boy, do I need a drink," he expects you to fix him *one*

(28) A: George Washington slept here
B: *He* did not
(29) A: I need a drink
B: Shall I fix you *one*?

(*b*) *ellipsis* (cf. also (11a) and (28))

(30) "I talk better English than the both of youse!" shouted Charles, thereby convincing me that he didn't
(31) A: I talk better English than the both of youse!
B: You obviously don't

(*c*) *"semantic anaphora"*

(32) What he actually said was, "It's clear that you've given this problem a great deal of thought," but he meant quite *the opposite*
(33) A: Did you know that northern magnolias are deciduous and southern ones are evergreen?
B: No, I thought it was just *the opposite*

Furthermore, the language/metalanguage distinction explicit in (21) (repeated here as (34)) is also paralleled in discourses, as in (35):

(34) When you said, "You won't be able to answer three of the questions," I guess
I took it the wrong way
(35) A: Flying planes can be dangerous
B: Which way do you mean that?

Not much has been said in the transformational literature about cross-discourse
syntactic phenomena. The usual justification for limiting attention to sentences is that
anything that can happen in discourse can happen within a single sentence; but the
converse is clearly false, and limitations need to be explored. Sometimes people write
as if all discourses were just conjunctions of sentences, and certainly some discourses
could be analyzed that way (particularly, but not exclusively, some monologs). But
clearly none of the discourses just presented can be analyzed as a conjunction. The
central problem, then, is what basis the *B* speaker in each of those dialogs has for
making his pronominalization, ellipsis, or semantic anaphora. It appears that the
basic principle is that, in understanding *A*'s sentence, *B* must impose enough structure
on it to perceive structurally significant relations between *A*'s sentence and his own.
And apparently *B* can do this even if he cannot generate *A*'s sentence himself (as
could be the case in (31)). Although I do not know how to state these principles at all
precisely, I think it must be significant that there is such a close match between the
permissible dialog phenomena and the phenomena that occur in direct quotation.

The conclusion I would draw from this observation is that it lends further support
to Davidson's claim that the quoted sentence is not syntactically or semantically a
part of the sentence that contains it. Furthermore, we can now resurrect part of our
earliest straw man and say that the (two-sentence) representation of a quotation needs
to include only the surface structure of the quoted sentence; moreover, all the apparent
evidence for deeper syntactic and semantic structure is a result of the main sentence
speaker's understanding and analyzing the noises he is quoting as a sentence, just as
he understands and analyzes a sentence, a string of noises, that comes to him from
someone else. It is in this process that the language/metalanguage distinction is
crucially involved.

REFERENCES

Anscombe, G. E. M. (1957a), "Names of words: a reply to Dr. Whitely," *Analysis, 18,* 17–19.
Anscombe, G. E. M. (1957b), "Report on *Analysis* 'problem' no. 10," *Analysis, 17,* 49–52
Davidson, D. (1968–69), "On saying that," *Synthese, 19,* 130–146.
Davidson, D. (forthcoming), "Quotation," draft of a chapter of a forthcoming book.
Geach, P. T. (1948–49), "Mr. Ill-named," *Analysis, 9,* 14–16.
Geach, P. T. (1958–59), "Is it right to say *or* is a conjunction?" *Analysis, 19,* 143–144.
Geach, P. T. (1963), "Quantification theory and the problem of identifying objects of
reference," *Acta Phil. Fennica, 16,* 41–52.
Kaplan, D. (1971), "Dthat," unpublished paper, UCLA.
Katz, J., and P. Postal (1964), *An Integrated Theory of Linguistic Descriptions,* Cambridge,
Mass.: M.I.T. Press.
Partee, B. H. (forthcoming), "The Semantics of Belief-Sentences," to appear in P. Suppes
and J. Moravcsik, eds., *Approaches to Natural Language: Proceedings of the 1970
Stanford Workshop on Grammar and Semantics.*
Quine, W. V. (1960), *Word and Object,* Cambridge, Mass.: M.I.T. Press.

language-particular rules and explanation in syntax[1]

David M. Perlmutter
Massachusetts Institute of Technology

Janez Orešnik
University of Ljubljana

PART ONE: Analysis of the Orphan Accusative in Slovenian

1. THE ACCUSATIVE PREDICTION RULE

In Slovenian, masculine and feminine nouns and adjectives have the forms shown in (1) in the nominative, accusative, and genitive singular:[2]

(1)	MASCULINE INANIMATE	MASCULINE ANIMATE	FEMININE
Nominative	*navaden ječmen*	*navaden človek*	*navadna ajda*
Accusative	*navaden ječmen*	*navadnega človeka*	*navadno ajdo*
Genitive	*navadnega ječmena*	*navadnega človeka*	*navadne ajde*
	'ordinary barley'	'ordinary man'	'ordinary buckwheat'

[1] This paper is really about how work in linguistics in done. It is therefore a great pleasure for us to dedicate it to Morris Halle, from whom we have learned so much about what one does in linguistic analysis and why.

This work was supported in part by a grant from the National Institutes of Health (5T01 HD00111-07) and a grant from the National Institute of Mental Health (5 P01 MH13390-05) to the Massachusetts Institute of Technology and a grant from the United States Office of Education (OEC-0-70-4986(823)) to the Language Research Foundation. The authors are indebted to Stephen Anderson, Wayles Browne, Janez Dular, Jorge Hankamer, Franc Jakopin, Breda Pogorelec, Paul Postal, John Ross, and Jože Toporišič, who read an earlier version of the manuscript and suggested many improvements. Responsibility for errors rests with the authors.

[2] Additional facts, such as the existence of other declensional classes and a definite (as opposed to indefinite) adjective ending, are not relevant to the subject of this paper and are therefore ignored here.

For feminines, the three cases are distinct. For masculines, however, the form of the accusative can be predicted by the rule in (2) (with a few exceptions, which are discussed briefly in Section 6):

(2) Accusative Prediction Rule
  (a) For animates, the accusative is like the genitive
  (b) For inanimates, the accusative is like the nominative

2. THE ORPHAN ACCUSATIVE

In answer to the question (3) one can say (4a) or simply (4b), without the head noun *ajdo*:

(3) *Katero   ajdo   hočete?*
     which   buckwheat   you want
     'Which buckwheat do you want?'
(4) (a) *Hočem   navadno   ajdo*
         I want   ordinary   buckwheat
         'I want ordinary buckwheat'
    (b) *Hočem navadno*
         'I want ordinary'

Similarly, one can answer (3) with either (5) or (6), where the latter again does not include *ajdo*:

(5) *Navadno ajdo*
     'Ordinary buckwheat'
(6) *Navadno*
     'Ordinary'

In reply to the question (7) one can say (8), parallel to (4a):

(7) *Kateri ječmen hočete?*
     'Which barley do you want?'
(8) *Hočem navaden ječmen*
     'I want ordinary barley'

However, the answer (9), which is the counterpart of (4b), is ungrammatical:

(9) **Hočem navaden*
     'I want ordinary'

Instead of (9), one must say (10):

(10) *Hočem navadnega*
      'I want ordinary'

Similarly, one can answer (7) with (11), the parallel to (5):

(11) *Navaden ječmen*
      'Ordinary barley'

But instead of (12), the parallel to (6), one must answer with (13):

(12) *Navaden
     'Ordinary'
(13) *Navadnega*
     'Ordinary'

When the head noun is not present, the adjective has the genitive form instead of the nominative form that is the usual accusative form for inanimates. Because the genitivelike accusative form *navadnega* appears in the absence of the head noun, we will refer to it as the "Orphan Accusative."

The Orphan Accusative occurs not only with mass nouns like *ječmen* 'barley', but also with count nouns. Thus, in answer to the question (14) one can say (15) but not (16):

(14) *Kakšen*   *površnik hočete?*
     what kind of overcoat you want
     'What kind of overcoat do you want?'
(15) *Hočem navaden površnik*
     'I want an ordinary overcoat'
(16) *Hočem navaden

Instead, one must say (17):

(17) *Hočem navadnega*
     'I want an ordinary one'

Similarly, one could answer (14) with (18) but not with (19):

(18) *Navaden površnik*
     'An ordinary overcoat'
(19) *Navaden

Instead, one would have to say (20):

(20) *Navadnega*
     'An ordinary one'

The key fact is that inanimate masculines have an Orphan Accusative form distinct from their ordinary accusative while feminines do not.[3] The Orphan Accusative therefore cannot be treated as a partitive genitive since this would not explain why it occurs with masculines but not with feminines. Furthermore, while the other Slavic languages have paradigms like (1), in which the accusative of the masculine is like the genitive if it is animate and like the nominative if it is inanimate, the Orphan Accusative, as far as we know, is unique to Slovenian. It is a language-particular phenomenon, and we are faced with the question of how it is to be dealt with in an explicit grammar of Slovenian.

Using a rewrite rule of the type one finds in the linguistic literature, we could state the facts as in (21):

---

[3] Since animate masculines have their accusative like their genitive anyway, there is no overt distinction between the Orphan Accusative and the ordinary accusative.

(21) Orphan Accusative Rule

$$\begin{bmatrix} +\text{adjective} \\ +\text{masculine} \\ +\text{accusative} \end{bmatrix} \rightarrow [+\text{genitive}] \ / \ \text{in the absence of the head noun}$$

We might then claim that we had accounted for the Orphan Accusative in Slovenian.

What is striking about the Orphan Accusative Rule (21) is the fact that it states outright the class that it applies to (masculine accusative adjectives), the change that they undergo (they become genitive), and the environment in which this happens (in the absence of the head noun). However, because the rule *states* these facts, it does not *explain* them. It is the purpose of this paper to show that pseudo-rules like (21) serve only to make us aware of the facts that need to be explained.

3. SOME QUESTIONS RAISED BY THE ORPHAN ACCUSATIVE

Examination of the Orphan Accusative Rule (21) immediately leads one to ask a number of questions.

Question One. Why is it that the special form found in the Orphan Accusative is not an arbitrary ending such as -uruburu *or* -on *but rather an ending that exists elsewhere in the adjectival desinential paradigm?*

Question Two. Why is the Orphan Accusative form the same as that of the genitive case rather than, say, the dative or instrumental?

Question Three. Why do all constituents with adjectival endings, rather than just quantifiers or demonstratives or just those adjectives that refer to inherent rather than transitory properties, have a special form for the Orphan Accusative?

Question Four. Why is it that masculines have a special form for the Orphan Accusative and feminines do not?

Question Five. Why is it the accusative that has a special orphan form, rather than some other case?

Question Six. Why is there a special form in the absence of the head noun rather than in some other environment, such as the presence of a demonstrative or the absence of a quantifier or when the head noun designates a stick-shaped or leafy object?

The proposed Orphan Accusative Rule (21) gives rise to another question that derives not from its content but from its very existence. Why should there be such a rule in Slovenian, but not in, say, Latin or Finnish? There is a more general formulation of this question:

Question Seven. What is particular to Slovenian in the Orphan Accusative phenomenon, and what is more general?

Viewing this situation from the point of view of linguistic theory, we see that a theory that allows the formulation of language-particular rules such as the Orphan Accusative Rule (21) in the grammars of particular languages thereby makes a wide range of similar rules available to particular grammars. In the absence of additional constraints on the form and content of syntactic rules, a theory that allows the Orphan Accusative Rule would also allow, among others, the rules in (22)–(24):

(22) A feminine plural accusative adjective takes the masculine singular instrumental

ending if the head noun is not deleted (and the usual feminine plural accusative ending otherwise)

(23) A masculine singular dative adjective takes the ending *-buni* if there is only one adjective modifying the head noun

(24) A masculine plural genitive or feminine singular locative demonstrative takes the feminine singular genitive ending in the absence of the head noun

But it seems that no language has rules like (22)–(24). A theory of language that permits such rules therefore fails to constrain sufficiently the notion "possible syntactic rule" and therefore also fails to constrain sufficiently the notion "possible human language." Thus, a linguistic theory that allows rules like the Orphan Accusative Rule and (22)–(24) is inadequate as a theory of language.

The immediate problem here is to replace the Orphan Accusative Rule by another analysis that will be able to answer Questions One through Seven. The more difficult problem is to construct a theory of language that will provide a principled basis for choosing this analysis over the Orphan Accusative Rule and for excluding rules like (22)–(24), thus limiting the notions "possible syntactic rule" and "possible human language."

4. IDENTITY OF SENSE PRONOMINALIZATION

The difference between Identity of Reference Pronominalization and Identity of Sense Pronominalization in English is illustrated by the contrast between the sentences (25) and (26):

(25) Bill saw a blue car and Tom saw it too
(26) Bill saw a blue car and Tom saw one too

The pronoun *it* in (25) indicates Identity of Reference (coreferentiality) between the car that Tom saw and the car that Bill saw, while the anaphoric element *one* in (26) indicates only that Tom saw a blue car, which was not necessarily the same one that Bill saw.

The Slovenian sentence (27) is ambiguous:

(27) *Stane je videl plav avto in tudi Tone ga je videl*
       saw blue car and too   it saw
    'Stane saw a blue car and Tone saw it too'
    'Stane saw a blue car and Tone saw one too'

The pronoun *ga* in (27) could be used either for Identity of Reference Pronominalization or for Identity of Sense Pronominalization. The fact that definite pronouns like *ga* can be used for Identity of Sense Pronominalization can be seen clearly from the fact that they appear in sentences such as (28), in which Identity of Reference Pronominalization would be impossible:

(28) *Stane ima pametnega otroka in   tudi Tone ga   ima*
       has bright   child and too   him has
    'Stane has a bright child and Tone has one too'
    (Literally: 'Stane has a bright child and Tone has him too')

(29) *Stane ima pametno ženo in   tudi Tone jo   ima*
          has bright   wife and too   her has
      'Stane has a bright wife, and Tone has one too'
      (Literally: 'Stane has a bright wife and Tone has her too')

Slovenian thus appears not to distinguish between Identity of Sense Pronominalization and Identity of Reference Pronominalization, at least in surface structure. When we look deeper, however, we find that the definite pronouns like *ga* and *jo* are not used in all cases of Identity of Sense Pronominalization. Consider the sentences in (30):

(30) (a) *Stane ima staro rjavo   hišo,   Tone pa ima novo belo*
              has old   brown house   has new   white
          'Stane has an old brown house and Tone has a new white one'
       (b) *Stane ima staro rjavo   hišo,   Tone pa ima novo*
              has old   brown house   has new
          'Stane has an old brown house and Tone has a new one'[4]
       (c) *Stane ima staro rjavo hišo   in   tudi Tone jo ima*
              has old   brown house and too   it has
          'Stane has an old brown house and Tone has one too'

Comparing the anaphoric elements in (30) with their meanings, we find the correspondences in (31):

(31) EXAMPLE   ANAPHORIC ELEMENT   MEANING
     (30a)   *novo belo*   *novo belo hišo*
     (30b)   *novo*   *novo (rjavo) hišo*
     (30c)   *jo*   *staro rjavo hišo*

A grammar of Slovenian must associate the anaphoric elements in (31) with their meanings.

In each case, that part of the meaning that is identical to something in the first conjunct is not present in the second conjunct in surface structure. It is only in the case where the entire noun phrase is identical to the antecedent that the pronoun *jo* appears.

It is possible to account for these facts by postulating that Identity of Sense Pronominalization in Slovenian proceeds in two stages, as sketched in (32):

(32) Identity of Sense Pronominalization
     STAGE ONE (Pronominalization): A noun phrase identical to an antecedent noun
        phrase is replaced by a pronoun
     STAGE TWO (Pronoun Deletion): The pronoun is deleted if it follows a modifier

Under this analysis, the anaphoric elements in (30)–(31) would have the derivations in (33):[5]

---

[4] The Slovenian example, like its English translation, is ambiguous: *novo* here can mean either 'new brown house' or 'new house'.

[5] The trees given in (33) as "underlying forms" are not necessarily the "deepest" level of representation. Thus, if adjectives are derived from underlying relative clauses, these "underlying forms" are derived structures. However, the question of whether these underlying structures are deep or derived is not relevant here.

(33)

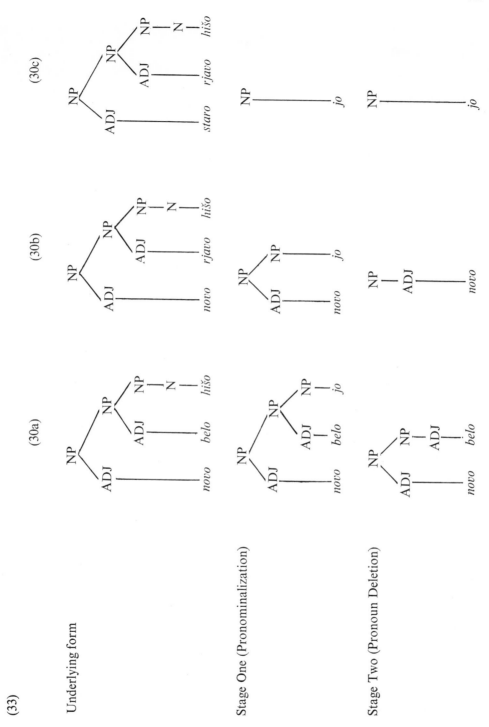

We propose, then, that Identity of Sense Pronominalization in Slovenian proceeds in the two stages outlined in (32).[6] This analysis is motivated by the necessity of matching the anaphoric elements in (30)-(31) with their meanings. The meanings are represented in the underlying forms, and the surface forms are then derived from them.

There are at least two other possibilities: the structures produced by our Stage One (Pronominalization) might be taken to be the underlying forms, or the structures produced by our Stage Two (Pronoun Deletion) might be so taken. In the second case, the underlying and surface forms of the anaphoric elements in (30)-(31) would be identical. Under either of these approaches, some other kind of mechanism would be necessary to associate the underlying forms with their meanings.

We will not argue either for or against the proposal that our Stage One be taken as the underlying form since that issue is not relevant to the topic of this paper. We will, however, present very strong arguments against taking our Stage Two (that is, the surface forms) as the structure underlying the anaphoric elements in (30)-(31).

5. THE CONCORD HYPOTHESIS

Consider Identity of Sense Pronominalization with an accusative masculine noun. From the structure underlying (34a), Identity of Sense Pronominalization as sketched in (32) will produce (34b):

(34) (a) *Stane ima rjav   površnik in   tudi Tone ima rjav   površnik*
              has brown overcoat and too   has brown overcoat
         'Stane has a brown overcoat and Tone has a brown overcoat too'
     (b) *Stane ima rjav   površnik in   tudi Tone ga ima*
              has brown overcoat and too   it has
         'Stane has a brown overcoat and Tone has one too'

From the structure underlying (35), Identity of Sense Pronominalization will produce (36):

(35) *Stane ima rjav   površnik, Tone pa ima črn   površnik*
           has brown overcoat   has black overcoat
      'Stane has a brown overcoat and Tone has a black overcoat'

(36) *Stane ima rjav   površnik, Tone pa ima črnega*
           has brown overcoat   has black
      'Stane has a brown overcoat and Tone has a black one'

In (36) we find the Orphan Accusative form *črnega*. The ordinary accusative *črn* would be ungrammatical in (36), as would the Orphan Accusative *črnega* in (35). This is like the examples considered in Section 2, where the Orphan Accusative appeared in the absence of the head noun. In (36), too, the head noun is absent, and we find the Orphan Accusative. However, we now know more about the derivation of (36). In particular, we know that Identity of Sense Pronominalization takes

---

[6] No explanation is offered here for why the second stage, that is, deletion of the pronoun, depends on the presence of a modifier. This fact, too, requires explanation.

place in two stages, Pronominalization followed by Pronoun Deletion. The last noun phrase in (36) would therefore have to undergo the derivation in (37):

(37)

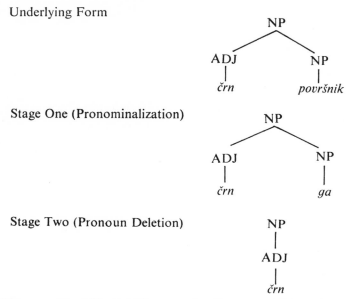

Underlying Form

Stage One (Pronominalization)

Stage Two (Pronoun Deletion)

However, if nothing else happens in the course of the derivation, we will get the incorrect *črn* in (36) instead of the Orphan Accusative form *črnega*. We propose that the Orphan Accusative is produced by the rule of "Concord within the Noun Phrase" (henceforth simply "Concord") applying between Stage One and Stage Two of the derivation. Such a rule is needed in the grammar anyway, completely independently of the cases at issue here. Concord makes adjectives agree with the head noun in gender, number, and case, as the examples in (38) illustrate:

(38) (a) *Stane ima staro rjavo hišo*
'Stane has an old brown house'
   (b) *Stane ima star rjav površnik*
'Stane has an old brown overcoat'

We are now proposing that the Orphan Accusative arises from the application of the rule of Concord at the stage of derivations at which the underlying head noun has been replaced by a pronoun. Agreement of the adjective *črn* with the pronominal head *ga* at this stage of derivation (37) will produce the Orphan Accusative form *črnega*. The mechanism by which Concord produces *črnega* will be discussed in Section 6. Here we will limit ourselves to testing the consequences of the hypothesis that the Orphan Accusative is due to Concord rather than to a special Orphan Accusative Rule.

After Concord has applied, the pronoun *ga* that causes Concord to produce the orphan form *črnega* will be deleted by Pronoun Deletion, leaving the Orphan Accusative form *črnega*. The entire derivation will therefore be as shown in (39):

(39)

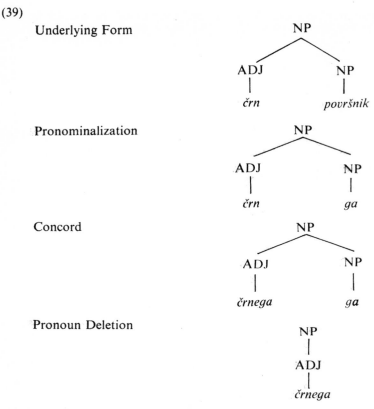

Underlying Form

Pronominalization

Concord

Pronoun Deletion

The most obvious consequence of using the rule of Concord to produce the Orphan Accusative in Slovenian is that the grammar is thereby simplified: there will be no special Orphan Accusative Rule at all since the independently needed rule of Concord will do its work. More importantly, such an approach makes two clear predictions that the Orphan Accusative Rule (21) does not make.

First of all, rule (21) is silent on the question of what happens to a masculine accusative noun phrase which contains more than one adjective if the head noun is absent. A priori, there are many possibilities, including those in (40):

(40) (a) Only the first adjective goes into the Orphan Accusative
     (b) Only the last adjective goes into the Orphan Accusative
     (c) Every second adjective goes into the Orphan Accusative
     (d) Every third adjective goes into the Orphan Accusative
     (e) All adjectives go into the Orphan Accusative

The Concord hypothesis, on the other hand, makes the prediction that all modifying adjectives will go into the Orphan Accusative since they all agree with the head noun when there is one. And this prediction is correct. Thus, alongside (36) we find (41), with both adjectives *novega* and *črnega* in the Orphan Accusative:

(41) *Stane ima star rjav   površnik, Tone pa ima novega črnega*
            has old brown overcoat   has new   black
      'Stane has an old brown overcoat and Tone has a new black one'

Similarly, in answer to the question (42) one can say (43), in which not only the adjectives *starega* and *rjavega* are in the Orphan Accusative but so is the number 'one' *enega*, which always undergoes Concord to agree with the head noun:

(42) *Koliko   površnikov ima Stane?*
     how many overcoats has
     'How many overcoats does Stane have?'

(43) *Samo enega starega rjavega*
     only one old   brown
     'Only one old brown one'

Now consider how the facts illustrated by (41) and (43) might be incorporated into a rule like the Orphan Accusative Rule (21). It would be necessary to say that *all* adjectives in the noun phrase whose head is absent go into the Orphan Accusative. But closer inspection reveals that this is not the case. To see this, consider sentence (44):

(44) *Videl sem velik zemljevid, obsegajoč hrvatski okraj, in majhen zemljevid,*
     saw   large map   comprising Croatian district and small   map
     obsegajoč slovenski okraj
     comprising Slovene   district

   'I saw a large map, comprising a Croatian district, and a small map, comprising a Slovene district'

The head noun in the second conjunct of (44) is *zemljevid* 'map', and its modifiers are *majhen* 'small', on the one hand, and *obsegajoč slovenski okraj* 'comprising a Slovene district', on the other. What will happen if the head noun *zemljevid* is deleted? Will *all* masculine singular accusative adjectives go into the Orphan Accusative? The answer to the latter question is no, for (45) is ungrammatical:

(45) **Videl sem velik zemljevid, obsegajoč hrvatski okraj, in majhnega, obsegajočega slovenskega okraj*

The correct version of (44) with the second occurrence of *zemljevid* deleted is not (45) but rather (46):

(46) *Videl sem velik zemljevid, obsegajoč hrvatski okraj, in majhnega,*
     saw   large map   comprising Croatian district and small
     obsegajočega slovenski okraj
     comprising   Slovene   district
   'I saw a large map, comprising a Croatian district, and a small one, comprising a Slovene district'

Crucially, the masculine singular accusative adjective *slovenski* in (46) does not go into the Orphan Accusative. And this fact is predicted automatically by the Concord hypothesis since *slovenski* in (44) and (46) agrees not with *zemljevid* but rather with its own head noun *okraj* 'district'. This can readily be seen by substituting the neuter noun *mesto* 'town' for *okraj* in (46), giving (47):

(47) *Videl sem velik zemljevid, obsegajoč hrvatski okraj, in majhnega, obsegajočega slovensko mesto*
   I saw a large map, comprising a Croatian district, and a small one, comprising a Slovene town'

In (47) we have the neuter form *slovensko*, in agreement with *mesto*.

If the grammar contained a special Orphan Accusative Rule, it would have to include a condition something like (48):

(48) In the absence of the head noun, all modifying masculine singular accusative adjectives go into the Orphan Accusative if they modify the deleted head noun.

This statement, however, duplicates the rule of Concord itself, and immediately leads to the following question:

Question Eight. Why do all adjectives (rather than just one, or some) that modify the absent head go into the Orphan Accusative and why does this happen only to adjectives that actually modify the absent head? By using the mechanism of Concord to produce the Orphan Accusative, the Concord hypothesis answers this question. Furthermore, it gives automatic answers to two of the questions posed in Section 3, namely, Questions Three and Six.

Question Three. Why do all constituents with adjectival endings, rather than just quantifiers or demonstratives or just those adjectives that refer to inherent rather than transitory properties, have a special form for the Orphan Accusative? It is all constituents with adjectival endings that have a special form for the Orphan Accusative, rather than any others, because they are the constituents that agree with the head noun. A rewrite rule such as (21) is perfectly capable of applying to any subclass of adjectives or to any class of constituents other than adjectives, but using Concord to produce the Orphan Accusative automatically predicts that whatever class of constituents agrees with the head noun will be the class that has a special form for the Orphan Accusative.

Question Six. Why is there a special form in the absence of the head noun rather than in some other environment, such as the presence of a demonstrative or the absence of a quantifier or when the head noun designates a stick-shaped or leafy object? The Orphan Accusative is produced by Concord with a pronominal head: it can arise only in an environment in which the head is pronominal. We have seen that Pronominalization is an intermediate stage in the process of deletion. Therefore we find the Orphan Accusative when the head noun has been deleted. There can be no Orphan Accusative in any environment in which there is no pronominal head.

By answering Question Three and Question Six, the proposal to use the mechanism of Concord to produce the Orphan Accusative provides an *explanation* of the facts.

6. THE MECHANICS OF CONCORD

We will now attempt to make precise how the rule of Concord produces the Orphan Accusative.

The conception of pronominalization that was dominant in generative grammar in the mid-1960's received its clearest formulation in Postal (1966). Under this theory constituents were conceived of as bundles of features, and pronominalization consisted of adding the feature [+pro] to the noun undergoing the process. The presence of this feature would then affect the operation of late "spell-out rules" or "segmentalization rules" that gave morphemes their phonological shape.

It is easy to see that this conception of pronominalization makes it impossible to use the rule of Concord to produce the Orphan Accusative in Slovenian in a natural way. In the sentence (49) the noun *površnik* would be represented as the bundle of features (50):

(49) *Tone ima črn   površnik*
            has black overcoat
      'Tone has a black overcoat'

(50) $\begin{bmatrix} +\text{noun} \\ -\text{animate} \\ +\text{singular} \\ +\text{accusative} \\ +\text{masculine} \\ \vdots \end{bmatrix}$

The rule of Concord would give the modifying adjective the features in (51):

(51) $\begin{bmatrix} -\text{animate} \\ +\text{singular} \\ +\text{accusative} \\ +\text{masculine} \end{bmatrix}$

Then spell-out or segmentalization rules that actualize these features in terms of phonological shape would spell out the feature bundle (51) on the adjective *črn* with the zero ending, yielding the correct form *črn* in (49).

If the pronominalization rule merely adds the feature [+pro] to a feature bundle, however, how will the Orphan Accusative form *črnega* be produced in (52):

(52) *Stane ima rjav   površnik, Tone pa ima črnega*
            has brown overcoat   has black
      'Stane has a brown overcoat and Tone has a black one'

The structure underlying (52) will have (49) as its second conjunct. *Površnik* will be marked as in (50), and the addition of [+pro] to this feature bundle will in no way affect the adjective's being given the features in (51) by the rule of Concord. When the spell-out or segmentalization rules apply, the adjective will again receive the zero ending, as it did in (49), resulting not in (52) but in the ungrammatical sentence (53):

(53) **Stane ima rjav površnik, Tone pa ima črn*

In order to use the mechanism of Concord to account for the Orphan Accusative, we propose that the pronoun *ga* be marked in the lexicon with the feature [+animate] and that this pronoun actually be present in post-Pronominalization trees. If Pronominalization is a transformation, it consists not of adding the feature [+pro], but rather of replacing a noun phrase by a pronoun with its own feature bundle. If, on the other hand, Pronominalization is not a transformation but pronouns are already present in underlying structures, then *ga* will of course already be present in trees. Our solution requires only that the pronoun *ga* be actually present in post-Pronominalization trees; it does not matter whether the pronoun was already present in underlying structures or produced by a transformation.

If the pronoun *ga* is lexically marked as [+animate] and is actually present in post-Pronominalization trees, then the rule of Concord, applying before Pronoun Deletion, will make adjectives that modify *ga* [+animate] as well. These adjectives will therefore not have the features in (51), but rather those in (54):

(54) $\begin{bmatrix} +\text{animate} \\ +\text{singular} \\ +\text{accusative} \\ +\text{masculine} \end{bmatrix}$

Then, the application of the Accusative Prediction Rule (2) to adjectives with the features in (54) will give them the accusative ending *-ega*, which is their genitive ending as well. The result will be the grammatical sentence (52) but not (53).

With respect to our proposal that the pronoun *ga* is marked [+animate], it should be noted that neither this feature nor the device of marking lexical items idiosyncratically for this feature is ad hoc. The feature [±animate] exists in Slovenian grammar independently of the Orphan Accusative since the Accusative Prediction Rule (2) makes crucial use of it. And although the feature [±animate] with regard to a particular noun is, in the overwhelming majority of cases, predictable from the semantic representation of that noun, there are a few nouns which idiosyncratically act as animates with respect to the Accusative Prediction Rule, even though they are semantically inanimate. For example, *rak* 'cancer' and *as* 'ace' have their accusative like their genitive (*raka* and *asa*, respectively) instead of like their nominative (*rak* and *as*), even though they are semantically inanimate. They must therefore be marked as inherently [+animate] in the lexicon. Thus the device of marking particular lexical items [+animate] is needed in the grammar of Slovenian independently of the Orphan Accusative, and, in proposing that the pronoun *ga* be lexically marked [+animate], we are only suggesting another use for a device that is needed anyway.

The proposal to account for the Orphan Accusative by marking *ga* as [+animate] in the lexicon and letting the rule of Concord and the Accusative Prediction Rule produce the Orphan Accusative constitutes our answer to Question Seven posed in Section 3: *What is particular to Slovenian in the Orphan Accusative phenomenon, and what is more general?* What is particular to Slovenian is the fact that the pronoun *ga* is inherently marked with the feature [+animate] (although we shall see that even this is related to a more general phenomenon). Everything else is perfectly general. The Accusative Prediction Rule (2), the rule of Concord, and the breakdown of Identity of Sense Pronominalization into Pronominalization and Pronoun Deletion as in (32) are needed in the grammar of Slovenian independently of the Orphan Accusative. Furthermore, our solution to the problem of the Orphan Accusative does not involve any restrictions on the operation of transformations. Rules apply in a perfectly general fashion. With the pronoun *ga* marked [+animate], the application of independently motivated rules automatically produces the Orphan Accusative. Our solution is therefore in accord with the view that the rules of a language express regularities, while idiosyncrasies are to be found in the lexicon.

We now turn to the remaining questions in Section 3 to show how this proposal answers them automatically, thereby providing an explanation of the facts in each case.

Question One. Why is it that the special form found in the Orphan Accusative is not an arbitrary ending such as -uruburu *or* -on, *but rather an ending that exists elsewhere in the adjectival desinential paradigm?* A rewrite rule such as (21) would be capable of producing an arbitrary ending such as *-uruburu* or *-on* for the Orphan Accusative. Under our hypothesis, however, the Orphan Accusative arises from Concord with a pronoun marked [+animate]. The Orphan Accusative form is therefore the usual form of adjectives that agree with an animate accusative head.

Question Two. Why is the Orphan Accusative form the same as that of the genitive case rather than, say, the dative or instrumental? The form for animate masculines in the accusative singular is like the genitive. Since the Orphan Accusative is produced by agreement with an animate head, its ending is like the genitive.

Question Four. Why is it that masculines have a special form for the Orphan Accusative and feminines do not? Under our hypothesis, the Orphan Accusative is the result of the Accusative Prediction Rule (2) applying to adjectives that have acquired the feature [+animate] by Concord. Since rule (2) applies to masculines but not to feminines, it follows automatically that masculines have a special Orphan Accusative form and feminines do not.

Question Five. Why is it the accusative that has a special orphan form, rather than some other case? Since the Orphan Accusative results from the application of the Accusative Prediction Rule to [+animate] adjectives, and since the Accusative Prediction Rule specifies accusative endings rather than those of some other case, it is the accusative and not some other case that has a special orphan form.

The proposal to mark the pronoun *ga* with the feature [+animate] and to let the rule of Concord distribute this feature to adjectives and the Accusative Prediction Rule spell it out as a genitive ending thus answers automatically the remaining questions of Section 3. It therefore gives an explanation of why Slovenian has the particular distribution of the Orphan Accusative that it has, rather than some other imaginable distribution.[7]

7. THE NONOCCURRENCE OF THE ORPHAN ACCUSATIVE IN THE PLURAL AND DUAL

While the accusative singular has a special orphan form that is like the genitive, this is not the case in the plural and the dual. Thus, in answer to the question (55) one could say either (56) or (57):

(55)　*Katere površnike hočete?*
　　　'Which overcoats do you want?
(56)　*Hočem navadne površnike*
　　　'I want ordinary overcoats'
(57)　*Hočem navadne*
　　　'I want ordinary ones'

Use of the genitive form of the adjective, as in (58), would be ungrammatical:

(58)　**Hočem navadnih*

Similarly, one could answer (55) with either (59) or (60) but not with (61):

(59)　*Navadne površnike*
　　　'Ordinary overcoats'
(60)　*Navadne*
　　　'Ordinary ones'
(61)　**Navadnih*

It is the same in the dual. In answer to (62) one can use any of the responses in

---

[7] It is interesting to note that Toporišič (1968; 1972) and Orzechowska (1971), in discussing the historical origin of the Orphan Accusative, state that it was probably due to the influence of the pronouns "which have the same genitive and accusative singular" (Toporišič (1968)).

(63) but not those in (64), which have the genitive form *navadnih* rather than the ordinary accusative *navadna*:

(62)   *Katera površnika hočete?*
       'Which (two) overcoats do you want?'
(63) (a)   *Hočem navadna površnika*
           'I want (two) ordinary overcoats'
     (b)   *Hočem navadna*
           'I want (two) ordinary ones'
     (c)   *Navadna*
           '(Two) ordinary ones'
(64) (a)   **Hočem navadnih*
     (b)   **Navadnih*

This immediately gives rise to another question:

Question Nine. Why is the Orphan Accusative found only in the singular and not in the plural or dual?

A rule such as the Orphan Accusative Rule (21) would simply add the specification [+singular] on the left-hand side of the arrow to take care of the facts under discussion. But the hypothesis proposed here provides an explanation. According to this proposal, the Orphan Accusative arises only as the result of the confluence of two factors: a [+animate] marking on the pronominal head when Concord applies, and the application of the Accusative Prediction Rule to give animate accusatives genitive endings. Our hypothesis therefore predicts that Orphan Accusatives will occur only in those morphological categories in which the Accusative Prediction Rule applies. If there are morphological categories in which this rule does *not* apply, then, even if a particular pronoun is marked [+animate], there will be no Orphan Accusative.

In the plural, we find the paradigms in (65):[8]

(65) | | ANIMATE PLURAL | INANIMATE PLURAL |
     |------------|---------------------|----------------------|
     | Nominative | *navadni Slovenci* | *navadni površniki* |
     | Accusative | *navadne Slovence* | *navadne površnike* |
     | Genitive | *navadnih Slovencev*| *navadnih površnikov*|
     | | 'ordinary Slovenes' | 'ordinary overcoats' |

These paradigms show that the Accusative Prediction Rule (2) does not apply in the plural. Thus, even if the accusative plural pronoun *jih* is marked [+animate] and this marking is placed on modifying adjectives by the Concord Rule, the Accusative Prediction Rule will not apply to plural forms to spell out the [+animate] marking as a genitive ending. Our hypothesis thus automatically predicts that there can be no Orphan Accusative in the plural.

The dual paradigms are given in (66):

(66) | | ANIMATE DUAL | INANIMATE DUAL |
     |------------|---------------------|----------------------|
     | Nominative | *navadna Slovenca* | *navadna površnika* |
     | Accusative | *navadna Slovenca* | *navadna površnika* |
     | Genitive | *navadnih Slovencev*| *navadnih površnikov*|
     | | 'ordinary Slovenes' | 'ordinary overcoats' |

---

[8] The *e* in the *-ev* ending of *Slovencev* is due to a phonological rule that is sensitive to the preceding consonant; there is no difference between the underlying forms of the animate and inanimate endings.

These paradigms show that the Accusative Prediction Rule has to be reformulated so that rule (2) will apply only in the masculine singular. The exact reformulation does not concern us here. What is important are the consequences of this reformulation for the Orphan Accusative. Under our hypothesis, the Orphan Accusative results whenever the Accusative Prediction Rule spells out animate accusative endings as genitive. Since the Accusative Prediction Rule does not do this in the dual (or the plural), it follows automatically that, even if the accusative dual pronoun *ju* is marked [+animate], there will be no Orphan Accusative in the dual.

Note that, with the limitations that have been observed on the domain of the Accusative Prediction Rule, it is possible that the [+animate] marking is not confined to the masculine singular accusative pronoun *ga* but is to be found on *all* pronouns in Slovenian;[9] it would then be only the restricted domain of the Accusative Prediction Rule that is responsible for the restricted distribution of a special Orphan Accusative form. In the next section evidence will be presented to show that this is in fact the case.

It has been shown in this section that, since our hypothesis makes use of the Accusative Prediction Rule to produce the Orphan Accusative by the same mechanism that makes the animate accusative like the genitive, and since the Accusative Prediction Rule does not apply in the plural and dual, we automatically answer Question Nine and provide an explanation of why there is no Orphan Accusative in the plural and dual.

8. THE ORPHAN ACCUSATIVE IN THE NEUTER SINGULAR

We illustrate the neuter singular with the noun *proso* 'millet'. In answer to the question (67) one can say (a) or (b) of (68):

(67) *Katero proso hočete?*
'Which millet do you want?'
(68) (a) *Hočem navadno proso*
'I want ordinary millet'
(b) *Navadno proso*
'Ordinary millet'

It is also possible to delete the head noun *proso*, but Slovenes tend to be hesitant to do this if the head is neuter. The reason is an uncertainty about what to do with the resulting orphaned adjective. Should one use one of the replies in (69), with the ordinary accusative, or one of those in (70), with the Orphan Accusative?

(69) (a) *Hočem navadno*
'I want ordinary'
(b) *Navadno*
'Ordinary'
(70) (a) *Hočem navadnega*
'I want ordinary'
(b) *Navadnega*
'Ordinary'

---

[9] We are indebted to Wayles Browne for this suggestion. This is possible because there is no way, aside from the Accusative Prediction Rule, that animacy shows up morphologically in Slovenian.

The situation here has two interesting properties: first, when they are asked about it, speakers are uncertain as to whether to use the ordinary accusative ((69a), (69b)) or the Orphan Accusative ((70a), (70b)), and upon reflection they tend to accept both as grammatical. Second, in actual usage one hears both forms. The situation in the neuter singular therefore differs from that in the masculine singular. In the masculine, Slovenes are not hesitant and uncertain, and the Orphan Accusative is obligatory and not optional: the question (71) can be answered by the forms in (72), with the Orphan Accusative, but not by those in (73), with the ordinary accusative:

(71) *Kateri ječmen hočete?*
      'Which barley do you want?'
(72) (a) *Hočem navadnega*
           'I want ordinary'
      (b) *Navadnega*
           'Ordinary'
(73) (a) **Hočem navaden*
      (b) **Navaden*

This difference between the masculine singular and neuter singular must be explained:

Question Ten. Why are speakers uncertain as to whether to use the Orphan Accusative in the neuter singular, and why is its use there optional?

If the neuter singular accusative pronoun *ga* is marked [+animate], our hypothesis answers Question Ten automatically, without any additional machinery. Given our proposal, if the pronoun is marked [+animate], an Orphan Accusative form will show up precisely where the Accusative Prediction Rule gives [+animate, +accusative] endings the same shape as genitives. In order to find out what our hypothesis predicts about the neuter singular, it is therefore necessary to see whether or not the Accusative Prediction Rule operates in the neuter singular. Inanimate neuter nouns have their accusative like their nominative, but it is the *animate* neuter nouns that are crucial here. There are only a handful of them, and, when asked about their form in the accusative, Slovenes tend to be uncertain as to whether it is like the nominative or like the genitive. After thinking it over, most speakers tend to accept both forms as grammatical. And in actual usage one hears both forms. Thus we find the paradigms in (74) with animate neuter singular nouns:

(74) Nominative   *navadno dekle*   *navadno ščene*
      Accusative   *navadno dekle/*   *navadno ščene/*
                   navadnega dekleta   *navadnega ščeneta*
      Genitive   *navadnega dekleta*   *navadnega ščeneta*
                   'ordinary girl'   'ordinary cur'

Regardless of what the precise reason may be,[10] the fact is that Slovenes tend

---

[10] Two facts of Slovenian morphology are relevant here. First, in the dual and plural, the accusative of neuters is like the nominative. Second, throughout the singular paradigm, neuter endings are the same as masculine endings (except for the nominative case, which is the citation form from which gender is in general predictable, and the accusative, which is under discussion here). In neuter singular, then, the conflict is between the generalization that neuter endings are like masculine endings in the singular, as a result of which the Accusative Prediction Rule (2) should apply in the neuter singular and yield *navadnega dekleta* and *navadnega ščeneta*, and the generalization that the accusative of neuters is like the nominative throughout the paradigm, which would yield *navadno dekle* and *navadno ščene* as accusative singular forms.

to be uncertain as to whether or not the accusative of animate neuter singular nouns is like the nominative or like the genitive, and they tend to accept both forms as grammatical and to use them both.

The feeling of uncertainty and the acceptance and use of both possibilities is precisely what characterizes the situation with respect to the Orphan Accusative in the neuter singular. If the neuter singular accusative pronoun *ga* is marked [+animate], both the uncertainty and the acceptability of both forms will follow automatically from our hypothesis. Consider the derivation of an answer to the question (75):

(75) *Katero proso hočete?*
'Which millet do you want?'

At the relevant stage of derivation, the answer will have the form in (76):

(76)
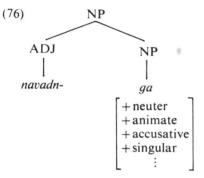

Concord will place the features [+neuter, +animate, +accusative, +singular] on the adjective, and after Pronoun Deletion we will be left with (77):

(77)
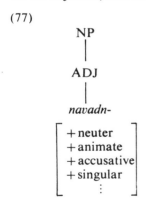

The Accusative Prediction Rule should now apply to (77). But, as we have seen from the paradigms of *dekle* and *ščene*, people are uncertain as to whether or not this rule applies to animate neuters. If it does, (77) will be actualized as (78):

(78) *Navadnega*

If it does not, we will get (79):

(79) *Navadno*

Speakers' uncertainty as to whether or not the accusative is like the genitive in the paradigms of *dekle* and *ščene* is automatically translated by our hypothesis into their uncertainty as to whether to answer (75) by (78) or by (79), and their acceptance and use of both *navadno dekle* and *navadnega dekleta* is translated into their acceptance and use of both (78) and (79). The initially strange behavior of neuter singulars with respect to the Orphan Accusative thus follows as an automatic consequence of their strange behavior with respect to the Accusative Prediction Rule.

It should be noted that the masculine singular accusative pronoun *ga* and the neuter singular accusative pronoun *ga* are not the same entity, as might be thought, but rather are distinct. The evidence for this comes from the derivation of (78) and (79) from (77). The adjective in (77) must be marked [+neuter] in order for it to evoke uncertainty and optionality with respect to the Accusative Prediction Rule. If it were the same as the masculine pronoun, there would be no uncertainty, and *navadnega* would be the only possible grammatical output. Note also that (79) has the neuter ending *-o*. The conclusion is inescapable that the masculine accusative pronoun *ga* and the neuter accusative pronoun *ga* are distinct.

Both pronouns, however, must be marked [+animate] if the appearance of the Orphan Accusative in both genders is to be accounted for. It would be strange enough for two pronouns to have ad hoc feature markings but even stranger for them both to have the *same* ad hoc markings. A grammar in which the animacy of the masculine pronoun and that of the neuter pronoun are two separate and unrelated facts is missing a generalization. However, there is a way that the relevant generalization can be captured, namely, by saying that *all* pronouns in Slovenian are marked [+animate].[11] Since the only place in Slovenian where animacy shows up morphologically is where the Accusative Prediction Rule makes the accusative of animates like their genitive, and since, as we have seen, this rule applies only in the masculine singular and, with uncertainty and optionality, in the neuter singular, the animacy markings on the other pronouns will cause no difficulty; there are no other syntactic rules that refer to animacy.

Although Slovenian pronouns must be marked [+animate] to account for the appearance of the Orphan Accusative, they can still refer to inanimate objects, as in (80), where the pronoun *ga* refers to the inanimate *površnik* 'overcoat':

(80) *Kar zadeva površnik, sem ga videl včeraj*
      'As far as the overcoat is concerned, I saw it yesterday'

But it is only the "weak" or "clitic" forms of the pronouns that can refer to inanimate objects; the corresponding "strong" forms cannot. Thus, in the sentence (81), in which we have the strong form *njega* instead of the clitic *ga*, *njega* can only have animate reference:

(81) *Včeraj sem videl samo njega*
      'Yesterday I saw only him'

This is true not only of the strong form *njega*, which corresponds to the clitic *ga*,

---

[11] Once all pronouns are marked [+animate], the argument given in Section 6 against a feature treatment of Pronominalization (as consisting of marking constituents with the feature [+pro]) loses force, as Charles Fillmore has pointed out to us, for it could then be argued that the way to mark pronouns for animacy is by means of a rule of the form [+pro] → [+animate]. Since pronouns in many languages behave like animates, the ultimate resolution of this question will depend on how the animatelike behavior of pronouns is to be captured in universal grammar.

but also of all other strong form pronouns in Slovenian. Thus, the feminine singular strong form *njo* in (82) can only have animate reference:

(82) *Včeraj sem videl samo njo*
'Yesterday I saw only her'

This fact is of interest in connection with our conclusion that it is not just the masculine and neuter accusative singular pronouns but all pronouns in Slovenian that are marked for animacy. The [+animate] marking that triggers the Orphan Accusative is no doubt related to the fact that the strong forms of the pronouns can only have animate reference. It is not clear, however, how this can be captured in the present theory of grammar. The question of how this is to be incorporated in a grammar and the concomitant question of why pronouns that are marked [+animate] can refer to inanimate objects must be left for future research.

In this section it has been shown how the status of the Orphan Accusative in the neuter singular follows automatically from the status of the Accusative Prediction Rule in the neuter singular. It follows from this that the neuter pronoun *ga* is distinct from the masculine pronoun *ga* but is also marked [+animate]. Indeed the correct generalization appears to be that all Slovenian pronouns are marked [+animate].

9. DIRECT EVIDENCE FOR THE STAGE OF DERIVATIONS AT WHICH CONCORD APPLIES

All of the questions concerning the distribution of the Orphan Accusative have now been answered. This has been accomplished merely by marking pronouns as [+animate], without adding any new rules or apparatus to the grammar.

The stage of derivations at which noun phrases consist of modifiers and a pronominal head (for example, *črn ga*) is crucial to the hypothesis since it is at this point that Concord produces *črnega ga*, which Pronoun Deletion then reduces to *črnega*, the Orphan Accusative form that appears in surface structure. Since Pronoun Deletion is obligatory if the pronoun is preceded by a modifier, the evidence for this stage of derivations has been indirect: it has enabled us to explain the distribution of the Orphan Accusative.

It would be possible to find direct evidence for the stage of derivations at which Concord applies if there is a rule which separates the pronominal head from its modifiers after Concord has applied but before the application of Pronoun Deletion. Under such circumstances, if our hypothesis is correct, a modifier that agrees with the masculine singular accusative pronominal head *ga* should have the *-ega* ending characteristic of the Orphan Accusative, with the head *ga* that triggered Concord still present in surface structure. Two additional properties of Slovenian—Clitic Movement and the behavior of *ves* 'all'—make it possible to find the relevant evidence.

In Slovenian, clitic pronouns are obligatorily moved to second position in the clause.[12] Thus, while 'I wanted to find Jože' is expressed by the sentence (83), 'I wanted to find him' is expressed by (84), in which the clitic pronoun *ga* has been

---

[12] This is actually an oversimplification, for the facts of clitic placement in Slovenian are more complex. For discussion of this question, see Toporišič (1970, pp. 176 ff.)

moved from the position of *Jožeta* in (83) to second position, where it joins the auxiliary verb *sem*, the other clitic:[13]

(83) *Želel sem najti Jožeta*
     wanted   find
     'I wanted to find Jože'
(84) *Želel sem ga   najti*
     wanted   him find
     'I wanted to find him'

Ves 'all' and *cel* 'whole' are floating quantifiers which can occupy a number of different positions in sentences. As a result they become separated from the clitic pronoun heads of their noun phrases. The clitic heads move out to second position in the sentence. Thus, while 'I wanted to eat up all the buckwheat' would be expressed as (85), 'I wanted to eat up all of it' would be rendered as (86), in which the clitic pronoun *jo* has joined *sem* in second position, leaving behind the modifier *vso*:[14]

(85) *Želel sem pojesti vso ajdo*
     wanted   eat up all buckwheat
     'I wanted to eat up all the buckwheat'
(86) *Želel sem jo pojesti vso*
     wanted   it eat up all
     'I wanted to eat up all of it'

Now consider an example like (87), in which the head is masculine:

(87) *Želel sem pojesti ves riž*
     wanted   eat up all rice
     'I wanted to eat up all the rice'

To say 'I wanted to eat up all of it', referring to *riž* 'rice', one would say (88):

(88) *Želel sem ga pojesti vsega*
     wanted   it eat up all
     'I wanted to eat up all of it'

The clitic pronoun *ga* has moved into second position, leaving behind the modifier *vsega*. The sentence (89), in which the modifier has been left in the ordinary accusative, is ungrammatical:

(89) **Želel sem ga pojesti ves*

This is a remarkable fact. And it shows that, completely independently of the Orphan Accusative, the pronoun *ga* must be marked in some way so that Concord will produce the genitivelike form *vsega* instead of the ordinary accusative *ves* if (88) and (89) are to be accounted for. Thus the device we have posited to account for the Orphan Accusative is needed in the grammar anyway. Sentences (88) and (89) show clearly that when a modifier agrees with the pronominal head *ga*, the modifier takes on the *-ega* ending that shows up in the Orphan Accusative. This is striking confirmation of our hypothesis.

---

[13] The two clitics *sem* and *ga*, as a group, are in second position. Clitic order constraints of the type discussed in Perlmutter (1971, Chapter 2) specify that within the clitic group *sem* precedes *ga*.
[14] *Jo* is the feminine singular accusative pronoun, and *vso* is the feminine singular accusative form of *ves* 'all'.

10. PREDICATE ATTRIBUTE AGREEMENT WITH A PRONOMINAL TRIGGER

Implicit in our hypothesis that the Orphan Accusative is produced by Concord with a pronominal head is another prediction: any adjective that agrees with a pronoun will acquire the feature [+animate], which, as a result of the Accusative Prediction Rule, will have the accusative ending characteristic of animates, *regardless of which agreement rule puts the [+animate] feature on the adjective.* Our discussion so far has been confined to examples where the relevant agreement rule has been Concord (within the noun phrase), but there is another agreement rule which can be used to test this prediction—the rule we will refer to as Predicate Attribute Agreement or simply Attribute Agreement. This rule is responsible for the agreement of *pomazan* 'stained' in (90) and (91):

(90) *Včeraj   smo našli mizo pomazano s   krvjo*
     yesterday   found table stained   with blood
     'Yesterday we found the table stained with blood'

(91) *Včeraj smo našli stol   pomazan s krvjo*
                       chair
     'Yesterday we found the chair stained with blood'

In (90) *pomazano* is feminine singular accusative, in agreement with its antecedent *mizo*; in (91), *pomazan* is masculine singular accusative, in agreement with its antecedent *stol*.[15] What our hypothesis predicts is that if the antecedent of *pomazan* is the pronoun *ga*, it will have the animate accusative *-ega* ending that is characteristic of the Orphan Accusative. And this is exactly what happens, as we see from (92):

(92) *Včeraj smo ga našli pomazanega s krvjo*
     'Yesterday we found it stained with blood'

The ordinary masculine singular accusative form *pomazan*, which is grammatical in (91), would not be in (92), as we see from (93):

(93) **Včeraj smo ga našli pomazan s krvjo*

This is further confirmation of our claim that it is agreement with the pronoun *ga* that produces the *-ega* ending of the Orphan Accusative. The phenomenon is now seen not to be confined to cases of Concord within the noun phrase; it extends to all sentences in which a modifier agrees with a pronoun. Thus, there can be no language (or dialect of Slovenian) in which adjectives have the Orphan Accusative found in Slovenian but do not assume the same endings under agreement with an overt pronoun. It is this claim that is supported by (92) and (93).

PART TWO: Consequences for Linguistic Theory

11. ON DELETION

11.1. A Pronominal Stage in Deletion

Postal (1970b) argues that the constituents deleted by Equi-NP Deletion in English are pronouns, rather than full noun phrases, at the stage of derivations at which deletion occurs. He suggests that this is but a particular consequence of a universal

---

[15] We will not be concerned here with the problem of specifying which noun phrase is the "antecedent" of the predicate attribute. For an important study of this problem, see Andrews (1971).

principle that the process of deletion of a noun phrase which is subject to the existence of a coreferent noun phrase in the same structure always passes through a pronominal stage. We have shown here that, in Slovenian, identity of sense deletion also goes through a pronominal stage. This suggests that the universal proposed by Postal may be but a special case of a more general principle: any deletion of a noun phrase under identity to another noun phrase (whether identity of sense or identity of reference) passes through a pronominal stage. It remains to be seen whether a universal principle as strong as this one will survive empirical test.

11.2. The Domain of Deletion

It has been shown here that at some stage of derivation certain noun phrases in Slovenian have a pronominal head that is subsequently deleted. Nothing has been said as to whether such pronominal heads are already present in underlying structures or are produced transformationally. Whichever is the case, however, these noun phrases with pronominal heads are possible only if preceded by an identical noun phrase. Thus, a sentence like (94) is not possible in isolation:

(94) *Ima samo enega starega rjavega*
       has only one   old   brown
       'He has only one old brown one'

However, it is natural as an answer to the question (95):

(95) *Koliko površnikov ima Stane?*
       'How many overcoats does Stane have?'

Thus the antecedent of a pronominal head can lie in a previous sentence in the discourse.

A question that has not been resolved here is which of the two phenomena involved in the derivation of sentences like (94)—Pronominalization (whether or not it is a transformation) and Pronoun Deletion—is the one that requires the presence of an antecedent. It seems likely that the antecedent requirement can be placed on Pronominalization in view of the fact that identity-of-reference pronouns require antecedents too. If this is correct, the rule of Pronoun Deletion can be a rather local rule that can be formulated roughly as (96):

(96) Pronoun Deletion $[X \text{ Adj Pro}]_{\textbf{NP}}$
                                    $\downarrow$
                                    ϕ

The other possibility is that it is the deletion rule itself rather than Pronominalization that requires an antecedent noun phrase. The resolution of this issue must be left for future research.

11.3. Directionality of Deletion

Consider a sentence like (97), with a conjoined noun phrase in the accusative case:

(97) *Videl sem očiščen ječmen in   navaden ječmen*
       seen   cleaned barley and ordinary
       'I saw cleaned barley and ordinary barley'

The conjoined noun phrase can be reduced in either of two ways. If the second instance of *ječmen* disappears we get (98), with *navadnega* in the Orphan Accusative:

(98) *Videl sem očiščen ječmen in navadnega*
      'I saw cleaned barley and ordinary'

Failure to use the Orphan Accusative in (98) results in the ungrammatical (99):

(99) **Videl sem očiščen ječmen in navaden*

This means that the object NP in (98) passes through the derivational stages in (100):

(100) (a) *očiščen ječmen in navadn-ga*
       (b) *očiščen ječmen in navadnega ga*
       (c) *očiščen ječmen in navadnega*

Since the deletion process passes through a pronominal stage, with Concord applying when the head is a pronoun, we can conclude that (98) arises through deletion of the second instance of *ječmen*.

It is also possible to reduce the object in (97) in such a way that the first instance of *ječmen* disappears. But then the facts are quite different. We get (101), in which *očiščen* is not in the Orphan Accusative:

(101) *Videl sem očiščen in navaden ječmen*
       'I saw cleaned and regular barley'

Using the Orphan Accusative in (101) results in the ungrammatical (102):

(102) **Videl sem očiščenega in navaden ječmen*

This is a striking fact. Why is there an asymmetry between (98) and (101) in the appearance of the Orphan Accusative?

We have already seen that the deletion process passes through a pronominal stage, allowing Concord to produce the Orphan Accusative along the way. The fact that the Orphan Accusative does not appear in (101) therefore indicates that the reduction is not accomplished by deletion. We propose that (101) is instead derived by means of the independently necessary rule of Right-Node Raising. This rule, as formulated by Lakoff and Ross, takes any constituent that is an end constituent in all conjuncts and removes it from all the conjuncts, Chomsky-adjoining a copy of it to the coordinating node. Right-Node Raising will thus operate on the structure (103), which is the object noun phrase in (97):

(103)

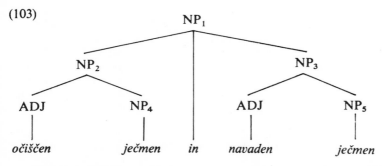

Since the NP *ječmen* is at the right end of both conjuncts, Right-Node Raising will remove NP$_4$ and NP$_5$ from their conjuncts and Chomsky-adjoin a copy to the coordinating node NP$_1$ to produce the structure (104):

(104)

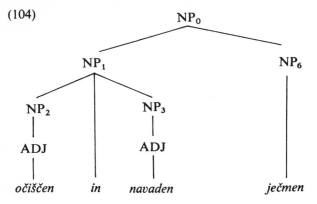

Under Lakoff and Ross's proposal, necessary principles of derived constituent structure will then convert (104) into the structure (105):

(105)

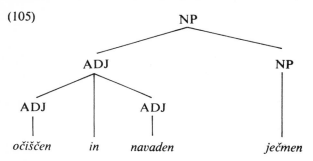

At no point in the derivation does *očiščen* modify a pronominal head. As a result, Concord will not put it in the Orphan Accusative, and we end up with the grammatical sentence (101).

The proposal that reduction of the first instance of *ječmen* in (97) is accomplished by Right-Node Raising and reduction of the second by deletion thus accounts for both the appearance of the Orphan Accusative in (98) and its ungrammaticality in (102).

Since reduction, whether by deletion or Right-Node Raising, is optional, something additional is needed to assure that the right rule applies in each case. Thus, if Right-Node Raising produced a structure in which *ječmen* remained on the left and disappeared on the right, the ungrammatical (99) would be generated. But Right-Node Raising is formulated in such a way that it cannot produce this output. Consider, however, the question of deletion. Forward deletion produces (98), with the Orphan Accusative. But what prevents backward deletion, which would produce (102)? The ungrammaticality of (102) leads to the conclusion in (106):

(106) The No-Backward-Deletion Constraint
      Deletion does not operate backward (from right to left) in coordinate structures

The constraint (106) is needed in the grammar of Slovenian to prevent (102). But (106) is exactly what Hankamer (1971) postulates as a linguistic universal, on totally independent grounds. The distribution of the Orphan Accusative in coordinate structures thus furnishes additional support for this proposed universal principle.

12. IDENTITY OF SENSE PRONOMINALIZATION IN UNIVERSAL GRAMMAR

In many languages Identity of Sense Pronominalization appears to be a simple process of deletion. In Spanish, for example, we find both (107) and (108):

(107) *Ramón tiene dos caballos negros y   Manuel tiene uno blanco*
           has two horses black and   has one white
        'Ramon has two black horses and Manuel has one white one'
(108) *Ramón tiene dos caballos negros y Manuel tiene uno*
        'Ramon has two black horses and Manuel has one'

It seems that in the derivation of (107) *caballo* has been deleted, while in (108) *caballo negro* has been. However our examination of Slovenian has led us to propose that the deletion of a noun phrase under identity with another noun phrase universally passes through a pronominal stage. If this is correct, the Spanish sentences (107) and (108) are not derived by simple deletion but also go through a pronominal stage like that shown for Slovenian.

The claim that noun phrase deletion under identity universally goes through a pronominal stage has two testable empirical consequences. First, if the claim is correct, there will be no languages with direct evidence *against* such a pronominal stage. Second, there should be some languages other than Slovenian that provide evidence *for* an intermediate pronominal stage in Identity of Sense Pronominalization. While Spanish furnishes no evidence either for or against such a stage, as far as we are aware, one language that does provide relevant evidence is Czech.[16]

In Czech, Identity of Sense Pronominalization paradigms are much like those in Slovenian (see (30)), with the pronoun remaining in surface structure if it has no modifiers. In the presence of modifiers, the pronoun is generally deleted, as in (109):

(109) *Tomáš má černý kabát a   Honza má bílý*
          has black coat   and   has white
        'Tomas has a black coat and Honza has a white one'

In informal, colloquial style, however, it is possible to say (110):

(110) *Tomáš má černý kabát a   Honza ho má bílý*
          has black coat   and   it has white
        'Tomas has a black coat and Honza has a white one'

Similarly, we find sentence pairs like (111):

(111) (a) *Tonda má košili s   proužkama, zatímco Ferda ji má jednobarevnou*
            has shirt with stripes   whereas   it has solid-colored
                                                              (*Continued*)

---

[16] We are indebted to K. Kovanda for this information about Czech.

(b) *Tonda má košili s proužkama, zatímco Ferda má jednobarevnou*
      'Tonda has a shirt with stripes whereas Ferda has a solid-colored one'

In (110) and (111a) the pronouns *ho* and *ji*, respectively, have been left in the surface string, whereas in (109) and (111b) they have been deleted. The conditions under which deletion takes place do not concern us here. The point is that whereas in Slovenian the pronouns that we postulated as playing a role in Identity of Sense Pronominalization show up with the modifiers *ves* 'all' and *cel* 'whole', in Czech they appear in surface structure in a wider class of environments. Both languages thus furnish evidence for a pronominal stage in Identity of Sense anaphora.

French also provides interesting data in this connection. Whereas Spanish exhibits what appears to be deletion in sentences (107) and (108), in French we find examples such as (112) and (113):

(112) *Jean-Pierre a   deux chevaux noirs et   Maurice en   a   un blanc*
              has two   horses   black and   of-them has a   white
        'Jean-Pierre has two black horses and Maurice has a white one'
(113) *Jean-Pierre a deux chevaux noirs et Maurice en a un*
        'Jean-Pierre has two black horses and Maurice has one'

That is, the French sentences are just like the Spanish ones except that French has the clitic pronoun *en* in preverbal position. The *en* is a pro-PP of the form *de* + NP.[17] This suggests that underlying *un cheval* 'a horse' is *un de chevaux* 'one of horses'.[18] What is of interest here, however, is the fact that although the pronominal form that shows up in Identity of Sense Pronominalization in French is a pro-PP rather than a pro-NP as in Slovenian and Czech, the stage of derivations involving this pro-form, which is an intermediate one in most cases in Slovenian and Czech, appears on the surface in French.

If linguists are content to describe each language completely in its own terms, a multiplicity of different descriptions will result. Identity of Sense anaphora will be treated as purely a deletion phenomenon in Spanish, while in French, Czech, and Slovenian pronominalization will be involved. A linguistic theory built on such descriptions will allow too much latitude for inter-language differences, and as a result the theory will be too weak, doing little to constrain the notion "human language" and thus making few substantive claims about the nature of language. When dealing with a particular phenomenon in one language, therefore, it is desirable to try to see how this phenomenon manifests itself in other languages as well and attempt to arrive at a canonical form for the process that will be universal. Such a universal statement should leave as little room for languages to differ as is consistent with the known facts, thereby constraining most strictly the notion "human language."

This is what we are attempting to do here by positing that Identity of Sense anaphora works universally by means of Pronominalization (whatever the exact nature of this phenomenon may be) and possible subsequent deletion of pro-forms, as has been shown to be necessary for Slovenian (and Czech). It remains to be seen whether this proposal can handle the full range of facts involving Identity of Sense anaphora in human languages, including phenomena like the pro-form *one(s)* in English and Identity of Sense anaphora involving constituents other than noun phrases.

[17] Evidence for this is provided by Kayne (1969).
[18] This proposal will be modified somewhat in Section 14.

13. RELATIVE PRONOUNS

Studies of relativization in generative grammar have generally viewed relative pronouns such as *which* in English as arising from underlying full noun phrases by attachment of *wh* and Pronominalization or, equivalently, by addition of the features [+*wh*] and [+pro] to full noun phrases.[19] Low-level spell-out rules have been assumed to give these pronominal *wh*-constituents phonological shape as *which*, *who*, and so on.

In some languages there is morphological evidence that the relative pronoun is not a replacement for an entire noun phrase but is merely a modifier: the relative pronoun has adjective endings rather than noun endings. This is the case in Slovenian, as the examples in (114) show:

(114) (a) *človek, brez katerega ne bi dobila dovoljenja*
            'the person without whom she would not have received permission'
       (b) *človek, kljub kateremu je končno dobila dovoljenje*
            'the person in spite of whom she finally received permission'
       (c) *človek, s katerim je govorila dolgo časa*
            'the man with whom she spoke for a long time'

The relative pronoun *kateri* has the adjectival endings *-ega*, *-emu*, and *-im* in (114) for the genitive, dative, and instrumental cases, respectively;[20] the corresponding endings for nouns would be *-a*, *-u*, and *-om*. The relative pronoun *kateri* must therefore be a modifier of the relativized noun and not a replacement for that noun.

Further evidence for this conclusion is provided by the Orphan Accusative in examples such as those in (115) and (116):

(115) (a) *princip, v katerega verjamem*
            'the principle in which I believe'
       (b) **princip, v kateri verjamem*
(116) (a) *okraj, v katerega sem prišel*
            'the district to which I came'
       (b) **okraj, v kateri sem prišel*

The relative pronoun *kateri* must be in the Orphan Accusative form, as in (115a) and (116a), and not in the ordinary accusative, as in (115b) and (116b).[21] Since the Orphan Accusative arises through Concord with a pronominal head, the relative pronoun *kateri* must be a modifier that agrees with the head and not the head itself. Relativization must therefore involve not pronominalization of an underlying noun phrase in such a way that it ends up as the relative pronoun *kateri*, but rather deletion of an underlying noun phrase in such a way that the modifier *kateri* is left behind. The fact that *kateri* appears in the Orphan Accusative, as in (115) and (116), shows that the deletion of the relativized noun phrase, like the other deletions discussed in this paper, passes through a pronominal stage.

---

[19] This is essentially the proposal made by Smith (1961), and it has been assumed in generative grammar ever since (as can be seen in Ross (1967), for example). The only change has been that since the appearance of Chomsky (1965) relativization has been conceived of in terms of the syntactic features [+wh] and [+pro] being added to the relativized noun phrase.

Of relevance here is the analysis of Kuroda (1969), in which the relative pronouns *who* and *which* are related to the interrogatives *who* and *which*.

[20] The preposition *brez* 'without' takes its object in the genitive case, *kljub* 'in spite of' governs the dative, and *z* 'with' (written *s* before a voiceless consonant) governs the instrumental.

[21] The preposition *v* in these examples takes its object in the accusative case.

That the interrogative pronoun *kateri* 'which' is a modifier is more obvious. It modifies the head in surface structure, having adjective endings that agree with the head in case, gender, and number, as shown in (117):

(117) *Kateri ječmen hočete?*
       'Which barley do you want?

The conclusion that the relative pronoun *kateri* is also a modifier gives it the same status as the interrogative pronoun *kateri*. Surely this is not an accident. The fact that interrogative modifiers such as *which* also serve as "relative pronouns" in many languages shows that there is a cross-linguistic generalization to be captured here.

It is possible, of course, that in some languages relativization deletes the relativized noun phrase, passing through a pronominal stage, and in others it converts it into a relative pronoun. But in the absence of any facts that force us to accept such a weaker theory, there is no reason to adopt it. We therefore propose that it is a universal of human language that, if a language has a relativization rule, the relativized noun phrase is pronominalized. This pronominalized noun phrase may then undergo deletion subsequently. Since there are languages in which the pronominalized noun phrase appears in surface structure, universal grammar must make the subsequent deletion of the pronominalized noun phrase optional. Particular languages may or may not have such deletion; and it may be optional or obligatory in particular languages, or its application may be governed by other, language-particular conditions.

What we are proposing, then, is that relativization can involve pronominalization and, depending on language-particular circumstances, subsequent deletion of the relativized noun phrase, and that this pronominalization and deletion can leave behind a modifier like *which* that has traditionally been called a "relative pronoun."

14. INTERNAL STRUCTURE OF THE NOUN PHRASE

14.1. Introduction

In Section 14.2 we shall show how the Orphan Accusative provides evidence that the structure underlying noun phrases such as (118) is, roughly, (119):

(118) one of those boats

(119)

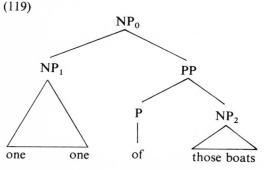

In (119) the second instance of *one* in NP_1 is the prop-word *one* that shows up in

Identity of Sense Pronominalization in English. The important point is that noun phrases such as (118) are derived from structures that contain two noun phrases.[22]

In Sections 14.3 through 14.7 further evidence from several languages will be presented to show that underlying structures like (119) enable us to account for a number of facts about noun phrases that would otherwise be mysterious. Of course, one could always devise an ad hoc way of accounting for each fact in isolation, but what is interesting is that by postulating that structures like (119) universally underlie noun phrases, it is possible to account for the whole range of ostensibly disparate facts by means of a single hypothesis.

So that all the facts to be presented here can be accounted for, structures like (119) are assumed to underlie not only noun phrases like (118) but also those like (120) and (121):

(120) a boat
(121) three boats

The structure underlying (121) would be, roughly, (122):

(122)

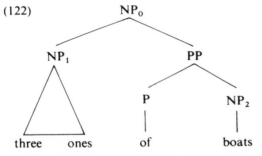

We propose that there is a process of NP Reduction that reduces (122) to the derived structure (121). Although the exact mechanism does not concern us here, it seems likely that it consists of substitution of NP_2 for the pro-form *one(s)* in (122).

In Slovenian, the equivalent of (118) is (123):

(123) *eden tistih čolnov*
       'one of those boats'

Here, instead of a prepositional phrase, we find the noun phrase *tistih čolnov* in the genitive case. If this genitive form is taken to be basic, the Slovenian equivalent of (122) will be (124):[23]

(124)

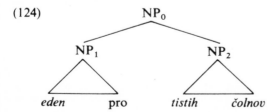

---

[22] While we claim that (118) is derived from (119), we do not claim that (119) is necessarily the "deepest" level of representation; (119) could itself be a derived rather than a basic structure.

[23] "Pro" and "gen" are used in these structures as symbols for entities that must be defined in linguistic theory for use by the grammars of particular languages.

But (124) does not make NP$_2$ subordinate, as it is in (119); in (124) NP$_1$ and NP$_2$ are instead coordinate. To avoid this undesirable consequence, we propose that cases other than nominative and accusative in languages with case be treated in the same way that prepositional and postpositional phrases are treated in languages with such overt phrases. We will represent the genitive in Slovenian phrases like (123) as a prepositional phrase, as shown in (125):

(125)

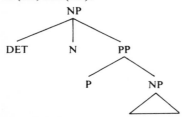

This presupposes a rule of Case Formation in Slovenian that will convert the PP into a genitive NP, giving (123) from (125).

The structure that is like (125) except that it lacks the demonstrative *tist-* 'that' will undergo NP Reduction, resulting in (126), just as in English (122) results in (121):

(126)   *en čoln*
        'a boat'

We will not be concerned with the exact mechanism of the relevant rules or with derivations that include them, but rather with the kinds of facts that show structures like (119), (122), and (125), which contain more than one noun phrase, to underlie surface noun phrases like (118), (120), (121), (123), and (126).[24]

---

[24] Jackendoff (1968) deals with structures underlying noun phrases like those in (118). Although he does not say so explicitly, it appears that he intends his proposal to cover only noun phrases with overt quantifiers, although he gives no reason why noun phrases without overt quantifiers in surface structure should not have the same underlying structure. His proposal resembles our proposal for all noun phrases in certain respects. He assumes underlying structures of the following form, similar to (119) and (122):

```
              NP
        _____|_____
       /      |      \
     DET      N      PP
                    __|__
                   /     \
                  P      NP
                        /\
                       /__\
```

The chief defect of this proposal is that Jackendoff's DET and N nodes do not together constitute an NP. In a phrase such as *a box of candy*, then, *a box* would not be an NP—a counterintuitive result that fails to capture the sameness of the phrase *a box* in *a box of candy* and other instances of *a box*. Jackendoff's structure would therefore make it impossible to capture the generalization between the operation of Concord to produce the Orphan Accusative in *enega tistih čolnov* and the operation of Concord to produce the Orphan Accusative in NPs (see Section 14.2) or to explain the failure of *one* to reduce in *one of those boats* (see Section 14.3) and of *eden* to reduce in *eden tistih čolnov* (see Section 14.4) by virtue of *one* and *eden* being alone in their respective NPs.

14.2. The Orphan Accusative in Slovenian

The Orphan Accusative furnishes evidence for underlying structures like (125) because of sentences like (127), in which *enega* 'one' is in the Orphan Accusative:

(127) *Videl sem enega tistih čolnov*
     seen   one   those boats
     'I saw one of those boats'

The use of an ordinary accusative here, as in (128), would be ungrammatical:

(128) **Videl sem eden tistih čolnov*

Since the Orphan Accusative arises through Concord with the pronominal head *ga*, *enega tistih čolnov* in (127) must pass through a stage in its derivation in which it is *enega ga tistih čolnov*. This means that *ga* is the head of a noun phrase with the modifier *enega*, just as *čolnov* is the head of a noun phrase with the modifier *tistih*. The noun phrase *enega ga tistih čolnov* must therefore have an internal structure with two noun phrases, as is provided by the underlying structure (125).

14.3. Reduction of *one* to *an* in English

In Perlmutter (1970) it is argued that the indefinite article in English is a reduction of the numeral *one* in proclitic position in the noun phrase. Stress on *one* prevents it from reducing to *an*, as in (129):

(129) one boat

But the fact that reduction is possible in this position, as in (130), shows that proclisis is possible here:

(130) a boat

The notion "proclitic" must be defined in linguistic theory. We will not attempt a definition here but will assume only that the correct definition will involve the statement that a constituent cannot be proclitic if there is no following constituent for it to lean on. Thus, if the remainder of the noun phrase is deleted, leaving only the numeral *one*, *one* has nothing to lean on and therefore cannot be proclitic. It therefore cannot reduce to *an*. As a result we find the situation illustrated in (131):

(131) (a)   Mike has three horses and Jerry has one
      (b) *Mike has three horses and Jerry has an

The final NP in (131) is left with the structure in (132) and therefore cannot reduce:

(132) $[_{NP}\text{one}]_{NP}$

Now note (133):

(133) (a)   one of those boats
      (b) *an of those boats

Why can't *one* reduce to *an* in (133)? The structure (119) provides an explanation. With (119) underlying (133), deletion of the pro-form *one* in NP_1 results in the derived constituent structure (134):

(134)

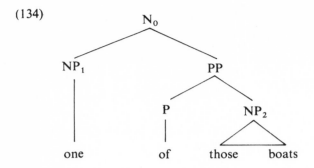

The numeral *one* constitutes an entire NP and therefore is not proclitic. It cannot reduce in (133) for the same reason that it cannot reduce in (131). The underlying structure (119) thus provides an explanation of this otherwise mysterious fact.

14.4. Reduction of *eden* to *en* in Slovenian

The Slovenian morpheme *en* in (135) corresponds both to the numeral 'one' and to the indefinite article in English, being able to appear both stressed and stressless:

(135) *en čoln*
       'one boat, a boat'

In the masculine singular nominative, however, there are two forms of the numeral 'one', namely, *en* and *eden*. If the numeral is alone in its noun phrase, we find *eden* instead of *en*. Both forms are illustrated in (136):

(136) (a) *En čoln je prišel   pravočasno, in   eden ni*
           one boat arrived on time   and one didn't
           'One boat arrived on time and one didn't'
      (b) **En čoln je prišel pravočasno, in en ni*

The distribution of *eden* and *en* in Slovenian is somewhat different from that of *one* and *a(n)* in English, as shown in (137):

(137)   ENGLISH   SLOVENIAN
      Standing alone   *one*   *eden*
      Modifying, under stress *one*   *en*
      Modifying, stressless   *an*   *en*

The fact that *eden* appears alone in the noun phrase provides evidence for two underlying noun phrases in cases like *one of those boats*. Note the examples in (138):

(138) (a) *Eden tistih čolnov je prišel pravočasno*
           'One of those boats arrived on time'
      (b) **En tistih čolnov je prišel pravočasno*

With (125) as the structure underlying such noun phrases, deletion of the pro-form in NP₁ leaves the derived structure (139):

(139)

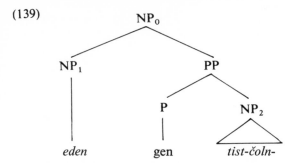

In this structure *eden* by itself constitutes an entire noun phrase. We therefore find *eden* instead of *en* in (138) for the same reason that we find it in the second clause of (136). The structure (125) provides an explanation of this fact.

14.5. Numeral Classifiers

Many languages have "classifiers" that must accompany numerals in the noun phrase. These are typically pro-forms for a semantic class of nouns. Thus, there may be a classifier for stick-shaped objects, a classifier for flat objects, and so on. The number and semantic range of classifiers differ from language to language; what is constant is their appearance together with numerals. Linguistic theory needs a way of accounting for these numeral classifiers which is not ad hoc, and the hypothesis that noun phrases have underlying structures like (119) provides just this.

So far we have discussed only examples in which the head of NP₁ was a general pro-form like *one* in English. But if a wider range of head nouns can appear in NP₁, we automatically have the numeral classifiers. We propose, then, that numeral classifiers are simply the heads of NP₁ in structures like (119). In fact, such forms exist in English, as in the quantified expressions in (140):

(140) (a) an ear of corn   (c) three rashers of bacon
      (b) twenty head of cattle   (d) two flights of stairs

Here *ear, head, rashers*, and *flights* perform the same function that numeral classifiers do in the languages that have them.

The dependence of choice of noun on physical shape can also be seen in English in examples like those in (141) and (142):

(141) (a) a stick of chewing gum
      (b) a stick of dynamite
(142) (a) a sheet of paper
      (b) a sheet of steel

The universal structure for noun phrases (119) automatically provides the structure both for these expressions in English and for classifiers in other languages.

14.6. *en* in French

The structure we have proposed for noun phrases also provides a framework in which it is possible to explain why *en* appears in Identity of Sense Pronominalization in French, as noted in Section 12. The noun phrase (143) has, at an earlier stage of derivation, the structure (144):

(143)   *trois des chevaux*
        'three of the horses'

(144)

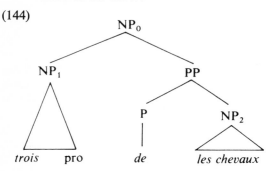

Note that the noun phrase in the prepositional phrase is definite—*les chevaux* 'the horses'.[25] There must therefore be another structure in which this noun phrase is indefinite, such as that in (145):

(145)

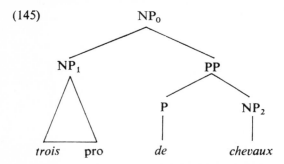

Whereas deletion of the pro-form in NP_1 reduces (144) to (143), the same operation applied to (145) would produce the ungrammatical string (146) instead of the grammatical (147):

(146)   *trois de chevaux
        'three of horses'
(147)   *trois chevaux*
        'three horses'

Therefore (147) must be derived from (146).

Similarly, the structure that would otherwise end up as (148) is reduced to (149):

(148)   *un de chevaux
        'one of horses'

---

[25] *De* + *les* becomes *des*.

(149) *un cheval*
'one horse, a horse'

The rule of NP Reduction proposed in Section 14.1 will accomplish this reduction.[26]

With the underlying structure we have proposed for *trois chevaux* and *un cheval*, there is an automatic explanation of why *en* appears in Identity of Sense Pronominalization in French. Consider (150):

(150) *Jean-Pierre a un cheval et Maurice en a trois*
'Jean-Pierre has a horse and Maurice has three'

Underlying the second conjunct is the structure (145). Now, what is particular to French is the fact that it has the pronoun *en* which replaces structures of the form *de* + NP and is moved to preverbal position with the other clitics. The proposed universal structure for noun phrases automatically provides a source for *en* in (150); thus the ostensibly strange appearance of this pronoun in Identity of Sense Pronominalization in French is completely regular.

14.7. Pronominal Anaphora

The structure that we have proposed to underlie noun phrases also provides a framework in which certain initially puzzling facts of pronominal anaphora can be accounted for. We will restrict ourselves here to examples from English, but analogous facts can be found in other languages.

Consider the sentence (151):

(151) Jerry has three horses and Roger has two of them

Here the pronoun *them* refers to *horses*. Note, however, that *them* is not "coreferential" with the antecedent *horses* but is rather understood in a "generic" sense: Roger has two horses but not two of the same horses Jerry has.

Now consider the sentence (152):

(152) Jerry has a horse and Roger has two of them

Here, too, the pronoun *them* refers to *horses* in the generic sense. Neither (151) nor (152) contains, at least in surface structure, a generic antecedent *horses* for *them* to refer to, and in (152) there is not even a plural antecedent to which *them* can refer. But the plural pronouns *they* and *them*, when anaphoric, require plural antecedents. Thus, consider (153):

(153) (a) The girl ran in, but I didn't see them
         (b) The girl ran in, and they started to scream

---

[26] Although we do not wish to go into the details of the mechanism of NP Reduction, it should be noted that simply deleting the pro-form in NP_1 and the preposition would be inadequate. In examples in Slovenian and English in which the quantifier in NP_1 is *eden* and *one*, respectively, such deletion would leave the quantifier alone in NP_1, thereby preventing reduction of *eden* to *en* in *en čoln* and reduction of *one* to the indefinite article in *a boat*. That is why we suggested in Section 14.1 that NP Reduction probably consists of substituting NP_2 for the pro-form in NP_1 with concomitant deletion of the preposition. It should also be noted that if the quantifier of NP_1 is one of a small set that includes *one* and *each* (and their equivalents in various languages), the noun in head position after NP Reduction must be singular.

In these sentences *them* and *they* are not anaphoric since there is no plural antecedent for them to refer to. A feminine singular pronoun in the same position could be anaphoric, since it could refer to the feminine singular noun phrase *the girl*, as in (154):

(154) (a) The girl ran in, but I didn't see her
     (b) The girl ran in, and she started to scream

How is it, then, that *them* in (151) and (152) is anaphoric, and understood as generic? The structure that we have proposed for noun phrases can account for this phenomenon. Underlying *three horses* in (151) is a structure like (155):

(155)

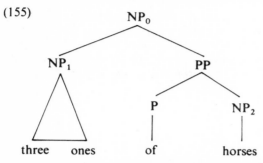

And underlying *a horse* in (152) is a structure like (156):

(156)

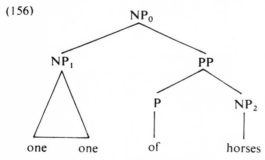

The underlying noun phrase in the second conjunct of both (151) and (152) has something like the structure in (157):

(157)

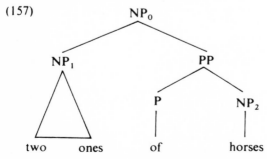

The generic *horses* in the prepositional phrase in (155) and (156) provides an antecedent for the plural pronoun *them* in (151) and (152).

Note that this phenomenon is not restricted to phrases like *two of them*. Consider the sentence (158):

(158) Jerry has a horse because they don't cause much pollution

Here the plural pronoun *they* again refers to a generic noun phrase *horses*, which antecedent is provided by the underlying structure (156). Determining the conditions under which NP$_2$ structures can serve as a pronominal antecedent and the conditions under which it cannot is an interesting problem but one that must be left to future research.

14.8. Summary

It has not been our purpose here to go into detail on the rules that convert underlying structures like (119), (122), and (125) into grammatical surface structures. What we wish to point out is the fact that the occurrence of the Orphan Accusative in Slovenian in examples like (127) led us to hypothesize that what appear to be simple noun phrases in surface structure actually contain two constituent noun phrases at a deeper level of representation. Hypothesizing that such structures exist universally, we were able to explain a number of ostensibly disparate facts in several languages.

15. CONCLUSION: LANGUAGE-PARTICULAR RULES AND EXPLANATION IN SYNTAX

It has been the purpose of this paper to investigate a language-particular phenomenon—the Orphan Accusative in Slovenian. We sought to determine how this phenomenon should be accounted for in the grammar of Slovenian and how to separate what was particular to Slovenian in the Orphan Accusative from what was more general. We then considered some of the implications of our analysis for general linguistic theory.

The point we wish to stress here is that when one is confronted with a language-particular fact in syntax, although the course of least resistance would be to write a language-particular rule to state it, such a rule only gives rise to questions like those posed in Section 3, which a proper account of the phenomenon must answer; unless such questions are answered, the phenomenon has not been explained.

In the case of the Orphan Accusative in Slovenian, it has been shown that under the correct analysis the only thing that is particular to Slovenian is the marking [+animate] on pronouns. Everything else concerning the Orphan Accusative follows from more general principles that automatically answer questions like those in Section 3, thereby providing an explanation of the facts that gave rise to them.

More difficult is the problem of how to construct linguistic theory so that incorrect solutions that give rise to questions like those considered here are excluded in principle. In the case of the Orphan Accusative, we were faced with a choice between including the Orphan Accusative Rule (21) and marking pronouns as [+animate]. One might argue that an explicit simplicity metric would choose the latter solution over the former, since the former involves adding an additional rule to the grammar. But at the present stage of the study of syntax, any talk of a simplicity metric is quite premature, since there are very few concrete proposals concerning the relative "cost" of different available grammatical devices. In the case at hand, there is no explicit proposal for a simplicity metric according to which a grammar with animacy markings on pronouns is "simpler" than one without such markings but with an additional rule.

What seems to be the most promising approach to the problem appears in Postal (1970a), Ross (1970), Bach (1971), and Hankamer (1971). These studies take the view that languages are not free to construct transformations at will (confining themselves, to be sure, to certain universally prescribed formal devices), but rather that there is a fixed inventory of transformations available to the grammars of particular languages, which they may or may not actually make use of. Transformations therefore will not vary from one language to another. The effect of this proposal is to go beyond the attempt to constrain transformaticns by purely formal means and to place strong substantive constraints on them as well. In this theoretical framework, the question of the Orphan Accusative Rule (21) would not even arise, for language-particular rules of this kind would be prevented on general theoretical grounds. The fact that rule (21) would be excluded on principled grounds is a merit of the theory.

In conclusion, we hope to have shown that any language-particular transformation is suspect when its structural description is rich in stating where it does and does not apply; such rules fail to explain why they apply where they do. In the absence of a general theory that predicts what rules can and cannot state, whatever a rule states it cannot explain.

REFERENCES

Andrews, A. (1971), "Case agreement of predicate modifiers in ancient Greek," *Linguistic Inquiry*, *2*, 127–151.

Bach, E. (1971), "Questions," *Linguistic Inquiry*, *2*, 153–166.

Bierwisch, M., and K. Heidolph (1970), *Progress in Linguistics*, The Hague: Mouton.

Chomsky, N. (1965), *Aspects of the Theory of Syntax*, Cambridge, Mass.: M.I.T. Press.

Hankamer, J. (1971), *Constraints on Deletion in Syntax*, unpublished Ph.D. dissertation, Yale University.

Jackendoff, R. (1968), "Quantifiers in English," *Foundations of Language*, *4*, 422–442.

Kayne, R. (1969), *The Transformational Cycle in French Syntax*, unpublished Ph.D. dissertation, M.I.T.

Kuroda, S.-Y. (1969), "English Relativization and Certain Related Problems," in Reibel and Schane.

Orzechowska, H. (1971), "Rodilnik pridevnikov in zaimkov kot formalni eksponent pri navezavi," *Jezik in slovstvo*, *17*, 57–64.

Perlmutter, D. (1970), "On the Article in English," in Bierwisch and Heidolph.

Perlmutter, D. (1971), *Deep and Surface Structure Constraints in Syntax*, New York: Holt, Rinehart and Winston.

Postal, P. (1966), "On So-Called 'Pronouns' in English," in *Report of the Seventeenth Annual Round Table Meeting on Linguistics and Language Studies*, Washington, D.C.: Georgetown University Press; reprinted in Reibel and Schane (1969).

Postal, P. (1970a), "The Method of Universal Grammar," in P. Garvin, ed., *Method and Theory in Linguistics*, The Hague: Mouton.

Postal, P. (1970b), "On coreferential complement subject deletion," *Linguistic Inquiry*, *1*, 439–500.

Reibel, D., and S. Schane (1969), *Modern Studies in English*, Englewood Cliffs, N.J.: Prentice-Hall.

Ross, J. R. (1967), *Constraints on Variables in Syntax*, unpublished Ph.D. dissertation, M.I.T.

Ross, J. R. (1970), "Gapping and the Order of Constituents," in Bierwisch and Heidolph.

Smith, C. (1961), "A class of complex modifiers in English," *Language*, *37*, 342–365.

Toporišič, J. (1968), "Končnica -ega v tožilniku srednjega in moškega spola ednine pri pridevniških besedah in še to in ono," *Jezik in slovstvo*, *13*, cover.

Toporišič, J. (1970), *Slovenski knjižni jezik*, *4*, Maribor: Založba Obzorja.

Toporišič, J. (1972), "Pripomba h končnici -ega za tožilnik ednine moškega in srednjega spola," *Jezik in slovstvo*, *17*, 116–117.

SEX, GENDER,
and the OCTOBER REVOLUTION[1]

Robert A. Rothstein

University of Massachusetts at Amherst

On November 7, 1917 (October 25 according to the Julian calendar), a salvo from the cruiser "Aurora" in Petrograd harbor marked the beginning of the Bolshevik Revolution, an event which, among other things, altered the surface structure of Russian sentences. In particular, the relative liberation of women after 1917 produced a need for new terminology to refer to women occupying certain jobs or positions, as, for example, *obsledovatel'nica* 'female investigator', *syrovarka* 'female cheesemaker', *frezerovščica* 'female milling-machine operator'. In this paper I shall try to connect this area of diachronic sociolinguistics with consideration of the "meaning" of gender in Russian.[2] My conclusions are rather tentative and are formulated here primarily to stimulate further study and discussion of the place of the traditional grammatical categories (gender, tense, aspect, and so on) in generative grammar.

Russian nouns are traditionally assigned to one of three genders—masculine, feminine, or neuter—on the basis of agreement. The assignments are by and large unmotivated semantically, but there is some correlation between gender and declension type. There are syntactic as well as semantic grounds for distinguishing animate and inanimate nouns. Finally, there are more than two hundred nouns referring to human beings that are said to be of common gender: their agreement depends on their sex

---

[1] The present work is a revised version of a paper given at the first meeting of the New England Linguistic Society on November 7, 1970, the fifty-third anniversary of the October Revolution. It is here dedicated to my teacher, Morris Halle, who bears part of the blame for making me a Slavist.

[2] A large body of data on current usage was compiled for a collective monograph (Panov (1968a, b, c, d)) on the state of the Russian language fifty years after the Revolution. Problems of gender are also discussed in individual papers (Mučnik (1963), Protčenko (1964), Janko-Trinickaja (1966)) published in a series of volumes preparatory to the Panov work.

reference (for example, *bednyj sirota* 'poor orphan' if the orphan in question is male, but *bednaja sirota* if the orphan is female).[3]

Many discussions of Slavic gender have included Jakobson's observation that the opposition of masculine and feminine gender is privative, with feminine gender the marked member of the opposition.[4] In his most precise formulation, given in the 1939 paper "Signe zéro," Jakobson defines the opposition only for nouns referring to human beings:

> Le féminin indique que, si le désigné est une personne ou se prête à la personnification, c'est à coup sûr au sexe féminin que cette personne appartient . . . Au contraire, la signification générale du masculin ne spécifie pas nécessairement le sexe (p. 110).

Thus, even in English, *congressman* could refer either to Father Robert Drinan or to Louise Day Hicks, but *congresswoman* could refer only to Mrs. Hicks.[5]

In nineteenth-century Russia there were few professions open to women, and for these there usually existed parallel terminology: *učitel'/učitel'nica* 'teacher', *tkač/tkačixa* 'weaver', *akušër/akušerka* 'midwife'. Here the opposition was not privative: each term was sex-specific. There was, however, some tendency to use the masculine form generically, especially in the predicate. Thus the architect V. P. Stasov wrote to his wife in 1882 about how good it was for a mother to become the "teacher and mentor of her children" (*učitelem i nastavnikom detej svoix*),[6] using the masculine terms for 'teacher' and 'mentor'. That such generic usage was not the rule (or at least that it could be willfully ignored) is illustrated in a case cited by Baudouin de Courtenay (1929, p. 239). Shortly before World War I, a female doctor of medicine applied to Moscow University for certification as a Privatdozent. The university was willing, but Education Minister Kasso refused his approval on the grounds that the statutes provided only for *docenty*, and not *docentki*.

With the opening of almost all professions to women after 1917, there was, initially, a tendency to create parallel terminology, following established morphological patterns, as in *obsledovatel'nica* and the other examples cited earlier. Gradually, however, many of the feminine terms were replaced by their masculine counterparts or took on a clear colloquial coloring as opposed to their stylistically neutral and semantically unmarked masculine counterparts. Official language uses the masculine forms, except in special cases such as *sportsmen/sportsmenka*, where there is a need to make the distinction (in this case because different standards apply to male and female athletes). A female Hero of the Soviet Union could only be called *Geroj Sovetskogo Sojuza*, the masculine form; calling her *Geroinja Sovetskogo Sojuza* would have to be a joke.

Attitudes toward the use of the marked and unmarked forms vary. On the one hand there are the customers of a Moscow department store who complained about a display labeled *Podarok pervoklassniku* 'Gifts for the first-grader': what about the

---

[3] On common gender see Kopeliovič (1970) and the literature cited therein.
[4] On privative oppositions and markedness see Jakobson (1932) and Trubetzkoy (1939).
I shall generally ignore the neuter here since it is not central to the discussion.
[5] The restriction to nouns referring to human beings is essential. Thus the word *lošad'* 'horse' is of feminine gender and can refer equally well to a stallion (*žerebec*, masculine gender) or a mare (*kobyla*, feminine gender). The relationships are slightly different in the pig family: *svin'ja* 'pig' (feminine gender) is both the generic term and the word for 'sow'; there is a separate word of masculine gender, *borov* 'hog'.
[6] Cited in Janko-Trinickaja (1966, p. 168).

pervoklassnica?[7] On the other hand, there is the head chef of a Leningrad restaurant, a young woman, who burst into tears when an American colleague of mine tried to compliment her by telling her that she was "*otličnaja povarixa*" 'an excellent cook', feminine form. She considered herself to be a *povar*.

With the widespread use of the unmarked masculine form to refer to women, problems of agreement arise. Do forms that show gender agreement (adjectives and the preterite forms of verbs) agree in such cases according to grammatical gender or according to sex reference? Recent surveys (Panov (1968c)) indicate a growing tendency for verbs to agree according to sex reference (preferred by about 52 percent of the respondents to one questionnaire, with about 10 percent undecided), while the tendency is for adjectives used attributively to agree according to gender (although 25 percent of those questioned preferred sex agreement here too). In both cases younger speakers and less educated speakers (blue-collar and white-collar workers with no higher education) had higher percentages. Writers and journalists were the most conservative.[8]

Given these various facts, the problem is to translate them into lexical representations and rules. I would suggest something like the following analysis. Among the lexical properties of Russian nouns are the binary features [±masculine gender], [±feminine gender], [±personal], [±male sex reference], [±female sex reference]. Sample (partial) lexical representations might then be as shown in the following table:

	učitel'nica 'female teacher'	*vrač* 'physician'	*moskvič* 'male Muskovite'	*sirota* 'orphan'	*stena* 'wall'	*stol* 'table'	*okno* 'window'
m gender	−	+	+	+	−	+	−
f gender	+	−	−	+	+	−	−
personal	+	+	+	+	−	−	−
m sex ref	(−)		+		(−)	(−)	(−)
f sex ref	(+)		(−)		(−)	(−)	(−)

Sex reference is possible only for [+personal] nouns; hence the redundant minuses for the [−personal] nouns. For most masculine personal nouns (for example, *vrač*) and for all the nouns of common gender, that is, nouns that are [+masculine gender, +feminine gender], sex reference is specified not in the lexicon, but rather in whatever manner pronominal reference is specified. Some masculine nouns, however (for example, *moskvič*), are lexically specified [+male sex reference]. That is to say, most speakers will accept (1) or (2):

(1) *Moja sestra — vrač*
    'My sister is a physician'
(2) *Moja sestra — traktorist*
    'My sister is a tractor operator'

---

[7] Cited in Mučnik (1963, pp. 42–43n).

[8] The question of the form of an adjective modifying a masculine word referring to a woman became the subject of polemics in the Soviet journal *Voprosy kul'tury reči*. Panfilov (1965) cites constructions like the following, with a feminine adjective, masculine noun, and woman's name:

    (a) *uvažaemaja tovarišč Ivanova*
       'respected comrade Ivanova'

He blames the spread of such constructions on the misguided scholasticism of certain normativists. In reply, Janko-Trinickaja (1967) argues that there is a difference between (b) and (c):

    (b) *Uvažaemaja (tovarišč Ivanova)*
    (c) *(Uvažaemyj tovarišč) Ivanova*

But they will reject (3) in favor of (4):

(3) *Moja sestra — moskvič
    'My sister is a Muskovite'
(4) Moja sestra — moskvička

Such nouns are exceptions to the general statement that masculine personal nouns are unmarked for sex reference. Feminine personal nouns, on the other hand, that is, nouns that are [−masculine gender, +feminine gender, +personal], necessarily have female sex reference. This is what is meant by the markedness of feminine gender.[9] Notice that a plus value for either sex reference feature implies a minus for the other, but the converse is not true.

The rules for agreement (I shall beg here the question of their precise formulation) will have to have at least three parts:

(a) If the noun is neither [+masculine gender] nor [+feminine gender], there is neuter agreement. This applies to all nouns traditionally classified as neuter gender as well as to nonnominal elements functioning syntactically as nouns, as in (5):

(5) Poslyšalos' gromkoe "Ja te pokažu!"
    'A loud "I'll show you!" was heard'

(b) If the noun is [−personal], agreement is by gender.[10]

[9] There are a few apparent counterexamples, including nouns like osoba and persona 'person', ličnost' 'individual', žertva 'victim', which are of feminine gender but can refer to a male or a female. See also note 14.

[10] There is one class of problems here. Nonnative names of animals that do not fit into any Russian declensional type (for example, kenguru 'kangaroo', šimpanze 'chimpanzee') are not declined and show masculine agreement except in contexts that clearly specify a female referent. Hence a female verb form is used in the following:

(a) Kenguru nesla v sumke kengurënka
    'The kangaroo was carrying a baby kangaroo in (its) pouch'

(See Rozental' (1965, p. 74).)
Notice that such words behave differently than words of common gender. The latter have agreement by sex reference; the former have such agreement only if sex is relevant. Perhaps words like kenguru should be treated as paired homonyms — kenguru$_1$ [+masculine gender, −feminine gender] and kenguru$_2$ [−masculine gender, +feminine gender], parallel to tigr 'tiger' and tigrica 'tigress', respectively. Consider the sentence in (b), however:

(b) Tigrica kormila tigrënka
    'The tigress was nursing the baby tiger'

There still remains the problem of accounting for the way in which the predicate in such a sentence requires that the subject be feminine, which in turn requires feminine agreement in the verb. Notice that this is not the same as ruling out (c):

(c) *John was nursing the baby

Tigr is not marked for male sex reference while John presumably is so marked.
What is apparently involved is the well-known ability of the unmarked member of a privative opposition to assume a negative marking in the appropriate context. Consider the classic example from Dostoevsky given in (d):

(d) Kolumb byl ščastliv ne togda, kogda otkryl Ameriku, a kogda otkryval eë
    'Columbus was happy not when he had discovered America but when he was discovering it'

Here the imperfective verb otkryval, generally unmarked for completion, takes on the negative marking 'noncompletion' in a context that contrasts it with the perfective otkryl, which is marked for completion.

(c) If the noun is [+personal], then

   (i) adjective agreement is by gender, if that is unambiguous; otherwise, by sex reference;
   (ii) verb agreement is optional, that is, it may be by gender or by sex reference.

Thus, by (b) we have the sentences in (6):

(6) (a) *Bol'šaja stena razvalilas'*
        'The big wall collapsed'
    (b) *Bol'šoj stol razvalilsja*
        'The big table collapsed'

By (c) we have the examples in (7):

(7) (a) *Staryj vrač ušël*
        'The old doctor (male or female) left'
    (b) *Staryj vrač ušla*
        'The old doctor (female) left'
    (c) *Bednyj sirota ušël*
        'The poor orphan (male) left'
    (d) *Bednaja sirota ušla*
        'The poor orphan (female) left'

Both (7a) and (7b) are accepted by normativists for the case where the doctor is a woman (as most Soviet physicians are), although (7b), as we have seen, is gaining in usage, with some speakers undoubtedly alternating between the two forms.

I have omitted from consideration the less common case of adjective agreement by sex reference for nouns unambiguous with respect to gender, which is illustrated in (8):

(8) *Staraja vrač ušla*

A speaker for whom (8) is possible presumably has shifted words like *vrač* to the common gender category, to which *sirota*, for example, belongs, that is, to the category specified as [+masculine gender, +feminine gender].[11]

There are two kinds of systematic violations of the rules given here, or, more precisely, of the principles underlying the suggested lexical representations. Both types of violation are used for stylistic ends. First, there is the expressive use of nouns of feminine gender, essentially hostile epithets, to apply to male human beings. Thus, it is more effective to call a man *dura* 'idiot', the form with feminine gender, than *durak*. This would seem to be a violation of the markedness of feminine gender.

Second, there is personification. A Russian is surprised to find death portrayed as an old man in English-language tradition since in Russian *smert'* 'death' is of feminine gender and is personified as a woman. In essence, personification is a process whereby gender is translated into sex reference. Thus, consider (9)–(12):[12]

(9)   *Žizn' — lučšij sovetčik*
      'Life is the best advisor'
(10) *Žizn' — lučšaja sovetčica*

---

[11] This may not be quite correct since the examples quoted seem to be almost all limited to the nominative case. Mučnik (1963, p. 77) does cite one example with an accusative, although that is in a participial construction.

[12] From Janko-Trinickaja (1966, p. 209).

(11)   *Opyt — lučšij sovetčik*
'Experience is the best advisor'
(12) **Opyt — lučšaja sovetčica*

The word *žizn'* is of feminine gender: when personified, it can be referred to by an (unmarked) masculine form as in (9) or a (marked) feminine form as in (10). The word *opyt* is of masculine gender: when personified, it can be referred to only by a masculine form as in (11); (12) is not possible.

Both kinds of systematic violation illustrate a more general phenomenon, namely, stylistic or expressive effects, poetic use of language, if you will, achieved by violating rules of the grammar.[13]

A third, more complicated violation may be partly explainable in the same way. At least some of the common gender nouns can occur with either masculine or feminine agreement when referring to a male but only with feminine agreement when referring to a female. Thus, while both (13) and (14) are possible, we can have only (15) and not (16):

(13)   *On — staryj p'janica*
'He's an old drunkard'
(14)   *On — staraja p'janica*
(15)   *Ona — staraja p'janica*
'She's an old drunkard'
(16) **Ona — staryj p'janica*

Our rules predict the grammaticality of (13) and (15) and the ungrammaticality of (16) but not the grammaticality of (14). It has been claimed (for example, Kopeliovič (1970)) that sentences like (14) are more expressive than sentences like (13), but a small sample of informants has failed to confirm this. One problem is that the words involved are already part of the expressive lexicon, and judgments on degrees of expressiveness may be somewhat unclear. This particular phenomenon needs further study.

I have wittingly begged some questions and skirted some issues, for example, the mechanism of reference[14] and problems connected with the small number of

---

[13] Compare, for example, the lines from the poetry of Gumilëv cited by Scholz (1965, p. 283):

Selestjat parusa korablej.
Bystrokrylyx vedut kapitany, . . .
'Ships' sails rustle.
The swift-winged ones are steered by captains, . . .'

Here the ships are personified through the use of the animate accusative (= genitive) *bystrokrylyx* instead of the inanimate accusative (= nominative), a violation of the rules of the grammar.

[14] Included in this omission is the problem of pronominal reference and the gender of anaphoric pronouns. While Russian anaphoric pronouns seem generally to take their gender according to sex reference, there are various kinds of exceptions. Thus, a female author, referring to herself in the third person as *avtor* 'the author' (a word of masculine gender with no stylistically neutral feminine counterpart), will use masculine third person pronouns:

Avtor budet blagodaren za vse kritičeskie zamečanija, kotorye pomogut emu v dal'nejšej rabote nad knigoj
'The author will be grateful for all critical observations, which will help him in further work on the book'

The author in question here is the Soviet phonetician Elena Andreevna Bryzgunova (1963, p. 8).

On the other hand, when the antecedent is one of the feminine words mentioned in note 9 but the referent is male, the choice of gender for the anaphoric pronoun may be determined by properties of the surface structure, such as the distance between pronoun and antecedent and/or between pronoun and last explicit mention of the referent.

neuter personal nouns. I may seem to have been suggesting that words such as *učitel'* 'male teacher' and *učitel'nica* 'female teacher' have separate lexical entries. Although I do not really believe that, I do not yet see the ideal solution. I hope to return to these questions, as well as to the more general question of grammatical categories in generative grammar.

REFERENCES

Baudouin de Courtenay, J. (1929), "Einfluss der Sprache auf Weltanschauung und Stimmung," *Prace filologiczne, 14,* 184–255.

Bryzgunova, E. A. (1963), *Praktičeskaja fonetika i intonacija russkogo jazyka,* Moscow: Izdatel'stvo Moskovskogo universiteta.

Hamp, E. P., F. W. Householder, and R. Austerlitz, eds. (1966), *Readings in Linguistics II,* Chicago: University of Chicago Press.

Jakobson, R. (1932), "Zur Struktur des russischen Verbums," in *Charisteria V. Mathesio oblata,* Prague: Cercle Linguistique de Prague; reprinted in Hamp, *et al.* (1966).

Jakobson, R. (1939), "Signe zéro," in *Mélanges de linguistique offerts à Charles Bally,* Geneva: Georg; reprinted in Hamp, *et al.* (1966).

Janko-Trinickaja, N. A. (1966), "Naimenovanie lic ženskogo pola suščestvitel'nymi ženskogo i mužskogo roda," in E. A. Zemskaja and D. N. Šmelev, eds., *Razvitie slovoobrazovanija sovremennogo russkogo jazyka,* Moscow: Nauka.

Janko-Trinickaja, N. A. (1967), "I *uvažaemyj . . . i uvažaemaja . . .*," *Voprosy kul'tury reči, 8,* 240–244.

Kopeliovič, A. B. (1970), "K voprosu ob opredelenii kategorii obščego roda v sovremennom russkom jazykoznanii," *Učënye zapiski Vladimirskogo gosudarstvennogo pedagogičeskogo instituta, 21,* 87–115.

Mučnik, I. P. (1963), "Kategorija roda i eë razvitie v sovremennom russkom literaturnom jazyke," in S. I. Ožegov and M. V. Panov, eds., *Razvitie sovremennogo russkogo jazyka,* Moscow: Izdatel'stvo AN SSSR.

Panfilov, A. K. (1965), "*Uvažaemyj* tovarišč ili *uvažaemaja* tovarišč?" *Voprosy kul'tury reči, 6,* 189–195.

Panov, M. V., ed. (1968a), *Russkij jazyk i sovetskoe obščestvo: Leksika sovremennogo russkogo literaturnogo jazyka,* Moscow: Nauka.

Panov, M. V., ed. (1968b), *Russkij jazyk i sovetskoe obščestvo: Slovoobrazovanije sovremennogo russkogo literaturnogo jazyka,* Moscow: Nauka.

Panov, M. V., ed. (1968c), *Russkij jazyk i sovetskoe obščestvo: Morfologija i sintaksis sovremennogo russkogo literaturnogo jazyka,* Moscow: Nauka.

Panov, M. V., ed. (1968d), *Russkij jazyk i sovetskoe obščestvo: Fonetika sovremennogo russkogo literaturnogo jazyka,* Moscow: Nauka.

Protčenko, I. F. (1964), "O rodovoj sootnositel'nosti nazvanij lic," in I. P. Mučnik and M. V. Panov, eds., *Razvitie grammatiki i leksiki sovremennogo russkogo jazyka,* Moscow: Nauka.

Rozental', D. E. (1965), *Praktičeskaja stilistika russkogo jazyka,* Moscow: Vysšaja škola.

Scholz, F. (1965), "Genre, Genus und Person im Russischen," *Die Welt der Slaven, 10,* 281–304.

Trubetzkoy, N. S. (1939), *Grundzüge der Phonologie, Travaux du Cercle Linguistique de Prague, 7.*

Linguistics as chemistry: the substance theory of semantic primes[1]

Arnold M. Zwicky

The Ohio State University

1. INTRODUCTION

The aims of this paper are (*a*) to place theoretical principles in linguistics in a larger conceptual framework, in particular, to note similarities between linguistics and various natural sciences (not only chemistry, but also physics and biology), and (*b*) to draw a parallel between a particular organizing hypothesis in semantics (the *Substance Theory*) and assumptions of the classical theory of chemical elements, for the purpose of arguing that this parallel is one of structure and that the chemical case can suggest interesting lines of inquiry for the semantic case. I should emphasize at the outset that I am not asserting any *overall* parallel, structural or otherwise, between linguistics and chemistry. In the principal sections of this paper, I am concerned with only one area of chemistry, the theory of substances and elements, and only one area of linguistics, the theory of words and semantic primes.

[1] This work was supported in part by the 1970 MSSB Advanced Research Seminar in Mathematical Linguistics, sponsored by the National Science Foundation through a grant to the Center for Advanced Study in the Behavioral Sciences, Stanford, California, and held at The Ohio State University, and in part by National Science Foundation Grant GN-534 to the Computer and Information Science Research Center of The Ohio State University. Versions of this paper were read at The Ohio State University in November 1970 and before the Chicago Linguistic Society in December 1970 and were greeted by a spirited rejection of some of my claims on the part of several listeners.

Many people have provided useful comments and criticisms. I am especially indebted to Gaberell Drachman, James Heringer, Jerrold Sadock, and Ann Zwicky. The Substance Theory (independent of the chemical analog) was first suggested to me in 1965 by George Boolos. In the intervening years I have had the opportunity to reconsider my initial skepticism toward the idea.

2. TYPES OF PRINCIPLES IN LINGUISTICS

Before we proceed to a treatment of elements, chemical and linguistic, it is necessary to distinguish a number of different types of "theoretical principles" in linguistics. My intent here is first to separate *methodological principles* from *systematic principles*, the latter being my real concern, and then to categorize systematic principles by level, from "descriptive" or "observational" statements to *organizing hypotheses*, central assumptions which, while capable of empirical test, tend to define an area of investigation.

2.1. Methodological Principles

Methodological principles, or "rules of thumb," are not assumptions capable of verification or falsification in any ordinary sense. Instead, their function is to suggest what the most likely state of affairs is in a given situation, in the absence of evidence of the usual sort. This being the case, the indication given by a methodological principle is always outweighed by pertinent evidence. Methodological principles can therefore be stated in an extreme form. A few linguistic examples will perhaps make these points clearer.

First, there is the Majority Vote Principle in comparative reconstruction, the guideline that says that if the majority of daughter languages agree in having a certain feature, then that feature is to be attributed to the protolanguage. Certainly, no one involved in reconstruction believes this to be valid in general, but when there is no special evidence on the point, the majority will carry the day. If there are other facts that bear on the point, these will prevail, of course.

Second, there is the Contrast Principle in phonology, which says that if segments are in contrast, then they are underlyingly distinct. In the context of structuralist linguistics, the Contrast Principle is an organizing hypothesis rather than a methodological one (see Section 2.2.2). Within the framework of generative phonology, however, it functions as a methodological principle: if there is no contravening evidence, surface contrasts are taken to be underlying contrasts as well.

A third example of a methodological principle is the Surfacist Principle, a syntactic analog of the Contrast Principle. This is the rule that, *ceteris paribus*, the syntactic structure of a sentence is its surface constituent structure. In other words, if you claim that some sentence has a remote syntactic representation, that is, one different from its bracketing into labeled constituents, you have to prove it.

These examples are familiar enough not to require an extended justification of the principles involved. In each case, the methodological principle provides a kind of background assumption, a position taken when no other is especially supported.

Instead of being verified or falsified, methodological principles are judged as useless or useful, and the basis for the judgment is whether the descriptions they recommend are confirmed or not. To defend a methodological principle, one provides numerous illustrations of cases where it chooses a description that turns out to be well supported on other evidence. To refute a methodological principle, one adduces cases where it selects a description that turns out to be unsatisfactory for independent reasons. In either direction, such arguments are not easy. (For the beginning of a negative argument, see Zwicky (1970b) on the Free Ride Principle, a methodological principle opting for longer derivations over shorter ones, other things being equal.)

Examples of methodological principles from other sciences are not hard to find.

In this category are the widespread preferences for round numbers, for equations of degree *n* over those of degree *n* + 1, and for circles over other conic sections, among many other preferences for "simple" accounts.

2.2. Systematic Principles

In contrast to methodological principles, which are apt to be termed "rules" (in one sense) or "guidelines," systematic principles are "descriptions," "observations," "regularities," "rules" (in another sense), "laws," "assumptions," or "hypotheses," depending upon their extent and their abstractness. I assume here that the different terms represent differences of degree, especially in view of the observations of many philosophers (for example, Hanson, Kuhn, and Toulmin) that "theoretical" assumptions infect observation in significant ways. That is, I assume that there is a cline from (*a*) through (*e*) (and beyond):

(*a*) observations that someone said a particular thing on some occasion or made a particular judgment about an utterance on some occasion
(*b*) observations that the members of some speech community usually make the same judgment on some point
(*c*) claims about the existence of a particular rule in English
(*d*) hypotheses about constraints limiting the applicability of rules in a particular language, or universally
(*e*) hypotheses about the range of possible rules in natural languages

My concern in the following sections is with the more "theoretical" statements (like (*d*) and (*e*)) than with the more "descriptive" ones (like (*a*) and (*b*)). But even these "theoretical" assertions range from relatively low-level assumptions, typically capable of precise formulation and usually subject to tests of some standard kind, to much more abstract propositions, often stated rather vaguely and not amenable to straightforward tests and argumentation. The more abstract propositions tend to act as organizing principles defining a field of investigation. Although the deeper principles are in some sense open to empirical verification or falsification, the tests required are quite indirect or involve extremely complex chains of inference in which various fundamental assumptions function. Without intending to claim that the deeper principles are untestable, I have termed the lower-level statements *arguable propositions* and the more abstract ones *organizing hypotheses*.

2.2.1. ARGUABLE PROPOSITIONS

Any "natural law" would serve as an example of an arguable proposition. Let us take an illustration from physics—Newton's Inverse Square Law, which states that the gravitational force between two bodies is inversely proportional to the square of the distance between them (*R* is the distance between the two bodies and *k* is a constant associated with the two bodies):

$$F = \frac{k}{R^2}$$

How do we tell that this is an inverse square law, rather than, say, an inverse cube law? A methodological principle chooses squares over cubes so long as the observations on the matter are reasonably consistent with this assumption. Aside from this, the two positions are indistinguishable so long as (*a*) the *range* of evidence is narrow, (*b*) the *accuracy* of the measuring device is low, and (*c*) *outside effects* cannot be discounted. If we have measurements only over a narrow range for *R*, then we may not be able to distinguish the squares hypothesis from the cubes hypothesis, given the accuracy of our measuring devices and the fact that small perturbations may be random, as a result of experimenter's error or outside effects that were not allowed for. Similarly, very accurate measurements may be worthless if they cannot be made over a sufficient range of values.

The garden-variety arguable propositions of current linguistics are universal hypotheses, most of them *exclusions*, restrictions on the use of certain notational conventions. A typical example is "There are no curly brackets (that is, braces) in syntax," a claim intended to illegitimize references to

$$\text{TENSE} \left(\left\{ \begin{array}{c} \text{M} \\ \text{have} \\ \text{be} \end{array} \right\} \right)$$

and the like in syntactic rules. This particular use of curly brackets, or braces, is criticized first by Ross (1969a); it is treated from a broader perspective by Zwicky (1968) and assimilated to the general exclusion principle by McCawley (1970a). To be effective, the exclusion hypothesis must be supported by observations over the appropriate *range*; these observations must be suitably *accurate*, and there must be some assurance that *outside effects* are not interfering significantly with the evidence. That is, there must be arguments that different phenomena, in different languages, which might have been thought to require the use of curly brackets, do not in fact do so; there must be arguments supporting the general adequacy and completeness of the grammars referred to (for if features of the rules in question were dependent on minor changes in other rules, the evidence from these descriptions would not be worth much), and there must be reason to believe that the supporting evidence is not seriously affected by external facts (difficulty in understanding sentences, for example).

Arguable propositions like Newton's Inverse Square Law or the No Curly Brackets Proposal may also be defended or attacked through arguments of a deeper sort, arguments that refer to general principles of scientific explanation (falsifiability, simplicity, plausibility, for example). Thus, the naturalness argument described in Zwicky (1968) in favor of the No Curly Brackets Proposal is an appeal to theoretical simplicity, as was the argument favoring the elegance of the Copernican heliocentric theory over the complexity of the epicycles in the geocentric theory.

Other examples of arguable propositions from linguistics include the following: (*a*) a proposal by Chomsky that no transformational rule insert material from one S into a lower S; (*b*) an unpublished but much discussed suggestion of Kiparsky's that rules effecting absolute neutralizations in phonology be prohibited; (*c*) the hypothesis that syntactic rules cannot be conditioned by phonological features (the Principle of Phonology-Free Syntax, treated in Zwicky (1969)); (*d*) the assumption that all the information required for the conditioning of phonological rules is available in superficial syntactic structure (the Principle of Superficial Constraints in Phonology, mentioned in Zwicky (1970a)); (*e*) a proposal in Zwicky (1970c) for limitations on the use of Greek-letter variables in phonological rules; and (*f*) a hypothesis, put forward tentatively by Chomsky and Halle (1968), that the phonological cycle is restricted to prosodic phenomena.

The linguistic cases that come first to mind are all exclusive principles, thanks to the emphasis within transformational generative grammar on restricting the range of notational conventions and their uses as a way of specifying as narrowly as possible the notion "possible natural language." Arguable propositions in the natural sciences are customarily stated positively, but they can easily be converted into exclusive principles. Newton's Inverse Square Law, for example, can be interpreted as a ban on physical systems in which the gravitational attraction between bodies is any function of R besides $1/R^2$. The difference, then, between the linguistic examples and the physical example is simply one of degree: physical principles are typically much more specific in their exclusions than are linguistic hypotheses.

There are, however, many sorts of specific, positively stated arguable propositions in linguistics. Putative linguistic universals, such as those treated by various authors in Greenberg (1963), are cases, as are claims that particular rules, phonological or syntactic, are universal in character (as has been argued by Bach (1971), Foley (1970), and Stampe).

2.2.2. ORGANIZING HYPOTHESES

Organizing hypotheses are high-level assumptions, fundamental empirical hypotheses. Various principles of linguistic change have this character—the Neogrammarian hypothesis of the regularity of sound change, for instance, and Kiparsky's (1968) proposal that rules reorder in time so as to reduce markedness. Also of this character are assumptions about the directionality of the relationship between syntactic and semantic representations. The most salient fact about such assumptions is that they are not easily given up, even in the face of apparent counterexamples, which will be treated as manifestations of minor complicating principles or as outright anomalies (see Kuhn (1962)). It is this resistance to disproof that gives organizing hypotheses their "field-defining" nature. They are testable, in some sense, and they can be abandoned after argument, but the tests are not simple nor the arguments straightforward.

As was emphasized earlier, there is no sharp break between arguable propositions and organizing hypotheses. The Principle of Phonology-Free Syntax and the Principle of Superficial Constraints in Phonology, which were mentioned in the preceding section, are fairly high-level assumptions and might be taken to be organizing hypotheses. I have listed them as arguable propositions because that is the way they are viewed in the articles cited, but it would be possible to consider them as being more fundamental, as together asserting a basic "separation of levels" between syntax and phonology.

Before continuing with examples from linguistics, let us look at two celebrated cases of organizing hypotheses in the physical sciences. The first is the Newtonian (originally, Galilean) inertial principle of motion versus the Aristotelian or resistance conception. Toulmin (1963) observes that

> Aristotle concentrated his attention on the motion of bodies against appreciable resistance, and on the length of time required for a complete change of position from one place to another. For a variety of reasons, he never really tackled the problem of defining 'velocity' in the case when one considers progressively shorter and shorter periods of time—i.e. instantaneous velocity. Nor was he prepared to pay serious attention to the question how bodies would move if all resisting agencies were effectively or completely removed. As things turned out, his hesitations were unfortunate; yet his reasons for hesitating are understandable, and in their way laudable . . . Leaving aside free fall for the moment as a special case, all the motions we observe going on close around us happen as they do (he saw) through a more-or-less complete balance between

two sets of forces: those tending to maintain the motion and those tending to resist it. In real life, too, a body always takes a definite time to go a definite distance. So the question of instantaneous velocity would have struck him as over-abstract; and he felt the same way about the idea of a completely unresisted motion, which he dismissed as unreal (pp. 50–51).

Here we have a sympathetic exposition of an organizing hypothesis formulated by Aristotle. In Aristotle's commonsensical view, bodies move only while they are impelled. A wagon on a country road, not a freely falling ball, is the paradigm for dynamics. The position is, ultimately, empirical. However, it is easier to imagine tests of Newton's Inverse Square Law (given that there is *some* attractive force between bodies) than to construct experiments bearing on the Aristotelian Resistance Hypothesis. In time, Aristotle's hypothesis was abandoned in favor of a different organizing hypothesis, namely, Newton's First Law, which holds that every particle continues in a state of rest, or in motion with constant speed in a straight line, unless acted upon by an outside force. Both hypotheses are difficult to formulate precisely, and the change from one to the other was accompanied by changes in other fundamental assumptions and was supported by arguments of many different types, including experimental evidence bearing indirectly upon the question and general considerations of adequacy of explanation.

The second example comes from astronomy—Kepler's First Law that the orbit of each planet about the sun is elliptical, with the sun at one of the foci of the ellipse. This organizing hypothesis replaced the theory that the orbits are circular, a proposition that seems to many (as it seemed to Aristotle) so self-evident that it scarcely would require support. The example is especially interesting because it illustrates a change from an organizing hypothesis that asserts circular motion to the present state of affairs, a methodological principle which prefers circles to ellipses, other things being equal. The same evolution from organizing hypothesis to methodological principle can be seen in the history of the Contrast Principle in phonology (mentioned briefly in Section 2.1). The reverse development, from methodological principle to organizing hypothesis, is not unknown either; I shall suggest an example shortly.

The history of Kepler's First Law illustrates another sort of evolution as well—a change from an organizing hypothesis to an arguable proposition of the ordinary sort. Clearly, when first put forth, Kepler's First Law was a fundamental thesis about astronomy, revolutionary in its content. Once accurate instruments of the required type had been developed, however, the difference between circular and elliptic motion could be detected by normal methods, and soon it became possible to derive Kepler's laws of planetary motion from Newton's laws, so that Kepler's First Law became a relatively low-level hypothesis in a network of assumptions.

Now let us return to examples of organizing hypotheses in linguistics. First we examine the "requirement that transformations preserve meaning," as Partee (1971) phrases it. I shall refer to this hypothesis as the *Post Office Principle*, on the grounds that it treats syntax as an elaborate delivery system, a system designed to get messages to an addressee without changing their content. As Partee notes, the Post Office Principle is viewed as a methodological principle by Katz and Postal (1964), who stress that the principle is "not . . . a statement in linguistic theory, but rather . . . a rule of thumb based on the general character of linguistic descriptions" (p. 157). But, in case after case, the Post Office Principle seemed to recommend analyses that were later confirmed by independent evidence, and it was thus elevated from a methodological principle to an organizing hypothesis. As Partee puts it, the principle "gained support very quickly, to the point where it was widely accepted as one of the more solidly established generalizations in linguistic theory and used as a criterion for transformational rules" (p. 2).

As is typically the case with organizing hypotheses, it is difficult to formulate the Post Office Principle precisely: as Partee points out, it involves in an essential way the difficult but fundamental notion of "synonymy," just as Newton's First Law involves in an essential way the difficult but fundamental notions of "motion" and "force." As is also typical of organizing hypotheses, it is hard to adduce convincing evidence for or against the Post Office Principle. The problem is that it is almost always possible to fix up a description so that it will conform to the principle. Accordingly, whether or not an analyst will make the required adjustments tends to depend on whether or not he believes in the Post Office Principle.

The final example of an organizing hypothesis that I will give is the one referred to in the title of this article, namely, the Substance Theory of Semantic Primes. In the form I shall use in the remainder of this paper, the hypothesis is: *every semantic prime is realizable as a lexical unit (root, inflection, or derivational affix) in some natural language.* A stronger version might be suggested: in any language, most semantic primes are realized as lexical units. The strongest form of the hypothesis—in any language, all semantic primes are realized as lexical units—seems clearly too much to hope for. I shall be content to defend the weak, or simple existential, form of the hypothesis in the sections to follow.

The idea behind the name "Substance Theory of Semantic Primes" is that every semantic prime is a real substance (a root, inflection, or derivational affix), not merely a principle manifested by real substances. The analogy here is with chemical elements, which, on the modern view, are assumed to be realizable as substances, as opposed to the ancient "elements" fire, air, earth, and water, or the alchemical "elements" salt, sulphur, and mercury, which were "not substances at all, but metaphysical abstractions of properties, typifying the natures of bodies" (Partington (1948, p. 113)).

Clearly, the Substance Theory is an organizing hypothesis rather than a methodological principle or an arguable proposition of the usual sort. It is difficult to see how one could construct a straightforward argument for or against the idea. And the reference to "realization" in the statement of the hypothesis makes its precise formulation a formidable task.

3. THE SUBSTANCE THEORY

In the remaining part of this paper, I review briefly the (very sparse) literature on semantic primes, preparatory to considering uses of the Substance Theory in discussions of semantics. Next, I take up the analogy with chemistry and argue that the analogy is material, to use Hesse's (1966) term. Finally, I supply a more general discussion of metaphor and analogy in linguistics, with additional examples of material analogies.

3.1. Semantic Primes

The statement of the Substance Theory in Section 2.2.2 refers specifically to "semantic primes" and therefore locates the hypothesis within the broad framework of generative semantics. This restriction is unnecessary, however, for the hypothesis is equally appropriate within theories that assume that the semantic readings of lexical units are constructs of primes called "features," "markers," "specifications," or the like. That is, I intend my remarks to apply not only to systems like those of McCawley (1968) and Lakoff (1970), in which semantic structures are of the same type as syntactic structures, but also to standard Katz-Fodor semantics (as presented in Katz (1966), for example), in which semantic representations of lexical units are sets of markers, as well as to various intermediate positions in which semantic representations of lexical units are more or less complex structures containing markers (as in such extensions of, variants of, or alternatives to the Katz-Fodor position as Gruber (1965), Weinreich (1966), Leech (1969), and Chafe (1970)).

Within none of these frameworks has there been any extended discussion of the character of the atomic units that appear in semantic descriptions. The following remarks by Katz (1966) are representative:

> Just as the meaning of a word is not atomic, a sense of a word is not an undiffer-entiated whole, but, rather, has a complex conceptual structure. The reading which represents a sense provides an analysis of the structure of that sense which decomposes it into conceptual elements and their interrelations. Semantic markers represent the conceptual elements into which a reading decomposes a sense. They thus provide the theoretical constructs needed to reconstruct the interrelations holding between such conceptual elements in the structure of a sense.
>
> ... Just as syntactic markers enable us to formulate empirical generalizations about the syntactic structure of linguistic constructions, so semantic markers enable us to construct empirical generalizations about the meaning of linguistic constructions. For example, the English words 'bachelor', 'man', 'priest', 'bull', 'uncle', 'boy', etc., have a semantic feature in common which is not part of the meaning of any of the words 'child', 'mole', 'mother', 'classmate', 'nuts', 'bolts', 'cow', etc. The first set of words, but not the second, are similar in meaning in that the meaning of each member contains the concept of maleness. If we include the semantic marker (Male) in the lexical readings for each of the words in the first set and exclude it from the lexical entries for each of the words in the second, we thereby express this empirical generalization. Thus, semantic markers make it possible to formulate such generalizations by providing us with the elements in terms of which these generalizations can be stated (pp. 155–157).

In practice, primes are set up within some narrow area that is of interest to the investigator, as a way of giving an account of the semantic relationships he perceives in that area (see, for example, Fillmore (1969)). There is virtually no attempt to argue for one system of primes over various possible alternatives. The only areas which have been "mapped" well in this way are inflectional categories and a few fields that are of interest to anthropologists as well as linguists—folk taxonomies, kinship systems, and color terms. Otherwise, these investigations are in their infancy. And surely the most-quoted words on the subject are those of Bendix (1966, p. 17): "a rough road into the empirical semantic wilderness is preferable to a well-paved one timidly skirting the borders."

For my purposes here, the most notable gap in existing treatments of semantic primes is the absence of assertions of formal or substantive universals involving them.[2] There are the same few exceptions as before, kinship and color terms especially.

---

[2] Chomsky's (1965) references to semantic universals are quite brief: "A theory of substantive universals might hold, for example, that certain designative functions must be carried out in a specified way in each language. Thus it might assert that each language will contain terms that designate persons or lexical items referring to specific kinds of objects, feelings, behavior, and so on" (p. 28); as formal universals, he suggests "the assumption that proper names, in any language, must designate objects meeting a condition of spatiotemporal contiguity [a footnote here illustrates the hypothesis], and that the same is true of other terms designating objects; or the condition that the color words of any language must subdivide the color spectrum into continuous segments; or the condition that artifacts are defined in terms of certain human goals, needs, and functions instead of solely in terms of physical qualities" (p. 29). In the same vein, James Heringer has suggested to me the hypothesis that words in natural (as opposed to technical) languages never refer to absolute measurements.

Given the lack of such assertions, we must try to infer general principles from whatever practices there have been.

First, however, a few words are necessary about the differences between words and semantic primes. There is a reasonably clear illustration of the distinction in Postal (1970):

I have claimed that the underlying structure of *remind* clauses is of the form:

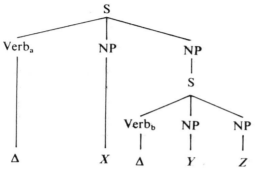

where Verb$_a$ is an element like *strike*, Verb$_b$ an element with the properties of a Similarity Predicate. In the context of the discussion of Generative Semantics, it is clear that there is no suggestion that these underlying verbals are *lexical items*, in particular none that they are the lexical *strike*, *resemble*, etc. The idea is that the underlying elements are *semantic* verbs, that is, predicates. Consequently, the claim is only that the underlying elements of *remind* clauses are those predicates which are lawfully connected to the various regularities documented for *strike* and Similarity Predicates. In particular, I would like to emphasize that it is not excluded that the actual lexical verb *strike* may have certain special properties not associated with the underlying predicate or predicate complex which shows up as the Surface Verb *remind*. Just so, the particular predicate of similarity which underlies *remind* may lack some ad hoc features of any or all of the verbals *similar*, *resemble*, *like*. In short, I have not intended to claim that *remind* is in any sense derived from underlying structures which contain the lexical verbs *strike*, or *resemble/similar/like*. Rather, I have argued that the derivation must be from elements whose properties are *included* in these lexical elements (pp. 113–114).

The crucial notion in discussions of primes and words is that of "realization," or "correspondence to": English *and*, in one of its senses, realizes the prime AND[3] because, aside from any syntactic or stylistic peculiarities associated with this sense of English *and*, its properties are those of an entity which bears certain specific relations to other entities (for example, OR, NOT, IF, ONE) which, taken together, form the basis for a semantic description of English. Among the relations in question is the duality of AND and OR—that AND is equivalent to NOT-OR-NOT and, conversely, that OR is equivalent to NOT-AND-NOT, or, stated precisely, that R AND S is equivalent to NOT $((\text{NOT } R)$ OR $(\text{NOT } S))$ and that R OR S is equivalent to NOT $((\text{NOT } R)$ AND $(\text{NOT } S))$. Just as one sense of *and* corresponds to AND, so one sense of *similar* corresponds to (realizes) LIKE, *become* and *-en* correspond to INCHOATIVE, and *say* corresponds to ASSERT.

3.1.1. *THE SUBSTANCE THEORY IN THE LITERATURE*

A run through semantic descriptions in the literature has turned up no primes which strike me as being incapable of realization in a word or affix; in nearly every case, in fact, there is an obvious English lexical item corresponding to the prime. In addition, it

---

[3] I shall follow the custom of using small capital letters for primes, as contrasted with italics for words or other lexical units.

is undoubtedly significant (as James Heringer has pointed out to me) that the factors governing selectional restrictions in English seem always to have easy "English translations"—(*concrete*) *object, feminine, human, activity*, to cite a few. If there is not necessarily a lexical unit corresponding to each prime, then we should expect to come across "inexpressible" selectional restrictions, which would require the invention of new technical terms for the purposes of linguistic description.

Although there are no examples now available of semantic primes that are not realizable in a word or affix, both Katz and Lakoff have taken pains *not* to subscribe to the Substance Theory. Both assume that the set of semantic primes, like the set of phonological features, is universal, but neither is willing to assert more than that the set of primes together is sufficient to provide an adequate account of the internal meaning relationships in the lexicon of any language. Katz (1966) even supplies the chemical analog:

> It is important to stress that, although the semantic markers are given in the orthography of a natural language, they cannot be identified with the words or expressions of the language used to provide them with suggestive labels. Rather, they are to be regarded as constructs of a linguistic theory, just as terms such as 'force' are regarded as labels for constructs in natural science. There is an analogy between the formula for a chemical compound and a reading (which may be thought of as a formula for a semantic compound). The formula for the chemical compound ethyl alcohol,

$$\begin{array}{ccc} \text{H} & \text{H} & \\ | & | & \\ \text{H--C--C--O--H} \\ | & | & \\ \text{H} & \text{H} & \end{array}$$

> represents the structure of an alcohol molecule in a way analogous to that in which a reading for 'bachelor' represents the conceptual structure of one of its senses. Both representations exhibit the elements out of which the compound is formed and the relations that form it. In the former case, the formula employs the chemical constructs 'Hydrogen molecule', 'Chemical bond', 'Oxygen molecule', etc., while in the latter the formula employs the linguistic concepts '(Physical Object)', '(Male)', '⟨Selection Restriction⟩', etc. (p. 156).

Lakoff (1970) finds himself asking whether there are two semantic primes WURF and GLIP with certain specified properties; he concludes:

> In an arbitrary system, one could always make up such predicates, but that is beside the point. The question here is an empirical one. Is there any evidence that such atomic predicates actually exist in the logical forms of sentences of natural language? This does not necessarily mean that there must actually be in some language single lexical items directly corresponding to these predicates. However, it is required, at the very least, that such predicates appear elsewhere. For example, there might be a number of other verbs which can be decomposed in terms of one or the other of these predicates (p. 351).

Lakoff does not claim that the Substance Theory is invalid; he merely withholds judgment on the matter and proposes a weaker condition on the universality of primes. The only thing that his condition rules out is the positing of a prime on the basis of properties of one lexical item in one language—surely a minimal constraint on the content of semantic theory.

In one instance, Lakoff (1970) uses the existence of a word corresponding to a putative prime as evidence for the prime's existence. In connection with the proposed decomposition of one sense of *persuade* into CAUSE-INCHOATIVE-INTEND, he writes:

Aside from the rule of predicate-lifting, all of the rules used in this derivation and in similar derivations are needed anyway in English grammar. Moreover, structures like [the one proposed for *persuade*] are also needed independently in English grammar. That is, there must be a verb "cause" which is a two-place predicate, a verb "come about" which is a one-place predicate, and a verb "intend" which is a two-place predicate (p. 342).

If there were no reason to suppose that primes were realized as words, then the existence of a verb *cause* in English would be irrelevant to the analysis of *persuade* as containing the prime CAUSE.

Since Katz and Lakoff do not suggest any analyses that violate the Substance Theory, we must turn to others for examples. As it happens, some relevant work has been done by logicians.

3.1.2. LOGICALLY ADEQUATE BUT LINGUISTICALLY UNNATURAL SYSTEMS

It has been the goal of logic to construct precise and satisfying accounts of a few areas of form and meaning that are of independent philosophical or mathematical interest. One of the criteria for satisfaction is systematic elegance—parsimony in primitive symbols or concepts, in sets of axioms, and so on. Logicians have been extremely ingenious in their parsimony. And their systems are often quite unnatural linguistically. Linguistic judgments of unnaturalness, in combination with predictions made by the Substance Theory, allow us to conclude that the logician's primes cannot be linguistic primes. I provide two cases here.

First, we consider the example of the Sheffer stroke.[4] A classic result of symbolic logic is that the logical connectives $\sim$ 'not', & 'and', $\vee$ 'or', $\supset$ 'implies', and $\equiv$ 'if and only if' can all be defined from one connective (either one of two different connectives, in fact). This is the Sheffer stroke | 'not both . . . and . . .'. The remaining connectives are definable in several ways, for instance:

$\sim P$ *defined as* $P \mid P$
$P \vee Q$ *defined as* $\sim P \mid \sim Q$
$P \supset Q$ *defined as* $\sim P \vee Q$
$P \,\&\, Q$ *defined as* $\sim (\sim P \vee \sim Q)$
$P \equiv Q$ *defined as* $(P \supset Q) \,\&\, (Q \supset P)$

What is linguistically interesting about this logician's strategy is that no language seems to have a conjunctive root *nub*, with the property that *A nub B* means 'not both A and B', and I would view with considerable suspicion any report of a language with such a conjunction. If no language has a lexical unit *nub*, then according to the Substance Theory, the Sheffer stroke cannot represent a semantic prime for linguistic, as opposed to logical, purposes.

An example of a somewhat different type is provided by Prior (1960), whose object is to assail the notion that the meaning of the word *and* is completely given by an account of the role it plays in deductions (that from *P and Q* we can infer *P*, that from *P and Q* we can infer *Q*, and that from *P* and *Q* we can infer *P and Q*). He affects to claim that any statement *Y* can be inferred from any other, *X*, by citing an inference of the form:

X
X tonk Y
$\therefore Y$

---

[4] Almost every standard logic text treats this subject; see, for example, Copi (1967, p. 201).

Prior adds:

> There may well be readers who have not previously encountered the conjunction 'tonk',
> it being a comparatively recent addition to the language; but it is the simplest matter in
> the world to explain what it means. Its meaning is completely given by the rules that
> (i) from any statement P we can infer any statement formed by joining P to any statement
> Q by 'tonk' . . . and that (ii) from any 'contonktive' statement P-tonk-Q we can infer the
> contained statement Q.

Not only is *tonk* not a "comparatively recent addition to the language," it is not part
of *any* language. Consequently, according to the Substance Theory, whatever it
might be, it is no semantic prime. Belnap (1962) has observed that the definition of
tonk is inconsistent, thereby providing an explanation for its unnaturalness.

The point of cases like the two just considered is that the Substance Theory can
link with observations about what sort of lexical items occur in the world's languages
to yield predictions about possible semantic primes. Without the mediation of the
Substance Theory, there is no reason for there to be a relation between the kinds of
lexical units that occur in languages and the semantic primes that are proposed for
them.

3.2. The Analogy with Chemistry

The Substance Theory of Semantic Primes, as I have already pointed out, is analogous
to Boyle's requirement, in the "Sceptical Chymist" of 1661, that chemical elements
be isolable substances and not abstract principles. We have also seen, in Section 3.1.1,
Katz's comparison of semantic structure to chemical structure. In this section I will
press this analogy further, with the intention of using the chemical case to suggest
useful lines of inquiry in the linguistic case. That is, I will be claiming that the parallels
between chemical structure and semantic structure are deep ones. This is not to say,
of course, that the two subfields of the different disciplines are isomorphic in every
detail. I do not anticipate the discovery of a set of deep principles from which the
properties of chemical structure and those of semantic structure will both be derivable.
Indeed, there are aspects of each subfield which are without obvious analogs in the
other; for instance, there is nothing in the chemical case that is a natural correspondent
of the phonological identity that unites the two senses of *persuade* (CAUSE-INCHOATIVE-
INTEND and CAUSE-INCHOATIVE-BELIEVE) or the distinct senses (each a separate lexical
unit) of many other words.

The initial analogy is of language to matter. The strategy of the disciplines,
linguistics and chemistry, respectively, is to analyze heterogeneous physical material
(speech, materials) into its parts (words, substances) and then to treat these parts as
either elemental substances (semantic primes, elements) or compounds of such
elemental substances. These analytic preliminaries require the identification and
removal of various kinds of intrusive factors.

The central part of the analogy, then, is an occurrence of a semantic prime in
some language, on the one hand, and an atom of some chemical element, on the other.
Corresponding to lexical entries are molecules.[5] Certain molecules, hydrogen molecules
for instance, are composed of only one sort of atom. In the same way, certain lexical
entries, the entry for *cause* for instance, are composed of only one sort of prime.

---

[5] This much of the parallel is echoed by Postal (1970, pp. 100–101), who speaks of "semantic
atoms" and "semantic molecules" but does not take the terms to be more than simple metaphors.

Other molecules, the sulfuric acid molecule for one, possess an internal structure in which more than one sort of atom (hydrogen, sulfur, oxygen) occurs. Just so, some lexical entries, the entry for *kill* among them, possess an internal structure with more than one sort of prime (CAUSE, INCHOATIVE, NOT, ALIVE).

In both linguistics and chemistry, the great majority of the known substances (or words) are complex. In each field, the number of actually occurring substances is quite large, and the number of possible substances is infinite in principle, though limited in fact by external factors (the physical instability of the molecules, the psychological complexity of the words).

Also, in both linguistics and chemistry, there are molecular properties which are "emergent," in the sense that they are not predictable by known principles from the character of the constituents of the molecule. Broad (1925) writes of a familiar chemical example:

> Oxygen has certain properties and Hydrogen has certain other properties. They combine to form water, and the proportions in which they do this are fixed. Nothing that we know about Oxygen itself or in combination with anything but Hydrogen could give us the least reason to suppose that it could combine with Hydrogen at all . . . And most of the chemical and physical properties of water have no known connexion, either quantitative or qualitative, with those of Oxygen and Hydrogen. Here we have a clear instance where, so far as we can tell, the properties of a whole composed of two constituents could not have been predicted from a knowledge of these properties taken separately, or from this combined with a knowledge of the properties of other wholes which contain these constituents (pp. 62–63).

The linguistic analog is the apparent impossibility of predicting the full range of syntactic properties of a lexical item given its decomposition into primes. From what semantic analysis of the verb *question* could one predict that it can be used performatively when its direct object is a simple NP (as in *I question that statement*) or a *whether*-clause (as in *I question whether we should do this*) but not when it is any other sort of *wh*-clause (**I question where he lives*) or a *that*-clause (**I question that he was responsible*) or an *if*-clause (**I question if we should do this*)?

In the quantitative atomic theory proposed by Dalton, it is assumed that the atoms of the same element are identical, in the sense that they have identical masses, and that atoms of different elements have different masses. The corresponding assumptions in semantics are that instances of the same semantic prime are associated with the same cognitive meaning (that is, that the cognitive meaning of a semantic prime is invariant across languages) and that different semantic primes have different meanings.

The tasks of chemistry are partly analytical (to devise methods for isolating and identifying substances), partly descriptive (to say what sorts of substances occur and what their properties are), and partly explanatory (to give an account of chemical structure from which the observed phenomena could be predicted). The analytical and descriptive aspects of elemental theory are summarized well in Weeks (1968), from which I conclude that semantics is a few hundred years behind chemistry simply in the matter of listing elements, not to mention explaining their properties. It is as if we were really sure of only a dozen or so chemical elements. Semantics has had no Mendeleev to organize the elements in a periodic table according to their salient common properties; and the linguistic analog of the Bohr atom, from which the groupings in the periodic table could be predicted, is scarcely imaginable.

If the structural analogy between chemistry and semantics is deep, what sorts of developments can we expect in semantics? Three, at least: the discovery of isotopes, a theory of valence, and the hypothesis of subatomic structure. I believe that there are indications that all three of these expectations are met.

First, there is the matter of isotopes. The discovery of different atoms of the "same" element with different masses (and even of atoms of "different" elements with the same mass) is an obvious embarrassment for a theory which takes an invariant mass to be criterial for a given element. The existence of isotopes, especially those which (like light and heavy hydrogen) have quite distinct properties, makes the study of subatomic structure inevitable. What are the semantic analogs of isotopes? They are occurrences of the "same" semantic prime with different meanings. Just this sort of situation is exhibited by lexical items which are "denotatively" distinct but do not differ in any independently motivated semantic feature; these are terms for correlative species, for example *rose*, *chrysanthemum*, and *pansy*, or *snap*, *crackle*, *thud*, and *rumble*. (The latter set of cases is from the discussion in Leech (1969, pp. 85–89).) It is natural to say that these two sets of items represent only two semantic primes—(SPECIFIC) FLOWER and MAKE A (SPECIFIC) NOISE—and that the individual lexical items differ subatomically.

Next, we turn to a theory of valence, a set of combinatory principles for semantic primes. Among these principles in semantics are conditions stating that a certain predicate "takes" so many arguments, of such and such a type; these conditions have been much studied by Fillmore ((1970), for example), among others. Also relevant here are conditions governing the embedding of one S in another—the deep structure constraints of Perlmutter (1971), restrictions on the occurrence of special classes of predicates, such as the stative and activity predicates, constraints against certain predicates embedding themselves (*TRY *to* TRY, *INTEND *to* INTEND), and the like.

Finally, there is subatomic structure. This is already called for by the isotope cases and might serve to explain the valence phenomena. It could also provide an account of the way in which primes fall into subclasses having properties in common (a set of connectives, like AND and OR, a set of modal elements, like NECESSARY and POSSIBLE, and so on). There are in addition a number of relationships among primes that might be accounted for by means of subatomic structure—the duality relation of NECESSARY-POSSIBLE, REQUIRE-PERMIT, AND-OR, and SOME-EVERY, for instance, or the relation between nonepistemic BE FREE TO and epistemic POSSIBLE (both realized as English *can*) and between nonepistemic HAVE TO and epistemic NECESSARY (both realized as English *must*). In his treatment of semantic primes, Grosu (1970) adopts a theory of subatomic structure without comment by deciding "to represent them as bundles of semantic and syntactic properties" (p. 41); he includes (pp. 84–89) a tentative list of such properties (or types already mentioned) for seven putative primes—CAUSE, INCHOATIVE, TRY, INTEND, BE ABLE TO, BE FREE TO, and HAVE TO.

In his discussion of the sort of emergence illustrated earlier in this section, Nagel (1961, pp. 366–374) observes that emergence is relative to a particular theory, so that as theories change, it may become possible to predict properties that were inexplicable within a previous theory. He notes that a change of this sort has occurred in chemistry, where properties of substances which were formerly thought to be emergent now can be predicted from an electronic theory of atomic composition. It is even possible to imagine that all properties of interest to chemists and still considered emergent might be predictable. The rather breathtaking linguistic analog is that there might turn out to be no syntactic exceptions, that the behavior of every lexical item with respect to syntactic rules and constraints might be predictable in some way from its semantic structure.[6]

[6] Exactly this hypothesis has been made to me by Georgia Green in conversation.

3.3. Analogy and Metaphor

I have claimed that the parallel between chemical structure and semantic structure is systematic enough to merit study, hence, that it is like the parallel between water waves and electromagnetic phenomena, which is treated at length by Hesse (1966) in her very interesting work on models and analogies. She draws a distinction between metaphors, which are suggestive but not productive, and material analogies, which function to provide models for inquiry.

Merely metaphoric are such names as the "Post Office Principle" and the "Free Ride Principle," as well as Ross's "tree-pruning" (1969b) and "Pied Piping" (1967, Section 4.3). More information about the way the post office operates is not likely to further the study of the requirement that transformations preserve meaning,[7] and arboricultural research will not elucidate problems of derived constituent structure.

To round out this discussion, I will contrast some instance of merely metaphorical writing with examples of more illuminating analogies, choosing now nontransformational illustrations.

For the unsatisfying cases, I have selected ideas of two of the most original and inspiring traditional grammarians, Noreen and Jespersen. Lotz (1966) summarizes Noreen's theory of the structure of grammar as follows:

> Thus, grammar should have three branches, each of which should view the entire speech phenomenon from a special angle: *phonology*, which should treat the articulated sound; *semology*, which should deal with the linguistically formed psychological content; and *morphology*, which should account for the way in which the sound material is formed to express the semantic content. He attempted to elucidate these distinctions by analogies, e.g., a certain object can be regarded as a piece of bone (material), having the shape of a cube (content), and serving as a dice (form); or, as a building composed of bricks (material), in Moorish style (content), and serving as a café (form). But these analogies are rather far-fetched and not very illuminating (pp. 58–59).

And McCawley (1970b) attacks Jespersen's poetic attempts in *Analytic Syntax* (1969, pp. 120–121) to distinguish the notions "nexus" and "junction":

> In *AS*, his characterizations of nexus and junction rest heavily on analogies which I find unenlightening (p. 447).

Compare the corresponding analogies in Jespersen (1924):

> Comparisons, of course, are always to some extent inadequate, still as these things are very hard to express in a completely logical or scientific way, we may be allowed to say that the way in which the adjunct is joined to its primary is like the way in which the nose and the ears are fixed on the head, while an adnex rests on its primary as the head on the trunk or a door on the wall. A junction is here like a picture, a nexus like a process or drama (p. 116).

In the same work, Jespersen strives to account for the relationships of modifiers by means of an analogy less striking than he had hoped it would be:

> . . . it is really most natural that a less special term is used in order further to specialize what is already to some extent special: the method of attaining a high degree of specialization is analogous to that of reaching the roof of a building by means of ladders: if one ladder will not do, you first take the tallest ladder you have and tie the second tallest to the top of it, and if that is not enough, you tie on the next in length, etc. In the same way,

---

[7] Although I cannot resist pointing out that structures in violation of derivational constraints are the analogs of pieces of mail returned to the sender.

if *widow* is not special enough, you add *poor*, which is less special than *widow*, and yet, if it is added, enables you to reach farther in specialization; if that does not suffice, you add the subjunct *very*, which in itself is much more general than *poor* (p. 108).

For an instance of a more productive analogy, consider the parallel between replacement of vocabulary items in a language over time and the decay of radioactive elements, a parallel first emphasized by Swadesh and discussed clearly by Lees (1953):

> The members of the chosen subset may be likened to the (indistinguishable) atoms in a given mass of a radioactive element. Since the rate of disintegration is predictable at any time during observation of the sample, the mass (or number of remaining atoms) of the element remaining among the decay products at any time in the sample is a measure of how long the sample has been decaying. The analysis of decay products in mineral samples permits the calculation of the age of the earth's crust. Similarly, analyses of morpheme decay products should provide an absolute chronology for lexical history (pp. 113–114).

This analogy turns out to have several faults: morpheme decay probably does not proceed at a constant rate, and, even if it did, the resulting estimates of absolute chronologies would normally not be exact enough for ordinary linguistic purposes. Nevertheless, the analogy is close enough to have inspired some important research, and in special cases glottochronological methods are still useful.

Analogies of many kinds were a fancy of nineteenth-century writers on language. In the following passage, Whitney (1867) spoke more truly than he could have known:[8]

> There is a yet closer parallelism between the life of language and that of the animal kingdom in general. The speech of each person is, as it were, an individual of a species, with its general inherited conformity to the specific type, but also with its individual peculiarities, its tendency to variation and the formation of a new species. The dialects, languages, groups, families, stocks, set up by the linguistic student, correspond with the varieties, species, genera, and so on, of the zoölogist. And the questions which the students of nature are so excitedly discussing at the present day—the nature of specific distinctions, the derivation of species by individual variation and natural selection, the unity of origin of animal life—all are closely akin with those which the linguistic student has constant occasion to treat. We need not here dwell further upon the comparison: it is so naturally suggested, and so fruitful of interesting and instructive analogies, that it has been repeatedly drawn out and employed, by students both of nature and of language (pp. 46–47).

Whitney cites Lyell and Schleicher as additional proponents of the proportion

species : variety = language : dialect

and of the related parallels between genetic classification in linguistics and biological taxonomy, although Whitney nevertheless castigates Schleicher for attempting "to prove by [this proportion's] aid the truth of the Darwinian theory, overlooking the fact that the relation between the two classes of phenomena is one of analogy only, not of essential agreement" (p. 47).

In fact, the analogy is a deep one. There is a population of individuals, who vary in a number of characteristics (linguistic or morphological). The individuals form themselves into a number of groups on the basis of their similarities. There is also an ability for certain pairs of individuals to interact in a special way, if they are brought

---

[8] The passage is sandwiched between an analogy relating linguistic history and organic growth and decay and one associating earlier stages of a language with geological strata.

together. (Their speech is mutually intelligible, in the linguistic case, or they can (inter)breed, in the biological case.) The interactive ability is then used scientifically as a necessary and sufficient test for determining groups within the population. (In the linguistic case, mutual intelligibility is used as a stringent criterion for a *language*, and in the biological case, ability to interbreed is used as a stringent criterion for a *species*.)

Several developments of these notions can be predicted. First, it will frequently not be possible to bring together the appropriate pairs in order to test relationships. Thus, biological specimens may be dead, or geographically separated, or ecologically separated; languages may be defunct or far-flung. In both fields, the consequence is the development of an independent notion of relationship, one based solely on the characteristics. In the case of biology, this is the "morphological" species, as opposed to the "biological" species (see, *inter alia*, Cain (1954)). In the case of linguistics, this is the Stammbaum principle of genetic classification, as opposed to a sociolinguistic classification. The new, or "strict," theory is easily seen to be unsatisfactory because the characteristics will show a considerable degree of independence, hence, a Wellen-theorie in linguistics and a theory of diffusion of characters through gene pools in biology.

Another, less predictable characteristic of the systems we are considering is that the stringent criterion turns out not to characterize a transitive relation. That is, evidence will arise indicating that the criterion is not necessary but merely sufficient. In the case of biology, we have animal chains in which each animal can breed with the animals in the adjoining territory, although the animals at the extremes cannot interbreed (a readable exposition occurs in Dobzhansky (1955, Chapter 8)); in the case of a "species" of gulls surrounding the North Pole, the extremes happen to occur in the same area and cannot interbreed. The linguistic analogies are well-known cases where groups of speakers find their dialect mutually intelligible with their neighbors' but the extreme dialects are not mutually intelligible. Indeed, knowing the case of the gulls, we might have been able to predict the existence of problematical dialect chains.

The analogy between linguistic and biological classification is a systematic one: in most respects, there is a point-to-point correspondence between the two fields. The claim made in this paper is that the correspondence between semantic and chemical structure is of the same sort.

REfERENCES

Bach, E. (1971), "Questions," *Linguistic Inquiry*, 2, 153–166.
Bach, E., and R. T. Harms (1968), *Universals in Linguistic Theory*, New York: Holt, Rinehart and Winston.
Belnap, N. D. (1962), "Tonk, plonk and plink," *Analysis*, 22, 130–134; reprinted in Strawson (1967).
Bendix, E. H. (1966), *Componential Analysis of General Vocabulary*, IJAL, 32, Part II (IURAFL Publ. 41).
Broad, C. D. (1925), *The Mind and Its Place in Nature*, London.
Cain, A. J. (1954), *Animal Species and Their Evolution*, London: Hutchinson; Harper Torchbooks edition, 1960.
Campbell, M. A., *et al.*, eds. (1970), *Papers from the Sixth Regional Meeting, Chicago Linguistic Society*, Chicago Linguistic Society.

Chafe, W. L. (1970), *Meaning and the Structure of Language*, Chicago: University of Chicago Press.

Chomsky, N. (1965), *Aspects of the Theory of Syntax*, Cambridge, Mass.: M.I.T. Press.

Chomsky, N., and M. Halle (1968), *The Sound Pattern of English*, New York: Harper & Row.

Copi, I. M. (1967), *Symbolic Logic*, 3rd ed., New York: Macmillan.

Darden, B. J., *et al.*, eds. (1968), *Papers from the Fourth Regional Meeting, Chicago Linguistic Society*, Chicago Linguistic Society.

Dobzhansky, T. (1955), *Evolution, Genetics, and Man*, New York: Wiley.

Fillmore, C. J. (1969), "Verbs of judging: an exercise in semantic description," *Papers in Linguistics*, *1*, 91–115.

Fillmore, C. J. (1970), "The Grammar of *Hitting* and *Breaking*," in Jacobs and Rosenbaum.

Fillmore, C. J., and D. T. Langendoen, eds. (1971), *Studies in Linguistic Semantics*, New York: Holt, Rinehart and Winston.

Foley, J. (1970), *Systematic Morphophonology*, ms.

Greenberg, J. H., ed. (1963), *Universals of Language*, Cambridge, Mass.: M.I.T. Press.

Grosu, A. (1970), *On Coreferentiality Constraints and EQUI-NP-DELETION in English*, unpublished Master's thesis, The Ohio State University.

Gruber, J. (1965), *Studies in Lexical Relations*, unpublished Ph.D. dissertation, M.I.T.

Hanson, N. R. (1958), *Patterns of Discovery*, London: Cambridge University Press.

Hesse, M. B. (1966), *Models and Analogies in Science*, Notre Dame: University of Notre Dame Press.

Jacobs, R. A., and P. S. Rosenbaum, eds. (1970), *Readings in English Transformational Grammar*, Waltham, Mass.: Ginn.

Jespersen, O. (1924), *Philosophy of Grammar*, London: George Allen & Unwin.

Jespersen, O. (1969), *Analytic Syntax*, photographic reprint of 1937 edition, New York: Holt, Rinehart and Winston.

Katz, J. J. (1966), *The Philosophy of Language*, New York: Harper & Row.

Katz, J. J., and P. M. Postal (1964), *An Integrated Theory of Linguistic Descriptions*, Cambridge, Mass.: M.I.T. Press.

Kiparsky, P. (1968), "Linguistic Universals and Linguistic Change," in Bach and Harms.

Kuhn, T. S. (1962), *The Structure of Scientific Revolutions*, Chicago: University of Chicago Press.

Lakoff, G. (1970), "Natural Logic and Lexical Decomposition," in Campbell, *et al.*

Leech, G. N. (1969), *Towards a Semantic Description of English*, Bloomington: Indiana University Press.

Lees, R. B. (1953), "The basis of glottochronology," *Language*, *29*, 113–127.

Lotz, J. (1966), "Plan and Publication of Noreen's *Vårt Språk*," in Sebeok (1966b), Vol. 2; originally published in *Studia Linguistica*, *8*, 82–91.

McCawley, J. D. (1967), "Meaning and the description of languages," *Kotoba no uchū*, *2*, 10–18, 38–48, 51–57.

McCawley, J. D. (1968), "Lexical Insertion in a Transformational Grammar without Deep Structure," in Darden, *et al.*

McCawley, J. D. (1970a), "English as a VSO language," *Language*, *46*, 286–299.

McCawley, J. D. (1970b), Review of Jespersen, (1969), *Language*, *46*, 442–449.

Nagel, E. (1961), *The Structure of Science*, New York: Harcourt Brace Jovanovich.

Partee, B. H. (1971), "On the Requirement That Transformations Preserve Meaning," in Fillmore and Langendoen.

Partington, J. R. (1948), "The concepts of substance and chemical element," *Chymia*, *1*, 109–121.

Perlmutter, D. M. (1971), *Deep and Surface Structure Constraints in Syntax*, New York: Holt, Rinehart and Winston.

Postal, P. M. (1970), "On the surface verb 'remind'," *Linguistic Inquiry*, *1*, 37–120; reprinted in Fillmore and Langendoen (1971).

Prior, A. N. (1960), "The runabout inference-ticket," *Analysis*, *21*, 38–39; reprinted in Strawson (1967).

Reibel, D. A., and S. A. Schane, eds. (1969), *Modern Studies in English*, Englewood Cliffs, N.J.: Prentice-Hall.

Ross, J. R. (1967), *Constraints on Variables in Syntax*, unpublished Ph.D. dissertation, M.I.T.

Ross, J. R. (1969a), "Auxiliaries as Main Verbs," *Studies in Philosophical Linguistics*, Series One, 77–102.

Ross, J. R. (1969b), "A Proposed Rule of Tree-Pruning," in Reibel and Schane; originally in Report NSF-17 (1966), Harvard Computation Laboratory, Section IV.

Sebeok, T. A., ed. (1966a), *Current Trends in Linguistics, II: Theoretical Foundations*, The Hague: Mouton.

Sebeok, T. A., ed. (1966b), *Portraits of Linguists*, Bloomington: Indiana University Press.

Strawson, P. F., ed. (1967), *Philosophical Logic*, Oxford: Oxford University Press.

Toulmin, S. (1963), *Foresight and Understanding: An Inquiry into the Aims of Science*, New York: Harper & Row.

Weeks, M. E. (1968), *Discovery of the Elements*, 7th ed. (rev. and expanded by Henry M. Leicester), Easton, Pa.: Journal of Chemical Education.

Weinreich, U. (1966), "Explorations in Semantic Theory," in Sebeok (1966a).

Whitney, W. D. (1867), *Language and the Study of Language*, New York: Scribner.

Zwicky, A. M. (1968), "Naturalness Arguments in Syntax," in Darden, *et al.*

Zwicky, A. M. (1969), "Phonological constraints in syntactic descriptions," *Papers in Linguistics*, *1*, 411–463.

Zwicky, A. M. (1970a), "Auxiliary reduction in English," *Linguistic Inquiry*, *1*, 323–336.

Zwicky, A. M. (1970b), "The Free-Ride Principle and Two Rules of Complete Assimilation in English," in Campbell, *et al.*

Zwicky, A. M. (1970c), "Greek-letter variables and the Sanskrit *ruki* class," *Linguistic Inquiry*, *1*, 549–555.